The Developing Child

Tenth Edition

Holly E. Brisbane

 **Glencoe**

New York, New York   Columbus, Ohio   Chicago, Illinois   Peoria, Illinois   Woodland Hills, California

The McGraw·Hill Companies

Copyright © 2006 by The McGraw-Hill Companies, Inc.
All rights reserved. Except as permitted under the United States Copyright Act,
no part of this publication may be reproduced or distributed in any form or by any
means, or stored in a database or retrieval system, without prior written permission
of the publisher, Glencoe/McGraw-Hill.

Send all inquiries to:
Glencoe/McGraw-Hill
3008 W. Willow Knolls Drive
Peoria, IL 61614

ISBN 0-07-868968-6 Student Edition
ISBN 0-07-868969-4 Teacher Wraparound Edition

Printed in the United States of America
6 7 8 9 10 071 09 08 07

CONTENTS IN BRIEF

Unit 1 | Children and Parenting

Chapter 1: Learning About Children..20
Chapter 2: The Challenges of Parenting....................................46
Chapter 3: Building Strong Families 70

Unit 2 | Pregnancy and Childbirth

Chapter 4: Prenatal Development 104
Chapter 5: Preparing for Birth..146
Chapter 6: The Baby's Arrival 178

Unit 3 | The Baby's First Year

Chapter 7: Physical Development of Infants................................208
Chapter 8: Emotional and Social Development of Infants 252
Chapter 9: Intellectual Development in Infants.............................278

Unit 4 | The Child from One to Three

Chapter 10: Physical Development from One to Three 310
Chapter 11: Emotional and Social Development from One to Three 342
Chapter 12: Intellectual Development from One to Three 380

Unit 5 | The Child from Four to Six

Chapter 13: Physical Development from Four to Six................................408
Chapter 14: Emotional and Social Development from Four to Six 428
Chapter 15: Intellectual Development from Four to Six 452

Unit 6 | The Child from Seven to Twelve

Chapter 16: Physical Development from Seven to Twelve 476
Chapter 17: Emotional and Social Development from Seven to Twelve 494
Chapter 18: Intellectual Development from Seven to Twelve 520

Unit 7 | Additional Topics of Study

Chapter 19: Adolescence 544
Chapter 20: Children's Health and Safety.................................574
Chapter 21: Family Challenges 598
Chapter 22: Child Care and Early Education 626
Chapter 23: Careers Working with Children 656

Technical Reviewers

Gayle Mindes, M.S., Ed.D.
Chair, Department of Teacher Education
DePaul University
Chicago, Illinois

Ann Kennedy, M.A., Ed.D.
Adjunct Instructor: Graduate School of Education
Reading Specialist
Arlington, Virginia

Teacher Reviewers

Mary Kay Anderson, M.Ed.
FACS Instructor
Shorewood Public Schools
Shorewood, Wisconsin

Anne Beal, M.Ed.
FACS Department Chair
Emmaus High School
Emmaus, Pennsylvania

Alice M. Bristle
FACS Instructor
Lake Fenton High School
Linden, Michigan

Carol Crowder
FACS Instructor
Douglas S. Freeman High School
Richmond, Virginia

Karen Feltz, M.Ed.
FACS Instructor
St. Henry Consolidated
School District
St. Henry, Ohio

Karleen Fossum
Special Education Teacher
Glasgow High School
Glasgow, Montana

Christine Bunte Halweg
FACS Instructor
Peotone CUSD 207U
Peotone, Illinois

Janet Hartline
FACS Instructor
Fort Payne High School
Fort Payne, Alabama

Eleanor L. Keppler, M.S., CFCS
FACS Department Chair
Lawrence Central High School
Indianapolis, Indiana

Kathleen A. Murer Libby, MAT, BSE
FACS Department Chair
Affton High School
St. Louis, Missouri

Patricia Lynn
FACS Department Chair
Charles Herbert Flowers
High School
Springdale, Maryland

Patricia Martin
FACS Instructor
South Western High School
Hanover, Pennsylvania

Stephanie M. Meinke
Vocational Coordinator,
FACS Instructor
Farmington High School
Farmington, Minnesota

Jonie S. Nock
FACS Instructor
Greeneview Schools
Jamestown, Ohio

Nancy Plowman
FACS Instructor
Davis County Community School
Bloomfield, Iowa

Karin C. Ohr Pyskaty
Career & Technical Education
Department Chair
Lyman Hall High School
Wallingford, Connecticut

Shirley P. Rauh
FACS Department Chair
Lutheran High School South
St. Louis, Missouri

Mary Kay Roesch
FACS Instructor
Bradford Area High School
Bradford, Pennsylvania

Becky F. Roseberry
FACS Instructor
Pulaski County High School
Dublin, Virginia

Ann D. U'Halie
FACS Instructor
Sharon High School
Sharon, Pennsylvania

CONTENTS

Unit 1 | Children and Parenting

Chapter 1: Learning About Children   20

Section 1-1: Making a Difference in Children's Lives 21

Your Impact on Children • Views of Childhood • Comparing Childhood Past and Present • Living What You Learn

Section 1-2: Studying Children 27

Why Is Childhood Crucial? • The Developing Brain • Theories About Development • What Researchers Have Found • Lifelong Growth and Development

Section 1-3: Observing and Interacting with Children 35

Why Observe Children? • How to Observe Young Children • Using Observations

Chapter 2: The Challenges of Parenting   46

Section 2-1: Parenting and Families 47

Parenting: A Learning Process • The Changes That Parenthood Brings • Making Decisions About Parenthood

Section 2-2: Teen Parenthood 58

Teen Sexuality • When Teen Pregnancy Occurs • Thinking It Through

Chapter 3: Building Strong Families   70

Section 3-1: Families: The Context for Parenting 71

Functions of the Family • Family Structure • Joining a Family • The Family Life Cycle • Trends Affecting Families • Sources of Family Support • Building a Strong Family

Section 3-2: Effective Parenting Skills 83

Meeting Children's Needs • Parenting Styles • Guiding Children's Behavior

Unit 2 | Pregnancy and Childbirth

Chapter 4: Prenatal Development — 104

Section 4-1: The Developing Baby 105

Conception • The Germinal Stage • The Embryonic Stage • The Fetal Stage • Preparing for Birth

Section 4-2: A Closer Look at Conception 114

The Genetic Package • Multiple Births • Family Planning • Infertility

Section 4-3: Problems in Prenatal Development 122

Losing a Baby • Types of Birth Defects • Causes of Birth Defects • Prevention and Diagnosis of Birth Defects

Section 4-4: Avoiding Dangers to the Baby 133

Alcohol and Pregnancy • Other Drugs • X Rays • Hazardous Substances and Chemicals • Infections • Sexually Transmitted Diseases (STDs)

Chapter 5: Preparing for Birth — 146

Section 5-1: A Healthy Pregnancy 147

Early Signs of Pregnancy • Medical Care During Pregnancy • Discomforts of Pregnancy • Nutrition During Pregnancy • The Developing Brain • Personal Care and Activities • Emotional Health During Pregnancy

Section 5-2: Preparing for the Baby's Arrival 161

Preparing for Parenthood • Clothes, Equipment, and Space • Decisions About Feeding • Choosing a Pediatrician • Making a Budget • Balancing Work and Family

Section 5-3: Childbirth Options 171

What Is Prepared Childbirth? • Who Will Deliver the Baby? • Where Will the Baby Be Born?

Chapter 6: The Baby's Arrival 178

Section 6-1: Labor and Birth.. 179

The Beginning of Labor • Stages of Labor • Cesarean Birth
• Premature Birth

Section 6-2: The Newborn.. 190

A Newborn Baby Arrives • The Developing Brain • Examining
the Newborn • Later Tests

Section 6-3: The Postnatal Period 195

Bonding • The Hospital Stay • Caring for Premature Babies
• Postnatal Care of the Mother

Unit 3 | The Baby's First Year

Chapter 7: Physical Development of Infants 208

Section 7-1: Infant Growth and Development 209

Patterns of Physical Development • Influences on Growth and
Development • The Developing Brain • Growth During the
First Year • Development During the First Year

Section 7-2: Infant Care Skills.. 225

Handling Babies • Ensuring Adequate Sleep • Feeding Babies
• Dressing a Baby

Section 7-3: Infant Health and Wellness 240

Bathing a Baby • Diapering • Baby's Teeth • Regular Checkups

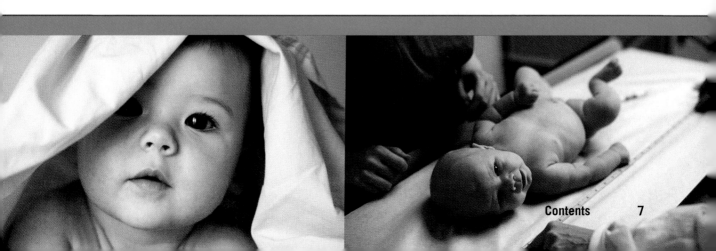

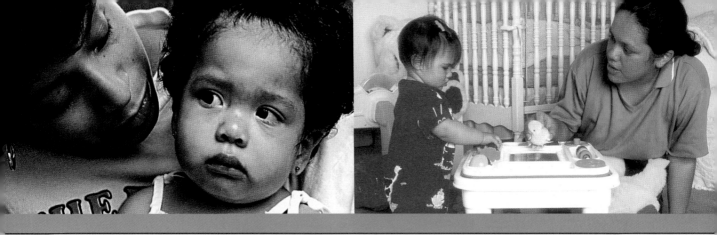

Chapter 8: Emotional and Social Development of Infants   252

Section 8-1: Understanding Emotional Development of Infants 253

Comparing Emotional and Social Development • Emotions in Infancy • Building Bonds of Attachment • The Developing Brain • Understanding Temperament • Crying and Comforting • Emotional Climate of the Home

Section 8-2: Understanding Social Development of Infants 266

Signs of Social Development • Stranger Anxiety • How Behavior Is Learned • Social Development Through Play • A Play Environment for Infants • The Difference Between Exploration and Play

Chapter 9: Intellectual Development in Infants   278

Section 9-1: Early Brain Development 279

The Study of the Brain • The Structure of the Brain • The Developing Brain • Building the Brain • Is the Brain Organized Only Once?

Section 9-2: Intellectual Development During the First Year 288

Learning in the First Year • The Developing Brain • Piaget's Theories • Stimulating Infants' Senses • Beginnings of Concept Development

Section 9-3: Helping Infants Learn 296

Encouraging Learning • The Importance of Play • Developing Communication

Unit 4 | The Child from One to Three

Chapter 10: Physical Development from One to Three   310

Section 10-1: Growth and Development from One to Three 311

Toddlers to Preschoolers • Influences on Growth and Development • Growth from One to Three • Motor Development from One to Three • The Developing Brain

Section 10-2: Caring for Children from One to Three 321

Sleeping • Nutritional Needs and Eating • Hygiene • Dressing • Health, Illness, and Safety

Chapter 11: Emotional and Social Development from One to Three   342

Section 11-1: Emotional Development from One to Three 343

General Emotional Patterns • Specific Emotions • Individual Differences • Developing a Positive Self-Concept • Evaluating Emotional Adjustment • Sleep, Emotions, and Behavior

Section 11-2: Social Development from One to Three 361

General Social Patterns • Making Friends • Promoting Sharing • Possible Behavioral Problems

Chapter 12: Intellectual Development from One to Three   380

Section 12-1: Brain Development from One to Three 381

The Study of the Brain • The Role of Intelligence • Methods of Learning • Concept Development • The Mind at Work • The Developing Brain

Section 12-2: Encouraging Learning from One to Three 392

Readiness for Learning • Guiding Learning • Play Activities and Toys

Unit 5 | The Child from Four to Six

Chapter 13: Physical Development from Four to Six   408

Section 13-1: Growth and Development from Four to Six 409

Height and Weight • Posture and Body Shape • Teeth • Motor Skills

Section 13-2: Caring for Children from Four to Six 415

Providing Good Nutrition • Nutritional Concerns
• Teaching Self-Care Skills

Chapter 14: Emotional and Social Development from Four to Six   428

Section 14-1: Emotional Development from Four to Six 429

General Emotional Patterns • Specific Emotions • The Developing
Brain • Children and Stress • Encouragement

Section 14-2: Social and Moral Development from Four to Six 439

General Social Patterns • Resolving Conflicts • Family Relationships
• Moral Development

Chapter 15: Intellectual Development from Four to Six   452

Section 15-1: The Developing Brain from Four to Six 453

What Is Intelligence? • Signs of Intellectual Development
• Piagets's Theory of Preoperational Thinking • Vygotsky's Theory
• Montessori's Theory of Learning

Section 15-2: Learning from Four to Six 461

Helping Children Learn • The Developing Brain • The School
Experience • Speech Development

Unit 6 | The Child from Seven to Twelve

Chapter 16: Physical Development from Seven to Twelve — 476

Section 16-1: Growth and Development from Seven to Twelve 477
Height and Weight • Proportion and Posture • Permanent Teeth
• Onset of Puberty • The Developing Brain • Motor Skills

Section 16-2: Caring for Children from Seven to Twelve 482
Nutrition • Physical Fitness • Sleep • Caring for Teeth
• Personal Hygiene • Checkups and Vaccines

Chapter 17: Emotional and Social Development from Seven to Twelve — 494

Section 17-1: Emotional Development from Seven to Twelve 495
A Sense of Self • The Developing Brain • Emotional Changes
• Specific Emotions • Living with Children Seven to Twelve

Section 17-2: Social and Moral Development from Seven to Twelve 505
Relationships with Peers • Family Relationships
• Moral Development

Chapter 18: Intellectual Development from Seven to Twelve — 520

Section 18-1: The Developing Brain from Seven to Twelve 521
Signs of Increased Intellectual Growth • Theories of How
Children Learn

Section 18-2: Learning from Seven to Twelve 531
Learning Methods • Middle School—A Place for Transition
• Measuring Students' Intellectual Development

Unit 7 | Additional Topics of Study

Chapter 19: Adolescence   544

Section 19-1: Physical Development of Adolescents 545

A Time of Many Changes • Physical Development During Adolescence • Healthy Habits • The Developing Brain

Section 19-2: Emotional and Social Development of Adolescents 553

Emotional Development of Adolescents • Social Relationships in Adolescence • Opportunities for Social Interaction

Section 19-3: Moral Development of Adolescents 561

Developing a Moral Compass • Kohlberg's Levels of Moral Development • Social and Cultural Influences on Moral Development • Linking Behavior to Personal Values

Section 19-4: Intellectual Development of Adolescents 566

Getting Older and Smarter • Two Theories of Teen Intellectual Development • The Impact of Educational Experiences

Chapter 20: Children's Health and Safety   574

Section 20-1: Childhood Illnesses 575

Regular Health Care • Immunization • Common Childhood Conditions • Caring for a Sick Child • Comforting a Sick Child • Going to the Hospital

Section 20-2: Accidents and Emergencies 583

Safety • Guidelines for Fast Action • First Aid • Rescue Techniques

Chapter 21: Family Challenges   598

Section 21-1: Family Stresses 599

Children and Stress • Situational Stress

Section 21-2: Exceptional Children 608

Children with Special Needs • Types of Disabilities • The Developing
Brain • Educating Children with Special Needs • Raising Children
with Disabilities • Gifted Children

Section 21-3: Child Abuse and Neglect 617

Types of Maltreatment • Why Does Abuse Occur? • What Can Be Done?

Chapter 22: Child Care and Early Education   626

Section 22-1: Child Care Options 627

The Need for Substitute Care • Types of Substitute Care
• The Developing Brain • Choosing Substitute Child Care

Section 22-2: Participating in Early Childhood Education 639

The Early Childhood Classroom • Health and Safety • Planning
Appropriate Activities • Promoting Positive Behavior

Chapter 23: Careers Working with Children   656

Section 23-1: Preparing for a Career 657

Career Options • Finding Career Information • Analyzing Careers
• Preparing for Career Success

Section 23-2: Beginning Your Career 667

Looking for a Job • Building Career Skills • Leaving a Job
• Ongoing Employability

Glossary 684

Credits 698

Index 700

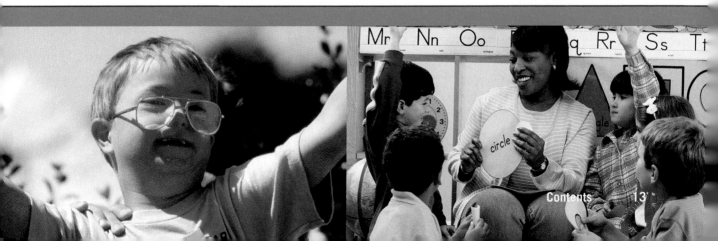

Health & Safety

Keeping Children Safe: An Observer's Role 41
Car Seat Safety.. 169
NICUs and Their Expertise in Caring for Premature Babies 200
Food-Related Hazards 232
Infant Safety Concerns 245
RSV.. 246
Tempting Toys... 300
Brushing Teeth.. 330
Safety Concerns, Ages One to Three.. 337
Separation Anxiety.. 352
Outdoor Safety, Ages Four to Six 421
ADHD 432
Personal Safety, Ages Seven to Twelve 488
Internet Safety.. 513
Self-Destructive Behaviors 569
Food Safety Routines.. 644

Learning Through PLAY

Comparing Toys 23
Play as a Family 72
Playing with Babies 213
Face-to-Face 262
Sensory Play 293
Changes in Play.................................317
Memory Games...................................386

Taking on Roles 413
Social Rules and Play 440
Playing Grown-Up 465
Problem Solving Through Play..........510
Children's Museums..........................526
Bicycle Safety Classes....................584
Play in a Montessori School.............646

HOW TO

Take Notes During an Observation 40

Balance School and Parenting 64

Give Children Effective Directions 89

Understand Genetic Traits 116

Reduce Stress During Pregnancy 158

Choose a Crib 167

Cope with Labor 185

Bond with a Baby 197

Burp a Baby 234

Bathe a Baby 241

Help a Baby Develop a Sense of Trust 259

Cope with Stranger Anxiety 267

Stimulate Brain Development in an Infant 286

Manage Transitions in a Child's Routine 323

Childproof a Home 335

Manage Misbehavior 356

Help Young Children Develop Social Skills 366

Encourage Imagination and Creativity 390

Encourage Physical Activity 419

Guide Children's Behavior 447

Know When a Child Is Ready for School 467

Emphasize Enjoyment in Organized Sports 479

Help a Child Work Through a Difficult Situation 503

Stay Involved in a Child's Education 536

Encourage Good Nutrition and Self-Image 549

Provide Good Nutrition During Illness 581

Help a Child Cope with Divorce 603

Tell if a Child Is Doing Well in Child Care 633

Choose Early Childhood Materials 648

Write a Follow-Up Letter After an Interview 676

THE DEVELOPING BRAIN

These short excerpts on brain development provide additional information at the point of use.

LOOKING AT REAL LIFE

These case studies provide examples of the child development content being applied in real-life situations.

Parenting Q&A

How Can We Help Children Develop Self-Esteem?................................ 33
How Can I Make a Positive Difference in a Child's Life? 48
What Is the Controversy About Spanking?.. 97
What Can a Concerned Couple Do About Genetic Birth Defects?............ 123
How Do Caffeine and Alcohol Affect a Fetus? 136
What Are Diet Guidelines for an Expectant Mother?............................ 155
What Physical Changes Occur in a Newborn? 193
What Is Sudden Infant Death Syndrome? 228
Why Is Consistent Feedback Important? 271
How Does Reading to Infants Help Them Develop Language Skills? 302
What Are Some Ways to Calm a Toddler Who Is Having a Temper Tantrum? 374
What Are Some Signs of Language Development? 401
What Is the Best Way to Handle Bedwetting?..................................... 423
Why Do Young Children Lie? 445
How Much Television Is Too Much? 462
How Can Parents Help an Overweight Child? 484
How Can Parents Teach a Child Tolerance? 514
How Much Should I Help My Child with Homework?........................... 534
How Much Independence Should a Teen Be Allowed? 559
What Rights Do Children with Disabilities and Their Parents Have?........ 613

Children
Around the World

Development Is Similar Around the World 30
Giving New Parents a Break in Finland 75
Where Neighbors Are Few, Genetic Diseases Affect Many 117
Korea Taegyo 159
What's in a Name? 187
Preventing Infant Death in Australia 247
Carrying a Baby on Your Back 257
Speaking Without Words 301
Dexterity Among the Navajos 318
Preschool in France 395
"Health Clubs" in Singapore 418
Raising a Child in Austria 437
Lessons You Can Eat 515
Analyzing the Media's Messages 528
Child Care in Denmark 642
A School Where Teachers Fly to Work 659

Career Opportunities

Actor in Children's Theater 43
Parent Educator 67
Adoption Consultant 99
Genetic Counselor 143
Obstetric Sonographer 175
Pediatric Nurse 203
Pediatrician 249
Storyteller 275
Child Development Researcher 305
Child Life Specialist 339
Puppeteer 377
Play Therapist 403

Speech-Language Pathologist 425
Family Court Judge 449
Toy Designer 471
Children's Activities Director
  for City Parks 491
Animator 517
Gymnastics Coach 539
Camp Counselor 571
Emergency Medical Technician 595
Wildlife Educator 623
Child Care Worker 653
Kindergarten Teacher 681

Children and Parenting

Chapter 1
Learning About Children

Chapter 2
The Challenges of Parenting

Chapter 3
Building Strong Families

1 Learning About Children

Thoughtful Reading:

As you read this chapter:

- Ask questions about what you are reading.
- Identify new information you learn from what you read.
- Connect what you read to your personal experiences.

Section 1-1
Making a Difference in Children's Lives

Section 1-2
Studying Children

Section 1-3
Observing and Interacting with Children

Making a Difference in Children's Lives

Why do babies like to chew on books? Why do toddlers throw their toys again after you've just retrieved them? What should you do when a three-year-old lies? Children's behavior can be both fascinating and frustrating, especially when you don't understand it. As you study child development, you'll find answers to questions such as these. You'll also learn that taking care of children is one of the most important responsibilities you can have.

Objectives

- Summarize the benefits of studying children.
- Explain how learning about typical behaviors can help you better understand children.
- Describe how childhood today differs from childhood in the past.

Key Terms

typical behaviors
caregivers

Your Impact on Children

Have you ever really thought about the process by which children grow up and become independent adults? You might never have realized that you have an impact on children's lives. People and events shape who children become. When you live with children, you influence them every day. If your contact with children is less frequent, what you say and how you act still matter. Even if you don't interact with children regularly, you can be sure that younger children are watching you and paying attention to how you behave. Do you think that you are a good role model? Studying child development will help you learn how you can make a positive difference in a child's life.

Benefits of Studying Children

As you learn more about how children grow and develop, you will understand them better. You will also improve your understanding of yourself.

Many experts have written about how children learn and how best to care for them. No two children are alike, however, and no expert can explain every aspect of their behavior. As with many subjects, the best way to learn about children is through your active involvement with them. As you study children, you will:

- **Learn why children feel, think, and act the way they do.** It is not always easy to understand children's behavior, particularly before they learn to talk. However, there is a set of **typical behaviors**—ways of acting or responding that are common at each stage of childhood. Understanding these behaviors can help you respond to children more appropriately. For example, Cassie was puzzled because her brother Brett and his neighbor Curtis, both two-year-olds, never interacted when they played. Brett and Curtis usually sat near each other, but they played with different toys. In a child development class, Cassie learned that two-year-olds typically play *alongside* each other but not *with* each other. Cassie understood that her brother's style of play was typical for his age.

- **Discover caregivers' importance.** Parents and others who tend to children are called their **caregivers**. As you learn more about how children develop, you will see why they are dependent upon others for many years. Caregivers provide more than food and clothes. They give the affection children need to grow emotionally. They stimulate learning, teach children to get along with others and how to know right from wrong.

- **Enjoy children more.** Learning about children can help you discover what a joy they can be. Spending time with them will give you opportunities to experience their honesty, humor, energy, and curiosity. Caring for children can be very rewarding! See Fig. 1-1.

- **Learn about career opportunities.** Throughout this book, you will be introduced to people in many jobs related to children. You may find one that interests you.

Fig. 1-1 **Interacting with children is the best way to learn about them.**

Learning Through  P**L**AY

Comparing Toys

For our country's settlers, a primary concern was survival. Children helped greatly with chores, gathering wood, sewing, and even plowing. However, toys were still an important part of their lives. Parents showed their love for their children by making them toys out of the materials at hand. A child might have had a doll made of cloth or an animal carved from wood. Toys were simple, and they encouraged children to use their imagination. Today, many toys are electronic, and they don't involve as much use of the imagination. However, children still enjoy books and other traditional toys that have been favorites for generations.

Following Up

What is the role of toys in children's lives?

Views of Childhood

Childhood means different things to different people. The way you think about childhood depends in part on what your own childhood was like. If your childhood was fairly easy and comfortable, you may think of it as a carefree time of security. If your parents struggled to provide for you, you may think of childhood as a time of hardship. For everyone, childhood is a period of rapid development, dependence on caregivers, and preparation for adult life.

Researchers and scholars have made a special study of childhood and its phases. They have looked at how children develop, what their needs are, and how those needs can best be met. Perhaps one of their most important findings is that childhood has a profound influence on later life.

Childhood has not always been considered a separate, important stage of life. In fact, childhood—as it is now known—is a fairly recent "discovery."

Comparing Childhood Past and Present

Until the twentieth century, some people believed that there was nothing special or important about the early years of life. Some adults said children were meant to be "seen and not heard." Little was known about the emotional and intellectual needs of children. Changing attitudes, social changes, and advances in technology and medicine have changed views about childhood.

- **Health.** Before the twentieth century, it was common for parents to lose a child due to illness. Diseases caused deaths in almost every family, and particularly among children. Today, many deadly diseases can be controlled, and better nutrition has helped children to grow and thrive as never before. However, not all children eat well. Some simply don't have enough food. Others have plenty of food but eat too many high-fat, high-sugar foods. In addition, lack of sufficient regular exercise is increasingly common. Poor food choices plus insufficient exercise have increased the rate of childhood obesity and related problems.

- **Education.** Public education for all children did not become widespread in this country until the early 1800s. Schools were small, and they often included children of different ages and abilities in the same classroom. In today's schools, students are grouped according to age and sometimes learning levels. Computers and other technology have enhanced learning options. Schools work to meet the special needs of individual students.

- **Love.** Although childhood in the past was different in many ways from childhood today, one thing that hasn't changed is children's need for love. Most parents and other caregivers work hard to build a good life for their children and to raise them as moral, responsible, and independent people. See Fig. 1-2.

- **Work.** Up until the twentieth century, children were expected to work—at adult jobs—at an early age. Then laws were enacted banning children from working in factories or other adult workplaces. Today, most young children are still expected to work—but at growing, learning, and playing. Teens may hold jobs,

Fig. 1-2 Do you think the ways parents show their children love today is different from the past? Explain your answer.

Fig. 1-3 **One noticeable difference between children today and children in the past is how they dress.** What are some other differences?

but laws specify the minimum working age, and most dangerous jobs are banned. Most children are expected to help out at home, however. Children may be responsible for cleaning their rooms, feeding pets, helping with yard work, or helping care for siblings.

- **Play.** Play has always been important to children. It's how they learn. How much children play and what they play with have changed. In the past, children had far fewer toys, they were simple, and they were often homemade. Baseball wasn't developed until the 1800s. Video and computer games first became available in the 1970s. Today, the variety of toys seems endless. Children spend much of their time playing.

- **Dress.** If you look at old pictures, you will quickly notice that children dressed more formally. Infants and toddlers of both genders often wore long gowns. Older boys wore suits, while girls wore dresses. Today, casual clothes for boys and girls are often similar in style. They are washable, comfortable, and loose enough to allow freedom of movement. See Fig. 1-3.

Living What You Learn

You are in an excellent position to study child development. You are close enough to adulthood to think critically, but still young enough to remember clearly what being a child felt like. As you learn about children, some of your views about childhood and childrearing may be reinforced, while new information may cause you to rethink your ideas. You may be left with questions. Opportunities to interact and work with children can help you answer them.

Gaining New Skills

As you learn about children and ways to meet their needs, try to find opportunities to apply your knowledge. You might spend your summers working at a local park or pool, or looking after a younger sibling or a neighbor's child. Knowing how to bathe a baby, prepare a healthy meal for a toddler, or encourage a four-year-old to settle down for a nap will give you confidence—which will in turn make the children you care for feel more secure in your care.

Understanding Yourself

As you acquire a fuller understanding of children, you will also come to know yourself better. You may begin to see your own childhood differently. Try to recall your significant childhood experiences. Think about how they revealed aspects of your personality, or how they influenced whom you have become.

Building for the Future

If you want to work with children, many career paths—from teacher to children's librarian or pediatric nurse—are open to you.

You may not intend to work with children as an occupation, but there's a good chance you will be a parent someday.

SECTION 1-1 Review and Activities

Reviewing the Section

1. Why are teens often role models for younger children?
2. Summarize the benefits of studying children.
3. Give an example of how play is different today than it was fifty or a hundred years ago.
4. What are *typical behaviors*? How can knowing them help you care for children effectively?
5. State briefly how you might immediately apply what you learn about children.
6. Name two reasons why you are in a good position to study children.

Observing and Interacting

Watch a child or children interacting with a caregiver at a nearby public place such as a park or supermarket. Make a list of at least three behaviors you observe. For each behavior, evaluate how knowing about child development can help the caregiver deal with the behavior.

Studying Children

Imagine spending your entire career doing research on child development. By the time you retired, do you think you could solve all its mysteries? The answer is no. Many researchers have devoted their professional careers to the study of children, yet there are still many unanswered questions. What has been learned, however, has dramatically changed how parents raise children, how educators teach them, and how we think of development today—as a lifelong process.

Objectives

- Explain why childhood is an important time of development.
- Compare and contrast the leading theories about how children develop.
- Identify and give examples of the five characteristics of child development.
- Explain the impact that heredity and environment each has on development.
- List and define the stages of development after childhood.
- Describe how self-esteem and development are interrelated.

Key Terms

stimulation
sequence
heredity
environment
human life cycle
developmental tasks
self-esteem

Why Is Childhood Crucial?

Childhood is a time of preparation for adulthood. Recent research has shown that early childhood may be the most important life stage for brain development. Children's brains are not yet fully developed at birth—in fact, the brain is the least developed of the organs. A baby's brain is about one-quarter the size of an adult's. By age three, it has produced hundreds of trillions of connections among the brain cells. Scientists have found that babies' brains develop in response to **stimulation**, which includes activities that arouse a baby's sense of sight, sound, touch, taste, and smell. Such activities can improve a baby's curiosity, attention span, memory, and nervous system development. In addition, babies who are stimulated develop more quickly and have a more secure self-image.

By the time babies are three to four months old, they are beginning to connect what they see with what they smell, feel, and taste. By the time toddlers start walking, the brain is sending messages faster and more clearly. Repetition of actions, such as throwing a ball, reinforces pathways in the brain, making it easier to perform the same action the next time.

THE DEVELOPING BRAIN

Why do babies learn so much so fast in the first three years of life? Newborn babies' brains contain about 100 billion nerve cells, called *neurons*. Those neurons have about 50 trillion connections. These connections increase rapidly, and by the age of three, a child has twice as many connections as an adult. As a child matures, unused pathways are eliminated. This also means that babies who live in an environment where they learn more retain a greater number of connections.

Theories About Development

Child development theorists have provided valuable information about how children learn and develop skills. Some perform experiments involving children to test their theories. For example, children's perceptions of volume can be tested using the same amount of water in containers of various shapes. Other theories cannot be tested, such as Erik Erikson's belief that each stage of development includes a personal crisis. Not everyone agrees on how parents, caregivers, and educators should apply theories and research findings. Figure 1-4 summarizes the study and research findings of some of the major child development theorists.

What Researchers Have Found

Although they don't always agree, scientific researchers have given us insight about how best to nurture and educate children. They have also laid the foundations upon which future researchers can build.

Characteristics of Development

Researchers have found that child development follows five general rules:

- **Development is similar for each individual.** Children go through the same stages in about the same order. For example, all babies lift their heads before they lift their bodies.

- **Development builds upon earlier learning.** Development follows a **sequence**, or an order of steps. The skills a child learns at one stage build on those mastered earlier. For example, a child learns to say single words before speaking in phrases or complete sentences.

- **Development proceeds at an individual rate.** While all children pass through the same stages of development, each child goes through these stages at his or her own pace.

- **The different areas of development are interrelated.** Even though researchers tend to focus on one area of development at a time, changes occur in many areas—body, mind, emotions—at the same time.

- **Development is a lifelong process.** The rate of development varies. Sometimes it is rapid and sometimes less so. No matter what the pace is, development doesn't stop.

Fig. 1-4 Major Child Development Theorists

These are some of the researchers who have made a significant contribution to the study of child development.

Theorist	Findings or Ideas	Significance
Sigmund Freud (1856–1939)	Believed that personality develops through a series of stages. Experiences in childhood profoundly affect adult life.	Childhood is much more important than previously thought, and its effects are longer lasting.
Jean Piaget (1896–1980)	The first to study children scientifically. Focused on how children learned. Believed that children go through four stages of learning.	Children must be given learning tasks appropriate to their level of development.
Lev Vygotsky (1896–1934)	Wrote that biological development and cultural experience both influenced children's ability to learn. Believed social contact was essential to intellectual development.	Children should be given the opportunity for frequent social interaction.
Erik Erikson (1902–1994)	Like Freud, said that personality develops in stages. Thought that each stage includes a unique psychological crisis. If that crisis is met in a positive way, the individual develops normally.	Parents and other caregivers must be aware of, and sensitive to, children's needs at each stage of development and support them through crises.
B. F. Skinner (1904–1990)	Argued that when a child's actions have positive results, they will be repeated. Negative results will make the actions stop.	Parents and other caregivers can affect a child's behavior through the use of negative and positive feedback.
Albert Bandura (1925–)	Said that children learn by imitating others. Disagreed with Skinner. Pointed out that although the environment shapes behavior, behavior also affects environment.	Caregivers must provide good examples for children to follow.
Urie Bronfenbrenner (1917–)	Outlined layers of environment that affect a child's development, such as the child's own biology, family/community environment, and society.	Child's primary relationship with a caregiver needs to be stable, loving, and lasting.

Influences on Development

Children develop at different rates because each has a unique combination of factors influencing their development. These factors fall into one of two categories:

- **Heredity. Heredity** is the biological transfer of certain characteristics from earlier generations. Blood type, eye color, and hair color are just a few of the characteristics determined by heredity.

- **Environment. Environment** refers to the people, places, and things that surround and influence a person, including family, home, school, and community.

Heredity is often referred to as *nature*. For example, if someone says, "Dylan is musically talented—it's in his nature," they mean that he was born with this gift. *Nurture* is used to refer to influences and conditions in a child's environment. Dylan may also play the piano well because his parents make

Children Around the World

Development Is Similar Around the World

If you traveled the world visiting families in various countries, you would see that babies are cared for in different ways in different cultures and environments. However, all infants follow an orderly, predictable sequence of development at approximately the same ages. When learning to talk, they first express their needs or feelings by crying, then babbling before they utter their first words. Babies must learn to lift their heads before they can sit, crawl, stand, and eventually walk. While the sequence remains largely the same, however, the rate babies progress at each step varies.

Investigating Culture

1. What aspects of babies' lives might influence their rates of development through the various stages of childhood?
2. Do you think babies everywhere babble the same way? Why or why not?

Fig. 1-5 **Heredity plays a major role in physical characteristics and development.** What are some ways environment might affect development?

him practice each day. For years, scientists and philosophers have debated whether nature or nurture has more influence. Most agree that they work together.

Children inherit certain physical characteristics from their parents and ancestors. For example, Alejandra has brown hair and eyes, as do her parents. Children also learn attitudes and beliefs from their environment. Samira's parents take helping family and friends very seriously, and so does she. Children are greatly influenced by the wider world around them. What they read, the music they listen to, the type of community in which they grow up—all these and many other influences play a part in who they become. If you spend time around children, you can count yourself as one of these influences.

Of course, children don't always copy the attitudes and actions of others, and no two children are exactly alike. They react to outside influences in their own ways. That's one reason that brothers and sisters who grow up in the same home may experience life differently, and why they may become different people. No two children have exactly the same environment—even those who grow up in the same home. Their choice of friends, food, and activities will differ, and so will they.

During infancy and early childhood, environment plays a particularly important role in development. That is why working with young children is such an important responsibility—and such a challenging opportunity. See Fig. 1-5.

Anne, a pediatric nurse, has two nine-year-old patients, Ian and Seth, who have asthma. Aside from their age and diagnosis, their situations are different.

"Seth has been to the hospital only once for an asthma attack," Anne says. "His mom also has asthma, so they have learned together how to manage their symptoms. They keep emergency medication on hand and clean their house often to reduce dust.

"Ian, on the other hand, spends a lot of time in the hospital for asthma attacks," Anne continues. "Two conditions in his home can make his asthma worse: his family has a cat and one of his parents smokes. Ian's parents asked how to help reduce his number of attacks. I told them that keeping the cat out of Ian's bedroom and eliminating his exposure to smoke would be very helpful."

▶▶PERSONAL APPLICATION

1. What steps can you take to avoid getting common illnesses, such as colds?
2. Think of some health hazards that you might find in your environment. How could you go about eliminating one of them?

Lifelong Growth and Development

Development doesn't end when childhood does. It continues through life—from birth to death—in stages called the **human life cycle**. Each stage of the cycle presents different challenges that must be met or skills to be acquired. These **developmental tasks**, such as starting a career, occur at different stages in life. Of course, individuals differ in how they approach these challenges. Mastering the tasks of one stage prepares a person for the next.

Development Beyond Childhood

- **Adolescence.** This is the stage of life between childhood and adulthood. During this time, teens work on three developmental tasks: creating an identity, becoming independent, and pursuing education and career opportunities.

- **Young adulthood.** This stage refers to people in their twenties, when many young adults finish their education and begin working. Many marry in this period.

- **The Thirties.** This stage presents the challenges of establishing roots, reevaluating life choices made earlier, and finding stability in career and relationships.

- **Middle age.** This stage lasts from about ages 40–55. Parents adjust as their children become more independent. Adults in this stage typically ask themselves if they are satisfied with the life they have built. If not, they may make changes, such as starting a new career.

- **Late adulthood.** At some point during this stage (ages 55–75), most adults retire. They may become more politically or socially active, travel, take classes, or enjoy other activities they didn't have time for before. Others enjoy having more time with their grandchildren. Health issues may arise.

- **Very late adulthood.** It is in this stage (beyond age 75) when health problems become more common. However, many older adults are still active, and they contribute their knowledge and experience to society. Those in fragile health often need more assistance or care.

Parenting Q&A

How Can We Help Children Develop Self-Esteem?

Parents and other caregivers play a major role in developing a child's sense of self-worth, or self-esteem. Here are a few ways to have a positive effect.

- **Give praise.** Praise children for their accomplishments or real effort. Praise builds confidence.
- **Don't be overly critical.** Remember that they are still learning. When children don't do things quite right, don't yell or belittle them. Instead, try to find the good in what they have done and discuss how they can do better the next time.
- **Set realistic goals.** Help children set goals that they can reach. When children try activities that are too difficult, they become discouraged. Reaching smaller, more realistic goals makes them feel good about their accomplishments and want to try more.
- **Encourage new activities.** Help children learn to enjoy trying new things. Explain that life is not always about winning; it is also about the adventure.
- **Model self-esteem.** Children learn by example. If the adults in their lives say negative things about themselves, children will learn to imitate this negative behavior.
- **Be honest about mistakes.** Children need to see that adults have faults and make mistakes, too. It is reassuring to know that no one is perfect.

THINKING IT THROUGH

1. Identify the characteristics of someone with high self-esteem. With low self-esteem.
2. Think of a time when someone's criticism lowered your self-esteem. How might that person have encouraged you instead?

The Role of Self-Esteem in Development

Self-esteem, or self-worth, refers to the value people place on themselves. Self-esteem plays a role in people's ability to face and overcome the challenges of each developmental stage, including those of young childhood.

People with low self-esteem often feel that they are failing or constantly disappointing others. Researchers have found a link between low self-esteem and poor school performance, truancy, and criminal behavior.

A sense of self-worth is critical to children's development. Research has shown that the level of self-esteem that is developed in childhood changes little over time. Children who feel good about themselves are more likely to show enthusiasm for learning, form friendships, and make healthy choices. Having a sense of self-worth can help children deal with life's frustrations and disappointments as well as its successes.

SECTION 1-2 Review and Activities

Reviewing the Section

1. Explain why early childhood is considered the most important period for brain development.
2. What are the five characteristics of child development?
3. Compare the major theories of Erikson and Freud. How are they alike and different?
4. Explain what is meant by "nature" and "nurture." Why do scientists believe that they work together to influence development?
5. Identify the six stages of adolescent and adult development, and choose one to explain in detail.
6. How can positive *self-esteem* help a child?

Observing and Interacting

Think of a time when your self-esteem was especially high.

1. Describe what took place.
2. What steps could you take to maintain a strong sense of self-worth? You may need to do some additional research to find out. Researching some of the development theorists may be a good starting point.

Observing and Interacting with Children

Child development comes to life when you observe children in action. Learning how to observe children is an important skill for teachers, parents, and other caregivers. Sandy uses her observation skills when she babysits. She is constantly learning about how children grow and develop from what she sees. Sandy uses the information from her observations to learn more about her own babysitting methods.

Objectives

- Explain why observation is important in the study of child development.
- Compare subjective and objective interpretations.
- Evaluate four methods of observation, and give examples of situations in which they might be used.
- List specific guidelines to follow when observing young children.

Key Terms

subjective
objective
running record
anecdotal record
frequency count
baseline
developmental checklist
interpretation
confidentiality

Why Observe Children?

While you can learn a great deal from reading about children, observing them is even more helpful. Observing offers you the chance to see children as individuals, meeting the challenges of development in their own ways and in their own time.

Observing young children and interpreting their behavior are skills that take time to learn. Developing these skills will bring to life what you learn in this course.

You'll see how one stage leads to the next, for example, as an infant learns to sit up, then pull up, then stand alone, and finally walk. Caregivers who are familiar with the various stages of development can help and encourage children as they progress.

Observing an individual child will acquaint you with his or her unique personality. If you get to know a child, you will be able to tailor activities to that child's needs. Caregivers who are careful observers often can identify children who may have disabilities or require extra care. Children developing slowly can be evaluated and treated. Researchers have found that children whose special needs are spotted and treated early do better over the long term.

Finally, observing children provides caregivers with useful feedback. Watch how children respond to your attempts at guiding their behavior, and you'll see how successful your methods are. If you stick to what works, you will be more effective at earning children's cooperation and trust.

How to Observe Young Children

Knowing how to record what you observe and analyze it later will give you insight into children's development. Observing means more than just watching. It means following certain steps so that your observations will be useful.

Objective Versus Subjective Observations

When observing, you must learn to separate fact from opinion. Compare the two observations of the same event in Fig. 1-6.

Observation A is **subjective**—it relies on personal opinions and feelings, rather than facts, to judge the event. From reading the observation, it is hard to tell what really happened between Ethan and Cody. The observer in this example recorded an opinion about how Ethan felt.

An **objective** record is factual, and leaves aside personal feelings and prejudices. The observer describes only what was actually seen and heard. Observation B is objective.

Subjective observations are based on the false assumption that the observer knows what is going on in the child's mind. Subjective observations can be misleading. Ethan might not have been acting selfishly; instead, he might have had an earlier agreement with Cody about taking turns. He might be angry because Cody isn't holding up his end of the bargain. Subjective observations don't record facts, so they are hard for others to use. A teacher who knew that Ethan was generally shy at school would probably prefer to hear the objective facts presented in Observation B. The teacher might interpret Ethan's behavior as a sign of growing self-assertion: Ethan might not be behaving appropriately, but the teacher might be pleased that he is sticking up for himself.

Writing objective observations takes practice. An observer can note that a child smiled or laughed, for example, but should avoid saying that this means the child is happy. That is an interpretation. Remember to record only what you see and hear, without making judgments, whenever you are observing.

Types of Observation Records

While there are many ways to observe children, four methods are particularly useful:

- **Running record.** When observers create a **running record**, they write down everything observed for a set period, such as 15 minutes. This method is useful for observers who are just getting to know a child or group of children. A running record is also appropriate when you are concentrating on a certain area of development, such as social interaction.

Fig. 1-6 Examples of Observations

Observation A

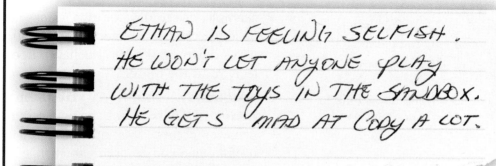

ETHAN IS FEELING SELFISH. HE WON'T LET ANYONE PLAY WITH THE TOYS IN THE SANDBOX. HE GETS MAD AT CODY A LOT.

Observation B

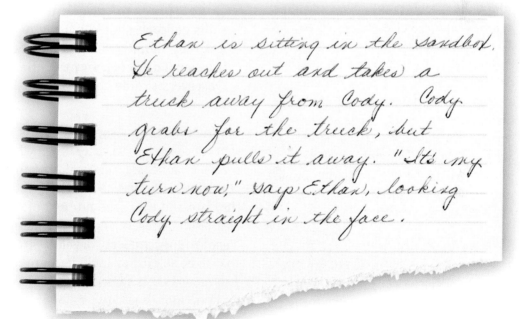

Ethan is sitting in the sandbox. He reaches out and takes a truck away from Cody. Cody grabs for the truck, but Ethan pulls it away. "It's my turn now," says Ethan, looking Cody straight in the face.

Observations can be subjective or objective. What are the differences you see between these two observations?

Sam teaches at a child care center. He has fifteen children in his care and one assistant. Occasionally, Sam asks his assistant to lead the group so that he can observe. He is amazed that no matter how often he observes the children in this way, he never fails to discover something new, something he couldn't see if he was leading the class.

Today while observing, Sam notices that Maggie has problems interacting positively with her classmates. She grabs toys, draws on other children's papers, and says hurtful things. Sam knows Maggie is often involved in spats with her classmates. Usually the stories of who did what become so complicated that Sam simply helps both children work it out together.

Now that Sam has been able to carefully observe several examples of Maggie's behaviors, he can try to understand the cause. Does she lack good social skills? Might she be trying to get her classmates upset on purpose? If so, why? Sam's attempts to understand and help Maggie will help her classmates as well.

▶▶ PERSONAL APPLICATION

1. Have you ever observed children in a school setting? If so, what types of behaviors did you observe? If not, what might you look for?
2. If you were a teacher in that setting, how would you use the information you gathered?

- **Anecdotal record.** An **anecdotal record** is similar to a running record in that the observer can concentrate on a specific area of development, such as adjustment to a new child care center. The time is not limited, however. For example, every day for two weeks an observer can use an anecdotal record to write down how a child behaves upon arriving at the center.

- **Frequency count.** A **frequency count** is a tally of how often a certain behavior occurs. This kind of record is useful when you are trying to change an unwanted behavior. First, the observer finds a **baseline**—a count made before any steps are taken to try to change the behavior. As attempts are made to change the behavior, additional frequency counts can be made. The observer can then determine whether the methods are working.

- **Developmental checklist.** A list of skills children should master, or behaviors they should exhibit at a certain age, is called a **developmental checklist**. Observers simply check off the skills or behaviors they see.

When making observations, it is important for observers to write down what they see as it happens. If they wait, they may forget details. Begin each record by recording the date and time, the number of children and adults present, and their names and ages. Young children develop so quickly that it is helpful to include months when you record their ages. A child of two years and one month is quite different from one who is two years and eleven months of age. The record should also note the setting (school or home, for example) and exactly where the observation occurred (on the jungle gym, for example). See Fig. 1-7.

Fig. 1-7 **Observing young children is an important way to learn about child development.** Why do you need to have a specific focus or purpose for an observation?

How to Act While Observing

There are two different ways you can observe young children: formally and informally. A formal observation might be something you set up with a child care center or a family. An informal observation is one where you don't make yourself so obvious—like observing at the mall. When you make informal observations, you will have to estimate the ages of the children you observe. Avoid making quick judgments about children, since you are only getting glimpses of their abilities and behavior.

Whether you observe children formally or informally, you don't want to be noticed. When you observe children, it is generally important to try to blend into the environment as much as possible and avoid calling attention to yourself. If your presence affects the children's behavior, it may not be possible to gather objective information. Sit or stand slightly outside the area where the children are, and be ready to take notes. Make sure you clearly understand your observation assignment before you have begun and noted the basic information.

Children are naturally curious, and they will want to find out who you are and what you are doing. Answer questions honestly but briefly. Avoid asking questions, which will encourage conversation. If the children need to be persuaded to return to their activities, you might say, "I am writing a story about how children play. If you go back to playing, I can write about you in my story."

Take Notes During an Observation

When you are observing children, things happen very quickly. Here are some tips for taking the kind of notes that will be useful for later analysis:

- **Know your purpose.** Before you do your observation, define the purpose of your observation. Ask yourself what you are supposed to observe.

- **Identify the *when, where, who,* and *what.*** Take note of the physical features of the setting. Who is there? What activities are going on? Make a record of the time and place of the observation, and be specific.

- **Be descriptive.** You can use words and phrases to capture the moment. Think of it as giving a picture of what you see.

- **Make comparisons.** Look for similarities and differences. If you are watching groups of children, evaluate what each group is doing. If you are focusing your observation on one child, how do his or her skills compare to those of another child of the same age?

- **Uncover the data.** Record as much factual information as you can, focusing on the evidence at hand.

If you are observing specific children, note not only what they are doing but also what evidence you see of learning taking place.

- **Review and clarify.** At the end of your observation, read through your comments, make clarifications or corrections, and add any additional notes. It is important to review your notes while the observation is still fresh.

YOUR TURN

Preparation. You are watching a group of children to record their social interactions. How might you prepare your paper in advance to help you complete all the aspects of your observation?

Health & Safety

Keeping Children Safe: An Observer's Role

Children often don't have the judgment or skills to realize that they are in danger. If, while observing, you see a child in a dangerous situation, you must intervene and get help from a teacher or caregiver. For example, you are observing children at a child care center and you notice a young toddler putting a small puzzle piece in his mouth. You should get help from a child care worker immediately. Getting help quickly often prevents more harm from coming to children.

Check-Up

Give an example of a situation in which you would intervene immediately. Choose a situation in which you would alert the child's caregiver or teacher.

In some situations, you may need to interact with a child. For example, if you are updating a developmental checklist you might need to find out how well a child can catch and throw a ball. You could pull the child aside for a few minutes and test for these skills. The "Health and Safety" feature on this page describes other reasons you might need to step in.

Using Observations

Before you use your observation, you will want to finalize your paperwork. In many cases, you will need to transfer your notes to another sheet or use your notes to write a longer observation record. Some observations are kept in a child's file for future reference, so make sure that your final report appears neat and professional.

Simply having a half-hour's running record of a child's behavior is of little use unless you analyze it. This is called **interpretation**. In recording the information, it was your job to remain objective. Now it's time to form and express ideas about what you saw. Your study of child development will help you do so.

Anyone who observes children and interprets information about them must maintain **confidentiality** (CON-fuh-den-shee-AL-uh-tee). This means that you protect the child's and family's privacy. You may share your information only with the child's parents or your child development teacher. It isn't ethical to discuss children outside of class.

Remember that most observations are brief. For this reason, your interpretation may not be accurate. You are just developing your observation skills, so your interpretation may not match that of a professional. For these reasons, you must avoid discussing the child's behavior with your friends. Comments such as "Lauren is spoiled" or "Caleb is a slow learner" might lead to gossip that could hurt the child or the family.

If you have questions or concerns about a child you observed, discuss them only with your child development teacher.

SECTION 1-3 Review and Activities

Reviewing the Section

1. Give at least two reasons why observing children is helpful to your study of their development.
2. Offer a one-sentence example of a *subjective* observation and a one-sentence example of an *objective* observation. Explain why one is more useful than the other.
3. Describe situations in which subjective and objective observations would each be appropriate.
4. What basic facts should an observation record include?
5. Give an example of a situation in which you would have to stop being just an observer and interact with the child you're observing.
6. Discuss how you would go about interpreting a child's behavior. What steps would you take after recording your information?

Observing and Interacting

With a partner, observe one child for at least ten minutes. One of you will write a running record of all the behaviors observed. The other will write an anecdotal record, concentrating on one aspect of behavior, such as attitude toward learning. How do your records differ? How are they similar?

Actor in Children's Theater

Actors have been performing in plays since ancient times, but theater for children is relatively new in this country. In contrast, Chinese and Russian actors have a long history of performing children's theater. Children often respond more candidly to theater than adults do. If they love a play, the performers will know it! This is one reason many actors find performing for younger audiences especially rewarding.

▸ Job Responsibilities

Because it can be hard to find steady work, many actors hold other jobs. Actors are artists, and their task on stage is to bring characters to life. Acting can be physically demanding and requires good coordination skills as well as stamina.

▸ Work Environment

Theater companies perform one or more shows daily, so the hours are long. Many companies take their shows on the road, so travel is common. Some performances take place on holidays.

▸ Education and Training

Aspiring actors can take small roles in community theater productions, take acting classes, or pursue a performing arts degree at a college or university.

▸ Skills and Aptitudes

- Ability to memorize lines
- Creative instincts
- Ability to improvise
- A love of entertaining others
- A wide range of skills such as singing and dancing

WORKPLACE CONNECTION

1. **Thinking Skills.** How could a children's theater actor benefit from taking a child development course?

2. **Resource Skills.** If acting interests you, what can you do to gain experience?

CHAPTER 1

Review and Activities

SECTION SUMMARIES

- By studying children, you can learn why they act the way they do, discover why caregivers are an important influence, and enjoy children more. (1-1)
- As more has been learned about children over the years through research, attitudes and practices have changed. (1-1)
- Experiences in the first years of life promote rapid brain development. (1-2)
- Heredity and environment both impact development. (1-2)
- Self-esteem—a feeling of self-worth—influences a person's ability to face life's challenges. (1-2)
- Through observing children you can learn things you can't learn from a book. (1-3)
- There are several types of observation methods. Whichever is used, observations should be conducted carefully and kept confidential. (1-3)

REVIEWING THE CHAPTER

1. How do teens have an influence on children? (1-1)
2. Identify the two benefits of studying children that you think will be most important to you and explain why. (1-1)
3. Compare the significance of the theories of Skinner and Bandura. (1-2)
4. Name the five characteristics of child development and give examples of each. (1-2)
5. Which do you think affects development more, heredity or environment? Explain your answer. (1-2)
6. Prepare a chart showing the stages of the human life cycle after childhood and each stage's developmental tasks. (1-2)
7. How does self-esteem affect development? (1-2)
8. Imagine that someone said, "You don't need to observe children. You were one yourself—didn't that teach you what you need to know?" Write how you would explain the importance of observing children. (1-3)
9. If you are trying not to talk with the child you are observing, how can you find out the child's age? (1-3)
10. Give an example of a kindergartener's behavior that might be assessed through a frequency count. (1-3)

THINKING CRITICALLY

1. **Drawing Conclusions.** What are some reasons why adults might feel freer as they settle into middle age?
2. **Making Inferences.** Why might the conclusions of scientific studies, such as those in child development, perhaps later be viewed as invalid?

MAKING CONNECTIONS

1. **Writing.** Imagine that you are campaigning to prevent children from being put to work. Write a letter to the editor of a newspaper arguing against child labor. Use your child development information to support your arguments.

2. **Social Studies.** Research childhood in any other country. What is expected of children in that society? What do parents believe their responsibilities are toward their children?

APPLYING YOUR LEARNING

1. **Analyzing Behaviors.** Create a chart that shows attitudes and behaviors associated with high and low self-esteem. In small groups, use your charts to develop a checklist of questions that could be used to evaluate a person's level of self-esteem.

2. **Interpersonal Skills.** A three-year-old child consistently tries to get in the front of the line for the playground slide. What observations can you make about the child's behavior? What are some ways to help this child learn to take turns?

3. **Researching Theories.** Search online for more information about one of the child development theorists mentioned in this chapter. Compile your findings in a report.

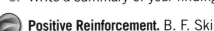

Learning from Research

1. Choose one of the research findings listed below to investigate.
2. How can your research findings affect your interactions with young children?
3. Write a summary of your findings.

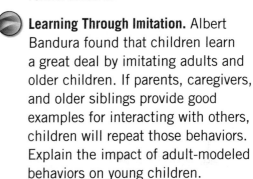

Positive Reinforcement. B. F. Skinner found that when children are given *positive reinforcement,* or a reward they like for a behavior, they will repeat that behavior. If they receive *negative reinforcement,* or a response that they don't like for a behavior, children will stop the behavior. Contrast the use of positive and negative reinforcement.

Learning Through Imitation. Albert Bandura found that children learn a great deal by imitating adults and older children. If parents, caregivers, and older siblings provide good examples for interacting with others, children will repeat those behaviors. Explain the impact of adult-modeled behaviors on young children.

Stages of Development. Erik Erikson believed that people pass through eight stages of development. Each stage involves a conflict. For example, in the period between "industry and inferiority," children must cope with demands that they learn new skills. Otherwise, they may feel a sense of failure. Explain the impact of Erikson's stages on child development theory.

2 The Challenges of Parenting

Thoughtful Reading:

As you read this chapter:

- Make a prediction about what you are reading.
- Visualize what you are reading and describe it.
- Reflect by writing four sentences about what you have read.

Section 2-1
Parenting and Families

Section 2-2
Teen Parenthood

Parenting and Families

Parenting is a job unlike any other. Parents work hard but are not paid. They are on call 24 hours a day, seven days a week. Fortunately, being a parent can bring unique rewards. Parents cherish those times when the family seems especially close or has fun together. They watch with pride as their children become adults, ready to start independent lives of their own. For most parents, the joys outweigh the challenges.

Objectives

- Explain how a knowledge of child development can help parents.
- Identify and describe Galinsky's six stages of parenthood.
- Describe the challenges and rewards of parenthood.
- Develop a self-assessment for judging a person's readiness for parenthood.
- Explain how good resource management skills relate to parenting.

Key Terms

parenting
emotional maturity

Parenting: A Learning Process

Parenting—caring for children and helping them grow and develop—is complicated. It requires understanding a child's needs and meeting those needs. It also requires good judgment.

- There are times when parents need to know when to help and when to let children try a task on their own—even if it means they will fail. Children have to learn how to bounce back after setbacks and try again.

- Parents need to decide when to encourage children to try different activities. It is important to allow children the freedom to explore their own likes and dislikes. While parents want to avoid pushing children into activities they are not yet ready for, they need to encourage children to engage in enjoyable activities.

- The skills parents need change as their children get older. Parents must adapt their parenting skills to each stage of their children's development.

It's not just parents who need parenting skills. Anyone who lives or works with children can benefit from knowing about child development and parenting. By learning about these skills and how to apply them, people who interact with children have a positive influence on them.

Having Reasonable Expectations

"Act your age." "How old are you, anyway?" "Would you grow up?" Do these sound familiar? Many parents have made remarks like these to their children. What

Parenting Q&A

How Can I Make a Positive Difference in a Child's Life?

There are many ways to make a positive difference. If there are younger children in your family, you are probably well aware that they pick up cues on how *they* should act by watching *your* behavior. Make sure you are sending appropriate, positive cues! Treat others with kindness and consideration. Make time in your day for younger siblings. Pay attention to what's important to them and to what's going on in their lives. Ask about school, friends, and activities they're involved in. Support them by attending their school or sporting events.

Some neighborhood children, especially those with single or working parents, can benefit from having a teen friend. You might be able to help

a new, struggling reader by loaning your old books and listening to him or her practice reading. You might work on a craft project with a group of neighborhood children.

Volunteer work and paid jobs also provide opportunities to work with children. Volunteer jobs might include tutoring at an after-school program or helping with a Scout troop, religious education class, or a sports program. Some hospital child care centers welcome summer volunteers. Possible paid jobs include babysitting, working as a mother's helper, teaching swimming or dance lessons, and working as a camp counselor. Whatever the job, don't be surprised if interaction with children enriches your own life as much as it makes a difference in the children's lives.

THINKING IT THROUGH

1. As you were growing up, were there teens who made a positive difference in your life?
2. Describe a time when you were a positive influence for a child.
   How might working with children as a teen prepare you for parenthood one day?

adults often don't realize is that children usually do act their age. It is adults who don't always know what to expect from children at different ages. That is why understanding child development is so important. Having reasonable expectations for children is an essential first step in effective parenting. For example, Kristin grew increasingly frustrated when two-year-old Adam said "no" to everything. Then her mother told her that children usually go through a negative stage at that age. Relieved that Adam would outgrow the behavior, she was better able to handle it.

Even when parents and caregivers know what children are like at different ages, it is important for them to remember that each child is an individual. Some children learn to walk earlier than others. Some need extra encouragement in making friends. Some children immediately respond when given directions, while others may need gentle reminders and more time to complete tasks. It's important to accept and respect the differences among children. See Fig. 2-1.

Fig. 2-1 **Knowing how children develop helps caregivers have reasonable expectations about what a child can do.** How can this help prevent some parenting frustrations?

Developing Parenting Skills

Can parenting be learned? Absolutely! There are many different ways to gain these skills. Classes in child development and parenting are good sources of information and help. Hospitals, schools, community groups, and private instructors offer courses or workshops on parenting skills. Some courses are targeted to age-related issues of children. Others may focus on certain behavioral or health challenges.

Still other courses may focus on helping a parent cope with difficult personal issues that can affect family life, such as financial stress and relationship problems.

There are other ways to build parenting skills, too:

- Read reliable books, magazine articles, and online information about parenting.
- Gain experience working with or caring for children, informally or as a job.
- Ask the advice of family and friends who have parenting experience.
- Observe parents and children wherever possible.

Take advantage of as many learning opportunities as possible. Because each child is different, ideas or techniques that work with some don't work with every child. By learning different strategies, you are more likely to find one to match a particular child and situation.

The Stages of Parenthood

In her book, *Between Generations: The Six Stages of Parenthood*, psychologist Ellen Galinsky describes how parents typically develop through their interactions with their children. Her findings were based on interviews with parents.

Stages of parenthood Galinsky identified are important because they describe how parents themselves develop and change as their children do. When parents are aware of these stages, they can be more prepared for parenthood. By being prepared, they are more likely to be effective parents, leading happier, more satisfied lives. Figure 2-2 below summarizes Galinsky's six stages.

The Changes That Parenthood Brings

When a new child joins the family—whether by birth, remarriage, or adoption—parents feel great joy. Some also feel that a great burden has been placed on their shoulders. The decision to become a parent is a serious one. Being a parent radically changes a person's life and creates new long-term responsibilities.

When Dominique and Ross adopted baby Tanya from Russia, they were thrilled. The

Fig. 2-2 Galinsky's Stages of Parenthood		
Stage	**Time Period**	**Parents' Tasks**
Image-Making	Pregnancy	• Begin to imagine themselves as parents
Nurturing	Birth to Age 2	• Become emotionally attached to child • May question relative worth of other priorities
Authority	Age 2 to Ages 4–5	• Determine rules • Clarify role as authority figure
Interpretive	Ages 4–5 to Age 13	• Rethink their role as parents • Decide what knowledge, skills, and values child needs
Interdependent	Adolescence	• Establish boundaries • Find disciplinary methods appropriate for teens
Departure	Child Leaves Home	• Evaluate their parenting

waiting was finally over. Everything felt right. At first, Dominique's parents stayed with them for a week to help with the baby's care. Life with Tanya seemed relatively easy. However, after the baby's grandparents left, the challenges and responsibility of raising a child began to feel overwhelming.

Tanya hardly slept at night, so Dominique and Ross didn't get much sleep, either. Ross dragged himself to work each day feeling exhausted. Meanwhile, Dominique was left with the baby—feeling alone and uncertain. They both wondered how so many people managed to raise families. It was clearly not as easy as it seemed.

Fig. 2-3 **Raising a baby takes patience and dedication. It also brings rewards.**

The Challenges of Parenthood

Many new parents say that having children changes everything. Becoming a parent does present many challenges. However, as the "newness" of parenthood passes, many parents adjust to the changes and find that their lives are enriched by the presence of a child.

New Responsibilities

Once people become parents, they can no longer think of only their own needs. They have considerably less time for themselves. They must always consider their child's needs—first and foremost. Children need physical care, financial support, love, and guidance.

First-time parents can feel overwhelmed by these new responsibilities. Family and friends can help in many ways, from watching the baby while the parent goes shopping to just listening or helping solve a problem.

Communities have many resources too, including religious organizations, government agencies, and support groups.

Changes in Lifestyle

New parents have to adjust to major changes in their daily lives. Caring for a child—especially a newborn—takes a huge amount of time and energy. A newborn needs to be fed every few hours—day and night. In addition, babies must be diapered, played with, comforted, and supervised for safety. See Fig. 2-3.

With children of any age, parents have limits placed on their personal freedom. They have less time to spend with friends. Instead of unwinding after work, they have to fix dinner, spend time with their children, bathe them, and put them to bed. While it can be disappointing, sometimes plans have to be changed. Dennis and Shawna had looked forward to his brother's party for weeks, but had to cancel at the last minute. Their toddler was sick, and they didn't feel right leaving him with a babysitter.

Parents are better able to adjust to these changes if they prepare for them. Taking classes and caring for the child of a friend or relative can help give an idea of what it is really like to live with a child. There is no substitute for the experience of parenting, but making an effort to learn about child development and parenthood can make the demands of the job less surprising and unsettling.

Emotional Adjustments

Parenthood requires many emotional adjustments. Going through so many changes is stressful in itself. On top of that, many parents feel conflicting—and sometimes difficult—emotions, such as:

- **Fear** of not being a good parent.
- **Frustration** at the loss of personal freedom and the addition of new responsibilities.
- **Worry** over money matters.
- **Jealousy** of the baby and the attention he or she gets from the other parent, friends, and relatives.
- **Depression** due to exhaustion or to the physical changes of pregnancy and birth.

Parents can feel confused and troubled by these negative emotions, but, in time, most get over these rough spots. They learn that these emotions are common among new parents, and they learn how to handle them. If these feelings persist, however, it's important to tell someone and get the help needed.

Changes in Relationships

When people become parents, they are likely to notice changes in how they interact with each other and with other family members. This is especially true for first-time parents.

The birth of a baby is an exciting time. Sometimes, though, parents may feel overwhelmed by concerns, negative emotions, and lack of sleep. They may argue with one another. Having patience and trying to be understanding can reduce the danger of frustration boiling over into anger. One key to getting past such trouble spots is for the couple to communicate effectively.

A new baby changes the relationship between the new parents and their own parents. Most grandparents feel love and joy of their own and want to spend time with their grandchild. Some may offer to help with child care or household chores. Some freely share

Fig. 2-4 **Some parents change their work situation once they have a child.**

Fig. 2-5 **Raising children is especially rewarding when parents can share in the excitement of reaching special goals.**

advice based on their own parenting experience. Sometimes, however, offers of help or advice cause friction. New parents may resent advice that they perceive as criticism. At the same time, the grandparents may feel hurt if their suggestions or offers of help are rejected.

On the other hand, new parents often find that having a baby brings them closer to their own parents. Understanding the sacrifices and work involved in parenting, they now appreciate their own parents more.

Employment

Having children can have an impact on careers. Some parents stop working or cut back on their hours to care for their children. People who were accustomed to working overtime and weekends or traveling for their jobs may be less willing to do so once they become parents.

Some employers have policies to help working parents. They may offer flexible hours, part-time work, or work-at-home options. Others have child care facilities at or near the workplace. See Fig. 2-4.

The Rewards of Parenthood

While parenthood is a lot of work and responsibility, it brings many joys as well. There is nothing quite like a baby's first smile or hearing a toddler say, "I love you, Daddy." Parents feel happiness, pride, and love that they have never felt before.

By helping children discover the world, parents often see it with new eyes themselves. Having children can also enrich an already strong marriage. Finally, raising children can give parents a great sense of accomplishment. Getting a first-hand look at the growing and learning process of a child is very rewarding for a parent. As shown in Fig. 2-5, graduation is one of these times.

Making Decisions About Parenthood

People considering parenthood should take a close look at what parenting involves. This includes looking at their own emotional maturity as well as health considerations, financial concerns, and how skilled they are at managing personal resources.

Emotional Maturity

To handle the changes and demands that parenthood brings, a person needs **emotional maturity.** People who are emotionally mature are responsible enough to consistently put someone else's needs before their own needs. They are secure enough to devote their attention to a child without expecting anything in return. They can control their temper when an infant cries for hours on end or a child breaks a favorite possession. They are able to handle being constantly on call.

Prospective parents should take an inventory of their own emotional maturity. Are they truly equipped to handle the challenges of parenthood? If there are doubts, it is best to put aside the desire for a child until they are convinced they have the maturity it takes to raise one.

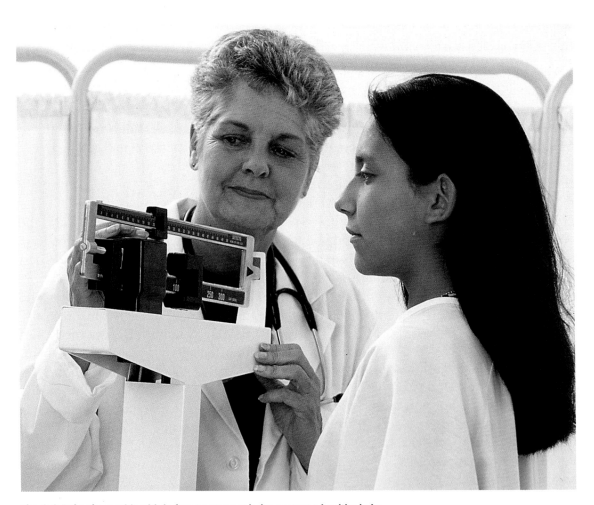

Fig. 2-6 **Being in good health before pregnancy helps assure a healthy baby.**

Desire for Parenthood

Some prospective parents hope that having a child will help them solve some personal problems, such as low self-esteem or marriage difficulties. Not all the reasons for wanting children show a real readiness for parenthood.

Health Considerations

Before pregnancy, it is best for both prospective parents to have a medical checkup. Some medical problems can affect the health of a baby or the parent's ability to care for a child. The age of the prospective mother is another consideration. If she is under 17 or over 35, pregnancy is riskier for both her and the baby.

Pregnant teens, for example, are less likely to have proper nutrition, gain adequate weight, and seek good prenatal care than older expectant mothers. These issues can adversely affect the teen's health as well as her baby's. Women over 35 are at greater risk for developing diabetes and a potentially dangerous type of high blood pressure during pregnancy. There are also higher rates of birth defects among children born to older mothers. See Fig. 2-6.

Financial Concerns

Raising a child is expensive. It requires the financial resources to pay for clothes, health care, food, equipment, and other expenses. Before deciding on parenthood, couples should consider the costs of having a child during the first year and in the years ahead. It is not unusual for couples to have to change their way of life in order to meet these expenses.

If both prospective parents work, they need to think about what they will do after the baby arrives. Will one parent stop working to care for the baby? If so, how will they cope with the drop in family income? If both parents continue working, how will they arrange for reliable child care and have the money to pay for it? See Fig. 2-7.

Resource Management Skills

Parents need to use the resources they have available wisely to provide for their families. Money is just one resource. Time, skills, and energy are others. Because most resources are limited, applying a process for managing them can help parents do their best for all family members. There are five key steps to good resource management:

1. **Set goals.** Decide what is important and then turn those things into personal goals. For example, Sara considered preschool an important learning opportunity for her son, Eli. Although the family budget was tight, her goal was to send him to preschool when he was four years old.
2. **Identify resources.** Make a list of the resources needed to achieve the goal. Sara checked into the cost of a local preschool program. She had some savings that could pay for part of the tuition, but would need to work part time to earn the rest.

Fig. 2-7 **Parents must learn to handle money wisely.** What are some expenses that must be considered when planning to meet a child's needs?

3. **Make a plan.** Decide how to use the identified resources to achieve the desired goal. Sara realized she needed more money to afford Eli's preschool. Because that was two years away, she figured out how much she would need to save each month to have the tuition by the time Eli turned four. To achieve her goal, she also started looking for a job she could do at home.

4. **Put the plan into action.** Start working toward the goals using the steps outlined in the plan. Sara started watching her neighbor's kindergartener after school. Before the money could be spent on other things, she put it into a savings account.

5. **Reevaluate from time to time.** Step back and take stock of progress. Are more or different resources needed? Was the goal achieved? What are some new goals to work toward? That August after Eli's fourth birthday, Sara was pleased to be able to take him to preschool. She had already decided on a new savings goal—saving for a family vacation.

SECTION 2-1 Review and Activities

Reviewing the Section

1. Why do parents have to change the way they parent over the years?
2. What are three ways to build parenting skills?
3. Identify and describe three of Galinsky's stages of parenthood.
4. Describe the adjustment that people face when they become parents.
5. What is *emotional maturity*? Why is it vital to parenting success?
6. Name two steps to good resource management, and tell how these steps relate to parenting.

Observing and Interacting

Think of a time when you experienced something for the first time.

1. What were some of the challenges you faced? What were some of the rewards?
2. List the steps you had to take to accomplish the task.

Teen Parenthood

A very real consequence of sexual activity is pregnancy. While teen pregnancy has declined somewhat, nearly two million U.S. teens become pregnant each year. Once a teen finds out she is pregnant, she and the baby's father must make responsible plans and carefully consider their options. For many reasons, the teen years aren't the best time to have a baby. However, with support from friends and family, motivation, realistic expectations, and hard work, teen parents can succeed at parenthood and raise a healthy, happy baby.

Objectives

- Distinguish between sexuality and sexual activity.
- Summarize what people consider when making responsible decisions about sexual activity.
- Describe the possible consequences of sexual activity.
- Evaluate the challenges of teen pregnancy.

Key Terms

sexuality
hormones
sexually transmitted disease (STD)
abstinence
paternity
confidential adoption
open adoption

Teen Sexuality

Sexuality and sexual activity are not the same thing. **Sexuality** refers to a person's view of himself or herself as a male or female. It involves more than physical maturity or the ability to be sexually active. Sexuality includes how people feel about themselves and their sense of responsibility for and understanding of other people and their feelings. Thus, sexuality has physical, intellectual, emotional, and social aspects.

Individuals show their sexuality in various ways. They show their maleness or femaleness in their attitudes, in the way they walk, talk, move, and dress.

During adolescence boys and girls begin to develop a sense of their own sexuality. Chemicals in the body called **hormones** dictate changes as teens become sexually mature. These changes often have an emotional, as well as physical, impact. They can cause mood swings and emotional ups and downs.

Social development also shifts into high gear during puberty. There are attractions to new friends. Relationships with family members often change as teens become more independent, want to spend more time with friends, and sometimes question parental authority.

In the midst of these changes, messages about sexual activity seem to be everywhere. Music, television, radio, movies, and advertising often convey the messages that sexual activity is a necessary part of sexuality. Peer pressure, the influence of friends and other teens, may come with the mind-set of "Everyone's doing it—why aren't you?"

With such pressures, it's easy to lose sight of what is important. Dating—as couples or in groups—can help teens discover which qualities or characteristics in another person they find desirable. They can learn more about building relationships. Dating can be fun without the hazards of becoming sexually active. See Fig. 2-8.

Fig. 2-8 **Dating doesn't have to include sexual activity. It can be just getting to know someone.** What can people learn about one another by going on dates?

Making Responsible Decisions About Sexuality

Decisions related to sexuality are too important to be made casually. They deserve careful consideration, because they have serious lifelong consequences.

It can be helpful to discuss decisions about sexuality with other people. While teens often turn to friends for advice, most teens can benefit from talking to a responsible adult. Trusted adults—a parent, an older family member, a religious leader, an adult friend, a school counselor, or a doctor—can be valuable resources.

Values and Sexuality

One role of families is to pass on the family's and society's values. These are the principles they consider important—the rules they use to guide their lives. They include trust, self-respect, respect for others, commitment, and loyalty. Family can help answer questions about sexuality based on values. For example, who am I as a male or female? How should I treat people of the opposite sex? How can I balance old friendships and new relationships with someone of the other sex?

Values help shape each person's response to these questions.

By drawing on their values, teens can choose to build a sense of their own sexuality without becoming sexually active. A look at the consequences of sexual activity shows the wisdom of this decision.

The Consequences of Sexual Activity

Teens who become sexually active often regret that step. Sexual activity can cause serious problems, including diseases and emotional and social stress. With these problems comes a loss of self-respect.

Sexually Transmitted Diseases

A **sexually transmitted disease**— STD (sometimes called a *sexually transmitted infection*—STI) is spread from one person to another by sexual contact. It is estimated that one in five people in the United States has an STD—and 25 percent of new cases of STDs are infected teens. All STDs are preventable. The only way to completely prevent STDs is through **abstinence**— avoiding sexual activity altogether.

Some STDs can be treated. Others last a person's entire life. The chart, Fig. 2-9, describes the most common STDs.

AIDS

One STD has deadly results. Acquired immune deficiency syndrome (AIDS) is caused by the human immunodeficiency virus (HIV). HIV can remain in a person's blood for many years before it develops into AIDS. Although AIDS doesn't directly kill its victims, it allows other diseases to invade the body. Eventually, one or more of these diseases usually causes the person's death. There is no known cure for AIDS at this time, although research is continuing.

Pregnancy

Another possible consequence of sexual activity, of course, is pregnancy. Pregnancy causes many problems—and they affect both the teen mother and father. When Tracy became pregnant, she and Parker married. Parker took a job, planning to finish high school after a year. Before that could happen, their car broke down and he needed to work overtime to pay for the repairs. Soon after, Tracy became pregnant again. By the time their second child was a year old, Parker had been out of high school almost three years. He didn't feel like going back—although he knew that he could earn more with a diploma or a GED.

Teen pregnancy creates four types of problems:

- **Health risks.** Pregnancy presents special health risks for both a teen mother and her baby. A teen is not yet physically or emotionally mature and may not be ready for the extra demands of pregnancy. Teens are also at greater risk than adult women for experiencing serious medical complications from a pregnancy. These include significant iron deficiency, which can deprive the baby and mother of oxygen, and a dangerous condition called *toxemia*, which can lead to the premature delivery of the baby.

  A female teen has high nutritional needs. If she becomes pregnant and there is no extra emphasis on nutrition, her body may not be able to provide the nutrients that she and her growing baby both need. In addition, a critical period of development occurs before most mothers are even aware they are pregnant. Babies of teen mothers are more likely to be born early and have low birth weights. These conditions are linked to other problems, including learning difficulties.

Fig. 2-9 Sexually Transmitted Diseases

Some of these symptoms may indicate other diseases or conditions as well. Anyone who experiences any of these symptoms should be tested so that his or her exact condition can be determined and treatment begun.

Disease	Symptoms	Treatment	Effects
Chlamydia (kluh-MIH-dee-uh)	Pain when urinating. Women may feel abdominal pain, nausea, and low fever. Note: Some people show no symptoms.	Can be cured with antibiotics.	Can cause sterility—the inability to have children.
Genital herpes (JEN-uh-tuhl HER-pees)	Open sores on sex organs, which go away in a few weeks. Painful urination, fever.	There is no cure. Symptoms can be treated.	Can cause brain damage or death if passed to the baby during childbirth.
Genital warts	Small growths on the sex organs, which cause discomfort and itching.	There is no cure, but a doctor can remove them.	If left alone, they may become cancerous.
Hepatitis B (hep-uh-TY-tuhs)	Causes flu-like symptoms.	There is no cure, but a vaccine is available. It can prevent the disease.	Can lead to liver disease or cancer.
Gonorrhea (gon-uh-REE-uh)	Burning, itching, and the discharge of liquids from infected areas.	Can be treated with antibiotics.	Can cause sterility in females. A baby born to an infected mother can suffer eye damage.
Syphilis (SIF-uh-luhs)	In early stages: sores on the sex organs, fever, rash, and hair loss.	Can be cured with antibiotics.	Can cause insanity and death.
AIDS	Caused by the human immunodeficiency virus (HIV), which can remain undetected in the bloodstream for many years.	Once HIV develops into AIDS, there is no cure. Some medicines can delay the development of AIDS.	AIDS lessens immunity to other illnesses, which cause death.

- **Education.** It is important for pregnant teens to complete their schooling—at least through high school. Unfortunately, many drop out of school. Nearly half of the teen mothers who leave school—even those who planned to return—never finish their education. Without a high school diploma, it is hard to find a job, particularly one with a salary that will support even a small family. See Fig. 2-10.

  Pregnant and parenting teens can work with school counselors and social service agencies to find solutions to such problems. These resources can help find ways to provide care for the babies while their parents take classes. Graduating needs to be a high-priority goal for young mothers and fathers.

- **Financial problems.** Most teen parents experience financial problems. To help reduce the health risks associated with teen pregnancy, teen mothers need good medical care. That care costs money, as does childbirth. Teen parents who keep their child must provide food, clothing, housing, and health care. This continues for at least 18 years.

  Even when teen parents don't marry, both are legally responsible for providing financially for their child. If the father chooses not to stay involved with the child, it is especially important to establish **paternity**. This legally identifies the man as the father and his responsibilities toward the child. A medical test can prove paternity.

  For many teen couples, the financial burden of child care expenses becomes overwhelming. In order to accommodate financial needs, a young couple's goals and plans for the future need to be changed. This tension can lead to arguments. The stress from financial issues can spill over from their relationship to other family members and even to the baby.

- **Emotional and social stress.** Adjusting to new relationships can cause great stress. So, too, can changes to old relationships. Teen parents may miss their old friends but find that they no longer have much in common with them. Teens who enjoyed sports or other after-school activities may find that they have to give them up or cut back. Teen parents realize quickly that their lives have changed in profound ways.

Deciding to Abstain

"It can't happen to me." Countless teens have thought that—and they were wrong. The threat of STDs is very real, as is the threat of pregnancy. There is only one guaranteed way of avoiding these problems—abstaining from sexual activity.

Fig. 2-10 **The birth of a child prompts many teens to drop out of school.** Why is it so important to stay in school?

Fig. 2-11 **The decision to abstain can be a difficult one.** Besides pregnancy, what are some other hazards of becoming sexually active?

This is a decision that each individual needs to take time to think through thoroughly before encountering a sexual situation. It's much more difficult to reach the decision to abstain in a moment of passion. Once a person has decided to abstain, it's important to stick to the decision, remembering why the decision was made in the first place.

Fig. 2-12 **If a teen thinks she may be pregnant, she should see a doctor.** What are some of the early symptoms of pregnancy?

When Teen Pregnancy Occurs

Teens can and do get pregnant—although many have trouble believing and acknowledging the symptoms when it happens. A girl who fears she might be pregnant may try to ignore the possibility. However, for her health and the baby's health, it is essential that she confirm the pregnancy and get good prenatal care as soon as possible. See Fig. 2-11 and Fig. 2-12.

A teen who suspects she is pregnant should discuss her concerns with someone close—a parent or other family member, her boyfriend, a trusted friend, or a special teacher or counselor.

Balance School and Parenting

Balancing school with other activities and responsibilities is always a challenge. For teen parents, the balancing act is even more demanding. However, with planning, help, and management skills, teens can succeed both as students *and* as parents. Here are some suggestions.

- **Manage time.** Get the baby into a routine. When the baby sleeps, do homework. If possible have someone watch the baby so you can study at the library.

- **Prioritize assignments.** Tackle your most important assignments first. Break big projects into smaller steps. Use study halls to finish as much work as possible at school.

- **Find help at school.** If your school offers a child care center, use it. Guidance counselors can help students adjust to changes. Tutors can help boost grades and confidence.

- **Involve relatives.** Ask willing family members to babysit. Other relatives may be able to help in other ways.

- **Reach out.** Family doctors, religious leaders, counselors, and social workers know a lot about community services. They can offer advice about parenting, child development, and time management, too. As professionals, they keep personal information confidential.

- **Connect with others.** Find a peer group for support. Teen parents are not alone.

- **Think ahead.** By setting goals, teen parents can work toward the future.

YOUR TURN

Time Management. Identify at least ten time management techniques all teens could use. Compile a class list and choose three to try to incorporate into your life.

Once her pregnancy has been confirmed, a teen can begin to make plans. Her partner should be involved, too. After all, the father has rights and responsibilities, and the pregnancy will have a long-lasting effect on his life, too. Family can be a good resource for support and guidance at this time as well. In order to make responsible plans, they will have to carefully consider the options and their consequences.

Weighing the Options

When faced with pregnancy, teens have several options. Each one must be considered seriously. There are several factors that must be considered for each option.

- **Single parenthood.** Having a tiny baby to cuddle and love can seem very appealing. Indeed, it can be rewarding to care for someone who is so small, helpless, and dependent. However, caring for a newborn is a huge responsibility, and becoming a parent is a lifelong commitment.

  All these responsibilities can be draining for an adult—and even more so for a teen. Not surprisingly, many teen parents suffer from burnout or depression and need to find support.

  Teens considering single parenthood need to be realistic and ask a lot of questions. How much help—emotional and financial—can one teen parent expect from the other? From his or her own parents and other family members? A teen considering single parenthood must guard against romanticizing the situation. For example, a teen who isn't interested in marriage during the pregnancy is unlikely to change his or her mind after the birth. Parents, counselors, and other adults can help teens develop realistic expectations for their own situations as single parents.

LOOKING AT REAL LIFE

Derrick never thought he could feel this much love. When Sandra said she was pregnant, Derrick was scared. He admits that he thought about running away. They were only eighteen! But he knew the baby was his responsibility. The baby needed a father. He didn't want to leave Sandra; he loved her and wanted to build a life with her. Now that Derrick Jr., or DJ, is part of their lives, Derrick couldn't be happier. Their life is not easy. To make ends meet, Derrick works nights and Sandra works days. Derrick takes care of DJ during the day and sleeps when he can. Derrick knows that someday their hard work will pay off and they will be able to enjoy spending more time together as a family.

▸▸ **PERSONAL APPLICATION**

1. Describe how this example presents both challenges and rewards that a teen father may face.
2. Imagine how Sandra's life would have been impacted if Derrick had chosen to try not to take responsibility for their child. Explain how their lives would have been different.

- **Marriage.** Marriage has many benefits for both the teen parents and their child. At any age, however, marriage isn't easy. It takes a special commitment, responsibility, and work.

  Married teens face a special set of problems. As the initial excitement of marriage wears off, the strains of responsibility and the new social situation set in. Teens who marry because of a pregnancy face an additional problem. They have to adjust to parenthood at the same time they are adjusting to being married.

Married teens who meet these challenges can find themselves with a strong and rewarding relationship. Having two people share the child care lessens the work of each. Finally, married teens can build a caring home for a child.

• **Adoption.** Adoption is another option for pregnant teens. In adoption, the birth mother and father legally give up their rights and responsibilities for raising the child to another family.

The decision to place a baby for adoption is not easy. Teens considering adoption need to think it through carefully, because it's a permanent decision. Many teens choose adoption because they feel they are giving their child an opportunity for more care, guidance, and love than they are able to provide at this stage of their lives. Placing a baby for adoption for these reasons is an act of love. However, even when the decision is made with careful thought and consideration, it is an emotional decision.

There are two types of adoption. In a **confidential adoption**, the birth parents don't know the names of the adoptive parents. In an **open adoption**, birth parents and adoptive parents know something about each other. There are different levels of open adoption based on how much information is shared with both sets of parents.

Thinking It Through

Parenthood is a challenging and rewarding time of life, but it can be especially challenging for teens. When people wait to have children until they are physically, emotionally, and financially prepared, it helps assure a bright future for both the children and the parents.

SECTION 2-2 Review and Activities

Reviewing the Section

1. What is the difference between *sexuality* and sexual activity?
2. How do values influence a person's decision to become sexually active?
3. What are the possible consequences of being sexually active? How can these consequences affect a teen's life?
4. What pressures can affect a teen marriage?
5. Distinguish between confidential and open adoption.

Observing and Interacting

Suppose a seventeen-year-old unmarried friend confided to you that she suspected she was pregnant. How would you respond? What advice would you give your friend?

Parent Educator

Sometimes parents want to do more for their children outside of the home and classroom. Parent educators are informal teachers that help with child development. Most parent educators are parents themselves. They can provide assistance, instruction, and materials in academic areas such as language, reading, and math. Parent educators can demonstrate techniques to enhance parent-child growth.

▸ Job Responsibilities

One primary responsibility of a parent educator is to educate parents about resources available to them. They provide referral information, along with working with children to promote academic development.

▸ Work Environment

Depending on the area in which they specialize, parent educators have the flexibility of working in schools, community centers, and hospitals. Some parent educators visit the homes of the people they work with.

▸ Education and Training

Most parent educators are parents, and most have bachelor's degrees with an emphasis in early childhood education or psychology. Some hold master's degrees in fields such as social work or developmental psychology.

▸ Skills and Aptitudes

- Interpersonal communication and language skills
- Knowledge of early childhood behavior, characteristics, and development
- Effective parenting skills
- Mentoring abilities
- Record-keeping abilities

WORKPLACE CONNECTION

1. **Thinking Skills.** Why would it be beneficial for a parent educator to also be a parent?

2. **Resource Skills.** Where can you find more information on being a parent educator?

2 Review and Activities

SECTION SUMMARIES

- Parenting is a learning process, and offers many challenges and rewards. (2-1)
- Before deciding to become parents, it is important to seriously consider one's readiness for parenthood. (2-1)
- Parents need effective resource-management skills. (2-1)
- Decisions related to sexuality are too important to be made casually. (2-2)
- Abstinence is the only guaranteed way to prevent pregnancy and sexually transmitted diseases. (2-2)
- Teen pregnancy is not ideal, but with motivation and support, teen parents can be effective parents. (2-2)

REVIEWING THE CHAPTER

1. Explain why having reasonable expectations is important prior to becoming a parent. (2-1)
2. Identify three challenges of parenthood. Identify three rewards. (2-1)
3. How can resource management skills help a parent, and ultimately a family? (2-1)
4. Name two negative consequences of sexual activity. (2-2)
5. Identify two common STDs and how they are treated. What are possible long-term effects? (2-2)
6. What is paternity? (2-2)
7. How can teens benefit by abstaining from sexual activity? (2-2)
8. What should a teen do if she suspects she is pregnant? (2-2)
9. What is the difference between confidential and open adoption? (2-2)

THINKING CRITICALLY

1. **Analyzing.** Knowing that you hope to spend as much time as possible with your child, how might you approach a career path? Why?
2. **Synthesizing.** Galinsky presents six stages of parenthood. How do parents develop during each of these stages?
3. **Applying.** A teen has decided to abstain from sexual activity until he is married. How might he explain this decision to his girlfriend?
4. **Analyzing.** What are the worst reasons for wanting to become a parent?

MAKING CONNECTIONS

1. **Writing.** Write a scene for a play in which a young couple discusses whether to start a family at this time. You can end the scene with either decision, but make sure both characters show good communication skills as they talk about the issue.

2. **Math.** Find an ad or visit a store that sells diapers. Find the size that would fit a 15-pound baby and record the price of a box. If a baby uses seven of these diapers a day, how much would it cost per day to diaper the baby? How much per week? Per year?

APPLYING YOUR LEARNING

1. **Developing an Evaluation.** Using the information on pages 54–57, "Making Decisions About Parenthood," work in a group to develop questions for a self-assessment test for potential parents. Include at least 25 questions and a scoring system.

2. **Healthy Babies.** Use the Internet to find out more about the health concerns related to teen pregnancy. What can teens do to ensure that they will remain healthy and deliver a healthy baby?

Learning from Research

1. Choose one of the following research claims to investigate.
2. How can this research finding be useful to parents and other caregivers?
3. Summarize what you have learned about teens and pregnancy.

Teen Mothers Are Less Likely to Complete High School. Many teen mothers are unable to continue attending high school once they have a baby to care for. Statistics show that the dropout rate is higher for teen mothers than for other female teens. Identify programs that help teen mothers stay in school while they raise their child.

Pregnant Teens Are More Likely to Deliver Prematurely. A teenager's body is still developing. This fact increases the likelihood of premature birth. Research other possible pregnancy complications that may occur in teens.

Pregnant Teens Are Less Likely to Receive Prenatal Care. Some pregnant teens do not receive prenatal care throughout pregnancy. One reason for this is that prenatal care can be expensive, and teens have no way to pay for that care. Identify programs that are available to help teens pay for quality prenatal care.

3 Building Strong Families

Thoughtful Reading:

As you read this chapter:

- What do you wonder? Note each of your questions and the page number.
- What opinions do you have about what you read?
- Summarize what you read in a short paragraph.

Section 3-1
Families: The Context for Parenting

Section 3-2
Effective Parenting Skills

Families: The Context for Parenting

Within every culture, there are families. A family can be different from group to group. In some cultures, "family" includes only parents and children. In others, aunts, uncles, grandmothers, and grandfathers are important parts of the family. Families are the foundation on which every human culture is built.

Objectives

- Describe the functions of the family.
- Identify the basic needs of children and how parents meet those needs.
- Compare different types of family structures.
- List the stages of the family life cycle.
- Describe trends that affect families.
- List sources of support that are available to families.
- Identify ways people can help build strong families.

Key Terms

nuclear family
single-parent family
custodial parent
blended family
extended family
legal guardian
foster children
intergenerational

Functions of the Family

Each day after band practice, Marisa picks up her little brother from the after-care program at his elementary school. When they arrive home, they share a snack and then read, do homework, or watch television together. While this may sound routine, underlying Marisa's actions is the key to the importance of family. Family members help meet each other's basic needs.

Meeting Basic Needs

Everyone needs food, clothing, and shelter. Families need to make sure that these basics, along with health and safety needs, are met. Family members care for one another when they are sick. They teach children basic rules about safety, such as how to cross the street safely.

Strong families meet emotional and social needs, too. Family members have the chance to love and be loved, to care and be cared for, to help others and receive help. Living in a family teaches how to share, take turns, and work to achieve common goals.

Strong families meet their members' intellectual needs as well. The family is a child's first teacher, teaching concepts such as language, numbers, and colors. The family's expectations, support, and involvement in learning affect success in school.

Preparing Children to Live in Society

Author Robert Fulghum wrote a book called *All I Really Need to Know I Learned in Kindergarten*. His point was that children learn the basic rules of life in kindergarten, such as: "share everything," "play fair," and "don't hit people." Fulghum could have said the same thing about family. By learning how to live with others in the family, children are prepared to live with others in society.

Adults teach children what is important to people in their society. They pass on these values in three ways:

- **Through example.** When adults treat children and each other with respect, they show children how to behave.

- **Through communication.** Parents who explain to toddlers why hitting is wrong, or talk to teens about respecting others' individuality, are passing on values through communication.

- **Through religious training.** In houses of worship, of whatever faith, children learn the principles of what is right and what is wrong as taught by people of that faith.

Each society has its own way of life revealed through its art and music, its cooking and clothing styles, and its views of work and play. Families introduce children to their society's way of life.

Adults teach children about the traditions of their society, such as holidays. Adults also explain and demonstrate acceptable

Learning Through PLAY

Play as a Family

One of the many rewards of parenthood is being able to play again! Play is more than just a time for fun, however. It is also a great learning experience for children. Play teaches children about trust, honesty, cooperation, taking turns, following rules, counting, colors, and having fun. With so much to learn, it is no wonder children need plenty of opportunities for play. Parents can do their part by setting aside time for play and having a variety of toys and games available.

Here are some ideas for engaging in family play:

- Sing or say nursery rhymes together.
- Use puppets, dolls, or action figures for pretend play.
- Do puzzles and sorting games together.

Exactly what a parent and child play is not important. What truly matters is that families spend time together playing, learning, and enjoying each other.

Following Up

What activities and games does your family do together? Share your experiences with the class.

behavior. What kind of language is appropriate? How should children speak to adults? These and similar questions are first answered in families.

Family Structure

While each family has individual characteristics, most can be categorized as nuclear, single-parent, or blended families.

Nuclear Families

A **nuclear family** includes a mother and father and at least one child. In a nuclear family there are two parents to help raise the children. The families may differ depending on how many children there are, whether the parents work outside the home, and other characteristics.

Single-Parent Families

A **single-parent family** includes either a mother or a father and at least one child. The absent parent might have died or left after a divorce, or the parents may never have married. While single parenting presents special challenges, it can still be effective.

Raising a child alone is a demanding job. A single parent typically has little free time, since there is no one with whom to share the work or to help solve problems related to parenthood. Single-parent families usually have less income than two-parent families, and the added cost of child care for a working single mother or father can increase the challenges of parenting.

Many single parents receive help from friends or relatives. They may provide child care while the parent works. They

Fig. 3-1 **When parents remarry, what can they do to make the transition easier for their children?**

may help simply by giving the parent a sounding board—someone to talk to about frustrations, problems, or challenges, as well as rewards and successes. In the case of a divorce, many children make scheduled visits to the parent who doesn't live with them. These visits give the **custodial parent**, the one with whom the child resides, a necessary break from the challenges of single parenthood. It also preserves the relationship between the other parent and child.

Blended Families

A **blended family** is formed when a single parent marries another person, who may or may not have children. To a child, the parent's new spouse becomes a stepparent. To the couple, each child of the new spouse is a stepchild. If both spouses have children when they marry, these children become stepbrothers or stepsisters to each other. See Fig. 3-1.

Becoming a strong family unit can be a challenge for a blended family. Parents and children need time to adjust to one another. Everyone has to learn about and adapt to each other's habits, likes, and dislikes. Even topics such as how to celebrate holidays can cause conflict. Patience, tolerance for different opinions and habits, and a sense of humor can help families overcome the challenges they face.

Extended Families

An **extended family** includes a parent or parents, at least one child, and relatives other than a parent or child who live with them. For example, a grandparent may live with a nuclear family or an aunt or uncle may live with a single-parent family.

Sometimes the term *extended family* is also used to refer to family members who don't live with the core family but play important roles in the child's life.

Joining a Family

A child can join a family in many ways. In the majority of cases, a child is born into a family, or is a biological child. In other cases, a child joins a family through a legal process. A **legal guardian** is a person who is designated by a legal process to assume responsibility for raising a child.

Adoption is a legal process in which children enter a family they weren't born into. The adopted child has the same rights as any biological children those parents have. See Fig. 3-2.

Fig. 3-2 Adoption pairs children who need parents with those who want to build a family.

Giving New Parents a Break in Finland

New parents need all the help they can get from family, community, and society. In Finland, one parent (mother or father) has the right to 10 months' fully paid leave from work after the birth of a child, or couples can split the time. Even a Prime Minister took two weeks off from work after the birth of his child.

Researchers have discovered that longer, paid parental leaves are associated with lower rates of infant death, but they aren't sure why. When parents are paid while on leave, they can usually maintain their standard of living. When a parent stays home with a child, he or she may be more likely to take the child for regular doctor's visits. Finally, women who take paid leaves may be more likely to breastfeed. Research has shown that breastfeeding decreases infant mortality rates. Longer leaves may, however, make it harder for parents with children to advance in their careers.

Investigating Culture

1. Parents in this country do not get parental leaves that are as long. What effect do you think this has on children?
2. In industrialized nations, women are the parents who most often take parental leaves from work. If parents were given the right to even longer paid leaves, what impact might this have on women in the workforce?

In the past, children were matched closely with the families adopting them. Adoption agencies looked carefully at the child's and parents' race, ethnic and religious background, and physical characteristics. Today the emphasis is more on finding a good home rather than a home with parents who match the child in some outward ways.

At some time or other, most adopted children ask why their biological parents gave them up for adoption. They may feel rejected and need reassurance. Showing adopted children that they are loved and wanted helps them realize that they truly belong in the family.

Bree is a typical nine-year-old girl. She lives with Mr. and Mrs. Mason, her foster parents. When Bree was seven, her biological mother and father weren't able to care for her, so they allowed her to be adopted. Bree lived with several families before she came to stay with the Masons. Many families who want to adopt are looking for a baby. Sometimes it's more difficult for an older child to find an adoptive family. Moving from family to family and home to home has been hard for Bree. Sometimes she has had to change schools and make new friends. Bree has lived with the Masons for a year now, and they are seeking to formally adopt her. Nothing would make her happier.

▶▶**PERSONAL APPLICATION**

Do you know anyone who has foster parents? What were his or her experiences like? Were they similar to or different from your own?

Some children join a family as **foster children**. These children typically come from troubled families, or those in difficult circumstances. Foster parents care for foster children, giving them a home while their parents solve their problems, or sometimes until a permanent adoptive home can be found. Adults apply to the state government to become licensed foster parents. They receive payment to help with the expense of caring for the child.

The Family Life Cycle

There are many differences between families, but there are many similarities, too. Families go through a series of six stages called the family life cycle.

- **Beginning Stage.** In this stage, a couple works to establish a home and their marriage relationship.

- **Parental Stage 1.** This is the expanding stage. The couple prepares for and adjusts to parenthood.

- **Parental Stage 2.** This is the developing stage. As children grow, parents work to meet children's changing needs and help them develop independence.

- **Parental Stage 3.** This is the launching stage. Children gradually leave home to support themselves. Parents help their children adapt to life on their own.

- **Middle Age.** In this stage, a couple renews their relationship and prepares for retirement. If they had children who have left home, this is called the "empty nest" stage.

- **Retirement.** In this stage, the couple stops full-time work and adjusts to having more free time.

Of course, families differ in how they experience these stages. Families spend different amounts of time in the same stage. Some may return to a stage after they had left it. The Bensons, for instance, adopted a baby after their last child moved out of the home. This put them in the expanding stage all over again. Changes such as divorce or remarriage have an effect on the cycle too. See Fig. 3-3.

Fig. 3-3 **Each stage in the family life cycle presents special challenges and rewards.**

Trends Affecting Families

All families are affected by trends in the society around them. These trends may support or put additional pressure on families. Some current trends include mobility, an aging population, fluctuations in the economy, workplace changes, and the impact of technology.

Mobility

Today many adults move from the community where they were raised. As a result, many families lack close, supportive connections with extended family. Grandparents, aunts and uncles, and cousins may be spread out across the globe. In this situation, families must rely on themselves, neighbors, and close friends for support and assistance.

When an extended family is far away, it takes time and effort to remain close. However, many families value a strong family connection and find it is worth an extra effort to maintain bonds. Such connections help build traditions and reinforce the importance of family history.

Aging Population

People are living longer than they used to. Advances in medicine and nutrition have contributed to the longer average lifespan. As a result, more people find themselves caring not only for children, but also helping and caring for aging parents. This can create stress as well as opportunities for **intergenerational** interaction—relationships between older and younger age groups. A related trend is that more grandparents are helping to raise their grandchildren because their children aren't able to parent on their own. See Fig. 3-4.

Economic Changes

Many families struggle to make ends meet. This is particularly true in times of economic downturn. Finances are often the primary reason why both parents in a nuclear family are employed. This trend has had a significant impact on families. Many are smaller than they used to be, and some couples are having their first child later in life. The rise in two-income families has also added to the demand for child care, including before- and after-school care for school-age children.

Workplace Changes

The working world is changing rapidly. Many companies employ fewer workers. The types of available jobs are shifting. For example, the number of manufacturing jobs in this country has declined, while jobs in health and technology have expanded. Such changes affect families. After a layoff, a parent may be unemployed for a time. New jobs available may pay less or may not have health insurance as a benefit.

In a changing work environment, there's a continuing need to learn new skills. Many workers invest time and money in additional education. When Marianna's mother

Fig. 3-4 What are some benefits of having a grandparent involved in a child's life?

Fig. 3-5 **It is important for parents to find help when they need it. Sometimes just having someone to listen to you or give another point of view helps a parent get through a difficult time.**

needed to learn more advanced computer skills, she decided to take a night course. Marianna was happy for her mother, but she also missed having her at home.

Another trend is the growing number of people who work out of their homes. This arrangement has both benefits and drawbacks for families.

Technology

Advances in technology continue to make family life both easier and more complicated. With cellular phones and the Internet, there is a growing need to be sure children use these tools safely and within reasonable limits. Critics claim that these innovations tend to isolate people from one another. Linda felt that way when she took her niece on a shopping trip. Thirteen-year-old Ashley passed the time in the car by punching buttons on her cell phone, text-messaging her friends at home and playing games. Linda had hoped they would spend the day talking to each other.

Sources of Family Support

With all the demands and stresses put on families, parents need to have a support system to help get them through rough spots and sometimes just everyday life. Talking to a sympathetic friend, relative, or coworker helps. These same people may be willing to watch the children so a parent can have a short break.

When stress causes health or relationship problems, it is helpful to consult a professional such as a family doctor, counselor, social worker, or religious advisor. Seeking additional sources of support can help a parent get through the more difficult times. See Fig. 3-5.

Some families may feel as though they don't have a support system, but there are people and services ready to help. Besides communicating with friends, neighbors, coworkers, and relatives, a parent can talk to caregivers, teachers, religious leaders, or school counselors. A local hospital or place of worship may provide lists of support groups, and local family service agencies are also available for support. By using one or more of these sources of support, parents can help strengthen family relationships and relieve some of their stress.

Building a Strong Family

Families aren't just a group of individuals who happen to be related. They are a group where all members can feel accepted and safe. In families, adults and children can learn and grow together. Families provide children with a sense of belonging. They provide emotional support, nurturing, protection, and security. As families spend more time together, they form stronger bonds and traditions. Families also give children their first lessons in values and acceptable social behavior; lessons they will carry with them throughout their lives.

Developing family relationships isn't an easy task, especially when families are spread out. However, just living together under one roof doesn't guarantee smooth relationships. When individuals need to work together as a group, there are going to be differences of opinion, problems, and conflict. Each family member can help make a family stronger.

Strong families have a variety of characteristics. Family members spend time together, share responsibilities, and work together to resolve differences. They listen to each other with an open mind and allow each person to express opinions and share feelings. Families share goals and values and also show appreciation for each other. These are vital lessons for life. See Fig. 3-6.

Forming Traditions

Spending time together—whether doing special activities such as a family vacation or following everyday routines such as eating dinner together—is the foundation to building a strong family. These activities or ways that families do things are what become family traditions. Families that form many traditions form strong ties with each other.

Traditions provide a sense of continuity, understanding, and appreciation that brings a family together. They are also opportunities for families to have fun times and establish good memories that will carry them through tough times. Traditions provide a family with time together to communicate, heal from a loss, adapt to new events, affirm family values, celebrate, and connect to the past.

There are three types of traditions that families form:

- **Celebration traditions** are activities or events formed around special occasions, such as holidays and birthdays.
- **Family traditions** include events and special activities created to fit a family's lifestyle, such as vacations or family meetings.
- **Patterned family interactions** are actions that are centered on the daily routines in life, such as dinner time and bedtime.

Traditions are the threads of life that create a sense of togetherness and appreciation in families. It is the "little things" done together that not only create strong family ties, but also memories to last a lifetime.

Fig. 3-6 **Even when family members live far away, many make spending time together a priority.**

Shared Values

Values are the beliefs held by an individual, family, community, or society. They include feelings about the importance of acceptable behavior in terms of honesty, respect, responsibility, friendliness, kindness, and tolerance. The values that parents pass on to their children are largely shaped by the values that their parents passed on to them as children, their own life experiences, and their religious beliefs. Society also helps shape a family's values. For example, it is wrong to lie, steal, and hurt others. Societies rely on these values to keep order and to function effectively.

In a strong family everyone is committed to one another. The family is built on a foundation of shared values. For example, when parents and other caregivers teach children the value of honesty, they foster that trait in their children. When a problem or conflict arises, their children have learned to be honest and that the family will not judge or criticize them. Their children then communicate more openly, and, as a family, they work together to solve the problem.

With a strong foundation of shared values, children feel more at ease. They experience more success when they venture away from the family to meet new people, take on challenges, and become valuable members of society.

Handling Family Conflict

There is no way around it: Families argue. Sometimes they bicker over seemingly minor issues such as what show to watch or whose turn it is to take out the trash. Other times the conflicts are more serious. Many families may have conflicts about money or curfews, for example.

No matter what the issue—big or small—families need to know how to resolve their differences. Parents and children need to try to understand each other's viewpoints and feelings. When families can resolve their conflicts successfully, the whole family is stronger.

Here are some tips for handling conflicts effectively:

- **Keep cool.** When emotions run high, people say and do things they don't really mean. It is always a good idea to calm down before trying to resolve a conflict. Physical conflict, such as hitting, should never be a part of teen or adult relationships.

- **Be an active listener.** Even in the middle of a conflict it is important to listen carefully to each other's concerns without immediately judging them. It helps to repeat back what was heard in an effort to avoid confusion about feelings and attitudes. Often people are so concerned about what they will say next that they fail to really listen. Active listening encourages problem solving and better communication.

- **Use positive body language.** People who make eye contact and sit up straight send the message that they are truly listening and do care about the other person. When appropriate, a pat on the back or a hug can do wonders to help break the tension and make the other person feel loved and more at ease.

How would you rate your family's conflict resolution skills? Which technique could you use to improve your own?

SECTION 3-1 Review and Activities

Reviewing the Section

1. What are two functions of families?
2. Give an example of how families meet each of a child's basic needs—physical, intellectual, social, and emotional.
3. Analyze the similarities and differences among the four family structures described.
4. Identify the stages of the family life cycle.
5. Identify three trends that affect families.
6. Identify a trend that might negatively impact a family. Where might the family turn for help?
7. Describe at least three ways that people can build strong families.

Observing and Interacting

Think of two people you know who come from a different family structure than your own. What would you consider the advantages and disadvantages of each type?

Effective Parenting Skills

Having a child makes a person a parent, but it doesn't necessarily make a person an effective parent. Parenting skills don't always come naturally or easily. For most people, parenting is a learning process—one that occurs each and every day. Parents must work to develop the skills required to meet their children's needs, guide their behavior, and help them develop positive relationships. It takes time to figure out what works for each parent, each child, and each family. Sometimes effective parenting means learning from mistakes and trying to do better each day.

Objectives

- Identify the basic types of children's needs.
- Describe the three parenting styles and some characteristics of each.
- Give examples of effective techniques for encouraging appropriate behavior.
- Explain how to set limits and why they are important.
- Identify ways of dealing with inappropriate behavior.
- Explain the importance of consistency when guiding children.

Key Terms

deprivation
parenting style
guidance
self-discipline
conscience
positive
   reinforcement
negative
   reinforcement
time-out

Meeting Children's Needs

Maria wakes up to Brett's cries at 4:30 in the morning. She changes his diaper, warms a bottle, and feeds him. Although she is ready to go back to sleep, Brett is wide awake and wants to play. She puts him in his bouncy seat on the floor and talks to him about his colorful toys. After an hour, Brett seems sleepy, so Maria rocks him a bit and returns him to his crib. Just as she is ready to go back to bed, Maria hears, "Mommy?" Two-year-old Karenna is awake and ready for a fresh diaper herself. Unfortunately, Maria won't be going back to sleep, so she goes to the kitchen instead to make breakfast and start the day.

Parents often must put their own needs aside to take care of their children. The list of parenting tasks is seemingly endless. In addition, all children are different, with individual characteristics and needs. Ask a group of parents what it takes to raise happy, healthy, well-adjusted children, and you hear many different opinions.

Children's needs can be grouped into three categories:

- **Physical needs.** These include food, clothing, and shelter. See Fig. 3-7.

- **Emotional** and **social needs**. Fulfilling these needs means making sure that children feel safe, loved, and cared for. In turn, they learn how to make friends and work with other people.

- **Intellectual needs.** All children need their minds stimulated and the opportunity to learn about the world and become educated. By fulfilling this need, parents and caregivers help prepare children for life as independent adults.

Unfortunately, some parents can't or don't meet all of their children's physical, emotional, social, or intellectual needs. These children tend to lag behind other children in their overall development. They suffer from **deprivation**, or a lack of the critical needs and an encouraging environment that are essential for physical, emotional, and intellectual well-being. Some people mistakenly believe that deprivation and poverty are the same things. This is not true. Deprived children can come from wealthy or poor families—or anywhere in between. Money isn't the only factor; what matters most is whether a child's basic needs are being met.

Physical Needs

The most important and obvious task of parenthood is meeting children's basic physical needs. Parents are responsible for providing nourishing meals for their children. For clothing, children don't need the latest and most expensive styles, but they do need to be clean and dry and comfortable. In addition, children should have a safe, clean place to call home.

Parents are also responsible for the health and safety of their children. They schedule regular health checkups and provide care when children are sick or hurt. Ensuring children's safety includes

Fig. 3-7 **Meeting children's physical needs includes providing nutritious food that will fuel their growing bodies.** Why can't small children live on junk food?

Fig. 3-8 **Children need plenty of opportunities to play.** How does play help children develop social skills?

using a car seat and/or seat belt while in a vehicle, making sure toys are safe and appropriate for the child's age, and eliminating hazards in the home so that children can safely explore their environment. In addition, parents should always make an effort to know where their children are, whom they are with, and what they are doing.

Emotional and Social Needs

A major parenting goal is to raise children who will become happy, independent adults who can support themselves. They may even go on to raise children themselves. To become independent, children need to learn how to function in the world and get along with others. For example, children need to learn how to show respect for figures of authority and concern for people who are hurt. Children learn these lessons through relationships with people who nurture them.

Nurturing children means giving them plenty of love, support, concern, and opportunities for enrichment. These factors help to meet children's emotional and social needs and help prepare them for their own adult lives. Parents and other caregivers can also aid in children's emotional and social development by removing as many barriers as possible that prevent children from exploring the world on their own, and yet still keep them safe. For an infant, this means providing a safe environment to explore. For a preschooler, this might mean her playing in the sandbox without worrying about whether clothes will get dirty. With reassurance and freedom to explore, a child develops a healthy emotional well-being. See Fig. 3-8.

Parents can show children love and support in many different ways—a hug, kiss, or a smile. Unfortunately, some parents have difficulty showing affection for their children. They may be embarrassed or feel that affection will make their children "too soft." When a parent fails to recognize their accomplishments, children may feel insecure and worthless. Over the course of life, they may have a difficult time forming healthy relationships, because they didn't learn how to give and receive love.

Communicating and giving time and attention show children love and support. Actively listening is one way to show children that they are important. See Fig. 3-9.

Some parents become overprotective or over attentive, or both. They shower a child with too much attention, too many toys, and too many treats. They may try to shield the child from all unpleasant experiences. This can harm children, too. Children learn from trial and error. They need to make mistakes so they can learn from them. They must also learn to deal with the ups and downs of life.

Fig. 3-9 **Children need plenty of love and attention.**

Intellectual Needs

 With parents as their first teachers, children begin learning at birth. Researchers have found that with stimulation, the brain undergoes tremendous growth during a child's first years. In the past, it was thought that a baby couldn't learn much in the first few months of life. Researchers now know that infancy can be a time of constant learning if a baby is given opportunities to learn. Early on, their lessons come through touching, tasting, and looking at the objects around them. Parents can nurture this early learning by playing with their children and filling their environment with interesting sounds, smells, sights, and things to touch. When parents stimulate young children in these ways, they help encourage brain development and a lifetime love of learning.

As children grow older, their intellectual needs also expand. They want to play games and explore more of their environment. Parents meet these intellectual needs by continuing to provide opportunities for play and learning. These can be as simple as playing ball in the park or borrowing books from the library.

Learning to read and enjoying books are keys to intellectual development. Sharing books together can begin at birth. Infants simply enjoy the sound of the reader's voice. As they grow a bit older, they enjoy the pictures and story, and soon learn that the words on the page have meaning. Sharing books with children helps foster a love of books and a joy for reading. It also helps them learn about the world around them.

It is a myth that children need a lot of expensive toys. Everyday objects and experiences with nurturing adults can provide great opportunities for learning. Allowing children to explore in a safe environment is the best way to get children ready and excited about learning. When their intellectual needs are met at an early age, children are better prepared for school. See Fig. 3-10.

Parenting Styles

How parents and other caregivers care for and discipline children is known as their **parenting style**. Effective parents use a style they feel comfortable with—one that matches their personality and values. For this reason, no one parenting style is considered "right" or "best," and no one style works best with all children. In addition, parents often need to adapt their parenting style somewhat as each child grows and changes.

There are three main styles of parenting:

• **Authoritarian.** An authoritarian parent believes children should obey their parents without question. The parent tells a child what to do, and the child's responsibility is to do it. When rules are broken, the authoritarian parent typically responds quickly and firmly.

• **Assertive-Democratic.** In this style, children have more input into the rules and limits of the home. Learning to take responsibility is important, so children are given a certain amount of independence and freedom of choice within those rules. When rules are broken, the assertive-democratic parent believes children learn best from accepting the results of their actions or by problem solving with the child to find an acceptable punishment.

• **Permissive.** In the permissive style, parents give children a wide range of freedom. Children of permissive parents may set their own rules. They are

Fig. 3-10 **Reading together helps children develop a love of reading. Older children can practice reading with a parent.**

encouraged to think for themselves and not follow trends. Permissive parents typically ignore rule breaking.

Few parents follow just one style at all times. A parent may use a more authoritarian style on some issues—say, where health or safety is involved—and be more assertive-democratic on others, such as clothing or hairstyles. Parents also may change their style as children age. They may feel that before children become teens, they need firm rules, but that as teens they should be allowed the freedom to make more of their own choices.

Fig. 3-11 **Learning to share toys is a difficult lesson for children to learn.**

Guiding Children's Behavior

Amy was frustrated because Jenny, age four, never put her toys away. She tried reminding Jenny, scolding her, and even banning television until the toys were picked up. Nothing seemed to work. She didn't know what to do.

Whether it is putting toys away, getting along with a sibling, or saying please and thank you, acceptable behavior doesn't come naturally to children. They need to be taught what is acceptable, what isn't acceptable, and what is expected of them. As children grow, they develop minds of their own and test limits. Doing so helps them to learn about the world and their place in it. See Fig. 3-11.

Guiding children's behavior can be both the hardest and the most rewarding task of parenting. For years, Cara felt as though she was constantly reminding her children to get along with each other and showing them effective ways to settle their disputes—without results. Then one day—finally—her message seemed to click, and the two managed to settle a disagreement on their own without it escalating into a shouting match. Although the children continued to bicker, they became increasingly more effective at avoiding disputes and finding better ways to resolve their differences than arguing. Cara's guidance, patience, and persistence had paid off, and all three of them were able to benefit from it.

Understanding Guidance

Guidance means using firmness and understanding to help children learn how to behave. With effective guidance, children learn **self-discipline**—the ability to control their own behavior. They also learn how to get along with others and how to handle their feelings in acceptable ways. Guidance promotes security and positive self-esteem, and it helps children learn the difference between what is right and wrong. Very young children understand right from wrong only in terms of being praised or scolded. Gradually, they develop a **conscience**, or an inner sense of what is right. As they mature, they use this conscience to decide how to act in new situations.

Give Children Effective Directions

Parents and other caregivers often need to tell children what to do. At times children don't seem to listen, but often the real problem is lack of understanding. Here are some tips for making it easier for children to understand and follow your directions:

- **Be sure you have the child's attention.** Make eye contact. You may have to stoop down or sit beside a young child to do so.

- **Be polite.** A child will respond better if you speak politely in a normal voice.

- **Use positive statements.** Say, "Please walk," rather than, "Don't run."

- **Use specific words that the child can understand.** Say, "Be sure to keep the paint on the paper," not, "Don't be sloppy."

- **Begin with an action verb.** Beginning this way helps keep directions simple. Say, "Pick up your socks" or "Get ready for bed."

- **Give a limited number of directions at a time.** Very young children can only remember one step. Adjust the number as the child's memory improves, but remember that

fewer are easier to understand, remember, and follow.

- **Be clear.** Think in terms of the child's point of view as you decide what to say.

- **Give praise and love.** All people need to hear good things about themselves—especially young children. Praise encourages cooperation.

YOUR TURN

Guidance. Read the following direction: "Go upstairs, get undressed, take a bath, and don't waste time." Why might this be an ineffective direction? How would you word it differently so that it can be effective?

Parents can successfully guide their children in three basic ways. They can be positive role models. They can set limits and redirect their children's behavior. Finally, they can use positive reinforcement to let children know when their behavior is on the right track.

Being a Role Model

Children are great imitators. They learn best by being shown what to do rather than by simply being told what to do. Parents and others in a child's life serve as role models. Children constantly watch those around them and then imitate the behaviors they see. The old saying is true: Actions speak louder than words. That is why parents need to demonstrate at all times those behaviors they would like to see in their own children. For instance, parents who want their child to talk politely to others need to speak politely themselves.

The desire to imitate applies to all behaviors—not just the acceptable ones, or those that parents want their children to imitate. Five-year-old Mark sees his older brothers yell at each other when they disagree. It is little wonder then that Mark yells at his friends when he is upset with them. Parents need to model respect, honesty, and kindness. See Fig. 3-12.

Setting Limits

Setting limits is another way to guide children toward appropriate, safe behavior. Limits include physical restrictions, such as preventing a child from crossing the street alone. Another kind of limit is a rule of behavior: "We don't hit other people," or "we don't use that word."

Children need limits to grow into responsible adults. Setting limits helps them to understand expectations and acceptable behavior, and to develop self-control. Children of any age will test limits, but parents should be consistent in enforcing them.

Fig. 3-12 **Children adopt the behavior they see.** What positive behaviors have been modeled in your family?

In setting limits, parents and other caregivers often follow this general guideline: Limits should keep children from hurting themselves, other people, or property. Children will respect and follow guidelines if they are reasonable.

The following questions can help parents determine limits:

- **Does the limit allow the child to learn, explore, and grow?** Too much restriction hinders development.

- **Is the limit fair and appropriate for the child's age?** A toddler might be restricted to a fenced-in yard. A school-age child might be permitted to visit a friend living down the street.

- **Does the limit benefit the child, or is it merely for the adult's convenience?** Restrictions should be for the child's good, not because they fit a routine.

Children must be told what is expected of them in ways they can understand. Limits should be stated simply and briefly and in a calm, direct tone of voice. For example, "We don't throw toys," stated calmly is a simple limit that is easily understood. If a young child throws a toy, for example, he or she should be reminded of the rule and then redirected to an acceptable behavior. "We don't throw toys. You can go outside to throw a ball." Redirection is important because it helps the child to do something other than the unacceptable behavior and it suggests another, acceptable behavior. However, the redirection must be appropriate for the child's age. Infants, for example, may need to be physically moved to another, acceptable activity.

Limits must also be clear. Telling three-year-old Madeline that she can have a little snack is not a clear limit. She might not know what makes a snack "little." A better

Fig. 3-13 **Parenting involves setting various types of limits. Some must be designed to keep children safe.**

limit suggests a specific snack Madeline can have, such as half an apple.

Limits often have to be repeated each time the situation arises. Children, especially young ones, don't always remember limits from one day to the next. They may not realize that limits stated one day still apply another day. See Fig. 3-13.

With very young children, it isn't necessary to explain the reasons for expected behaviors. For a one-year-old, the instruction "Be gentle with the kitty," combined with modeling of gentle handling, is enough. Around age three, however, children begin to understand simple reasoning. Then they can understand limits that include the

Fig. 3-14 **Preschoolers are capable of learning appropriate behavior.** How can caregivers encourage that behavior?

wrong without noting what they do right. Instead of changing children's behavior, constant scolding makes them feel as though they can't do anything right. After a while, they may decide to stop trying.

Children, like all people, are more likely to change their behavior when they are praised for the things they do right. Giving children attention when their actions are appropriate is an example of **positive reinforcement**, a response that encourages a particular behavior. When children learn that an action wins attention and approval from adults, they are likely to repeat that action. Positive reinforcement can be used to help change a problem behavior and to strengthen good behavior. See Fig. 3-15.

Use these guidelines to encourage appropriate behavior:

- **Be specific.** Clearly comment on the behavior being acknowledged: "That was such a nice letter you wrote to Grandpa."

- **Comment on the behavior as soon as possible.** Recognize the behavior right away to help the child link the action and the praise.

- **Recognize small steps.** Encourage steps in the right direction. Don't wait for perfect behavior. If a child usually leaves toys all over the floor, acknowledge the effort of even putting some toys back where they belong.

- **Help children take pride in their actions.** Saying "That was hard work to get dressed by yourself, but you did it!" helps a young child feel competent.

- **Tailor the encouragement to the needs of the child.** Praise behaviors that are difficult for that child. The child who usually forgets to wash his hands should be rewarded with approval for remembering to do so.

reason for them: "It hurts the kitty when you pull his tail. If you want to play with him, you need to be gentle." See Fig. 3-14.

Once established and explained, limits should be firmly and consistently enforced. Parents who are not consistent with limits teach their children that they don't mean what they say. Children take rules more seriously if they are enforced at all times.

Positive Reinforcement

"You didn't clean your room—again." "Why do you always make such a mess?" "How many times do I have to tell you to pick up your toys?" All too often, parents remind children of all the things they do

- **Use positive reinforcement wisely.** If children are praised for everything they do, it no longer motivates them.

Dealing with Inappropriate Behavior

No matter how hard adults try to encourage appropriate behavior, children—all children—misbehave from time to time. When this happens, adults must deal with the situation appropriately and effectively.

The child's age should shape an adult's response to inappropriate behavior. A one-year-old who bites another child can be told "We don't bite," but the child cannot be expected to understand the meaning of his or her action. A four-year-old certainly understands that biting is unacceptable.

When considering how to respond to misbehavior, parents and other caregivers should think about these questions:

1. Is the expected behavior appropriate, given the child's age and development?
2. Does the child understand that the behavior was wrong?
3. Did the child do the behavior knowingly and deliberately, or was it beyond the child's control?

Unintentional Misbehavior

With children of any age, misbehavior is sometimes unintentional. A young child may drop a glass of milk that is too heavy or accidentally break something. Such unintentional actions shouldn't be punished.

Misbehavior is also unintentional if the child had no way of knowing it was wrong. For example, Ana picked a flower in the park and brought it to her father. People shouldn't pick flowers in parks, but Ana had never been told that. Rather than scolding, Ana's father simply explained that she shouldn't have done it, explaining that

Fig. 3-15 **Children should be praised for positive behavior.** Do you think it's possible for a parent to praise a child too much?

flowers in the park are there for everyone's enjoyment. He asked her to draw a picture of a flower.

Using Punishment Effectively

By guiding children's behavior, parents and other caregivers are more likely to teach a child acceptable behavior. Still, when children test the limits and misbehave, punishment—used thoughtfully and with good judgment—can be effective.

Punishment can help remind children that appropriate behavior is important and teach them that there are consequences for poor choices.

When using punishment, parents should clearly show that they disapprove of the behavior but that they still love the child. They can do this by avoiding blame and criticism. See Fig. 3-16.

The first time a child breaks a rule, parents may choose to give a warning rather than a punishment. Even a child with good self-control makes an occasional mistake. A warning reminds the child of the rule and why it is important. It also gives the child a chance to regain self-control.

Fig. 3-16 Even when being punished, children should still understand that they are loved. What types of misbehavior should not be punished?

After a rule has been broken another time, punishment is appropriate. However, the punishment given should be in proportion to and/or related to the misbehavior. Forgetting to put dirty clothes in the hamper one day doesn't call for severe punishment. In this case, a simple reminder would be sufficient. Repeated failure to stop throwing sand in the sandbox calls for more action, such as leaving the park or not visiting the park for a few days.

Negative Reinforcement

A response aimed at discouraging children from repeating an inappropriate or unacceptable behavior is called **negative reinforcement**. Several different methods can be used. They include natural consequences, logical consequences, loss of privileges, and time-out.

- **Natural consequences.** With natural consequences, children suffer from the actual result of their action. For example, suppose Kwan loses his new jacket. Using natural consequences, his parents don't replace it and he has to wear his old one.

  When a natural consequence occurs, parents should not lecture. For children, it is often difficult enough to have to live with the consequences. Nor should parents attempt to remedy a situation for their children. This defeats the purpose of the consequence. Children who are rescued from their choices will expect to be saved whenever they make poor choices.

- **Logical consequences.** Parents may choose to address a child's misbehavior with consequences that have a connection to the misbehavior. Parents often choose logical consequences when natural consequences are inappropriate. For example, when Katie colored on the table with crayons, the natural consequence—a messy table—bothered her mother more than it bothered Katie. Her mother told Katie that she was taking the crayons away for the day—a logical consequence.

Parents who use logical consequences need to be prepared to follow through. They should think about the logical consequence before giving it and ask themselves "Am I ready to do this?" After all, lack of follow-through shows children that they don't need to take their parents or their limits seriously.

- **Loss of privileges.** Sometimes using natural or logical consequences is not appropriate. If a child runs into the street, the natural consequence—being hit by a car—is far too dangerous. A parent might take away a privilege instead. This type of punishment is most effective for children age five and older. It works best if the privilege taken away is related to the misbehavior. That way, the child is likely to associate the two. See Fig. 3-17.

- **Time-out.** Another way to respond to misbehavior is with a time-out. A **time-out** is a short period of time in which a child sits away from other people and the center of activity. The purpose of a time-out is to give children a chance to calm down and regain self-control. Time-outs can be especially effective when emotions are running high and the child (and everyone else) simply needs a break. One minute of time-out for each year of a child's age is generally a good length of time.

Five-year-old Teresa, for example, continued to grab pretzels away from her playmates even after her teacher gave her a warning and redirected her to other activities. The third time it happened, her

Fig. 3-17 **Sometimes it is necessary to take something away when a child does not use the item appropriately.**

teacher immediately intervened, explained again why the behavior was inappropriate, and instructed Teresa to sit in the "thinking chair" for five minutes. After five minutes, Teresa had calmed down, and her teacher invited her to do a puzzle.

When deciding which method of negative reinforcement to use, parents and other caregivers often find that what works for one child may not be effective for another. The same method may not work every time for the same child—or for the same child at different ages. See Fig. 3-18.

Parents need to think about which method of negative reinforcement is most appropriate for the child's personality and their own values. For the method to be effective, they must also be consistent in their use of it. Ideally, the punishment should be linked to a child's age and emotional, social, and intellectual development.

Poor Disciplinary Measures

Well-meaning parents and caregivers sometimes use disciplinary methods that are less effective than others—and sometimes even harmful. Those who follow the positive discipline techniques already described in this chapter will likely find that they don't need to use the following measures.

- **Bribing.** Bribing children so they stop misbehaving can backfire. Instead of learning self-control, children learn to expect rewards for ending inappropriate behavior. Children may even misbehave on purpose, knowing that by stopping they will earn a treat or privilege. Bribing and rewarding desirable behavior are not the same things. Positive reinforcement for acceptable behavior is a more effective way to guide children's behavior.

- **Making children promise to behave.** In the process of learning to control their behavior, children naturally make mistakes. When promises are made, children may feel forced to lie about misbehavior rather than disappointing someone they love.

- **Shouting or yelling.** When children misbehave, parents and caregivers should

Fig. 3-18 **A time-out can be a good way for a child to regain self-control. How long should a time-out be for a four-year-old?**

Parenting Q&A

What Is the Controversy About Spanking?

Few parenting issues are as controversial as spanking. While it has long been a common form of discipline, it is used less often today. Some parents and caregivers believe that spanking is an effective way to punish children and teach them how to behave. Other parents feel that certain misbehaviors call for spanking, such as when children hit someone or push the limits of safety.

Most child development experts believe that there are much more effective ways to get children to behave appropriately. They argue that there are a few problems with spanking, such as:

- Spanking can physically harm children.
- Parents who spank serve as role models for hitting and other aggressive behaviors.
- Spanking doesn't teach lessons about behavior.
- Children younger than two are unable to make the connection between their behavior and a spanking.

Parents need to set firm limits and follow through with warnings, redirection, and if necessary, punishment. This helps children make a connection between their actions and the consequences. Until they develop self-control, children are motivated more by approval and the risk of losing privileges than by the fear of a spanking.

THINKING IT THROUGH

1. Do you think spanking is ever an appropriate way to discipline a child? Why or why not?
2. Why should parents discuss discipline with their child's other caregivers?

---

talk to them in a calm, reasonable voice. A loud, harsh voice can frighten young children. Older children may learn to "tune out" yelling. In addition, adults who yell aren't modeling acceptable behavior.

- **Shaming or belittling.** Parents and caregivers shouldn't ridicule children's mistakes or make comments such as "If you chew with your mouth open, no one will want to sit with you at the lunch table!"

- **Threatening to withhold love.** Statements such as "I won't love you anymore if you don't start treating your brother better" create the fear of being rejected or abandoned.

- **Exaggerating the consequences.** Parents and caregivers sometimes hastily threaten wildly impractical consequences. For example, if two children refuse to leave a toy aisle in a department store, a tired parent might say "If you don't come with me now, I'm going to leave you at the store." Such statements can not only frighten children, they can also cause a parent to lose credibility. When children see that a parent won't follow through on such exaggerated claims, they may begin to doubt that what a parent states will actually be done as a consequence.

Consistency in Guidance

Being consistent is the key to guiding children's behavior. Consistency is a matter of clearly making rules and applying them in the same way whenever the situation occurs. Consistency helps children know what is expected of them and what responses they can expect from parents.

Children lose trust and confidence in caregivers who constantly change rules or fail to enforce them in a consistent way. If parents permit a behavior one day and punish children for the same behavior the next, children will feel confused and insecure. They will pay little attention to the next limits that are set.

Consistency becomes an important issue when more than one person cares for a child. All caregivers need to agree in advance on rules and ways to enforce them. Each one also needs to be careful not to undercut the other's decisions. If caregivers don't agree, children can use the inconsistency to their advantage, playing one adult against the other.

SECTION 3-2 Review and Activities

Reviewing the Section
1. What are the three main areas of children's needs?
2. Describe the three styles of parenting and name a characteristic of each one.
3. What is one example of an effective technique for encouraging appropriate behavior?
4. How can a parent set limits? Why is it important to set limits?
5. List two ways to deal with inappropriate behavior.
6. Why is consistency in guiding children's behavior important?

Observing and Interacting
Visit a place where adults and children interact, such as a playground or supermarket.
1. What parenting styles described in this chapter do you observe?
2. What kind of guidance do you observe?
3. If you observe any inappropriate behavior by a child, how did the parent or caregiver handle it? Was the technique effective?

Adoption Consultant

Some parents cannot care for their children and decide to allow other people to adopt them. This is usually a difficult decision. Adoption consultants make it easier.

▶ Job Responsibilities

Depending on their areas of expertise, adoption consultants may visit the homes of people who want to adopt and interview them, or match birth parents to families. If they studied law, they may give legal advice or counseling. People with social work or counseling backgrounds train parents on how to adjust to having an adopted son or daughter.

▶ Work Environment

Consultants usually work within an adoption or other social service agency. Some countries allow children to be adopted by people who live in other countries, so some consultants must travel or live overseas.

▶ Education and Training

Most adoption consultants have a bachelor's degree in social work. Often they have training in counseling. Some have degrees in law and specialize in adoption. Most have experience helping protect children from abuse, neglect, and other forms of harm. In many cases, adoption consultants have adopted children themselves.

▶ Skills & Aptitudes

- Sensitivity to others' feelings
- Good communication skills
- Love of children
- Respect for cultural differences

WORKPLACE CONNECTION

1. **Thinking Skills.** What types of work experience do adoption consultants need?

2. **Resource Skills.** If you wanted to volunteer at a child welfare agency, where could you find out how?

3 Review and Activities

SECTION SUMMARIES

- Families meet children's basic needs and prepare them to live in society. (3-1)
- Nuclear, single-parent, and blended families are common family structures today. (3-1)
- Families typically follow a series of stages called the family life cycle. (3-1)
- Trends in society affect families. Sometimes they need support. (3-1)
- Children have physical, emotional, social, and intellectual needs that should be met by a family. (3-2)
- Parents should find the parenting style that works best for them and their children. (3-2)
- There are positive ways to guide children's behavior and deal effectively with inappropriate behavior. (3-2)

REVIEWING THE CHAPTER

1. What are the functions of a family? (3-1)
2. Give an example of each basic need a family provides. (3-1)
3. What difficulties do *blended families* face that are different from those of *nuclear families?* (3-1)
4. How might a parent's new job affect a family? (3-1)
5. Is it appropriate for parents to change their parenting style? Why or why not? (3-2)
6. While running errands with her children, Rachel is polite to the bank teller and the librarian. Why are her actions so important? (3-2)
7. What are three ways of disciplining that parents should not use? Why? (3-2)
8. Why is consistency so important when guiding children's behavior? (3-2)

THINKING CRITICALLY

1. **Analyzing.** The chapter notes that traditions help to strengthen a family. Why do you think this is so?
2. **Comparing.** How does guidance differ from punishment?
3. **Applying.** Nathan lost a library book and his father says they can no longer check out books from the library. Do you think this is an appropriate punishment? Why or why not?

MAKING CONNECTIONS

1. **Writing.** Write a dialogue between two parents whose child refuses to eat dinner. One parent has an authoritarian parenting style, and the other has a permissive parenting style. Describe how they might compromise to find a solution.

2. **Social Studies.** If a family adopts an older child from a culture very different from their own, how might the parents help the child maintain his or her culture's traditions?

APPLYING YOUR LEARNING

1. **Analyzing Behaviors.** Observe a parent or other caregiver interacting with a child. How would you describe the parenting style you observe? Give specific examples to back up your choice.

2. **Interpersonal Skills.** A friend is frustrated because she fights with her brother all the time. What advice can you give her about dealing with family conflict?

3. **Strong Families.** Interview a couple who have been married at least 20 years. What attracted them to one another? How do they settle conflicts? What advice would they give engaged couples?

4. **Family Relations.** Talk to people who are part of a blended family. Ask what they like and dislike about their situation. What did they do to help everyone get along?

Learning from Research

1. Choose one of the following research claims to investigate.
2. How can this research finding be useful to parents and other caregivers?
3. Summarize what help is available for people who want to become more effective parents.

Children Learn from Positive Reinforcement. Many child development experts believe that the best way to teach children how to behave is by providing positive reinforcement for appropriate behaviors. Identify positive reinforcement techniques and explain how families can use them effectively.

Parenting Classes Help Parents with Tough Issues. Parents have to make hard decisions about raising their children. Many parents take classes to learn strategies for handling difficult situations. Identify parenting programs that offer such classes.

Parenting in Blended Families Presents Challenges. The emotional balance in blended families is often fragile. Parents must build effective relationships with stepchildren, among stepchildren, and between themselves. Identify strategies that can help parents create harmony in blended families.

Pregnancy and Childbirth

Chapter 4
Prenatal Development

Chapter 5
Preparing for Birth

Chapter 6
The Baby's Arrival

4 Prenatal Development

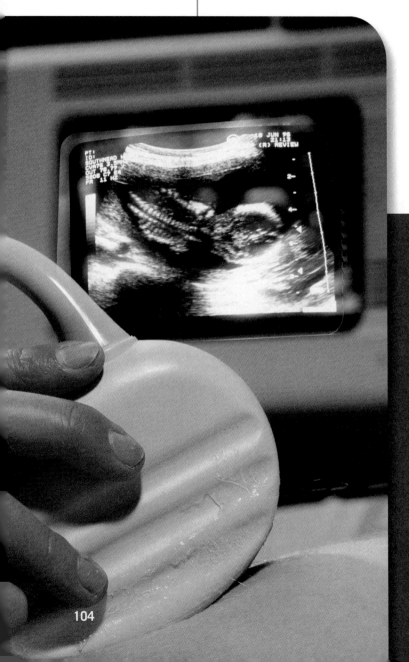

Thoughtful Reading:

As you read this chapter:

- Ask clarifying questions such as who, what, when, and where.
- Ask follow-up questions such as how and why.
- Find sources to answer all your reading questions.

Section 4-1
The Developing Baby

Section 4-2
A Closer Look at Conception

Section 4-3
Problems in Prenatal Development

Section 4-4
Avoiding Dangers to the Baby

The Developing Baby

During pregnancy, a single cell grows and develops into a human being capable of life outside the mother's body. This amazing process takes only about nine months. Different developmental milestones are reached during each of the three stages of pregnancy. These developmental milestones are signs that changes and development are taking place.

Objectives

- Explain how conception occurs.
- Identify and explain what occurs during each of the three stages of prenatal development.
- Describe the changes that affect a woman during each stage of pregnancy.

Key Terms

ovum
uterus
Fallopian tube
sperm
conception
prenatal development
zygote
embryo
amniotic fluid
placenta
umbilical cord
fetus

Conception

About once every 28 days, an **ovum** (OH-vum)—an egg cell—is released by one of a woman's two ovaries. This occurs as part of a woman's menstrual cycle and is called *ovulation*. At the same time, a woman's body releases specific hormones. These prepare the uterus in the event that the ovum is fertilized. The **uterus** is the organ in a woman's body in which a baby develops during pregnancy. It is a pear-shaped muscle able to expand during pregnancy.

During ovulation, the inner lining of the uterus grows and thickens. If the ovum is not fertilized, the lining breaks down and passes out of the body. This is the bleeding that women experience as a menstrual period.

When an ovum is released from the ovary, it moves through the **Fallopian tube**, which connects the ovary to the uterus. The journey from the ovary to the uterus takes about two or three days.

When the ovum reaches the uterus, it usually disintegrates and leaves the body

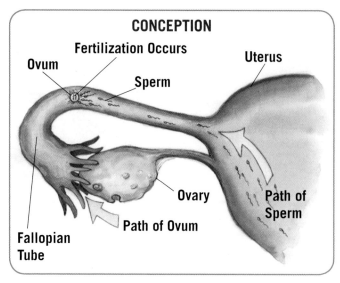

CONCEPTION

Ovum
Fertilization Occurs
Sperm
Uterus
Ovary
Path of Sperm
Path of Ovum
Fallopian Tube

Fig. 4-1 **For conception to occur, a sperm cell must penetrate an egg cell in the Fallopian tube.**

with the menstrual flow. When a **sperm**, or male cell, reaches the Fallopian tube, it may penetrate and fertilize the ovum. This process is called **conception**. Pregnancy begins at that time. See Fig. 4-1.

An ovum usually lives 12 to 24 hours, while a sperm is capable of fertilizing an ovum for approximately 48 to 72 hours. During a woman's menstrual cycle, there

are approximately three to four days during which intercourse could lead to conception.

The Germinal Stage

The baby's development during a pregnancy is called **prenatal development.** It is often grouped into three stages, called the germinal stage, embryonic stage, and fetal stage. The fetal development chart on pages 108–109 outlines month-by-month development of these stages.

The germinal stage is the first stage in a baby's development. It includes the formation of the **zygote** (ZIE-gote), or fertilized egg. This stage lasts only about two weeks, but includes the key steps in establishing a pregnancy.

- **Cell division.** While the zygote is still in the Fallopian tube, it begins to grow by cell division. The single cell splits into two cells, then the two cells rapidly multiply to four, then to eight, and so on.

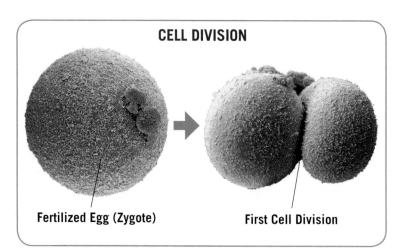

CELL DIVISION

Fertilized Egg (Zygote)
First Cell Division

Fig. 4-2 **Between conception and birth, a baby grows from a single cell through the process of cell division.**

EMBRYO ATTACHES TO UTERUS

Fallopian Tube — Embryo

Ovary

Uterus

Fig. 4-3 **The embryo must become implanted in the lining of the uterus in order to grow.** What stage does this occur in?

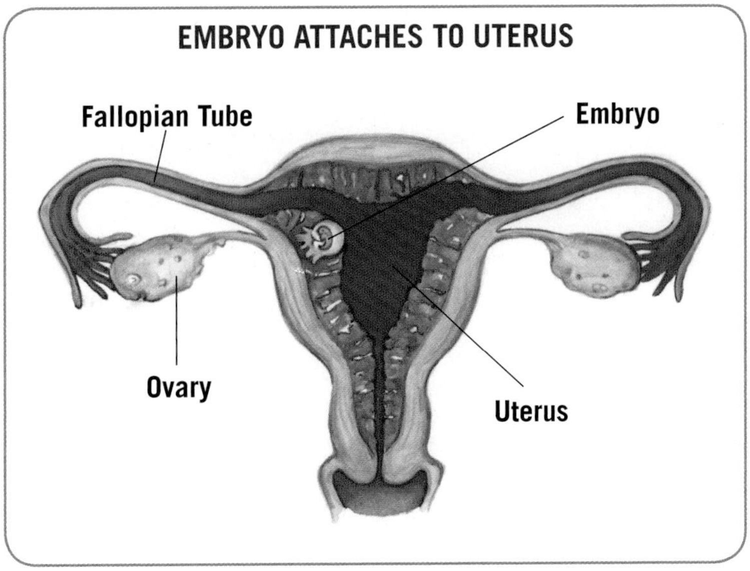

After about four days of growth and slow movement, the zygote reaches the opening to the uterus. See Fig. 4-2.

- **Implantation.** By this time, the lining of the uterus has thickened enough to provide a place for the zygote to attach itself and continue to grow. The zygote usually implants in the lining of the uterus and is covered over by that lining. See Fig. 4-3. Despite the rapid growth of the zygote during the two weeks after fertilization, it is only the size of the head of a pin.

The Embryonic Stage

The second stage of pregnancy is the embryonic stage. The **embryo** is what the developing baby is called from about the third week of pregnancy through the eighth week. During this time, the embryo grows rapidly. It is also during this stage that several important and amazing changes

occur. They are outlined in Fig. 4-4, the fetal development chart on pages 108–109.

- **Organs and body systems.** First, the cells begin to separate and develop into the major systems of the human body—heart and lungs, bones and muscles. These internal organs and their systems are not ready to function yet, however. They continue to develop throughout the pregnancy. Approximately 27 days after conception, the *neural tube,* a tube in the back of the developing baby that will become the brain and spinal cord, has closed. At this point, the brain begins to take control of the various body systems. By about the sixth week after conception, the connections between the brain and the spine allow the first movements of the embryo. The developing brain is sensitive to damage from any drugs or alcohol the mother might take, especially at this crucial stage. It is vital that a pregnant woman avoid these substances throughout her pregnancy.

Fig. 4-4

Fetal Development

Month by Month

Month 1

- Size: At two weeks, the size of a pin head.
- Egg attaches to lining of uterus.
- Critical stage for brain and spinal cord development.
- Internal organs and circulatory system begin to form.
- The heart begins to beat.

Month 2

- Size: About ¼ inch (6 mm) long as month begins.
- Face, eyes, ears, and limbs take shape.
- Bones begin to form.

Month 3

- Size: About 1 inch (25 mm) long as month begins.
- Nostrils, mouth, lips, teeth buds, and eyelids form.
- Fingers and toes almost complete.
- All organs present, although immature.

Month 4

- Size: About 3 inches (7.6 cm) long, 1 ounce (28 g) as month begins.
- Can suck its thumb, swallow, hiccup, and move around.
- Facial features become clearer.

Month 5

- Size: About 6½–7 inches (16–18 cm) long, about 4–5 ounces (113–142 g) as month begins.
- Hair, eyelashes, and eyebrows appear.
- Teeth continue to develop.
- Organs are maturing.
- Becomes more active.

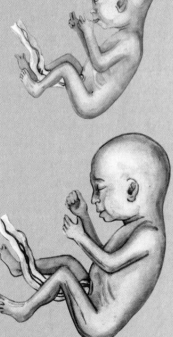
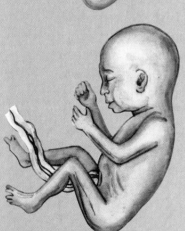

Month 6

- Size: About 8–10 inches (21–25 cm) long, about 8–12 ounces (227–340 g) as month begins.
- Fat deposits under skin, but fetus appears wrinkled.
- Breathing movements begin.

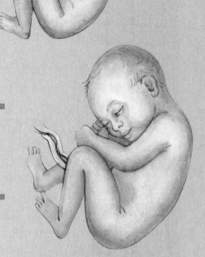

Month 7

- Size: About 10–12 inches (25–31 cm) long, about 1½–2 pounds (680–907 g) as month begins.
- Periods of activity followed by periods of rest and quiet.

Month 8

- Size: About 14–16 inches (36–41 cm) long, about 2½–3 pounds (1.0–1.4 kg) as month begins.
- Weight gain continues rapidly.
- May react to loud noises with a reflex jerking action.
- Moves into a head-down position.

Month 9

- Size: About 17–18 inches (43–46 cm) long, 5–6 pounds (2.3–2.7 kg) as month begins.
- Weight gain continues until the week before birth.
- Skin becomes smooth as fat deposits continue.
- Movements decrease as the fetus has less room to move around.
- Acquires disease-fighting antibodies from the mother's blood.
- Descends into pelvis, ready for birth.

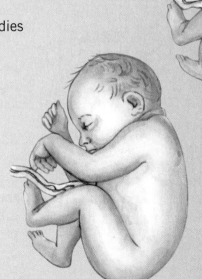

- **Amniotic sac.** Second, a sac filled with fluid forms around the embryo. This **amniotic** (AM-knee-AH-tik) **fluid** protects the developing baby. The amniotic sac is formed from special layers of cells in the uterus. It cushions the embryo from any bumps or falls that the mother might have. At this point in development, the embryo is still very small (about 1 inch or 2.5 cm long) and can float freely in the amniotic fluid.

- **The placenta and umbilical cord.** Third, a tissue called the **placenta** (pluh-SEN-tuh) develops. The placenta is also formed from special layers of cells in the uterus. It is rich in blood vessels and attached to the wall of the uterus.

  The mother's bloodstream carries food and oxygen to the placenta. The placenta's job is to absorb oxygen and nourishment from the mother's blood to be transmitted to the baby through the **umbilical cord**, which connects the baby to the placenta. In addition, the umbilical cord takes carbon dioxide and other waste products away from the baby and to the placenta, which releases those wastes into the mother's bloodstream.

The umbilical cord is usually stiff and firm, like a garden hose filled with water. It is generally not flexible enough to loop around the fetus, although this may occur in rare cases. The placenta and umbilical cord provide everything a baby needs until birth.

The Fetal Stage

The third and final stage of development, the fetal stage, is also the longest. It begins around the eighth or ninth week of pregnancy and lasts until birth. During this stage, the developing baby is called a **fetus** (FEE-tuhs). At this time, the buds for all 20 "baby" teeth appear. The vocal cords develop, and the digestive system and kidneys begin to function. By the end of the third month, spontaneous movements are possible.

- **Making movements.** Sometime during the fourth or fifth month, the kicks and other movements of the fetus touch the wall of the uterus. These movements are faint and infrequent at first. These are usually the first fetal movements that the mother can feel. She may feel her baby's movement as a kind of fluttering, like a butterfly. Gradually, these sensations become stronger and more frequent, telling the mother that she is indeed carrying a live child within her. See Fig. 4-5.

  A pregnant woman's doctor usually asks her when she first felt these movements. This information helps the doctor estimate the baby's age and make sure the baby is developing normally. This information can also be used to help project an accurate due date.

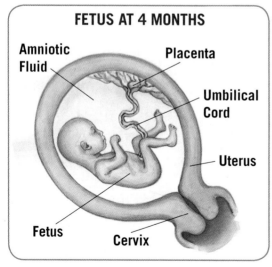

FETUS AT 4 MONTHS

Amniotic Fluid

Placenta

Umbilical Cord

Uterus

Fetus

Cervix

Fig. 4-5 The fetus is nourished through the umbilical cord.

- **Completing development.** During the last few months of pregnancy, development continues, preparing the fetus to live independently. By the seventh month, the baby is capable of living outside the uterus, but not without a great deal of medical help. The body's major organs become ready to function without any help from the mother's body. The fetus also gains weight rapidly. Fat deposits, which will help the baby maintain body heat after delivery, are formed under the skin. The fetus, which had been thin and wrinkled, takes on the smoother, rounder appearance of a baby. During this time, the fetus also stores nutrients and builds immunity to diseases and infections.

- **Staying active.** The fetus can do a surprising number of things—suck its thumb, cough, sneeze, yawn, kick, and hiccup. A fetus can even cry. Even though the uterus is crowded, the fetus is still very active and can change positions.

- **Growing bigger.** As the fetus grows, so does the amount of surrounding amniotic fluid. The uterus also expands, causing the woman's abdomen to grow. When the fetus grows large during the last few months of pregnancy, it no longer has room to stretch out. It curls up inside the uterus in what is called the *fetal position*. See Fig. 4-6.

Preparing for Birth

The common length of pregnancy is about 40 weeks, or 280 days, from the first day of the last menstrual cycle. By this time, the fetus is fully developed and can usually survive outside the mother's body without a great deal of medical assistance. Some babies are born either a few weeks early or a few weeks late. This is generally not a problem. See Fig. 4-7 on page 112.

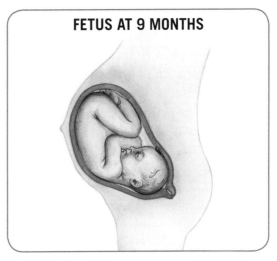

FETUS AT 9 MONTHS

Fig. 4-6 **As the end of pregnancy nears the fetus is folded in the fetal position.**

LOOKING AT REAL LIFE

Melissa is in her 35th week of pregnancy, and she is eager to deliver her first baby. She and her husband Mark have been attending parenting classes at the hospital. Overall, her pregnancy has not been a smooth one. In the first few months, she expected some nausea and discomfort, but she has been surprised at how often she has felt sick. She has been tired most of the time and experienced lower back pain, especially in the last month. Melissa asked her doctor about her symptoms. She was relieved to know that what she has been going through is considered normal. Every woman's body and each pregnancy is different.

▸▸**PERSONAL APPLICATION**

Do you know someone who has been through a difficult pregnancy? What symptoms did the mother have?

Fig. 4-7
Pregnancy Development
Month by Month

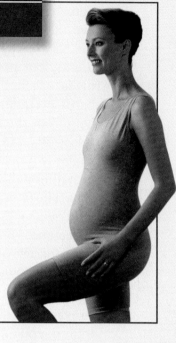

Month 1
- Missed menstrual period.
- Other signs of pregnancy may not yet be noticeable.

Month 2
- Breasts begin to swell.
- Pressure on bladder from enlarging uterus results in need to urinate more frequently.
- Possible nausea ("morning sickness").
- Fatigue is common.

Month 3
- Breasts become firmer and fuller, may ache.
- Nausea, fatigue, and frequent urination may continue.
- Abdomen becomes slightly larger. The uterus is about the size of an orange.
- Weight gain may total 2–4 pounds (0.9–1.8 kg).

Month 4
- Abdomen continues to grow slowly.
- Most discomforts of early pregnancy, such as morning sickness, usually gone.
- Appetite increases.

Month 5
- Enlarged abdomen becomes apparent.
- Slight fetal movements felt.
- Increased size may begin to affect posture.

Month 6
- Fetal movements sensed as strong kicks, thumps, and bumps. Some may be visible.
- Weight gain by the beginning of this month may total 10–12 pounds (4.5–5.4 kg).

Month 7
- Increased size may affect posture.

Month 8
- Discomfort may result from increased size. Backache, leg cramps, shortness of breath, and fatigue are common.
- Fetal kicks may disturb the mother's rest.
- At the beginning of this month, weight gain totals about 18–20 pounds (8.2–9.1 kg).

Month 9
- "Lightening" felt as the fetus drops into the pelvis. Breathing becomes easier.
- Other discomforts may continue.
- A total weight gain of 25–35 pounds (11.3–15.9 kg) is typical.
- False labor pains may be experienced.

Physical Changes for the Mother

Toward the end of the 40 weeks, the baby's weight seems to shift downward, and most mothers feel more comfortable in their upper abdomen. This shift is called *lightening*. Sometimes there is a visible change in the shape of the mother's abdomen, giving signs that the baby has dropped into the birth canal—the channel through which the baby passes during birth.

In the majority of births, the fetus is usually upside down at this point, with the head nestled in the mother's pelvis. This is the easiest and safest position for birth because the baby's head is the largest part of the body. If the head can be expelled from the mother's body easily, the rest of the body usually delivers easily as well. The baby is generally less active because there is very little space to move.

In some cases, the fetus does not turn to the head-down position in the last few weeks. Instead, the fetus is in a seat-down or feet-down position in the mother's pelvis. This is called a "breech presentation." In many of these instances, a doctor uses a surgical procedure called a *cesarean section* to deliver the baby. A complete discussion of cesarean birth appears in Chapter 6.

The skin of the mother's abdomen appears stretched to capacity. The muscles of the uterus and abdomen can be stretched to many times their original size during pregnancy. At the end of pregnancy, the muscles of the uterus contract to expel the baby during delivery. The mother's abdominal and uterine muscles generally return to near-normal sizes approximately six weeks after delivery.

SECTION 4-1 Review and Activities

Reviewing the Section

1. What cells join together to cause *conception*?
2. What happens during the germinal stage? How long does this stage last?
3. What changes might a pregnant woman feel in the germinal and embryonic stages?
4. What major changes take place in the developing baby during the embryonic stage?
5. What are some characteristics of a fetus at five months' development?
6. Why do babies born at full term have a better chance for survival than babies born a few months early?
7. When a mother feels *lightening*, what does this tell her about the fetus?

Observing and Interacting

Visit a store that sells maternity clothes. Look at how the clothes are designed to accommodate a growing fetus. What features of the clothing make them more comfortable for expectant mothers?

A Closer Look at Conception

Have you ever looked at old photographs of your relatives and compared their looks to your own? Maybe you looked a lot like your father when you were both seven years old. Maybe your face resembles your Aunt Mary's when she was a teen. It can be fascinating to study why people resemble other members of their family.

Objectives

- Describe how personal characteristics are inherited.
- Explain the causes of multiple births.
- Evaluate different possible solutions for infertility.

Key Terms

chromosomes
genes
genome
DNA
dominant gene
recessive gene
infertility
surrogate

The Genetic Package

People inherit many physical traits from their parents. These characteristics may include physical build; skin color; hair texture and color; eye color and shape; the size and shape of ears, hands, and feet; and blood type. Parents can pass on to their children a predisposition for certain talents, such as musical or athletic ability. Some medical conditions are inherited as well. How does this happen? Scientists are continually learning more and more about how *heredity*—the passing on of characteristics—works.

At the moment of conception, every human baby receives 46 **chromosomes**, tiny threadlike structures in the nucleus of every cell. These chromosomes come in 23 pairs. The father's sperm and mother's ovum each contribute one chromosome to each pair. Each chromosome has hundreds to thousands of **genes**, the units that determine a human's inherited characteristics. The complete blueprint for the creation of a person is called a **genome**. Genes are made up of a complex molecule called **DNA**—deoxyribonucleic acid. A human's 46 chromosomes form that person's unique DNA. No two people, except identical twins, have identical DNA.

Dominant and Recessive Genes

For every inherited characteristic, a person receives two copies of a gene—one from the mother and one from the father. When both genes are the same, the child automatically has that characteristic. In many cases, a person receives two different genes. What factors determine the characteristic that person will express? The characteristic expressed is controlled by the **dominant gene**, or stronger gene. The **recessive gene**, or weaker gene, will not be expressed. Of course, the terms *dominant* and *recessive* only refer to the relationship of genes to each other, not that one characteristic is actually weaker than another.

Most traits are influenced by multiple genes. Height, weight, personality, and intelligence are examples of these. These traits are determined by a specific combination of genes that are brought together at conception. See "How to Understand Genetic Traits" on page 116 for more information.

Making a Unique Person

Heredity explains why people in the same family often resemble each other. You may have a friend who looks a lot like his or her sibling. Heredity also explains why two people in the same family can look quite different. Every sperm and egg cell contains a different combination of genes. When these genes combine, they produce a unique individual. That is why one child in a family can have light brown hair and another can have black or blonde hair. If each child in a family inherited the exact same genes from the father and the mother as his or her siblings inherited, all of the children in the family would look exactly the same.

The sex of the child is determined at conception. The sex chromosomes come in two types, X and Y. Each ovum in the woman's ovaries carries an X chromosome. Each sperm cell in the man's body

carries either an X or a Y chromosome. If the sperm that fertilizes the egg carries an X chromosome, the child receives an X chromosome from each parent. A child with the XX combination is a girl. If the sperm carries a Y chromosome, the child receives an X chromosome from the mother and a Y chromosome from the father. A child with the XY combination is a boy.

Understand Genetic Traits

Why do I have this hair color? Why do I have blue eyes like my mom instead of brown eyes like my dad? Figuring out why people have certain traits can be confusing. All people have physical traits that are controlled by the genes they inherit. For each trait, there is one gene that comes from the father, and one that comes from the mother. It's how these genes are combined that determines the chances of having one trait over another.

Some people may not look much like their mother or father, but may look a lot like one of their grandparents. Certain physical traits may skip a generation when recessive genes are inherited. For example, red hair often skips a generation, because the gene for red hair is recessive. If two parents each have a dominant gene for black hair and a recessive gene for red hair (Br), they will both have black hair. The chart below shows the four possible gene combinations for the children of these parents. Statistically, only one of every four (25 percent) of their children would inherit the two recessive red hair genes needed to have red hair.

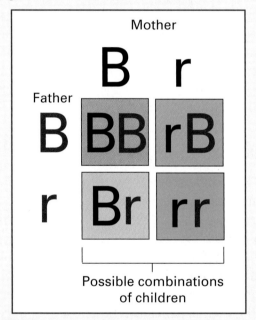

Possible combinations of children

YOUR TURN

What physical traits do you share with your parents? Do some research on dominant and recessive genes to determine how you inherited one of those traits.

Where Neighbors Are Few, Genetic Diseases Affect Many

Isolated communities, especially those on islands, often have small populations and few immigrants. This means that most residents are at least distant relatives. The South Atlantic island of Tristan da Cunha—known to residents simply as Tristan—is one such community. All 300 residents of Tristan are cousins. Genetic disease is widespread, and over half of Tristan's residents have asthma. The rate of asthma is at least three times the rate in other communities.

Close relatives are likely to have similar genetic combinations, which means that their children are more likely to be born with defects. Harmful genetic mutations are less likely to appear in large populations in which individuals reproduce with unrelated partners.

Iceland is another isolated island community. It has a population of 270,000 people who are at least distantly related. Icelanders have kept

excellent historical records. Researchers can compare the DNA of people who have suffered diseases to the DNA of those who have not. This helps them locate the genes that play a role in diseases.

Investigating Culture

1. Find out which genetic research projects are taking place in Iceland. Do you think that a country such as Iceland should make its genetic information available for scientific research?
2. What are the privacy issues that are involved?

Multiple Births

The number of children a woman will give birth to at one time is determined at conception or soon after. When a woman gives birth to more than one child at a time, it is called a *multiple birth*. The most common instance of multiple births is twins.

There are two types of twins, identical and fraternal. When a sperm fertilizes a woman's ovum, the cell begins to divide right away. As the cells continue to divide, the mass of cells may split in half, creating two separate cell masses. Each cell mass continues to divide and grow into a separate embryo. The result is identical twins. Because only one ovum and sperm were involved in conception, identical twins have very similar physical characteristics and are always the same sex.

Fraternal twins form when two eggs are released from the ovaries at the same time and are fertilized by two different sperm.

Because of the different eggs and sperm, fraternal twins may not look any more alike than other siblings do. They just happen to be in the mother's uterus at the same time. It is common for fraternal twins to be opposite sexes.

In a general population, three in 100, or about 3 percent of all births, are twins. The chances of having identical twins are less than that of fraternal twins. Out of 1,000 births, about 23 will be fraternal twins and about four will be identical twins. See Fig. 4-8.

The birth of three or more babies is much more rare. However, a rise in the use of treatments to help women become pregnant has increased the frequency of multiple births. In fact, one potential drawback to some of these treatments is that they can cause more than one egg to be released at a time, making multiple births more likely. The more children a pregnant woman carries, the more difficult it is for all of them to survive.

Fig. 4-8 **Multiple births may be identical or fraternal.** What is the difference between the two?

Family Planning

Anytime a couple has sexual intercourse, a conception may take place. The only sure way to prevent pregnancy is abstinence—avoiding sexual activity. There are various other methods of contraception, which help prevent pregnancy.

Most methods do not prevent sexually transmitted diseases (STDs). Abstinence also prevents STDs.

Most family planning methods have possible side effects. These problems develop among some, but not all, users. The chart below compares various methods of family planning and indicates if there are side effects. Check medical reference books for complete listings of side effects.

Effectiveness is given as a percentage. A method that is 100 percent effective—such as abstinence—works all the time. If a method is 80 percent effective, there is a one in five chance that a pregnancy could occur when that method is used.

Fig. 4-9 Methods of Family Planning

Method	Characteristics
Abstinence	Only method that is 100% effective.
Birth control pills	Some side effects; 95–98% effective.
Cervical cap	Small latex thimble must remain in place 8 hours; increased risk of infection; 60–91% effective.
Condom	Available for females, but more frequently used by males. Helps reduce spread of STDs. Effectiveness 86% to 97%; should be used with spermicide.
Diaphragm	Diaphragm is used with spermicide; increases risk of urinary infections; 80–94% effective.
Hormonal implants	Capsules placed under skin of upper arm; 99% effective for up to 5 years.
Hormonal injections	Hormones given by physician monthly or once every 3 months; may cause irregular bleeding; up to 99% effective.
Hormonal patch	Thin patch worn on skin 3 weeks each month; similar side effects to birth control pills; 99% effective.
Intrauterine device (IUD) and Uterine implant	May cause discomfort and side effects first 3 months of use; up to 99% effective.
Natural family planning	Known as the rhythm method, 53% to 80% effective.
Spermicide	Foams, creams, gels may cause allergic reactions; 72% effective; should be used with condom, diaphragm, cervical cap.
Vaginal implant	Ring worn internally for 3 weeks each month; 95–99% effective.

Fig. 4-10 **Consulting a doctor is the first step for couples who suspect a problem with infertility.**

Infertility

Not all couples who want to become parents are able to conceive. These couples are considered infertile. There are many causes of **infertility**—the inability to become pregnant—in both men and women. Male infertility is the major factor in about 40 percent of infertility cases, while about 40 percent are due to female infertility. The rest have unknown causes or are linked to both partners.

People with infertility problems often feel isolated and abnormal. There are support groups available to help couples in this situation. In addition, advances in medicine have helped couples overcome infertility. The treatments used depend on the cause. For example, a doctor can prescribe medication when a woman's ovaries do not release an ovum each month. Some fertility medications, however, can cause uncomfortable or potentially serious side effects, and require the careful supervision of a doctor. As time passes, researchers are improving the safety and effectiveness of a variety of infertility treatments. See Fig. 4-10.

Options for Infertile Couples

After attempts to treat infertility, some couples still cannot conceive a child. There are several other options they may discuss with each other and their doctors:

- **Adoption.** By adopting a child, a couple legally takes on all responsibilities and rights for raising, loving, and caring for a child in need of a permanent home.

- **Artificial insemination.** In this process, a doctor injects sperm into a woman's uterus. This procedure is timed to take place when a woman's ovary releases an ovum. Often, the sperm is from the woman's husband. If the spouse has a genetic disorder that prevents his sperm from being used, sperm from a male donor can be used.

- **In vitro fertilization.** This process is used to treat many causes of infertility, including when a woman has damaged Fallopian tubes that will not allow an ovum to pass through to the uterus. With the help of a microscope, the doctor combines a mature ovum from the woman with sperm from her husband.

If the ovum becomes fertilized, the doctor places the new zygote in the woman's uterus. If the zygote attaches itself to the uterus, pregnancy takes place.

- **Ovum transfer.** This procedure is similar to in vitro fertilization, except an ovum has been donated by another woman. The ovum is fertilized in a laboratory and placed in the mother's uterus. This procedure is an option for women who lack working ovaries, have poor ovum quality, or who have inherited disorders.

- **Surrogate mother.** A **surrogate** (SIR-ug-get), or substitute, mother is a woman who becomes pregnant to have a baby for another woman. This option requires legal arrangements be made for all of the people involved, including the child. Each state has laws regarding surrogate motherhood that must be followed.

Questions Raised

As technology and knowledge continue to advance, other options for the treatment of infertility may become available. However, personal beliefs may limit a couple's options. Not everyone believes that these alternatives are acceptable. For example, the use of surrogate mothers and sperm and ovum donors is considered controversial. These practices raise many ethical questions, as will new procedures in the future.

Sophisticated medical procedures for infertile couples require access to specialists. Not all couples can afford the costs involved. Most medical insurance plans exclude or limit coverage for infertility treatment, which is often very expensive.

SECTION 4-2 Review and Activities

Reviewing the Section

1. List at least five traits that are inherited.
2. What is a *genome*?
3. Explain how dominant and recessive genes work.
4. What is the difference between fraternal and identical twins?
5. What is one potential drawback to fertility treatments?
6. Explain one of the options an infertile couple has if infertility treatment does not work.

Observing and Interacting

Log on to the web sites of several adoption agencies. Record and then compare their requirements for people who are looking to adopt children. If you know parents who have adopted a child, interview them about the process they went through. Share what you have learned with the class.

Problems in Prenatal Development

Will the baby be healthy? This is a major concern for all expectant parents. Fortunately, most babies develop normally and are born healthy. There are many things medical professionals and expectant parents can do to monitor the health of a baby as they wait for its arrival. However, prenatal development does not always proceed as expected.

Objectives

- Contrast miscarriage and stillbirth.
- Identify some major birth defects.
- Compare and contrast the four causes of birth defects.
- Explain why genetic counseling may be helpful to some couples.
- Describe how birth defects can be diagnosed and prevented.

Key Terms

miscarriage
stillbirth
birth defect
ultrasound
amniocentesis
**chorionic villi
  sampling**

Losing a Baby

Sometimes a pregnancy begins, but the baby doesn't develop normally. In some of those cases, the developing baby dies. If this happens prior to the 20th week of pregnancy, the event is called a **miscarriage**. If the baby dies after that time, it is called a **stillbirth**.

Unfortunately, miscarriages are not all that uncommon. Approximately 15 to 20 percent of recognized pregnancies end in miscarriage. Medical professionals don't completely understand the causes.

Stillbirth occurs in about two percent of pregnancies. The most common causes are problems with the placenta, abnormal chromosomes, poor growth, and infections.

Dealing with Grief

The loss of a child by miscarriage or stillbirth can be very unexpected and painful for the parents. Most couples look forward to a baby's birth and feel a great sense of attachment long before the birth. When they lose their baby, they may go through stages of grief similar to those experienced by the loss of a child that was already born. Sometimes these parents feel terribly alone and may blame themselves for the death. In most cases, however, these tragedies are completely beyond the parents' control. Couples may need support to work through their grief. Most couples who suffer a miscarriage or stillbirth are later able to have healthy children.

What Can a Concerned Couple Do About Genetic Birth Defects?

For some couples, considering having a baby brings up concerns about genetic birth defects. This typically happens if the inherited diseases seem to occur in the family of one or both of the couple. The first step would be for the couple to share their concerns with their family doctor or obstetrician. If there is a family history of one specific disease or symptoms of a genetic disorder, individuals may wish to be tested. There are different types of genetic testing. Prior to pregnancy, testing can show whether a person carries the traits for cystic fibrosis, Tay-Sachs disease, or sickle cell. If necessary, the doctor can refer the couple to a genetic counselor.

THINKING IT THROUGH

1. Reasearch the ethical, legal, and social issues regarding genetic testing.
2. How do you feel about these issues?

Types of Birth Defects

Some babies survive pregnancy, but are born with serious problems that threaten their health or even their lives. These problems are called **birth defects**. There are hundreds of types of birth defects, each with its own set of symptoms. Some are so mild that no one would ever know the child has a birth defect. Others can result in severe lifelong disabilities or even death. Approximately 150,000 babies around the world are born each year with a birth defect. Scientists and medical professionals are working diligently to understand the causes of birth defects, decrease their incidence, and improve the lives of those affected by a birth defect.

Some birth defects cause an abnormality in the structure of the body. For example, an affected baby might have a misshapen foot or an extra or missing finger. Other birth defects cause one or more systems of the body to not function properly. Blindness, deafness, and mental retardation are examples.

Not all birth defects are apparent at birth. Sometimes the abnormality isn't discovered until months—or even years—have passed. Figure 4-11 on pages 124–126 describes types of birth defects as well as the causes, how to detect them, and treatment for them.

Fig. 4-11 **Birth Defects**

Cerebral Palsy
- **Description:** Cerebral palsy is a general term for a variety of problems of the motor system. The symptoms can include lack of coordination, stiffness, jerkiness, difficulty with speech, and paralysis.
- **Causes:** Cerebral palsy results from damage to the brain before, during, or shortly after birth. The causes vary.
- **Detection:** The symptoms usually appear during the first year of life. The child usually does not develop motor skills as quickly as other babies.
- **Treatment:** The damage caused to the brain is irreversible. However, physical therapy, speech therapy, surgery, and medication can often lessen the effects of this damage.

Cleft Lip and/or Cleft Palate
- **Description:** A gap in the upper lip or palate (the roof of the mouth) causes problems with eating, swallowing, speech, and appearance.
- **Causes:** Condition may be caused by hereditary or environmental factors or both.
- **Detection:** Both cleft lip and cleft palate are apparent at birth. They can often be detected by ultrasound before birth.
- **Treatment:** Surgery corrects the gap and helps eliminate the problems associated with it.

Cystic Fibrosis
- **Description:** Cystic fibrosis (CF) affects the respiratory and digestive systems. Many with CF die before reaching adulthood, although treatment now allows sufferers with the condition to live longer than in the past.
- **Cause:** It is far more likely to affect Caucasians than African or Asian Americans. CF is caused by inheriting defective recessive genes from both parents.
- **Detection:** Symptoms include very salty sweat and a cough that doesn't go away. Blood tests can identify carriers of the gene and sweat tests can diagnose an affected child.
- **Treatment:** There is no known cure. Those with CF can be helped through special diets, lung exercises, and therapies and medication to treat symptoms.

Down Syndrome
- **Description:** A group of problems that may include, among other conditions, mental retardation; problems of the heart, blood, and digestive system; and poor muscle tone.
- **Cause:** Down syndrome is caused by the presence of an extra chromosome 21.
- **Detection:** It can be detected in a fetus by amniocentesis or chorionic villi sampling, or after birth by a blood test.
- **Treatment:** Treatment includes therapy, special educational assistance, and in some cases corrective surgery. The earlier treatment begins, the better for the child.

Fig. 4-11 **Birth Defects** continued

Muscular Dystrophy

- **Description:** There are many different types of muscular dystrophy; all involve a progressive weakness and shrinking of the muscles. The most common form begins between the ages of two and six.
- **Causes:** Most types of muscular dystrophy are hereditary. The most common form is transmitted by female carriers of the gene but affects only males.
- **Detection:** The disease is recognized once symptoms appear. Genetic counseling can identify carriers.
- **Treatment:** There is no known cure. Physical therapy can minimize the disabilities.

PKU

- **Description:** PKU (phenylketonuria) is a condition in which the body is unable to process and use a specific protein that is present in nearly all foods. Brain damage and mental retardation can result.
- **Cause:** A child with PKU inherits defective recessive genes from both parents.
- **Detection:** Newborns are tested for PKU, as required by law in all states.
- **Treatment:** There is no known cure for PKU. If it is diagnosed early, a special diet can reduce or prevent brain damage.

Sickle Cell Anemia

- **Description:** Malformed red blood cells interfere with the supply of oxygen to all parts of the body. The symptoms include tiredness, lack of appetite, and pain. Sickle cell anemia can lead to early death.
- **Cause:** Sickle cell anemia is caused by inheriting defective recessive genes from both parents. African Americans are more likely to have this condition than any other group.
- **Detection:** Amniocentesis or chorionic villi sampling can identify sickle cell anemia in a fetus. Genetic counseling can identify parents who carry the gene. Blood tests can show the presence of the condition after birth.
- **Treatment:** There is no known cure for sickle cell anemia. Medication can treat the symptoms.

Spina Bifida and Hydrocephalus

- **Description:** In spina bifida, an incompletely formed spinal cord may lead to stiff joints, difficulty moving the legs, partial paralysis, and problems with the kidneys and urinary tract. Seventy of every 100 children with spina bifida also have hydrocephalus, in which an excess of fluid surrounds the brain.
- **Causes:** The problem seems to be caused by a combination of hereditary and environmental factors. Taking a folic acid supplement during pregnancy may help reduce incidence.
- **Detection:** Spina bifida is apparent at birth. Hydrocephalus is indicated by overly rapid growth of the head. Tests of the mother's blood, amniocentesis, and ultrasound can reveal suspected cases in a fetus.

(continued on next page)

Fig. 4-11 **Birth Defects** continued

Spina Bifida and Hydrocephalus (continued)
- **Treatment:** Corrective surgery, physical therapy, and special schooling can minimize disabilities caused by spina bifida. Hydrocephalus can be helped by surgically implanting a shunt that relieves the fluid that has built up.

Tay-Sachs Disease
- **Description:** Babies born with Tay-Sachs disease lack a certain chemical in their blood that makes their bodies unable to process and use certain fats in the brain and nerve cells. The condition leads to severe brain damage and to death, usually by the age of four.
- **Cause:** Tay-Sachs disease is caused by inheriting defective recessive genes from both parents. It is most common in families of eastern European Jewish descent.
- **Detection:** Amniocentesis or chorionic villi sampling can identify Tay-Sachs disease in a fetus. Blood tests can identify those who carry the defective gene and can test for the condition after birth.
- **Treatment:** There is no known cure for this disease. Treatment consists of doing everything possible to make the child comfortable.

Causes of Birth Defects

At this time, scientists don't fully understand the exact causes of most birth defects. However, they are constantly working to understand why they occur, which they hope will lead to cures for these conditions. So far, they have determined that there are four main causes for birth defects, and research is continuing in each area. Factors in the environment of the developing baby cause some birth defects. Hereditary factors cause others. Abnormal genes or chromosomal errors can also cause birth defects, and some are caused by a combination of environmental and hereditary factors.

Environmental Causes

During the first few weeks after conception, a baby develops all the bodily systems needed for survival and a healthy, normal life. During this time, the developing baby depends completely on the mother's body for nourishment and oxygen.

This early development is critical, and many choices the mother makes, possibly even before she knows she is pregnant, can affect the lifelong health of her baby. There may also be environmental factors that the mother is unaware of that can affect the development of the baby. Some environmental causes of birth defects include the following:

- The nutritional balance of the mother's diet.
- Any diseases or infections the mother has during pregnancy.
- Harmful substances the mother consumes, including alcohol, over-the-counter medications, and illegal drugs.
- Some medicines that benefit the mother, but hurt the baby.
- Exposure to hazards, such as certain chemicals, high levels of radiation, and X rays, especially early in pregnancy.

Hereditary Causes

Every person has approximately 20,000 to 25,000 genes that not only determine traits such as eye color and height, but also direct the growth and development of every system in the body. Half of each child's genes come from the mother and half from the father. Children typically get five or six imperfect recessive genes passed on to them. In the majority of cases, though, a single copy of an imperfect recessive gene will have no effect on the development of the baby. However, sometimes both parents will pass on the same imperfect recessive gene, causing the baby to have a birth defect. This is called *recessive inheritance*. Two examples of conditions caused by recessive inheritance are Tay-Sachs disease and cystic fibrosis.

Sometimes a child inherits a defective gene that is dominant. It is only necessary for this gene to be passed on by one parent for the child to have the birth defect. This is called *dominant inheritance*. Huntington's disease is a condition caused by dominant inheritance. Some inherited conditions only affect one sex. Hemophilia, a condition that prevents the blood from clotting, is passed on from the mother only to her sons. Like color blindness and Duchenne muscular dystrophy, hemophilia usually only affects males. See Fig. 4-12.

Fig. 4-12 **Duchenne muscular dystrophy is caused by a defective dominant gene.** What is the difference between a dominant and a recessive gene?

Errors in Chromosomes

Several types of birth defects are caused by problems in the number or structure of chromosomes. An error may occur when an egg or sperm cell is developing, causing a baby to have too many or too few chromosomes or to have broken or rearranged chromosomes. These are not hereditary defects because neither parent has the abnormal chromosome.

The most common birth defect of this type is *Down syndrome*. A child with Down syndrome may have some degree of mental retardation, plus physical problems. One in 800 to 1,000 babies has this condition. Under normal conditions, each sperm and egg cell carries 23 chromosomes. Sometimes an error occurs when an egg or sperm cell is forming, causing there to be an extra copy of chromosome 21. Instead of having two copies of chromosome 21, the child has three. Because each chromosome carries hundreds of genes, the defect can interfere with development in many ways, including an increased risk of heart defects and leukemia, poor muscle tone, problems with vision and hearing, delayed physical growth and motor development, and distinctive physical characteristics. The risk for having a child with Down syndrome is higher for older mothers.

Interaction of Heredity and Environment

Some birth defects are caused by a combination of heredity and the environment. For example, a child may inherit the tendency that may later lead to a heart defect. If a factor such as a drug or virus affects the baby during pregnancy, the baby will have the heart defect. If the baby did not inherit the gene for the heart defect, or did not get exposed to the drug or virus, the heart would be normal. Because both the inherited factor and the environmental factor were present, the baby's heart had a defect.

Birth defects such as cleft lip, cleft palate, and spina bifida may be caused by a combination of hereditary and environmental factors. See Fig. 4-11 on pages 124–126 for more information on these birth defects. Both cleft lip and cleft palate may be caused by a number of inherited genes in combination with exposure during pregnancy to certain medications, infections, illnesses, and tobacco or alcohol. A genetic predisposition for spina bifida, combined with the use of medications for the treatment of diabetes and seizure disorders during pregnancy, increase the likelihood of a child having the defect.

Prevention and Diagnosis of Birth Defects

It can be challenging for a child born with a serious birth defect to lead a normal, productive life. Other family members are affected by the emotional and financial strain the defect causes. However, advances in treatment and support groups are helping children and their families cope. While not all causes of birth defects can be anticipated or controlled, there are several things that couples can do to minimize the chances of having a child with birth defects. See Fig. 4-13.

Before even trying to conceive, prospective parents can schedule a checkup to evaluate their overall health. They can discuss lifestyle changes that may improve their chances for a successful pregnancy and healthy baby. For example, women should stop using tobacco and alcohol prior to pregnancy, as these substances can lead to health problems and birth defects. Because many women do not know they are pregnant in the early weeks, it is safer to quit smoking and drinking before there is even the possibility of pregnancy. Men, too, are advised to either cut back on or avoid alcohol, as it has been linked to low sperm count.

Once she is pregnant, the expectant mother can visit her doctor for prenatal care. Such care goes a long way toward a successful pregnancy, as her doctor can monitor her health and the baby's growth and development. The mother can also continue to abstain from alcohol, illegal drugs, and tobacco. She can talk to her doctor about the effects of any over-the-counter and prescription medications on her baby. She should not take any medication that is not approved by her doctor.

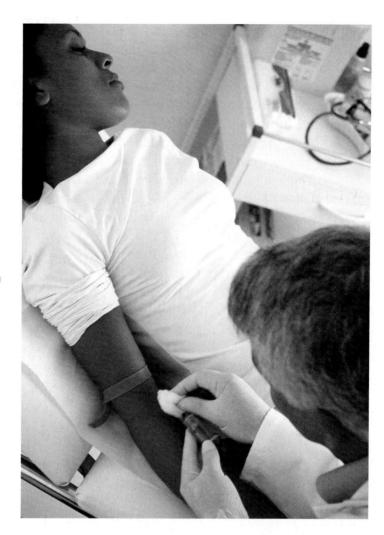

Fig. 4-13 **A genetic counselor will usually request a physical examination, including a blood sample, for both parents.**

Genetic Counseling

Some people seek genetic counseling to assess their risk of having a child with a birth defect that is caused by a defect in the genes. The patients might be a couple who wish to have a child but are concerned about having a child with serious birth defects. There may be a history of birth defects in the family. Some couples may already have a child with a birth defect and want to learn more about the risks for subsequent children. Genetic counselors don't tell people what to do about the information they receive; they only explain the options and risks.

Family doctors can perform genetic counseling, but most patients are referred to a genetic counselor. This specialist usually begins working with a couple by evaluating the family history of both the mother and the father. This includes information relating to the medical histories, diseases, and causes of death of all known family members. To learn more about what a genetic counselor does, see the "Career Opportunities" feature on page 143.

Along with the family history, a genetic counselor will usually request a complete physical examination for both parents. If specific birth defects are of concern, some other members of the family may receive physical examinations as well. Special laboratory tests may also be performed. Small samples of blood and body tissue may be analyzed. For example, a blood sample can be tested to determine whether the parents are carriers for the gene that causes cystic fibrosis.

Once all of the testing is complete, the genetic counselor can usually tell the couple what their risks are for having a child with certain genetic birth defects. It is the couple's decision whether or not to have children. If they do, they will be aware of extra testing that may be needed during pregnancy to closely monitor the development of the baby.

Prenatal Tests

More than 100 kinds of birth defects can now be detected before a baby is born. There are many tests that are standard for prenatal care in this country that help a

doctor decide whether or not a baby might have a birth defect. These tests can help determine what treatments, if any, are necessary for the child before or after birth.

Sometimes prenatal tests are simple blood tests. Other tests involve procedures that carry more risks. The couple must weigh the potential value of the information to be gained against possible risks for the developing baby or the mother. Prenatal tests include:

- **Alpha-fetoprotein (AFP).** This blood test is performed on the expectant mother between weeks 15 and 20 of a pregnancy. AFP is a protein produced in the liver of the fetus that is detectable in the mother's blood. Abnormal AFP levels can indicate a possible birth defect. Further testing can be done to determine if a birth defect does exist and what it might be.

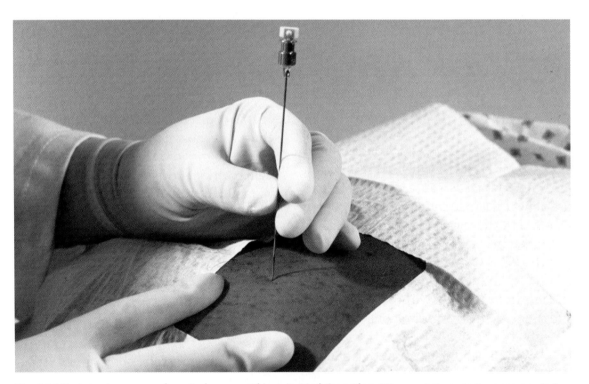

Fig. 4-14 **Tests such as an amniocentesis can provide valuable information.** Why aren't these tests recommended for all pregnant women?

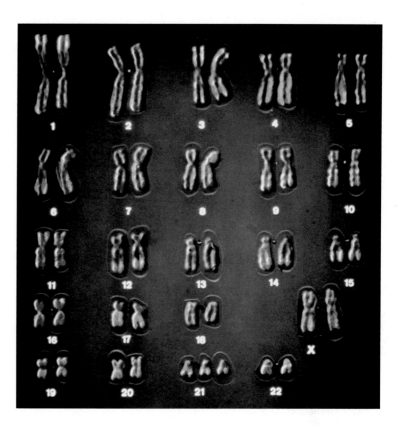

Fig. 4-15 **The fluid obtained from amniocentesis can be used to check chromosomes.** In this case, Down syndrome is shown by what unusual circumstance in chromosome 21?

- **Ultrasound. Ultrasound** uses sound waves to make a video image, called a *sonogram*, of an unborn baby. It can help the doctor monitor the development of the baby, pinpoint the baby's age, and detect certain birth defects. Problems with the baby's skeletal, circulatory, or nervous system may be detected during an ultrasound. The sonogram also helps confirm the due date and the presence of more than one fetus.

  Many women will have an ultrasound during their pregnancy, usually near the 20th week. Many doctors now perform 3D ultrasounds, which provide more detailed images and information about the baby's development. While research has shown that an ultrasound poses no threat to the unborn child or the mother, it should be performed only when there is a real medical reason for doing so.

- **Amniocentesis.** The process of withdrawing a sample of the amniotic fluid surrounding the unborn baby is called **amniocentesis** (AM-knee-oh-sen-TEE-sis). The doctor uses the view from an ultrasound to guide a needle through the mother's abdomen into the amniotic sac. Some cells from the fetus are in the amniotic fluid. The sample is taken to a lab and tested for evidence of birth defects and other health problems. See Fig. 4-14.

  Amniocentesis is most often used as a test for Down syndrome when the expectant mother is over age 35. The test may also be performed after questionable results have been obtained through an ultrasound or the AFP blood test. Amniocentesis involves some risk to the fetus and is performed only when there is a strong medical reason to do so. See Fig. 4-15.

- **Chorionic villi** (CORE-ee-ON-ik VI-lie) **sampling. Chorionic villi sampling** uses a sample of the tissue from the membrane that encases the fetus to check for specific birth defects. Samples of the tissue are snipped or suctioned off and analyzed.

Chorionic villi sampling tests for the same disorders as amniocentesis, but it is used less often because its risks are much greater. One advantage is that it can be performed much earlier in the pregnancy than amniocentesis.

Several other methods of prenatal diagnosis are now in the experimental stages. These may someday provide more accurate information at earlier stages of development. For example, it is possible to view the fetus directly through a special instrument called a laparoscope. Doctors can also obtain samples of fetal blood and tissue and even perform surgery on an unborn child. Currently, these procedures carry a risk. Further advances in medical research and technology may make these procedures safe enough for widespread use.

SECTION 4-3 Review and Activities

Reviewing the Section

1. How are a *miscarriage* and a *stillbirth* similar? How are they different?
2. What is the cause of Down syndrome? What is one factor that increases the risk of Down syndrome?
3. What group is most likely to have sickle cell anemia?
4. What are the four categories of *birth defects*?
5. Why might a person who has a parent with a genetic birth defect want to consult with a genetic counselor?
6. What steps are involved in the genetic counseling process?
7. What are the two most common tests that check for possible birth defects during pregnancy?

Observing and Interacting

Search the Internet or consult a local hospital or phone book to find an organization that helps people with birth defects, such as the March of Dimes or the Special Olympics. Find out what they do and how they help people with birth defects. What services do they provide? Do they provide treatment? What type of treatment? Report your findings to the class.

Avoiding Dangers to the Baby

From the beginning to the end of her pregnancy, the mother-to-be has an enormous responsibility. She must do everything possible to increase the chances of having a healthy baby. She needs to consider the effects of her actions on her unborn child. It is vital that she take care of herself physically and emotionally, and avoid potential dangers. An essential part of good prenatal care is avoiding hazards such as alcohol and other drugs, smoking, X rays, hazardous chemicals and other substances, and infections.

Objectives

- Describe the hazards that alcohol and other drugs pose to prenatal development.
- Explain why other environmental hazards, including hazardous substances and chemicals, must be avoided during pregnancy.
- Compare and contrast how a fetus can be affected by certain illnesses the mother may contract.

Key Terms

fetal alcohol syndrome (FAS)
fetal alcohol effects
low birth weight
SIDS
toxoplasmosis

Alcohol and Pregnancy

Sometimes people forget that alcohol is a drug—an especially dangerous one for unborn children. When a pregnant woman consumes alcohol, she puts her baby at great risk. The alcohol, as with anything else the mother consumes or inhales, is passed directly to her child through the placenta. Even a small amount of alcohol can harm the developing systems of the baby.

Doctors don't know just how much alcohol it takes to endanger a developing baby. There is no known "safe" amount of alcohol that a pregnant woman can drink. For this reason, doctors recommend that women consume no alcohol when they are trying to become pregnant and throughout the pregnancy. This will prevent any negative effects on the baby related to alcohol.

Fetal alcohol syndrome (FAS) is an incurable condition found in some children of mothers who consumed alcohol during pregnancy. FAS includes a wide range of physical and mental disabilities that last a lifetime.

One in five babies born with FAS does not live to see his or her first birthday. Those who survive suffer a variety of possible problems, such as facial deformity, delayed physical growth, heart defects, and hyperactivity. Some are mentally retarded or have severe learning problems. Alcohol interferes with tissue growth and development, and brain tissue is easily injured by alcohol. Other common problems include poor coordination and difficulty controlling behavior.

Some children may suffer from **fetal alcohol effects**. This condition is less severe than fetal alcohol syndrome. To a lesser degree, the child suffers from many of the same ailments as with FAS.

The extent of damage to the child is usually directly related to the amount of alcohol the mother consumed during pregnancy. It may also be affected by her stage of pregnancy when she drank. For example, women who engage in binge drinking in the early stages of pregnancy may have an increased risk of having a baby with FAS. The combination of alcohol with other drugs also affects the degree of damage to the child.

Other Drugs

Researchers and physicians believe very strongly that drugs consumed during pregnancy are among the major causes of birth defects linked to environmental factors. See Fig. 4-16. In addition to alcohol, other substances include:

- Medicines, including both those that doctors prescribe and over-the-counter types.
- Caffeine, found in some foods (such as chocolate) and beverages. While the safety of caffeine during pregnancy has been controversial, until researchers know more about its effects, it is wise to avoid caffeine.
- Nicotine and other toxic chemicals found in cigarettes.
- Illegal drugs such as heroin, LSD, ecstasy, marijuana, and all forms of cocaine.
- Inhalants—fumes that are inhaled into the lungs.

Fig. 4-16 **Birth defects caused by drinking, smoking, and other drugs are preventable.** How do you think a mother feels if she finds out her behavior caused her child's birth defect?

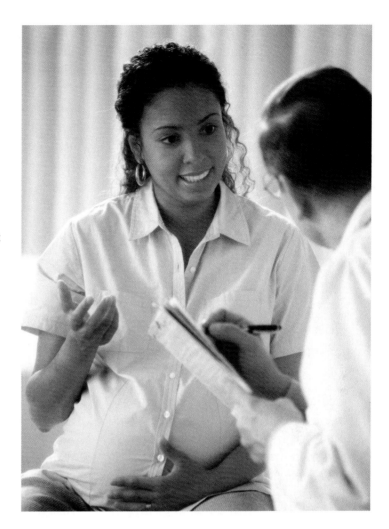

Fig. 4-17 **Even common medicines that are sold in pharmacies and super-markets may be unsafe for an unborn baby.** How can a pregnant woman be sure that a medicine is safe?

Prescription Drugs and Over-the-Counter Drugs

Every time an expectant mother considers using any type of medication, vitamin, or herbal supplement, she should check with her doctor. There is no such thing as a completely safe drug for a developing fetus. See Fig. 4-17.

An extreme example of an unsafe medication is thalidomide. This drug was prescribed to women in the 1950s to relieve morning sickness. Before its devastating effects were discovered, more than 5,000 babies were born with severe birth defects, such as missing or deformed arms and legs. Had doctors known the effects of this drug, they never would have prescribed it.

More recently, a prescription medicine for acne proved harmful to unborn children. When taken during pregnancy, the drug can cause serious birth defects. Therefore, it is not prescribed for pregnant women or those who may become pregnant.

The first three months of pregnancy are the most critical because the baby's body systems, including the brain, are being formed. The chemicals found in some medications can cause severe harm, including mental retardation.

In the fourth through ninth months of pregnancy, harmful substances that reach the fetus may cause slow growth, infections, or bleeding at birth. Drugs taken shortly before delivery will still be in the baby's bloodstream after birth.

In some instances, the expectant mother needs medication for a specific medical condition. For example, some women may need to take medications daily for epilepsy, diabetes, or high blood pressure. It is acceptable for a pregnant woman to take these necessary medications, as long as her doctor prescribes them and she takes them correctly. Medications that are not absolutely necessary should be avoided.

Parenting Q&A

How Do Caffeine and Alcohol Affect a Fetus?

While the dangers of caffeine and alcohol to an unborn fetus may seem like common sense, many people are unaware just how dangerous these common drugs can be.

- **Caffeine passes from a mother to her fetus easily through the placenta.** With its immature metabolism, the fetus may have higher blood levels of caffeine than the mother.
- **Caffeine can increase fetal heart rate and movement.** It can also contribute to premature birth and low birth weight, putting a baby at risk for further problems.

- **Consuming alcohol during pregnancy can also cause serious health problems for the baby.** The alcohol passes directly to the baby through the placenta and may cause problems in development, especially that of the brain.
- **While even small amounts of alcohol may harm the baby, greater amounts have been linked to fetal alcohol syndrome (FAS).** FAS causes physical and mental disabilities that last a lifetime.

Expectant mothers can avoid these risks by completely avoiding alcohol during pregnancy.

THINKING IT THROUGH

1. Does a fetus eliminate caffeine from its system as quickly as its mother does? Why or why not?
2. What information would you share with a pregnant friend or relative who feels that drinking alcohol on weekends is acceptable?

Caffeine

Caffeine is found in beverages many people consume several times a day, such as coffee, tea, cocoa, and most soft drinks. It is also present in some foods and many over-the-counter medications. Because it is consumed so frequently, caffeine is often not considered a drug—but it is.

Small amounts of caffeine, such as two cups of coffee or caffeinated soft drinks per day, don't appear to pose great pregnancy risks. However, larger quantities have been associated with a variety of prenatal problems. That is why most doctors advise women to avoid caffeine during pregnancy.

When women consume large amounts of caffeine during pregnancy, there is an increased risk of miscarriage and low birth weight, as well as a higher risk of infant death. Birth weight is a critical factor to a baby's survival. **Low birth weight** is a weight of less than 5 pounds, 8 ounces (2.5 kg) at birth. Babies with low birth weight may have serious health problems as newborns and are at greater risk of long-term problems.

Tobacco

Many studies have proven that nicotine found in tobacco is harmful to the health of any person. It is exceptionally harmful to a baby's development before birth. Smoking has been proven to cause low birth weights. The more a mother smokes, the smaller her baby is likely to be at birth. Heavy smoking is believed to cause premature birth as well. Finally, smoking during pregnancy is linked to respiratory infections and allergies among children after they are born. Nicotine from secondhand smoke has similar effects.

LOOKING AT REAL LIFE

Lori has been a smoker for several years. She and her husband want to have a baby, so Lori is going to try to quit. Lori's friend Beth explains that finding out that she was pregnant was what made her give up smoking. "I had smoked for so many years and tried almost everything—the nicotine patch, other over-the-counter treatments, classes—nothing worked. Once my husband and I found out we were having a baby, I found the motivation to quit."

"I never thought about it that way, Beth," Lori said. "Protecting my baby's health is reason enough to quit. I know about all the risks involved, not to mention the possibility of pregnancy complications. I've just needed something to motivate me enough to do it."

▸▸ PERSONAL APPLICATION

Have you ever worked to change a habit? What helped you achieve your goal?

Illegal Drugs

The use of illegal drugs, including cocaine, marijuana, and other illegal substances, can have devastating effects for an unborn baby. A mother who is addicted to a drug usually passes the addiction on to her baby. All drugs in the mother's bloodstream pass through the placenta directly to the baby. As a result, addicted newborns may suffer the consequences throughout their lives.

Right after birth, these infants must go through a painful period of withdrawal, as the body no longer receives the drug upon which it depends.

Babies that survive withdrawal have an uncertain future. Many experts believe that the long-term effects of prenatal addiction can be severe. Many of these children have a multitude of learning and behavioral difficulties.

Cocaine has been proven to increase the risk of miscarriage when used early during a pregnancy. It may also cause stillbirth or premature birth. Cocaine use may cause the unborn child to have a stroke that results in brain damage, a heart attack, serious birth defects, or even die. Babies exposed to cocaine tend to have a low birth weight, smaller heads than other newborns, and a risk of seizures and *sudden infant death syndrome* (**SIDS**). SIDS is the sudden death of a baby under one year of age with no clear cause.

Babies exposed to cocaine may also have tremors, exaggerated startle response, irritability, sleep and feeding difficulties, and developmental delay—all of which may persist into the early school years.

Currently, researchers are learning more about the effects of the drug ecstasy on unborn children, and the results are not good. Recent studies have shown that babies of women who take ecstasy are more likely to have congenital heart disease or a physical abnormality. This drug is not safe to take any time, but it is especially unsafe during pregnancy.

X Rays

X rays present another potential danger to the unborn baby. Radiation from X rays, or from other sources, can cause birth defects. There has been a great deal of debate about the safety of X rays during pregnancy. If an X ray is absolutely necessary due to an accident, illness, or dental work, the mother should inform the medical staff that she is pregnant. Special precautions can be taken to make sure the fetus is not exposed to much radiation. Dental X rays are generally considered safe, because they are focused very far from the uterus. Even so, many dentists delay routine X rays for a patient until after she has given birth.

Patients should always wear abdominal shields during an X ray to reduce the amount of radiation they are exposed to. See Fig. 4-18.

Hazardous Substances and Chemicals

A pregnant woman must be careful about hazardous substances in her home and work environment. Some include:

- Paint—low-odor latex paint in a well ventilated area may not pose a problem. A woman should check with her doctor before any exposure.
- Pesticides used to exterminate bugs
- Lead (in water and paint)
- Carbon monoxide
- Mercury (found in fish, such as swordfish and shark).
- Solvents, paint thinners, and formaldehyde (used in some workplaces)

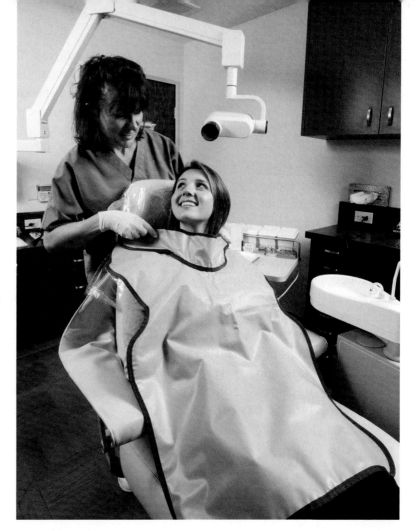

Fig. 4-18 **When X rays are suggested, a pregnant woman should inform the medical staff that she is pregnant so precautions can be taken.**

If a pregnant woman must live or work around some of these substances, she should consult her doctor immediately. She should also take extra precautions to minimize her exposure to any of these substances.

Infections

Occasionally, an expectant mother might get an infection during the course of her pregnancy. Some of these infections pose more of a risk to a fetus than others. The timing of an infection may have an effect on the risk level to a fetus as well. Some infections can be treated without any harm to the unborn baby if they are caught early and treated properly.

Rubella

If a pregnant woman contracts rubella, also known as German measles, it can have terrible consequences for her unborn baby. The infection can cause severe birth defects, especially in the first three months of pregnancy. These can include blindness, deafness, heart disease, and mental retardation.

A vaccine for rubella is available, and millions of children have been vaccinated. The vaccine may be dangerous, however, for women who are pregnant or who become pregnant shortly after receiving it. A woman who is unsure whether she has been vaccinated can check her health records or ask her doctor to test her. Every woman should be sure she is immune to rubella before she considers becoming pregnant. See Fig. 4-19.

Toxoplasmosis

Toxoplasmosis (TOX-o-plaz-MO-sis) is an infection caused by a parasite. This parasite is found all over the world, so the infection is quite common. It is estimated that as many as 60 million people in the United States carry the parasite, but most people have immune systems that are strong enough to prevent them from feeling any ill effects. However, developing babies are at risk if their mothers get the disease. Toxoplasmosis can cause blindness, hearing loss, and learning disabilities. Some cases are so severe that a baby dies shortly after birth or has long-term mental disabilities. Toxoplasmosis can also cause miscarriage or stillbirth.

An expectant mother can take several precautions to avoid exposing her baby to toxoplasmosis. She should never clean a cat's litter box, because cats carry the parasite that causes the infection. She shouldn't eat undercooked meat and should wash her hands immediately and thoroughly after touching raw meat.

Chicken Pox

Varicella, more commonly known as chicken pox, is a viral infection that commonly occurs in childhood. Some women who have not had chicken pox will get the infection during pregnancy. Depending upon when the infection occurs, there can be serious consequences to the fetus. If an

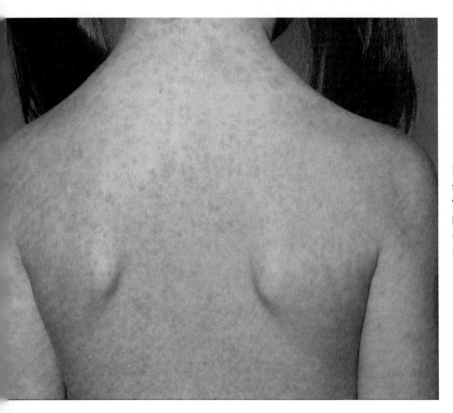

Fig. 4-19 Women need to make sure they have received a rubella vaccination before becoming pregnant. What are some possible effects on the unborn baby if the mother becomes infected?

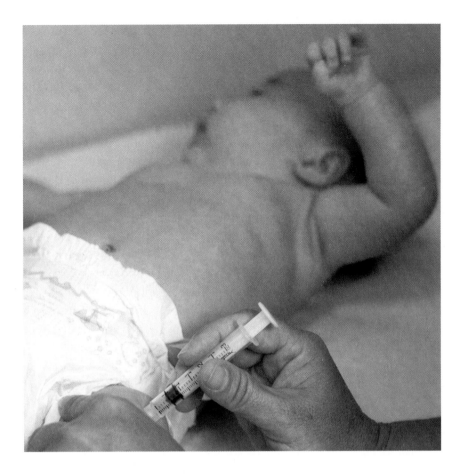

Fig. 4-20 **Many children receive vaccinations for chicken pox each year.** What other vaccinations are available?

expectant mother gets chicken pox during the first half of her pregnancy, her baby is at a slight risk of getting a condition called congenital varicella syndrome. This condition can cause scarring of the skin, limb defects, eye problems, and other serious abnormalities. In a very small number of cases, it can cause miscarriage.

Women who haven't had chicken pox should get the vaccine before getting pregnant and/or should avoid people with chicken pox. See Fig. 4-20.

Sexually Transmitted Diseases (STDs)

As with rubella, sexually transmitted diseases can do great harm to unborn babies, and in some instances may be passed to the child during the birth process. As you read in Chapter 2, some STDs include syphilis, gonorrhea, hepatitis B, genital herpes, acquired immune deficiency syndrome (AIDS), and chlamydia.

Many of these diseases can be passed on from the pregnant woman to the unborn child in the same way that the child receives nutrients from the mother. Some can result in serious illnesses, physical disabilities, or even death.

People can be infected with a sexually transmitted disease without realizing it. They may never even have any symptoms to indicate a problem. For this reason, special measures are usually taken to protect babies from the effects of STDs. Most doctors routinely test pregnant women for syphilis and group B streptococcus. In fact, many states require these tests by law. In addition, doctors usually treat the eyes of newborns with a solution that will kill any gonorrhea germs that could cause blindness.

Medical treatment can cure syphilis and gonorrhea and can relieve the symptoms of herpes in adults. No drug can cure the damage to a newborn that results from a delay in diagnosis and treatment. Any pregnant woman who suspects she might have been exposed to an STD should discuss this possibility frankly with her doctor.

AIDS

When an expectant mother has AIDS, there can be serious consequences for her unborn baby. There is a 35 to 65 percent risk that the virus will be passed on to the baby. AIDS attacks the brain, and infected babies often have seizures and retarded mental development. Most states now require an AIDS test early in a pregnancy. If a doctor knows that a pregnant woman has AIDS or the virus that causes it, special measures can be taken to reduce the baby's exposure to the disease. For example, the mother can take medication that reduces the chance that the baby will be infected with the virus. Also, most babies exposed to the AIDS virus and other STDs are delivered by cesarean section. This avoids exposure to the disease that may exist in the birth canal. AIDS testing also helps doctors to prepare for a newborn infected with the HIV virus that causes AIDS.

SECTION 4-4 Review and Activities

Reviewing the Section

1. What causes *FAS*? How can it be prevented?
2. What kinds of drugs, other than alcohol, can harm a developing baby?
3. What should a pregnant woman do before taking any over-the-counter medications?
4. Why should a woman tell a dentist when she is pregnant?
5. Why should a woman be vaccinated against rubella and chicken pox before becoming pregnant?
6. What is *toxoplasmosis*? How can it be avoided?

Observing and Interacting

Talk to parents you know about things they were told to avoid during pregnancy. What new information have doctors learned about things that can harm a baby since their children were born? How has testing for diseases changed since then?

Genetic Counselor

If you could find out before birth what chance your child had of having a genetic disease, would you? Many parents take tests to learn whether they carry diseases that may be passed along to their children. Genetic counselors help families understand what test results mean. They also provide emotional support.

▸ Job Responsibilities

Genetic counselors work with families who may be at risk for genetic diseases and ask questions about the family's medical history. They go over the test results with the family and talk about what it might be like to have a child who has an inherited condition. This gives people more control and helps them make better decisions about the future.

▸ Work Environment

Most genetic counselors work as part of a team. They also work in private offices or in hospitals. Some also conduct genetics research.

▸ Education and Training

Genetic counselors hold master's degrees in genetic counseling. Many have experience in other fields, such as social work or nursing. If they hold a master's degree and have counseling experience, they can take exams to become certified.

▸ Skills and Aptitudes

- Scientific skills and knowledge
- Compassion
- Respect for patients' privacy
- Ability to explain difficult concepts

WORKPLACE CONNECTION

1. **Thinking Skills.** Why is it important for professionals to be certified?

2. **Resource Skills.** If you could talk to a genetic counselor, what questions would you ask about the profession?

4 Review and Activities

SECTION SUMMARIES

- Prenatal development begins with conception and moves through three stages during the 40 weeks of pregnancy. (4-1)
- Specific changes take place just before birth signaling delivery is near. (4-1)
- Chromosomes from each parent carry the genes that determine all the traits a person inherits. (4-2)
- Couples who can't conceive may seek infertility treatment or adopt a child. (4-2)
- Grieving parents must deal with miscarriage or stillbirth. (4-3)
- Birth defects have a variety of causes. There are tests to help diagnose potential problems. (4-3)
- Everything a pregnant woman eats, drinks, and breathes affects her developing baby. (4-4)
- A pregnant woman should avoid alcohol, tobacco, and other drugs, including over-the-counter medications. (4-4)

REVIEWING THE CHAPTER

1. Use five "Key Terms" to describe how conception occurs. (4-1)
2. How long is each of the three stages of pregnancy? (4-1)
3. What changes occur in the fetus in the ninth month of prenatal development? (4-1)
4. How do genes shape the inheritance of physical characteristics? (4-2)
5. Name three options an infertile couple can use to help them have children. (4-2)
6. Identify the four general causes of *birth defects*, and give an example of a birth defect caused by each. (4-3)
7. How can genetic counseling help a couple concerned about possible birth defects? (4-3)
8. Compare and contrast recessive genes and dominant genes. (4-3)
9. What is the best advice for pregnant women regarding the use of any drugs? (4-4)
10. Why should even small amounts of alcohol be avoided during pregnancy? (4-4)

THINKING CRITICALLY

1. **Predicting Outcomes.** What could be the consequences of a teen denying that she is pregnant and not seeking any medical care?
2. **Synthesizing.** If identical twins have the exact same genetic blueprint, will they have the exact same personalities? Why or why not?

MAKING CONNECTIONS

1. **Social Studies.** Research the occurrence of birth defects in this country. How many people are born with birth defects? What are the social, economic, and political effects of birth defects?

2. **Science.** Research the latest advances in ultrasound technology. How can these advances help with the diagnosis of birth defects? What else can these new technologies reveal about a developing fetus?

APPLYING YOUR LEARNING

1. **Analyzing Development.** Create a quiz to share with the class. List specific events that occur during development, such as when finger- and toenails form, and leave blank spaces next to each one. Share the quiz and see if your classmates can fill in the blanks.

2. **Interpersonal Skills.** Women who become pregnant for the first time are often nervous about the well-being of their babies. However, they don't always know what questions to ask during their first prenatal visit. If you were an obstetrician, what communication techniques would you use to make sure important information is understood?

3. **Categorizing Causes.** Develop a chart that divides birth defects mentioned in the chapter by the four general causes.

Learning from Research

1. Choose one of the following research claims to investigate.
2. How is this research finding useful to prenatal development?
3. Summarize what you have learned about how over-the-counter medications affect a fetus.

Acetaminophen and Prenatal Development. Acetaminophen is a pain killer and fever reducer that is sold over the counter. Research has shown that, with a doctor's approval, this medication is safe to take during pregnancy in small amounts. Find out what amounts of acetaminophen are considered safe to consume during pregnancy.

Ibuprofen and Prenatal Development. Ibuprofen is a pain killer and fever reducer that is sold over the counter. Research has proven that this medication is not safe for a developing fetus when taken during pregnancy. It can cause birth defects. Find out which birth defects can be triggered by using ibuprofen during pregnancy.

Vitamins and Prenatal Development. Research has shown that before and during pregnancy, with a doctor's approval, a woman should take a vitamin that contains folic acid. Prenatal vitamins can help prevent birth defects. These vitamins are sold over the counter. Identify the amounts of folic acid recommended for each stage of prenatal development.

5 Preparing for Birth

Thoughtful Reading:

As you read this chapter:

- Identify three phrases that remind you of background knowledge.
- Reread the passages.
- Write three "I connect to ____?____ on page _____" statements about what you read.

Section 5-1
A Healthy Pregnancy

Section 5-2
Preparing for the Baby's Arrival

Section 5-3
Childbirth Options

A Healthy Pregnancy

A pregnant woman's responsibilities grow along with her baby. What happens to a baby during prenatal development can affect both the baby's and parents' lives. For their babies' health and their own, mothers-to-be need to eat a well-balanced diet, exercise moderately, get plenty of sleep, and manage stress.

Objectives

- List the early signs of pregnancy.
- Assess the importance of good medical care throughout pregnancy.
- Identify possible discomforts and complications of pregnancy.
- Plan a nutritious diet for expectant mothers.
- Explain the importance of stress management during pregnancy.

Key Terms

obstetrician
anemia
Rh factor
gestational diabetes
preeclampsia
lactose intolerance
lactase

Early Signs of Pregnancy

How do women discover that they are pregnant? Within a few weeks of conception, women usually experience one or more of the following signs of pregnancy:

- A missed menstrual period (often the first indicator)
- A full feeling or mild ache in the lower abdomen
- Feeling tired or faint
- A frequent, urgent need to urinate
- Swollen breasts causing discomfort or tenderness
- Nausea and/or vomiting, particularly in the morning

These symptoms are common, but they don't always mean that a woman is pregnant. If she believes she is pregnant, she should take a pregnancy test as soon as possible. Doctors can conduct tests to confirm pregnancy. There are also a variety of home pregnancy tests available. They are easy to use and very accurate. Early detection of pregnancy is crucial to the health of the expectant mother and her baby.

Medical Care During Pregnancy

Once pregnancy is determined, it is important for a woman to schedule a doctor's visit. Most pregnant women choose an

obstetrician (ahb-ste-TRISH-un)—a doctor who specializes in pregnancy and childbirth—for medical care during pregnancy.

Most doctors schedule regular checkups during pregnancy, then assist during childbirth and examine the newborn. It is important that expectant mothers find a doctor they like, feel comfortable with, and trust.

Many obstetricians work as part of a team with other doctors, taking turns caring for patients at night and on weekends. Although pregnant women usually have a primary doctor, they typically meet all the doctors who work in the same office so they know and feel comfortable with them. If the primary doctor is not on duty when they are ready to deliver, another doctor on the team will deliver the baby. However, the primary doctor performs most of the woman's checkups. See Fig. 5-1.

Some women believe they will save money by seeing a doctor only when the baby is ready to be born. This is not the case. Most obstetricians set a fee for all the services they provide throughout the pregnancy, from the first exam to the follow-up visits after the baby is born. Nothing is more important to the health of the baby than for the mother to get regular medical care and advice from the beginning to the end of the pregnancy.

The First Exam

When pregnancy is confirmed, the woman receives a thorough examination that includes the following:

- A check of her blood pressure, pulse, respiration, and weight. See Fig. 5-2.
- A discussion of her medical history, including existing medical conditions, such as high blood pressure, that may require special treatment or observation during pregnancy.

Fig. 5-1 **A pregnant woman often meets all the doctors in a medical office, in case her primary doctor isn't available when she goes into labor.** How can meeting the other doctors help a woman prepare for childbirth?

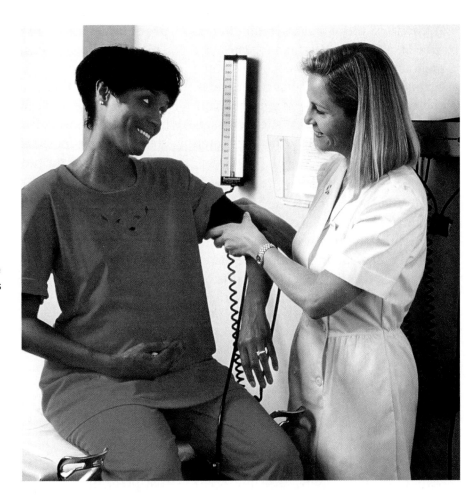

Fig. 5-2 **Blood pressure is checked regularly during pregnancy. An increase in pressure may signal a serious problem.**

- A measurement of her pelvis to determine whether it is wide enough to allow a baby of normal size to pass through.
- An analysis of her urine for signs of infection or diabetes, a condition characterized by excessive amounts of urine. Diabetes develops when the body is not able to produce enough insulin to keep blood sugar (glucose) within an acceptable range. This condition affects the body's ability to burn energy.
- Blood tests to rule out **anemia**, a condition that results from not having enough red blood cells. Symptoms include fatigue, shortness of breath, and rapid heartbeat. People with anemia often report feeling cold and weak. The blood test also determines whether or not the mother's blood contains a certain protein, known as the **Rh factor**. Knowing about the presence (Rh positive) or absence (Rh negative) of this protein is very important. The Rh factor is determined genetically. If the mother's blood doesn't have the protein and the fetus's blood does, the mother's blood builds up antibodies that attack the protein in the fetus's blood, as it would an invading germ. This doesn't affect a first pregnancy, but it can endanger any later pregnancies. However, once identified, the mother can receive an injection that will prevent the antibodies from forming, thus protecting any Rh positive fetus.

- A check of the woman's immunity to rubella, also called German measles. If a pregnant woman hasn't been vaccinated against this disease and has never had it, she must be especially careful to avoid anyone who has it. If she contracts rubella during pregnancy, the fetus could be harmed.

One question every pregnant woman has is "When will my baby be born?" The approximate birth date is easy to calculate. Nine months and one week after the first day of her final period before pregnancy is her baby's due date. Of course, doctors know that even in a typical pregnancy a variation of up to two weeks before or after that date can be expected.

Later Checkups

Expectant mothers have checkups, or prenatal visits, once a month until the sixth or seventh month of pregnancy. After that point, women see the doctor twice a month. In the final month, checkups occur once a week. During these visits, doctors monitor the baby's development and the mother's health.

Between the 24th and 28th weeks of the pregnancy, most women take a glucose tolerance test to check for signs of **gestational diabetes**, a form of diabetes that occurs only during pregnancy. If left untreated during pregnancy, diabetes can cause the baby to be heavier than is normal or healthy. Some women who don't normally have diabetes develop the condition when they are pregnant. This type of diabetes usually goes away after the baby is born. Gestational diabetes can usually be controlled by a special diet or may require medication.

Another serious condition that can occur during the second half of pregnancy is **preeclampsia** (pre-ee-CLAMP-see-ah). This condition is characterized by high blood pressure and the presence of protein in the mother's urine. Preeclampsia can prevent the baby from getting enough blood, which provides oxygen and food. Treatment for preeclampsia depends on how far along in the pregnancy a woman is. Her doctor can recommend the appropriate treatment, such as bed rest or medication, for this condition.

Most doctors welcome the father or another person who will be attending the birth to accompany the pregnant woman at prenatal visits. This gives the support person a chance to meet the doctor and follow the baby's growth. Sometimes it is helpful to have someone else ask questions and remember key information.

Discomforts of Pregnancy

Most women experience few problems during pregnancy. In fact, some women say that pregnancy is a time of robust health. Other women feel some discomfort, which usually doesn't indicate serious problems. If a woman experiences one or more of the following symptoms, however, she should report it to her doctor:

- **Nausea and/or vomiting.** While this is commonly called "morning sickness," it can occur at any time of the day. Morning sickness is the most common complaint of pregnant women. It rarely lasts beyond the fourth month of pregnancy. If it is severe and prolonged, however, women should alert their doctors.

- **Sleepiness.** Due to hormonal changes, sleepiness is quite common early in pregnancy. Many women feel more energetic in the middle months of pregnancy. For most, however, fatigue returns in the

Fig. 5-3 Why shouldn't pregnant women who experience common problems such as headaches take over-the-counter remedies?

final months, since the baby weighs more and takes up more room.

- **Heartburn.** This is a burning feeling in the upper abdomen. Women with heartburn—which has nothing to do with the heart—should ask their doctors about safe forms of relief.

- **Shortness of breath.** Pressure on the lungs from the baby can cause shortness of breath. This is particularly common late in pregnancy. See Fig. 5-3.

- **Varicose (swollen) veins.** When there is pressure on the blood vessels in the legs, varicose veins can appear.

Varicose veins are twisted, enlarged veins, or blood vessels, that are close to the skin's surface. Getting plenty of exercise, resting with the legs elevated, and using support stockings can help relieve the swelling.

- **Muscle cramps in the legs.** Gentle stretches, rest, and a diet rich in calcium may alleviate the pain of these cramps.

- **Lower back pain.** Wearing low-heeled shoes and learning to lift properly (or avoiding it altogether) can minimize back problems. Exercises that strengthen the back can also help.

Possible Serious Complications

A few women experience more serious problems during pregnancy. Any of the following symptoms should be reported to a doctor immediately:

- Vaginal bleeding
- Unusual weight gain or loss
- Excessive thirst
- Diminished need to urinate or pain during urination
- Severe abdominal pain
- Persistent headaches
- Severe vomiting
- Fever
- Increased vaginal mucus
- Swelling of the face, hands, or ankles
- Blurred vision or dizziness
- Prolonged backache

Nutrition During Pregnancy

 Good nutrition is the single most important requirement during pregnancy. The baby's growth and development, including crucial brain development, depend on nutrients from the mother. By eating a nutritious, balanced diet, a pregnant woman promotes her baby's development and maintains her own health. See Fig. 5-4.

The Role of Nutrients

There are five types of nutrients a body needs. Each nutrient plays a special role in promoting a healthy diet:

- **Protein.** Meat, poultry, fish, dried beans, nuts, eggs, milk, and cheese provide protein, which is vital to the baby's growth and development of bones and teeth. It also helps keep the mother's body in good condition. Expectant mothers need more protein than they did before they were pregnant.

- **Vitamins.** Research has determined some birth defects, such as spina bifida, are linked to vitamin deficiency. Women usually need more vitamins during pregnancy, including twice the usual amount of folic acid for normal spinal development. Women who are considering becoming pregnant should also increase their intake of folic acid. Pregnant women should take vitamins and other supplements only when their doctors approve them.

  Vitamins help to maintain a healthy pregnancy. Vitamin A ensures proper eye development. Vitamin B assists in general fetal development. Vitamin C helps build healthy teeth and gums and helps form the connective tissue of skin, bone, and organs. Vitamin D aids in the creation of bones and teeth.

  Fresh fruits and vegetables, whole-grain breads and cereals, and fortified milk and other dairy products are great sources of vitamins. Milk is often enriched with vitamins A and D.

- **Minerals.** These nutrients help produce strong bones and teeth and ensure regular elimination of waste from the body. Doctors may instruct pregnant women to take mineral supplements.

  Pregnant women particularly need iron, a mineral that helps prevent anemia and assists in developing the baby's own blood supply. Extra iron is stored in the baby's liver and is used in the months right after birth. During this period, a baby who lives on breast milk lacks iron in the diet. Good sources of iron include dried beans, raisins, dates, meat, and leafy green vegetables.

Calcium and phosphorous are also important minerals during pregnancy. They work together to keep the mother's bones and teeth strong and build the baby's. Milk and other dairy products are key sources of calcium and phosphorous.

• **Carbohydrates and fats.** These nutrients provide the body with energy and perform many other important functions that keep the body running smoothly. Whole-grain breads and cereals, fruits, and starchy vegetables such as potatoes all provide carbohydrates. Sugars are also carbohydrates, but should be eaten in moderation. The body also needs some fats, though the average diet is more likely to contain too much fat rather than too little. Foods high in fats, such as those fried in oil, should be avoided.

Fig. 5-4 **Eating nutritiously is one of the best gifts a pregnant mother can give her unborn baby.**

 THE DEVELOPING BRAIN

Some pregnant women fail to follow a sensible and balanced diet. Others, wrongly concerned about gaining weight, severely restrict their food intake. Either way, the developing fetus is put in serious danger. One possible outcome of failing to supply adequate nutrition to the fetus is that brain development will be stunted and the baby will be mentally retarded. Alcohol consumption, cigarette smoking, and drug abuse during pregnancy can have similar results.

Making Wise Food Choices

Everywhere you look, there seems to be conflicting advice about what you should eat. Much is still being studied in the science of nutrition. However, guidelines for healthy eating have been established. These are summarized in Fig. 5-5 on page 154. These recommendations emphasize choosing a variety of foods high in key nutrients. Less nutritious foods can be eaten occasionally. Pregnant women have a special responsibility to make good food choices.

Fig. 5-5

Guidelines for Healthy Eating

Focus on fruits. Eat a variety of fruits—whether fresh, frozen, canned, or dried—rather than fruit juice for most of your fruit choices. For a 2,000-calorie diet, you will need 2 cups of fruit each day (for example, 1 small banana, 1 large orange, and ¼ cup of dried apricots or peaches).

Vary your veggies. Eat more dark green veggies, such as broccoli, kale, and other dark leafy greens; orange veggies, such as carrots, sweet potatoes, pumpkin, and winter squash; and beans and peas, such as pinto beans, kidney beans, black beans, garbanzo beans, split peas, and lentils.

Get your calcium-rich foods. Get 3 cups of low-fat or fat-free milk—or an equivalent amount of low-fat yogurt and/or low-fat cheese (1½ ounces of cheese equals 1 cup of milk)—every day. For kids ages 2 to 8, it's 2 cups of milk. If you don't or can't consume milk, choose lactose-free milk products and/or calcium-fortified foods and beverages.

Make half your grains whole. Eat at least 3 ounces of whole-grain cereals, breads, crackers, rice, or pasta every day. One ounce is about 1 slice of bread, 1 cup of breakfast cereal, or ½ cup of cooked rice or pasta. Look to see that grains such as wheat, rice, oats, or corn are referred to as "whole" in the list of ingredients.

Go lean with protein. Choose lean meats and poultry. Bake it, broil it, or grill it. And vary your protein choices—with more fish, beans, peas, nuts, and seeds.

Know the limits on fats, salt, and sugars. Read the Nutrition Facts label on foods. Look for foods low in saturated fats and *trans* fats. Choose and prepare foods and beverages with little salt (sodium) and/or added sugars (caloric sweeteners).

Parenting Q&A

What Are Diet Guidelines for an Expectant Mother?

Pregnant women who eat a diet low in nutrients, or who smoke, drink alcohol, or use drugs, risk giving birth to babies with serious physical and mental defects.

What pregnant women need:
- About 300 extra calories per day.
- Six to eleven servings of whole-grain or fortified foods such as bread, cereal, and pasta.
- Five servings of fruits and vegetables every day, including juices or fruit rich in vitamin C.
- Oranges and leafy green vegetables for folic acid. Adequate amounts of this nutrient reduce the risk of brain and spinal defects.

- Three to four servings of protein per day, such as beans or lean meat.
- Six to eight glasses of water per day.

What pregnant women should avoid:
- Supplements that contain more than the recommended daily value of vitamins and minerals. Too much Vitamin A can harm a baby.
- Raw eggs and milk or cheeses that are not pasteurized and certain fish.
- Alcohol, which can lead to mental retardation in babies.
- Smoke, because mothers who smoke don't get enough oxygen, and their baby may not develop properly.

THINKING IT THROUGH

1. Do you know anyone who is or has been pregnant? Did she adjust her diet to include or exclude certain things?
2. Do you have a good diet? If not, how could you improve it?

Nutrition and Pregnant Teens

Teens' bodies have special nutritional needs because they are still developing. Pregnancy places significant additional strain on the body. While many teens fill up on high-calorie, low-nutrient foods, pregnant teens must be particularly careful to eat nutritious meals and snacks. It is essential for a teen's own body—and her growing baby—to get all the necessary nutrients for proper growth and development. It's especially important for pregnant teens to get enough calcium and iron. Calcium is essential for growing bones, and iron helps the blood carry oxygen to every part of the body. During pregnancy, a woman has more blood moving around her body, so iron is even more important to her health.

Special Diets

Milk and other dairy products are a rich source of calcium, protein, and other key nutrients. Expectant mothers who can't tolerate milk products need special eating strategies. One alternative is to eat larger amounts of other calcium-rich foods, such as broccoli, tofu, and leafy green vegetables. Protein can come from meat, poultry, fish, and dried beans. If milk products cause symptoms such as abdominal pain and gas, the problem is usually **lactose intolerance**. (Lactose is a type of sugar found in milk.) Cultured yogurt contains **lactase**, an enzyme that helps in the digestion of lactose. This works for some. Many people who have problems digesting lactose can still eat dairy foods, as long as they are served in small quantities or eaten with other foods. Taking lactase in liquid or tablet form can also relieve symptoms. Before taking lactase or any other dietary supplement, pregnant women should consult their doctors.

Vegetarians don't eat meat, which is high in protein. Some vegetarians, called *vegans*, don't eat any animal products at all, including eggs and milk. By eating enough tofu and other soybean products, dried beans, nuts, and nut butters such as peanut butter, pregnant vegetarians and vegans can get the protein they need.

Weight Gain During Pregnancy

Women typically gain about 24 to 30 pounds during pregnancy. Figure 5-6 shows how that weight is usually distributed.

In the first three months of pregnancy, some women don't gain any weight and may even lose a few pounds. Morning sickness sometimes contributes to this, and it is not a cause for concern unless it is severe and a woman begins to lose weight. Recommended weight gain is about a pound a month during the first three months. In the fourth through sixth months, weight gain should be about half a pound a week.

Gaining too little weight can increase the risk of fetal death or premature birth. Women who begin a pregnancy underweight or overweight will require special monitoring.

Fig. 5-6 Weight Gain During Pregnancy	
	Pounds
Weight of average baby at birth	7–8
Placenta	1–2
Amniotic fluid	1½–2
Increased size of uterus and supporting muscles	2
Increase in breast tissue	1
Increase in blood volume	1½–3
Increase in fat stores	5
Increase in body fluids	5–7
Total	24–30

Personal Care and Activities

In addition to practicing good nutrition, pregnant women can take care of themselves in other ways. While pregnant women can usually follow some of the same daily routines they had before pregnancy, they should also do the following:

- **Get plenty of rest.** Taking frequent breaks during the day may provide more energy.

- **Exercise.** While pregnancy is not the time to start a strenuous exercise routine, moderate exercise is important to everyone, including pregnant women. Doctors may recommend walking, biking, or swimming. There may be exercise classes available that are planned specifically for pregnant women.

- **Practice good hygiene.** Keeping the skin clean helps the body to maintain a healthy temperature and eliminate waste. A warm bath or shower before bedtime also may help pregnant women relax.

Pregnant women don't need to radically change their activities during pregnancy. While moderation is advised, they can usually continue their activities as before.

Maternity Clothes

By around the fourth or fifth month, a pregnant woman needs looser clothing to allow for freedom of movement and circulation as the baby grows. Maternity pants often have a stretch panel in the front. Shirts, too, are made looser to accommodate the growing baby. When choosing clothing, an expectant mother should consider how garments will fit during her ninth month.

LOOKING AT REAL LIFE

"I guess you'll have to stop exercising with me now that you're pregnant," Gwen said to her friend Holly, who just found out she was pregnant. "I don't know, actually," Holly told Gwen. "I'll give Dr. Wallace a call."

From the doctor, Holly learned that a woman *can* and *should* exercise while pregnant, although some aspects of her usual exercise regimen might need to be adjusted to her changing body. She and Dr. Wallace came up with a workout plan suited to her needs. She would perform light aerobic activity, such as swimming or walking. Dr. Wallace said, "If you were exercising before becoming pregnant, it's okay to continue your routine with modifications. Always drink plenty of water. After the first trimester, don't do any exercises that require you to be on your back or do any abdominal work. You can use any sitting exercise machine, such as the seated leg curl." "That sounds great," said Holly. "The better shape I'm in, the easier it will be to cope with the birth."

▸▸PERSONAL APPLICATION

What are some physical conditions that would limit your fitness routine? What adjustments might you make to stay fit?

Reduce Stress During Pregnancy

If you have experienced stress, you know how it affects you. You may feel moody, anxious, annoyed, or afraid. Perhaps you lose your appetite, have nightmares, or feel sweaty and shaky. Pregnancy can be a stressful time, but it is important that pregnant women find ways to ease the pressure—for themselves and their babies. There are many ways to cope with stress while pregnant.

- **Avoiding sugary foods and caffeine.** These can make pregnant women jittery.

- **Exercising.** Gentle exercises such as stretching and moderate physical activity such as walking can help pregnant women feel lighter and more energetic.

- **Taking a time-out.** Taking time to relax and enjoy a favorite activity can help relieve stress.

- **Practicing relaxation techniques.** Pregnant women can easily learn breathing or visualization exercises through books or classes.

- **Talking about concerns.** Mothers-to-be can benefit from talking to supportive friends or family members, particularly those who have children.

- **Taking a class for expectant parents.** The more pregnant women know about the birth process, the greater their sense of control. Feeling prepared reduces stress.

YOUR TURN

A friend in need. Imagine you have a friend who is expecting a baby. She is very fearful about giving birth. How can you help her reduce the tension in her life and prepare for labor and delivery?

Emotional Health During Pregnancy

Pregnancy and birth are major events in a couple's life. They are also times of emotional adjustments. It is vital to talk things out. Spending time alone together can help. Family and friends can also be sources of information and support.

Pregnancy causes hormonal changes that may lead to mood swings. Every woman feels upset and worried at times during pregnancy, and effective stress-reduction techniques are important. See "How to

Children Around the World

Korea *Taegyo*

In Korea, pregnant women learn a set of practices that have been transmitted to women by word of mouth and through literature and folklore for centuries. The word for these practices is *taegyo* (TAYG-yo), which literally means "fetal education." There is a saying in Korea that fetal education is more important than the first ten years of a child's schooling. Pregnant women are taught to read inspiring books; eat colorful, attractive foods; sit or stand straight; and listen to beautiful music. They are not supposed to go outside in bad weather, deceive anyone, or dwell on anything unpleasant. These practices stem from the belief that the fetus is extremely sensitive to what the mother feels.

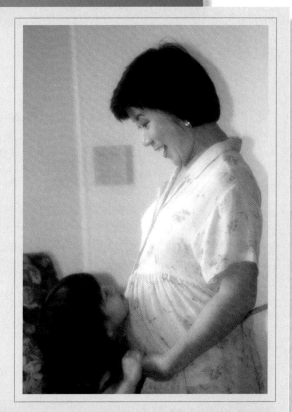

Investigating Culture

1. Korean women believe that what happens to their unborn babies can affect the course of their babies' entire lives. In what ways do you think this is true?
2. What role does recreation play in helping pregnant women cope with stress?

Reduce Stress During Pregnancy" on page 158 for ways in which pregnant women can alleviate stress.

Depression

Emotional and physical stress can lead to depression, deep and lasting feelings of sadness. Expectant mothers who feel overwhelmed need to seek help. There are a number of ways they can find support. A woman's doctor may recommend a professional counselor or local support group. Often, women who are going through, or have been through, similar experiences can help the expectant mother. The Internet is another tool for finding support groups. Even relevant books can help expectant mothers understand their concerns and improve their outlook.

SECTION 5-1 Review and Activities

Reviewing the Section

1. What are three early signs of pregnancy? Do these signs always mean a woman is pregnant?
2. If a pregnant woman's last period began on April 10th, what would her expected due date be?
3. Why is it so important for a pregnant woman to receive prenatal care from the beginning through the end of her pregnancy?
4. Give at least three examples of the common discomforts in the first few months of pregnancy. Which are more common later?
5. Name five symptoms that pregnant women should report to their doctors right away.
6. What is a glucose tolerance test?
7. Which nutrients are more important during pregnancy than other times?
8. About how much weight should women gain during pregnancy if they are of normal weight?
9. If a pregnant women is feeling stressed, what are three ways she could alleviate her stress?

Observing and Interacting

Suppose a pregnant woman wants to buy clothing so that she has something different to wear five days of the week, whether she is at home or working in an office or going out to dinner. Make a list of what she would need to buy. Then visit a maternity clothing store or a department store that sells maternity clothes or search Web sites that sell maternity clothes. Determine how much she would have to spend to get five outfits.

Preparing for the Baby's Arrival

Pregnancy is a time of anticipation and preparation. It is also a time for expectant parents to think about what their baby's physical, emotional, and intellectual needs will be and how they are going to meet them. Having practical plans in place can help things go more smoothly once the baby arrives.

Objectives

- Describe the decisions and preparations expectant parents must make for the physical needs of their baby.
- Explain why a budget is important and list the items parents need to include in a budget.
- Identify the considerations involved in making a decision about who will care for a new baby.

Key Terms

formula
pediatrician
fixed expenses
flexible expenses
maternity leave
paternity leave

Preparing for Parenthood

Many expectant parents—especially first-time parents—worry that they may not be up to the demands of raising a child. However, before the baby's arrival is the time for parents to discuss their hopes, fears, worries, and other aspects of parenting. How will they handle guidance and discipline? How will parenting tasks be shared? How will they manage all the new expenses? Of course, no one can plan for every situation, and parents' ideas often change somewhat as they gain parenting experience. Agreeing on certain ground rules, however, can reduce confusion and conflict in relationships later on.

Parents-to-be must also prepare for their changing responsibilities. In addition to their current roles, perhaps as spouses, employees, students, volunteers, sisters or brothers, daughters or sons, they will become parents. It is clear that some of these existing responsibilities will change due to the time and energy that parenthood demands.

Everyone can benefit from good time-management skills, but they are especially important for parents. Developing a basic daily schedule helps keep things on track. Routines also help infants and young children know what to expect when, which helps them feel secure. Using time wisely can help make sticking to a schedule easier. For example, combining errands or taking advantage of naptimes can help parents feel less overwhelmed.

Diana and Brent have a three-year-old son, Charlie. They are having another child, but they are concerned about how their son will react to a new baby brother or sister.

"Charlie, guess what?" Diana asks. "Mommy is going to have a baby. That means that you are going to have a little brother or sister." Charlie looks confused. "Where are you going to get the baby? From the store?" "No," says Diana. "The baby is growing inside Mommy's tummy." She points to her belly. "Do I have to give him my toys?" Charlie asks. "Well, we'll get some new toys for the baby, but do you think you'll be able to share your toys with him, too? The two of you could play together and you could help him. You can help Mommy and Daddy take care of him, since you're going to be his big brother." "I don't want a baby," Charlie says. "I want a dog!"

▶▶PERSONAL APPLICATION

How would you have told Charlie about the baby coming?

Other Children in the Family

It is not always easy for children to accept a new baby in their lives. Older siblings may not be as excited as their parents about the new addition to the family. Who can blame them? All of a sudden their world is turned upside down. They have to share their parents' attention, their own toys, and space. It is a big adjustment. Of course, many children are also happy to have a sibling. They look forward to helping care for the new baby and to showing their sibling the ropes.

How children react to a new sister or brother depends in large part on how well prepared they were before the baby's arrival, how they typically react to change, and their age. Parents should be prepared for a wide range of attitudes—from jealousy and confusion to excitement and love. A two-year-old doesn't really understand what is happening. Adjusting takes time. Talking about concerns and acceptance of a child's feelings can help foster a positive relationship between siblings.

Clothes, Equipment, and Space

The list of basic supplies for a baby can be overwhelming for many new parents. Babies need clothes, bedding, bath supplies, and travel equipment such as a stroller. Parents who choose bottle-feeding need bottles, plastic nipples, and lids. Figure 5-7 describes basic baby supplies. Parents can get specific suggestions from doctors, family, friends, and magazines and books that test products.

Fig. 5-7
Basic Baby Supplies

Diapering Needs
- A changing table or some surface to use for changing the baby
- If using disposable diapers: About 70 (a week's supply)
- If using cloth diapers: 3–4 dozen diapers; diaper pins; waterproof pants; a covered diaper pail; 8–10 disposable diapers for occasional use
- 6–10 washcloths
- Diaper rash ointment

Clothing
- 6–8 undershirts; 4–6 one-piece footed sleepers; 4–6 gowns
- 6 cotton receiving blankets; 1 warm outer wrapping blanket
- 1 dress-up outfit (optional)
- 1 sweater
- 1–2 sun hats or bonnets; warmer hat if needed for cooler weather
- Coat and mittens (optional)

Feeding Equipment
- If breast-feeding and mother works: Breast pump and pads; plastic bottles for storing breast milk
- If bottle-feeding: 6–8 large bottles (8-ounce or 237-mL); nipples and bottle caps (the same number as bottles, plus a few extra); bottle and nipple brush
- Bibs
- High chair

Bedding/Bedroom
- Crib and waterproof mattress (if the baby will sleep alone); bumper pad (fits around inside of crib just above mattress; keeps baby's arms and legs in, drafts out)
- Waterproof mattress cover; 2–4 absorbent pads
- 4 fitted crib sheets
- 2–3 lightweight blankets or spreads; heavier crib blanket
- Storage space, such as chest of drawers
- Wastebasket

Bathing and Other Supplies
- Baby bathtub or other container
- Rubbing alcohol (for umbilical cord)
- Mild, pure soap; baby shampoo
- Several soft washcloths, 2 soft cotton bath towels
- Cotton balls
- Baby oil and baby lotion
- Blunt-tipped nail scissors; baby comb and brush set
- Thermometer

Travel Equipment
- Car seat which meets the latest safety standards
- Tote bag for carrying supplies
- Stroller, carriage, or infant carrier (optional)

Baby's Room

Newborns may sleep as many as 18 to 22 hours a day. During the first six months, most babies sleep 15 to 18 hours a day. Some parents believe that babies sleep better in their parents' room. This arrangement makes late-night feedings easier. Others think that babies need a quiet space of their own in which to sleep. Of course, many babies share a sibling's room. Comfortable conditions are more important than a large amount of space. If the baby doesn't have a separate room, curtains or other room dividers can be used to create a quieter, private space.

A safe crib is one basic need. If a friend or relative offers to pass on a pre-owned crib, check it carefully to be sure it works properly and meets the current government standards for safety. See "How to Choose a Crib" on page 167 for specific features to be checked. While soft bedding may look cute and comfortable, it can be a suffocation hazard. Basic bumper pads around the crib, just above the mattress, can be used. When a baby is in a crib, remove pillows, fluffy blankets, and stuffed toys.

Some parents put a baby monitor near the crib. The device picks up sounds from the room and sends them to a speaker in another part of the home. This system lets parents know if the baby needs attention.

The Diaper-Changing Area

Parents need to set aside a space where the baby can be changed and dressed. While they can buy a changing table, almost any sturdy, flat surface—except those used for eating—will do. Whatever surface is used, it should be covered with a cloth or towel that can be washed regularly.

Even young babies can wiggle, roll, or move quickly. That is why a baby should never be left unattended on any elevated surface such as a changing table or a bed. Falls can occur very quickly—within seconds.

Decisions About Feeding

All parents must decide whether to breast- or bottle-feed their baby. There are several factors for parents to consider when making that choice. Figure 5-8 lists the advantages and disadvantages of breast-feeding and bottle-feeding.

Breast milk has many benefits, and health-care professionals recommend it whenever possible, even for a short time. Many mothers successfully breast-feed when they are at home with their babies and provide breast milk so that other caregivers can feed the baby when the mother is not available.

Using bottles enables the baby's father or others to enjoy time alone with the baby. Babies who are bottle-fed drink **formula**—a mixture of milk or milk substitutes, water, and essential nutrients. Formula comes in powdered form, which is mixed with water, or in liquid form.

Whether a baby is bottle-fed or breast-fed, the nurturing and touch that comes with being held and fed is as important as the food itself.

Choosing a Pediatrician

Before the baby is born, parents should choose a doctor to care for the child. Often this doctor is a **pediatrician**, a doctor who specializes in treating children. This doctor may be the child's primary doctor for years. Some families choose a family practice medical group so the whole family can go to one place for medical care. A family practice physician may treat children of all ages, or the medical group may include a pediatrician to care for children.

Fig. 5-8

Comparing Breast-Feeding and Bottle-Feeding

Breast-Feeding

Advantages

- Best source of nutrition for baby.
- Gives the baby some immunity against diseases.
- Creates a bond through physical closeness with the mother.
- May boost brain development.
- Reduces baby's risk of allergies.
- Causes fewer digestive upsets.
- Speeds the return of the mother's uterus to normal size.
- Reduces the mother's risk of later having breast or ovarian cancer.
- Reduces the risk that the mother will feel depressed.
- Is conveniently available at all times.
- Is free, though a nursing mother needs additional food.

Disadvantages

- Prevents father from participating in feeding.
- Baby has to be fed more often.
- In rare cases, may be medical reasons that suggest breast-feeding is not desirable.
- May be painful for some mothers.
- May be difficult because of work schedule.

Bottle-Feeding

Advantages

- Allows father to participate in feeding.
- Allows mother to have a more flexible schedule.
- Eliminates concern about mother's diet or medications she takes.
- Babies need feeding less often.

Disadvantages

- Can be expensive.
- Does not give the baby any natural immunities to disease.
- Involves a greater chance of baby developing allergies.
- Creates risk that baby may not be given close physical contact during feeding.

Parents can ask their own doctors or friends who have children for recommendations for pediatricians. Once they have a few names, they should interview each doctor to see if they like the doctor and agree with his or her ideas about caring for children. Most pediatricians welcome this opportunity to talk with prospective patients.

When choosing a doctor, some considerations are practical. Where is the doctor's office? What are the office hours? What are the fees for checkups, tests, and vaccinations? Which insurance plans are accepted?

Making a Budget

Prenatal care—an important expense—can be quite costly. Add these costs to the additional expenses involved with having a baby, and the amount of money needed to support a baby climbs higher than most new parents may anticipate. Planning can help parents meet these expenses, and creating a budget is one way to do this.

A budget is simply a spending plan that people use to help estimate their present and future income and expenses. A budget allows people to set goals for saving and develop a spending plan that meets their needs. Budgets are helpful for everyone, but especially for expectant and new parents.

The first step in making a budget is to identify income, such as money from jobs. The next step is to list where that income currently goes. **Fixed expenses**, such as car payments, housing payments and expenses, and taxes, generally can't be changed. **Flexible expenses**, such as food costs, household items, clothes, and entertainment, can be reduced if necessary.

Estimating Health Care Expenses

Health care costs during pregnancy and for childbirth can be high. This includes doctors' fees and the cost of staying in the hospital or birthing center. Hospitals charge different fees based on the care provided to the mother and baby. Most health insurance plans will cover these expenses—but only if the woman has insurance coverage at the time she becomes pregnant. If a pregnant woman isn't covered by insurance, some large hospitals have free or lower-cost clinics to help people who cannot pay the full fees or will make arrangements for payment plans. There are also government programs that offer financial assistance for health care costs.

Many employers offer health insurance to their employees, and these plans often cover their spouses and children, too. Workers should find out what part of the expenses they must pay on their own.

Even if employers don't provide insurance, people can purchase their own health insurance. It is always a good idea to shop around for a health care plan before buying into one. Insurance companies charge different amounts, and people can save money by making comparisons. As part of this process, it is important to carefully check the cost of the insurance and exactly what services it will cover. Some insurance plans pay doctors and hospitals directly. Others require the insured persons to pay bills themselves and then submit a claim for reimbursement.

Choose a Crib

Babies spend countless hours alone in a crib. That means crib safety should be a high priority. Here are the characteristics of a safe crib:

- **Slats.** Slats should be no more than $2\frac{3}{8}$ inches apart. If they are wider than this, a baby's head could become trapped between them.

- **Paint.** If the crib is painted, the paint should not contain lead and should be smooth, with no flaking.

- **Structure.** Corner posts should all be the same height. If some corner posts are taller than the sides of the crib, the baby's clothing or bedding could catch on the posts.

- **Sides.** When lowered, crib sides should be about 9 inches above the mattress to keep the baby from falling out. When they are raised, they should be at least 26 inches above the mattress.

- **Latch.** The latch to raise and lower the sides should lock securely. Never use a crib with a broken latch.

- **Mattress.** The mattress should be firm and fit the crib exactly, with no gaps. Infants can get trapped if there is space between the crib and mattress.

- **End panels.** If the end panels have decorative cutouts, they should be very small, so the baby's head, arms, and legs can't become caught in them.

- **Age.** If the crib was pre-owned, it should be carefully checked to be sure it meets these current safety standards.

YOUR TURN

Safe bedding for babies. Some parents buy cribs that meet the safety guidelines but fill them with objects that can be dangerous to babies. Why might placing quilts, pillows, and stuffed toys in a baby's crib be unsafe?

Estimating Other Expenses

Expectant parents must also consider other costs, including the following:

- Maternity clothes
- The supplies listed in Fig. 5-7 on page 163
- Formula, if a baby is bottle-fed, which can cost between $1,200 and $2,200 per year
- A crib or other necessary furniture
- Substitute child care, if needed

Making a Plan

Once parents have a list of all anticipated expenses, they then compare these to their income and savings. If the couple's monthly income is less than their projected monthly expenses, it may be necessary to cut back or explore other sources of income. If the mother works outside of the home, they will also need to consider whether her income will be disrupted when the baby arrives and she is off work. Parents who have saved money will have an easier time. Even those with no savings should include saving a regular amount in their budget. This cushion helps families deal with unexpected expenses and future needs. See Fig. 5-9.

Reducing Expenses

There are several ways to cut costs. Shopping for baby clothes at store sales, garage sales, or secondhand stores can save

Fig. 5-9 **If a mother leaves her job to stay home with her baby, a couple must be able to live on one income.**

Health & Safety

Car Seat Safety

One of the most important pieces of equipment parents buy is a child safety seat. Restraining a child properly while traveling in a car is the best way to prevent injuries in a crash. Children should be restrained using the appropriate car seats for their size and weight.

The safest place for an infant is facing the rear of the car in the middle of the back seat. This helps support the baby's head and back. Two kinds of seats are made for babies—infant-only seats and convertible seats. Infant-only seats fit babies up to 22 pounds. A convertible seat fits children from birth to about 40 pounds. It is used facing the back of the car for the first year, then can be turned to face the front when the baby is at least 1 year old and weighs at least 20 pounds. Children between 4 and 8 years use booster seats locked in place with seat belts. Check that the restraint is fitted correctly and tightly every time you put the child in the car. The forward-facing car seat is attached using an adult seat belt and an upper tether strap. To avoid injury, never put a child age 12 or under in the front seat in a car that has passenger-side airbags. Buckle them up in the back seat with both the lap and shoulder belts on every trip.

money. Using coupons can help stretch the family's food budget. Borrowing baby equipment and clothes is another way to save money. However, all used or borrowed items should be carefully cleaned.

Balancing Work and Family

Once expectant parents have developed their budget, they need to review their options for child care. Parents must consider many factors, including each other's goals, skills, and time available when deciding how to care for their child. Will one parent be able to cut back on working hours or stay at home full-time to care for the child? What other child care options are available, and what are their costs?

Many new parents who work take **maternity** or **paternity leave**. Under a federal law called the Family Medical Leave Act, employers with more than 50 workers must offer 12 weeks of unpaid family or medical leave to new mothers and fathers. Many workers don't take the entire 12 weeks of leave for financial reasons.

Couples sometimes decide that one parent will care for the child and not work outside the home. In the past, this was usually the mother. Today, many fathers are full-time caregivers.

Regardless of who takes primary responsibility for daily caregiving, both parents should share the work of caring for their children. In many families, both parents decide to return to work. In others, there is just one parent to support the family. These single parents have to consider child care options.

SECTION 5-2 Review and Activities

Reviewing the Section

1. Why are time-management skills important for parents?
2. What factors play a role in how siblings react to a new baby?
3. What are two ways expectant parents can reduce the costs of baby supplies and equipment?
4. What are the advantages of breast-feeding? What are the benefits of bottle-feeding?
5. Why should expectant parents make a budget?
6. What is the Family Medical Leave Act?
7. Identify factors expectant parents must consider when deciding about child care.

Observing and Interacting

Look at the list of basic baby supplies in Fig. 5-7 on page 163. Then look through the classified ads of your local paper, shop at a secondhand store, search Web sites, or visit some garage sales in your area. How many items from the list are you able to find used?

Childbirth Options

Years ago, most babies were born at home. Mothers didn't have the option of going to a hospital or the availability of today's lifesaving technology. Today, there are a variety of options for childbirth. With the help of their doctor, expectant parents can choose the best possible birth situation for the mother and baby.

Objectives

- Compare and contrast the qualifications of health care professionals who deliver babies.
- Outline ways expectant parents can prepare for birth.
- Analyze the benefits of childbirth classes.
- Evaluate the benefits and drawbacks of the different types of delivery.

Key Terms

prepared childbirth
labor
delivery
midwife
alternative birth center

What Is Prepared Childbirth?

Prepared childbirth involves reducing pain and fear during the birth process through education and breathing and conditioning exercises. Many expectant parents attend childbirth education classes to help them prepare for **labor**—the process by which the baby gradually moves out of the uterus and into the vagina to be born—and **delivery**—the birth itself. The father—or someone else who can support the mother during birth—functions as a "coach" for the mother.

Childbirth education classes may be offered by hospitals, health care providers, and private teachers. In addition to learning breathing techniques, participants learn so much more, including the following:

- How the baby develops throughout pregnancy.
- Warning signs that may indicate a potentially serious problem during pregnancy.
- What to expect during labor and delivery, including the stages of labor.
- The role of the coach.
- Breathing and conditioning exercises to make pregnancy, labor, and delivery more comfortable, including pain relief.

Fig. 5-10 **Many hospitals offer childbirth education classes.** How can taking a class help reduce expectant parents' fears?

- How to make a plan for the labor and delivery, also called a *birth plan*. This tells the medical staff what the couple would like to have happen throughout the childbirth process, including the possible use of pain medication.

- What to expect after the baby is born. See Fig. 5-10.

Who Will Deliver the Baby?

The following health care professionals are qualified to deliver babies:

- **Obstetricians.** Because these doctors specialize in the care of mothers and babies both before and right after birth, they are qualified to handle any emergencies or complications.

- **Family doctors.** Some family doctors provide prenatal care and deliver babies. If complications arise, however, they may call in an obstetrician.

- **Licensed midwives.** A **midwife** is trained to assist women in childbirth. There are two types of midwives: certified nurse-midwives (CNMs) and certified midwives. CNMs are registered nurses. Both have advanced training in normal pregnancy and birth and must pass a certification exam before they can practice.

Where Will the Baby Be Born?

It is only in the last 100 years that most babies have been born in hospitals. Some women still choose a home birth. However, for safety's sake, this option is only possible for women with uncomplicated pregnancies and a low risk of complications during delivery. Unfortunately, it is not possible to know what problems might arise. For example, a baby's umbilical cord may become compressed, threatening the baby's oxygen supply. No one can predict these types of problems. Newborns born at home are twice as likely to die as those born in hospitals. The mother is also at higher risk with a home birth. If a woman does decide on this option, medical personnel should be notified in advance of the birth.

Some couples choose **alternative birth centers** that are not part of hospitals. These provide a more homelike environment for labor and delivery. These centers emphasize prepared, natural childbirth and so do not offer pain medication during labor. Midwives generally handle births in these centers. Most accept only mothers at low risk of complications. A nearby hospital is on call to handle any problems that may develop. These centers typically charge less than hospitals do. Time spent at the facility is usually shorter. Parents and their baby typically leave the center within 24 hours if there are no complications.

Depending on health insurance and other issues, new mothers and their babies may spend two to three days in a hospital if the delivery was routine and up to a week if there are complications. The government requires insurance companies to cover at least two days in the hospital after delivery for women who have routine, vaginal births.

LOOKING AT REAL LIFE

With books about childbirth piled around their house and friends and family calling to offer advice, Gabrielle and Antoine, who are expecting a baby in four months, are feeling overwhelmed. Gabrielle wants to have a natural childbirth, but she is worried about the pain. She and Antoine haven't decided where to have the baby. They recently toured a birthing center at a nearby hospital that was comfortably furnished with a large bed, living area, and even kitchen facilities. There was even a place for Antoine to sleep in the same room as Gabrielle and the baby. Another hospital a little further away, however, offered tubs for water birth in its birthing center. A nurse told Gabrielle that the warm water relaxes the muscles and takes the weight off the mother's back and hips during birth. The nurse said that she thought the water worked as well as drugs in certain women. The nurse explained what kinds of anesthesia were available, too. At the end of the visit, Gabrielle and Antoine chose the second hospital for the baby's birth. Gabrielle was reconsidering anesthesia. She would try to give birth without it, but she wouldn't consider it a setback if she had to take something for her pain.

▶▶ **PERSONAL APPLICATION**

Where can you learn about childbirth options that are available in your area?

Trained personnel, sanitary conditions, and the presence of high-tech medical equipment make hospital births safer than home births. Hospitals may offer several types of services to meet the needs of expectant parents, including:

- Classes that prepare parents for delivery and infant care.
- Programs for young siblings and expectant fathers.
- Private rooms that provide soft lighting, music, and comfortable furniture. Mothers and their families can stay in these rooms for labor, delivery, and recovery, unless complications arise. Additional medical equipment is kept out of sight but is ready for immediate use.
- The option for mother and baby to room together during their time in the hospital.

When making a decision about where to have their baby, expectant parents should explore the hospitals in their area. Their options may be limited by their health insurance or by which hospital their doctor uses, so they need to investigate this as well. Many hospitals offer tours and will gladly discuss concerns and special needs.

Couples should discuss the benefits and drawbacks of each type of delivery with each other and with their doctor.

SECTION 5-3 Review and Activities

Reviewing the Section

1. What is *prepared childbirth*?
2. What can expectant parents gain from taking a childbirth education class?
3. Compare and contrast the qualifications of three kinds of health care professionals who can deliver babies.
4. Describe at least two places where babies are born. What are the advantages and disadvantages of each?
5. Why are home births not always recommended?

Observing and Interacting

Talk to your mother or another relative or friend about her childbirth experience. Find out where she delivered the baby and who delivered the baby. Who was with her when she gave birth? Compare and contrast the information you gather with the information you learned here.

Obstetric Sonographer

When a pregnant woman has an ultrasound, radio waves are used to make pictures of her baby's soft tissues. This can show whether a baby is male or female, and whether the fetus's spine and internal organs are developing properly. Obstetric sonographers perform ultrasounds and other scans.

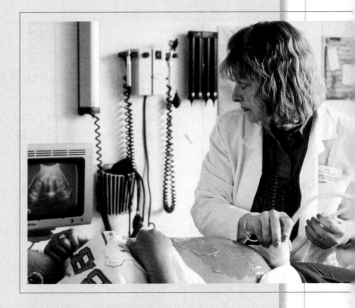

▶ Job Responsibilities

Obstetric sonographers review their patients' medical histories, perform ultrasound scans, and talk to doctors about the results. Strength is required to help pregnant women on and off of the table they lie on during scans.

▶ Work Environment

Sonographers work in hospitals and doctors' offices. After several years of work experience, sonographers may become administrators in medical imaging departments.

▶ Education and Training

Many obstetric sonographers hold a bachelor's or associate's degree. Others take a year-long course in obstetric sonography to earn a certificate. Some courses of study are designed for people from other areas of health care who are changing fields. Courses in diagnostic medical sonography include classes in anatomy, physics, patient care, and medical ethics.

▶ Skills and Aptitudes

- Attention to detail
- Physical strength
- Strong interpersonal abilities
- Ability to work on a medical team

WORKPLACE CONNECTION

1. **Thinking Skills.** How would having medical experience help you get a job as an obstetric sonographer?

2. **Resource Skills.** How could you get experience working with pregnant women?

SECTION SUMMARIES

- A woman should see a doctor once she thinks she is pregnant and receive regular prenatal care during her pregnancy. (5-1)
- Good nutrition, moderate exercise, and stress management are essential to the health of both the developing baby and the mother during pregnancy. (5-1)
- Expectant parents should prepare their home for the birth of the child and have basic supplies ready. (5-2)
- Expectant parents need to figure out how they will balance their lives after the baby is born. (5-2)
- Prepared childbirth helps expectant parents get ready for labor and delivery. (5-3)
- Expectant parents have to choose who will help deliver their baby and where the baby will be born. (5-3)

REVIEWING THE CHAPTER

1. What is prenatal care and why is it so important? (5-1)
2. What is the *Rh factor* and why is it important? (5-1)
3. What role do calcium and iron play in the diet? (5-1)
4. Why should pregnant women eat a variety of nutritious food? (5-1)
5. Why should expectant parents interview *pediatricians*? (5-2)
6. How can parents save money on basic baby supplies? (5-2)
7. What are *maternity* and *paternity leave*? (5-2)
8. What factors should expectant parents consider in determining whether both parents will work? (5-2)
9. What are *alternative birth centers*? (5-3)
10. Why might it be safer to have a baby in a hospital instead of at home? (5-3)

THINKING CRITICALLY

1. **Drawing Conclusions.** Why do you think older siblings might have trouble accepting a new baby?
2. **Making Inferences.** Why do some pregnant women choose an alternative birth center over a hospital?

MAKING CONNECTIONS

1. **Writing.** Imagine you are the father or mother of a new baby. Write a letter to your child to read when she or he is older describing what you did to keep the baby safe and healthy during pregnancy.

2. **Math.** Determine the cost of bottle-feeding a newborn for the first month, assuming a newborn eats three ounces of formula every two hours and that the formula costs $18.99 for a 25.7 ounce can.

APPLYING YOUR LEARNING

1. **Analyzing Behaviors.** Explain the importance of the following behaviors to the health and safety of pregnant women and their babies.
   - Getting enough folic acid
   - Avoiding alcohol
   - Getting exercise

2. **Interpersonal Skills.** Think about the kinds of highs and lows that women experience when pregnant. Imagine that your older cousin is pregnant, and she feels tired and uncomfortable. How might you help her to lift her spirits?

3. **Positive Messages.** Write a list of three things you could say to a pregnant woman to encourage her to eat a nutritious diet.

4. **Certified Nurse Midwives.** Search online for information about certified nurse midwives. What kind of training do they need? Why would someone choose a midwife over a doctor to deliver her baby?

Learning from Research

1. Choose one of the research claims listed below to investigate.
2. How is this research useful to expectant mothers and their families?
3. Summarize what you have learned about how breast-feeding affects a baby's health.

Breast-feeding and the Brain. Research has shown that certain amino acids–the building blocks of protein—in breast milk can help brain development. One day, these amino acids may be added to infant formula. What impact might this addition make on the practice of breast-feeding?

Breast-feeding and Allergies. The number of children with allergies has increased in the last 20 years. Studies have shown that being breast-fed reduces childhood allergies. Breast milk does this in part by coating the walls of the intestines and preventing the absorption of foreign substances that may cause allergic reactions. Give an example of an allergy that researchers believe has been reduced by breast-feeding.

Breast-feeding and Obesity. More children are overweight today than ever. As you will learn later, obesity in children is a problem with serious health consequences. Breast-feeding for the first six months of life has been shown to help prevent obesity in children. Explain why researchers believe this to be true.

Thoughtful Reading:

As you read this chapter:

- Write down any questions you have about what you read.
- Identify at least three phrases that you question.
- Find answers in the text or in outside sources.

Section 6-1
Labor and Birth

Section 6-2
The Newborn

Section 6-3
The Postnatal Period

Labor and Birth

Nine months is a long time to wait to hold a new baby. Many an expectant mother has felt as though her due date would never come. Finally, though, it does. A nervous, excited woman goes into labor, and her baby arrives. Giving birth is a powerful physical and emotional experience—one that leaves many new mothers feeling both exhausted and exhilarated.

Objectives

- Describe signs that indicate labor may have begun.
- Contrast false labor and premature labor.
- Summarize the three stages of labor.
- Explain what happens during a cesarean birth.
- List what factors can contribute to a premature birth.

Key Terms

cervix
contractions
fetal monitoring
dilate
cord blood
stem cells
cesarean birth
incubator

The Beginning of Labor

During the last few weeks of pregnancy, time seems to slow down. Many women become anxious for the baby to be born. During this time, they feel what is called *lightening*. This occurs when the baby settles deep in the pelvis near the time of birth. The pressure on the woman's upper abdomen is reduced. With a first pregnancy, lightening may occur days or weeks before labor. A woman who has already had a baby may experience this change just before labor begins.

Early Signs of Labor

There are many signals that the baby is on its way. One is commonly called the "show" or "bloody show." This refers to the few drops of blood or a pinkish vaginal stain that occurs when the mucus that plugs the uterus during pregnancy dissolves. This plug seals the **cervix** (SIR-viks), the lower part of the uterus, and prevents bacteria from moving into the uterus. This may occur as early as a few days prior to birth.

Some women realize that they are in labor when they feel a trickle—or even a gush—of warm fluid from the vagina. This indicates that the membrane, or amniotic sac, holding the amniotic fluid surrounding the baby has broken. Often, the membrane does not rupture until much later in labor. This is what is meant when a woman says that her "water has broken."

If the mother experiences this, she should note the time, the amount of fluid, and the color and odor of the fluid. She should call her doctor or midwife and report this information. Once the membrane has broken, delivery should be within 24 to 48 hours to protect the baby from infection.

Contractions, the tightening and releasing of the muscles of the uterus, are also signs of labor. When the uterus contracts, it shortens and closes, pushing the fetus against the cervix. Then the uterus relaxes before the next contraction. This is why contractions may last a few minutes. Earlier in labor, the period between them is longer. This time gets shorter as labor advances. See Fig. 6-1.

Mothers often report that contractions are painful but bearable. There is time between them to rest and recover. After the baby is born and the placenta is also pushed out, contractions end and there is no lingering pain.

As labor and contractions begin, the baby's heart can be monitored. **Fetal monitoring**, watching the baby's heart rate for indicators of stress, is usually done during labor and birth. There are different types of fetal monitoring, though one of the most common methods is done by using an ultrasound device. This method provides a beat-to-beat picture of the baby's heart in relationship to the mother's contractions.

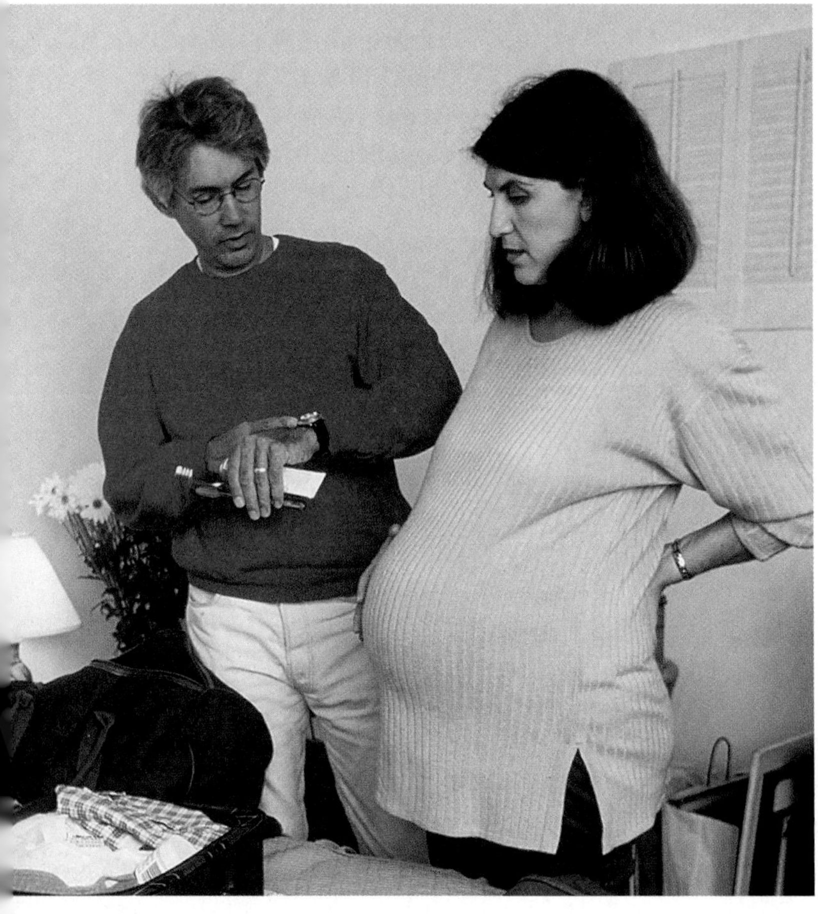

Premature Labor

A full-term pregnancy usually lasts 40 weeks, although giving birth a week or two earlier or later is still considered normal. Premature, or *preterm*, labor occurs when the fetus has been developing in the womb for 37 weeks or less. Warning signs of premature labor include having contractions every ten minutes or less, feeling a dull backache, and leaking fluid or blood. Doctors can give medication to stop premature labor.

Fig. 6-1 As labor begins, many women practice breathing techniques they learned.

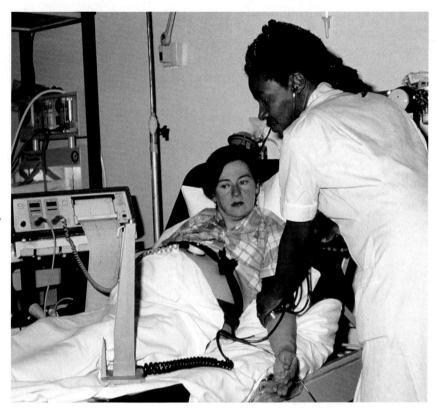

Fig. 6-2 Many doctors advise patients to go to the hospital when contractons become strong, regular, and closer together.

False Labor

Some women feel what is called "false labor" hours or even days before their actual labor starts. They begin to feel strong contractions and believe that labor may have begun. Doctors look for three signs that indicate false labor:

- Contractions aren't regular or rhythmic.
- Contractions don't become stronger over time.
- Contractions end with light exercise, such as walking.

When contractions follow a regular pattern and grow in intensity, a woman is having real labor. The woman and her labor coach should time the contractions—how long they are lasting and how frequently they are occurring.

It can be difficult to determine the right time to go to the hospital or birthing center. The doctor or the nurses at the obstetrician's office or medical center can provide guidance. See Fig. 6-2.

Inducing Labor

If necessary, labor can be started by artificial means, such as by using medication or puncturing the amniotic sac. Often, labor is induced for medical reasons or in emergencies. If the baby has been slow to develop or is still in the womb after 42 weeks, the physician may decide to induce labor. This is also the case if the amniotic sac has broken and labor doesn't begin on its own. Having labor induced doesn't significantly change the process. The labor probably won't be longer, more painful, or more difficult than natural labor.

Fig. 6-3

The Stages of Labor

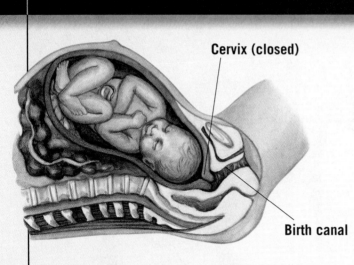

Cervix (closed)

Birth canal

Before Labor Begins

Before labor begins, the cervix is its normal size and shape.

First Stage of Labor

Contractions make the cervix **dilate**, or widen. The cervix also becomes thinner, changing from its usual thickness of about ¾ inch (19 mm) to become as thin as a sheet of paper. This thinning is called "effacement."

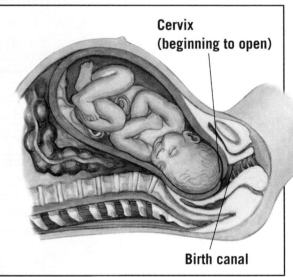

Cervix (beginning to open)

Birth canal

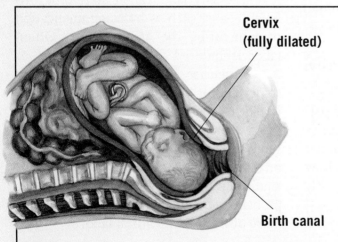

Cervix (fully dilated)

Birth canal

Transition

Transition completes the work of the first stage. The cervix becomes fully dilated to a size of 4 inches (10 cm) and the baby's head slips out of the uterus into the birth canal.

Second Stage of Labor: Crowning

First the top of the head appears at the opening of the birth canal.

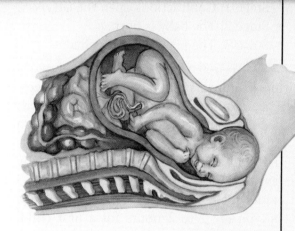

Second Stage of Labor: Head Emerges

The baby's head emerges first. The head has changed its shape to ease passage through the birth canal. It will later return to normal. After the head, the shoulders follow. The rest of the baby slips out easily.

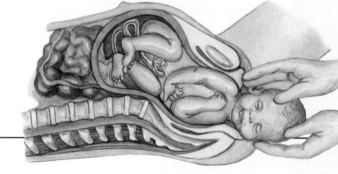

Third Stage of Labor

The woman gives birth to the placenta, no longer needed by the baby.

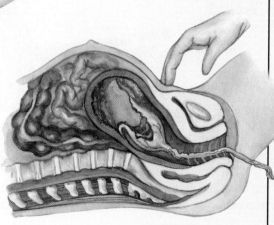

Stages of Labor

Labor moves through three stages:

- Stage 1: Contractions open the cervix.
- Stage 2: The baby is born.
- Stage 3: The placenta is expelled.

Figure 6-3 on pages 182–183 provides more information about these stages. The amount of time it takes to give birth depends on the mother and baby. It often takes longer if the baby is the woman's first. For a first birth, the initial stage may last from 6 to 18 hours. It may be 2 to 5 hours for a later child. The second stage is typically 1 to 2 hours for a first child, but might last 15 to 30 minutes for a later child. The third stage, the shortest, can take anywhere from 10 to 30 minutes.

Fig. 6-4 **During the first stage of labor, the mother should try to relax as much as possible, both between and during contractions.**

The First Stage

In the first stage of labor, contractions in the uterine muscle pull up on the cervix, slowly softening and thinning it and allowing it to open. Contractions increase in strength, length (lasting about 60 seconds), and frequency (5 to 6 minutes apart). The woman begins to turn inward, searching for the strength to deal with the demands of labor. She becomes more focused and needs support from her coach. See Fig. 6-4.

As the cervix opens, or dilates, the baby moves into the lower pelvis. Most babies enter the world headfirst, but some enter the pelvis with their feet or buttocks first, a position known as *breech presentation*. Babies in these positions may have a difficult time moving through the pelvis. The doctor will decide whether a normal delivery is possible.

The first stage concludes with a period called transition when the cervix becomes fully dilated to a diameter of about 10 centimeters (about 4 inches). Strong contractions that last up to 90 seconds and are more frequent—2 to 3 minutes apart—mark this period. This is the more difficult part of labor. A woman needs encouragement and reassurance from her coach at this time.

The Second Stage

Contractions during the second stage are more productive, pushing the baby through the pelvis and out of the vagina, or birth canal. During this period, it is safe for a woman to push—to use her muscles to expel the baby. Earlier pushing might have resulted in tearing of delicate tissues, or other types of injuries.

Cope with Labor

Most first-time mothers worry about how much pain is involved in the birth process. The truth is, it varies. Some women find it very painful and tiring, while others don't. There are many ways to cope with the pain, including medication. About 20 percent of North American women give birth without drugs. There are different options available to help expectant parents cope with labor.

- **Childbirth classes.** Mothers and fathers can learn breathing and relaxation techniques and focusing exercises that may help distract a woman from pain. Some classes teach a form of self-hypnosis that can significantly reduce pain.

- **Pain relief.** There are several types of anesthesia used for childbirth. Some are injected into veins or muscles, where they act on the entire body. These don't slow labor but may make women and their babies sleepy. Others, called *epidural* (eh-pi-DUR-al) *blocks*, are injected into the lower back, where they numb the lower half of the body. Epidural blocks still allow women to feel some pressure as the baby's head descends. Sometimes, if the pain is worse than expected, or there are other problems, more medication may be necessary.

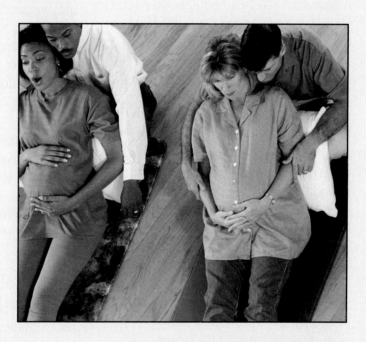

How can a baby fit through such a narrow space? Ligaments, or connective tissue, join the bones of the mother's pelvis. During labor, a hormone called *relaxin* allows this tissue to stretch like rubber bands, moving apart the pelvic bones. Relaxin also makes it possible for the walls of the vagina to stretch so that the baby can safely pass through.

A baby's body is designed for this journey, with a soft skull that enables the baby's head to become longer and narrower than usual. The skull consists of five separate bones that move together and allow for the baby's head to fit through the pelvis and vagina.

Sometimes the opening in the mother's body is too small to accommodate the baby's passage. In this case, the doctor may widen it with a surgical cut called an *episiotomy*.

As the baby's head emerges, the doctor or midwife provides gentle support. The head is followed by one shoulder, and then the other. The rest of the baby follows quickly.

Sometimes doctors use surgical tongs called *forceps* to grasp the baby's body and guide its movement. A vacuum extractor that applies suction to the baby's head once it appears may be used if the baby needs to be moved through the birth canal quickly.

The Third Stage

After birth, the mother may be able to rest briefly, and then may feel a few contractions and a desire to push. These contractions usually are not painful. They help the placenta, the organ that develops in the mother and helps supply oxygen to the fetus, separate from the uterine wall. When the mother pushes the placenta out of her body, the birth process is complete. The final stage of labor is brief but important. See Fig. 6-3 on pages 182–183 for more information on the stages of labor.

Scientists have discovered that **cord blood**, the blood left behind in the umbilical

---

LOOKING AT REAL LIFE

Adriana is tired. It's been twelve hours since her labor began, and still she has not given birth. Adriana and her husband Lorenzo decided weeks earlier that, if possible, she would not take pain medication. She always disliked taking medicine, and it's important to her to feel every sensation of her child's birth. Fortunately, Lorenzo is at her side, feeding her chips of ice and massaging her back between contractions. When she says she can't go on, he reminds her of how far she's come already. He says he's proud of her. He coaches her through breathing exercises during contractions and tells her that she's doing great—really making progress. Lorenzo is right: Two hours later, their baby Isabella is born.

▶▶ **PERSONAL APPLICATION**

1. Has anyone in your family had a baby? Did you go to the hospital after the birth?
2. Where might a pregnant woman learn relaxation techniques to help with labor?

What's in a Name?

What is the best way to choose a name for a baby? Children are often named after relatives, living or deceased. In China, parents' hopes for a healthy, prosperous life for their children are reflected in the names they choose. Girls' names typically include words relating to elements of beauty or composure, such as *ting* (graceful) or *hua* (flower). Boys' names are designed to honor ancestors or indicate strength, such as *shaozu* (bring honor to our ancestors) and *gang* (steel). Some Chinese names are combinations of elements, such as *po yee*, meaning "treasured child."

Investigating Culture

1. Discuss how people use names to link children to past generations.
2. The number of last names in China is small, but there are billions of first names. Why might the number of first names be so large?

cord and placenta following birth, contains **stem cells**. These stem cells are capable of producing all types of blood cells. The stem cells can be used to treat many serious blood-related illnesses in the baby or other family members. Parents can arrange to have the cord blood stored for later use in case there is a future medical need. It may also be donated for use by others.

Cesarean Birth

Not all births progress through these stages of labor. If complications arise during pregnancy or labor, a **cesarean birth** (si-ZARE-ee-uhn), also known as a *cesarean section* or *c-section*, may become necessary. In this case, the baby is delivered through a surgical incision in the mother's

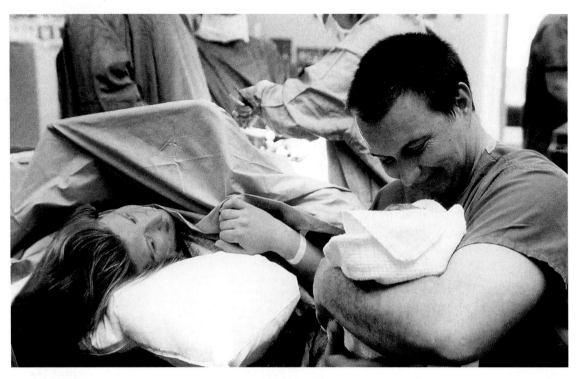

Fig. 6-5 **A cesarean birth may be necessary when complications arise during labor.** How does a cesarean birth differ from natural birth?

abdomen. Reasons for cesarean delivery can include lack of normal progress during labor, discovering that the baby is in distress or turned in the wrong direction, or having multiple babies. If a cesarean birth is anticipated during pregnancy, special childbirth classes can help parents prepare. See Fig. 6-5.

Pain medication is used for cesarean births. With certain types of medication, such as an epidural, women can remain awake during the surgery. In other situations, general anesthesia that puts the mother to sleep is used. With the physician's permission, the father or other labor coach may be present. (For more information on managing the pain of labor, see "How to Cope with Labor" on page 185.)

Because a cesarean birth is surgery, it carries some risks. However, when necessary, it can relieve stress on the baby, speed up delivery, and allow the doctor to better control the birth process.

After a cesarean delivery, mothers are taken to a recovery area where they stay for a few hours. They may be able to hold their babies during this time. They are encouraged to stand or walk with help as soon as possible to help speed the healing process. Women who have had cesareans may need up to six weeks to fully recover.

Premature Birth

Between 5 and 6 percent of all babies are born prematurely. Premature babies are those born before reaching 37 weeks of development and weighing less than 5 pounds, 8 ounces (2.5 kg). The earlier babies are born, the less developed their organs are and the lower their birth weight.

Why are babies born prematurely? No one knows for sure, but mothers who have had other premature births, are carrying more than one baby (as with twins or triplets), or have other medical problems are more likely to have premature babies. Teen mothers are more likely to give birth prematurely. Women can reduce their risks by eating properly and getting proper prenatal care.

 Premature babies require special care. They are not really ready to live outside their mother's body. Their systems for controlling body temperature, breathing, and feeding are not yet mature. These systems are under control of the brain. At this point, a premature baby's brain is not yet ready to control these systems. To help control them, a premature baby is usually placed in an **incubator**. In this special enclosed crib, the oxygen supply, temperature, and humidity can be closely controlled. Advances in medical technology allow many premature infants—some weighing as little as 1 pound (454 g)—to survive and grow to be healthy. Others have long-term health problems, learning problems, or even brain damage.

SECTION 6-1 Review and Activities

Reviewing the Section

1. Name two early signs of labor.
2. What is the purpose of *fetal monitoring*?
3. Why must a baby be delivered within 24 to 48 hours after the mother's water has broken?
4. How do premature labor and false labor differ?
5. Why is it sometimes necessary to induce labor?
6. What happens during the first stage of labor?
7. Why is the third stage of labor important?
8. What is relaxin, and what does it do?
9. Name three reasons why a baby might be delivered by *cesarean birth.*
10. What are *stem cells*?
11. Why do premature babies require special care?

Observing and Interacting

Think about when you have seen babies being born on television or at the movies.

1. How was labor shown to happen?
2. After reading this section, do the labors you have seen in the media seem realistic?

The Newborn

At birth, a newborn goes through physical changes that are necessary for the baby's survival outside of the mother's body. Before birth, parents often wonder, "What will my baby look like?" When parents imagine the answers to this question, they usually imagine a sturdy, smiling baby of about six months. Newborns look nothing like that. It will take some time before they are picture perfect.

Objectives

- Describe the newborn's appearance immediately after birth.
- Identify the physical changes that prepare the newborn for life outside the uterus.
- Explain the purpose of common hospital procedures following birth.

Key Terms

fontanel
lanugo
vernix
Apgar scale

A Newborn Baby Arrives

A newborn baby has a tiny measure of independence. No longer reliant on the mother for basic needs, the baby will take a first breath. During the pregnancy, the baby's lungs are collapsed. Oxygen is delivered through the mother's blood, and the lungs are not used.

During delivery, the lungs fill with the amniotic fluid that was in the baby's trachea, the tube that delivers air from the mouth to the lungs. Most of the fluid is squeezed out during the trip through the birth canal. Whatever remains in the mouth is suctioned out immediately after birth. Usually, newborns breathe naturally. If the baby needs help, medical personnel gently rub the baby's back to encourage breathing. Once the lungs have begun to take in oxygen, the baby's circulatory system changes. Blood now circulates to and from the lungs, rather than bypassing them as before.

The umbilical cord once provided the baby with nourishment and oxygen, but now it isn't needed. Within a few minutes of birth, the cord stops pulsing with the mother's heartbeat and begins to shrink. The cord is clamped and cut off, leaving a small stump at the baby's navel that falls off in a few days.

How Does the Newborn Look?

Most people think of bright eyes and plump arms and legs when they picture babies, but newborns tend to look a little different. Their limbs may be skinny, and their features sometimes appear flattened.

The newborn's head is wobbly and looks too large for the body. The baby's skull may appear pointed or lopsided due to the passage through the birth canal. A baby's skull bones are not fully fused. Open spaces known as **fontanels** can be found on the baby's head where the bones are not yet joined. One of these soft spots is just above the baby's forehead, and the other is toward the back of the skull. Fontanels allow the bones to move together during birth. As the baby develops during the first year and a half of life, the bones grow together and fuse, covering the fontanels. In the meantime, a thick layer of skin covers them and protects the brain.

 THE DEVELOPING BRAIN

At birth, a baby's head is about one-fourth of the baby's total height, which averages about 20 inches (50 centimeters). That is twice the size, compared to the rest of the body, of an adult's head. An infant's head is big because the brain is big. After birth, the head and brain grow much less than the rest of the baby's body.

The face of the newborn may be swollen or puffy after the birth process. Typically, newborns have fat cheeks; short, flat noses; and receding chins. The small features make it easier for the baby to nurse at the mother's breasts. At birth, babies' eyes are nearly adult-size.

LOOKING AT REAL LIFE

Colleen's parents had heard the saying: "A baby whose sweat tastes salty will have a miserable life." What they didn't know was that very salty sweat is one of the signs of a genetic disease called cystic fibrosis. While it affects all racial groups, the disease is most common in Caucasians, and affects both boys and girls equally. Doctors tested Colleen, a newborn, by taking a few drops of her sweat and measuring the chloride (a body salt) in it. The test was painless, and the results came back the same day. Colleen tested positive for the disease. This didn't mean, however, she would have a miserable life. Some people with the disease have breathing problems and trouble digesting food, while others show no signs of the disease except very salty sweat. Currently, there is no cure for cystic fibrosis, but there are many promising treatments in use.

▶▶ **PERSONAL APPLICATION**

Do you or does anyone you know have a genetic disease? What are some of the symptoms?

Babies of African, Asian, and Hispanic descent often have brown eyes at birth, and they remain this color. Caucasian babies' eyes are usually a dark grayish-blue at birth, but the color may change before becoming permanent at three to six months.

Babies' circulatory systems must make adjustments to the fluctuating temperatures of the outside world. Tiny fingers and toes may be slightly cooler than the rest of the body for the first 24 hours. Keeping babies wrapped in blankets makes them feel more secure; a knitted cap keeps their heads warm. Hospitals often put babies under warming lamps immediately after birth. See Fig. 6-6.

Some babies, particularly those born prematurely, have fine, downy hair called **lanugo** (la-NEW-go) growing on their foreheads, backs, and shoulders. This hair soon disappears.

While in the uterus, the baby is floating in amniotic fluid, and is covered with a thick, white, pasty substance called **vernix** (VIRN-ix). Vernix is made up of the fetus's shed skin cells and the secretions of skin glands. It acts as a protection against constant exposure to the fluid. Any remaining vernix is washed off during the baby's first bath.

Many babies have tiny, white bumps called *milia* (MILL-ee-ah) on their nose and cheeks. These bumps are also known as "baby acne." They are plugged oil ducts caused by stimulation from the mother's hormones, which remain in the baby's system for a short time after delivery. The milia disappear in a week or so.

Examining the Newborn

When babies are born, their condition is usually evaluated using the **Apgar scale**, a system of rating the physical condition of a newborn baby. Five factors are checked at

Fig. 6-6 The outside world is colder than the womb. Incubators keep newborns warm.

What Physical Changes Occur in a Newborn?

Newborns have a big adjustment to make. For nine months, their world has been warm and dark. Outside the uterus, things are bright and strange. To survive in the world, a baby's circulation, heart, lung function, and blood must all change. The biggest adjustment for babies is breathing air instead of receiving oxygen through the umbilical cord.

In order for newborns to breathe:

- Their circulatory systems must deliver a great deal of blood to the lungs.
- Their hearts must pump harder to get more blood to the lungs.

The heart changes, too:

- Two small openings in the heart begin to close.
- A new type of hemoglobin, a part of the red blood cell that delivers oxygen to the body, develops.

For the first few months, newborns breathe through their noses and may even pause briefly in their breathing while they sleep. Newborns may sneeze often in order to clear mucus from their noses. A newborn's breathing becomes regular a month or two after birth.

THINKING IT THROUGH

1. Have you ever spent time with a newborn baby? What surprised you about the baby's appearance?
2. Many parents become scared when their newborns stop breathing briefly. What should they do if a baby stops breathing and doesn't start again?

---

one minute, and again five minutes after birth. The scale rates the five areas on a scale from zero to two. They are: heart rate, breathing, muscle tone, response to stimulation, and clear skin color. A normal total score is in the six-to-ten range. Ten is a perfect score. A lower score indicates that the baby may need medical assistance. Nurses also examine the baby, checking especially for any condition that might require special care. They weigh, measure, and dry off the baby. They apply antibiotic drops or ointment to the baby's eyes to prevent infection. The baby often receives an injection of vitamin K to prevent a rare bleeding disorder.

Shortly after birth, certain records are created. The baby's foot is printed in ink for the public record. Plastic bands with the baby's last name are fastened to the mother's wrist, to the baby's wrist or ankle, and to the wrist of someone of the mother's choosing. The bands have matching numbers and are checked each time the baby leaves the mother's room. In most hospitals, only hospital staff members with the appropriate identification are permitted into the hospital nursery after the baby is transferred there.

Later Tests

Newborns are given several other tests and medical procedures during their first few days of life.

Most newborns also receive at least one and often two hearing screenings. Blood is taken from the umbilical cord immediately after birth to check the baby's blood type and to screen for certain diseases.

SECTION 6-2 Review and Activities

Reviewing the Section

1. What happens to the baby's lungs during delivery? What happens to them after delivery?
2. Why do many babies appear to have a pointed head after birth?
3. Why might the face of a newborn be swollen after birth?
4. How are babies kept warm after birth?
5. What is *vernix*? What is its purpose?
6. What are the five characteristics that are rated on the *Apgar scale*? Why are these important?
7. Why do you think hospitals are so careful with babies' identification records?

Observing and Interacting

Talk to someone you know who is a mother.

1. How long was she in the hospital after the birth of her baby?
2. What did her son or daughter look like after the birth?
3. What procedures were followed at the hospital? Why?

The Postnatal Period

Once the baby has finally arrived, parents quickly begin forming emotional ties with their newborn. This enjoyable process not only plays an important role in the emotional and physical development of the baby but also helps the parents. Mothers go through emotional changes, and it's important that they receive support from their families, friends, and health care professionals.

Objectives

- Explain what bonding is and how to promote it.
- Identify problems that often accompany prematurity.
- Summarize the physical and emotional needs of a mother and baby.

Key Terms

bonding
colostrum
neonatal period
jaundice
bilirubin
lactation consultant
rooming-in
postnatal period
postpartum
   depression

Bonding

In recent years, many researchers have devoted attention to the emotional needs of the newborn. They have emphasized **bonding**—forming emotional ties between parents and child. Having learned how important bonding is, most hospitals now delay some of the routine procedures after birth, if there are no complications, and let the parents hold the child and begin forming an attachment.

Immediately following birth, nurses may place the baby on the mother's abdomen to feel the warmth of her skin and to hear her voice and the heartbeat that became so familiar in the uterus. At this point, many fathers examine their newborn's tiny toes and fingers. Parents usually begin touching and talking to the baby, looking into the baby's eyes and stroking the baby's cheeks. The newborn instinctively focuses on the human face, which in turn helps the newborn bond. Research has shown that newborns are even drawn toward rough sketches of the human face.

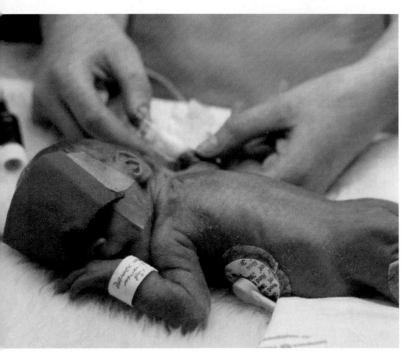

Fig. 6-7 In phototherapy, a newborn with jaundice is placed in an incubator under a special ultraviolet light that is absorbed by the baby's skin. The light changes the bilirubin into a form that can be eliminated from the baby's kidneys.

 Bonding also helps a baby's brain development. During the first year, a baby's brain cells are making millions of connections. Parents' efforts to bond with their baby help build connections in the brain. Through simple bonding interactions, such as holding, rocking, or singing to the baby, parents help strengthen the development of their baby's brain.

If the baby will be breast-fed, the mother may begin nursing the baby right away. Newborns are born with a strong sucking reflex and are usually alert immediately after delivery. Breast-feeding is important because each feeding session stimulates the mother's body to continue producing milk. Also, early feeding helps the uterus contract after birth, stopping any bleeding.

High-calorie, high-protein early breast milk called **colostrum** (cole-UH-strum) satisfies the baby's appetite and provides protection from illnesses. Babies may gradually become too sleepy to nurse. The father or another relative can then hold the baby while the mother rests.

The Hospital Stay

The neonatal period involves major adjustments for mother and baby. The **neonatal period** refers to the first month after the baby is born. Labor and delivery are tiring, and mothers and babies need time to rest and recover. In some facilities, such as alternative birth centers, a healthy mother and baby may go home as soon as 12 hours after birth. In hospitals, the average stay following birth is about two and one half days. The average stay in the hospital following birth has risen slightly in recent years.

Jaundice (JAWN-diss), a condition that occurs in over 50 percent of newborns, causes the baby's skin and eyes to look slightly yellow. Jaundice occurs when the liver can't remove **bilirubin** (bill-ih-ROO-bin), a substance produced by the breakdown of red blood cells. The baby's body may be producing too much of this by-product, or the baby's liver, which is still developing, isn't able to remove it quickly enough. If left untreated, jaundice can damage the nervous system.

In the hospital, doctors may prescribe *phototherapy*—the use of ultraviolet light to help the liver do its job. See Fig. 6-7. Sometimes the treatment is continued at home.

Bond with a Baby

Caring for a newborn can mean so much more than endless rounds of feeding and changing diapers. Babies crave close physical touch, and close emotional ties help their brains and bodies develop. By taking the time to include the baby in their usual activities, parents and other caregivers give their babies varied experiences while cementing their own relationship. Here are a few practical ways to promote bonding.

- **Use a baby carrier.** Being comfortably strapped to a parent's body keeps the baby close to the heart. The rhythm of a heartbeat comforts babies.

- **Sing or read to the baby.** It isn't necessary to wait until the baby is old enough to understand what is being read. The sound of a familiar voice can be very comforting to a baby.

- **Routines.** Fathers who spend time alone with their babies get to know them better. Giving a late-night bottle, changing diapers, and going for walks can enhance the bonding experience.

- **Let the baby handle you.** Babies are interested in different textures, like beards and long hair. But be careful—babies have a tight grasp and don't like to let go!

YOUR TURN

Playtime. Playing with babies is another way for parents and babies to become familiar with one another. Can you think of some ways to play with a baby that would promote bonding?

Hillary was worried whether Daniel, her one-month-old, was getting enough milk. She decided to call Dr. Lopez, Daniel's pediatrician, to talk about his eating habits. Dr. Lopez asked her how many diapers Daniel went through each day. "About ten a day," Hillary answered. Dr. Lopez asked if the diapers were wet when Hillary took them off. "They're always wet," Hillary said. She was a bit surprised when Dr. Lopez asked about the color of Daniel's urine, but she responded, "It's pale, almost clear." Dr. Lopez assured Hillary that if Daniel appeared content after feedings and was gaining weight steadily, then it seemed that he was getting plenty to eat. Hillary felt relieved and thanked the pediatrician for her help. Just then, Daniel started to fuss. It was almost lunch time, and he was hungry.

▶▶**PERSONAL APPLICATION**

Have you ever fed, or watched someone feed a baby? How did you know the baby had had enough to eat?

Help with Feeding

All babies lose weight during the first few days of life, but gain it back later. By the third or fourth day, breast-feeding mothers begin producing more milk.

Some mothers have difficulty with breast- or bottle-feeding. Parents can get help with feedings while they are still in the hospital. Many hospitals offer **lactation consultants**, professional breast-feeding specialists who show breast-feeding mothers how to encourage adequate milk and how to position babies properly so that they can nurse. Nurses can also help. During the first few days of life, some babies are too sleepy to eat. To wake them, mothers can try unwrapping their babies to expose them to the air in the room. A little stimulation, such as light massage, can also wake the baby for a feeding.

Rooming-In

Many hospitals offer the option of full or partial **rooming-in**. Full rooming-in means that the baby remains with the mother in her room during the entire hospital stay. Partial rooming-in means that the baby stays in the nursery part of the time, such as during the night. Mothers can ask that their babies be brought to their rooms for night feedings. Hospitals that offer rooming-in generally allow the father to visit whenever he wishes.

Rooming-in programs have advantages for the entire family. Typically, rooming-in babies have only one main caregiver, usually a nurse, attending to their needs, so they seem to cry less. As a result, a rooming-in mother gets more rest and doesn't worry about her baby in the nursery. When babies room in, parents start learning how to take care of them right away.

Legal Documents

A birth certificate is the most important piece of personal identification anyone has. It is required for entrance into school. Getting one is simple. The parents fill out a form provided by the hospital or birthing center, at which time a temporary certificate is issued. Several weeks later, the parents receive one copy of the birth certificate, while another is sent to a government office to be filed.

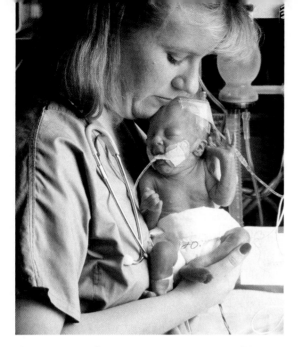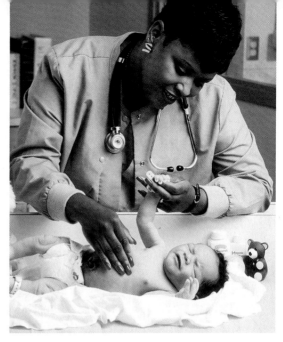

Fig. 6-8 **A preemie, or premature baby, looks different than a full-term baby. As preemies gain weight, they have the same appearance as full-term babies.**

The federal government recommends that a baby receive a Social Security number in the first year. Hospitals also provide new parents with the necessary Social Security forms to fill out. Parents should fill out the forms to obtain a number for their child. They can then claim an exemption on their income taxes, obtain medical coverage for the child, and take part in government programs.

Caring for Premature Babies

As you read earlier, premature babies are those that are born before 37 weeks of development. Many premature babies spend time in a hospital's *neonatal intensive-care unit (NICU)*, which has special equipment and highly trained nurses. Not all hospitals have these units. In many areas, babies are transferred to a larger hospital that has a NICU.

Premature babies stay in the hospital until their internal organs develop enough to function independently. This may take anywhere from a few days to a month or more. Premature babies are usually fed through a tube in the stomach because they lack the ability to coordinate sucking and swallowing milk. Breathing machines are often used to help babies whose lungs are immature. The NICU also cares for newborns with other serious medical conditions. See Fig. 6-8.

While the outlook for premature babies has improved significantly over the years, they still have an increased risk of medical and developmental problems. How well a premature baby thrives often depends on how close the baby was born to the original due date. Premature babies can experience long-term difficulties such as cerebral palsy and developmental delays. The more premature the baby is, the more risks the baby faces. Those born between 23 and 26 weeks have the highest risk of complications. The risk of difficulties decreases for those babies born between 28 and 30 weeks.

NICUs and Their Expertise in Caring for Premature Babies

When babies are born prematurely (before 37 weeks of development), specialists must decide how best to care for them. They must choose a level of care appropriate for the baby's needs.

A neonatal intensive care unit, or NICU, is a special nursery for newborns. There are three levels of NICU care. Level I facilities provide routine care for premature newborns, or *preemies*, including keeping them warm and nourished. Level II facilities are for preemies who need to be monitored closely. Some states have only one or two hospitals that have Level III facilities, which provide care for very premature (less than 34 weeks) and full-term infants who have serious or life-threatening conditions. A baby born far from a Level III facility may be transported there by ambulance or helicopter, depending on the baby's condition.

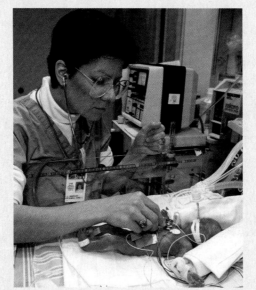

Premature babies don't have enough body fat to maintain their temperature, even with blankets. NICUs have incubators and special warmers for preemies. These decrease the chance of infection and surround the baby with warmed air.

Preemies also need special types of nourishment because they grow more quickly than full-term babies. Their digestive systems are immature. Most preemies are fed breast milk through feeding tubes. Breast milk contains substances that protect against infection and disease. Many preemies receive extra vitamins and nutrients. Once they are in stable condition and show signs of sucking, doctors determine whether they can breast-feed. Sometimes preemies need special pacifiers that help them learn how to suck properly.

Babies in the NICU are frequently tested for infections and blood cell and blood sugar levels. Nurses and doctors monitor them carefully, changing their individual care plans to reflect each baby's needs.

Check-Up

Where is the nearest NICU unit in your area?

As premature babies grow, doctors determine when they can leave incubators and be placed in open cribs. When these babies are able to breathe without a machine, drink, maintain a steady body temperature, and maintain a weight of 5 pounds or more, they can leave the hospital unless other problems require a longer stay.

Premature babies need constant monitoring, which can disrupt parent-child bonding. Incubators and machines can be intimidating to parents. If a baby is extremely premature, the parents may touch the baby through the openings in the incubator. As their babies grow, parents can hold, sing, talk to, and bathe them. As with full-term babies, this contact helps babies develop more quickly. Breast-feeding mothers can provide milk for their babies.

Postnatal Care of the Mother

In the time following the baby's birth—the **postnatal period**—a new mother has special needs. She may be physically exhausted from birth, and is now responsible for the well-being of a newborn. Nurses will explain how the new mother should care for herself as she meets the needs of her baby. Mothers who give birth by cesarean section have a longer recovery time since they have had major surgery.

Physical Needs

Recovery from pregnancy and childbirth takes time. The new mother's hormone levels change and her sleep may be interrupted by the baby's feedings. Breast-feeding mothers experience additional changes related to producing milk. Women who have had a cesarean section require additional care. They are generally required to stay in the hospital longer and will be more fatigued. The physical needs of the new mother are:

- **Rest.** During the first few weeks, she may be tired. She should try to sleep whenever the baby does. Relatives and friends can help by preparing meals, offering to do household chores, or looking after the baby for a few hours.

- **Exercise.** With her physician's approval, a new mother can generally begin exercising gently. Stretching and walking short distances can help her lose weight and feel more energetic.

- **Good nutrition.** As during pregnancy, eating right is important for new mothers. They should continue to follow the Guidelines for Healthy Eating on page 154. Breast-feeding mothers are naturally hungrier. They are providing nutrition for their own bodies as well as for their babies. They need about 300 more calories per day than before pregnancy. They also need to drink plenty of fluids.

- **Medical checkups.** Four to six weeks after birth, a new mother should have a postnatal checkup. Her doctor makes sure her uterus is returning to normal and there are no other problems.

Emotional Needs

In addition to physical changes, a new mother goes through emotional changes as well. Many women feel confused a few days after birth. Some have mood swings. These "baby blues" are very common. The mother may cry for no reason, or feel irritable, lonely, anxious, or sad. Joining a support group for new mothers or talking with other mothers often helps.

A small percentage of new mothers experience these symptoms to a greater degree. The "blues" do not go away, but rather worsen. Symptoms of **postpartum depression** may include feeling sad or crying a lot, having no energy, being overly anxious about the baby, having little interest in the baby, and thinking of causing harm.

Treatment is available for postpartum depression. It is very important for women who have such symptoms to talk with their doctors about treatment. Talking to a therapist can help, as can medication. See Fig. 6-9.

Fig. 6-9 **Some new mothers experience severe depression and need treatment.** How does this differ from the "baby blues"?

SECTION 6-3 Review and Activities

Reviewing the Section

1. How is *bonding* promoted between parents and their baby?
2. What is the danger of a baby having an excess of *bilirubin*?
3. Name two reasons why newborns might not eat.
4. Why is *rooming-in* beneficial to the baby? How can it benefit the father?
5. Why should babies have Social Security numbers?
6. List three requirements that a premature baby must meet before being allowed to go home.
7. What issues are involved in a mother's postnatal care?

Observing and Interacting

Some people say that premature babies look like baby birds. Compare the photographs on page 199 of a premature and a full-term baby.

1. What differences do you see?
2. How might you feel if you were that baby's parent?

Pediatric Nurse

Children who receive proper care often recover from illnesses and injuries more quickly than adults. Seeing children heal is one of the joys of being a pediatric nurse. Nurses can educate worried parents about their children's health and chances of recovery. Caring for a dying child is one of the hardest parts of the job.

▸ Job Responsibilities

Pediatric nurses administer medications and use instruments to check children's health. They teach parents how to care for ill or injured children. Nurses also help children deal with illness by answering questions and maintaining a positive outlook.

▸ Work Environment

Pediatric nurses who work in hospitals usually have a choice of shifts. Some work every weekday, while others work weekends only. Others prefer to work three long shifts per week. Nurses who work in doctors' offices and clinics often only work during the day.

▸ Education and Training

Nurses can earn a bachelor's degree in nursing or study at nursing schools. The kind of work nurses are allowed to do depends on the type of college degree they earn. Pediatric nurses must pass state board exams in order to work.

▸ Skills and Aptitudes

- Attention to detail
- Keen observation abilities
- Compassion
- Ability to communicate clearly
- Energy and stamina

WORKPLACE CONNECTION

1. **Thinking Skills.** What kinds of experience would help you prepare to be a nurse?

2. **Resource Skills.** Where could you get experience caring for children?

6 Review and Activities

SECTION SUMMARIES

- There are three main stages of labor. (6-1)
- A cesarean birth may be necessary when the mother's or baby's health is in danger. (6-1)
- Premature babies require special medical care. (6-1)
- The birth process often makes newborns look different than older babies. (6-2)
- Immediately after birth, a newborn's physical condition is evaluated through a variety of tests. (6-2)
- Bonding after birth strengthens the emotional connection between parents and their child. (6-3)
- Mothers and babies recover from birth during the postnatal period. (6-3)
- Premature babies need specialized care. (6-3)
- New mothers need rest, good nutrition, and follow-up medical care. (6-3)

REVIEWING THE CHAPTER

1. How can you tell the difference between real and false labor? (6-1)
2. What happens during each of the three main stages of labor? (6-1)
3. What occurs during a *cesarean birth*? (6-1)
4. How do newborn babies look? Why do they look this way? (6-2)
5. What are *fontanels* and what is their purpose? (6-2)
6. What tests are performed on a newborn baby? (6-2)
7. How do hospitals promote *bonding*? (6-3)
8. What causes *jaundice* and how is it treated? (6-3)
9. What are the benefits of *rooming-in* at the hospital? (6-3)
10. What is a neonatal intensive care unit? (6-3)
11. What is postpartum depression and why does it require treatment? (6-3)

THINKING CRITICALLY

1. **Drawing Conclusions.** What are some of the reasons that women might choose labor without pain medication?
2. **Making Inferences.** What feelings might a new mother have during the postnatal period? Why?

MAKING CONNECTIONS

1. **Math.** Look online for information about infant mortality rates in other countries. Which nation has the highest rate? The lowest? Where does the United States rank? Compile your findings into a graph.

2. **Writing.** A new mother is worried because her baby's face isn't round and chubby like babies on television. She writes an e-mail to her sister expressing her concern. Her sister volunteers in a hospital maternity ward. Write a reassuring e-mail reply from the perspective of her sister.

APPLYING YOUR LEARNING

1. **Analyzing Behaviors.** In each scenario, determine what type of labor a woman is in:
   - Contractions become stronger with time.
   - At 36 weeks, the woman feels a dull pain in her back.
   - After the woman walks for a while, the contractions stop.

2. **Interpersonal Skills.** Imagine that a relative or friend is having a baby. List at least six ways you could help just before and after the birth.

3. **Determining Effects.** Research how prematurity in babies affects their families. How are the families' home lives affected by a premature birth? Are premature births usually more costly than normal births? What impact might a premature birth have on work schedules or routines?

Learning from Research

1. Choose one of the following research claims to investigate.
2. How can this research finding be useful to expectant mothers?
3. Summarize what you have learned about conditions or procedures that affect pregnant women or newborns.

Inducing Labor. Inducing labor is a common obstetric procedure. Inducing labor for elective reasons has increased at a higher rate than for medical reasons. What are the risks involved in inducing labor for elective reasons?

Congenital Heart Defects. In about 6 to 8 out of every 1,000 live births, the newborn has some kind of congenital heart defect. Which of these defects are mild? Which of them are severe? What are their possible causes and treatments? Which defect is more likely to affect premature babies?

Postpartum Depression. Postpartum depression is a serious complication in 10 percent to 15 percent of all deliveries. For adolescents who give birth, the incidence is between 26 and 32 percent. Why is the percentage higher in adolescents? What are some of the warning signs of postpartum depression? Identify treatment alternatives.

The Baby's First Year

Chapter 7
Physical Development of Infants

Chapter 8
Emotional and Social Development
of Infants

Chapter 9
Intellectual Development in Infants

7 Physical Development of Infants

Thoughtful Reading:

As you read this chapter:
- Ask questions about what you are reading.
- Identify new information you learn from what you read.
- Connect what you read to your personal experiences.

Section 7-1
Infant Growth and Development

Section 7-2
Infant Care Skills

Section 7-3
Infant Health and Wellness

Infant Growth and Development

Babies experience a tremendous amount of physical growth and development in their first year of life. In just twelve months, babies who begin as helpless newborns learn to stand alone, feed themselves, and even walk. While babies typically follow the same development patterns, they do so at their own rate. Parents have the responsibility to do what they can to help their baby grow and develop normally.

Objectives

- Describe the three patterns that a baby's physical development follows.
- Explain the effects that heredity, nutrition, health, experiences, and environment have on an infant's growth and development.
- Describe how a typical baby grows in the first year.
- Classify the different movements a baby makes as reflexes, gross motor skills, or fine motor skills.

Key Terms

developmental milestones
stimulating environment
growth chart
proportion
depth perception
reflexes
gross motor skills
fine motor skills
hand-eye coordination

Patterns of Physical Development

The terms *growth* and *development* are often used interchangeably, but they are not the same things. *Growth* refers to changes in size, such as weight and length. *Development* refers to increases and changes in physical, emotional, social, or intellectual skills.

An infant's physical development follows three basic patterns: from head to foot, near to far, and simple to complex. Understanding these patterns can help you understand and follow the sequence of a typical baby's development.

Head to Foot

This pattern of development begins long before birth. It starts during the prenatal stage, when a baby's head takes the lead in development. This pattern continues after birth and can be seen in the increasing control that babies gain over their body. Babies first develop some control of head movement. For example, they will raise their head to see an object. Control of muscles then moves down the body to the arms and hands. Control of the baby's legs and feet occurs more slowly. It isn't until about the age of one that a baby develops all the skills needed to walk.

Near to Far

An infant's development also starts close to the trunk of the body and moves outward. First, babies simply wave their arms when they see an object they want. Later, they develop more precise hand and finger control and can reach out and grasp for an object with their fingers.

Simple to Complex

In the developmental pattern of simple to complex, babies first develop their large muscle groups—such as those in the legs, neck, arms, and torso (the trunk of the body). As they strengthen and gain control over these muscles, they learn to do increasingly complex tasks. These tasks begin with controlling the head, rolling, reaching, crawling, and continue through to walking. Even more complex movements that require small muscle development come later. Coloring, for example, requires good control of the fingers to grasp, hold, and direct a crayon.

Influences on Growth and Development

Researchers have found that both heredity and environment play significant roles in a baby's growth and development. Heredity—

or "nature"—includes the physical makeup that a baby inherits from his or her parents. Environment—or "nurture"—is a more complex concept. It includes influences such as nutrition, amount of stimulation, health, and relationships. All these factors work together to influence a baby's physical growth and development. However, at various times one or more of these factors can play a larger role than the others in an infant's growth and development.

During an infant's first year, he or she gains specific skills and abilities. Child development experts have studied the range of ages to determine the average ages at which children acquire certain skills. These key skills used to check a child's progress are called **developmental milestones**. For example, Jeffrey may inherit a strong, healthy body from his parents. But if Jeffrey becomes sick for an extended period, he may miss out on opportunities for active play that would strengthen the large muscles of his legs. As a result, he may reach developmental milestones—such as learning to walk or climb steps—later than a healthy baby. Another baby, Aisha, inherits a strong, healthy body and enjoys good health. She therefore has more opportunities for physical play than Jeffrey had and will more likely develop at a normal rate.

Heredity

As explained in Chapter 4, genes provide a "blueprint" for the development of the human body and how it functions throughout life. Children inherit a unique combination of genes from their parents. This combination of genes determines traits such as eye and hair color, when the teeth first emerge, whether certain diseases are likely to develop, and much

Fig. 7-1 **Children inherit many physical characteristics from their parents.** What other factors influence a baby's growth and development?

more. The genes also shape or influence larger traits, such as a person's intellectual potential or artistic abilities. Having certain genes, though, does not mean a person will automatically exhibit those traits. Nature and nurture both play a role in determining how a child grows and develops. For example, a girl's genes may give her the potential to be musically gifted, but if she is never given the opportunity to sing or play an instrument, her talent may never emerge. Think of people you know who seem to have inherited physical characteristics or artistic abilities. See Fig. 7-1.

Nutrition

Eating foods that contain the essential nutrients the body needs to grow and develop is key to a child's lifelong health. Even newborns who spend most of their time sleeping are growing and developing. Proper nutrition fuels that development. In fact, research has shown that nutrition affects many aspects of a baby's physical growth and development, including bone strength, brain development, and height. Not getting enough calories or necessary nutrients places a baby at risk for illness, delayed growth, or even death.

Health

Staying healthy is closely linked to other factors that influence growth and development. A baby who is healthy is more likely to eat well and have the energy to be active. A healthy baby is more likely to have varied experiences that stimulate the brain and aid in muscle development. An infant with poor health is at risk of falling behind developmentally. See Fig. 7-2.

Parents and other caregivers must guard children's health. In addition to providing good nutrition, they must provide a safe environment. Children also need regular medical checkups and care.

Experiences

 An infant's experiences are also an important key to development. Brain development, which impacts all areas of development, is linked to the quantity and variety of experiences a child has. Infancy is a critical period. Failure to achieve normal brain development at this stage can have lifelong effects.

Fig. 7-2 **Proper health and nutrition are important to a baby's physical growth.** How is a healthy baby likely to grow and develop?

Learning Through  PLAY

Playing with Babies

Babies may seem too young to play games, but even a six-month-old infant can enjoy simple interactive play. All that's usually needed is an adult, a baby, and some creativity. Peek-a-boo and hide-and-seek with toys are old favorites. Babies also enjoy listening to music and clapping hands together or hearing an adult sing nursery rhymes or mimic animal sounds. Whatever the activity, it is important to remember that it's not the type of play that matters; it is the benefits that count. Playing with babies is not only fun, it helps promote physical development, brain development, and social interaction. The contact that occurs during play also helps nurture a baby's sense of security and well-being.

Following Up

Create two play activities for babies six to twelve months old. Share your activities with the class.

Environment

A **stimulating environment**—one in which the baby has a wide variety of things to see, taste, smell, hear, and touch—enhances brain development. A world with plenty of ways to use all the senses provides wonderful opportunities for an infant. While investigating their world, all that they experience is stored in the brain. As associations form (the high chair means food), additional brain connections are made.

An environment lacking in stimulation can result in fewer or weaker connections in the brain and delayed or slow development in other areas. For example, infants aren't born with language skills. During the first few months of life, connections form in the part of the brain responsible for language, eventually enabling the child to begin speaking. If the child is not exposed to language and not encouraged to speak during this time, there will be fewer connections in the brain. This can delay normal language development.

THE DEVELOPING BRAIN

Some people think, "How silly!" when they see adults talking to newborns. Is it a waste of time? How can a baby possibly understand? In fact, talking to and playing with infants are important for brain development and learning. These activities help babies to learn language and to develop social skills.

Other environmental factors can have an impact on a child's development as well. For example, children who breathe secondhand smoke are more likely to suffer from poor health, including respiratory infections, ear infections, and asthma. These conditions can make it more difficult for a child to develop normally. For more information on how pollutants and tobacco smoke can affect development, see page 137.

Growth During the First Year

From birth to age one, babies typically triple their birth weight. They usually increase their length by about 50 percent. One way doctors can judge whether a baby is growing at a healthy pace is by using growth charts. **Growth charts** show the average weight and height of girls and boys at various ages. Figure 7-3 focuses on average heights and weights for boys and girls from birth to age one. Boys and girls are plotted separately because their growth rates and patterns differ.

Very few babies match the average measurements on growth charts. That's because children grow at their own rate. Instead of focusing on any one measurement, doctors watch for a steady pattern of growth. Sudden drops in a baby's weight could indicate health concerns.

Fig. 7-3 Average Lengths and Weights: Birth to 12 Months				
	MALES		FEMALES	
Age	Length / Inches	Weight / Pounds	Length / Inches	Weight / Pounds
Birth	19¾	7½	19½	7½
3 months	24	13	23½	12¼
6 months	26½	17½	25½	15½
9 months	28	20½	27½	18¾
12 months	29	22½	29	21

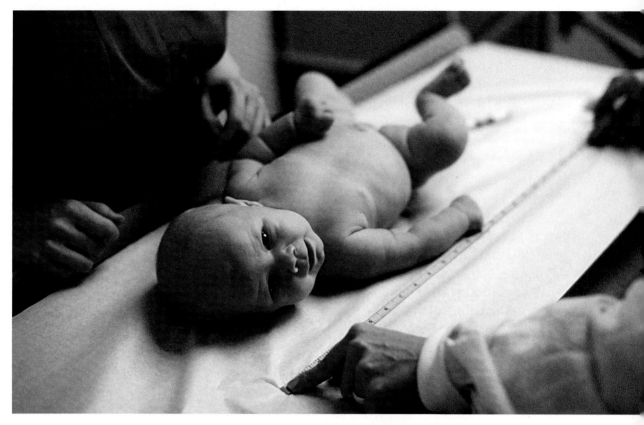

Fig. 7-4 During the first year, physicians talk about and track an infant's length rather than height.

Weight

Weight gain is one of the best signs of good health. Most newborns lose about 10 percent of their birth weight in the first five days of life. After that, they begin to gain weight rapidly. In the first six months, a healthy baby gains about 1 to 2 pounds (0.45 to 0.9 kilograms) per month. In the following six months, the average monthly weight gain is about 1 pound (0.45 kilograms). A baby's birth weight usually doubles in the first few months and triples by the end of the first year. The average weight of a one-year-old is 20 to 22 pounds (9 to 10 kilograms). However, boys tend to weigh slightly more than girls during babyhood.

Length

In the first year, physicians talk about the "length" of a baby rather than the "height," because babies are measured while lying down. See Fig. 7-4. Babies steadily grow in length during the first year, in part because bone growth is rapid at that time. For example, the average newborn measures 20 inches (51 cm) long. One year later, the average is about 30 inches (76 cm) long. Again, not all babies grow at the same rate, and boys tend to be slightly longer than girls.

Heredity more strongly influences height than weight. A baby with tall parents is more likely to be tall as an adult than a baby with short parents.

Body Shape

Newborns hold themselves in a tightly curled position with their fists clenched, legs curved, and feet curved inward. The head may have an elongated shape from moving through the birth canal. Arms and legs are skinny, and the abdomen is large. The umbilical cord stump usually dries up and drops off within about three weeks after birth, revealing the navel. Gradually, babies stretch out their arms and legs and uncurl their fingers. Their legs and feet generally straighten out over about the first six months.

Babies typically look chubby by three months of age, but they usually lose that look as they grow longer and become more active. After about eight months, when babies begin to practice standing, their typical posture includes a protruding belly and a slight lean forward. See Fig. 7-5.

Proportion

In child development, **proportion** refers to the size relationship between different parts of the body. Compared to the rest of the body, a baby's head and abdomen are large, and the legs and arms are short and small. A baby's head grows rapidly during the first year to accommodate the swiftly developing brain. More than half the total growth of the head occurs during this time. As you learned in Chapter 6, the bones of a newborn's skull have gaps called fontanels, where bones of the skull have not yet joined permanently.

Fig. 7-5 **The growth and development of a child during the first year of life is dramatic.** What changes are obvious from these photos?

During birth, these gaps allowed the head to change shape to pass through the birth canal. During infancy, they allow the head to grow as the brain develops. They later close up permanently.

Development During the First Year

A baby goes through remarkable changes during his or her first year. The baby's growth and development are both quite rapid. Each month brings changes and new abilities. Growth and development are not nearly as obvious in older children. In a group of teens, you could probably tell older teens from younger ones, but it would be difficult to pinpoint their exact age. A fifteen-year-old and a sixteen-year-old sister look and act much alike.

Vision

A baby's eyesight improves rapidly during the first year. At first, vision is blurry, but within a week or so, a newborn is increasingly aware of the environment and can focus on objects that are 7 to 10 inches away. Babies' eyes can also follow an object moved slowly past their face. By one month, babies can focus on objects as far away as 3 feet. By six months, their eyesight reaches the clarity and sharpness of the adult level.

At first, the world a baby sees is two-dimensional—like looking at a picture. In the second month, however, infants begin to demonstrate **depth perception**. This is the ability to perceive objects that are three-dimensional. This ability significantly impacts children's interaction with the world. They can track people's movements. They also learn to reach for objects by judging how far away they are.

Patterns and colors are also important to a baby's world. Young babies seem to prefer patterns that show high contrast, such as alternating stripes, bull's-eyes, or simple faces. When shown the same object in different colors, they typically look at red or blue objects the most often.

Aside from an inability to focus in the early days, some babies appear to have eyes that are slightly crossed, or one eye that seems to wander outward. This condition typically improves by the fourth month as the eye muscles strengthen.

Hearing

The sense of hearing develops even before birth. Unborn babies often respond to sounds with changes in heart rate or activity level. A young pregnant woman who attended a loud concert found that out first hand. For an hour after the concert, the baby continued to move to the beat of the music.

At birth, a full-term baby can already tell the general direction that a sound comes from. Newborns also respond to the tone of a voice rather than to the words. A soothing, loving voice calms them, and an angry or loud voice alarms them. By the age of seven months, babies recognize their parents and other caregivers by their voices.

Language development begins with hearing spoken words, then imitating and understanding them. Premature babies and those who have had frequent ear infections tend to have more hearing problems that can delay language acquisition.

Touch

Newborns lack both sufficient brain development and movement skills to explore their world through the sense of touch. However, they rely on the touch of others to teach them about their environment. Meeting a young baby's needs promptly and with a gentle touch builds trust.

Touch becomes a more important sense for learning as the first year progresses. At first a baby may begin to notice different textures—a soft blanket or a father's scratchy chin. Later, as the ability to reach and grab objects develops, a baby uses touch for exploration.

Smell and Taste

Since babies are surrounded by amniotic fluid until birth, their sense of smell doesn't have an opportunity to develop until after birth. A study has shown, however, that even newborns have some sense of smell because they respond differently to different scents. Within ten days, they can distinguish their mother from another person by smell.

The sense of taste develops rapidly in children. Research studies have found that even two-week-old babies can taste the difference between water, sour liquids, sugar solutions, salt solutions, and milk. Even at this early age, babies show a preference for sweet tastes.

Throughout the first year, babies put anything and everything into their mouths. This is a primary way of learning about their world. It is important to be sure that anything a baby grabs is clean, not sharp, and not so small that it could cause choking. Any object that can fit into a paper towel tube is likely too small for a baby to play with. See Fig. 7-6.

Voice

The newborn's cry is shrill, but it softens as the baby's lungs mature. The change in the voice of the child also results from the physical growth of the throat muscles, tongue, lips, teeth, and vocal cords. The tongue and the inside of the mouth change in shape and proportion during the first months of life. This growth makes speech development possible. Babies prepare for speech by making word-related sounds. They begin babbling vowel sounds, such as "ooh" and "ah" as early as three months of age. By the age of one, many babies can imitate some speech sounds and understand simple phrases.

Motor Skills

At birth, babies have little control over their muscles. Most movements are due to **reflexes**—instinctive, automatic responses, such as grasping or sucking.

Much of a baby's physical development during the first year is in muscle movement, also called motor skills. These skills depend mainly on direct control and use of muscles, not reflexes. For example, the arms and legs must get stronger and become coordinated before a baby can crawl.

There are two basic types of motor skills, gross motor and fine motor skills. **Gross motor skills**, also called large motor skills, involve the large muscles of the body such as those of the legs and shoulders. Gross motor skills have to do with the ability to make large movements, such as jumping and running. **Fine motor skills**, also called small motor skills, involve the smaller muscles of the body such as those in the fingers. Fine motor skills require small, precise movements, such as using scissors or writing. During their first year, babies' gross motor skills develop more rapidly than fine motor skills. The chart on pages 222–223 shows some of the major gross motor and fine motor milestones during the first year.

Fig. 7-6 **For much of the first year, children explore the world through the senses of sight, sound, and taste. After they learn to grasp objects, they begin to explore more of the world through touch.** What kinds of small objects can present hazards for babies?

Reflexes

Newborns begin life with a set of automatic reflexes to help them survive in the first several weeks of life. For example:

- **The sucking reflex.** This reflex is stimulated when something is put in a baby's mouth.

- **The rooting reflex.** This happens when the baby's cheek is stroked. During the rooting reflex, Ella turns toward the side of her face that was stroked.

- **Other automatic reflexes.** These reflexes include shutting the eyes under bright lights, grabbing a finger when it is placed in the hand, stepping motions when the feet touch the floor, and throwing the arms back with fists clenched when the arms are held and suddenly released (the Moro reflex). See Fig. 7-7.

Most of these reflexes go away within a few months, and babies learn to control the muscles and develop motor skills.

Gross Motor Skills

The large muscles of the body involved in gross motor skills are primarily in the legs, arms, trunk, and neck. Newborns can turn their head, wave their arms, and kick their legs. However, these movements occur as the result of reflexes and not because the baby purposefully controls the muscles.

One of the first motor skills that infants acquire is control of the head. A newborn's head is large and heavy, and the neck muscles are weak. For example, by age one month, when Chen was placed on his stomach he could lift his head slightly. By three months, he was able to prop himself up with his arms and lift up his head and chest. Over the next few months, Chen learned to roll over from front to back, and keep his head steady when he was propped

Fig. 7-7 **A newborn shows an automatic reflex when grabbing a finger.** What are some other automatic reflexes?

Fig. 7-8 **The increased development of gross motor skills during the first year gives a child great mobility.** What can a caregiver do to allow a child to explore without getting hurt?

in a sitting position. By his first birthday, he could stand while holding on to something. This sequence of development is typical during a baby's first year.

By about nine months, many babies are crawling and beginning to explore their world. This is an exciting time for babies, who have more independence than ever before. This newfound mobility adds many new opportunities for learning. See Fig. 7-8.

Fine Motor Skills

Fine motor skills involve the smaller muscles of the body, such as those of the fingers. By three months of age, babies' clenched fists have relaxed and they can open and close their hands. This is an important milestone in the development of fine motor skills. It means the child can purposefully grasp objects. By about five or six months, babies can reach for toys and pass a block from one hand to the other. By about seven months, babies can pick up objects by "raking" at them with the fingers and hand. Between nine and twelve months, babies fine-tune the ability to self-feed and learn to drink from a cup and pick up food and other objects with the thumb and forefinger. For more on motor skills, see Fig. 7-9 on pages 222–223.

MONTH

- Lifts head and turns it from one side to the other when placed on stomach
- Focuses on objects from about 10 inches to up to 3 feet away
- Reacts to parent's voice

 MONTHS

- Makes sounds such as "ooh" and "aah"
- Watches objects moved about 6 inches away from face
- Responds to more sounds and different pitches of voice

3 MONTHS

- Opens and closes hands
- Holds head steadily when held up
- Lifts head and chest when on stomach
- Swipes at objects
- Brings hands together

4 MONTHS

- Supports upper body on hands when lying on stomach
- Shows preference for red and blue over yellow
- May begin to use vowels and consonants in babbling, such as "ah ga"
- Grasps rattle
- Puts hands in mouth
- Rolls from tummy to back

5 MONTHS

- Rocks on stomach while kicking legs and making swimming motions with arms
- Reaches out and grabs toys
- Turns head in direction of sound
- Knows positive speech from unhappy speech

6 MONTHS

- Passes a block from one hand to the other
- Puts objects to mouth with hand
- May begin creeping
- Recognizes basic sounds of native language

Fig. 7-9 Developmental Milestones—PHYSICAL   1st Year

7 MONTHS

- Rolls over both ways
- Sits up steadily
- Stands with assistance
- Knows parents and caregivers by their voices and by sight
- Can follow a path of moving objects with eyes
- Babbles with strings of vowels and consonants, such as "ba, ba, ba"
- Grabs for objects with raking motion

8 MONTHS

- Pulls self up to standing
- Bangs blocks together
- Propels self by arms, knees, or squirming motion
- Looks at objects with sustained attention

9 MONTHS

- Uses index finger to poke
- Puts objects in containers
- Leans forward to pick up toy
- Notices small objects
- May start associating sounds with objects

10 MONTHS

- Crawls well
- Can put objects in containers
- Uses index finger to start pointing
- Imitates new word sounds more frequently

11 MONTHS

- Walks while holding onto furniture or crib rails for support
- Uses gestures like shaking head for no
- Releases objects intentionally
- Grasps with thumb and forefinger

12 MONTHS

- May walk a few steps alone
- Stands alone for short time
- Picks up small objects using thumb and forefinger
- Puts objects into and takes them out of containers
- Holds and drinks from cup

Hand-Eye Coordination

The ability to move the hands and fingers precisely in relation to what is seen is called **hand-eye coordination**. This is an essential skill for many tasks in life. It is what allows people to eat, catch a ball, color pictures, and tie shoes.

Newborns have poor hand-eye coordination, but it develops as vision and motor skills improve. Around the age of three or four months, babies begin to reach and grab for objects they see and bring them to their mouths. By the end of their first year, babies can pick up an object and put it in another place.

SECTION 7-1 Review and Activities

Reviewing the Section

1. How does growth differ from development?
2. What is meant by the near-to-far pattern of development? Identify and describe the other two patterns of development.
3. What effect might an infant's health and environment have on his growth and development?
4. What are three major physical milestones that a baby should meet by twelve months of age?
5. If a newborn weighed 7 pounds, would it be reasonable to assume that she would weigh 15 pounds at her first birthday? Why or why not?
6. Contrast a typical baby's eyesight at birth and at the end of the first year.
7. List three *reflexes*, three *gross motor skills*, and three *fine motor skills* that a baby shows in the first year.

Observing and Interacting

Observe a baby under the age of twelve months. How interested is the baby in moving around independently? What signs of such interest do you see? Record the baby's actions, then share your findings with the class. Have the class try to guess the baby's age based on his or her actions.

Infant Care Skills

A baby requires a tremendous amount of physical care. Every simple need, from a clean diaper to being comforted, requires someone's help. Aside from tending to her physical needs, when parents and other caregivers pick up and hold a baby they have an opportunity to strengthen emotional bonds. In addition to all this, babies must be properly fed. Their nutritional needs must be met to fuel all the rapid physical and brain growth that takes place in the first year.

Objectives

- Demonstate how to safely handle a baby.
- Evaluate various ways of nurturing and bonding with babies while caring for them.
- Identify two possible sleep hazards.
- Identify a baby's nutritional needs as well as foods to avoid.
- Compare the benefits of breast milk and formula.
- Describe the best type of clothing suitable for a baby.

Key Terms

antibodies
malnutrition
shaken baby syndrome
weaning

Handling Babies

Babies need to be held for all sorts of reasons—to be changed, fed, bathed, dressed, cuddled, and hugged. When picking up and holding a baby, safety, physical care, and emotional bonding are all involved.

Newborns and very young babies require the most careful handling. A newborn's neck muscles aren't strong enough to support the head. For that reason, anyone picking up and holding a newborn must support the baby's neck and head at all times. By about four months of age, babies can hold up their head without support. Even then, handling babies gently and holding them close gives the babies a sense of security. See Fig. 7-10 on page 226.

Whenever picking up or putting down an infant, try to move smoothly and gently to avoid startling the baby. A crying baby can often be calmed by being picked up and held. Sometimes rocking the baby and gently patting the back can also be soothing.

Fig. 7-10
Handling a Newborn Safely

- **Lifting a newborn**—Slide one hand under the baby's bottom and the other under the shoulders and head. Use your forearm to support the neck and head as you raise your hands together to lift the newborn.

- **Holding a newborn in your arms**—Hold the baby upright, cradled in the curve of your arm. Your arm supports the baby's head and neck, and you can easily maintain eye contact with the baby.

- **Holding a newborn against your chest**—Hold the baby against your chest, so that the baby faces—or peeks over—your shoulder. Use your hand to support the baby's neck and head.

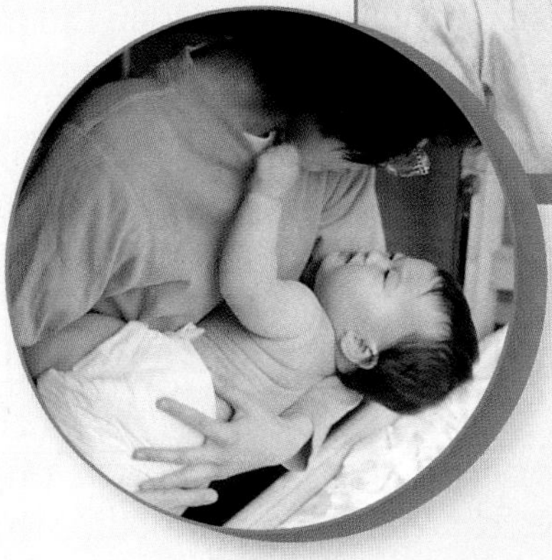

- **Putting a newborn down**—Continue to support the neck, head, and body. Bend over and rest the child on a surface that can support the baby's body. Then remove your arms.

Shaken Baby Syndrome

No one should ever vigorously shake or jiggle a baby. These actions are extremely dangerous. Every year thousands of babies suffer serious problems due to **shaken baby syndrome**. This condition occurs when someone severely shakes a baby, usually in an effort to make her stop crying. Shaken baby syndrome can lead to damage to the brain, including mental retardation, cerebral palsy, or blindness. Sometimes the shaking breaks bones or injures the neck and spine, or even causes death.

The baby cries and cries and nothing you do seems to help. You are scared, frustrated, and angry. You are afraid you will lose control and hurt the baby. You may think this could never happen to you, but it might. Even experienced adults sometimes come close to a breaking point. For new parents and child care providers, the odds are higher. What could you do in such a situation?

- Put the baby down in a safe place, go into another room, and take some deep breaths or look out the window to calm down.
- Ask a friend or relative to care for the baby for a few hours.
- Call someone and talk about the problem.
- Call a parenting hotline or take the baby to a crisis nursery if available in your area. Both can give immediate help and show you how to handle stress in the future.

Gently rocking or playfully bouncing a baby on the knee is not dangerous. However, shaking or hitting a baby can be deadly. A baby can't purposely aggravate a parent. If you or someone you know is ever in this situation, ask for help.

Ensuring Adequate Sleep

Sleep is essential for growth and development. It also appears to be necessary for the brain to work properly. In babies, children, and teens, sleep coincides with the release of chemicals in the body that contribute to growth. In addition, during sleep the body's cells are hard at work, building and repairing themselves.

Some infants sleep more than others. Generally, a baby who is active needs more sleep than an inactive baby. Babies also need more sleep on some days than on others.

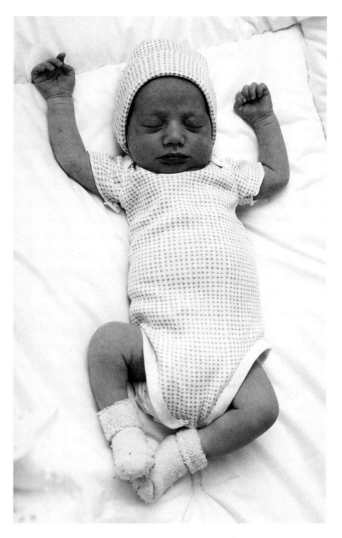

Fig. 7-11 **While a crib may seem like a safe place for infants to sleep, there are safety hazards to be aware of.** What are some safety precautions for putting a baby to sleep in a crib?

As harmless as sleeping may seem, there are safety precautions to follow when putting babies to sleep. Besides choosing a safe bed, pillows, fluffy blankets, puffy bumper pads, and stuffed toys need to be removed. They can cause suffocation. See Fig. 7-11.

Babies should be placed face up when put to bed. This is to help prevent a death from sudden infant death syndrome. Read more about this on page 228.

Bedtime Routines

Putting a baby to sleep should be a relaxed and pleasant experience. One of the best ways to help a baby settle down to sleep is to establish a consistent bedtime routine. Some common routines include a warm bath, reading a story, and rocking the baby gently. Put the baby in the crib, gently pat the baby goodnight, and leave the room. The baby may cry or whimper a bit but usually will fall asleep within a few minutes.

Lupe wants to begin a bedtime routine with her three-month-old son, Miguel. The first night, she gives Miguel a warm bath and puts a fresh diaper and some pajamas on him. She then rocks Miguel gently as she sings him a lullaby. After a few minutes, Miguel seems drowsy. Lupe gently lays him in his crib and creeps out of his room.

Parenting Q&A

What Is Sudden Infant Death Syndrome?

Sudden infant death syndrome (SIDS), or crib death, is the unexpected death of an infant with no obvious cause. The baby dies during sleep, with no crying out and no evidence of struggle. SIDS affects infants up to twelve months old, but the vast majority of children who die of SIDS are under six months old. SIDS strikes one or two children out of every thousand, and it most often occurs in winter.

The cause of SIDS is unknown. However, researchers have identified some groups who are at risk. Among those groups, the most likely victims are male babies who had a low birth weight. Premature babies, babies who live with a person who smokes, and babies who sleep on their stomachs are also at greater risk of SIDS.

To reduce the risk of SIDS:
- Put babies to sleep on their backs.
- Pregnant women should avoid smoking during pregnancy and after the baby is born.
- Avoid exposing the baby to smoke from others.

Parents who suffer the loss of a baby to SIDS often feel guilt as well as grief. Help is available through family and friends, grief counselors, physicians, and SIDS support groups.

THINKING IT THROUGH

1. What other dangerous effects does cigarette smoke have on babies?
2. Why might parents who lost a child to SIDS feel guilty?

Fig. 7-12 How Much Do Babies Sleep?

Age	Hours of Sleep	Description
Newborn	16	• Takes four or five naps a day, each about 3 to 4 hours. • Between each nap is a period of wakefulness that lasts a few hours.
3 months	14 to 15	• Total amount of sleep decreases but takes longer naps—about 4 to 5 hours long. • Longer sleeping periods at night.
4 months	12 to 14	• Takes naps midmorning and late afternoon. • Sleeps much of the night.
6 months	12 to 14	• Takes two long naps. • Sleeps about six hours at night.
1 year	12 hours	• May take one or two naps. • Has 9- to 10-hour sleeping periods at night.

Experts have varied in their advice about what to do if a baby continues to cry. Some recommend leaving the baby alone to "cry it out." Others say the baby should be comforted. Today, many experts say to go to the baby after a few minutes of crying, offer comfort without picking up the baby, and then leave the room. If the baby cries again, stay away a bit longer than before and repeat the sequence. This process reassures the baby that a parent will always be near. However, any baby who continues to cry for more than 15 minutes should be checked for a wet diaper, sickness, or other problems.

Sleep Patterns

The amount of time a baby spends sleeping decreases considerably during the first year. A newborn may sleep a total of 12 to 20 hours a day. By one year, however, a baby often has as few as two or three sleep periods, including naps. Figure 7-12 shows how much sleep babies typically need over the course of the first year.

Responding to Cries

It is important to respond to a baby's cries. Pediatricians say that a prompt response to a very young baby doesn't "spoil" the baby. As discussed earlier, the only time parents and other caregivers *may* be advised to let a baby cry is at bedtime, when they are trying to establish good sleep habits. At other times, the reason for crying may be as simple as a wet diaper or feeling cold or hungry. Pain or sickness may also cause crying. Some babies may simply be startled by loud noises. First, make sure a crying baby is comfortable, fed, and dry. Next, try rocking, talking, singing, or other comforting techniques to soothe the baby.

Feeding Babies

Mealtime provides babies with much more than the nutrients they need to grow and develop. It is also an opportunity for babies to interact with others, learn more about their world, and practice skills. The cuddling, body contact, and nurturing that go along with feeding babies are almost as important as the food.

Nutritional Needs

In the first year, a baby's basic source of nutrition is breast milk or formula. In fact, for the first six months of life, a healthy baby's nutritional needs can be met solely through breast milk or iron-fortified formula.

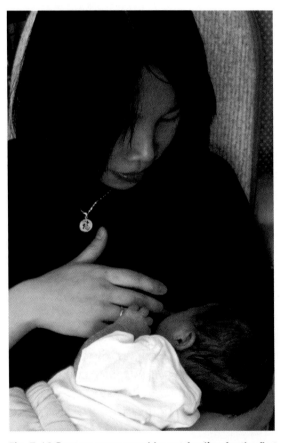

Fig. 7-13 Doctors recommend breast-feeding for the first 12 months. Why is breast-feeding sometimes difficult?

At about six months, parents can introduce solid foods. Watery rice cereal is often introduced first, followed by other thin cereals and strained fruits, vegetables, and cooked meats. These solid foods are an important source of calories, or food energy, needed for growth. After about eight months of age, babies should get about half of their calories from solid food and half from breast milk or formula. The proportion of solid food should continue to increase gradually. By a baby's first birthday, most nutrition should come from solid foods.

Babies under age one shouldn't be fed cow's milk because it is hard for them to digest. Never substitute cow's milk for breast milk or formula. It lacks important nutrients that breast milk and formula provide. Fruit juice seems like a nutritious food for infants. However, there are good reasons for limiting it. Fruit juice promotes tooth decay and may curb a child's appetite for more nutritious foods. It is usually best to wait until the baby is six months old before introducing fruit juice.

The Case for Breast-Feeding

If a mother is capable, nutrition experts recommend breast-feeding. There are many advantages to breast milk:

- It contains all the nutrients a baby needs.
- It also contains **antibodies**—substances produced by the body to fight off germs—from the mother. Antibodies boost a baby's defenses against infection. Colostrum, or the first breast milk, is especially rich in nutrients and these protective substances.
- It is germ-free and easy to digest.
- Breast-fed babies get fewer ear infections, respiratory infections, and allergies than formula-fed babies. They are also less likely to develop asthma.

Breast milk lacks vitamin D, a nutrient important for bone growth. Fortunately, the skin makes this vitamin when it is exposed to sunlight. Would a young baby in a cold climate get much sun in winter?

The World Health Organization encourages mothers to breast-feed for at least one year. This gives babies the best possible nutrition and a good start in life. See Fig. 7-13.

Baby Formula

Many babies are fed formula for part or all of their infancy. Not every mother is physically able to breast-feed. Other parents choose to use formula.

Baby formula is specially made to meet babies' nutritional needs. Milk-based formula is used most often. The cow's milk used as an ingredient has been modified to eliminate digestive problems. Soy-based formula is also available. Formula comes in three forms: ready to use, a concentrated liquid that is mixed with water, and a powder that is mixed with water.

Fig. 7-14 **Bottle-feeding, whether with breast milk or formula, gives a father an opportunity to participate in the closeness of feeding an infant.**

Feeding Schedules

A newborn's schedule of eating and sleeping is unpredictable. Pediatricians recommend that newborns be fed as much and as often as they want to eat.

Frequent feedings are necessary because a newborn's stomach can hold only a small amount. In the first few weeks of life, breast-fed babies may want to eat as many as eight to twelve times a day or more. Formula-fed babies may eat every three to four hours for the first few weeks. See Fig. 7-14.

By the second or third month, most babies are eating on a regular schedule. They may wake for a feeding every three or four hours. Eventually—typically when they weigh about 12 pounds (5.4 kg)—babies no longer need a late-night feeding. At this weight, their stomach is usually large enough to allow them to sleep through the night, about six hours.

Feeding Methods

Most babies under the age of six months eat only breast milk or formula, so there are only two ways they can be fed—by breast or bottle. With either method, babies should be allowed to eat until they are satisfied. Healthy babies usually eat only the amount they need, so overeating is generally not an issue with young babies.

Breast-Feeding

Breast-feeding is very natural, but it doesn't always come naturally. It can take practice. Many hospitals have consultants on staff to offer assistance if needed. They

Health & Safety

Food-Related Hazards

Watching children enjoy new foods for the first time can be a wonderful experience. But, there are some important things to keep in mind as new foods are introduced.

- **Food Allergies.** Babies should not be fed eggs, citrus fruits, honey, peanut butter, corn, or shellfish during their first year of life. All of these foods can cause allergic reactions.

- **Food Poisoning.** Botulism is a deadly form of food poisoning. Food poisoning can make children very sick. Some of the milder symptoms may include diarrhea, vomiting, nausea, stomachache, headache, weakness, and fever. Food poisoning is caused by eating foods that have not been handled properly, or by bacteria in the foods.

- **Choking Hazards.** When a baby begins self-feeding, it is important to avoid foods that could get lodged in a baby's throat. Some

of these foods include raw vegetables, hot dogs, nuts, scoops of peanut butter, whole grapes, candy, chips, pretzels, and popcorn. Any hard, round food can get stuck in a baby's throat.

Check-Up

Why do you think babies are most sensitive to foods during their first year?

Fig. 7-15 **It is important to check the temperature of the formula before feeding it to a baby.** Why is this important?

can help new mothers learn how to find the best way to hold the baby and get the baby to eat. They can also give advice on the mother's nutritional needs and how to deal with problems.

Bottle-Feeding

There are certain guidelines for bottle-feeding as well. The first deals with preparing the formula.

If using a powdered or concentrated formula, mix it with sterile (germ-free) bottled water or water that has been boiled. Bottles should be washed in a dishwasher or with hot, sudsy water followed by a boiling water rinse. Bottles with disposable liners are a popular alternative. Bottles can be prepared up to 24 hours ahead and stored in the refrigerator.

Most infants seem to prefer their bottles at room temperature or warm. To warm a bottle, place it in a pan of warm water. Heat the formula until it is lukewarm. Test the temperature by dripping a small amount of formula onto the inside of your wrist. If it is hot, allow it to cool down before feeding. A baby should never be given hot formula or formula that has been warmed in a microwave oven—the formula might contain pockets of hot liquid that will burn a baby's mouth. See Fig. 7-15.

For bottle-feeding, hold the baby close in a semi-upright position. The head needs support in the first few months. Propping up the baby and bottle and leaving the baby to drink alone is never a good idea. It deprives the baby of important physical contact. In addition, babies shouldn't be put to bed with a bottle. The milk can pool around the gums and cause decay in developing teeth. This practice also leads to an increased risk of ear infections.

If a baby doesn't finish the contents of the entire bottle, the remainder should be thrown away. Disease-causing bacteria can grow quickly in leftover formula and if eaten, could lead to illness.

Burping the Baby

A baby needs to be burped at least twice during each feeding. Page 234 gives step-by-step directions.

Burp a Baby

Babies often swallow air as they drink—whether they are bottle- or breast-fed. To feel comfortable, a baby must be burped periodically to expel the air. Without burping, a baby may spit up, become irritable, or have gas. It's a technique that anyone who cares for a baby needs to know.

- **Burp a baby at least twice during a feeding.** Depending on how much the baby is drinking, try burping at least once during a feeding and once after a feeding.

- **Find the most comfortable position to burp a baby.** Many caregivers lay the baby across their knees. Others hold the baby across their chests with the baby's head above their shoulders.

- **Pat the baby on the back to induce the burp.** A gentle tap works as well as a firmer one, so be very gentle.

- **Protect your clothing.** Put a towel or cloth under the baby's head to catch any liquid that comes up.

- **Remember that it is perfectly normal for a baby not to burp each time.** Each baby's liquid intake is different. Although a baby may not burp each time, it is important to try.

YOUR TURN

Perseverance. Sometimes a baby may not burp right away. Why is it important to continue trying to burp a baby during feeding?

Fig. 7-16 **By six months old, a baby can eat solid foods.** What is the first type of solid food a baby can eat?

It is also common for most babies to spit up from time to time. This may occur after the baby has eaten more than his or her stomach can hold. Sometimes a baby will spit up while burping. It's a good idea to protect your clothes with a cloth while holding or burping a baby. Avoid placing the baby in a seated position after eating because this can put pressure on the stomach and cause the baby to spit up. If a baby vomits forcefully, or doesn't appear to be gaining weight, consult a pediatrician.

Weaning

Sometime around their first birthday, many babies are ready for **weaning**, or changing from the bottle or breast to a cup. Weaning is an important sign of a baby's increasing independence.

There is no absolute time at which a baby should be weaned. Many babies show signs that they are ready. They may show less interest in breast- or bottle-feeding. Typically this occurs between nine and twelve months of age. Other signs that a baby is ready to be weaned include playing or looking around while feeding, pushing the breast or bottle away, or showing a preference for eating from a spoon.

It is best to approach the weaning gradually. If a mother is breast-feeding, her body can adjust to decreasing demands on milk production. The slower transition also gives children time to get used to drinking formula or milk, depending on their age. Forced weaning may result in other feeding or behavior problems for the child.

Some pediatricians recommend a transition directly from the breast-feeding to a cup if the child is old enough to drink from one. This avoids later transitions from bottles to cups. However, if an infant moves from breast-feeding to a bottle, the breast milk should slowly be replaced with formula or milk first.

Introducing Solid Foods

Babies are typically given their first solid foods around the age of four to six months. There is no rush to start, however. Once babies have started to eat cereal, other new foods can be introduced. It is not unusual for a baby to have a bad reaction to a certain food. It may cause a skin rash, digestive trouble, or an allergic reaction. By introducing new foods at least four days apart, it is easier to figure out which food is the problem. See Fig. 7-16.

Self-feeding

When babies can sit up steadily in a high chair—usually at about eight or ten months—they typically start to eat with their fingers and reach for a spoon. Being able to pick up food and self-feed is an important developmental milestone because it signals increased independence. Providing "finger foods," small pieces of food that can easily be picked up with the fingers and eaten, encourages self-feeding. Foods that break up easily in the mouth are best. This might include dry toast, cereal pieces, small pieces of chicken, small pieces of cooked pasta, and chunks of banana.

Fig. 7-17 **Older babies enjoy feeding themselves "finger foods," which are small pieces of food that can easily be picked up and eaten.** What are some appropriate finger foods for babies?

A baby's first efforts at self-feeding with a spoon will probably be fun for the baby but not very productive. At first, mealtime may consist of the baby trying to self-feed finger foods while the caregiver spoons in extra food whenever possible. Babies may not become expert spoon users until twelve to eighteen months of age. It takes patience—and a sense of humor—to reach this point. Allowing plenty of time for each meal and anticipating some messiness helps. See Fig. 7-17.

Nutritional Concerns

Just like adults, babies who are eating solid foods should eat nutritious, well-balanced meals that include grains, fruits or vegetables, and protein. They should be able to eat whenever they are hungry, rather than on a rigid schedule. Foods should be soft and easy to gum and swallow. Salty snack foods should be limited because they are likely low in nutritional value. Certain other foods may contain substances that aren't good for a baby. Babies have very specific nutritional needs. They include the following:

- Enough calories to provide for activity and rapid growth
- Foods that provide key nutrients, such as vitamins and minerals
- Adequate amounts of liquid

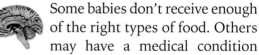 Some babies don't receive enough of the right types of food. Others may have a medical condition that prevents them from absorbing enough nutrients after they eat. **Malnutrition**—inadequate nutrition—during infancy can cause lasting physical problems. Poor nutrition is also linked to poor brain development, which can lead to learning difficulties.

There are many government and community programs working to eliminate infant and childhood malnutrition. Some of these programs provide food; others teach parents about making good nutritional choices for children.

While most babies eat the amount they need, it is possible to overfeed a baby. This is more common with bottle-fed babies. They may be encouraged to finish all the formula in their bottle, even if they are already full. See Fig. 7-18. A chubby baby will not necessarily grow up to be an obese adult. Research indicates that obesity in adulthood is linked to heredity. However, poor eating habits in the first year can lead to health problems later in life. Pediatricians can offer advice about finding the best ways to meet a baby's nutritional needs.

Allergies

An allergy is an oversensitivity to a particular common substance that is harmless to most people. When a person has an allergy, the body's immune system attacks the substance, and allergy symptoms are the side effects of the attack. People may have an allergic reaction when they eat, breathe in, are injected with, or touch the thing they are allergic to. The reaction may be as mild as puffy, itchy eyes or as severe as *anaphylactic* (ana-fih-LAK-tik) *shock*, a life-threatening condition that makes it difficult to breathe.

It is important to watch for signs of allergies in babies. Parents who have allergies themselves should be especially careful, since the tendency to develop allergies runs in families. Signs of food allergy in a baby may include excessive fussiness, vomiting almost all food after a feeding, or eight or more watery stools a day.

Fig. 7-18 **Parents and other caregivers should never overfeed a baby.** How might a caregiver know when a baby is full?

Children often outgrow allergies to eggs, milk, and soy, but other food allergies are likely to continue throughout life. The best treatment for a food allergy is to avoid the food. Breast-feeding mothers should also avoid foods to which a baby is allergic, because substances from the food can enter the breast milk.

Dressing a Baby

Have you ever seen babies who seem over- or under-dressed for the weather? Babies lose body heat more easily than adults do, but they are also sensitive to overheating. As a general rule, pediatricians recommend dressing babies in one more layer of clothing than an older child or an adult would wear.

Fig. 7-19 What characteristics should you look for when choosing clothes for babies?

Clothing size is determined by a baby's weight and age, although weight is typically the more reliable guide. In general, clothes shouldn't be so snug that the baby has trouble moving or so large that the clothes gets wrapped around or stuck under the baby.

When choosing baby clothes, comfort and ease in dressing are important. Features such as snaps along the inner legs help make changing diapers easy. Shirts that snap rather than go over the head are also easy to use with young babies. To get longer use out of clothes, look for clothes with cuffs or generous hems that can be let down, extra buttons on shoulder straps, and waistbands that allow for growth. See Fig. 7-19.

A new baby doesn't need a lot of fancy clothing. Babies do need diapers, undershirts, and simple outer garments. Socks and booties are usually not necessary for everyday wear. Many newborns spend their days and nights in a sleeper, a one-piece stretchy garment that has feet or a simple drawstring at the bottom. On hot days, just a diaper and an undershirt will do.

When babies begin to creep and crawl, they need more durable clothes that allow for movement. Some baby clothes have padded knees to add durability. Shoes aren't essential until a baby starts to walk outdoors. When babies are learning to walk, going barefoot gives them more flexibility at the ankle and allows them to grip the floor with the toes. Once the baby is ready for shoes, either flexible sneakers or soft leather shoes are good choices.

Choosing Clothing

Many clothes for infants are made of knit fabrics that are comfortable and stretchy, making it easy for baby to move around.

How to Dress a Baby

Dressing and undressing a baby quickly and smoothly takes some practice. See Fig. 7-20. It is easy to understand why babies don't really like the process. There is usually an abrupt change in temperature combined with being pushed and pulled through clothes. Here are some hints for dressing babies in different types of clothing:

- **Pullover garments.** These clothes have a stretchable neck opening. If the neck opening is large, put the opening around the baby's face first and pull it over the back of the head. If the opening is small, gather the garment into a loop and slip it over the back of the baby's head. Stretch the garment forward, down, and away from the face and ears. Put the baby's fist into the armhole and pull the arm through with the other hand. Repeat with the other arm, and then straighten out the bottom of the garment. When undressing the child, carefully stretch the garment away from the chin and face as it is lifted off.

- **Open-front shirt.** Lay the baby down on the shirt, face up. Gently pull the baby's arms through the sleeves. Fasten the front.

- **One-piece garment with feet.** Putting on this type of garment is easier when the zipper or the snaps go from neck to toes. Lay the baby on the open garment. Start with the bottom part of the garment. Put the baby's leg on the side without the zipper or snaps into the leg of the garment, followed by the other leg. Roll the baby onto one side and pull the garment up under the baby's shoulders. Roll the baby back onto the garment, and then gently pull the sleeves over the baby's arms. Finish by zipping or snapping the garment closed.

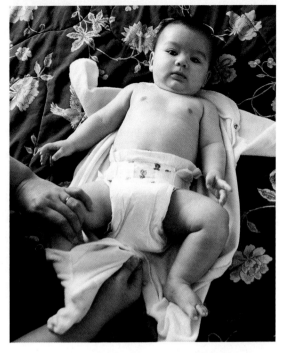

Fig. 7-20 **As you dress or undress a baby, it is important to work as quickly and smoothly as possible.**

SECTION 7-2 Review and Activities

Reviewing the Section

1. What are three things a frustrated parent or caregiver might do when a baby won't stop crying?
2. Why should pillows and stuffed toys be removed from the crib before a baby is put to sleep?
3. Describe a possible routine to use when putting a baby to bed at night.
4. About how much time does a newborn sleep daily? A 12-month-old?
5. Describe a baby's nutritional needs during the first year.
6. Compare the benefits of breast milk and formula. How are they different?
7. What solid foods are usually introduced to babies first? Why?
8. Describe three factors you would consider in choosing a clothing gift for a newborn.

Observing and Interacting

Go to a mall food court or other place where you can see young babies eating. Observe babies as they are fed or try to feed themselves. Note such things as the kinds of foods they are eating and how the parents interact with the baby. Prepare a written report of your experience.

Infant Health and Wellness

For parents, the first year of a baby's life can be very demanding. Beyond the everyday care of a baby, parents have to maintain their baby's overall wellness, from bathing their baby to keeping their baby safe. Their baby's health is in their hands, too. An infant should be taken to the doctor for regular checkups and vaccinations. Though the work can often feel overwhelming, it is vital to the health and well-being of the baby.

Objectives

- Demonstrate how to bathe a baby.
- Demonstrate how to diaper a baby.
- Describe the signs of teething.
- Describe at least five important ways to keep a baby safe at home.
- Explain why checkups and immunizations are important for babies.

Key Terms

cradle cap
diaper rash
teething
immunizations
vaccine

Bathing Baby

Regular baths help keep babies clean and healthy. There are two types of baby baths. Newborns should have sponge baths until the navel heals, about two or so weeks after birth. After that, the baby can be given a tub bath. Many parents use a portable baby bathtub, a large dishpan, or a sink. It is best to wait until a baby can sit up independently before using a full-size tub. For more information, refer to "How to Bathe a Baby."

A sponge bath can be used any time a baby needs to be clean. Around age two to three months, babies should have baths two or three times a week. By age seven to eight months, when most babies can sit up steadily in the bath, they really enjoy bath time. They love to splash and play in the water with floating toys and plastic cups. Through much of early childhood, the bathtub can be a favorite play place, where bath toys and a child's imagination merge for delightful play.

Bathe a Baby

Bath time can be a lot of fun for babies. Some like to kick and splash in the water or play with bath toys. Caregivers often talk, sing, or play games with a baby. At the same time, it's important to handle a slippery baby carefully.

- **Prepare for the baby's bath.** Gather everything needed for the baby's bath ahead of time. Set up the baby bathtub, towels, washcloths, shampoo, and other supplies. Put about two inches of warm water in the baby's bathtub. Test the temperature of the water with your arm. Undress the baby.

- **Put the baby in the tub.** Support a very young baby's head and neck with one hand and arm. Hold the baby's body with the other hand. Lower the baby into the tub feet first. Stay with the baby at all times.

- **Wash the baby's face.** Use clear water and a damp, soft washcloth to wash the baby's face. Then gently pat it dry.

- **Wash and rinse the baby's hair.** About twice a week, wash the baby's hair with baby shampoo. Wet the baby's hair. Add a bit of shampoo and rub gently. Rinse by pouring water toward the sides and back of the baby's head.

- **Wash the baby's body.** While supporting the baby's body, use your free hand to wash and rinse the baby.

- **Dry the baby's body.** To prevent chills, wrap the baby in a clean towel immediately. Pat the baby dry. Diaper and dress the baby right away.

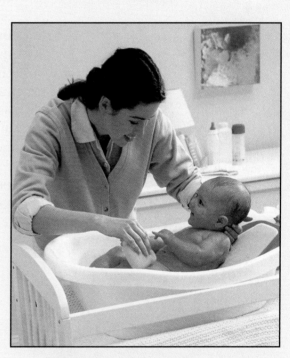

YOUR TURN

Bonding. If you were a caregiver, how do you think that bath time would help you bond with a baby?

Sometimes infants develop **cradle cap**, a skin condition known for yellowish, crusty patches on the scalp. Most cases disappear after a few weeks or months. Parents can treat it by washing the baby's scalp daily with a mild shampoo. Other treatments, such as baby oil or excessive shampooing, can worsen the scales or dry the skin.

Bath time is also a good time to trim a baby's nails, if needed, using baby nail clippers. Baby nails are soft but sharp, and they can scratch the baby's face.

Fig. 7-21 Keeping a baby clean helps prevent problems such as diaper rash.

Diapering

Diapers are the most essential part of a baby's wardrobe. A very young baby may need diaper changes 12 to 15 times each day. A newborn wets several times an hour but in small amounts that don't require changing each time. An older baby probably needs fewer diaper changes each day—and is more likely to let you know when a clean diaper is needed.

A common problem that occurs is **diaper rash**. Symptoms include patches of rough, irritated skin in the diaper area. Sometimes painful raw spots develop. Controlling bacteria in diapers helps prevent this condition. See Fig. 7-21. Mild cases of diaper rash can be treated by changing the diaper more frequently and being sure to thoroughly clean the baby at each changing. More severe cases call for a diaper rash treatment, such as a medicated cream. Exposing the area to air and avoiding waterproof pants can also help the rash heal.

It is a personal choice whether to use disposable or cloth diapers. Each has advantages and disadvantages.

- **Disposable diapers.** These are more convenient and more effective at keeping babies dry and comfortable than cloth diapers. Some babies develop a sensitivity to disposables, causing a rash. Infant care centers use disposable diapers for convenience and sanitation. Disposable diapers do add significantly to environmental waste.

- **Cloth diapers.** These are the most economical choice if they are washed at home. However, they cost more than disposable diapers if they are provided and cleaned by a commercial diaper service. Cloth diapers are more environmentally friendly.

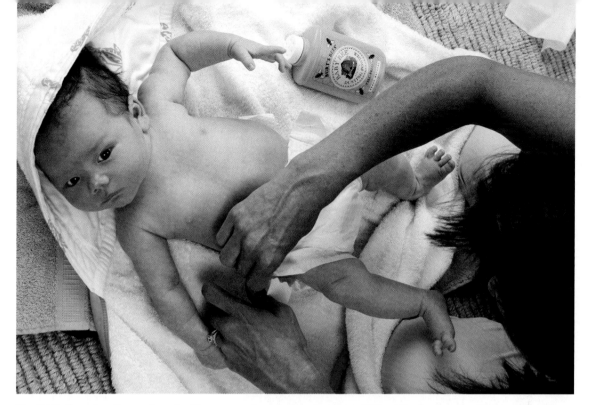

Fig. 7-22 **Changing diapers is a significant part of a caregiver's responsibility.** Why is changing diapers regularly important?

Designating a changing area makes it easy to keep diapers and other supplies close at hand. Any flat, clean surface may be used. However, it is never safe to leave a child alone on a raised surface. A changing table is a good choice because it has sides to keep the baby from rolling off. Diapering supplies may include wet washcloths, disposable wipes, soft tissues, and dry cloths for cleanup. For outings away from home, a diaper bag can hold diapers and supplies. It is also a good idea to include extra clothes and a plastic bag for diaper disposal.

Diapering a Baby

Diaper changes are an opportunity for positive interaction by talking and laughing with the baby while changing the baby's diaper. See Fig. 7-22. Here are the steps to changing a diaper:

1. **Remove the diaper and clean the baby.** Thoroughly clean the diaper area with a moist washcloth or disposable wipe.
2. **Put on a fresh diaper.** Hold the baby's ankles and lift the body to slide the diaper underneath the baby. With disposable diapers, be sure the adhesive tabs are on the back side of the diaper. With cloth diapers, place the folded side in the back for girls and in the front for boys. Then, bring the diaper up between the baby's legs. Fasten it together with the adhesive tabs, or with diaper pins or diaper tape on a cloth diaper. When using pins, keep a finger between the pin and the baby's skin. Parents using cloth diapers may choose to add plastic or cloth diaper covers, which help hold the diaper in place. Waterproof pants can help keep the baby's clothing dry.

soaked in a covered container that is filled with water, detergent, and bleach. Later, they should be washed in hot water with mild detergent.

Baby's Teeth

The development of a baby's teeth actually begins about the sixth week of pregnancy. However, a baby's teeth typically don't begin to break through the gums until about six months of age. The set of teeth a baby gets are called the *primary teeth* or "baby teeth." The complete set of primary teeth generally comes in by the time a child is twenty months old, though the timetable for when teeth appear varies somewhat for each child.

Teething refers to the process of the teeth pushing their way through the gums. The gums around the new teeth swell and become tender, so it can be a painful experience. During teething, a baby may become cranky, fuss during meals, drool a lot, develop a low-grade fever, and want to chew on something hard. Massaging the gums and allowing the baby to chew on a cold, hard, unbreakable object—such as a refrigerated teething ring—can bring relief to some. Physicians don't recommend using medications to soothe the pain. Teething medication doesn't bring much relief because it washes out of the mouth in minutes. If a baby develops a higher fever or can't be consoled, parents should check with a doctor. See Fig. 7-23.

Fig. 7-23 **Teething often causes discomfort.** How can parents and caregivers provide relief?

3. **Dispose of used supplies.** Throw out all used wipes and disposable diapers, preferably in a trash container with a lid. Disposable diapers clog plumbing, so never flush one down a toilet. Dirty cloth diapers should be rinsed in a clean, flushing toilet and

Infant Safety Concerns

Keeping children safe is one of a caregiver's greatest responsibilities. Caregivers can help prevent accidents before they happen by learning how to keep infants safe. The following are some safety guidelines for infants:

- **Choking.** Keep floors clear of small objects, such as buttons, coins, and safety pins.

- **Suffocation.** Soft, flexible objects that can cover an infant's nose and mouth may cause suffocation. Keep all plastic bags away from infants. Keep stuffed animals out of a child's crib.

- **Water.** Never leave a baby alone near or in water, such as a bucket, bathtub or wading pool.

- **Falls.** Don't leave a baby unattended on any raised area, including an adult bed or a changing table.

- **Poisoning.** Babies put everything into their mouths. Keep all medicines, household cleaners, paints, and other poisonous substances in locked storage areas.

- **Burns.** Never leave children alone around hot liquids, ovens, or irons.

Use safety covers on all electrical outlets. Keep the water heater set at no higher than 120°F (49°C).

- **Sun.** Infants should wear sunglasses and hats with a brim. Avoiding sun exposure and dressing babies in lightweight long pants and long-sleeved shirts are the best ways to protect them from sunburn. For infants younger than six months of age, sunscreen should be used when adequate clothing and shade are not available.

- **Animals.** Babies do not know how to act around animals, even pets. Never leave a child alone with any animal.

- **Clothing.** It is very important that a baby's clothing—especially sleepwear—be flame retardant. Check clothing labels for this information.

Check-Up

Why do infants require so much supervision?

RSV

Respiratory syncytial virus (RSV) affects nearly all babies by the age of two. In adults and children, RSV usually causes mild cold-like symptoms. In premature babies, it can even develop into a serious respiratory illness. Children born prematurely often have underdeveloped lungs and many have not received enough antibodies from their mother to help them fight off RSV disease once they have been exposed to it. High-risk children who are infected with RSV often need to be hospitalized. Parents and other caregivers of high-risk children should follow these steps to help the baby stay free of RSV.

- Always wash hands with warm water and soap directly before touching the baby, and make certain that relatives and other caregivers do the same.

- Anyone who has a runny nose, cold, or fever should be kept away from the baby.

- Avoid taking the baby to crowded areas such as shopping centers. The baby should not be around smoke.

Treatment for RSV can include cough and cold medicines, humidifiers, respiratory therapy, and fluids.

Once the baby's first teeth emerge, it is a good idea to begin cleaning them regularly. The best way is to wipe them with a soft, moist cloth or gently brush them with a soft baby's toothbrush. It's important for babies to get fluoride after six months of age to build healthy teeth. Usually babies can get fluoride from their drinking water or water used in formula. If their local drinking water doesn't contain fluoride, a pediatrician can determine if a baby needs fluoride supplements.

Regular Checkups

An infant's first checkup usually occurs within a day of birth. A pediatrician does a thorough check of the newborn, including all parts of the body, the baby's reflexes, the fontanels, the heart rate and breathing, the skin color, the umbilical stump, the nostrils and mouth, and the eyes. The health care staff will also record the first measurement of the baby's weight, length, and head circumference—measurements that will be tracked over the next year. A blood sample will be drawn to test for a range of disorders and diseases. A follow-up visit often occurs two or three days after a baby is born.

Additional checkups are typically scheduled at 1 month, 2 months, 4 months, 6 months, 9 months, and 12 months. During these exams, the pediatrician will continue to track the baby's growth and development, thoroughly examine the baby, and respond to parents' questions and concerns.

The Importance of Immunizations

Some checkups include **immunizations**. Immunizations, or shots, involve giving the body a small amount of a disease-carrying

Preventing Infant Death in Australia

Infant mortality refers to death that occurs before a child reaches the age of one. These deaths are usually the result of genetic diseases, birth defects, or diseases that can be transmitted to others. Infant mortality rates are thought to be an indicator of the overall health of a population. In Australia, the rate of infant death is lower than that of the United States. In fact, Australian rates of infant death sharply declined in the 20th century. Why?

In the first part of the century, the decline was linked to improvements in sanitation and health education, as well as the use of antibiotics and public campaigns to prevent disease

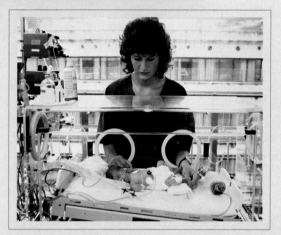

from spreading. In the second half of the 20th century, declines in infant mortality in Australia were attributed to improved medical technology, campaigns to prevent sudden infant death syndrome (SIDS), and improvements in hospitals' intensive care units for newborns.

Investigating Culture

1. Researchers believe that social support for a new mother may play a role in preventing infant death. Discuss how support systems—family, community or religious organizations, and friends—can help mothers and their babies stay healthy.
2. Find out the main causes of infant mortality in this country.

germ so that the body is able to build resistance to the disease. The most common way to immunize against a disease is with a **vaccine**. This is the disease-carrying germ that usually is injected in the body.

Immunizations are one of the most important ways parents and other caregivers can protect their children against certain diseases. After being immunized, the body produces antibodies to fight off the germs for that disease. If later exposed to the disease, the individual already has antibodies that fight it and will be unlikely to get the disease or will only get a mild form of it. Only in extremely rare cases does a child have a bad reaction to a vaccine.

State regulations and schools typically require that children have certain immunizations before being admitted to a school. It is up to parents and other caregivers to keep a record of their child's immunizations and to make sure that they receive important immunizations on time.

Watching for Illness

Because babies can't say when they don't feel well, it is important to watch for signs of illness. Such signs may include irritability, lack of energy, constipation, nasal congestion, persistent coughing, diarrhea, rashes, vomiting, and fever. Parents and caregivers should never hesitate to call the doctor if a child shows any significant symptoms that are of concern. For more information on illnesses, see Chapter 20.

SECTION 7-3 Review and Activities

Reviewing the Section

1. How is a sponge bath different from a tub bath?
2. What are the three main steps to follow when changing a diaper?
3. Why do babies need fewer diaper changes as they get older?
4. At what age might a baby be expected to get a first tooth? What signs may indicate that a baby is teething?
5. Describe what happens during a baby's regular checkup.
6. What are at least three important ways to keep babies safe at home?
7. How are antibodies related to immunizations?

Observing and Interacting

Review the infant safety concerns on page 245. Identify potential hazards in your home that don't pose a threat to older children and adults, but would to a baby.

Pediatrician

Pediatricians are doctors who specialize in treating children. Pediatricians work in offices, clinics, hospitals, and pharmaceutical companies. Some specialize in caring for children who have diseases such as cancer or diabetes.

▶ Job Responsibilities

Pediatricians keep track of children's growth and vaccinate them against disease. They diagnose and treat injured or sick children, and show their parents how to care for them. Many children are afraid of doctors, so pediatricians must be patient and kind.

▶ Work Environment

Most pediatricians see patients in their offices and visit them in the hospital. The hours can be long, and some pediatricians remain on duty when they are at home. If they are called, they must rush to the hospital to see patients or give advice to worried parents.

▶ Education and Training

Pediatricians earn two degrees: a bachelor's, usually in biology or chemistry, and a medical degree. Their education after high school can take eight years, followed by three years of training in pediatric medicine. Pediatricians must pass a state exam to earn their medical license.

▶ Skills and Aptitudes

- Strong communication skills
- Stamina
- Compassion
- Keen observation abilities
- Respect for patients' privacy

WORKPLACE CONNECTION

1. **Thinking Skills.** Why are students in medical school rotated through different areas of medicine?

2. **Resource Skills.** Where would you go to learn about volunteering in a hospital?

CHAPTER 7

Review and Activities

SECTION SUMMARIES

- Heredity, nutrition, health, experiences, and environment all play a role in a baby's growth and development. (7-1)
- Babies usually triple their birth weight and grow in length by 50 percent by their first birthday. (7–1)
- Babies must be handled carefully and never be shaken. (7–2)
- Breast milk or formula provides the nutrition a baby needs for the first six months. Other foods should be introduced gradually. (7-2)
- A baby's clothing should be comfortable and easy to put on and take off. (7-2)
- Babies should be bathed regularly but never be left alone in the bathtub. (7-3)
- Parents should follow a recommended schedule of checkups and immunizations to protect the health of their babies. (7-3)

REVIEWING THE CHAPTER

1. Describe one of the three basic patterns of growth. (7-1)
2. What role do heredity and nutrition have on an infant's growth and development? (7-1)
3. How do experiences affect brain development in babies? (7-1)
4. Describe the difference between *reflexes, gross motor skills,* and *fine motor skills.* (7-1)
5. How do experts recommend helping a baby fall asleep independently? (7-2)
6. Describe how to safely handle a newborn. (7-2)
7. What is sudden infant death syndrome? (7-2)
8. How can a baby's basic nutritional needs be met during the first six months of life? (7-2)
9. Is it acceptable for an eight-month-old to drink the same milk as the rest of the family? Why or why not? (7-2)
10. What are two possible signs of *teething*? (7-3)
11. Describe how to bathe a baby. (7-3)
12. How can a parent prevent *diaper rash*? (7-3)

THINKING CRITICALLY

1. **Drawing Conclusions.** Why do you think babies shouldn't sleep in bed with their parents?
2. **Making Inferences.** Why might certain household plants be dangerous to an eleven-month-old child?

MAKING CONNECTIONS

1. **Health.** Create a brochure or poster to help teach the importance of immunizations.
2. **Science.** Make a chart with headings for each of the five senses: sight, hearing, smell, taste, and touch. Under each heading of the senses, list activities that promote the development of that sense in infants.

APPLYING YOUR LEARNING

1. **Analyzing Behaviors.** You have been asked to babysit for two different neighbors' babies. One has a two-month-old; the other has an eight-month-old. Which one do you think will be easier to care for, and why? Write a list with examples of the types of responsibilities you would have with each baby.

2. **Demonstrating Skills.** Using a doll, demonstrate how to correctly hold, bathe, and diaper a baby. How would demonstrating these skills with a real baby be more challenging?

3. **Decision-Making Skills.** Suppose you are caring for a six-month-old baby. You put the baby in the crib at bedtime, but after 15 minutes the baby is still crying. What would you do?

Learning from Research

1. Choose one of the following research claims to investigate.
2. How is this research finding useful to parents of children ages twelve months and younger?
3. Summarize what you've learned about infant motor development.

Iron Deficiency and Motor Skills Development. Research has found that iron deficiency in infants leads to delays in their motor skill development. Infants need more iron as their growth accelerates during the second half of the first year. Identify good sources of iron for infants.

Confinement and Motor Skill Development. Research has found that infants who are confined to carriers, strollers, and play pens for extended periods of time roll over, crawl, and walk later than other children. What interactive activities help children develop motor skills?

Lying Position and Motor Skill Development. Research has found that infants who spend many of their waking hours lying on their backs may have delayed motor development. Pediatricians recommend placing babies on their tummies while awake to promote coordination and muscle control.

8 Emotional and Social Development of Infants

Section 8-1
Understanding Emotional Development of Infants

Section 8-2
Understanding Social Development of Infants

Understanding Emotional Development of Infants

Most babies show clear differences in their physical growth. One may weigh more or be longer than another. Differences also show in other areas of development. Some babies move happily from one person's lap to another, while others don't. One baby may squeal in delight while crawling on the grass in the park, another sits quietly, and still another is frightened by the unfamiliar environment. Each infant is becoming a unique individual.

Objectives

- Compare and contrast emotional and social development.
- Explain the importance of attachment to emotional development.
- Relate the care an infant receives to emotional development.
- Analyze people according to different temperament traits.
- Explain how the emotional environment in the home can affect a baby's development.

Key Terms

emotional development
social development
attachment
failure to thrive
temperament
colic
reflux

Comparing Emotional and Social Development

Emotional and social development begin at birth and continue throughout life. Development in these two closely linked areas is shaped by a variety of influences.

Emotional development is the process of learning to recognize and express feelings and establish a unique personal identity. Healthy emotional development helps a child become an adult who is self-confident, able to handle stress, and empathetic to the feelings and concerns of others.

Social development is the process of learning self-expression and how to interact with others. Healthy social development helps a child become an adult who communicates well with others, listens to different points of view before acting, and shows tolerance for other people. Emotional and social development are connected in that the feelings children have about themselves will be reflected in their behavior toward others.

The most important influences on emotional and social development are the bond formed between caregiver and child, the temperament of the child, and the atmosphere of the home.

Emotions in Infancy

Think about the range of different emotions that people experience: from excitement and joy to anger and fear. These emotions develop gradually, beginning in infancy.

Emotions become more specific with age. At birth, the range of emotion is limited. Pain or discomfort is expressed by crying. A newborn who is content is quiet. Between the end of the first and second months, however, babies show a welcome new emotion—delight, which is expressed by smiling. In the second month, babies also start to show different feelings by varying their types of cries. Parents eventually learn what each cry means. This enhances the baby's comfort, encourages the expression of emotions, and strengthens the parent-child bond. See Fig. 8-1.

Fig. 8-1

How Emotions Develop

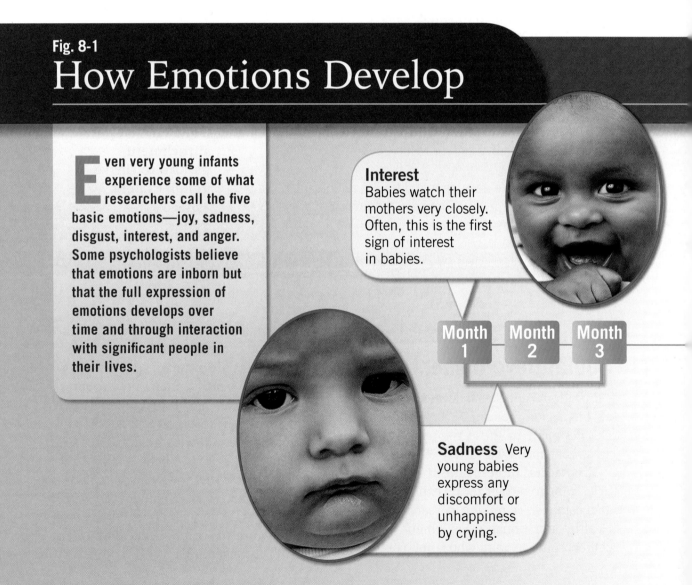

Even very young infants experience some of what researchers call the five basic emotions—joy, sadness, disgust, interest, and anger. Some psychologists believe that emotions are inborn but that the full expression of emotions develops over time and through interaction with significant people in their lives.

Interest Babies watch their mothers very closely. Often, this is the first sign of interest in babies.

Month 1   Month 2   Month 3

Sadness Very young babies express any discomfort or unhappiness by crying.

Building Bonds of Attachment

Infants have a basic need for physical contact. They need to be held and cuddled. Sometimes they may just need to be near someone they trust. Physical contact helps build the bond between a child and a parent or other primary caregivers. That's called **attachment**. Many psychological studies have shown that forming attachments is a crucial part of an infant's emotional development. See Fig. 8-2.

One of the first studies on attachment was conducted by American psychologist Harry Harlow with monkeys. Harlow created substitute "mothers" to raise baby monkeys. He made monkey-shaped forms out of chicken wire and also out of soft cloth. He discovered that the baby monkeys clung to the "mothers" made of soft cloth—even if the chicken-wire "mothers" held their feeding bottles. He concluded that the monkeys needed to feel physical closeness as well as receive a feeding. Harlow also realized that attachment

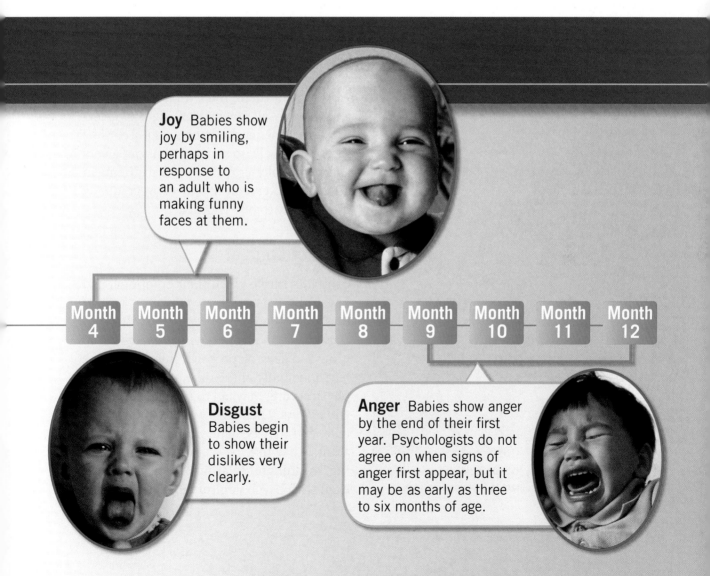

Joy Babies show joy by smiling, perhaps in response to an adult who is making funny faces at them.

Month 4 Month 5 Month 6 Month 7 Month 8 Month 9 Month 10 Month 11 Month 12

Disgust Babies begin to show their dislikes very clearly.

Anger Babies show anger by the end of their first year. Psychologists do not agree on when signs of anger first appear, but it may be as early as three to six months of age.

requires more than physical contact. As the baby monkeys grew up, they didn't know how to relate to other monkeys and form normal social relationships. Harlow believed this was caused by the lack of interaction between the baby monkeys and their real mothers.

Many psychologists believe that an infant's attachment to a parent, based on trust, sets the stage for healthy, loving relationships later in life. In the 1950s, psychologist Erik Erikson theorized that the first year of life is a time when infants learn to trust or mistrust the world. Love and affection from parents and other caregivers foster a baby's sense of trust.

Gentle touching strengthens that trust. A gentle massage or patting on the back can help to calm an infant.

Fig. 8-2 Babies not only like physical closeness, they actually *need* human contact to grow and develop normally.

The most critical period in the formation of a close emotional bond is in the first few months of life. Attachment is not fully formed until about age 2. A child who hasn't developed a strong attachment by then may experience difficulty in relationships later in life.

Communication

Communication between infants and parents or other caregivers is also important to building positive attachments. Even though infants can't yet understand words, they respond to the sound of a caregiver's voice, facial expressions, and eye contact.

Babies cry to signal they are hungry, need their diaper changed, or have other needs. They stop crying when their needs are met. They gaze into the eyes of those who care for them, track their movements, and cuddle—all of which are signs of growing attachment. As babies mature, they respond verbally to and hug their caregivers and eventually crawl or walk to them. In attachment, caregiver and baby gradually grow closer to one another.

Lack of Contact

Infants thrive when their emotional and physical needs are met. However, lack of love and attention may result in **failure to thrive**, a condition in which babies fail to grow and develop properly. Infants who are left alone most of the time, except for basic physical care, may fail to respond to people and objects. Their cries weaken, their smiles fade, and they become withdrawn. Even as adults, they may be unable to develop caring, meaningful relationships with others, even with psychological help.

Carrying a Baby on Your Back

People have been strapping babies to their bodies for thousands of years. In Somalia, women tie their babies securely to their backs with long, colorful scarves. In Nepal, mothers carry their babies in a garment that also holds money and tools. The Inuit people of the Canadian Arctic can snuggle their babies in the furry linings of their parkas. In this country, active parents take infants shopping and hiking in backpack carriers. Researchers have found that stimulating experiences, such as exposure to sounds, smells, and colors, actually help infants' brain connections grow.

Investigating Culture

1. "Wearing" a baby protects him or her from danger and promotes bonding. What other purposes might it serve?
2. How does being carried change a child's view of and interaction with the world?

In the 1990s, child care experts in Romania were alarmed to find many children in government orphanages suffering from failure to thrive. At the time, the conditions in the country were desperate. The children had received little personal attention from adults and were rarely touched in a caring way. Fortunately, such children can usually be helped. Many of the children in the Romanian institutions improved when they went to live in loving and supportive homes.

THE DEVELOPING BRAIN

A lack of contact can also affect brain development. Researchers have found that abused and neglected children who failed to receive love, touch, and opportunities for learning had brains 20 to 30 percent smaller than average.

Building Trust Through Care

The world is a strange place for newborns. Depending on a baby's early experiences, it may be a comfortable, secure place or a confusing, difficult one. The attitude newborns develop about their world depends on how their needs are met.

If the newborn's needs are met and she has bonding contact with adults, she comes to feel that the world is a comfortable place. She develops a sense of security. On the other hand, if the newborn is made to conform to a rigid schedule of feedings, and if crying brings no comfort from a caregiver, the world doesn't seem like a very friendly place. See Fig. 8-3.

Caregivers need to strive to be consistent in their care and responses toward an infant. If schedules change often, or if caregivers are patient and loving at times and impatient and harsh at other times, babies have difficulty building trust. Page 259 gives more details on how to establish trust.

Understanding Temperament

Every baby copes with life in a very personal way. For example, all infants react if the surface on which they are lying is suddenly shaken. However, each baby has a unique response to the situation. One may respond by screaming, while another may simply squirm a bit and then settle down.

These different responses are based on the baby's **temperament**. Temperament is a person's unique nature. It will determine how a baby reacts to others and to the world. Different temperaments are revealed in how children react to a situation. The characteristics of temperament evident in infants become more apparent as children grow and develop.

You can see clues to temperament whenever you watch children. Shana, for example, tries to reach the mobile above her crib. She keeps reaching and grabbing for it. Finally, when her father picks her up, she snatches it and giggles with delight. Luke, on the other hand, tries to grab a ball but gives up because it's out of reach. Instead he goes back to playing happily with a stacking toy.

Fig. 8-3 **Feeding a hungry baby is one way to build a sense of trust.** What are some other ways?

Anyone who cares for a baby has the responsibility to help the baby feel happy and secure—to feel a sense of trust. There are many ways to do so.

- **Follow a predictable routine.** Through routine care, a baby learns to trust a parent or caregiver. Having regular feeding times, baths, and naps provides a reassuring environment that makes a baby feel safe.

- **Get to know the baby.** Spend time nurturing and holding the baby. Learn about the baby's likes and dislikes. Anticipate hunger, tiredness, or boredom since infants can't communicate in words. Babies respond to caregivers who meet their needs.

- **Bond with the baby.** Use feeding time and diaper changing time to grow close to a baby. Talk to the baby in a soft, positive tone. Smile and establish eye contact. Physical closeness helps young babies develop a close relationship.

- **Meet the baby's needs.** Strive to meet a baby's physical, social, and emotional needs. Provide proper care and affection so the baby

learns trust. When they grow up, babies benefit tremendously from these early attachments.

YOUR TURN

Routine. Child development experts agree that babies benefit from a routine. If you were a parent, what kind of routine would you create to help a baby develop a sense of trust?

Researchers have identified nine different temperament traits. Every child has each trait to a greater or lesser degree. Each baby—each person—needs to be looked at in terms of all the traits together. See Fig. 8-4.

- **Intensity.** How strong or weak are a child's emotional responses to events or to other people? A highly intense child has deep and powerful responses. Intense children often react loudly. An intense baby may cry heartily, while a less intense one will cry more softly.

- **Persistence.** How determined is a child to complete an action? A persistent child may become very upset if unable to finish a task or a project. These children are goal-oriented and are unwilling to give up. A less persistent child can easily be persuaded to begin a new activity. A less persistent child accepts no for an answer, while a highly persistent one doesn't.

- **Sensitivity.** How strongly does a child react to his or her feelings? A child who is highly sensitive has strong reactions. Such a child may be a fussy eater or may complain about uncomfortable clothing. Highly sensitive children may be bothered by sights, sounds, or smells.

- **Perceptiveness.** Perceptive children are aware of all that's around them. These children can be easily distracted as they become involved in new experiences. They have a hard time following directions involving several different steps. Children lower in perceptiveness are less likely to notice what's going on around them. That makes it easier to follow through on multi-step tasks.

- **Adaptability.** Some children find it easier to adapt than others. Children who are low in adaptability resist change. A highly adaptable child isn't bothered by surprises.

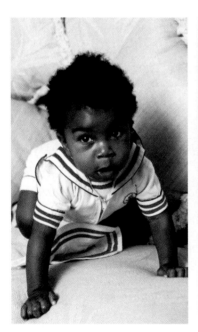  

Fig. 8-4 **Babies soon show that they are becoming unique individuals with a combination of temperament traits. What traits do you think each baby is showing?**

- **Regularity.** Does a child's behavior follow regular patterns? Children who are highly regular get tired and go to sleep at the same time each evening. They go to the bathroom at about the same time. They get hungry at the same time. Children who are low in regularity are just the opposite; each day's schedule is different for them.

- **Energy.** What is a child's energy level? High-energy children are physically active. Even when they are sitting, they often squirm and move around in their seats. Once they are able to walk, high-energy children seem to prefer running. Low-energy children move much less.

- **First reaction.** Children differ in how they face new situations. Some dive right in. These children are open to new activities and willing to try new foods. Others hold back and watch what others do before joining. They are less comfortable in unfamiliar situations.

- **Mood.** Is a child typically cheerful or cranky? One child may usually have a positive outlook while another is inclined to point out problems.

Parents and other caregivers have their own temperaments, too. Problems can arise if the adult's temperament conflicts with the child's. Understanding such differences can help prevent clashes. For example, a parent with a relatively low energy level needs to accept and find positive ways of dealing with the activity level of a high-energy child. When the child's high energy becomes bothersome, taking a trip to the park or finding other opportunities for vigorous play can help. One of a caregiver's responsibilities is to adapt to the temperament of the child. See Fig. 8-5.

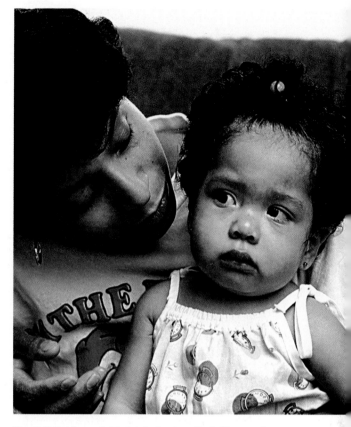

Fig. 8-5 **Babies quickly begin to show their likes and dislikes.** How can understanding their temperament help parents take care of them?

Crying and Comforting

The most obvious sign of an infant's emotions is crying. Newborns vary greatly in the amount and intensity of their crying. Some babies don't cry very often and are usually easy to comfort. Often they are labeled as "easy" or "good" babies. Other babies cry loudly and often, and it's usually hard to comfort them.

A young baby who is crying needs attention and care. The first step is to check for a physical problem. Is the baby hungry or in need of a diaper change? Is the infant cold or hot? Did the child not burp at the

Face-to-Face

When infants play, they are exploring their world. In face-to-face interactions with their caregivers, infants' play includes smiles, vocalizations, and movement. For example, a mother shakes a rattle as she moves it slowly back and forth. Her daughter hears the rattle and watches it move. She reaches for the rattle, grasps it, pulls it towards her mouth, and then smiles. Her mother smiles back at her and laughs. Whether the interaction is focused on the rattle or playing peek-a-boo, it gives pleasure to both.

Following Up

What are some other interactions a caregiver and baby can share?

last feeding? If none of these is the cause of the crying and the baby doesn't seem ill, he or she probably needs something else: company, cuddling, or comforting. Remember that these are real needs, too. See Fig. 8-6.

As parents and their baby get to know each other, parents will probably discover which comforting measures work best. These are a few time-tested ways that are worth trying:

- Cuddle up with the baby in a rocking chair. The combination of being held and rocked often soothes a crying baby. Sometimes holding the baby close while walking around helps.

- Move the baby to a new position. The baby may want to move to a different position but can't yet roll over. Maybe the baby wants to sit in an infant seat and see what is happening.

- Talk softly or sing to the baby. Even when caregivers aren't great singers, the tone and rhythm of their voices and the attention they indicate may comfort the unhappy baby.

- Offer a toy to interest and distract the baby. An infant may be bored and want something to do. A favorite toy may end the crying.

- Stroke or gently rub the baby's back to give comfort.

Babies develop their own techniques for comforting themselves. Many babies soothe themselves with soft objects such as a blanket or stuffed toy. They develop a special attachment to the object and use it for comfort when they are sleepy or anxious. Other babies comfort themselves by twisting their hair or by rocking themselves back and forth in their cribs. The most common comforting technique, however, is sucking. A baby will suck on a thumb, a fist, or a pacifier.

The special self-comforting techniques used by babies are indications of their individuality and rates of development. Children typically outgrow their need for such self-comforting techniques and, when they are ready, give up these habits.

Colic

Some babies who are extremely fussy every day may have a condition called **colic** (COL-ick). A baby with colic cries a lot and is inconsolable. The periods of crying usually come between six o'clock in the evening and midnight. The symptoms of colic are often the worst when the baby is about six weeks old. The fussy periods then begin to grow shorter until they finally end.

LOOKING AT REAL LIFE

Emily was worried when she was unable to calm her baby, Jared. It seemed like he had been crying for hours. Nothing Emily tried soothed him. Finally, Emily called her own mother. She advised Emily to try and remain calm. "Babies can sense when you're upset, so they think something is wrong and will continue to be upset, too." She also suggested taking Jared for a ride in his stroller or the car. She said, "Sometimes a change of scenery and the motion of a stroller or car can help soothe a baby." Emily's mother asked if Jared was ill or if he had a temperature. Emily said that Jared seemed fine just a few hours earlier, but she noticed that he was pulling on his ear a lot and thought that he felt a little warm. Emily decided to call the doctor because she suspected that Jared had an ear infection. Then she would try a walk in the neighborhood.

▶▶**PERSONAL APPLICATION**

Have you ever had difficulty calming a crying baby? What did you do?

Fig. 8-6 **A baby usually cries when something is wrong.** What are the first things to consider as the source of the problem?

If an infant cries constantly, the problem may be something else. It could be the baby is having trouble with partially digested food that rises in the throat. This problem, called **reflux**, can cause colic-like symptoms. Parents should discuss the matter with their pediatrician if they are in doubt about why a baby is constantly crying.

Doctors aren't sure why babies get colic. It may have to do with gas collecting in the stomach. The colic may stem from certain foods. The solution can sometimes be as simple as eliminating that food. If the baby is bottle-fed, pediatricians may recommend using a soy-based, rather than a milk-based, formula. If the baby is breast-fed, the colic could stem from something in the mother's diet. Breast-feeding mothers can experiment by avoiding foods such as cabbage and onions.

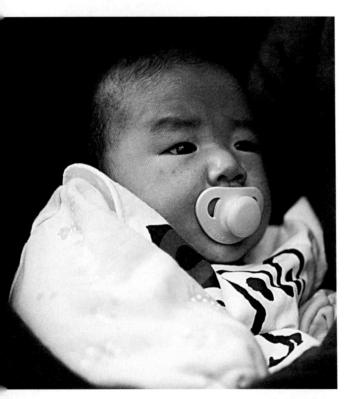

Fig. 8-7 **Many infants learn to comfort themselves by sucking on their thumbs, fingers, or a pacifier, a habit they usually grow out of.**

Thumb Sucking and Pacifiers

Almost all babies suck their thumbs or fingers. Sucking is a basic urge in infants. Parents usually need not be concerned about this behavior. Many babies stop sucking their thumbs on their own, usually at around six or seven months of age when their first teeth appear. See Fig. 8-7.

Thumb sucking can eventually become a cause for concern if it results in physical changes to the baby's mouth. A pediatrician can check the roof of the baby's mouth and the teeth once they begin to appear.

Many infants find comfort in sucking on a pacifier. Some parents and other caregivers, however, are opposed to using pacifiers. They fear a pacifier could cause physical or emotional harm. The American Academy of Pediatrics disagrees. The Academy recommends that parents use a pacifier that is the correct size and shape for their baby's age. The Academy also emphasizes that for safety and health reasons a pacifier should be washed frequently and never be tied around a baby's neck or hand with a string. Pacifiers should only be used for self-soothing and never as a replacement for food.

Emotional Climate of the Home

You probably have days when you feel grumpy. Have you ever noticed how contagious those feelings can be? If you snap at someone, chances are that person will snap back at you or at someone else. Babies react the same way. Long before they know the meanings of words, babies are influenced by adults' feelings. Worried or angry caregivers are likely to be tense in handling their babies. Babies sense these feelings and can become irritable and fussy.

Almost every family has ups and downs, and a baby adapts to them. It is essential, however, for a baby to feel that affection and caring are the basis of the family's interactions. Bitterness and mistrust can hinder an infant's healthy development.

Will and Sabrina were excited when Grace was born, but soon their feelings began to change. Will felt left out because Sabrina seemed closer to their daughter than he was. Sabrina loved the baby, but some days she felt trapped with a child who needed her constant attention. She barely had time to take a shower. One night, these feelings erupted into an argument. When Grace cried for more than an hour, Sabrina abruptly handed the baby to him, shouting, "Here! You take care of her for a change!" Sabrina stalked off into the bedroom.

What Will and Sabrina felt isn't unusual. Angry feelings toward a beloved child are normal. One outburst won't ruin the home's emotional climate for Grace. If her parents' negative feelings continue to fester, however, the trouble may become more serious. Sabrina and Will should talk about their frustrations when they are both calm.

The challenge can be even greater for single parents. With no other adult to share the work—or the worries—they may feel alone and overwhelmed. It's important that they find ways of releasing negative feelings away from their children. When they do, they can find the patience to create a caring environment. Having someone to talk to and provide support is crucial.

SECTION 8-1 Review and Activities

Check Your Understanding

1. Compare *emotional development* and *social development*. How are they alike? How are they different?
2. Why is it important to hold and cuddle a baby?
3. What is *failure to thrive* and how can it be helped?
4. Nine-month-old Alec loves to play and move about. He crawls around constantly and moves quickly. What *temperament* trait does he have? If Alec's caregiver has a different temperament, what should he or she do to prevent conflict?
5. Describe at least two ways to comfort a crying baby.
6. What is *colic*? At what age is it likely to occur?
7. Does it matter to a baby how the adults in the family get along? Why or why not?

Observing and Interacting

Look at the nine temperament traits described in the chapter. Rate yourself in each area on a scale of one (low in that characteristic) to five (high). Summarize your temperament.

Understanding Social Development of Infants

Jo remembers how sweet the feeling was when she first felt Franklin in her arms. He had just been born. After feeling immense relief that her labor was over, she was swept up in a powerful wave of love. She promised herself that she would never forget that feeling.

Objectives

- Identify signs of social development in infants.
- Describe how social behavior is learned.
- Explain the importance of play and how it affects social development.
- Analyze the relationship of play and exploration.

Key Terms

stranger anxiety
play environment
cause and effect

Signs of Social Development

Like physical and emotional development, social development in infants follows a pattern. There are common signs of social development in babies during the first year. These signs provide a general guide for what infants ordinarily go through.

The "Developmental Milestones" chart (Figure 8-8 on pages 268–269) highlights common signs of social development during the first year. However, this shouldn't be used as a checklist for evaluating a specific baby. Each child develops at his or her own pace.

Stranger Anxiety

Julia had just flown five hours to visit her nine-month-old grandson. She hadn't seen him since he was six weeks old. Julia was disappointed that Cory seemed afraid of her. Then Julia's daughter reminded her about stranger anxiety. **Stranger anxiety** is a fear of unfamiliar people, usually expressed by crying. This behavior develops sometime during the second half of the baby's first year, often around the age of eight months. During this period, a baby who used to sit cheerfully on a stranger's lap suddenly screams and bursts into tears when an unfamiliar person approaches. That's what happened when Cory saw his grandmother.

Cope with Stranger Anxiety

Beginning at around six months of age, many babies show some signs of stranger anxiety when faced with a person who is not familiar to them. They may pout and look very worried—or even burst into tears. Some simply bury their heads in a parent's shoulder as a new person approaches. While this is an entirely normal response, it can be awkward. Here are some ways to help introduce a new person to a baby.

- **Act welcoming toward the new person.** The baby will be watching your interactions and looking for guidance. Remind the baby if the person is a friend or relative who has been over to visit before.

- **Encourage friends and relatives to speak softly to the baby and let the baby get used to them.** Using a gentle tone of voice can help to put the baby at ease.

- **Never force a baby to be held by an unfamiliar person.** You can sit next to that person while holding the baby in order to introduce them to each other.

- **Stay close to the baby.** Always be around to provide comfort and reassurance.

- **Let the baby set the timetable for adjusting to a stranger.** It may take minutes, hours, or even multiple encounters before the baby will become comfortable.

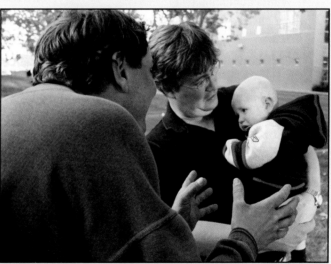

YOUR TURN

Comfort. If you were a child care provider about to begin caring for a one-year-old, what steps could you take to minimize the possibility of stranger anxiety?

1 MONTH

- Coos and babbles

- May cry a lot, but quiets down at sight of caregiver's face or sound of voice, or when lifted or touched

2-3 MONTHS

- Begins to smile and show excitement
- Eyes can follow moving objects
- Wants companionship
- May like being tickled

- Maintains brief eye contact while being fed
- Makes different crying sounds for different needs
- Can tell a smile from a frown

4-6 MONTHS

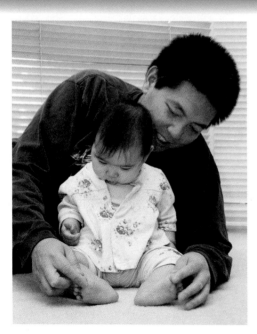

- Turns to sound of familiar voices
- Laughs, squeals, babbles
- Can tell the difference between family members
- Reaches out with hands and arms to play
- May cry when left alone

7-8 MONTHS

- Tries to imitate sounds made by adults
- Plays alone and plays longer with other people and toys
- Enjoys other children
- Begins to experience stranger anxiety and clings to familiar caregivers

9-10 MONTHS

- Responds to "no" and own name
- Says simple words, such as "no," "bye-bye," "dada," and "mama"

- Objects if a toy is taken away
- Crawls around to look for parents
- Enjoys playing "peek-a-boo" and sound games

11-12 MONTHS

- Uses the words "Dada" and "Mama" to refer to specific people
- Uses gestures as well as simple body language
- Shows stronger likes and dislikes
- Spends time looking in mirrors

Fig. 8-9 **Stranger anxiety is a normal part of a baby's development. Some babies experience it more than others.** How can a caregiver help a baby pass through this stage?

This stage in the baby's development will pass. In the meantime, suggest that unfamiliar people approach the baby slowly and give the baby time to adjust. Try to keep the baby's routine as regular as possible. This isn't a good time to make sudden changes in the baby's routine or to introduce a new caregiver. See Fig. 8-9.

How Behavior Is Learned

Studies show that infants learn how to behave through their relationships with others. The type of behavior babies learn depends on the messages they receive from caregivers.

Babies learn social behaviors in much the same way as they learn to anticipate physical care—by seeing that the same action brings about the same response every time. Running water signals that it's bath time. Rocking in a familiar chair signals that it's time for sleep. In their social development, babies learn that certain behaviors always earn a positive response from adults. When babies coo and smile, for example, they are rewarded with laughter, hugs, and praise. Love is important to babies, so they repeat these behaviors. Babies also learn that other behaviors bring scolding or frowning from adults.

Babies develop better social behaviors if they get more positive responses than negative ones. Always try to give a baby clear messages. Never frown while expressing love for the baby. Never smile while expressing disapproval of a certain behavior. Babies become confused if their behavior provokes a positive response one time and a negative response another time. Caregivers and parents must provide consistent responses to help a baby understand what behaviors are expected.

Social Development Through Play

The job of a baby is to play. Babies learn about the world around them through play. Play strengthens all areas of development.

Parenting Q&A

Why Is Consistent Feedback Important?

Parents and caregivers are a baby's most important teachers. As babies grow, they watch the behavior of important adults in their lives and imitate their actions. It's important for caregivers to model desirable behaviors, such as kindness and patience.

Babies also learn how to behave depending on another person's response to their actions. Caregivers can reward positive behaviors with smiles, hugs, and enthusiastic praise. When negative responses are necessary, it's important to remember that babies cannot understand scolding and other forms of discipline. The best way to deal with infants who are "misbehaving" is to redirect them to an appropriate activity.

Child care experts say that parents and caregivers should give far more positive responses than negative ones, and they should quickly respond to a baby's needs. This will make the baby feel secure and not "spoiled." A baby who feels secure will be happier. Experts also say caregivers should be clear and consistent in how they respond to a baby's behavior.

THINKING IT THROUGH

1. How should family members respond when the baby gently touches the family cat? What does this response teach the baby?
2. How should a caregiver respond to a ten-month-old who continually tries to dig in the potted plants?

Socially, it helps children learn to interact with other adults and children.

Baby's play activities provide an opportunity for interaction with the caregiver. From birth to about six months of age, caregivers can:

- Play games with toys or objects the baby can grasp.
- Place colorful toys where the baby can learn to recognize and reach them. Name the colors of the toy as the baby chooses one to play with.
- Make noise with a rattle or other toy.
- Gently shake, stretch, and exercise the baby's arms and legs while smiling and talking to the baby.
- Follow the baby's lead. Laugh and smile after the baby laughs and smiles.

Babies from six to twelve months of age are able to play somewhat more complicated games and handle more toys. From six to twelve months of age, caregivers can:

- Play peek-a-boo with the baby.
- Set toys just out of reach so that the baby has to crawl to them. Encourage the baby to crawl to the object and praise success.
- Read to the baby from simple books that have big pictures. Reading experts say it

is never too soon to start introducing a child to books.

- Give babies plastic buckets or other containers that they can fill up with water or sand and dump out. Talk the baby through the activity, describing what can be done.

After each play activity, reward the baby for successes by showing positive responses. Through play, caregivers can learn more about the baby while the baby learns more about them and the world they live in.

A Play Environment for Infants

It's up to parents and other caregivers to provide a safe **play environment**, a comfortable space with no dangers and with toys that are safe and interesting.

Infants love toys that are colorful, move around, and make noise. Hanging mobiles, rattles, and stuffed animals are wonderful toys for infants. Babies from six to twelve months of age enjoy more complicated toys, such as those they can push or pull.

It is important to choose toys that are safe and appropriate for the age of the baby. Toys should be big enough so that babies cannot put them all the way in their mouths. Choose toys that do not have small parts. Babies can swallow and choke on small parts or stick them in their nose or ears. Toys should also be sturdy. Go through a safety checklist to make sure the rooms where a baby plays do not have any hidden dangers. See Chapter 10 for tips on how to childproof a room. See Fig. 8-10.

Toys must be kept clean. Always wash a brand new toy with soap and water, and give it frequent washings after the baby plays with it.

LOOKING AT REAL LIFE

Shawna and Lara have been friends for years. They gave birth to their children just three months apart. They get together often to visit while their children play. Shawna's son Aaron is six months old, and Lara's daughter Ashley is nine months old. Both mothers enjoy talking about their children and comparing experiences. Shawna is excited that Aaron is finally sitting up by himself and showing a real interest in playing with his toys. Lara notes that while Ashley is constantly on the move and crawling around the house, she is concerned that she is not pulling herself up on furniture. Both babies have similar eating and sleeping habits, but Aaron still has trouble sleeping through the night. Ashley can manipulate her toys with ease and shows more curiosity than Aaron. Shawna and Lara feel that giving their children time together will help them develop social skills.

▶▶**PERSONAL APPLICATION**

How does spending time with other children help babies develop social skills?

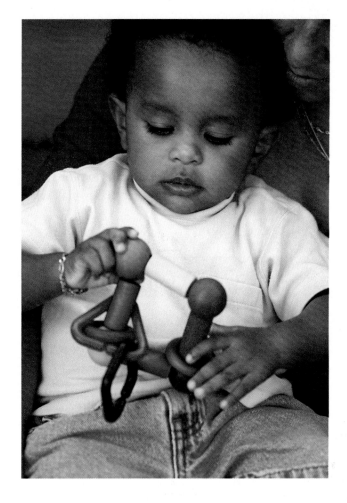

Fig. 8-10 **Babies learn about the world through play.** What kinds of skills do you think this baby is learning?

The Difference Between Exploration and Play

If you give a baby a toy or stuffed animal, its first stop is likely to be the baby's mouth. Babies do this to explore and discover. Babies have an inborn need to explore. They explore with all their senses—touch, vision, hearing, smell, and taste.

Sometimes it is difficult for a parent or caregiver to understand a baby's need to explore. Pulling everything out of a drawer, pouring cups of water on the floor, and squishing, pounding, and throwing food may seem to some adults like naughty behavior. The baby isn't trying to behave

badly but is trying to see what effects these actions cause. This is not misbehavior but curiosity. See Fig. 8-11.

Child experts say that babies explore and learn using **cause and effect**. This means that one event (the effect) is caused by another event. For example, infants learn that, by crying, they can get their needs for food and comfort met. They learn that letting go of a toy will cause it to fall.

Fig. 8-11 **Gates across stairs help create a safer environment for babies.** Why is it important for a baby to explore his or her surroundings?

Sometimes babies repeatedly throw or drop things just to see what happens. The more eager a baby is to explore, the more difficult these explorations can be on adults. Eager babies can get into everything.

Play and exploration are related. Babies use play to explore their world. They look at and play with toys to explore colors and textures. Blocks let babies explore how things stack up and balance. They play with household items the same way. Caregivers can help babies explore by giving them plastic spoons and cups and empty boxes they can fill.

Encouragement and positive responses from an adult motivate babies to explore and learn. Everything in the world is new to a baby. By participating in explorations with the baby, caregivers can deepen their attachment to their children.

SECTION 8-2 Review and Activities

Check Your Understanding

1. What are two signs of social development that are exhibited by many one-month-old babies?
2. What two signs of social development usually appear around the fifth month?
3. What is *stranger anxiety*? When does it usually develop?
4. How can parents' smiles and frowns help babies learn good behavior?
5. Give an example of a learned behavior.
6. How does play affect a baby's social development?
7. Describe how play and exploration are related.

Observing and Participating

Look in toy catalogs and online for examples of toys that encourage interaction between infants and caregivers. Look for examples of toys that would not involve interaction. Discuss with classmates which toys would be best for babies 12 months and younger.

Storyteller

Before societies had written historical records, they had storytellers who kept their traditions alive. Around a fire, a storyteller might describe how ancestors fought off outsiders, explored, and settled the wilderness. Today's storytellers also seek to educate and entertain as they practice an ancient art.

▶ Job Responsibilities

The best storytellers captivate their audiences, pacing their words to create suspense and changing their tone to enhance the story. Storytellers use their voices the way musicians use instruments. They must memorize many stories and tell each one with enthusiasm and conviction.

▶ Work Environment

Storytellers may travel to senior centers, schools, libraries, prisons, and hospitals. Some perform on the radio or on television. A few record and sell their stories.

▶ Education and Training

Many storytellers study literature, folklore, and drama. Any type of public speaking is also good preparation for storytelling. Although no college degree is required, many storytellers hold a degree in library science or literature. This allows them to pursue more than one career.

▶ Skills and Aptitudes

- Imagination
- Good memory
- Ability to communicate clearly
- Dramatic instincts
- Self-motivation

WORKPLACE CONNECTION

1. **Thinking Skills.** How could storytellers benefit from taking a public speaking course?

2. **Resource Skills.** How could you get experience performing in front of others?

---

8 Review and Activities

SECTION SUMMARIES

- Emotional development deals with expressing feelings. Social development deals with forming relationships with others. (8-1)
- Attachment between infant and parent or another primary caregiver is essential for a baby's healthy emotional and social development. (8-1)
- Babies have their own unique temperaments. (8-1)
- Babies learn how to behave by watching and interacting with others. (8-2)
- Stranger anxiety is a normal phase of a baby's emotional and social development. (8-2)
- Babies learn by playing and exploring. (8-2)

REVIEWING THE CHAPTER

1. What are two factors that could cause a baby to have poor *emotional development*? (8-1)
2. How are trust and *attachment* related in a baby's emotional development? (8-1)
3. What are three ways babies might soothe themselves? (8-1)
4. Describe *failure to thrive* and explain its causes. (8-1)
5. What can parents and other caregivers do to create a sense of trust in a baby? (8-1)
6. Describe two babies with different *temperaments* and how they might respond differently in the same situation. (8-1)
7. What progress in a baby's mental abilities brings about *stranger anxiety*? (8-2)
8. What kind of toys do babies one to six months of age like to play with? How can a caregiver be sure they are safe? (8-2)
9. Describe a situation in which a baby is learning from *cause and effect*. (8-2)

THINKING CRITICALLY

1. **Synthesizing.** Suppose a caregiver who is highly adaptable is in charge of a baby who is low in adaptability. Give an example of how the two temperaments might come into conflict. What things could the caregiver do to alleviate the problem?
2. **Drawing Conclusions.** What are the possible drawbacks to parents putting their 11-month-old in a playpen on a daily basis?

MAKING CONNECTIONS

1. **Writing.** Take the role of someone who writes an advice column. A young parent asks for advice on how to handle her nine-month-old son, who cries and acts terrified around friends and neighbors. Write an answer explaining why the baby is behaving this way and give some tips on how to handle the situation.

2. **Social Science.** Work with a partner to create a "Baby's Bill of Rights." List everything you believe a baby has a right to receive from parents and other caregivers.

APPLYING YOUR LEARNING

1. **Justifying Behavior.** Suppose you are a new parent and you have a relative visiting who fears that you are "spoiling" the baby. Write a possible dialogue between you and the relative.

2. **Giving Comfort.** Make a list of problems to check for to find out what might be making a baby cry. Suppose the baby continues to cry even though there is no sign of an obvious problem. List three things that a caregiver can do to try and comfort the baby.

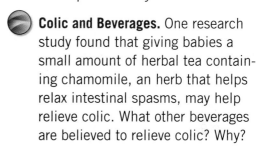

Learning from Research

1. Choose one of the following research claims to investigate.
2. How is this research finding useful to caregivers of babies with colic?
3. Summarize what you've learned about possible ways to relieve colic.

Colic and Beverages. One research study found that giving babies a small amount of herbal tea containing chamomile, an herb that helps relax intestinal spasms, may help relieve colic. What other beverages are believed to relieve colic? Why?

Colic and Spinal Joints. Research indicates that symptoms of colic may be related to mild disturbances of the spinal joints. In one study, when parents were taught a series of gentle fingertip spinal massage techniques, their babies experienced a significant reduction in colic symptoms. What can be done to prevent colic?

Colic and Tension. Researchers have found that the degree of tension in a baby's household may contribute to colic. The higher the emotional turmoil and tension in the household, the greater the likelihood of colic. Maternal depression or emotional turmoil during pregnancy may also increase the risk of colic. What role do other environmental factors play in colic? What can be done to address each of these factors?

Intellectual Development in Infants

Thoughtful Reading:

As you read this chapter:
- What do you wonder? Note each of your questions and the page number.
- What opinions do you have about what you read?
- Summarize what you read in a short paragraph.

Section 9-1
Early Brain Development

Section 9-2
Intellectual Development During the First Year

Section 9-3
Helping Infants Learn

Early Brain Development

Maya and Joe had watched six-month-old Abby's every twitch, gulp, burp, gurgle, and coo with rapt attention. They often worried whether Abby was developing as she should. The doctor said she was healthy, but they wanted her to be smart as well. Their families and friends offered lots of advice, but some was contradictory. Sometimes they tried to guess what Abby was thinking, if she was thinking. When they took a parenting class they were amazed to find out how much was already going on in a six-month-old's brain.

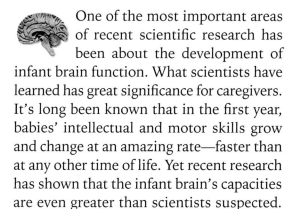

Objectives

- List the functions each part of the brain controls.
- Describe how brain cells work together.
- Explain how the brain becomes organized.
- Identify activities that support the development of brain pathways.
- Give an example of how neural pathways in the brain help a baby to acquire new skills.

Key Terms

neuron
neural pathways
cortex
axon
myelin
dendrite
synapse
neurotransmitter

The Study of the Brain

One of the most important areas of recent scientific research has been about the development of infant brain function. What scientists have learned has great significance for caregivers. It's long been known that in the first year, babies' intellectual and motor skills grow and change at an amazing rate—faster than at any other time of life. Yet recent research has shown that the infant brain's capacities are even greater than scientists suspected.

It is clear that by providing new activities, parents and other caregivers can stimulate, or awaken, a baby's senses of sight, sound, touch, taste, and smell. Doing so helps the infant's brain develop new abilities. In fact, it now appears that much of a baby's increased brain function is due not only to the capabilities of the brain itself, but also to the quantity and quality of experiences the baby has.

At birth, the brain has billions of nerve cells called **neurons**. In response to experiences, babies' brains immediately

Fig. 9-1 **One of the first skills a baby gains is the ability to visually track moving objects.** What experiences help a baby learn this skill?

begin to develop links between these neurons. See Fig. 9-1. These links, or **neural pathways**, "wire" the brain so that it can control different body functions and thinking processes. Neural pathways are created quickly. For example, babies just four days old have demonstrated that they are able to make fine distinctions in hearing, such as being able to distinguish between their parents' voices and other people's voices. This ability is the result of linkages in the brain that the baby has formed in the few days since birth. Such linkages form continuously during a child's early years; they reach their peak number at about age ten. See Fig. 9-2.

The Structure of the Brain

How the brain develops in a baby's first year of life has profound effects on the baby's whole life. Before birth, while still in the mother's womb, the fetus's world is warm and dark. At birth, this state of affairs changes radically. The newborn child is showered with input to the senses. Eyes closed for so long are exposed to bright lights, there are new sounds and smells, and the baby feels a sudden drop in temperature from the familiar 98.6°F. It's no wonder that so many babies cry when they come into the world! However, it is this variety of sensory input that the brain uses to build neural pathways and babies' brains will make use of every bit of noise and new sensations.

Newborns learn about the world through their senses—what they see, hear, smell, taste, and touch. A mobile moves when it is touched, and brightly colored objects move before the baby's eyes. Caregivers' voices sound familiar, and their smells are familiar too. A fist or a finger tastes different from milk. The blanket feels soft and warm.

In general, the responses of a newborn are reflexes. For example, the newborn will instinctively grasp a finger placed in its palm, and an overheated baby will kick until a blanket falls off. However, these are not deliberate actions that come from *learned* responses. They are only reflexes.

By the time the baby is six months old, he or she is aware that blankets and socks can be kicked, or even pulled off, when the child is uncomfortable. By the time a child is a year old, he or she has the ability to stack toys, stand up, and perhaps even walk. All these skills result from the brain's growing ability to direct the body's actions.

Parts of the Brain

The brain is divided into different sections, each controlling specific functions of the body. The major sections are shown in Fig. 9-2, along with the functions they control.

Fig. 9-2 **Parts of the Brain**

Cerebrum: Receives information from the senses and directs motor activities. Controls such functions as speech, memory, and problem solving. Most of these activities occur in the outer layer, called the "cortex," or "cerebral cortex."

Thalamus: Connects the spinal cord and cerebrum. Controls expression of emotions.

Cerebellum: Controls muscular coordination, balance, and posture.

Pituitary Gland: Secretes hormones that regulate growth, metabolism, and sexual development.

Brain Stem: Controls involuntary activities such as breathing, heart rate, and blood pressure.

Spinal Cord: Transmits information from the body to the brain and from the brain to the body. It coordinates the activities of the left and right sides of the body and controls simple reflexes that do not involve the brain.

One of the most important parts of the brain is the **cortex** (CORE-teks), which is part of the cerebrum. Growth in this outer layer of the brain permits more complex learning. After one year of life, a baby's cortex is far better developed than it was at birth. As babies experience more and more input from the world around them, their brains respond by forming more and more connections in the brain. It is in this way that the quality of caregiving affects brain growth. As caregivers hold, play with, and talk to an infant, the baby actually uses these experiences to build the brain's capacity.

How the Brain Works

The brain contains billions of nerve cells called neurons. An infant is born with all the neurons he or she will have—none are added during life. Although neurons aren't added, dramatic changes do take place in the brain after birth.

Neurons are connected by **axons** (ACKS-ons) and dendrites, which act as transmitters of information. Each axon is coated with a waxy, protein-based substance called **myelin** (MY-uh-lin). This substance helps transmit information from one nerve cell to another. At the end of

—————————— **Fig. 9-3 How Neurons Work** ——————————

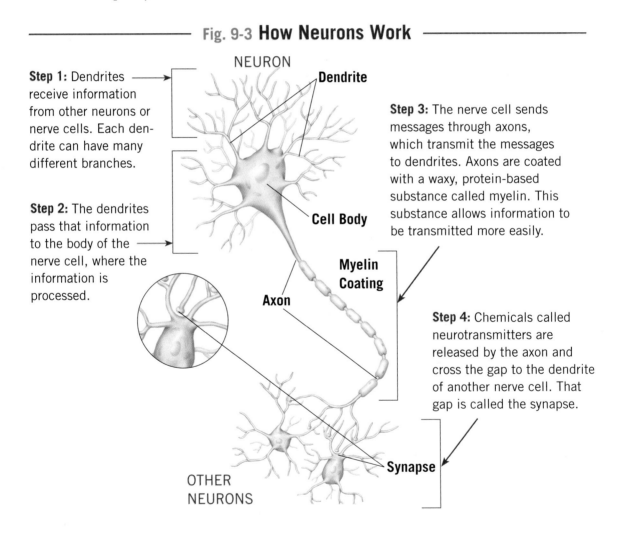

NEURON

Step 1: Dendrites receive information from other neurons or nerve cells. Each dendrite can have many different branches.

Dendrite

Step 3: The nerve cell sends messages through axons, which transmit the messages to dendrites. Axons are coated with a waxy, protein-based substance called myelin. This substance allows information to be transmitted more easily.

Step 2: The dendrites pass that information to the body of the nerve cell, where the information is processed.

Cell Body

Myelin Coating

Axon

Step 4: Chemicals called neurotransmitters are released by the axon and cross the gap to the dendrite of another nerve cell. That gap is called the synapse.

OTHER NEURONS

Synapse

(Newborn)   (2-year-old)

Fig. 9-4 The image at left shows the neurons of a newborn, with few dendrites. The image at right shows the greatly increased number of dendrites found in the brain of a two-year-old as a result of the child's experiences. More dendrites allow for faster thinking and indicate increased learning.

each axon are branchlike **dendrites** that receive the messages. This process actually begins when the baby is developing in the mother's uterus. After birth, it happens more quickly. As Fig. 9-3 shows, dendrites reach out toward the dendrites of other neurons. Although the dendrites don't touch, they come very close. At the tiny gaps between them—the **synapses** (SIN-ap-suhs)—messages are transmitted from one neuron to another. See Fig. 9-4.

The chemicals released by an axon are called **neurotransmitters** (NOOR-oh-tranz-mih-terz). These chemicals look for a dendrite to attach to—but they can only attach to those dendrites with the right kind of receptors. The more times the same axon and dendrite connect, the stronger the connection grows. As a result, they can send and receive messages more quickly.

 **THE DEVELOPING BRAIN**

The number of connections in an infant's developing brain can be increased by a stimulating environment or decreased by a lack of stimulation. The change can be as much as 25 percent in either direction. Babies love visual stimulation, and they have a preference for high-contrast images.

Building the Brain

The more dendrites that neurons grow and the more links that develop between neurons, the more neural pathways are created in the brain. More pathways give the brain more power—it can do more tasks and control more actions. Think of a road system around a city. The more roads there are, the more places a driver can go.

These increased numbers of connections also give the brain more flexibility. Again, this is like a road system. The more roads there are, the more choices a driver has. If one road is shut down, there are alternate routes.

Fig. 9-5 How does attention and experiences contribute to brain development?

This increase in connections is the direct result of sensory input. The more the baby interacts with the world, the more complex the brain's "wiring" becomes.

How the Brain Becomes Organized

Each child's brain becomes organized in a unique way. This is because the organization is based on the particular experiences unique to that child. As connections between dendrites and axons grow stronger, a group of neurons becomes linked together. They become systems of nerve cells that control a particular action or thinking task.

For instance, one group of neurons can work together to control drinking from a cup. Each time a ten-month-old drinks from a cup, this network of synaptic connections fires together, in a particular sequence. At first, the connections take time to move the muscles. Eventually, after many repetitions, the neurons work together so well that it becomes easy for the child to drink from a cup. The child's skills increase as a result of the increased number of neural pathways. The child learns.

These connections affect not only actions but all areas of behavior. Systems of neurons work together to influence how babies see and hear as well as think and remember. This process is how all learning takes place. The system is so flexible that humans are able to continue to learn new behaviors and form new ideas all their lives.

Note that the connections between neurons are not permanent. They can be broken when the behavior or idea is not repeated, and the synaptic pathways fade away if they are not used. People lose synapses in this way all through their lives; they forget what they have learned. At the same time that some connections are being lost, however, new ones are being added. The new connections become part of the brain as new skills are learned or new experiences are stored as memories.

Indeed, children form so many synaptic connections that they must lose some surplus connections in the process of refining a new skill and becoming proficient at it. Such neural "pruning" helps the brain focus only on useful connections, and thus acquire more skills.

Is the Brain Organized Only Once?

The answer is "no." There are a number of circumstances that prove that this isn't the case. Some children who suffered damage to the brain area that controls language have still learned to speak. Older people who suffer strokes—where neurons in an area of the brain die—can relearn skills by learning to use other areas of the brain. The brain can be reorganized. In practical terms, that means a child doesn't have to be exposed to every possible activity in the first year—or even few years—of life. What is important is to give young children a stimulating environment. By doing so, parents and other caregivers help children's brains develop many pathways and connections.

Speeding the Brain's Work

Myelin, a waxy substance that coats axons, makes it easier for axons to transmit signals—it speeds their work. When a baby is born only those nerves that control basic instincts such as nursing have this myelin coating. See Fig. 9-5.

Other axons acquire a coating of myelin as the child grows. This process continues until about age twenty. The myelin coating

LOOKING AT REAL LIFE

Donna has always loved music, so it was only natural that she began to share it with baby Michael as soon as he was born. Donna sings to Michael every night when she puts him to bed. Michael falls asleep right away after she sings him his favorite lullaby. Donna was pleased to learn that listening to music may even have a positive effect on certain thinking skills. Some researchers believe that musical training actually creates new pathways in the brain. Now Donna tries to include music in Michael's day in a number of ways that may help enhance his creativity and coordination. She enrolled Michael in a "Music for Tots" program at the park district. The musical stimulation helps strengthen the pathways in his brain, increasing his ability to learn. Music also helps him relax and fall asleep.

▸▸PERSONAL APPLICATION

1. Do you remember any songs or lullabies that you enjoyed when you were younger?
2. Do you think that listening to music can affect your brain development? Why or why not?

is added in different areas of the brain at different times. Axons in the area of the brain that controls such skills as motor abilities, vision, and hearing receive the coating the earliest. As a result, those are the areas in which babies first show development.

Stimulate Brain Development in an Infant

Brain development research suggests ways to help foster intellectual development:

- **Keep it simple and natural.** Everyday experiences such as changing a diaper or giving a bath build the pathways between neurons when combined with cuddling, talking, or singing to the baby. Experts urge parents to give children an environment rich with positive interaction and talking.

- **Match experiences to the child's mental abilities.** Babies need physical experiences—that is how they learn. It is important to provide experiences at their level of understanding. For example, a safe interactive toy can help infants learn. However, flashcards are too advanced for a three-month-old.

- **Practice makes perfect.** The more repetition, the stronger the connections between neurons. Establish routines with the baby so a baby learns what to expect. Include reading a bedtime story, even when the baby can't read. An infant will learn that sitting down with you and a book is important.

- **Actively involve the baby.** Provide experiences in which the child takes part. Children of all ages learn best by doing.

- **Provide variety, but avoid overload.** Some parents try to expose their baby to as many different experiences as possible to enhance brain development. Babies do benefit from a variety of experiences, but too many can overwhelm them.

- **Avoid pushing the child.** Children learn better if they are interested in what they are doing. Look for clues as to whether the child continues to show interest in the activity. If not, don't pursue it.

The rate at which axons receive this waxy coating may explain why some children have difficulty learning certain tasks. If the nerves handling a certain activity are not yet covered with myelin, it would be difficult for a child to learn the activity. The lack of myelin does not make it impossible to learn the task. The presence of myelin, however, makes learning much easier.

Indeed, myelin is so crucial to the speed at which nerves function that if this coating is lost, it affects the way the brain and body function. Multiple sclerosis is a disease in which the absence of myelin plays a role. Scientists are working hard to find new treatments for this and other diseases.

SECTION 9-1 Review and Activities

Reviewing the Section

1. In what part of the brain is the cerebral *cortex*?
2. What abilities does the cerebellum control?
3. How do *dendrites* and *axons* function together in the brain?
4. How does *myelin* help axons do their work?
5. How do repeated experiences help organize the brain?
6. What happens to *synapses* throughout life?
7. What impact on learning results from the rate of the spread of myelin?

Observing and Interacting

Compare photographs of newborn infants with pictures of babies at six, twelve, and eighteen months.

1. What differences in their abilities can you infer from what you see?
2. Write a caption for each photograph, summarizing the baby's abilities.

Intellectual Development During the First Year

During the first year of life, children undergo a greater change than they ever will again. In just 12 months, a helpless newborn becomes a whirlwind of energy and activity. From birth to one year, babies go from not being able to move to moving about by crawling or walking. As their social skills begin to emerge, a newborn communicates only by crying, whereas a one-year-old can use gestures or even words. By age one, a baby has likes and dislikes, an imagination, and a unique personality.

Objectives

- List four signs of intellectual growth in infants.
- Identify Piaget's first period of learning and describe specific abilities that babies learn during this period.
- Summarize the importance of sensory stimulation to the intellectual development of infants.
- Describe the progression of concept development in young children.

Key Terms

perception
attention span
sensorimotor period
object permanence
imaginative play
symbolic thinking
concepts

Learning in the First Year

 Right from birth, babies have a number of capabilities. Newborns can hear, see, taste, smell, and feel. They use these abilities as the building blocks of learning. A baby's brain is fed by what is experienced through the senses. Babies' ability to learn from sensory information, called **perception**, improves as experiences are repeated. The brain's neurons begin to become organized, increasing the baby's learning and skills. Newborns can't purposely grasp and lift objects, but a three-month-old can. In time, babies' hand-eye coordination improves further. They develop many skills. These developmental milestones of intellectual development are summarized on page 290.

In just the first year of life, babies also develop four abilities that show their growing intellectual abilities:

- **Remembering experiences.** In the first few months, babies develop the ability to remember. The information from the senses can be interpreted in light of past experiences. A two- or three-month-old baby may stop crying when someone enters the room because the baby anticipates being picked up.

- **Making associations.** This act—the baby's ceasing to cry—also indicates association. The baby associates a parent or other caregiver with receiving comfort.

- **Understanding cause and effect.** Babies also develop an understanding of cause and effect, the idea that one action results in another action or condition. Sucking causes milk to flow. If the baby stops sucking, the milk stops. In short, every time the infant does something, something else happens.

As babies' motor skills develop, cause-and-effect learning changes. By seven or eight months, babies can throw things deliberately. They can pull the cord on a toy and make the toy move. At this age, babies have a better understanding of their own power to make things happen.

- **Paying attention.** A baby's **attention span**—the length of time a person can concentrate on a task without getting bored—grows longer. If the same object is presented over and over again, the baby's response to the object will eventually become less enthusiastic. The baby's diminishing response is a way of saying, "That's old stuff. I've seen it before." Generally, bright babies have a short attention span—they tend to lose interest sooner than babies of average or below-average intelligence. (Beyond infancy, children with above-average intelligence typically have a longer attention span than others their age.) See Fig. 9-6 on page 290.

THE DEVELOPING BRAIN

When babies get bored, they often announce their boredom by letting out a loud wail. Parents can come to the rescue by giving the infant a toy to play with or by talking to or playing with the baby. Some parents and other caregivers use the television as a substitute. However, television can't take the place of live interaction. Researchers have found that language not connected to the events around an infant is nothing but noise to the child.

1-2 MONTHS

- Gains information through senses
- Makes eye contact
- Prefers faces to objects
- Can distinguish between familiar and unfamiliar voices

3-4 MONTHS

- Can distinguish between familiar and unfamiliar faces
- Makes vowel-consonant combinations such as "ah-goo"
- Can tell a smile from a frown

5-6 MONTHS

- Is alert for longer periods of time, up to two hours
- Studies objects carefully
- Recognizes own name
- Distinguishes between friendly and angry voices
- Recognizes basic sounds of native language

7-8 MONTHS

- Imitates the actions of others
- Begins to understand cause and effect
- Remembers things that have happened
- Sorts objects by size
- Solves simple problems
- Forms sounds such as *da, ga, ma, ba*
- Recognizes some words
- Babbling imitates speech inflections

9-10 MONTHS

- Looks for dropped objects
- Responds to some words and phrases, such as "no" and "all gone"
- Takes objects out of containers and puts them back in
- May say a few words

11-12 MONTHS

- Can point to and identify objects in books
- Fits blocks or boxes inside one another
- Says "Mama" and "Dada" for parents
- Understands simple words and phrases like "Come to Mommy"
- Speaks some words regularly

Fig. 9-7 Piaget's Four Periods of Learning

Period	Characteristics
Sensorimotor Birth–2 years	Children learn through their senses and own actions.
Preoperational 2–7 years	Children think in terms of their own activities and what they perceive at the moment.
Concrete operations 7–11 years	Children can think logically but still learn best through experience.
Formal operations 11–Adult	People are capable of abstract thinking.

Piaget's Theories

Jean Piaget, a Swiss psychologist who died in 1980, had a great influence on what is known about how children learn. In an effort to understand how children's intellectual skills developed, Piaget systematically observed infants and children and recorded his observations about the growth of their ability to reason—the increases in the level of their intellectual understanding. He found that intellectual development followed a pattern. His theory identified four major learning stages, or periods, that take place from birth to adulthood.

According to Piaget, these four periods appear in the same order in all children. They are the sensorimotor period, the preoperational period, the concrete operations period, and the formal operations period. Although the ages at which the periods emerge may vary from child to child, researchers have established average ages at which they appear. See Fig. 9-7.

Piaget determined that children must learn to master one thinking skill before they can move on to another. Children can't be forced to understand a concept or master a skill any faster than the speed at which their abilities mature. He also noted that children who don't get the opportunity to apply new skills during each stage of development might never reach their full potential. For this reason, it is important for children to have constant learning opportunities.

The Sensorimotor Period

The **sensorimotor period**, from birth to about age two, is Piaget's first stage of learning. During this period, babies learn primarily through their senses and their own actions. This period coincides with the period during which the neurons in the infant's brain establish pathways that enable learning. The exact role played by the brain in infant learning was not known when Piaget first developed his theories. Later scientific discoveries about neural pathways confirmed Piaget's observations that sensory stimulation in the first year of life was crucial to fostering a child's intellectual development.

Piaget noted that during the sensorimotor period, babies come to understand an important concept. Usually at about ten months of age, babies recognize that objects continue to exist even when they are out of sight. This concept is called **object permanence**. For example, at four months, when Megan drops her rubber ring toy and it rolls behind her, she simply looks for something else to play with. But at eleven months, when her ball rolls out of sight, Megan actively looks for it. She has learned the concept of object permanence.

Six Stages

The sensorimotor period can be broken down into six shorter stages. At each stage, a baby has specific intellectual abilities. See Fig. 9-8, which explains these six stages. It will help you better understand how learning occurs. Note that the child's abilities at each stage after Stage 1 build on the stage

before. For example, the inborn grasping reflex in Stage 1 establishes a pattern that permits learning to grasp and hold a desired object. At Stage 2, an infant has learned how to grasp a desired object—a piece of food or a teething ring—and bring it to the mouth. Acquiring these abilities permits an infant to move on to learn a more complex set of skills at each stage.

At the end of the sensorimotor period, by Stage 6, children have used their experiences of the physical world to construct a consistent view of the world they live in. At this point, especially if they have been read to regularly, children can hold an image in their minds of a period beyond the immediate moment. Words such as "soon" or "later" now have meaning because the child is able to conceptualize a time in the future.

Fig. 9-8 Piaget's Sensorimotor Period: Birth to Age Two		
Stage	**Approximate Ages**	**Characteristics**
Stage 1	Birth to 1 month	• Practices inborn reflexes. • Does not understand self as separate person.
Stage 2	1 to 4 months	• Combines two or more reflexes. • Develops hand-mouth coordination.
Stage 3	4 to 8 months	• Acts intentionally to produce results. • Improves hand-eye coordination.
Stage 4	8 to 12 months	• Begins to solve problems. • Finds partially hidden objects. • Imitates others.
Stage 5	12 to 18 months	• Finds hidden objects. • Explores and experiments. • Understands that objects exist independently.
Stage 6	18 to 24 months	• Solves problems by thinking through sequences. • Can think using symbols. • Begins imaginative thinking.

Learning Through  PLAY

Sensory Play

During the sensorimotor period of development, from birth to two years of age, children learn through their senses and their environment. In the first few months, babies learn about their own bodies—how to move hands and feet at will and handle bottles and small toys. At about eight months to one year, children learn to crawl and then to walk. This greatly expands the world they can explore. Everything in their path becomes an opportunity for learning. Besides seeing, touching, smelling, and listening, babies put almost everything into their mouths. Feedback from this sensory exploration teaches infants about their world. By providing everyday objects and toys that will stimulate the child's senses, parents and other caregivers can enhance learning.

As the baby grows, new objects and toys that stimulate all of the senses can be introduced.

Following Up

What concepts might a young child learn from playing in a sandbox?

Imaginative play—pretending—is also possible at Stage 6. The child can imagine things that have not happened but might happen. (Imaginative play is sometimes called *make-believe play* or *dramatic play*.) This is also the time when **symbolic thinking**, the use of words and numbers to stand for ideas, begins, and the foundations for reading are established. Children can begin to learn pre-reading skills, such as the letters of the alphabet, and are able to understand that a letter represents a sound.

Stimulating Infants' Senses

A child's senses can be easily stimulated each and every day. For example, a baby's senses of touch and taste are routinely stimulated as he or she is changed and fed.

Very young infants prefer looking at people, rather than things. They can focus on and follow objects and can see shapes and forms. Hanging a mobile in an infant's crib will help stimulate a baby's sense of sight. Mobiles should be hung about 12

Fig. 9-9 **There are many ways to provide an infant with sensory stimulation.** What are some safe toys a baby could play with while riding in a car?

inches from the baby's eyes. Infants will respond to brightly colored objects, perhaps soft stuffed dolls with smiling faces and large eyes. Change the baby's position from time to time to vary the view.

Infants are surprisingly sensitive to sound. They recognize the voices of family and friends and can be calmed by a loving voice even from another room. They are increasingly aware of their own voices and will babble back to an adult, mimicking the adult's tone of voice. Talking, reading, singing, and humming are wonderful ways to vary and stimulate an infant's hearing.

Touch is one of the most important ways to communicate love to an infant. The infant's sense of security and trust are built through cuddling, rocking, and patting. This also helps the infant gain a sense of his or her own body. This sense is crucial to the

development of motor skills. A slowly swaying rocking chair or baby swing is a deeply comforting sensation for a baby, and helps him or her develop an awareness of space. In some areas, infant massage classes are available for learning more formal techniques for using touch to stimulate a baby's sense of touch. See Fig. 9-9.

Beginnings of Concept Development

As they continue to learn, young children between ages one and three begin to organize the information they receive from their senses. They start to form **concepts**, general categories of objects and information. Concepts range from categories for objects such as "fruit" to qualities such as color or shape and to abstract ideas such as time.

Children learn words and concepts by using three principles:

- Children start by thinking that labels are for whole objects, not parts. Suppose Dwane's father points to an animal and says "dog." How does Dwane know that the label "dog" applies to that animal and not to its nose or its tail?
- Children believe that labels apply to the group to which the individual objects belong, not to the particular object. Any four-legged creature may elicit "doggy!" from Dwane.

- Young children tend to believe that an object can only have one label. That may be why it takes time for young children to learn to use pronouns—to recognize that "mommy" and "she" can mean the same person.

As a child matures, concepts become more accurate. Babies begin with two broad concepts—"the baby" and "not the baby." Later, children make very broad distinctions between people and things.

SECTION 9-2 Review and Activities

Reviewing the Section

1. What is a *perception*? Give an example of how a baby's perception changes during the first year of life.
2. How can pull-toys help a baby learn about cause and effect?
3. Explain what *attention span* means.
4. What are Piaget's four periods of learning, and what are their approximate age spans?
5. What do babies use to learn during Piaget's first period of development?
6. Explain how the loving touch of a caregiver helps a baby develop certain senses that are important to the development of motor skills.
7. Compare a baby's concept of the world to a three-year-old's concept of the world.

Observing and Interacting

Play the game peek-a-boo with a partner. How do you think this game contributes to the development of object permanence?

Helping Infants Learn

Intellectual development in an infant is closely linked with the responsiveness of others in the baby's environment. That is, babies learn more and learn faster when parents and caregivers comfort them, smile at them, talk to them, and play with them. A baby treated in this way is likely to progress more rapidly and develop more skills more quickly than a child who receives less interactive care. Babies' most important teachers are the people who care for them every day.

Objectives

- Describe ways parents and other caregivers can help babies' intellectual growth.
- Identify toys appropriate for a baby's age.
- Explain how babies develop communication skills.

Key Terms

age appropriate
childproof
manipulate

Encouraging Learning

Even the youngest babies learn about the world from the care they receive. When Tyler's stomach feels uncomfortable, he cries. Then his mother picks him up and nurses him, and he feels better. Everyday events—discomfort, crying, cuddling, being fed—are connected. The child learns to recognize this pattern. If the baby's cries are not answered, the baby sees no relationship between his or her needs and the caregiver's actions. There is no pattern to help the baby form new pathways, and therefore new abilities and associations, in the child's brain.

In addition to giving a child basic care, there are things that parents and other caregivers can do to help build and influence their child's learning, or intellectual development. Encouraging learning doesn't require money or special toys. Rather, it depends on the attention, knowledge, and time that parents and other caregivers can give to the child.

Here are some ways that parents and other caregivers can encourage learning:

- **Learn about child development.** Understanding how an average child develops can help caregivers provide toys and learning experiences that are age appropriate. (**Age appropriate** describes things that are suitable for the age and individual needs of a child.) Understanding age-appropriate behavior also helps caregivers have realistic expectations for what their child should be able to do.

- **Give the child time and attention.** No baby needs attention every waking moment. However, a caregiver can help a baby thrive—and learn—just by talking to and playing simple games with the baby.

- **Provide positive feedback.** When the baby demonstrates a new skill or tries out a new activity, showing pleasure and responding with praise will encourage the baby to keep trying new things.

- **Express love.** Caregivers who use their personal style to show their love for the baby are helping the baby grow in self-confidence, and encouraging him or her to try more—and to learn more.

- **Talk, talk, talk.** Talking has many benefits. When caregivers talk to infants, they help them learn about their environment. Current research shows that the more caregivers talk to a baby, the faster the child's brain develops. Talking builds feelings of security, too. See Fig. 9-10.

Safe Learning

To encourage learning, allow the baby as much freedom of movement at home as possible. In the first few months, move the baby from room to room to be with the family. A baby who spends time in different rooms and with the family as they go about their daily routine learns more than a baby who is kept alone in a crib.

Older babies who can crawl or walk shouldn't be restricted to playpens for long periods of time. It is better to **childproof** the home—take steps to protect the child from possible dangers—and monitor the child's activities. For more information about childproofing, see page 335.

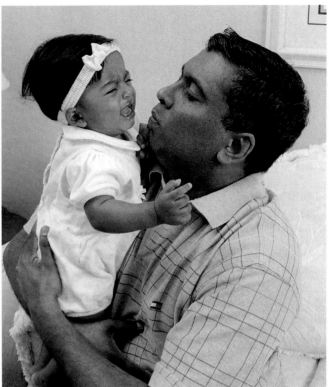

Fig. 9-10 **When a person responds to a baby's needs, the baby learns to make connections between the events.**

The Importance of Play

For children, play is work as well as pleasure. Researchers have clearly established that playtime is essential to intellectual development. Toys are the tools for learning.

Play is also a physical necessity through which development takes place. When a baby shakes a rattle, stacks blocks, throws a ball, or chews on a teething toy, it's not just for amusement. These are serious, absorbing tasks through which infants strengthen their muscles, refine their motor skills, and learn about the world.

Babies learn from listening, too. The familiar voice of the primary caregiver is the first sound a baby learns to recognize. Rattles and squeak toys introduce different sounds. Babies delight in music—from a

Kirk's mother peeked around his bed-room door. She found him awake, but happily playing alone in his crib. He played with his mobile, which played a tune as it turned, and dangled brightly colored stuffed animal shapes tempt-ingly over his crib. He reached eagerly for the animals and batted at them with his chubby fists as they swung above him. He giggled as they danced above his head. After a few minutes, Kirk's mother went in his room to greet her son. Later that day, they went to their playgroup at another member's home. Once they arrived, Kirk's mother placed him on the floor so that he and the other babies could play together. There was a large, soft, brightly colored blanket on the floor, which was covered with toys. The babies in the playgroup crawled all over the blanket, eagerly reaching for cloth books, large plastic blocks, and teething rings.

▶▶**PERSONAL APPLICATION**

Why do you think it is important for babies to play with stimulating toys?

wind-up toy, a CD, or a person's singing. They can also enjoy different rhythms. With exciting music, they can "dance" in the arms of a caring adult. With soothing music, they can cuddle and be rocked.

Different Toys for Different Ages

Because babies mature and change rap-idly during the first year, they will need dif-ferent toys to play with as they develop:

- **Birth to three months.** A baby at this age needs little more than things to look at and listen to. Bright colors, moving objects, and interesting sounds stimulate development of the senses. A mobile hung safely above the crib is interesting for the baby to watch, and allows him or her to practice following objects with the eyes. Brightly colored wallpaper and pictures can also provide interest.

- **Four to six months.** The sense of touch is important in this period. Babies need things to touch, handle, bang, shake, suck, and chew. Make certain that toys are small enough to handle easily but too large to swallow. All items and pieces should be at least 1½ inches across. Teething rings, cups, rattles, and plastic toys are good choices. Stuffed toys are fun to touch, and toys that squeak give results that baby can learn to purposely reproduce. Providing objects with different textures helps the child learn by touch. Babies this age like simple picture books, and learn to love being read to. Choose washable books with col-orful pictures of familiar objects.

- **Seven to nine months.** Babies still need things to handle, throw, pound, bang, and shake. Anything that makes a noise fascinates infants this age. Look for books that have inserts of different textures to feel, or places to press on the page that produce squeaking or squealing noises. Children of this age enjoy blocks, balls, large plastic beads that pop apart, and roly-poly toys that can be pushed or kicked. Safe house-hold items are just as interesting as purchased toys. Pots and pans with lids, and plastic containers to stack make great playthings.

- **Ten to twelve months.** By the end of their first year, babies need things to

Fig. 9-11 **At ten to twelve months, babies enjoy pushing toys on wheels.** What other types of toys do babies enjoy at this age?

crawl after. Those who are already walking enjoy toys that they can push or pull. During this period, children especially enjoy toys that they can **manipulate**, or work with their hands. Baskets, boxes, and other containers are fun. Babies like to put things into them and then dump them out again. Picture books are good for looking at alone or for brief story times during the day or before bed. Vinyl books are now available that can even withstand a trip to the tub; floating toys are also great choices. See Fig. 9-11.

Choosing Toys

When choosing playthings for a young child, look for toys that encourage participation and use. Younger children need simpler toys, but as a baby's abilities increase, toys can be more complex.

Toys, especially those labeled "educational," can be expensive. Sometimes they have limited usefulness. Parents can provide a baby with as much fun and learning by making common household items available. Items such as plastic measuring spoons, plastic measuring cups, a clean plastic bucket, plastic bowls, a metal pan or mixing bowl and a large wooden spoon, or a large cardboard box with a "window" cut in it all make great toys because young children can use them in many different ways. With any toy, however, supervision is important for safe play. See Fig. 9-12.

When buying toys, caregivers should look for ones that will remain interesting and appropriate for a number of years. A set of blocks is a good example. At the age of six months, Reynaldo grasped and inspected his blocks. By his first birthday,

Fig. 9-12 **Even simple household objects can make fun toys for babies.**

he could stack several blocks into a tower; and at the age of three, he used the blocks to make roads for his cars. Now, at age six, Reynaldo creates elaborate houses and castles, using every available block.

Developing Communication

One of an infant's major tasks is to learn to communicate with others. This skill depends on development in all areas— physical, emotional, social, and intellectual. There are wide differences in the rate of development from baby to baby. However, healthy babies should show steady improvement in communication skills.

Communicating Without Words

Babies communicate long before they can talk. By the end of the first year, they can effectively make most of their needs and wants known without words.

At first, crying is simply an automatic way to communicate discomfort. However, babies quickly learn that crying produces a response that someone will come and try to make them feel better. Within a month or so, the crying takes on a pattern. A cry is followed by a pause to listen for reactions. If no response arrives, the baby resumes crying. The baby soon develops different cries for different problems. A cry indicating hunger may be interrupted by wails of frustration as the baby learns to manipulate a bottle. A cry of pain may include groans and whimpers. Caregivers can learn to identify a baby's problem by the type of cry.

Babies also send messages with movements and gestures. It is clear that a wiggling baby doesn't want to get dressed. An eleven-month-old who pushes away a bowl of a usually favorite food has had enough to eat. The baby who clings with both arms to a parent's leg is showing a sure sign of anxiety. The use of gestures continues into adulthood, but they are used more to reinforce words than as a substitute for words.

Finally, a baby communicates by making special sounds. Some sounds, such as giggles and cooing, carry obvious messages.

Learning to Speak

 Before learning to talk, a baby must learn to associate meanings with words. This is a gradual process. It depends on caregivers talking to the baby, even when the baby doesn't appear to respond. For example, when taking the baby for a walk, caregivers can talk about what they see.

When talking to a baby, use simple words, but avoid baby talk. Children are

Children
Around the World

Speaking Without Words

In the United States and Canada, parents are using American Sign Language to communicate with babies between six and twelve months old. Experts say that babies as young as six months have the memory to recognize and remember signs their parents make, and to respond. Parents teach their babies to use hand signals for words such as "no," "eat," "more," "milk," and "dog," among many others.

Scientific studies have shown that signing enhances babies' language development by allowing them to learn language before they develop the ability to speak. The physical skills needed for speech (coordinating the movements of the tongue, jaw, and lips) don't develop until babies are between eleven and eighteen months of age, while the motor skills needed

to produce hand signals develop much sooner. Signing also helps children learn social skills by allowing them to express themselves.

Investigating Culture

1. Conduct some research on sign language. Do other countries have their own versions?
2. Do you know any sign language? Are you interested in learning? Find the signs for the words mentioned above. Are they difficult to make?

experts at repeating what they hear. If they learn baby talk first, regular speech is more difficult. Caregivers should speak clearly using simple words. In this way, the child will become accustomed to hearing real words. Although babies won't understand much of what caregivers say, they are beginning to establish an important habit. Listening to other people's talk—especially talk directed to the baby—is essential for an infant's language development. This interaction also helps build speech centers in the child's brain.

A newborn is physically unable to speak. Over the first year, physical changes take place that allow the baby to make the sounds necessary for speech. Babies get ready for real speech by babbling—repeating syllables and sounds. You may have heard babies endlessly repeating consonant and vowel sounds such as "bababababa" or "gogogogo." Babbling is a baby's preparation for saying recognizable words. To encourage babbling, respond to and imitate the baby's sounds. This encourages the baby to continue practicing. See Fig. 9-13.

Parenting Q&A

How Does Reading to Infants Help Them Develop Language Skills?

Children need to hear speech and learn that sounds have meanings before they can develop language skills of their own. Parents and caregivers can help with this by reading to children.

- Vivid pictures in children's books help infants connect the sounds they are hearing to concrete objects, and rhymes help children remember words.
- Repetition is key to children's learning. Reading favorite books over and over produces a familiar pattern of sounds. Children recognize these familiar patterns and attempt to repeat them, even if they don't know what the words mean.
- If children read with caregivers, they will start to associate books with attention and care. They will be much better prepared to learn to read when the time comes and will likely be more motivated to do so.
- Reading to young children also helps to increase their vocabularies and promotes their ability to read aloud.

THINKING IT THROUGH

1. How does reading favorite books over and over help infants develop language skills?
2. How do the pictures in a book help a young child develop language skills?

Birth-3 MONTHS

- Babbles
- Cries to express hunger, anger, pain, or discomfort

4-6 MONTHS

- Babbling sounds more like speech with different sounds such as *p*, *b*, and *m*
- Voices excitement and displeasure
- Gurgles

7 MONTHS – 1 YEAR

- Babbling has long and short groups of sounds
- Uses speech to get attention
- Imitates different speech sounds
- Says one or two words

1-2 YEARS

- Adds more words to vocabulary each month
- Asks one- to two-word questions, such as "Go bye-bye?"
- Puts two words together ("More juice.")

2-3 YEARS

- Has a word for almost everything
- Uses two- to three-word sentences to talk about and ask for things

3-4 YEARS

- Talks about activities
- Uses four- or more word sentences

4-5 YEARS

- Voice is clear
- Uses sentences with a lot of details
- Tells stories
- Says most sounds correctly

A child's first real words are usually understandable between the ages of eight and fifteen months. Because the infant typically has been babbling and coming close to real word sounds for some time, it isn't always easy to know exactly when a specific word is purposely spoken. First words are usually common, simple words that have special meaning for the baby, such as "mama," "dada," or "bye-bye." Most children don't have a large vocabulary or combine words into simple sentences until after their first birthday.

There are predictable stages that children progress through as they develop speech.

Figure 9-13 on page 303 outlines typical speech milestones. Of course, children vary in their development of speech, so these milestones serve only as a guide to normal development. They help doctors and caregivers determine when and if a child may need extra help to develop his or her speech.

A baby's first words are one of the most exciting milestones parents and other caregivers experience with their child. When a child learns to talk, it opens the door to a whole new world of communication and learning.

SECTION 9-3 Review and Activities

Reviewing the Section

1. How does a baby learn from the care he or she receives?
2. Why should caregivers choose toys that are *age appropriate*?
3. What are five guidelines for caregivers to help children learn?
4. List three things caregivers need to evaluate when deciding if a toy or other object is safe for a baby.
5. Why are bright colors and toys with sounds good for babies from birth to three months?
6. Before they learn to talk, do babies communicate? If so, how? If not, why not?
7. During what age span are young children able to say one or two words?

Observing and Interacting

Look at the list of developmental milestones in Fig. 9-6 on page 290. Based on the skills shown, create a list of four toys suitable for one age-span. Visit a store or check online to locate the toys on your list. Evaluate each toy, considering appropriateness, appeal, safety, and price. Which two would be the most appropriate purchases, and why?

Career Opportunities

Child Development Researcher

Children's development is of endless interest to scientists. How do babies learn to make sounds? Why do some children fall behind in school? Helping to answer these questions is the work of child development researchers.

▸ Job Responsibilities

Child development researchers plan and execute studies, analyze data, and explain their results in writing. Their findings are published in scientific journals, allowing other people to build on their work. Doctors and other professionals read these journals to get information that may help the children they work with.

▸ Work Environment

Most child development researchers teach in universities, often in psychology or education departments. Many work on research teams. Good communication skills and teamwork are key to their success.

▸ Education and Training

Child development researchers are required to have bachelor's degrees in psychology or child development, as well as master's degrees—or sometimes doctorates—in education or psychology. Most specialize in human development or early childhood education.

▸ Skills and Aptitudes

- Curiosity
- Persistence
- Research skills
- Ability to relate to children
- Ability to work in teams

WORKPLACE CONNECTION

1. **Thinking Skills.** How does the work of researchers affect your daily life?

2. **Resource Skills.** How could you use research to learn about child develoment?

Review and Activities

SECTION SUMMARIES

- Early in life, babies learn entirely through stimulation of their senses. An infant's brain undergoes major changes in response to stimulation. (9-1)
- Each part of the brain controls a different function of the body. (9-1)
- The transmission of information between nerve cells in the brain creates neural pathways that organize the brain. (9-1)
- Repeated actions strengthen the neural pathways in the brain that control motor skills such as sucking or grasping. (9-1)
- Based on his observations, Piaget said that all children go through the same four stages of learning. (9-2)
- A baby needs a safe and stimulating environment for proper brain development. (9-3)
- Play is a child's chief means of learning and practicing new skills. (9-3)
- Choosing appropriate toys can facilitate learning. (9-3)
- Children communicate well before they learn to talk, but reading to a child promotes reading readiness and vocabulary even before the child learns language skills. (9-3)

REVIEWING THE CHAPTER

1. How do axons and dendrites work together in the brain? (9-1)
2. What role does repetition play in brain development? (9-1)
3. Why is it important to read and talk to a baby even if the baby does not understand? (9-1)
4. What are four signs of the brain's development in a child's first year? (9-2)
5. Summarize Piaget's four periods of learning. (9-2)
6. Describe two ways a caregiver can stimulate an infant's senses. (9-2)
7. What three principles indicate how children learn concepts? (9-2)
8. Describe two toys or household objects that would be appropriate for a six-month-old baby to use as toys. (9-3)
9. Describe one way caregivers can help a baby communicate. (9-3)
10. Summarize the milestones of speech development in the first year. (9-3)

THINKING CRITICALLY

1. **Diagramming.** Create a flow chart showing how nerves send information to the brain and send instructions from it.
2. **Making Inferences.** A baby's first word is often "mama" or "dada." Why do you think so?

MAKING CONNECTIONS

1. **Writing.** Write a scene that shows how a caregiver can provide an infant with encouragement while the baby is trying to master a new skill in intellectual development.
2. **Science.** Which parts of the brain control each of the following: expression of anger, making sounds that will lead to speech, and a newborn's sucking reflex?

APPLYING YOUR LEARNING

1. **Evaluating Toys.** Evaluate a toy designed for a baby under the age of one. How is the toy designed to be safe? Present your findings to the class.
2. **Make a Poster.** Create a poster that would persuade caregivers to encourage learning in their children.
3. **Making a Mobile.** Infants enjoy mobiles. Design a mobile to hang above an infant's crib. Make the mobile or draw a diagram of it, describing the materials and labeling what colors you would use in making it.
4. **Newborn's Senses.** Research how one of an infant's senses improves during the first year.

Learning from Research

1. Choose one of the following research claims to investigate.
2. In what ways might infants who have been spoken or read to in the womb be developmentally ahead of infants who were not?
3. Summarize what you have learned about learning in the womb.

Prenatal Learning and Music. Many companies have recorded albums to be played to babies before birth. Makers of these recordings claim that mothers who listen to the recordings have easier births and calmer infants as a result. Identify at least two companies that offer music for prenatal learning.

Prenatal Learning and Mother's Voice. Proponents of prenatal learning assert that a baby can hear as early as 16 weeks into the pregnancy, and that the sound waves of the mother's voice are conducted to the baby directly through the mother's body. Studies suggest that newborn infants indicate a preference for the mother's voice over any other voice to which they are exposed. Identify at least two research studies that support this premise.

Prenatal Learning and Taste and Smell. Research suggests that babies perceive tastes and smells in the amniotic fluid. The structures for tasting develop at about 14 weeks. The nose develops between 11 and 15 weeks. Identify at least two research studies that support this premise.

The Child from One to Three

Chapter 10
Physical Development from One to Three

Chapter 11
Emotional and Social Development from One to Three

Chapter 12
Intellectual Development from One to Three

Physical Development from One to Three

Thoughtful Reading:

As you read this chapter:

- Ask clarifying questions such as who, what, when, and where.
- Ask follow-up questions such as how and why.
- Find sources to answer all your reading questions.

Section 10-1
Growth and Development from One to Three

Section 10-2
Caring for Children from One to Three

Growth and Development from One to Three

The growth and development of a child from babyhood to the preschool years is dramatic. A one-year-old still moves with some uncertainty, needs help dressing, and eats messily. A three-year-old can run and jump, get dressed alone, and eat fairly neatly with a fork and spoon.

Objectives

- Identify typical changes in height, weight, proportion, and posture from ages one through three.
- Describe how to keep one- to three-year-olds' teeth healthy.
- Compare fine and gross motor skills for this age period.

Key Terms

toddler
preschooler
developmentally appropriate
dexterity
sensory integration

Toddlers to Preschoolers

After the fast pace of the first year of life, physical growth slows somewhat, but children's skills improve dramatically between their first and fourth birthdays. At about the age of one, most children begin to walk a few unsteady steps. The term **toddlers** refers to one- and two-year-olds. By age three, however, children are typically far from toddling. Three-year-olds not only walk steadily but they also hop, skip, and run. Most of their other physical skills have advanced as well. From their third birthday until about age five—the age when most children start going to school—children are called **preschoolers**.

To build their physical skills, young children need plenty of space and room to move around. They need time each day for active play so they can exercise their muscles and use their stored-up energy. Although their attention span is longer than that of infants, they still want to change games and activities often. Each day brings new learning.

Influences on Growth and Development

A number of different influences impact the way children develop. Heredity plays a significant role in child development. As

Fig. 10-1 **A child could have the same color eyes or hair as a parent. These physical traits are passed on by genes.** What other factors influence a toddler's growth and development?

you learned in Chapter 3, heredity refers to the various characteristics that children inherit from their parents and ancestors through the genes. When people remark that a child has "her father's eyes" or "his mother's nose," they are describing what they perceive a child has inherited. Physical traits such as body size, eye color, and even disease risk can be passed on through genes. Genes don't determine growth and physical development on their own. Instead, they act as a general road map for

physical development while other factors fill in the rest of the picture. Other factors include nutrition, health, and life experiences. See Fig. 10-1.

Growth from One to Three

Watching a child's growth during the toddler years can be an amazing and informative time. At this stage, changes in a child's physical growth are evidenced mainly by height, weight, body proportion, stance, and teeth. Motor development and ability progress as a child's physical development progresses.

Height and Weight

Children from one to three gain less than half the average monthly weight they did during the first year of life. Growth in height also slows by about half. Figure 10-2 shows the average heights and weights for boys and girls from ages one to three.

Heredity and environment influence the rate at which children grow in height and weight. These influences are more noticeable among children one to three than among infants. After their first birthdays, children begin to show greater variation in size. Some are much larger than average, while others are smaller. These size differences often continue through life. A tall two-year-old often grows to be a tall adult, and an unusually short toddler will likely be shorter than average as an adult.

Proportion and Posture

Because of changes in physical proportions, a child's posture improves during the period from ages one to three. Until age two, the circumferences (measurement around) of a child's head, abdomen, and

Fig. 10-2 Average Heights and Weights: Ages One to Three

Age	BOYS		GIRLS	
	Height / Inches	Weight / Pounds	Height / Inches	Weight / Pounds
One year	29 to 30½	21 to 24½	28¼ to 29¾	19½ to 22½
Two years	33½ to 35¼	26 to 30	32¾ to 34¾	24½ to 28½
Three years	36¾ to 38¾	29¼ to 34	36¼ to 38½	28¼ to 33¼

chest are about the same. Between ages two and three, however, the chest becomes larger around than the head and abdomen. During this period, the arms, legs, and torso lengthen. These changes in proportion help improve the child's balance and motor skills.

By the age of two, a child's posture is straighter but the child still doesn't stand completely erect. The typical toddler still has a protruding abdomen. The head is still bent forward somewhat. The toddler's knees and elbows are also slightly bent. By their third birthdays, children stand straighter because their spines are stronger.

Teeth

A child's teeth emerge at different rates, but there are averages. One-year-olds typically have about eight teeth. During the second year of life, eight more teeth usually come in. For most children, the last four back teeth emerge early in the third year, giving them a complete set of 20 primary, or baby, teeth. These teeth will eventually fall out and be replaced by adult, or permanent, teeth.

Diet greatly influences the quality of a child's teeth. Teeth are formed before birth, so the mother's diet during pregnancy affects the quality of her baby's teeth. The child's diet during the first two years is also important because adult teeth are forming under the primary teeth. Dairy products, which are rich in calcium and phosphorus, are especially important to good dental health. The vitamin D in milk also helps in the development of strong and healthy teeth and bones. Children should drink water that contains fluoride. Most tap water contains fluoride but most bottled waters do not.

A poor diet can cause tooth decay. To promote good dental health, sweets should be limited in a child's diet. Gum-like candy, raisins, and fruit snacks that stick to the teeth are a particular problem. In addition to regular brushing, children should brush their teeth after eating sugary cereals. If left between the teeth, they can promote dental decay. Don't put a child to bed with a bottle unless it contains only water. When sweet liquids, including milk, are left in the mouth too long, they can cause tooth decay. In babies, it can lead to a condition called *baby bottle decay*, which destroys young children's teeth.

Heredity appears to play a role in tooth quality. Dentists have identified a protective mechanism that discourages decay. Some children inherit this trait from their parents.

It's important to take children to a dentist at the age of 18 months or so. This will help them become comfortable with dental visits from an early age and begin preventive care long before the permanent teeth come in. See Fig. 10-3.

Motor Development from One to Three

The three general patterns of physical development (from head to foot, from near to far, and from simple to complex) are evident in this age span. When you compare the skills of children at age one with those at the end of their third year, you can see major changes. Hand skills, for instance, show a pattern of development from simple to complex. At thirteen months, a child can bang blocks together or may manage to build a short stack of them. By age four, the same child can manipulate the blocks skillfully to create much more complex structures, such as towers, houses, and roads.

Tracking Development

It is not always predictable when children from ages one to three will acquire various physical skills. Although they were born just two weeks apart, Blake and his cousin Damon haven't mastered physical skills at the same pace. That's not surprising, because some children learn skills earlier or later than average. These variations can be caused by differences in a child's physical size, health and diet, interests, temperament, or opportunities for physical play.

Child development experts have studied the range of ages at which children acquire certain important skills and have determined average ages. These developmental milestones for physical development of one-, two-, and three-year-olds are shown in Fig. 10-4. These help compare the average abilities of children of different ages. They also help caregivers plan **developmentally appropriate** activities. For example, an 18-month-old can stack two blocks. That means activities that involve large building blocks would be developmentally appropriate for 18-month-olds.

Motor Skills

 During this period, both gross and fine motor skills improve dramatically. Keep in mind that not all children develop physical skills at the same rate.

Fig. 10-3 **During the second year of life, eight teeth usually come in, giving the two-year-old a set of sixteen teeth.** How many total primary teeth will there be?

Fine Motor Skills	Gross Motor Skills

 MONTHS

- Turns several pages of a book at a time
- Picks up small objects with thumb and forefinger
- Moves objects from hand to hand

- May walk alone or while holding a caregiver's hand
- Sits down without help
- Slides down stairs backwards, one step at a time

18-24 MONTHS

- Stacks from two to four blocks
- Grasps crayons with a fist and scribbles

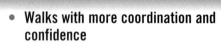

- Walks well
- Jumps in place
- Climbs up or down one stair
- Pull toys with wheels

2-2½ YEARS

- Stacks six blocks
- Turns one page of a book at a time
- Picks up objects from the floor without losing balance

- Walks with more coordination and confidence
- Jumps off the bottom step
- Pushes self on wheeled toys

2½-3 YEARS

- Stacks eight blocks
- Screws lids on and off containers
- Draws circles and horizontal and vertical lines

- Alternates feet going up stairs but not going down
- Runs but may not be able to stop smoothly
- Throws a ball overhead but inaccurately

3-4 YEARS

- Stacks nine or ten blocks
- Cuts with scissors
- Draws recognizable pictures
- Jumps up and down in place with both feet
- Catches a ball with arms straight
- Rides a tricycle

Gross Motor Skills

Physical exercise promotes the development of gross motor skills, those that involve the use and control of the large muscles of the back, legs, shoulders, and arms. As children exercise, they slowly build the confidence, strength, and coordination that helps them run, jump, and kick a ball.

Walking is a significant gross motor milestone for children. It gives them a feeling of pride and much more mobility for exploration. Most children begin to walk at about the age of one year. At first, children walk by holding on to furniture for stability. They are wobbly and uncertain. Their toes are pointed outward, their feet are spread apart, and their arms are held out for balance. After a few shaky steps, they collapse into a sitting position. With practice, children improve in steadiness, balance, and body control. See Fig. 10-5.

Climbing skills follow a similar sequence if the child has stairs to climb, but climbing isn't limited to stairs. Nothing is safe from the climbing toddler—furniture, counters, ledges, and even people are conquered like mountains! This motion, of course, makes safety an important concern for caregivers. The "How to Childproof a Home" feature on page 335 suggests ways to help make areas safer for children's exploration.

Fig. 10-5 Exercise is necessary for gross motor development. How does physical exercise promote the development of gross motor skills?

THE DEVELOPING BRAIN

Scientists have discovered that the learning of abilities, such as riding a bike, and the learning of facts, such as names and dates, are handled by different parts of the brain. Once a skill is learned, it forms a very durable memory. You never forget how to ride a bike. The same is not true of fact memories. Facts that are not used often slowly fade away until they are forgotten.

Fine Motor Skills

One of the major fine motor milestones that children reach at about age one is the ability to pick up small objects between their thumb and forefinger. This skill enables them to better grasp and lift small objects.

Between their first and second birthdays, children use fine motor skills as they learn to feed themselves and to drink from a cup. At first, young children frequently spill because they have poor hand-eye

Changes in Play

How children play changes as they grow and develop. By the time they are one, children are beginning to discover what objects are used for. A one-year-old will understand that a telephone is used for speaking to another person. However, by the time they are three, the role of imagination has begun to play a part in children's play. A telephone may no longer be a phone but could be used as a remote for turning on a pretend television. Many toys for young children are small versions of real things. A two-year-old will play with small plates and silverware. However, by the age of three, the same child might use her imagination to pretend that a piece of paper is a plate and a crayon is a spoon. During this time period, children go from being curious about objects to using their imagination with objects.

Following Up

What are some games that you could play with a child age one, two, or three to encourage imagination?

coordination, but with practice their success and neatness improve.

Toys offer the chance for children to practice fine motor skills. One-year-olds usually enjoy playing with blocks, large beads, and stacking games. They also like play phones, toys that roll, and musical toys.

Two-year-olds typically display greater **dexterity**, or skillful use of the hands and fingers. They can turn the pages of a book one at a time and turn on a faucet. They enjoy using crayons and typically color with such happy abandon that they leave marks running off the paper and on the table or floor. Another favorite activity of children in this age group is stacking blocks. They build small towers of blocks that usually topple after five or six blocks.

Three-year-olds show considerably more success than younger children at tasks and play that require fine motor skills. They typically delight in taking things apart and putting them back together. Children this age have enough dexterity to draw circles, lines, and crosses.

Before the age of two, it's difficult to determine whether a child will become left-handed or right-handed. After that age, some children make their preference clear by favoring one hand over the other. Others, however, may continue switching between hands well into their preschool years. Physicians say that such switching back and forth isn't a problem as long as it doesn't inhibit a child's ability to complete developmentally appropriate tasks.

Hand-Eye Coordination

Hand-eye coordination continues to improve among children in this age group, giving them the ability to zero in on small objects and pick them up for examination. Shortly after their first birthdays, children

Children Around the World

Dexterity Among the Navajos

At first, researchers were puzzled when they discovered that many Navajo children's fine motor skills were better developed than those of their peers. The Navajo children also displayed above average ability in visual perception. Then the researchers learned that many Navajo children are taught traditional handicrafts—painting, weaving, and working with silver—at a young age. The researchers realized that the Navajo children had refined their small motor skills by practicing these traditional crafts, many of which use intricate patterns that are kept in the mind and never written down.

Investigating Culture

1. Other studies found that Navajo children also excelled at spelling. Why do you think this is?
2. How would you recommend teachers present new information to Navajo children, based on what you have learned about them?

start picking up very small objects between their thumb and forefinger. At first, this is difficult. With practice, however, their skill improves, and by about eighteen months of age, children have mastered it. This milestone in hand-eye coordination and fine motor skills gives them greater ability in manipulating objects, poking fingers in holes, opening boxes, and playing with balls. It also aids them in building structures, sorting beads, and coloring with crayons. By their second birthdays, children's coordination and strength has increased so much that they can turn door-knobs and pick up small objects on the ground without losing their balance. See Fig. 10-6.

Fig. 10-6 Improved hand-eye coordination and fine motor skills give a child a greater ability to explore. What might this mean to parents and caregivers?

Sensory Integration

 As children grow, their senses develop, giving them greater awareness of their environment. Normally, the brain combines information taken in through the various senses to make a single whole picture of where they are and what is happening. This is called **sensory integration**. However, some children are unable to normally process all the information their senses take in. These children are said to have *sensory dysfunction*. They may react more strongly to some types of stimulation, such as noises or lights, and less strongly to other types. When this happens, a child may have learning and behavioral problems.

SECTION 10-1 Review and Activities

Reviewing the Section

1. Explain the difference in growth between the ages of one and three and growth during the first year of life.
2. Describe how a one-year-old stands and how a three-year-old stands.
3. Imagine that a parent said, "I can give my child whatever she wants to eat while she's little. Her baby teeth are going to fall out anyway." Explain what is wrong with this reasoning.
4. What is meant by *developmentally appropriate*?
5. Compare gross and fine motor skills. Give an example of each type of skill that a two-year-old could do.
6. What is *dexterity*?

Observing and Interacting

Watch a group of toddlers playing and notice the skills they are using. Try to gauge their ages by what they are doing.

Caring for Children from One to Three

By their first birthdays, children are already beginning to do things for themselves. Their skills and sense of self-care grow through practice. By age three, children can be responsible for some of their own needs. A typical three-year-old might dress, eat, brush teeth, and use the toilet independently.

Objectives

- Explain why children may feel fearful at night and how to comfort them.
- Plan nutritious meals and snacks for children.
- Identify ways to help children learn and practice good hygiene.
- Summarize the key considerations for choosing clothing for children.
- Describe how to protect children against hazards in the home.

Key Terms

night terrors
hygiene
sphincter muscles
synthetic fibers
flame-resistant

Sleeping

Changes in their sleeping needs and patterns are common for children at this age. Sleeping habits often change around a child's second birthday. Children usually require less sleep than before, and they may not fall asleep as easily. It's important for parents to make sure their children still get enough rest.

Sleep Patterns

Most one-year-olds continue the pattern of sleeping six or more hours at night. They typically take naps of several hours during the day. As they get older, daytime naps become shorter. The length of time they sleep at night slowly increases. By the age of two, most children no longer take a morning nap, while afternoon naps may continue for several years. In total, two- and three-year-olds sleep from about 10 to 14 hours a day.

Fears or anxiety about separation from parents can make falling asleep difficult for toddlers and preschoolers. Some may call parents back into their rooms again and again, asking for a drink of water, another story, or one more trip to the bathroom. What they usually want, however, is just comfort and reassurance.

Fig. 10-7 **Most children don't like to be rushed from one activity to the next. Reading can be a part of a child's bedtime routine to help transition from the day.**

Children feel more comfortable when their lives are predictable. A nightly routine such as brushing teeth, reading stories, singing, and choosing a soft toy to take to bed can help prepare children for sleep. When the routine is broken because of a late bedtime or a lost toy, it's more difficult for a child to fall asleep. It's common for children to use self-comforting techniques at bedtime, such as thumb sucking or cuddling a favorite blanket. See Fig. 10-7.

Sleep Disturbances

Sometimes the quantity or quality of a child's sleep is disrupted. When this happens, they may be tired and irritable the next day.

It's not unusual for toddlers to wake up briefly when sleeping. Some fall back to sleep, but others may begin to cry or try to get a caregiver's attention. The best response depends on the problem. For example, a trip to the bathroom may be needed.

Fear of the dark is common at ages two and three and may prevent a child from falling asleep. Calmly discussing fears or a nightlight may help. Never tease children about fears.

Nightmares and night terrors sometimes disrupt children's sleep. **Night terrors** are a type of sleep disturbance that occurs during the first few hours of sleep, when children are sleeping deeply. Children who aren't fully awake may sit up with their eyes open and scream. Such children are often very upset but unable to explain what's wrong. By morning, the child usually remembers nothing about the incident. In general, night terrors are not a cause for alarm. Children who experience them need reassurance.

Manage Transitions in a Child's Routine

Toddlers and preschoolers find a sense of security in a predictable routine. When their routine is changed, some become anxious. Transitions from one activity to the next are also difficult for some children this age. They may fuss when they must stop what they are doing or cry upon waking or going to sleep. The following tips can help those who care for children manage changes in a child's routine and smooth transitions from one activity to the next:

- **Make time for transitions.** Warn children ahead of time of changes in activities. For example, you might let a child know it will be time to leave for the store in five minutes. Such advance notice helps give children a sense of control and security, although it doesn't guarantee a smooth transition every time.

- **Familiarize children with the unfamiliar.** Give them time to check out new places and people. For example, if a child is going to a new preschool, visiting ahead of time gives the child a chance to explore the place and meet the people.

- **Be as clear and consistent as possible.** When transitioning from one activity to another with children, make sure the child knows what is expected. When the rules are clear and caregivers respond to them consistently, children will find security in the predictability of adults' reactions.

YOUR TURN

Routines. Think about how parents have to schedule their time in order to provide their children with predictable routines. How would you help the child make the transition from being awake to going to sleep?

Jamie, age two and one-half, kept climbing out of his crib even when he was tired. His parents were concerned that he could hurt himself, and they decided that it was time to get Jamie a bed.

On an afternoon visit to his grandmother's, Jamie napped in a bed for the first time. His grandmother let him choose a blanket to use and bring his favorite stuffed animal. She read a story to him, and Jamie fell asleep.

Back at home, Jamie's parents asked him about his visit to Grandma's house. He proudly talked about sleeping in the big bed. Jamie's mother said she wanted to get him a big bed, too. Jamie looked a little uncertain, but his mother quickly said she would need his help picking out sheets and a blanket to go with the bed, and he looked excited.

The new bed soon arrived. It had included a rail on one side to help prevent falls. Jamie talked about how big he was now. He climbed up on the bed and played on it for some time, getting on and off to bring up some of his favorite toys.

▶▶**PERSONAL APPLICATION**

1. How does it feel when you sleep in a bed different from your own?
2. Aside from getting a special toddler bed with a rail, how might you keep a child from getting hurt by falling out of bed?

Nightmares are frightening dreams that often seem real. Some children have difficulty separating dreams from reality. Experts recommend responding immediately with words of comfort to a child who has had a nightmare.

Nightmares may occur because of stress or significant changes in a child's life, such as starting preschool. Sometimes reassurance and reduction of pressure can help relieve a child's anxiety. Avoiding exposure to frightening images on television may also help.

Nutritional Needs and Eating

The habits and attitudes toward food that children learn at this stage will influence their eating habits throughout life. That's why it's vital to establish good eating habits early in life. Teaching good habits involves helping children learn to enjoy nutritious foods and to take appropriate portions of food.

Meals sometimes become a battle of wills between parents and young children. Experts recommend offering children a variety of healthy foods at mealtime and letting them choose what to eat. Like adults, children develop likes and dislikes. Children accept and try new foods more easily if they aren't pressured to try them.

Children this age like consistency at mealtimes. They may insist that a sandwich be cut just the right way or may become upset if they don't get lunch on a certain plate or a drink in a favorite cup.

Fig. 10-8 **It may be messy at first, but a child shows growing independence by drinking from a cup.**

Self-feeding

Self-feeding depends on a child's fine motor skills, and it also helps refine them.

- **One-year-olds.** Children at this age eat a variety of foods. Finger foods, such as slices of banana, are popular. They should avoid hard foods like raw carrots that can cause choking. (See page 327 for types of finger foods.) Using a spoon to eat usually begins before the age of one. Most children are about 18 months old before they can use a spoon with little spilling. When children first start drinking from a cup, a training cup is a good choice. This cup's handles, lid, spout, and weighted bottom minimize spills. By their second birthday, most children drink from a cup fairly well. See Fig. 10-8.

- **Two-year-olds.** Children in this age group can usually feed themselves and learn to use a fork, but they often take a long time to eat. They are still improving their fine motor skills as well as getting nutrition. At this age, a child should eat with the rest of the family.

- **Three-year-olds.** By age three, most children are quite skillful using a spoon and fork. Three-year-olds have a full set of primary teeth, so chewing foods isn't a problem. Meats and other tough foods should be cut into small pieces.

Fig. 10-9

Serving Sizes for Children Two and Three

Milk Group

Milk, yogurt—½ cup
Frozen yogurt, pudding—
   ¼ to ½ cup
Cheese, ½ to 1 oz.

Grain Group

Whole-grain bread—¼ to ½ slice
Ready-to-eat cereal—¼ to ⅓ cup
Spaghetti, rice, macaroni—¼ to ⅓ cup
Crackers—2 to 3
Hamburger bun—¼ to ½

Meat and Beans Group

Egg—1
   Chicken, hamburger,
      fish—1–2 oz.
      Baked beans—¼ cup
      Peanut butter—1–2 Tbsp.

Fruit Group

Apple, banana—¼ to ½
Fruit juice—⅓ cup
Grapes, strawberries,
   peaches—¼ cup

Vegetable Group

Carrots—¼ to ½
Corn, green beans,
   peas—¼ cup

Fig. 10-10 **Both adults and children find meals more appealing if there is variety with colors, textures, and shapes of foods on the plate.** What kinds of foods would be in a nutritious meal that is appealing?

Changes in Nutritional Needs

Since they are growing less rapidly than in their first year of life, children ages one to three don't eat as much. Because their stomachs are still small, most need food every three or four hours. However, the amount that children eat may vary greatly from day to day, depending on appetite and level of activity. Nutritious snacks, such as fresh fruit, can help bridge the gap between meals.

Nutritious Foods

An important means of establishing good health in children is to provide them with a variety of beneficial foods. Offer nutritious foods at both mealtimes and snack times, and avoid foods high in sugar, salt, and fat. Sticky foods such as raisins may cause tooth decay. Read the nutrition labels and ingredient lists on frozen, canned, and dried foods for help in making nutritious choices.

The *Guidelines for Healthy Eating* on page 154 are helpful for planning meals and snacks for children, as well as adults. The USDA's My Pyramid Plan recommends how much food children ages two and older should consume from each food group daily, depending upon their activity levels. Because their stomachs are smaller, young children need smaller servings, or portions, when they eat. Figure 10-9 on page 326 gives examples of a child-size serving for two- and three-year-olds in each food group. Children four and older need larger servings.

Meal Appeal

One way to promote interest in nutritious foods is to try to make meals appealing for children. Think about the following elements as you plan their meals. See Fig. 10-10.

- **Color.** Think about how dull a meal of fish, applesauce, milk, and vanilla pudding looks. Varying foods can add more color. Fresh fruits and vegetables are brightly colored and nutritious.

- **Texture.** Foods with different textures add variety to a meal. Try adding crackers, chewy cheese, or juicy grapes (be sure to cut them up) to a child's plate to provide different textures.

- **Shape.** Foods with a variety of shapes also add appeal. Your goal doesn't have to be to make a child's plate look like a circus, but you might cut sandwiches into rectangles or triangles or use large cookie cutters. Consider adding cucumber "cookies," zucchini sticks, or orange wedges to a plate. Help children identify the shapes.

- **Temperature.** Try serving both hot and cold foods at a meal, but always check the temperature of all hot foods before serving them. If a food has been cooked or warmed in the microwave, stir it thoroughly to even out the temperature. "Hot spots" from foods warmed in a microwave can burn a child's mouth.

- **Ease of eating.** Certain foods are easier than others for young children to eat. Ground beef, for example, is easier to chew and swallow than a pork chop. Many children like spaghetti, but they can handle it more easily when the strands are cut into short pieces.

Teaching Children Good Nutrition

Parents and other caregivers are role models for children when it comes to food choices and eating habits. Sharing nutritious meals with children, trying new foods together, and letting them help in the kitchen all promote good eating habits.

In addition to modeling good behavior, parents and other caregivers can encourage children to eat only when hungry and to eat slowly. They should keep in mind not to use food as a reward for behavior and not to withhold food as a punishment. Children can also be encouraged to drink water when thirsty rather than milk or sugary drinks. If parents have nutritional concerns, they should consult a physician. See Fig. 10-11.

Hygiene

Children in this age span also need to learn the basics of good **hygiene**—personal care and

Fig. 10-11 **Water is a good alternative to sugary juices.** Why do children need to drink water daily?

cleanliness. These range from using a tissue for a runny nose to bathing and effective hand washing. Also most children learn to use the toilet during this time.

Washing and Bathing

A daily bath helps children develop good hygiene skills. For most families, evening baths are the most practical. They can become an enjoyable part of the bedtime routine. Between the ages of one and three, many children enjoy splashing in the tub. Bath toys can add to the fun. Even simple plastic containers and measuring cups can become playthings at bath time.

Children often assert their independence at bath time. One-year-olds often want to wash themselves. At first, this means merely rubbing the washcloth over the face and stomach. By age two, however, most children can wash, rinse, and dry themselves fairly well, except for hard-to-reach places like the back. By age three, children can wash by themselves, with supervision.

Bathtub safety is very important. A child can drown in as little as 1 inch of water, so never leave a young child alone in the bath, not even for a minute. To prevent falls, use rough, no-slip stickers or a rubber mat on the bottom of the tub. See Fig. 10-12.

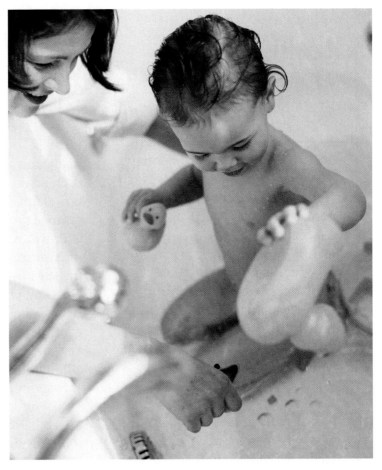

Fig. 10-12 **Bath time offers a child entertainment as well as an opportunity to get clean.** What should you do if the phone rings while you are bathing a child?

Caring for the Teeth

Experts recommend teaching good dental hygiene practices early. At age one, most children have eight teeth. These need to be brushed with a small soft toothbrush daily. By age two, children can begin practicing brushing their own teeth. Their first attempts to brush won't be very successful, but they will improve with encouragement and practice. For the most effective results, caregivers need to do most of the brushing for a toddler. Even three-year-olds may need adult help with this task. Children

Brushing Teeth

Tooth decay occurs faster in children than in adults. It's important to clean a child's teeth in the first few years of life. Young children don't have the ability to brush teeth effectively, but they need to learn. The key to getting a child to brush is to make it fun. Use only a pea-sized amount of mild-flavored toothpaste on the toothbrush. Brush gently and for at least one minute. Make sure the child spits out the toothpaste when finished instead of swallowing it. Swallowing toothpaste can lead to a condition called fluorosis, in which spots appear on the teeth. Helping a child learn to brush well and regularly can preserve a smile for a lifetime.

should brush their teeth at least twice a day with fluoride toothpaste to fight cavities.

Regular checkups at the dentist are an important part of good dental care. Dentists suggest that eighteen months is a good age for the first checkup. Preschoolers should visit the dentist every six months.

Toilet Teaching

Most children begin to learn to use the toilet sometime between their second and third birthdays. Some parents feel pressured by family or child care needs to launch into a training program before the age of two. Some experts say that when parents teach toileting too early, the process tends to take longer.

Readiness

To successfully learn toileting, a child must be both physically and emotionally ready. Physical readiness means that children are able to control their bladder and bowel functions. They must also be able to remove their clothes easily.

Bowel control involves the use of the **sphincter muscles** (SFINGK-tur), the muscles that help regulate elimination. Typically, children reach this level of maturity at about eighteen months of age. To control the bladder and bowel, a child must also be able to recognize the signals that elimination is necessary.

Emotional readiness means that the child shows an interest in wanting to be grown up and use the toilet. Starting to teach toileting during a calm period in family life increases the likelihood that it will go smoothly.

During Toilet Teaching

Caregivers' attitudes toward toilet teaching are very important. Calm encouragement is more effective than rules and punishment, and it helps build self-esteem. Remember that the child who is physically and emotionally ready for toilet learning genuinely wants to succeed. Even after a child is toilet trained, some "accidents" should be expected.

When children begin to use the toilet, they may prefer to use a child seat on the toilet or a potty chair. Using a child seat on the toilet eliminates the need for adjustments later. On the other hand, using a potty chair allows the young child more independence than the seat that fits the toilet. See Fig. 10-13.

Flushing toilets frighten some children. Unless the child is particularly interested in flushing, it may be better to flush the toilet after the child has left the bathroom.

Bowel training usually comes before bladder training. Most children are ready when they show awareness that a bowel movement is imminent. When caregivers see this awareness in the child's facial expressions or gestures, they should suggest that the child try sitting on the toilet seat or potty chair. They should be available and encouraging. If caregivers are too forceful or demanding, toilet learning will become more difficult.

Bladder training typically follows bowel training by several months, although some children learn both at the same time. Many young children are encouraged in toileting when they are given cloth or disposable *training pants*—heavy, absorbent underpants—in place of diapers. Wearing training pants makes it possible for a young child to use a toilet or potty chair independently. Most children also recognize that wearing underpants instead of diapers is a sign of maturity.

Dressing

Young children are eager to learn how to dress themselves and soon enjoy undressing as well. It's important to encourage self-dressing whenever a child begins to show interest. Dressing involves a number of gross and fine motor skills that must be learned one step at a time. These skills require frequent practice. Caregivers need to be patient and encouraging.

A child usually starts trying to help with dressing around the age of thirteen or fourteen months, perhaps by holding out an arm for the sleeve of a shirt. Next, the toddler may learn to push an arm through a sleeve. By two years of age, the child can pull up

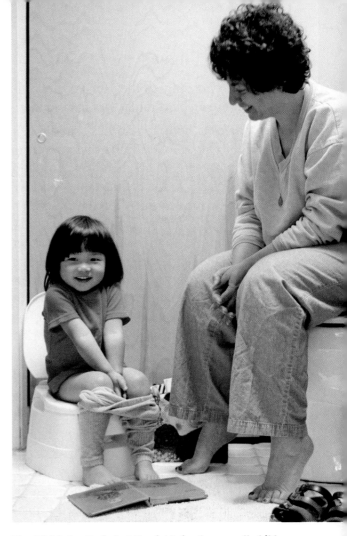

Fig. 10-13 **A potty is just the right size for a small child and can generally be used without assistance.** How can a potty help with toilet teaching?

pants, but putting on shirts continues to be difficult. Children may end up with their garments inside out or backwards. By age three, children can dress independently but require help with difficult fasteners like buttons and shoelaces. They may also put shoes on the wrong feet at this age.

With self-dressing, a child learns independence and responsibility, in turn boosting self-esteem. Caregivers can encourage self-dressing by choosing clothes that are easy to put on and take off. Shirts with loose necks and pants with elastic waists are easiest for young children to handle.

Choosing Clothes

When choosing clothes for young children, there are several factors to consider:

- **Comfort.** Look for clothes that allow a child to move freely. Knits that stretch as a child moves are good choices. Soft and sturdy fabrics are comfortable. Stiff or scratchy fabrics can bother children's skin. Size is an important factor in comfort. Clothes that are too small restrict movement, and clothes that are too large can get in the way. Look for clothes that are large enough to allow the child to move comfortably. Of course, all clothes labeled with the same size may not fit the same way. See Fig. 10-14.

- **Fabric.** Cotton is a comfortable natural fiber often used in children's clothing. It absorbs moisture, wears well, and washes well, though it may shrink. **Synthetic fibers** are those made from chemicals rather than natural sources. Fabrics made from synthetic fibers such as polyester and acrylic are durable, wrinkle resistant, and quick-drying. Unlike cotton, most synthetic fibers don't absorb moisture well and hold heat and perspiration against the body. This characteristic makes them a good choice for clothes that will be worn in cool weather. Often natural and synthetic fibers are blended to take advantage of the benefits of each. By law, all clothing must have a label that identifies the fibers used. Clothing labels also state how to care for each garment. Federal law requires that the fabric used in children's sleepwear be **flame-resistant**. This means that the fabric can still catch on fire, but will not burn as quickly as other fabrics.

- **Durability.** Children's clothes must withstand hard wear and repeated washings. Their durability is influenced by the quality of the fabric and the construction of the clothing. When you check the construction of the clothes, look for close, even stitching with strong thread. The stitching should be reinforced at points of strain, and all fasteners and trims should be firmly attached. Some pants have the knees reinforced with extra fabric which also helps improve durability.

- **Economy.** Young children grow rapidly and outgrow their clothes quickly. Many parents exchange outgrown clothes with other families in order to cut costs. Others find good used clothing at yard sales, secondhand stores, and thrift shops.

Fig. 10-14 **Young children don't care about designer labels. They like to be comfortable.**

Fig. 10-15 **Most children enjoy choosing new clothes.** What should parents look for on clothing labels?

When you shop for clothing, choose clothes that allow for growth. Look for deep hems or cuffs that can be let down. Check that the straps on overalls or jumpers are long enough to allow the buttons to be moved. Consider buying pants that are a size larger but will fit when you roll up the pant legs.

Whenever possible, let children help choose their own clothes. They usually love bright colors and tend to choose their clothes more by color than for any other reasons. Children also enjoy clothes printed with pictures of animals, toys, or familiar story characters. See Fig. 10-15.

Health, Illness, and Safety

Keeping a child healthy and safe is a top priority for parents and other caregivers. Doing so requires both knowing how to prevent problems and dealing with them when they do occur. Children ages one to three are particularly at risk for accidents. They are old enough to be mobile, but they are too young to understand the many hazards.

Checkups

Most children have a checkup at 12 months. The physician checks the child's growth and development. The doctor may

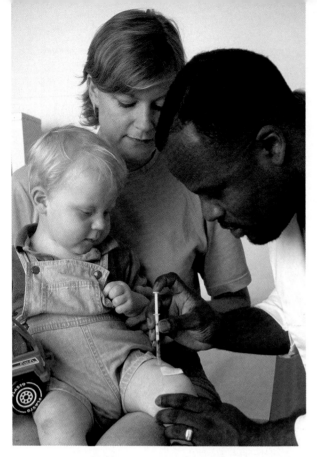

Fig. 10-16 **Regular checkups are important for the lifelong health of a child.** At what ages should children have checkups?

so that if a child is exposed to a certain disease, he or she can more easily fight infection. Children at this age are more prone to diseases since they spread easily in child care centers and preschools.

Some people are concerned about the safety of vaccines, but severe complications from vaccines are *very* rare. State law requires children to receive certain vaccinations before entering school, and physicians recommend that children receive most of their immunizations by age two. To find out what types of vaccines children need and when they need them, refer to the recommended schedule of immunizations in Chapter 20.

Illnesses

It's not uncommon for children between the ages of one and three to get sick. Some common illnesses are respiratory and ear infections. These illnesses are often mild and usually require no medical intervention, although chronic ear infections do require attention. Other illnesses, such as the flu, can cause more severe problems. They are preventable with vaccinations.

Environmental Influences on Health

Pollutants can be found in the home and outside it. One of the chief indoor pollutants is environmental tobacco smoke (ETS), also known as secondhand smoke. This smoke comes from burning cigarettes. Researchers have shown that environmental tobacco smoke puts children at increased risk for respiratory infections, middle ear infections, and problems with asthma. Adults can avoid these increased risks for health problems by keeping children away from smokers and smoky areas.

ask about the child's language ability, interest in learning and practicing new skills, and behavior. Additional checkups should be scheduled at 15, 18, and 24 months. These checkups will include growth measurements and routine examination of the eyes, ears, teeth, genitals, and other body parts. See Fig. 10-16.

Immunizations

Immunizations protect children from a particular disease, usually by giving a child a vaccine. When a child is given a vaccine, a small amount of disease-carrying germs is introduced to the body on purpose so that the body can build resistance to that disease. Vaccines bolster the immune system

Childproof a Home

Young children love to explore the world around them but the average home contains a variety of conditions that can be hazardous. To ensure children's safety while they explore, caregivers must childproof their homes.

Preventing Falls

- Are the floors and stairs clear of clutter? Make sure floors are clear and dry to avoid falls.
- Use safety gates on stairways until children learn to go up and down stairs safely.
- Check that open windows have screens with secure locks. Install window safety latches.
- Remove furniture that might tip.

Preventing Burns

- Teach children not to touch a range. Turn pot handles toward the range's center.
- Check the temperature of water from the faucet. Lower the water heater setting if it exceeds 120°F to 130°F (49° to 54°C).
- Place safety caps on unused electrical outlets.
- Keep toasters, irons, and other small appliances unplugged.

Other Safety Hazards

- Store cleaning supplies, paints, insecticides, and medicines in locked containers.
- Use window blinds with safety features. Keep blind cords away from children.
- Keep knives, razors, scissors, and matches away from children.
- Inspect toys and other play equipment regularly for broken parts or sharp edges.

YOUR TURN

Safety. What special safety concerns might you find in a bathroom? Make a list of solutions.

Fig. 10-17 **Lead can be found in old paint chips.** Why is lead even more harmful to children than adults?

Lead is another harmful substance that's found both inside and outside older homes, particularly in paint. Caregivers must prevent children from putting bits of dried paint in their mouths. Children under the age of six are vulnerable to high levels of lead because their brain and central nervous system are still forming. Exposure to lead affects children in many ways, from delayed growth and hearing loss to irritability and hyperactivity. See Fig. 10-17.

Safety

Children from one to three are interested in exploring their environment. They open drawers and cabinets, turn knobs, and put objects in their mouth. As they try to learn about their world, their probing and curiosity can often put them in danger's path. Rather than trying to curb a child's curious nature, it's better to childproof the home and make it as safe as possible for the child.

The following tips are a few ways a caregiver can help provide a safer environment for children:

- **Choking hazards.** To help prevent choking, make sure that children stay seated while eating. Parents and other caregivers should encourage children to take small bites of food during meals, to chew all food thoroughly, and to swallow before taking another bite.

- **Choosing safe toys.** Take time to select toys that are age appropriate. Small toys or toys with small, removable parts are choking hazards.

- **Handling poisons in the home.** Avoid using strong household cleaning products. Keep all poisonous substances and medications locked up. Learn what to do in case a child ingests a poisonous substance. Keep the phone numbers of the poison control center and your local hospital handy. See the chart in Chapter 20 for a list of common household poisons.

- **In case of fire and burns.** Keep children away from candles, fireplaces, matches, and lighters. Teach children the stop, drop, and roll technique for extinguishing fire on their clothes or in their hair. If a burn looks more serious than a slight reddening of the skin, consult a doctor immediately.

Safety Concerns, Ages One to Three

Water Safety

This is crucial at any age, but it is especially important for children ages one to three. Drowning is one of the leading causes of death for toddlers. Drowning can happen very quickly, in shallow water, bathtubs, swimming pools, backyard ponds, hot tubs, and even buckets of water and sinks. Toddlers ages one to three are at the highest risk because they are curious about their surroundings and don't understand the danger of water.

To reduce a child's risk of drowning:

- Never leave a child unattended in a bathtub or swimming pool.

- Empty bath water immediately.

- A child should always wear water wings or some other flotation device when in or around water other than a bathtub.

- If you have a pool, install fencing at least five feet high on all sides of the pool, as well as a gate that is a self-closing/self-latching gate. Don't leave anything close to the fence that would allow the child to climb over it.

- Teach a child who is old enough to swim.

Climbing

Another important safety concern for children ages one to three is climbing. Toddlers love to explore their environment by climbing stairs, climbing on furniture, and climbing on play equipment. Use safety gates near stairs so that children cannot go up or down without adult supervision. Bolt heavy bookcases to the wall to avoid tipping if a child tries to climb them. Insist that children sit instead of stand on furniture.

Check-Up

Imagine that you are a caregiver and you have a pool. What precautions would you take to keep children safe?

Fig. 10-18 **Children should always be safely buckled up in car seats when on the road.** What could happen to a child not secured in a car seat during an accident?

- **Motor vehicle safety.** Children must ride in a car seat that faces forward and is secured with seatbelts in the back seat of a vehicle. Always make sure children are wearing seatbelts while the vehicle is in motion. See Fig. 10-18.

- **Avoiding sunburn.** Have children wear protective hats and apply sunscreen to their skin. Reapply sunscreen every few hours, or more frequently.

- **Pet protection.** Young children should not be left alone with a dog or a cat because they are not mature enough to know how to behave with animals. Teach children to wash their hands after handling an animal.

Above all, always keep a watchful eye on young children. Accidents can occur in a matter of seconds.

SECTION 10-2 Review and Activities

Check Your Understanding

1. Compare the sleep needs of one-year-olds and three-year-olds.
2. What are *night terrors*? How should caregivers respond to them?
3. What is the most important consideration in preparing meals and snacks for young children?
4. List three ways children can develop good hygiene skills. How can parents encourage good hygiene with their children?
5. Explain why it is best to let a child help with dressing at an early age.
6. What characteristics would you look for when choosing an outfit for a young child to wear?
7. Imagine you are babysitting a two-year-old child. What can you do to prevent safety hazards such as choking or sunburn? What other safety hazards would you need to look out for?

Observing and Interacting

Go to the supermarket and list the items that you would buy to feed a two-year-old. Base your list on a plan for one day of healthy meals and snacks, taking into account color, shape, and other ways to add appeal. Share your plan with the class.

Career Opportunities

Child Life Specialist

Child life specialists are members of pediatric health care teams who focus on the emotional and social aspects of the lives of children who are sick. They help children make sense of what is happening in the hospital, ease anxiety, and provide emotional support to patients and families.

▶ Job Responsibilities

Child life specialists explain medical procedures in ways that make children feel safe. They offer children age-appropriate toys and teach them how to relax. Child life specialists also provide information to parents and siblings. They plan and host visits from musicians, clowns, and animals while children recuperate.

▶ Work Environment

Most child life specialists work in emergency rooms, surgical departments, and neonatal or pediatric intensive care units in children's hospitals.

▶ Education and Training

Child life specialists earn bachelor's degrees, usually in psychology or education. Their classes include human growth and development, education, and counseling. In addition to their studies, they must complete an internship, gain work experience, and pass an exam to become certified.

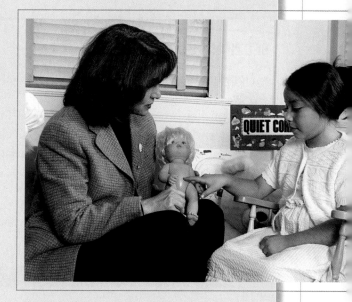

▶ Skills and Aptitudes

- Energy and stamina
- Ability to communicate clearly
- Resourcefulness
- Ability to relate to children
- Emotional stability
- Understanding of family dynamics

WORKPLACE CONNECTION

1. **Thinking Skills.** How would being a child care worker help you get a job as a child life specialist?

2. **Resource Skills.** If you interviewed a child life specialist, what would you ask?

SECTION SUMMARIES

- Heredity and environment play key roles in child development, affecting body size, eye color, and disease risk. (10-1)
- A poor diet can cause tooth decay. (10-1)
- Gross and fine motor skills improve as children get older. (10-1)
- Some toddlers experience sleep disturbances. (10-2)
- Children should be given nutritious foods and encouraged to feed themselves. (10-2)
- Toilet teaching shouldn't be attempted before a child is ready. (10-2)
- Parents should provide comfortable clothes and a daily bath. (10-2)
- Children at this stage need careful supervision. (10-2)

REVIEWING THE CHAPTER

1. What is the difference between a *toddler* and a *preschooler*? (10-1)
2. Describe how diet affects the health of teeth. (10-1)
3. What is meant by *developmentally appropriate*? Give at least three examples. (10-1)
4. Explain why physical and emotional factors play a role in toileting readiness. (10-1)
5. What is the difference between *night terrors* and nightmares? (10-2)
6. How does self-feeding differ for a one-year-old and a three-year-old? (10-2)
7. Point out problems with using food as a reward for good behavior. (10-2)
8. Why do young children need to eat more often than adults but eat smaller amounts at a time? (10-2)
9. How can parents and other caregivers keep children safe? List at least six ways. (10-2)

THINKING CRITICALLY

1. **Making Inferences.** What might a parent do if a child hasn't mastered large motor skills by the average ages listed in the chapter?
2. **Analyzing the Text.** The chapter notes that self-feeding both depends on and helps improve children's fine motor skills. Explain why this is true.

MAKING CONNECTIONS

1. **Writing.** Make a list of dos and don'ts for parents and caregivers to use for good dental health for their children.
2. **Math.** Research what clothes a two-year-old would need. Estimate their cost. Describe three ways that parents could save money on toddler clothes.

APPLYING YOUR LEARNING

1. **Appropriate Toys.** Using catalog photos, create a poster of toys that are developmentally appropriate for ages one to three. Put stars next to toys that help dexterity.
2. **Charting Information.** Make a chart of children's ages and the average fine and gross motor skills they develop.
3. **Interpersonal Skills.** Suppose a toddler is afraid of the dark. What might you suggest to help the child fall asleep more easily?

Learning from Research

1. Choose one of the following research claims to investigate.
2. How is this research finding useful to parents involved in toilet teaching?
3. Summarize what you've learned about how the factor you chose affects toilet teaching.

Toilet Teaching and Age. According to research, children who start toilet training at a younger age take longer to achieve daytime dryness than children who start later. This study involved children 18 months of age or older, so the results may not be due to a lack of emotional or physical readiness. Investigate the possible reasons for this finding.

Toilet Teaching and Child Care. Researchers have found that children who are in daycare centers or with caregivers outside the home complete toilet training at the same rate as other children. What other factors can affect the rate of toilet training?

Toilet Teaching and Gender. Research suggests that boys and girls show the initial signs of readiness for toilet teaching at about the same time. However, girls tend to complete toilet training sooner than boys do. According to researchers, what might be some reasons for this finding?

Emotional and Social Development from One to Three

Thoughtful Reading:

As you read this chapter:
- Identify three phrases that remind you of background knowledge.
- Reread the passages.
- Write three "I connect to ___?___ on page _____" statements about what you read.

Section 11-1
Emotional Development from One to Three

Section 11-2
Social Development from One to Three

Emotional Development from One to Three

Children undergo many emotional changes at the ages of one, two, and three. They develop new emotions, such as jealousy, that they had not felt before. At the beginning of this period, children display all their emotions very clearly. But by the end of their third year, they are learning to both control their emotions and express them in more socially acceptable ways. A child's emotional development depends upon brain development and personal experiences.

Objectives

- Describe common emotions and patterns of emotional development from ages one to three.
- Analyze how individual differences affect emotional development.
- Explain how self-concept develops.
- Assess the importance of sleep in emotional development.

Key Terms

self-centered
negativism
temper tantrums
phobias
separation anxiety
sibling rivalry
empathy
self-concept
sleep-deprived
REM sleep
NREM sleep

General Emotional Patterns

Emotional development tends to go in cycles all throughout childhood. The cycles are especially pronounced in children ages one through three years. They have periods of frustration and rebellion, but they also have periods of happiness, calmness, and stability. Negative periods tend to alternate with positive periods, and they are generally related to the age of the child.

Of course, each child is an individual. Claire may go through a negative period at eighteen months, while Jamal may not experience this until age two. Matthew may not seem to go through it at all. Generally, though, children can be expected to go through certain distinct emotional phases at certain ages.

Eighteen Months

By the age of eighteen months, children have become **self-centered**, meaning that they think about their own needs and wants, not those of others. This is not surprising, because during infancy caregivers promptly meet the child's needs and desires. This is appropriate for infants. By eighteen months, however, caregivers begin to teach the child that some desires will not be met immediately—and others never will be met. This is a difficult lesson for the eighteen-month-old to begin learning.

Spoken instructions are not always successful with children of this age. The young toddler is likely to do the opposite of what is requested. At this age, the child's favorite response to everything is "No." In part, this negative word allows the child to feel some control over his or her world.

Negativism, or doing the opposite of what others want, is normal for a young toddler. See Fig. 11-1. It has a number of causes:

- **The desire for independence.** Saying "no" is a way of saying, "Let me decide for myself." The child may even say "no" to things he or she would really like to do—just for the chance to make the decision!

- **Frustration.** Toddlers want to do more than their bodies are yet able to accomplish. They don't have the language skills yet to adequately express their feelings. The frustration that results is often expressed in a simple and emphatic "No!"

- **The child's realization of being a separate person.** This idea is both exciting and frightening. The child welcomes the power and independence of being a separate person but at times still wants a tight bond with a primary caregiver.

This negativism can produce a battle of wills between child and parent. Some strategies can help prevent clashes. One is to eliminate as many restrictions as possible. For example, rather than asking an eighteen-month-old not to touch certain objects, put them away. As the child gets older, they can be put back in place.

Fig. 11-1 **Toddlers go through negative periods as well as positive ones.** What are some causes of negativism?

Fig. 11-2 **Sometimes the "terrible twos" seems to be an unfair label placed on toddlers.**

Positive guidance can help handle a child who is negative:

- **Give choices.** Instead of saying "Pick up your books and toys," ask, "Which will you pick up first—the books or the toys?" Having choices allows the child to exercise control. Limit choices to two alternatives, however. Toddlers can't think about three or four things at a time.

- **Redirect the child.** If possible, distract the child's attention from the issue that is causing the negative response. You may be able to return to it later when the child is calmer.

- **Encourage talking.** You can help children learn to use words to communicate how they feel. Being able to talk will help both you and the child understand and deal with those feelings. Asking "What's wrong, Susie?" or "Don't you like that?" encourages children to share what they are feeling.

Around eighteen months, many children start to have **temper tantrums**. In tantrums, children release anger or frustration by screaming, crying, kicking, pounding, and sometimes holding their breath. These tantrums may occur until age three or four. Even seemingly minor frustrations can sometimes cause temper tantrums. Try to help the child find less explosive ways of expressing these feelings. For ways to calm a toddler who is having a temper tantrum, see page 374.

Two Years

Emotionally, two-year-olds are less at odds with the world than children who are eighteen months old. Their speech and motor skills have improved, relieving some sources of frustration. A two-year-old also understands more and is able to wait longer for various needs to be met. See Fig. 11-2.

At age two, a child expresses love and affection freely and seeks approval and praise. Though the child still has some emotional outbursts, they are fewer and less intense. Two-year-olds are easier to reason with. They usually get along better with parents and other children because they tend to be more outgoing and friendly, and less self-centered.

Two and One-Half Years

Just as parents and caregivers begin to adjust to a smoother, less intense toddler, the child enters another difficult stage. In fact, this period may seem even more difficult for caregivers than the eighteen-month-old stage. See Fig. 11-3. At two and one-half, toddlers aren't as easily distracted as they were at eighteen months.

Fig. 11-3
An Emotional Roller Coaster

Eighteen Months

The eighteen-month-old is defiant, trying to establish some control over her life.

Two Years

The two-year-old is affectionate—and may often be in the caregiver's way.

Children this age are learning so much that they often feel overwhelmed. Their desires and their ability to comprehend tasks exceed their physical ability to perform. For example, they may want their blocks stacked up in a certain way, but then fail to accomplish this before accidentally knocking the blocks over. They may know what they want to say but can't always make themselves understood.

These situations produce frustrations that may boil over.

At two and one-half, immaturity and a powerful need for independence clash head-on. Their drive for independence causes children to resist pressures to conform. They are sensitive about being bossed, shown, helped, or directed during this stage. They can be stubborn, demanding, and domineering. However,

Two and one-half years

At two and one-half, the child may feel overwhelmed, and frustration becomes anger.

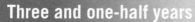

Three Years

The three-year-old is generally a happy child who is eager to help.

Three and one-half years

At three and one-half years, a child is often bothered by fears.

their moods change rapidly, and within a short time they can become lovable and completely charming. Children at this age have a need for consistency. They want the same routines, carried out the same way, every day. Following a routine is their way of coping with a confusing world. A routine helps them build confidence and a feeling of security.

At two and one-half, children feel both independent and dependent. Sometimes they seek help; at other times, they want to do things by themselves. They require love and patience, especially when their behavior is neither lovable nor patient. They need flexible limits rather than hard-and-fast rules.

Fig. 11-4 Children with special needs often begin early intervention programs as soon as a diagnosis is made. Why is this helpful?

Three Years

Three-year-olds generally have sunnier dispositions than two-year-olds. They are more cooperative and are learning to be considerate. As preschoolers, they are more physically capable, and, therefore, less frustrated than two-year-olds.

Three-year-olds become more willing to take directions from others. They will modify their behavior in order to win praise and affection—which they crave. Three-year-olds generally have fewer temper tantrums than younger children.

At three, children like to talk and are much better at it. They talk to their toys, their playmates, themselves, and even to their imaginary companions. They also respond when others talk to them, and they can be reasoned with and controlled by words. See Fig. 11-4.

Three and One-Half Years

The self-confident three-year-old suddenly becomes very insecure at age three and one-half. Parents may feel that the child is going backward rather than forward emotionally.

Fears are common at this age. The child may be afraid of the dark, imaginary lions and tigers, monsters, strangers, or loud noises—even though the child had no such fears before. Emotional tension and insecurity often show up in physical ways, too. Some children may start habits—such as thumb sucking or nail biting—to release tension or provide self-soothing. Others stumble or stutter.

At three and one-half, children try to ensure their own security by controlling their environment. They may issue insistent demands, such as "I want to sit on the floor to eat lunch!" or "Talk to me!"

Fig. 11-5 **All children feel anger, but how they express anger changes as they grow older.** What are the main differences in the ways an eighteen-month-old expresses anger compared to a three-year-old?

Specific Emotions

Even young babies have specific emotions. How children express emotions changes as they get older. Children express their emotions openly until the age of two or three. They begin to learn socially acceptable ways of displaying feelings after the age of three. For example, eighteen-month-old Marta shows anger by kicking and screaming. Jonathan, at age three and one-half, expresses anger through words. The specific emotions children between the ages of eighteen months and three years can feel include anger, fear, jealousy, love, affection, and empathy.

Anger

Anger is often the child's way of reacting to frustration. How children show that anger changes over the years. By the time children are three years old, they are less violent and explosive. They are less likely to hit or kick, and physical attacks give way to name-calling, pouting, or scolding.

The target of a child's anger changes in these years as well. An eighteen-month-old who has a tantrum usually doesn't direct the anger toward a particular person or thing. Beginning at ages two to three, children are more likely to aim their anger at the object or person they hold responsible for their frustration. See Fig. 11-5.

Some common causes of anger are temporary, and almost all children experience this kind of anger from time to time. If a child is sick, tired, uncomfortable, or hungry, frustration is more likely to turn into anger.

Children often feel angry when they can't get their way. Caregivers shouldn't make the child feel guilty about his or her anger—it is a normal emotion.

Sometimes anger gets expressed as aggression. Toddlers can become aggressive over toys. By hitting and otherwise acting aggressively, toddlers are trying out ways of getting along. They have not yet learned how to play with others and fully control powerful feelings, like anger.

Children can learn more acceptable ways of handling anger:

- **Use words.** Rather than hitting or lashing out, children—and adults—should express feelings with words.
- **Speak calmly.** Even when angry, people should speak calmly, not scream or yell.
- **Take deep breaths.** Have a child try to take a few deep breaths.

It may help to have the child rest for a while. Discuss the misbehavior and any punishment after the child has calmed down. Then help the child see what action was misbehavior and explain what the child should have done instead. See Fig. 11-6.

Certain factors can cause a child to be angry more often than normal. Angry outbursts are more frequent in anxious, insecure children. Children whose parents are overly critical or inconsistent become frustrated easily and show anger. A child who hasn't learned self-control also tends to have more frequent outbursts. It is important that the demands placed on children be limited and reasonable while children are learning self-control. Adults also need to respond to a child's anger in a controlled way. Reacting to a child's anger with anger will only make the situation worse and set a poor example.

Fear

Children have particular fears at different ages. While a one-year-old may be frightened of strangers, a three-year-old might be afraid of the dark. Some fears are actually useful since they keep the child from dangerous situations.

Fig. 11-6 Discussing misbehavior and punishment is easier once the child has calmed down.

Fig. 11-7 **It is common for children to feel fear, especially when they will be away from parents and familiar caregivers.** What are some things caregivers can do to help children who feel separation anxiety?

Other fears must be overcome in order for the child to develop in a healthy way. Abnormal fears are called **phobias**. These types of fears are more likely to develop in children who are shy and withdrawn. Parents who suspect a child might be developing a phobia should check with their pediatrician.

Adults sometimes communicate their own fears to children. Even if the fear is never discussed, a parent who runs away or crosses the street whenever a dog comes near may cause a child to become afraid of dogs. Do you have any of the same fears as your parents?

One common fear is **separation anxiety**. This is a fear of being away from parents, familiar caregivers, or the normal environment. Many children continue to experience this fear at this time of life.

Nicole cried when her parents left her with a new babysitter. Jake cried when his father left him on the first day of preschool. See Fig. 11-7.

Separation anxiety can upset parents and other caregivers. They may feel guilty about a child's tears and clinging when they try to leave the child with a babysitter or in a child care situation. The parents need to remind themselves that they have chosen a safe, secure caregiver for the child. Separation anxiety is simply a stage that children will go through—and grow out of. Parents can try to speed that process by spending special time with the child at home. They can also be specific about when they will return. Telling the child, "I'll be back after you've had your nap," gives the child a better sense of what to expect than "I'll be back at three o'clock." Sometimes parents give the child something special, such as a stuffed animal or blanket, for the child to keep nearby for "safe keeping" or comfort until the parent returns.

Many children who feel separation anxiety have trouble going to sleep at night. A bedtime routine and a reminder that a parent is nearby can help lessen these fears.

Here are some other ways to help toddlers deal with their fears:

- Offer support and understanding. Never make children feel ashamed of their fears.
- Encourage children to talk about their fears and listen intently. Often talking about fears diminishes their impact.
- In some cases, it is best to accept the fear and avoid trying to force the child to confront it. Often, it will simply go away on its own.

Health & Safety

Separation Anxiety

Babies can show signs of separation anxiety as early as six or seven months, but the crisis age for most babies is between twelve to eighteen months. Most commonly, separation anxiety strikes when parents leave a child to go to work or run an errand. Babies can also experience separation anxiety at night, safely tucked in their own cribs with Mom and Dad in the next room. It is important to be aware of the problem and help the child overcome it.

- Read books together about a child who experiences fear. Talking about the book may help relieve the child's fears.
- Make unfamiliar situations more secure. Discuss new experiences and events in advance to help the child know what to expect. If possible, accompany the child to new places.
- Teach the child how to control frightening situations. Getting in a swimming pool terrified Jacob, so his aunt showed him how to sit on the side and dangle his feet in the water.

Jealousy

Jealousy is an emotion that usually crops up some time during a child's second year. A twelve-month-old doesn't show any jealousy, but by the age of eighteen months, jealousy becomes very pronounced. It reaches its peak when a child is about three, and then becomes less intense as outside relationships begin to loosen a child's ties to home and parents. Sometimes parents become the target of a child's jealousy. For example, a toddler may resent any show of affection between parents because the child can't yet understand that parents have enough love for everyone. See Fig. 11-8.

Sibling rivalry, or competition between brothers or sisters for parents' affection and attention, is another common cause of jealousy. Children sometimes become jealous when a new baby is born. For example, a toddler finds that the attention once received is now focused on a new baby. Some young children react to a new baby by trying to get attention. They may show off, act in inappropriate ways, or revert to baby-like behaviors, such as wetting the bed or using baby talk. Some may behave aggressively towards the younger sibling.

Fig. 11-8 **A newborn baby sometimes causes jealousy in a toddler.** What are some other reasons that a toddler might be jealous?

- Avoid making comments that compare one child with another.
- Let the children take turns in choosing activities such as a game the family plays together or a movie they watch.
- Make clear that you will not accept one child tattling to get another one in trouble.
- Talk to children about their jealousy, how hard it can be to have siblings, as well as how lucky they are to have each other. See Fig. 11-9.

Love and Affection

The relationships that children have with others between the ages of one and three form the basis of their capacity for love and affection in later life. Young children must learn to love.

Parents should understand that fear of losing the parent's love caused the negative behavior in the first place. What the child needs is more affection and reassurance. Because of sibling rivalry, many experts say it is never safe to leave a baby alone with a toddler.

Sibling rivalry doesn't occur only when there is a newborn, however. One day Glen came home from work to find himself overwhelmed by hugs from both his four-year-old, Becky, and his three-year-old, Curt. Soon the children began pushing and shoving, trying to block the other child from getting near their father.

There are steps a parent can take to cut down on sibling rivalry:

- Make sure that each child feels love and appreciation.
- Set aside one-on-one time with each child.

Fig. 11-9 **Preschoolers are less likely to see younger siblings as rivals and may be protective of them.**

Babies first "love" those who satisfy their physical needs. Gradually, as children grow older, their affection expands to include siblings, pets, and people outside the home. See Fig. 11-10.

Loving relationships between parents or other caregivers and children need to be strong but not smothering. A child who depends entirely on caregivers for love has difficulty forming other relationships.

Empathy

For years, people believed that infants and toddlers were so self-centered that they couldn't feel anything toward someone who was unhappy. Research has overturned that view. While it's true that a toddler is mainly self-focused, the self is not their only focus. Between their first birthday and eighteen months, children begin to understand that their actions can hurt others. This is the first step toward developing **empathy**, or the ability to understand how another person feels. Children as young as one year old may pat and talk to another child who is unhappy. By age two, a child can show empathy. When two-year-old Antonio saw that little Nathan was upset, he offered Nathan his favorite stuffed animal as a way to cheer him up.

Caregivers can help teach children to show empathy. If a child in your care does something to hurt another's feelings—grabbing a toy, for instance—have the child give back the toy and apologize. Then ask the child to take an active step toward making the wronged child feel better, such as sharing another toy.

Individual Differences

Even though there are general patterns to how children develop emotionally, each child is unique and will develop in a special way. Individual differences can be very striking between the first and fourth birthdays and are caused in part by the different experiences that each child has. An only child, for example, will have different experiences from a child who is one of five children. The experiences of twins or triplets will be different from the experiences of other children.

Fig. 11-10 Have you seen a young child try to comfort someone who seemed unhappy?

Fig. 11-11 **Every child develops in a unique way because of his or her individual traits.** How can caregivers help children develop a positive self-concept?

Individual differences in emotional development also result from the child's temperament—the way the child naturally responds to other people and events. An intense child may become more frustrated than an adaptable child. A more perceptive child may show more empathy than one who is less perceptive.

Keeping in mind these differences in temperament is important when teaching children how to control their emotions. Connor, for example, is very perceptive. He is very aware of his environment and can be easily distracted. When his mother sees a temper tantrum coming on, she tries to turn his attention to something new, such as watching a squirrel play outside the window. Such a technique may not work on Nala, who adapts to change slowly. She dislikes surprises—even pleasant ones. Her parents have to give her plenty of warning and time to adjust before visitors arrive or any other change in her routine.

The unique combination of experiences and temperament blend together in a child's emotional development. Understanding these factors can help in dealing with such issues as negativism, tantrums, or sibling rivalry, and guiding a child to desirable behavior.

Developing a Positive Self-Concept

As they grow, children become more aware of their individual differences. The individual traits that make them special become part of their **self-concept**—how they see themselves. Self-concepts can be positive or negative. Children who see themselves as good and capable have a positive self-concept. Children who see themselves as bad or incapable have a negative self-concept. See Fig. 11-11.

Manage Misbehavior

Some parents worry that correcting misbehavior will damage their child's self-concept. However, a positive self-concept is based on actual achievement. By teaching and praising young children for appropriate behaviors, self-esteem is enhanced. Here are a few effective ways to discourage negative behaviors.

- **Explore feelings.** Read stories to a child and discuss ways that characters handle their feelings. After viewing children's videos together, talk about ways that the characters handle their problems.

- **Acknowledge feelings.** When a playmate takes a toddler's toy, grabbing or hitting may be a natural reaction. Caregivers should explain why this response isn't acceptable and give an alternative. They might say: "Everyone gets angry at times, but it's not okay to hurt people. Ask your friend for the toy back or choose another one."

- **Give choices.** Offer simple choices to empower children. Choosing what shirt to wear or what book to read makes a child feel important.

YOUR TURN

Empathy. Some young children act cruelly because they don't realize others have feelings. If you saw a child mistreating a playmate, what would you say to help the child develop empathy and learn to work through the problem?

Self-concept is different from self-esteem. Self-concept is what you think you are like as a person. Self-esteem is how highly you value yourself.

Children form their self-concept in response to the actions, attitudes, and comments of others. The years from one to three are crucial in the child's development of self-concept. Parents or a primary caregiver usually spend the most time with the young child during this time. They, therefore, have the strongest influence on the child's self-concept.

Young children believe what others say about them, and the opinions of others influence how the children behave. Often, when children hear adults say that they are good, they try to act the part. However, if they constantly hear that they are "bad" or "stupid," they will believe it and live up to that image. Even young toddlers who can't yet understand words are tuned in to the body language and tone of voice of adults. Adults' words and actions continue to have a strong influence on children until they are old enough to judge their own actions. By that time, however, their self-concept can be firmly established.

Another factor in building a positive self-concept is mastery of skills. For this reason, it is important to give infants and toddlers the chance to explore their world. Through exploration, they have the opportunity to master skills. Being able to learn such skills as finding toys and stacking blocks gives a sense of confidence, which leads to a positive self-concept.

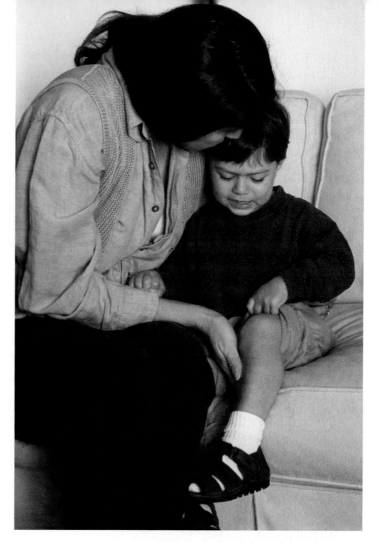

Fig. 11-12 It is important that young children have a good relationship with parents and other caregivers. What are some signs of a healthy relationship?

Evaluating Emotional Adjustment

How can parents tell whether a child's emotional development is on the right track? Between their first and fourth birthdays, the most important clue is the relationship of children with their parents or other primary caregivers. The early pattern established between the familiar adults and the child will shape the child's relationships later in life as a friend, coworker, and spouse. See Fig. 11-12.

These are signs of a healthy relationship between parents and child:

- Seeks approval and praise
- Turns to parents and caregivers for comfort and help

Jenny, the mother of two-year-old Amber, was baffled that her daughter fought going to bed every night. Amber would cry and beg to stay up. When she was carried into her bedroom, Amber would throw a temper tantrum.

Getting Amber up in the morning was almost equally as difficult. Jenny took Amber to child care at 7:00 a.m. every day. The child care workers reported that Amber had become aggressive, grabbing toys from other children and even hitting them on occasion.

On the way home from child care, Amber always fell asleep. The bedtime battle would begin later that night. Jenny looked up information about sleeping problems in children. She found some ideas for creating bedtime routines that would help Amber get to sleep. Now Amber takes a bath, brushes her teeth, and enjoys a story with her mom each night before going to sleep.

▸▸**PERSONAL APPLICATION**

1. How do you feel when you don't get enough sleep?
2. Do you notice a difference when you are well-rested?

- Tells caregivers about significant events so they can share in the joy and sorrow
- Accepts limits and discipline without too much resistance

Another indicator of emotional adjustment is a child's relationship with siblings. Some quarreling with brothers and sisters is bound to occur. However, the child who is continuously and bitterly at odds with brothers and sisters, in spite of parents' efforts to ease the friction, may need counseling. If emotional problems are dealt with early, it can make a difference for a lifetime.

Sleep, Emotions, and Behavior

A scream woke Joshua's parents in the middle of the night. It was not the first time that their three-year-old son had awakened terrified from a bad dream. Every time that Joshua woke up screaming, his parents rushed into his room and comforted him. Sometimes he was so frightened that one parent had to stay with him so that he could go back to sleep.

Most sleep problems in children are normal. In fact, they are one of the most common problems that children experience. Parents can help ease sleep problems by understanding what causes them.

Fears are a frequent cause of sleep problems, making it difficult for children to fall asleep. A bedtime routine and a reminder that a parent is nearby can help lessen these fears. Separation anxiety can also cause nightmares that wake the child. Asking the child to describe the nightmare can help calm him or her. It can be a relief for the child to talk about the bad dream. Also, by hearing about a dream, the parent may gain insight into the cause of the nightmare.

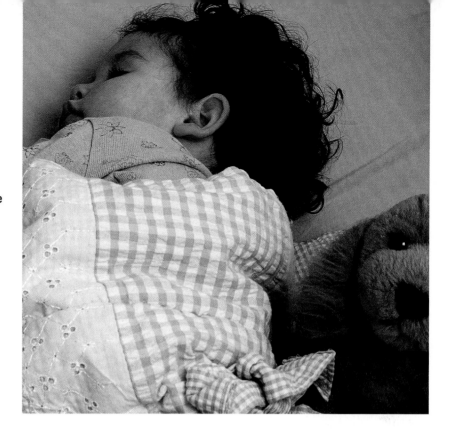

Fig. 11-13 **Children require more sleep than adults.** What steps can caregivers take to make sure a child gets enough sleep?

Some children find it hard to fall back asleep after waking in the night. Children may associate a certain routine, such as being rocked or hearing a lullaby, with sleeping. Parents may need to repeat bedtime routines in the middle of the night to restore sleep.

Sleep problems can be caused by something as simple as pajamas that are too tight or as serious as an ear infection or other illness. Parents concerned about the cause of a child's sleep problem should talk to their pediatrician.

The Importance of Adequate Sleep

 Adequate sleep, like adequate nutrition, is essential for good physical and emotional health. See Fig. 11-13. Without enough sleep, children can become **sleep deprived**. Lack of appropriate sleep may affect a child's temperament and ability to do even simple tasks during the day. Children may be less alert, inattentive, and even hyperactive. Children need to get adequate sleep in order to develop and function properly. One- to three-year-olds need lots of sleep—between twelve and fourteen hours each night.

Children, like adults, go through cycles of sleep each night. One cycle is called **REM sleep**, or rapid eye movement, and the other is called **NREM sleep**, or non-rapid eye movement. Sleep consists of cycles of REM and NREM sleep. NREM sleep is a deep sleep. REM sleep is a light sleep. Dreams occur during REM sleep, and children are more likely to wake up during this cycle.

Newborns have short sleep cycles and can go through an entire REM-NREM cycle in about an hour. By the time babies are about four months old, they sleep from six to eight hours at a time. This sleeping time increases to from ten to twelve hours by six months of age, although babies can still awaken during a sleep cycle.

What are signs of sleep deprivation? Children who don't get enough sleep must be awakened each morning and tend to be tired all day. They have trouble thinking and are at risk of hurting themselves while playing. They can also be cranky and hard to get along with. Sleep deprivation becomes more apparent once a child begins preschool or kindergarten and has to get up on a regular schedule. If the child doesn't go to sleep early enough and sleep well during the night, the child will end up being sleep deprived.

There are ways to help ensure that children get adequate sleep:

- **Determine a child's best bedtime.** People need differing amounts of sleep. Pay attention to when a child usually begins to get tired and sleepy, and use that as a guide. Children who stay up beyond this normal bedtime get a "second wind" and often have a hard time falling asleep.
- **Limit toys in the bed.** Toys might signal playtime rather than sleep time.
- **Establish a bedtime routine.** Every night, follow the same pattern such as a bath, brushing teeth, and a bedtime story.
- **Keep bedtime pleasant.** Talk and cuddle with the child or try giving a soothing backrub.

SECTION 11-1 Review and Activities

Reviewing the Section

1. What changes in emotions occur in children between ages three and three and one-half years?
2. Identify one common emotion a child experiences at this stage. How is this expressed from ages one to three?
3. Why are some children more likely than others to feel anger?
4. What is *sibling rivalry*?
5. What types of individual differences affect emotional development?
6. Explain the difference between *self-concept* and self-esteem.
7. What are three signs of healthy emotional adjustment?
8. How is adequate sleep related to emotional control?

Observing and Interacting

Observe one- to three-year-old children at a child care center, park, or shopping mall. Note the different emotions expressed by a younger child in this age group. Note the different emotions expressed by an older child in this age group. What are the similarities and differences?

Social Development from One to Three

Between the first and fourth birthdays, children develop attitudes and social skills that stay with them throughout their lives. Their experiences—especially with their families—help them learn how to get along with others.

Objectives

- Describe patterns of social development from ages one to three.
- Relate the importance of making friends to a child's social development.
- Compare and contrast different approaches to guidance.
- Describe ways to help children develop sharing skills.
- Identify common behavorial problems and effective methods of dealing with them.

Key Terms

socialization
parallel play
cooperative play
self-discipline
autonomy

General Social Patterns

Young children gradually learn how to get along with other people. First they learn how to get along with members of their own families and then with people in other groups. This process is called **socialization**. Through this process, children can be expected to learn various social skills by certain ages. Of course, as with other areas of development, individual differences may influence when, and in what order, social skills are learned.

Eighteen Months

By the time they are eighteen months old, children usually begin developing some independence from the family unit.

For most children, the closest relationships continue to be those with their families. However, toddlers need to learn about the outside world. This may mean trips to the playground or other opportunities to be with children and adults who aren't part of the family, such as at child care centers.

Children at this age, however, don't really interact with one another much, even when they are playing in the same area. Instead, children engage in **parallel play**, which means that they play near, but not actually with, other children. Each child plays independently. Two or more children may want—and grab for—the same toy, but the children are not really interacting with one another.

At eighteen months, toddlers often seem to treat other people more as objects than as human beings. At this stage, the toddler is intent on satisfying strong desires without regard for the person who interferes. There may be conflicts over toys that result in screaming, hitting, biting, or hair pulling.

Children of this age can understand that their actions have consequences for others, but this understanding is limited to actions that have direct, immediate, and physical results. When an eighteen-month-old hits another child, and that child cries, the first toddler can see the upset the action caused. See Fig. 11-14.

Two Years

By age two, children have begun to develop an impressive list of social skills. Two-year-olds are especially good at understanding and interacting with their main caregivers. Children can read their caregiver's moods and gauge what kind of behavior the caregiver is likely to accept. As their speech abilities develop, toddlers are increasingly able to communicate with others.

Two-year-olds find it is fun to play with someone else, though they usually continue to engage in parallel play. At two, they start to understand the idea of sharing or taking turns. Children this age like to please other people. Occasionally, they are willing to put the wishes of someone else (usually an adult) above their own wishes.

Two and One-Half Years

The negativism that characterizes the emotional development of the child at age two and one-half carries over into the child's social relationships. During this stage, a child may refuse to do anything at all for one person, while happily doing almost anything another person asks.

Fig. 11-14 **At eighteen months, toddlers will play in the same area, but they will not play together.** What kind of play is this called?

Fig. 11-15 **By the age of three, children engage in cooperative play.** What type of strategies do children use to resolve conflicts when playing together?

At this age, children are beginning to learn about the rights of others. They begin responding to the idea of fairness, although at first they are more concerned with what is fair to them. Social play is still parallel and works best with only two children. There are frequent, but brief, squabbles during play that children forget quickly.

Three Years

People become important to children of this age. A three-year-old will share, help, or do things another person's way just to please someone.

Three-year-olds begin **cooperative play**, actually playing with one another. See Fig. 11-15. They build sand castles together, push toy tractors down the same roads, and park their toy cars side by side in the same area. They can also work together in small groups to build with blocks, act out events for doll families, and fit puzzles together.

Parents or other main caregivers are still very important to three-year-olds, but they are no longer all-powerful in the children's social lives. Most toddlers of this age seek friends on their own. They also may prefer some children over others as friends.

Three and One-Half Years

By age three and one-half, children's play becomes more complex and includes more conversation. Disagreements with playmates occur less often. Because children this age enjoy the company of others, they realize they must share toys and accept some things they don't like in order to get along with friends.

At three and one-half, children can use several different strategies to resolve conflicts. Esteban tried to take a block that was behind Ramon, who was also playing with blocks. When Ramon said, "That's my block," Esteban replied, "Oh, okay" and put it down. Kelly and Rosa were playing with trucks. When Kelly reached for Rosa's yellow truck, Rosa objected and then said "You can have it if you give me that red one of yours."

There is an increasing ability to evaluate friendships. For example, a child may say, "I don't like to have Kevin come here. He doesn't play nice." Children who are closer friends begin to exclude others.

At this age, children also take more notice of what others are like. They become more likely to compare themselves to other children—not always to their own advantage. One day, Allison asked her mother, "Why does Libby always win when we race?" Her mother agreed that Libby was faster but also pointed out things that Allison did well. In this way, she acknowledged that Allison was not as skilled as Libby in one area but had other skills of her own.

Making Friends

The ability to make friends is important to normal social development. A child who is comfortable and friendly with others and who has at least one friend at a time is usually developing normally. However, if a child is unable or unwilling to make friends, it's important to discover the cause and take steps to help. For example, a shy child sometimes needs coaching on what to say or how to act so the child can join others in play. See Fig. 11-16.

Even very young children need contact with other people. This is how they learn the give-and-take of socializing. Children who begin to play with others at the age of one or two are less likely to be afraid in these early social

Fig. 11-16 **Making friends is an important aspect of a child's social development.** Why is it important for children to build friendships with other children?

Fig. 11-17 **Sometimes toddlers have disagreements and arguments.** When should a caregiver intervene to help children resolve a situation?

situations. They learn to cope with the occasional punches and toy snatching of other one- and two-year-olds.

When young children spend almost all of their time with adults, they may have difficulty interacting with others their own age. Adults are more polite and considerate than children. Children need to learn to enjoy the rough-and-tumble companionship of other children. If this learning is delayed until school age, the adjustment is more difficult. A five- or six-year-old's feelings are more easily hurt.

All children sometimes have disagreements and arguments. Whether or not a caregiver should step in depends on the situation. If two children are relatively evenly matched and there is no physical or emotional harm being done, the caregiver can simply observe the situation. Children need to learn how to solve social problems on their own, as in Fig. 11-17. If it looks as though someone might get hurt, the caregiver needs to help the children solve the problem. It is best for the children if the caregiver doesn't impose a solution but instead guides the children to find one for themselves.

Help Young Children Develop Social Skills

Knowing how to get along with others is key to success and happiness, and this depends upon social skills. There are many ways to help children develop social skills.

- **Establish a basic set of rules to guide social behavior.** The rules will probably center on teaching respect for self, for others, and for things.

- **Model good social skills.** Children are great imitators. They learn best by being shown what to do rather than by just being told. For instance, parents who talk politely to others are more likely to get their children to do so.

- **Help children understand and respect others' feelings.** You might show a child pictures of people's faces with a variety of expressions. Ask the child to tell how the person in the picture might be feeling, such as sad or angry. Talk about what these feelings mean to help the child develop empathy. Talk to them about how you are feeling.

- **Show respect for other people's belongings.** Tell a child, for example, not to touch grandma's flower vase, because it might get broken. This would make grandma very sad.

- **Show children how to use words rather than physically striking out.** Explain how using appropriate words when they are angry is better than hitting or shoving.

- **Help children learn specific social skills.** Demonstrate how to share a toy, wait their turn, and be kind to one another.

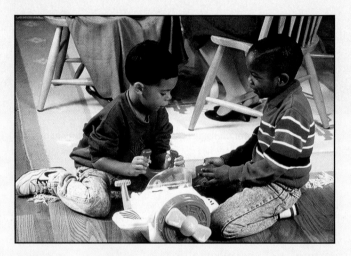

YOUR TURN

Respect. In helping children develop social skills, it is important to let them know that you respect them. Think of two ways you could communicate that you respect the feelings of a three-year-old. Make a list based on everyone's responses.

 YEAR

- Plays alone but often near others
- Dislikes sharing toys
- Desires approval
- Fears some strangers

2 YEARS

- Engages in parallel play
- Plays simple games with others
- Bosses other children
- Says "please" if prompted

3 YEARS

- Takes part in brief group activities (cooperative play)
- Takes turns
- Likes to help
- Shows affection

Imaginary Friends

Many toddlers begin to have imaginary friends. Some keep the same imaginary friend for a long time—from several months to a year. Others have several different imaginary friends. Some toddlers have imaginary animals rather than friends.

Imaginary friends may appear in a toddler's imagination as early as age two. These friends are even more common when a child is between ages three and four, a year during which children have rich imaginations and are interested in fantasy.

Some parents worry that children invent imaginary friends because they are unable to make real friends. They are concerned that an imaginary friend is a sign of unhappiness or problems coping with life.

In fact, an imaginary friend can be a very helpful way for a child to experiment with different feelings. Some children use an imaginary friend as a way of working through their negative feelings. For others, the friend mirrors everything the child does or experiences. Then the child talks to the family about how the imaginary friend felt about these experiences. In this way, children find a way to examine their own thoughts and feelings.

Imaginary friends usually fade away. Crystal simply stopped talking about her imaginary friend when she started school. Paul had an imaginary friend when he was three, but the friend was gone by the time Paul turned four. There is no cause for concern unless the imaginary friend continues into adolescence. For more information about social development, see Fig. 11-18.

Guidelines for Guidance

Guiding children's behavior doesn't simply mean "making children behave" and punishing them when they do something wrong. Punishment is only a small part of guidance. Guidance means using firmness and understanding to help children learn how to control their own behavior. The purpose of guidance is to help children learn **self-discipline**—the ability of children to control their own behavior.

Effective guidance helps children learn to get along with others and to handle their own feelings in acceptable ways. It promotes security and a positive feeling about self.

Guidance also helps children with moral development. Very young children understand right from wrong only in terms of being praised or scolded. Gradually, children develop a *conscience*—or an inner sense of what is right. As children mature, they use this conscience to act morally when facing new situations.

 Effective guidance depends upon a child's age and emotional and social development. There is no single best approach to guidance. Caregivers need to consider the individual personality of each child as well as each child's age, stage of development, and ability to understand. Different approaches may be especially effective at various ages.

Fig. 11-19 Children under the age of fifteen months cannot understand reasoning, so they should be removed from situations that could be dangerous to them.

Fig. 11-20 **Preschoolers begin to understand adult reasoning and more readily accept guidance.** What is a major factor in guiding a child's behavior?

- **One year to fifteen months.** Distracting children and physically removing them from forbidden activities or places works best for this age, because they can't yet understand adult reasoning. See Fig. 11-19. For example, Kareem tried to follow the lawn mower around the yard when his brother was cutting the grass. His older sister picked Kareem up and took him into the house, saying, "Let's see if we can find the book about the bear."

- **Fifteen months to two years.** Children this age require spoken restrictions as well as distraction and removal. Lee began playing with toy cars on the driveway. His father took him by the hand and said, "Let's take your cars into the backyard. You'll have more room there. The driveway isn't a safe place to play."

- **Two to three years.** By the age of two, children are usually able to understand spoken commands and simple explanations. Two-year-olds can begin to grasp the reasoning of adults. Caregivers who explain their reasons to children over age two get better results than those who only issue commands. When she saw that her two-and-one-half-year-old was still not dressed, Kerri's mother said, "Kerri, you need to get dressed now because Grandma will be here soon to go shopping with us. We can't go unless we are ready. Do you need any help?"

- **Three years.** Three-year-olds accept reasonable, loving guidance more readily than children of other ages. They like to please, and they may be quick to remind a parent that they are obedient. Marcus came inside on a rainy day and said, "I remembered to wear my boots today. See my clean shoes? I'm a good boy, right?" See Fig. 11-20.

Madison and Morgan are sisters and love to play together. Madison is two and Morgan is three. Because they are so close in age, they share everything, from a bedroom, to clothes, to toys. Madison gets clothes and toys that her sister has outgrown, which is fine with her. She is delighted when she can finally call a toy her own. This can create a problem, however. Sometimes if Madison is playing with a toy that once belonged to Morgan, Morgan wants it back. She tries to snatch it away from her little sister. While both girls have difficulty sharing, Morgan is better able to understand the concept of taking turns. But for two-year-old Madison, if someone else is playing with her toy, she cries until it is returned to her. Morgan learns more about sharing at preschool, where she must share things with eleven other children. It is during this time that Madison doesn't have to share with anyone!

▶▶PERSONAL APPLICATION

1. What would you say to children who are not sharing their toys?
2. Would you require children to share all their toys? Explain.

Being consistent is a major factor in guiding children's behavior. Make clear rules and apply them in the same way in all situations. Consistency helps children know what is expected of them and what responses they can expect from parents.

Consistency is especially important when more than one person cares for a child. Parents and other caregivers need to agree on rules and ways to enforce them.

Setting Limits

Parents can help children learn self-regulation and self-discipline by setting and enforcing limits. Setting limits is another way of guiding children toward appropriate, safe behavior. When parents and caregivers set limits, it helps children begin to set limits for themselves.

Make sure you state limits clearly. Telling three-year-old Kelly that she can have "a small snack" does not set a clear limit. Kelly isn't old enough to determine what makes a snack big or small. A clearer way to state the limit would be, "You can have either an apple or a banana." Speak in a calm, direct tone of voice to indicate that the limit is real and should be respected.

Here's how a caregiver might set limits about where a toddler can draw pictures. Setting limits includes four steps:

1. **Show an understanding of the child's desires.** "I know you think it's fun to draw on the wall."
2. **Set the limit and explain it.** "But you may not draw on the wall because it's hard to clean crayon marks off the wall."
3. **Acknowledge the child's feelings.** "I know you like drawing on the wall, but walls are not for drawing."

Fig. 11-21 **Setting limits goes a long way in helping children learn self-regulation.** What questions should a caregiver consider when setting limits?

4. **Give alternatives.** If possible, give the child a chance to continue the same activity in an acceptable way. "If you want to draw, you may draw on this paper, or you can play with your blocks. Which would you like to do?" See Fig. 11-21.

It is important to firmly and consistently enforce limits once they are set. If children beg to go beyond the limits and parents give in, the parents teach the children that they don't mean what they say. Parents who enforce limits strictly at some times and not at all at other times send an inconsistent message. Children are more likely to take rules seriously that remain in force at all times.

Encouraging Independence

"Me do it! Me do it!" insisted two-year-old Justine when her mother tried to pull socks over Justine's feet. Children from the ages of one through three long for more **autonomy**, or independence. They want to be able to do things for themselves, including bathing, dressing, and eating. Caregivers can help them achieve a degree of independence while still bearing the main responsibility of meeting the young children's basic needs.

It's important to have realistic expectations of what a child of a particular age can do. When a child begins learning to self-feed, the process will be messy, as shown in Fig. 11-22. Using unbreakable dishes, a child-size spoon and fork, and a cup with a spill-proof lid will minimize the mess. Give the child small servings of food that are cut into bite-size pieces and easy to handle.

When teaching toddlers how to dress themselves, choose clothes that are easy to put on and take off. Look for pants, skirts, and shorts with elastic waistbands and roomy tops that fasten in the front. Fasteners can cause problems for little fingers. Hook-and-loop fasteners, large buttons, and zippers are easiest for toddlers to manage. Learning to get dressed requires a whole set of skills. Let the child begin by helping with pulling up a zipper or slipping a foot into a shoe.

Providing toddlers with their own towel, washcloth, brush or comb, and toothbrush can encourage independence in staying clean and neat. These items should be within the child's reach. A step stool can help a child cope with an adult-size bathroom. Then set up and follow a daily routine that includes bathing, brushing teeth, combing hair, and washing hands before eating.

During this age span children can begin to help with simple household tasks. Putting toys away can start as a "picking-up" game. Also, let toddlers and preschoolers help you with simple chores, such as sweeping, gathering and folding laundry, and setting the table.

Remember to be patient. A child's efforts will always be slower and less efficient than your own. Jelly may get smeared on the table, shorts put on backwards, and tops fastened all askew. Learning self-help skills increases confidence and independence. However, skills can't be learned without lots of practice.

Fig. 11-22 **Toddlers learning to feed themselves are apt to be messy eaters at first.** What steps can a caregiver take to make the process less messy?

Fig. 11-23 **Caregivers can help children learn social skills to help them be happy and successful.** Name three rules of respect that children developing social skills should learn.

Promoting Sharing

How to share is one of the first social skills that toddlers should learn. Here are some ways to help them develop this skill:

- Engage children in activities that require them to share, such as playing on a see-saw. Place them in situations where they must take turns, such as going down a slide. See Fig. 11-23.

- Limit the materials available for an activity so that children have to share or take turns. For example, when making paper crafts, provide only one pair of scissors and one glue stick so the children will have to share.
- Have children take turns handing out snacks.
- Make clear what behavior you are trying to encourage. Call it "sharing" or "taking turns."

Parenting Q&A

What Are Some Ways to Calm a Toddler Who Is Having a Temper Tantrum?

Toddlers may have tantrums when they are tired or frustrated, especially when they are denied something they want. Giving in to tantrums teaches the child that tantrums are an effective way of getting what they want and makes the child more likely to have them. Here are some ways to deal with tantrums in toddlers.

- **If it is obvious that a tantrum is about to begin, try to head it off.** Distract the child with a toy or by pointing out some activity going on elsewhere. If the child is receptive to a hug, try giving one.
- **If a child has a tantrum at home, try ignoring it.** Children whose tantrums are ignored are less likely to have them.

- **If a child has a tantrum in public, take the child to a quiet spot to cool down.** If possible, take the child home or to the car.
- **Always remain calm and speak quietly yet firmly.** Resist the urge to respond with a loud or angry voice, as it will only add to the tension.
- **Acknowledge the child's feelings while restating why the child's demands can't be met.**
- **Adhere to set limits.**
- **Take care to protect toddlers having tantrums from hurting themselves or others.**
- **Once the tantrum is over, praise the child for having calmed down.**
- **Keep explanations short and remember that tantrums are a normal part of a toddler's attempts to assert independence.**

THINKING IT THROUGH

1. How should a caregiver respond to a screaming toddler demanding a certain DVD at the video store?
2. Why is the caregiver's tone of voice important when responding to a tantrum?

Not all sharing experiences are equal for a child. For example, a child may have a strong emotional attachment to a stuffed animal or be very happy with a new birthday toy. It can be much more difficult for the child to share these things than to take turns using scissors. If there's a reason not to share something, it's best to put it away when other children are around.

Parents of an only child should be sure to give their child opportunities to learn sharing. An only child who attends child care or play groups will quickly gain experience sharing and taking turns. It's also important for the adults and older siblings in children's lives to demonstrate and model sharing behavior.

Possible Behavioral Problems

Children at times behave in ways that are far different from their normal behavior. For example, an easygoing child may become aggressive—kicking, biting, or hitting. Behavioral problems among children one through three are quite common, and there is almost always a reason for their disruptive behavior.

Behavior is a form of communication, and inappropriate or aggressive behavior signals that a child is upset or that some need isn't being met. Young children can have a hard time using words to explain their feelings. On the other hand, sometimes children misbehave just because they enjoy the sensation; for example, repeatedly kicking a table leg.

Caregivers need to look for and understand the problem behind aggressive or otherwise inappropriate behavior. Finding the underlying cause of the behavioral problems can go a long way toward changing the behavior.

Biting

Marguerite was shocked when her two-year-old son ran up and bit her on the arm. He bit hard enough to leave a bruise.

It is not uncommon for young children to bite, and they bite for different reasons at different ages. Infants may bite because they fail to see any difference between chewing on a toy and chewing on a big brother or sister. One-year-olds may bite just to discover what happens when they do. Two- and three-year-olds may bite to get their way with other children or just to get attention. They may also bite when they are angry or frustrated.

Caregivers need to determine what is causing a child to bite, and then take steps to guide the child toward more appropriate behavior. A teething baby, for example, can be given a teething ring or a soft cloth to bite on to relieve the discomfort of cutting teeth.

Wilson discovered his eighteen-month-old daughter biting her brother in a tussle over a toy wagon. He set her on his knee, looked directly into her eyes, and calmly but firmly told her, "Do not bite. Biting hurts your brother. It makes him cry."

Hitting

Have you seen an adult react to a young child's aggressive behavior with anger? Unfortunately, this sends the message that anger and aggression are appropriate solutions to a problem.

 Two- and three-year-olds have trouble controlling these impulses, or aggressive reactions to emotions and situations. At these ages, the part of the child's brain that controls impulses is not well developed. In addition, children are still very self-centered and concerned mainly with fulfilling their own needs and desires. When something hinders them from getting their needs met, they become angry or frustrated.

Hitting, kicking, and shoving are aggressive behaviors often seen in toddlers. Anne wanted a ball that Juan was playing with. Juan refused to let go, so Anne began hitting him.

Anne's preschool teacher intervened when Anne began to hit Juan. "I know that you want to play with the ball. I can see that it makes you angry when Juan will not give it up, but you must not hit people. Use words to tell Juan you are angry." The teacher then guided Anne toward some choices. "You can wait your turn to play with the ball, or you can color a picture. Which would you like to do?"

Many child development experts believe that time-outs are an effective way to help children understand that certain behaviors are not acceptable. A time-out is another way of saying, "You cannot do that."

SECTION 11-2 Review and Activities

Reviewing the Section

1. What is *socialization*?
2. Compare *parallel play* and *cooperative play*. How are they different? When does cooperative play usually begin?
3. Describe the social development of a child who just turned two. How does it differ from that of a child six months older?
4. Explain why it's important to give young children opportunities to play with friends.
5. What guidance approach generally works best for a one-year-old? For a three-year-old?
6. What questions can caregivers ask themselves about the appropriateness of the limits they set for young children?
7. Give an example of how a parent could help a three-year-old practice sharing.
8. Name two common behavioral problems. How would a caregiver deal with those problems?

Observing and Interacting

Create a chart that shows the developmental milestones of a child's social development at eighteen months, two years, two and one-half years, three years, and three and one-half years. Evaluate how a child's social development changes. Observe a toddler or preschooler and watch for traits included in your chart.

Career Opportunities

Puppeteer

Puppeteers have been entertaining children for hundreds of years. They may manipulate hand-held puppets, wear a costume, or work the strings that make marionettes dance. Puppeteers often provide the voices for their characters. Some puppeteers design productions and create the puppets themselves. Even very young children can enjoy energetic and colorful puppet productions.

▶ Job Responsibilities

Puppeteers act out roles using their voices and gestures. Unlike actors, puppeteers are not limited by their body shape or looks. Creating a character from scratch is one of the joys of professional puppetry.

▶ Work Environment

Puppeteers perform in puppet theaters or on children's television programs. Some even set up stages in parks. Those wishing to gain experience in puppetry can arrange to give performances in shopping malls, community centers, and libraries.

▶ Education and Training

Many puppeteers study fine arts and drama at universities. If you want to be a puppeteer, attend puppetry workshops and as many public performances as you can.

▶ Skills and Aptitudes

- Creativity
- Interest in design
- Persistence
- Dramatic ability
- Attention to detail

WORKPLACE CONNECTION

1. **Thinking Skills.** How is being a puppeteer different from being another kind of artist?

2. **Resource Skills.** How could you get information about puppetry?

SECTION SUMMARIES

- Children go through a series of emotional stages, both positive and somewhat negative. (11-1)
- Each child develops emotionally in his or her own way. (11-1)
- Individual differences that make children special become part of their self-concept. (11-1)
- Adequate sleep is critical to many areas of a child's development. (11-1)
- The socialization process involves gradually developing social skills and learning to get along with others. (11-2)
- The ability to make friends is important to normal social development. (11-2)
- Behavior needs to be guided by caregivers, who set limits that help the children learn self-discipline. (11-2)

REVIEWING THE CHAPTER

1. What causes *negativism* in a toddler? (11-1)
2. Describe several emotional changes a child goes through at the ages of one, two, and three. (11-1)
3. In what ways might a toddler express *sibling rivalry* after the birth of a brother or sister? (11-1)
4. How might parents help a child form a positive *self-concept*? (11-1)
5. Distinguish between *REM sleep* and *NREM sleep*. (11-1)
6. Describe how a pair of two-year-olds might play together. How might a pair of three-and-one-half-year-olds play together? (11-2)
7. Explain why it's important for children to spend time with other children, not just with adults. (11-2)
8. Should having an imaginary friend be considered a problem? Explain. (11-2)
9. What are two common behavioral problems? How would you deal with them with three-year-olds? (11-2)

THINKING CRITCALLY

1. **Understanding Cause and Effect.** How might a child's family structure influence the child's emotional and social development?
2. **Predicting Consequences.** How might young children's emotions, such as anger and fear, be influenced by cartoons, television, and videos?

MAKING CONNECTIONS

1. **Writing.** Erik Erikson theorized that there are eight stages in a person's emotional and social development. The second stage involves children eighteen months to three years of age. Research the second stage of Erikson's theory and then write a summary.

2. **Social Studies.** Draw up a simple set of rules about getting along with other people. Base the rules on the principles of respecting self, respecting others, and respecting things. Word the rules so that two- and three-year-olds understand both the rules and the three principles.

APPLYING YOUR LEARNING

1. **Determining Appropriate Actions.** You have taken your two-year-old niece to the mall. Her mother said she could have only one snack at the food court. She chose cookies, but now wants ice cream too. You have explained that she can only have one snack. Because she didn't get her way, she has a tantrum. People are staring. How would you handle the situation?

2. **Modifying Outcomes.** Write six negative statements that someone might say to a child age one to three. Exchange papers with a partner. Turn each statement on the list into a more positive one, conveying the same message. Why are the positive messages a better choice?

Learning from Research

1. Choose one of the following research claims to investigate.
2. How is this research finding useful to parents and other caregivers of one- to three-year-olds?
3. Summarize what you have learned about how a caregiver's interactions with a child affect the child's social development.

Developing Social Skills Through Play. Parents of children with well-developed social skills engage in certain behaviors when playing with them. These include: responding positively to their ideas, smiling, and offering praise. Cite examples of how parents develop their children's social skills by interacting during play.

Developing Social Skills Through Conversation. Socially competent children have frequent conversations with their parents about their emotions and those of their peers. Explain how these conversations might help children develop social skills.

Developing Social Skills Through Positive Attitudes. Parents of children with strong social skills encourage positive attitudes toward others. Cite examples of how parents can develop their children's social skills by modeling a positive attitude toward others.

12 Intellectual Development from One to Three

Thoughtful Reading:

As you read this chapter:
- Write down any questions you have about what you read.
- Identify at least three phrases that you question.
- Find answers in the text or in outside sources.

Section 12-1
Brain Development from One to Three

Section 12-2
Encouraging Learning from One to Three

Brain Development from One to Three

Lisa, age two and one-half, revealed the growing power of her mind when she examined her doll with a toy stethoscope after returning from a visit to the pediatrician. A one-year-old is still much like a baby, just learning to make sense of the world. However, a child only a year or two older has learned so much that she can engage in imaginative play by imitating the actions of her doctor. In doing so, she develops her own ideas and extends her investigation of the world.

Objectives

- Relate the connection between brain research and learning.
- Describe how intelligence and environment affect learning.
- Differentiate among the four methods of learning used by young children.
- Explain how children develop concepts in stages.
- Summarize how one- to three-year-olds develop in seven areas of intellectual activity.

Key Terms

neuroscience
intelligence
incidental learning
trial-and-error learning
imitation
directed learning
creativity

The Study of the Brain

Most researchers agree that the brain plays a major part in directing behavior and determining intelligence. However, the exact functions of the brain were unknown until recent years. For a long time, people could do little but observe human behavior and theorize about exactly how the brain controlled human actions and abilities.

Cells from the nervous system, called neurons, were observed to have fibers radiating from them, called axons and dendrites. As you have learned, these fibers were found to conduct information to and from other neurons in the brain. Later, scientists discovered that connections between axons and dendrites formed pathways in the brain that controlled particular actions or thinking tasks.

Fig. 12-1 **Connections in the brain control actions and thinking tasks.** Why can't a one-year-old perform all the tasks a three-year-old can?

everyone is born with certain limits of possible intellectual development, the extent to which an individual's potential is actually developed is greatly influenced by that person's environment.

It is crucial for young children to have an environment that promotes learning and stimulates the senses. Such an environment includes interactions with caregivers, a variety of appropriate playthings, and plenty of encouragement. An enriched learning environment provides the best opportunity for learning during a child's early years. In fact, recent studies of the brain during development show that connections are made and the brain grows in complexity partly based on the opportunities for learning available to a child. A stimulating environment boosts learning.

Toddlers and preschoolers form attitudes about learning that can last a lifetime. If they are given many opportunities for learning, they are likely to develop a positive attitude toward learning.

Since then, the modern study of the brain, called **neuroscience**, has provided further important discoveries and insights about the functions of the human brain. These have greatly expanded the knowledge of how a child's brain develops. This, in turn, has had an impact on recommendations for care of children. See Fig. 12-1.

The Role of Intelligence

Intelligence is the ability to interpret and understand everyday situations and to use prior experiences when faced with new situations or problems. Intelligence is also the capacity to learn. Both heredity and environment shape intelligence. Although

Methods of Learning

Children learn much through everyday experiences and through play. Four different methods that children use for learning are incidental, trial-and-error, imitation, and directed learning. See Fig. 12-2.

Incidental Learning

Incidental learning is unplanned learning. For example, five-month-old Evan happens to push a button on a musical toy and discovers that this action causes music to play. After this occurs a few times, Evan recognizes a cause-and-effect situation. Then he pushes the button on purpose to hear the music.

Fig. 12-2 Piaget's Four Periods of Learning

Period	Characteristics
Sensorimotor Birth–2 years	Children learn through their senses and own actions.
Preoperational 2–7 years	Children think in terms of their own activities and what they perceive at the moment.
Concrete operations 7–11 years	Children can think logically but still learn best through experience.
Formal operations 11–Adult	People are capable of abstract thinking.

Trial-and-Error Learning

Trial-and-error learning takes place when a child tries several solutions before finding one that works. At twelve to eighteen months, this means experimenting. Trial-and-error learning may be more advanced for a three-year-old. For example, three-year-old Krista wants to play with her younger brother's toy robot. First, Krista grabs the robot from her brother. He screams, and her mother makes her give it back. Next, she tells her brother to go play in the sandbox, but he doesn't want to. Finally, Krista offers to let her brother play with her stuffed horse if she can play with his toy. He agrees to the trade, and Krista gets what she wants.

Imitation

Imitation is learning by watching and copying others. Older children are often annoyed when a younger sibling "copies" everything they do or say. The younger child uses the older as a model for behavior of all kinds. Both skills and attitudes can be learned by imitation.

Directed Learning

Learning that results from being taught, often by parents, other caregivers, teachers, or older siblings, is **directed learning**. Directed learning occurs in school or other places that offer formal instruction, as well as at home. Joel's kindergarten teacher helps him learn the letters of the alphabet by showing pictures of items that begin with each letter. At home, his sister demonstrates how to play "Go Fish" with playing cards. Directed learning begins in the early years and continues through years of formal schooling. It continues throughout life.

Concept Development

Children learn concepts—general categories of objects and information—and the words for those concepts in stages. It takes time for misconceptions that result from a toddler's broad generalizations to be sorted out. Young children often over-apply labels. For example, toddlers may think that any round food is a cookie. Young children also learn to categorize objects by shape, color, and size. Balls are round, and so are cookies and plates. Grass and leaves are both green. Size distinctions come in two steps. The relationship between two items—"big" and "little"—may be recognized as early as eighteen months. Not until age three, however, can children pick out the middle-sized ball from three possibilities. See Fig. 12-3.

Concepts concerning what is alive and what isn't are not learned until later. A young child believes that anything that moves or works is alive—clouds, toys, cartoon characters, and the washing machine!

Concepts of time improve during the second and third years. Two-year-olds may show more patience because they know what "soon" means and can wait a short time. They know the difference between "before" and "after." However, a child may not understand "today," "tomorrow," and "yesterday" until kindergarten.

The Mind at Work

Intellectual activity can be broken down into seven areas: attention, memory, perception, reasoning, imagination, creativity, and curiosity. Although these areas develop throughout life, their development from ages one to three is especially remarkable.

Fig. 12-3 **By age three, many children can classify items by size, shape, or color.**

Attention

At any given moment, the five senses are bombarded with information. Right now, for instance, you see the words on the page. You are aware of the size, shape, and color of the book and the amount of light in the room. You hear pages being turned, and perhaps you see other students jotting down notes. You feel the paper of the book; it is smooth and cool. If you were unable to screen out all of the extra information you take in, you wouldn't be able to read.

In order to function, adults must have the ability to focus their attention on the task at hand and block out much of the sensory information they receive. Infants and very young children are unable to do this. Their attention flits from one bit of sensory information to another as they try to make sense of it all. This is why toddlers are so easily distracted. A caregiver struggling to dress a toddler may find that while her back was turned, the child wandered away to investigate what was happening outside the window. It is very important for caregivers to understand how difficult it is for a child to pay attention to one thing at a time.

As children mature, they gradually develop the ability to ignore most sensory information they receive and to concentrate on one item of interest. Their learning becomes more focused on one particular topic at a time. One- to three-year-olds have short attention spans, but a three-year-old can focus on one activity for much longer than a one-year-old. The more children are able to screen out distractions, the more they can learn. See Fig. 12-4.

Memory

Without memory, there would be no learning. Experiences that are forgotten cannot affect later actions or thoughts.

Older children and adults have both short- and long-term memory. Short-term memory is brief and allows people to accomplish many everyday tasks without burdening the brain with storing unimportant information indefinitely. People use short-term memory when they look up a number in the phone book. They remember the number just long enough to place their call. Long-term memory is for more important data. First, this information must enter the short-term memory and be judged important enough to remember. Then it is stored in the long-term memory.

Fig. 12-4 **Toddlers are easily distracted by things going on around them.** At what age do young children begin to show the ability to concentrate?

Babies begin to demonstrate memory early. They quickly learn to recognize the faces of their primary caregivers, for example. Much of babies' memory abilities have to do with faces and foods. Between six months and a year, babies develop recall memory. This is the ability to remember more for longer periods of time, especially things that had a strong emotional impact. For example, by this time Kylie can remember that she didn't like cats because one scratched her.

As children develop, they become able to react to a situation by remembering similar experiences in the past. A one-year-old who was frightened by a dog may be afraid of all animals for a time. A three-year-old can remember the particular dog and compare it with others, or can recall a celebration and look forward to the next one. It is when children develop long-term memory beginning at age three that they can retain facts (the girl next door is named Keisha), observations (I love to go to the park), and their own personal history (I got a new puppy last year).

THE DEVELOPING BRAIN

Long-term memory—the ability to remember an event in one's life for a long period—depends on connections between neurons in two brain areas called the frontal lobe and the hippocampus. Research has shown that these parts of the brain do not become capable of forming long-term memories until a baby is seventeen to twenty-one months old. Even if a baby is too young to remember a story or a song, interactions with adults keep the child alert and interested and aid brain development.

Learning Through PLAY

Memory Games

As a toddler's intellectual abilities grow, so do the possibilities for play. A three-year-old is able to use his or her memory to play games. Do you remember playing card games where the object was to place cards face down, turn over one card, and then turn over another to find its match? Three-year-olds are able to play such a memory game successfully for two reasons. They are able to keep an idea in mind for longer periods of time than when they were younger. They can also complete a task without being easily distracted. Simple puzzles can be good for developing memory as well. Increasing a child's memory can help with later development of skills such as reading and writing.

Following Up

What do you think are good memory games for a one-year-old?

Perception

A newborn learns about the world through *perceptions*—the information received through the senses. This sensory information reinforces established connections in the brain and sparks new ones. Although a newborn's brain is developing these neural connections and pathways at a rapid rate, an infant is just beginning to interpret this information. Gradually, the brain organizes itself to handle increasingly complex learning as a child grows. This allows sensory information to be used more effectively.

If you care for young children, you can play a key role in the development of perception. By talking about what you and the children are doing, you encourage children's perception. Use descriptive observations that children can understand and expand on. For example, when playing with blocks, you might say, "Look at the blue block. Your shirt is blue, too. Let's see if we can build a tower using only blue blocks."

Two- and three-year-olds seem to ask questions constantly. Responding to questions of "Why?" "What's that?" and "How does it work?" helps improve a child's perception. It can be difficult for caregivers to answer these endless questions. However, when questions are ignored or brushed aside a child loses opportunities for learning. If the response is often an absent-minded "Uh-huh" or "Don't bother me right now; I'm busy," the child may stop asking questions.

Reasoning

Reasoning is necessary to gain the ability to solve problems and make decisions and is also important in recognizing relationships and forming concepts.

LOOKING AT REAL LIFE

Three-year-old Zack was curious about his surroundings, especially about other people. He wasn't at all shy, and his mother was happy that he so often smiled and greeted people. One day, Zack and his mother went grocery shopping. "What's wrong with her?" Zack said. "Why is she walking like that?" he asked loudly. Zack's mother drew him into a nearby aisle, and after a quick review of the use of "inside" and "outside" voices, she assured him that there was nothing wrong with the person he had seen. She was using crutches to help her walk because her legs might not work the way that Zack's do. On their way home, she reminded Zack that all people are different, and encouraged him to recognize that it might hurt people's feelings when he asks inappropriate questions.

▸▸**PERSONAL APPLICATION**

1. How might a parent prepare a child for encounters such as this one?
2. How can parents of young children begin to teach them to consider others' feelings?

Babies show the signs of simple problem-solving skills at about four to six months of age. One-, two-, and three-year-olds gradually learn more sophisticated reasoning skills. At fourteen months, Jason solves problems by actually trying out all possible solutions. When playing with a shape sorter box, he tries to fit each piece into each hole until one works. By his third birthday, Jason's problem solving is less physical and more mental. He can think through possible solutions and eliminate those that won't work without actually acting out each one. He can see that the square shape will fit in the square hole. See Fig. 12-5.

Making decisions involves choosing from different alternatives. Children learn to make good decisions through practice, so it's important to give young children plenty of opportunities to make real decisions. At first, these decisions should be based on choosing between two options in which neither choice could cause any harm. An eighteen-month-old can choose between two books to read at bedtime. At two, a child can choose between two different shirts. Parents of newly independent two-year-olds know that this approach has the added advantage of avoiding questions that may elicit a negative response, such as

Fig. 12-5 **At age one, children begin to learn more complex reasoning skills.** How might a three-year-old solve problems differently from a one-year-old?

1 YEAR

- Begins to put two words together
- Names common objects and people
- Understands "no" but ignores
- Finds hidden objects

2 YEARS

- Uses two- to three-word sentences
- Knows about 500 words
- Follows simple directions
- Identifies colors

3 YEARS

- Uses longer sentences
- Knows about 900 words
- Follows two-part directions
- Sorts by color and shape

"Would you like to have fish for dinner?" What kinds of decision-making opportunities might be appropriate to offer to a three-year-old? See Fig. 12-6 for more intellectual milestones.

Imagination

Imagination becomes very apparent at about two years of age. An active imagination enhances learning because it allows the child to try new things and to act out a variety of roles. Laundry baskets become planes, boxes are buildings, and closets are caves. The child becomes a ferocious lion or a busy airline pilot.

Children use their imagination to connect what they see and hear with themselves. A child may see an airplane, imagine that they *are* an airplane, and zoom around the backyard. Imagination can also help children cope with anxiety and frightening new concepts. For example, some children may pretend to throw a scary monster out the bedroom window as a way of managing their fear. Using a toy doctor's kit and pretending to be a doctor can help calm fears about an upcoming medical procedure.

It's important to respect a child's imagination and respond carefully. When three-year-old Emma makes up a story, she isn't lying—she's using her imagination. However, if Emma's mother says, "Don't be silly. You know that didn't really happen," Emma might be discouraged from using her imagination. In fact, until about the age of five, children are not always sure where reality ends and imagination begins.

Encourage Imagination and Creativity

Does it seem that some children are more creative than others? While some may naturally be more imaginative, all children need opportunities to control and direct creative play.

- **Encourage exploration.** Encourage play activities that depend on exploration and imagination. Drawing, playing with clay, building things, dressing up in grownup clothes, and telling stories are all examples. Try making up the beginning of a story and asking children to finish it.

- **Provide multipurpose toys.** Children need toys that can be used in more than one way. Small wooden blocks can become phones, cars, sandwiches, or the walls of a castle. Empty boxes can be semis, fire trucks, or doll beds.

- **Allow for unstructured time.** Children need uninterrupted time to themselves to use their imagination. The less television they watch, the more their imaginations will flourish.

- **Resist the inner critic.** Remember that the process of creating is more important than the product. At this stage, there's not one "right" way to draw, paint, or mold things from clay. Responding to

a child's drawing with, "Amanda, I've never seen a cat with three eyes before! I wonder what it would be like to have three eyes," will encourage Amanda to continue to think creatively.

- **Reward the young creator.** Praise the child's efforts with deeds as well as words. Display the child's pictures. Talk with family and friends about what the child has made.

YOUR TURN

Materials. Many caregivers worry about the mess resulting from creative play. How might you control the mess and still encourage children to work with art supplies?

Creativity

A related mental ability is **creativity**, in which the imagination is used to produce original ideas. These ideas are often displayed through an object that others can see, such as a drawing or finger painting. The creative product is sometimes not an object, as with daydreams, dramatic play, or silly stories. Creativity is most readily developed in early childhood and is an asset throughout life.

Curiosity

Children are curious about the world around them, and that curiosity helps brain development and learning. It's curiosity that causes children to wonder "why" and "how" about things or to try new activities. However, parents may sometimes stifle that curiosity by overprotecting a child. Although children need a safe environment, they also need the freedom to explore the world around them.

Most young children seem to be into everything. They peek into every corner and closet. They touch and examine everything within reach. It's often impossible to anticipate what a one-, two-, or three-year-old may do next. A doll may end up covered in bandages because "she fell down." Patience and a healthy dose of humor on the family's part are essential!

SECTION 12-1 Review and Activities

Reviewing the Section

1. What is *neuroscience*?
2. What is *intelligence*?
3. Identify and give your own examples of the four methods of learning.
4. Give an example of a concept that is only partially understood by a two-year-old.
5. Give an example of how a caregiver could help improve a child's perception.
6. How does an active imagination help children learn about the world around them?
7. Why is curiosity important?

Observing and Interacting

In writing, describe a learning situation that occurred in one of your classes this week. Identify the learning method the students used. Develop another version of the same situation in which a different learning method could have been used.

Encouraging Learning from One to Three

Learning begins very early in life. Those who care for children can help prepare a child for school and for life-long learning. Reading to a child every day helps develop the child's reading readiness skills. It's easy to incorporate simple math skills into routine activities by counting and categorizing items with a child. These activities that may seem very routine are important to a young child's intellectual development.

Objectives

- Identify the factors that affect a child's readiness to learn.
- Describe the skills necessary for learning reading and math.
- Explain ways parents and caregivers can guide the learning of young children.
- Give examples of the toys that are appropriate for children at different ages.
- Identify speech delays in young children, and describe how a speech-language pathologist can help.

Key Terms

reading readiness
math readiness
speech-language pathologist
articulation
stuttering

Readiness for Learning

Children can learn a new skill only when they are physically and intellectually ready. For example, it would be a waste of time trying to teach a six-month-old to put on a coat. The baby has neither the physical nor intellectual maturity that the skill requires. Most two-year-olds lack the fine motor skills and conceptual development necessary to learn to print letters and write words. Sometimes adults push children to learn things they aren't ready for. When children aren't able to succeed, feelings of frustration and failure may become stumbling blocks for learning. It is important to remember that children learn and grow at different rates. Therefore, worries such as "Evan is not talking as early as Mackenzie" should be minimized.

On the other hand, children should be taught skills they are ready to learn. For example, because he struggled with the task, Ben's mother dressed him every day, only to discover later that this "helping" caused problems. When Ben was well past the age when he should be able to dress himself, he continued to ask for help. He hadn't developed enough confidence to complete the task on his own. See Fig. 12-7.

Reading Readiness

A child's readiness to read depends in large part on the environment caregivers create. Enjoying books is key to learning to read. From early on, the act of being read to (even very brief sessions for very young children) should become a well-established, daily routine and a special time together. Interact with young children while reading to them. Let the children point at the pages and comment. Ask them to predict what will happen next. The more enthusiastic the reader is, the more enthusiastic children will become about story time. Before age three, **reading readiness**, or learning skills necessary for reading, focuses on children's excitement about reading. The bedtime story accomplishes more than many parents recognize.

- Children learn how to handle books and turn pages.
- They begin to associate written words that appear on the page with words being read aloud.
- Finishing a book creates a sense of accomplishment, especially when the child can choose what to read next.

The next stage of reading readiness involves letter recognition and the understanding that the letters of the alphabet combine to form words on a page. Some children are ready to recognize letters at age three. During reading time, you can encourage the child to name letters recognized on the page. You might respond, "You're right! That's a B—your name begins with a B—Brianna!"

Children's readiness to read on their own may vary widely, so don't expect a strict timetable for acquiring the preliminary

Fig. 12-7 **Children are ready to learn different skills at different times.** What skills do children usually learn before they walk?

skills necessary for reading. It is more important that children learn to enjoy the process. See Fig. 12-8.

Math Readiness

Math is a part of everyday life: counting out a dozen apples, measuring ingredients from a recipe, or counting out coins. People use math so often and so unconsciously, they may overlook experiences they could share with young children. **Math readiness** depends on an interest in learning basic math concepts. As with reading, math can become a welcome and pleasant part of everyday experiences. Children can explore sizes, shapes, amounts, and proportions long before they ever enter a classroom.

- To teach numbers, you can talk to children as they go about their daily routine. "Are there two bananas left this morning, or only one?" "How many plates are set out for dinner?" Counting and number recognition can be taught by making a game of finding numbers. How quickly can a child find a "3" on the signs in the grocery store?
- Blocks and puzzles can teach shape recognition and help in learning the shape names. Sorting is also a good mathematics skill. You can work with children to sort blocks and other items by shape, color, and size.
- Most importantly, children need plenty of time for undirected play and safe exploration. As children explore their environment and everything in it, they will naturally make many discoveries.

Fig. 12-8 **Reading to a young child can help them develop reading readiness skills.** Why is it helpful?

Children Around the World

Preschool in France

In France, nearly every child attends preschool, which is free of charge. It costs the French government about $3,300 per child per year. Preschools are staffed with highly trained teachers. The French government pays for teachers' education, and the government inspects each school every year. Preschool teachers in France earn salaries equal to those of elementary school teachers.

Investigating Culture

1. Do you think that children benefit more from attending preschool and socializing with others, or from staying at home with a parent? Why?
2. Some people argue that in order to create an equal society, high-quality preschool must be available to all children, regardless of their family's income. Do you agree?

Guiding Learning

There are many ways to help guide children's learning. As you read each suggestion, try to remember a time when someone helped enhance your learning in this way.

- **Give your time and attention.** Children learn best when a caring person pays attention to them and encourages them.

- **Allow time for thinking.** Solving problems and making decisions are new experiences for young children. They need time to consider choices and make decisions.

- **Give only as much help as the child needs.** If a toddler is struggling to put on a shirt, don't take over. Instead, just help slip the shirt over the child's head before it gets caught.

Children feel a sense of accomplishment when they achieve things on their own. When possible, let children do the final step in any task they are struggling with. See Fig. 12-9.

- **Encourage children to draw their own conclusions.** "Let's find out" is better than an explanation. Seeing and doing helps reinforce learning and allows for discoveries that prompt further curiosity.

- **Demonstrate how to solve problems.** When a toddler's tower of blocks keeps toppling, demonstrate that stacking one block directly on top of another provides the balance. Then leave building the tower to the toddler.

  - **Model problem solving.** Talk out loud as you solve everyday problems. That allows children to hear how it's possible to think your way to a solution.

  - **Maintain a positive attitude.** Express confidence in the child's abilities. One way is to praise the child's efforts. "Thank you for helping me plant the daisies. You did a great job!"

  - **Keep explanations simple and on the child's level.** Too much information can cause a young child to stop listening. When a child asks about why fish live in water, an appropriate explanation might be, "Fish breathe in water. People need air to breathe."

  - **Allow children to explore and discover.** Exploration is often a messy business. It's important to give children opportunities to roll in the grass, splash in puddles, and squeeze mud through their fingers and toes. Safety is important, but constantly saying "Don't do this" and "Don't touch that" limits the sensory and motor experiences that promote learning.

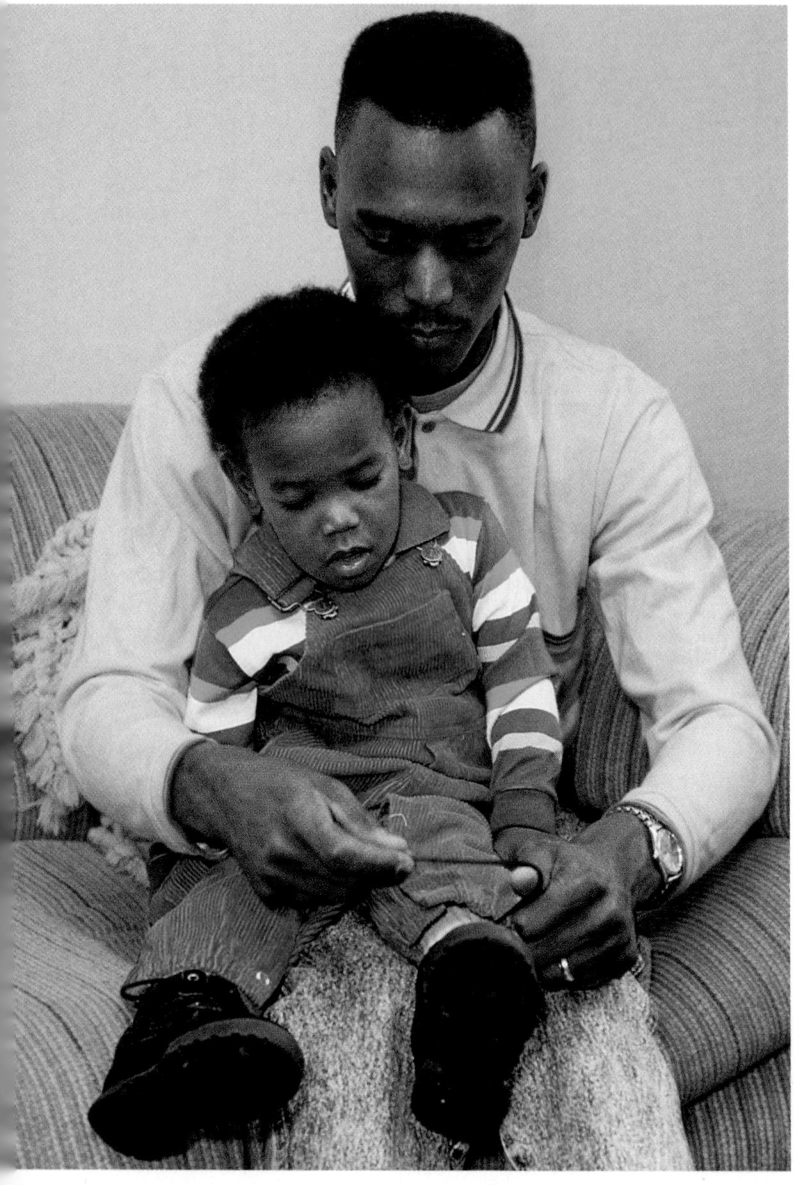

Fig. 12-9 **Don't give children more help than they need. A two-year-old needs more help than a three-year-old.**

- **Help children understand the world and how it works.** Take young children along, even on routine errands. On trips to the library, the supermarket, and the gas station, you could talk about what is happening and why it's happening. Helping out at home also boosts learning. While raking leaves together, for example, you might call attention to the different colors and the crackling sounds of the dried leaves.

- **Take frequent breaks.** A child needs stimulation, but also opportunities for unstructured play. Watch for clear signals that a child has had enough of an activity. Fussing, wiggling in a chair, or looking distracted all suggest that it's time to move on.

Play Activities and Toys

Toys are an important part of play. They help children to explore, imagine, and try out different roles. They encourage the development of motor skills and help children learn to share and cooperate with others, making further learning easier and more fun.

Stimulating Play Activities

Often a child's favorite "toy" is really a caregiver. After all, a toy can't respond as instantly and individually to the child's efforts at play and imagination. Some adults are reluctant to get down on the floor and play with children. Such interaction can expand the child's learning.

LOOKING AT REAL LIFE

Three-year-old Molly was excited when she woke up. Liz was taking care of her today! When Liz arrived that morning, Molly asked to have pancakes for breakfast. "I'll help you," said Molly confidently. While Liz got out the pancake mix, Molly watched. "How many cups of mix do we use, Molly?" asked Liz. "I know! Two!" said Molly. "You put it in a bowl." "That's exactly right. Let's use the big blue bowl today." Molly got out the bowl and handed it to Liz. "Thank you," said Liz. "Now I'll measure the mix." Liz filled a cup measure and let Molly level the cup with a spatula and put the mix in the blue bowl. Liz asked, "How many eggs?" "One!" "Right again!" Liz smiled at her helper. Liz measured the milk and Molly stirred it into the mix herself. Molly liked to count the pancakes in the pan as Liz cooked them and commented that the pancakes were the same color as the kitchen floor—brown!

▶▶**PERSONAL APPLICATION**

1. Were you allowed to help with chores or meals when you were Molly's age? What skills or concepts do you think you learned?
2. Make a list of the concepts and skills Molly was learning as she helped to make the pancakes. How do you think that Molly will be able to use these skills when she goes to school?

At the same time, the parent or caregiver can learn more about the child's interests and talents.

Evaluating Toys

With thousands of toys to choose from, knowing what to buy is important. See Fig. 12-10. Parents should ask themselves these questions:

- **Is the toy safe?** This is the single most important consideration. Check that there are no small parts that could be swallowed or sharp edges that could cut. Also check to make sure the toy is not flammable and indicates "nontoxic" when appropriate. The federal government's Consumer Products Safety Commission alerts the public about unsafe toys.

Fig. 12-10 How would you rate the toy in the photo based on the questions in this section?

- **Is it well-made and durable?** There is nothing more discouraging for a child—or an adult—than having a toy break the first time it's played with. Can the toy withstand the rough treatment it will receive?

- **Will it be easy to care for?** A well-loved stuffed animal needs to be washable. Similarly, books with hard pages and wipe-clean covers are the most practical choice for toddlers.

- **Does it encourage the use of a child's imagination?** Some toys do everything for the child. With no need to pretend, the child's imagination develops more slowly. Look for simple toys that can be used in a variety of ways. A talking doll may say ten phrases, but a child can make an ordinary doll say anything!

- **Is it colorful?** Young children respond more readily to colorful objects. These toys also encourage children to learn the names of colors.

- **Will it be easy for the child to handle?** Think about the size of the toy and its level of difficulty. The excitement of receiving a pink motorized car is quickly lost if the child is too young to operate it on her own.

- **Is it something the child will enjoy?** A toy that a child finds engaging is much better than a toy forced upon him by a well-intentioned parent or relative.

Age-Appropriate Toys

Toys should also be appropriate for a child's age. Infant toys are usually not challenging enough for three-year-olds, nor are an older child's toys able to hold the attention of most fourteen-month-olds. Children at different ages enjoy and learn from different kinds of toys. The following are some suggestions for age-appropriate toys. See Fig. 12-11.

- **One to two years.** At this age, a child practices motor control and learns through exploration. Some favorite toys are household items, such as metal pans, wooden spoons, and plastic storage containers. Pull toys, floating bath toys, pianos, and other toys that make music, and sorting toys are popular. Most toys that allow the child to use large muscles are also good choices. These items may include swings, riding toys with wheels, large balls, wagons, and cardboard boxes. One-year-olds also enjoy dolls and stuffed animals, sturdy books, simple puzzles, and toy cars. Physicians recommend avoiding toys with parts that are small enough to fit into the cardboard tube from a roll of toilet paper.

- **Two to three years.** Coordination and understanding improve greatly during this year. In addition, the child wants to do what adults are doing. The desire to imitate and role play provides ideas for a variety of toys: a child-size vacuum cleaner or lawn mower, shopping cart, telephone, plastic or wooden tools, play dishes and food, and empty food containers. Crayons, play dough, large beads to string, books, and large blocks are popular. A sandbox and a toy bucket and shovel can provide hours of enjoyment.

- **Three to four years.** Preschoolers' improved motor skills and increased imagination bring interest in more complex toys requiring fine motor skills. Dolls to dress, construction sets, and similar toys are popular. Three-year-olds love to mold play dough, color, cut with blunt scissors, and paint. Three-year-olds spend longer periods with books than younger children, and enjoy listening to

Fig. 12-11 **Toys should be age-appropriate and enjoyable for a child.**

music. They enjoy doing puzzles and using swings and slides. Most three-year-olds love to ride a tricycle.

Speech Development

 In the toddler and preschool years, language abilities grow at a very rapid pace. As with other areas of development, children's speech varies greatly. Brain development research has brought new insights into how children learn to use language. Children have an inborn ability to decipher sounds, words, sentences, and grammar from the language they hear. Most children develop language skills in the first three years of life.

Between their first and second birthdays, children work at learning new words. They like to learn the names of everything, and they enjoy listening to the sounds the words

Fig. 12-12 **Children's language development is influenced by how adults around them speak.**

make. At this point, rhyming books that tell stories are ideal. At twelve months of age, a child may speak two to eight words, but by age two, that jumps to about 200 words. During this period, most children use one or two words rather than a whole sentence to express a thought. For example, Charlene points to a jar on the counter and says "cookie" to mean "I want a cookie."

Encourage language development and learning by talking to young children about their lives. Speak clearly about children's everyday experiences. For example, take the time to describe and guide children by talking about whatever they are seeing or doing. "Look at the big bite you've taken out of that yellow banana. Does it taste sweet and yummy?" See Fig. 12-12.

At about age two, children usually start combining a few words to make short sentences: "Doggie bark." "Jimmy fall down." Between ages one and two, a child typically calls himself or herself by name. At about two years of age, children begin to use pronouns, such as "I," "we," "you," and "they."

At about two and a half, children begin to pick up some of the rules of grammar. They learn by listening to other people talk rather than by any formal teaching. For example, a child begins to add an *s* to words to make them plural. The child then—quite logically—applies this rule to all words; *foots* and *tooths* make as much sense as *hands* and *eyes*.

Speech Difficulties

Parents become concerned when they believe their child is a "late talker." Some make the mistake of pressuring the child, but this pressure just makes the child aware of the problem, possibly making it worse.

A child who doesn't seem to understand what is said, doesn't speak at all, or speaks very little should have a thorough examination. Local public school districts often provide free screenings by a **speech-language pathologist**, a specialist who is trained to detect and correct speech problems. Speech difficulties can often be treated beginning at age three. It is important to identify, as early as possible, any physical problem(s) that may be interfering with a child's language development. Hearing problems, learning disabilities, and mood disorders may all hinder a child's speech development.

Difficulty with **articulation**, the ability to use clear, distinct speech, is common until at least age three or four. Some children skip syllables or leave off the endings of words. These problems usually correct themselves over time. A speech-language pathologist can determine whether a problem is likely to go away on its own or if speech therapy is needed.

Instead of constantly correcting a child's pronunciation of words, it's important for adults to set a good example with their own speech. If a toddler says "ba" and reaches for a bottle, the caregiver can hand the bottle over, and say, "Bottle. Aurora wants her bottle."

Stuttering is a more serious speech difficulty for young children. This occurs

Parenting Q&A

What Are Some Signs of Language Development?

Early on, infants learn to recognize the speech of their parents and other caregivers. Shortly thereafter, infants begin practicing the sounds of speech by babbling. Beginning at around twelve months of age, babbling gradually transforms into a child's first words.

Between thirteen and twenty months, a toddler's brain becomes ever more focused in the way it responds to words. In this phase, a child acquires an understanding of the way words should sound and practices speaking.

At around age two, children begin absorbing vocabulary quickly, which is reflected in their growing language skills. Below are some general guidelines; bear in mind, though, that children's language abilities develop at different rates.

Most three-year-olds can:
- Say their name and age.
- Make all the vowel sounds and say the consonants P, B, M, W, H, D, T, and N.
- Speak without repeating a word or syllable.
- Use sentences of at least four words.
- Usually be understood by others, even strangers.
- Answer "what" and "where" questions.
- Understand what is meant by "on," "in," and "under."
- Follow a command with several parts.

THINKING IT THROUGH

1. Why is it important that a child be understood by strangers as well as caregivers?
2. What does a child's ability to follow a multi-step command say about his or her memory?

when a person speaks with sporadic repetition or prolonged sounds. However, many adults mistake normal speech hesitations for stuttering. A child may repeat whole words or phrases: "Johnny... Johnny... Johnny. He... he... he hit Zoe!" This isn't true stuttering. In this case, the child's speaking and thinking abilities are still immature, making it difficult to get the words out rapidly and smoothly.

True stuttering can be identified by the rhythm, pitch, and speed of speech. It is rapid, forced, and short and sharp in sound. Usually, the child repeats only the beginning sound of a word: "I c—c—c—can't g—g—g—go outside." The child often also shows tenseness in some way—with gasping, sputtering, or rapid blinking, for instance.

The cause or causes of stuttering are still not completely understood. Some children overcome the problem with speech therapy. However, most children who stutter outgrow it. Experts advise against finishing words for a child. Children who stutter need time to say the words on their own.

Children with speech difficulties need to be lovingly encouraged. Such an attitude will help the child cope with, and perhaps even overcome, the problem. Teasing or constant corrections only worsen the problem.

SECTION 12-2 Review and Activities

Reviewing the Section

1. Why can't a typical one-year-old be taught to write?
2. Define *reading* and *math readiness*.
3. Choose one of the principles for guiding a child's learning and give an example of a caregiver putting it into practice.
4. How does play promote physical, emotional, social, and intellectual development?
5. Recall a toy you enjoyed playing with as a child. Evaluate the benefits of that toy for young children.
6. List at least four toys the are appropriate and fun for toddlers between the ages of one and two.
7. Describe what children between the ages of two and three enjoy most.
8. Why is it better to use grammatically correct sentences when speaking to a child?
9. Identify two kinds of difficulties that might indicate that speech therapy is needed.

Observing and Interacting

Write a description of a routine chore such as putting away toys or clothes. Then describe how you would talk to a one-year-old, a two-year-old, or a three-year-old in your care about this chore. How could you get the child to help with the chore and make it a routine?

Play Therapist

Play is children's natural language. Troubled or abused children often have difficulty making sense of their experiences. Some are angry, lonely, or confused. Play therapists offer children a way to express themselves using dolls, animals, puppets, beanbags, and other familiar objects.

▸ Job Responsibilities

In play therapy, the child directs the action, choosing characters and setting stages. Play therapists believe that children's play reflects their wants, needs, and fears. They create a safe environment for play, interpret children's behavior, and help children overcome their fears.

▸ Work Environment

Play therapists often have private offices where they see children and families. Some work in hospitals or clinics.

▸ Education and Training

Play therapists usually hold bachelor's degrees in social work, psychology, or counseling. In order to become registered, play therapists must earn a master's degree and gain work experience. They must also take classes every few years in order to maintain and upgrade their skills.

▸ Aptitudes Needed

- Imagination
- Good communication skills
- Ability to express empathy
- Sense of fun
- Desire to help children

WORKPLACE CONNECTION

1. **Thinking Skills.** What kinds of experiences help people develop their ability to express empathy?

2. **Resource Skills.** Where could you go to get more information about working with troubled children?

CHAPTER 12

Review and Activities

SECTION SUMMARIES

- Intelligence is determined by heredity and environment. (12-1)
- Children learn concepts and the words for those concepts in stages. (12-1)
- Children use four different methods to learn. (12-1)
- There are seven areas of intellectual activity, ranging from memory to curiosity. (12-1)
- Caregivers can encourage reading and math readiness during play and everyday activities. (12-2)
- Toys should be safe, appealing, and appropriate to a child's age. (12-2)
- How caregivers speak to children can affect speech development. (12-2)

REVIEWING THE CHAPTER

1. What significance does brain research have for learning? (12-1)
2. What effects do *intelligence* and environment each have on learning? (12-1)
3. Compare an eighteen-month-old's ability to distinguish sizes to that of a three-year-old. What are the differences in development? (12-1)
4. Identify and give examples of at least five of the seven areas of intellectual activity. (12-1)
5. How can a caregiver help a child to develop *reading readiness* skills? (12-2)
6. Why is it important for a child to develop *math readiness* skills? (12-2)
7. What are three causes of speech delays in young children? (12-2)
8. What can parents investigate to determine whether their child has a speech delay? (12-2)
9. Identify three appropriate toys for a one-year-old. (12-2)

THINKING CRITICALLY

1. **Summarizing Information.** What method or methods of learning do children use as they acquire language skills? Explain how children use this method.
2. **Interpreting Data.** Make a chart showing the kinds of skills—gross motor, fine motor, social, or intellectual—that are developed by three of the toys listed on page 399. Keep in mind that a single toy can encourage more than one skill.

MAKING CONNECTIONS

1. **Art.** Create a poster that could help children learn a concept such as shape, color, or size.
2. **Science.** Research recent discoveries about how the brain makes and stores memories. What types of sights, sounds, colors, or words are most commonly remembered? What makes these memorable? Prepare a summary of your results.

APPLYING YOUR LEARNING

1. **Finding Resources.** You are a teacher of three-year-olds in a child care center. Choose one kind of activity related to art, music, or language, such as painting, and make a list of the kinds of play and toys that you would supply to promote that area of learning.
2. **Communicating Goals.** From the same point of view, write a brochure that presents to parents the guided learning goals of the child care center. Use the suggestions outlined on pages 395–397 to present your own ideas and examples. Make sure you address how the center builds learning readiness skills of children one to three years old.
3. **Learning at Home.** Identify an object that is found in most homes. List the ways in which this object could be used to help a young child learn. Offer at least one example for each of the four methods of learning.

Learning from Research

1. Choose one of the following research claims to investigate.
2. How is this research finding useful to parents of children who stutter?
3. Summarize what you've learned about factors that play a role in stuttering.

Stuttering and Genes. Most researchers believe that genetic, neurological, and social factors all play a role in stuttering. Cite examples of how researchers think genetic, neurological, and social factors are related to stuttering.

Stuttering and Anxiety. Researchers know that anxiety can make stuttering worse, and that anticipating each struggle to produce words leads to greater anxiety. Researchers have tested anti-anxiety drugs and found that they reduce stuttering in some patients. What other types of medication have researchers tested, and what did they find?

Stuttering and the Brain. Researchers have found differences in the ways the brains of people who stutter process information, even when they are not speaking. When people who stutter are given a language task, certain areas of their brains become more active, and response time is delayed. Find out which areas of the brain are affected and identify ways researchers can help stutterers speak more clearly.

The Child from Four to Six

Chapter 13
Physical Development from
Four to Six

Chapter 14
Emotional and Social Development
from Four to Six

Chapter 15
Intellectual Development from
Four to Six

13 Physical Development from Four to Six

Thoughtful Reading:

As you read this chapter:

- Ask questions about what you are reading.
- Identify new information you learn from what you read.
- Connect what you read to your personal experiences.

Section 13-1
Growth and Development from Four to Six

Section 13-2
Caring for Children from Four to Six

Growth and Development from Four to Six

If you've ever been around a four-, five-, or six-year-old, you know how active children are at this time of life. Instead of sitting still, they wiggle. Rather than walking, they run. It's sometimes hard to get them to stay in one place long enough to put on their clothes or eat. So what's the purpose behind all this activity? The answer is simple: Practice makes perfect. Children this age are constantly refining their physical skills.

Objectives

- Summarize how an average child's height, weight, posture, and body shape change from ages four to six.
- Explain the changes to a child's teeth that generally begin around age six.
- Identify when and why thumb sucking may become a problem for children.
- Compare average motor development of four-, five-, and six-year-olds.

Key Terms

permanent teeth
ambidextrous

Height and Weight

The rate of physical growth in children between the ages of four to six is only slightly slower than in children ages one to three. The average increase in height during these years is about 2½ to 3 inches (6.4 to 7.6 cm) per year. Most children gain about 4 to 5 pounds (1.8 to 2.3 kg) every year as well. Of course, these are just average gains among children, so larger or smaller gains are common, too.

Boys tend to be slightly taller and heavier than girls during this period. See Fig. 13-1 on page 410.

Most children will begin kindergarten at age five or six. Before they can attend school, however, they are typically required to receive a medical checkup and certain immunizations. Most schools require immunizations against hepatitis B, diphtheria, tetanus, pertussis (whooping cough), polio, measles, mumps, and rubella (German measles). More and more schools also require immunization against chicken pox. Parents and caregivers should check with the school to find out the specific requirements.

Posture and Body Shape

Children's posture changes noticeably between their fourth and seventh birthdays. Their bodies become straighter and slimmer, and the protruding tummy from babyhood flattens. Children this age hold their shoulders back and their upper bodies more erect. The chest, which had previously been rounded, broadens and flattens with improved abdominal strength. The legs also lengthen rapidly, growing straighter and firmer. Even the neck becomes longer.

Balance and coordination show improvement in these years as well. Four- to six-year-olds hold their arms nearer their body when they walk or run.

Teeth

School pictures of a six-year-old typically show a gaping hole in the child's smile. At about this time, larger **permanent teeth**, which will not be naturally replaced by another set, begin to appear. They replace the primary teeth that the child has lost. Children will eventually have a total of 32 teeth in the permanent set, to replace the 20 primary teeth.

The six-year-old molars, or "first molars," are the first permanent teeth to appear. These are new teeth, not replacements for primary teeth. There are four of them—two upper and two lower—positioned in back of the primary teeth. These molars act as an anchor, keeping all the teeth in front of them in place. The primary teeth are lost in the same order as they came in: the two lower front teeth first, then the two upper front teeth.

Thumb Sucking

Some four-, five-, and six-year-olds continue to suck their thumbs occasionally as a way to comfort themselves or handle stress. Adults may worry about this habit, but in most cases, it's best ignored. Trying to force a child to quit can cause more problems than the habit itself. Generally, children stop sucking their thumbs on their own.

If thumb sucking seems excessive, however, check with a dentist. After the child's fifth birthday, thumb sucking may cause changes in the shape of the roof of the mouth or in the way the teeth line up.

Fig. 13-1 Average Height and Weight: Ages Four to Six				
	BOYS		GIRLS	
Age	Height / Inches	Weight / Pounds	Height / Inches	Weight / Pounds
Four years	40½	36	39½	35½
Five years	43	40½	42½	39¾
Six years	45½	46	45¼	44½

Fig. 13-1 As children grow older, they experience significant differences in height and weight.

Motor Skills

From ages four to six, most basic gross and fine motor skills improve significantly in children. The timetable for the development of these skills varies. Just as in the earlier years, some children master one skill but are not as proficient at another. For example, one five-year-old may have the skills to put together complex puzzles but not yet be able to jump rope. Her neighbor may be comfortable with easier puzzles but excel at jumping rope. The "Developmental Milestones" chart, Fig. 13-2 on page 412, summarizes typical motor skills at each age.

Four-, five-, and six-year-olds are very energetic. Their favorite activities are usually physical—running, jumping, climbing, and turning somersaults. After age four, children are learning how to throw and catch both large and small balls. Five-year-olds show improved speed and coordination in all their activities. The movements of six-year-olds are even more smoothly coordinated. Six-year-olds enjoy balancing activities, such as walking on a curb or learning to ride a bicycle. Activities that involve rhythm appeal to them: they like keeping time to music and jumping rope to chanted songs.

Four- and five-year-olds show improved dexterity. They can use their hands and fingers skillfully. Most four-year-olds can learn to lace their shoes, but aren't able to tie them until they're five. Five-year-olds' hand-eye coordination has improved to the point that they can pour liquids from a pitcher—unless it's heavy or very full—into a glass. They enjoy cutting, pasting, and using glue. Five-year-olds also can print some letters but might have difficulty printing words. Six-year-olds show even greater fine motor skills and improved hand-eye coordination. Most children this age are able to draw detailed pictures, use scissors, and write their own names.

LOOKING AT REAL LIFE

Five-year-old Sean was upset that a first grader had called him a "baby" because he sucks his thumb. Tamisha, his nanny, assured him that he was not a baby. He was a big boy. Seeing that Sean was still obviously concerned, Tamisha reminded him he could always talk to her about anything that was bothering him. Sean said he still felt shy around the kids and the teacher. Tamisha agreed that it did take some time to get to know new classmates, and said that she could ask his teacher to set him up with a buddy tomorrow.

▶▶ PERSONAL APPLICATION

1. At what age do you think it's still appropriate for a child to suck his or her thumb? How could you encourage him or her to stop this behavior?
2. How can a teacher find ways to make sure all children feel included in activities and don't get left out simply because they are shy?

Fine Motor Skills	Gross Motor Skills

4 YEARS

- Dresses and undresses self
- Cuts on line with scissors
- Copies a circle and a cross

- Hops on one foot
- Throws ball overhand
- Alternates feet walking up and down stairs
- Walks backward easily

5 YEARS

- Draws a person with head, body, arms, and legs
- Prints some letters
- Buttons clothing
- Copies a triangle and a square
- Uses spoon and fork to eat, but still uses fingers for some foods

- Turns somersaults
- Skips with alternating feet
- Balances on each foot for short period

6 YEARS

- Cuts, pastes, and colors skillfully
- Writes entire words
- Ties shoes

- Can ride a two-wheel bicycle with training wheels
- Jumps rope
- Throws and catches a ball with more ease and accuracy (also requires fine motor skills and good hand-eye coordination)

Taking on Roles

Children of all ages frequently take on roles of other people when they play. Using dress-up clothes and other props, children love to pretend to be other people. Very young children choose roles in play that are close to their own experience. Children will frequently pretend to be a parent or teacher. However, as children learn more about the world, other characters become a part of their play. Children may not know these characters personally, but they have had some experience with them or have heard of them. Some of these characters include firefighters, police officers, nurses, or doctors. Children may begin to pretend by suggesting a plan, such as "Let's drive to the store and get something to eat." Playing different roles is a way for children to express their creativity and explore a world outside of their own.

Following Up

What could you provide to encourage this type of play when you care for children?

Children need plenty of opportunities to develop their motor skills. Giving them time and space to run, jump, and climb on play structures helps them develop their large motor skills. Activities such as making cards, painting pictures, drawing, tracing outlines, cutting, and playing games help them build small motor skills. Children with well-developed fine motor skills may be more successful at learning to print.

Hand Preference

As mentioned in Chapter 10, some children express a preference for using one hand over the other after the age of two. Others may continue to switch off during the preschool years. By about the second half of the fifth year, most children consistently use either their right or left hand for most activities. Naturally, whichever hand they choose becomes the stronger, more skillful one. Only a few people are **ambidextrous**, which means they are able to use both hands with equal skill.

Research continues on how a preference for one hand develops. Some people believe that heredity is probably the source of right- or left-handedness. Others think it depends on which hand parents usually put objects in during the child's early years. Whatever the cause, professionals agree that there's no reason to influence a child toward using one hand over the other.

SECTION 13-1 Review and Activities

Reviewing the Section

1. Describe the changes in a child's height and weight from ages four to six.
2. Describe how a six-year-old child's body shape and posture are different from those of a three-year-old.
3. What are two ways permanent teeth differ from primary teeth?
4. At what age might thumb-sucking be a problem for children? What concerns may a dentist have about a thumb-sucking habit at that age?
5. Name three motor skills that an average six-year-old has mastered that most three-year-olds would not be able to do.
6. Other than those mentioned in the chapter, what are three activities that can help children this age refine their small motor skills?

Observing and Interacting

Observe young children playing at a park or playground. Watch them, record what they are doing, and try to determine how old they are, based on their behavior. Write a report of your observation and conclusions.

Caring for Children from Four to Six

Four-, five-, and six-year-olds are more independent and need less physical care than younger children do. Many four-year-olds attend preschool programs, and most five-year-olds are in kindergarten for a full or half day. By age six, children are typically in school for a full day. Despite this new level of independence, four- to six-year-olds still need guidance in developing self-care skills.

Objectives

- Explain why good nutrition is essential for children ages four to six.
- Give examples of ways to encourage good nutrition and physical activity in children.
- Evaluate how poor nutrition may affect physical development.
- Describe the ways children from ages four to six develop good self-care habits.

Key Terms

fluoride
group identification

Providing Good Nutrition

A steady and varied supply of nutritious foods is the best fuel for children's physical and intellectual development. The recommendations in Guidelines for Healthy Eating on page 154 can help parents choose foods for good nutrition. The amount of food children need varies depending on their weight and level of physical activity.

For example, Stephanie spends hours kicking a soccer ball, running with her dog, and riding her bike. She needs more food energy than her cousin, who prefers coloring and building with blocks. Older or very active children need more food daily, while younger or less active children require less. USDA's MyPyramid Plan gives guidance.

Research has shown that children at this age fare better when they eat five or six small, nutritious meals and snacks a day instead of three large ones. Small meals and snacks are better suited to their small stomach size and provide a more constant level of energy. Snacks should be nutritious, appealing foods rather than convenience foods that are high in salt, sugar, or fat. Apple slices, grapes, cheese, yogurt, and raisins are nutritious and popular with this age group.

Parents and other caregivers can encourage good eating habits by making food appealing and by modeling good food habits themselves. Researchers have found that forcing a child to eat, making an issue of eating certain foods, or using foods as a reward may lead to poor eating habits and weight issues.

Fig. 13-3 **Children ages four to six are eager to help around the kitchen.** What are some tasks parents can ask them to perform?

Teaching Children About Nutrition

Nutrition lessons learned early in life can lay the foundation for a lifetime of better health and prepare children to make wise food choices at home and at school.

It's also important that parents keep tabs on how much time children spend in front of the television. Children may watch television instead of participating in physical activity. In addition, TV commercials try to persuade kids to choose high-fat snacks and high-sugar drinks and cereals. Parents should make children aware of these pressures. When they do, their children are more likely to make better choices.

At Home

Parents can take advantage of children's natural curiosity at this stage and use food as a rich resource for learning. See Fig. 13-3. Involving children in the ways their families obtain and prepare food can increase their interest in it. For example, children who visit or help tend a garden are often more willing to try new vegetables.

Children can tear lettuce for salads, stir orange juice concentrate, or mix batter. They enjoy cutting shapes out of bread. They can make mini pizzas by flattening pizza dough, pouring on tomato sauce, and sprinkling on cheese or other toppings.

Teaching children about food in this way offers other advantages as well. Children feel proud of the contributions they have made to family meals. Activities like these help children improve their fine motor skills. Spending time in the kitchen together adds to the amount of positive time that parents and children spend working together, which rewards both adults and children.

At School

Schools also use food as a learning tool, especially with younger children. Teachers might ask children questions about the texture, quantity, appearance, or nutrition of food. Consider a preschool snack of peanut butter, celery, and raisins. For preschoolers, spreading peanut butter on a celery stick and sprinkling raisins on the top provides a variety of lessons, as well as practice with fine motor skills. See Fig. 13-4.

Children can learn that these ingredients are good for them and help them grow, and that they come from different food groups. They can answer questions about the different textures of these foods, or a teacher might have them count the number of raisins they used.

For many children, school lunch will be the first time they will make an independent choice about what to eat. Children who are in school all day usually eat the lunch offered at school or bring lunch from home. However, what children are given to eat and what they actually eat may be quite different, as they often trade or throw food away.

Classmates or school lunch programs may introduce children to foods they never receive at home. Some of these foods may be high in sugar, fats, or salt. It's a good idea for parents to review which foods are more healthful than others—an apple over a candy bar, or pretzels over French fries, for example. In addition, children who bring their lunches will be less likely to trade foods if they already have nutritious, appealing foods of their own.

Nutritional Concerns

Two signs that children are meeting their nutritional needs for normal growth and development are gaining weight at an appropriate rate and eating a variety of nutritious foods. Even picky eaters can stay healthy and grow if their choices result in a well-balanced diet.

Poor Nutrition

Contrary to popular belief, lack of money to buy healthful foods is *not* the most common cause of poor nutrition.

Some parents and caregivers are simply not aware of the need for good nutrition, or they may not understand the basics of good nutrition. They may rely too heavily on convenience foods or foods from fast-food restaurants to save time. Although some of these foods may be nutritious, they are often very high in calories, salt, and fats.

Some adults set a poor example by frequently snacking on high-calorie foods. Some allow young children to choose their own food without guidance. It is the responsibility of parents and caregivers to provide children with healthful food and help them to learn to make appropriate choices.

Poor nutrition undermines the health of children. Children who lack essential nutrition have less resistance to illnesses, may not grow adequately, and may have learning difficulties.

Weight Problems

Children from four to six vary in their body type. They may look chunky or slim and still be healthy. If there are any concerns about a child's weight, parents and caregivers should consult the child's doctor before deciding that a child is overweight or underweight. If the doctor detects an issue with weight, there are many ways to help the child. Parents and caregivers might record the child's diet and physical activity over the course of a week. Often, this record alone will identify needed changes.

Children Around the World

"Health Clubs" in Singapore

More children are overweight or obese in the world today than ever before. Societies are tackling the problem in different ways. In Singapore, overweight schoolchildren must take part in a "health club" at school in which they exercise. Teachers monitor overweight students' height and weight every month. Schools don't restrict what students eat, but teachers do meet with overweight students' parents to discuss what they feed their children.

Investigating Culture

1. Do you think that Singapore's idea for its students is a good one?
2. Research other ways that societies are dealing with the problem of childhood obesity and summarize what you learned.

HOW TO

Encourage Physical Activity

Teaching young children to enjoy regular physical activity can bring lifelong health benefits. Here are some other ways to help get children up and moving:

- **Involve children in daily activities.** Children gain both exercise and a sense of accomplishment when they help out at home.

- **Enjoy fun activities together.** Activities such as biking, swimming, walking, hiking, and skating can involve the whole family.

- **Focus on age-appropriate activities.** Some sports and other physical activities are too challenging for young children and can discourage them from wanting to participate. Choose activities that are developmentally appropriate for the child.

- **Model active behavior in everyday activities.** Be a role model. Take the stairs instead of an escalator or an elevator. When possible, ride a bicycle or walk to get places. Limit such sedentary activities as television and computer games.

- **Find a team or individual sport that the child enjoys.** As children start school, sports are a natural way to engage in physical activity. If a child enjoys a sport, support that interest by playing the sport with the child or finding a team for the child to join.

- **Find friends to join the fun.** Children enjoy having a buddy with whom they can play. Bring along friends on a trip to the park.

YOUR TURN

Communication. Some parents work long hours and wonder how to find time to play with their children and to encourage physical activity. If you were a pediatrician, what ways would you recommend that busy parents could help encourage physical activity in their child?

The Guidelines for Healthy Eating are always a good place to start in planning healthful meals and snacks. If the problem is more severe, a dietitian or nutritionist can help parents and other caregivers design a program to promote changes in diet or activity level.

When a child eats more calories than the body uses through physical activity, the body stores the extra calories as fat. If this happens consistently over time, the child is at risk for being overweight. Conversely, a child who consistently eats fewer calories than his or her body needs may become underweight. Neither of these conditions typically occurs suddenly. Instead, both result from poor eating habits over time.

The number of overweight children has been rising. Overweight children are at increased risk of being overweight or obese as adults and developing life-threatening diseases, such as diabetes and heart disease.

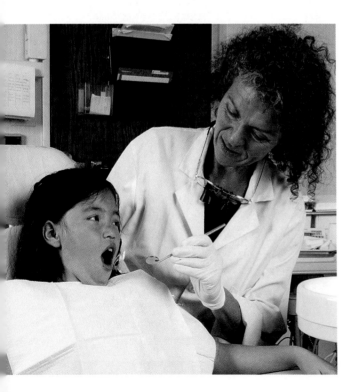

Teaching Self-Care Skills

As the physical strength and motor skills of four- to six-year-olds improve, they become increasingly able to care for themselves. They can wash and dress themselves, brush their teeth, and begin to care for their clothes.

Washing and Bathing

Although bath time continues to be fun for some children, many this age are less interested in washing and bathing regularly than they were when they were younger. Some children just don't like to take the time to stop playing to bathe.

Praising children for taking a bath or shower is much more effective than nagging them to do so. Setting up and maintaining hygiene routines helps children accept these tasks as expected behavior.

Caring for Teeth

Regular tooth brushing and flossing is another essential routine that parents can teach their children. Until a child handles a toothbrush well, at about the age of five, dentists recommend that parents help with brushing and flossing, especially at night.

Tooth decay is a special concern because permanent teeth are coming in. Regular dental checkups and cleanings are important. Sometimes dentists apply a coating of **fluoride** to children's teeth. Fluoride strengthens the enamel (the hard, outer coating) of teeth to help prevent decay. Fluoride is often added to drinking water and most toothpastes. See Fig. 13-5.

Fig. 13-5 **Regular tooth brushing helps children prevent tooth decay.** Why is tooth decay of greater concern at this age?

Health & Safety

Outdoor Safety, Ages Four to Six

Children ages four to six spend much of their time playing outside. For this reason, it is very important to teach children about outdoor safety. Here are some safety guidelines for outdoor play.

Bicycles can be fun for five- and six-year-olds, but can also pose dangers to the rider. A safety helmet should always be worn to protect the head from injury. Children should be taught the rules of the road when riding a bike. For more information on bicycle safety, see page 584.

Swings are the most common cause of injury from moving equipment on a playground. To reduce the risk of injuries on swings, children should always sit in the swing, not stand or kneel, and stay a safe distance away from other children who are swinging.

Slides are safe if children are careful when using them and hold onto the handrails when climbing ladders to the top. Children should also slide down feet-first and one at a time, not in groups.

Climbing equipment poses the greatest risk of any stationary equipment on public playgrounds. Falling is the most common cause of injury for children of all ages. Make sure there are not too many children on the equipment at once. Adult supervision is especially important for younger children, who might not have the arm strength necessary for play on climbing equipment.

Traffic is one of the most dangerous situations children can encounter when playing outside. Children must be taught to look both ways before crossing the street and not play near parked cars.

Strangers are not always people who will harm children. Nonetheless, children should be taught to avoid contact with people they don't know unless the stranger is accompanied by an adult whom they do know.

Check-Up

What are some other outdoor safety guidelines for this age group?

However, as children start school, two other factors become important in clothes selection. First, children this age have definite likes and dislikes. Some become attached to a favorite garment, as they do to a particular toy. Second, **group identification**—a feeling of belonging—becomes important at this age and may bring with it a desire to wear clothes like those of classmates.

Parents can help satisfy children's desire to wear certain clothes by allowing them to select some of their clothes. See Fig. 13-6.

Caring for Clothes

Once children begin to care about what they wear, they can learn basic clothing care. To start, they can fold and hang up clothes and put dirty items in the appropriate place. Putting clothes away is simpler if the child has storage within reach. Hooks at eye level, low rods, and handy shelves and containers are helpful.

Good habits for taking care of clothes won't develop overnight and will require consistent but gentle reminders. To many parents, it just seems easier to continue doing such tasks for their children. However, this is the stage of development when children need to increase their independence and sense of responsibility. Parents who continue to pick up and put away clothes for their children run the risk of having teens who expect the same service.

Sleeping

By the age of four, many children no longer take an afternoon nap. Some continue taking a daily nap until they begin a full day of school, depending on their needs. Without an afternoon nap, nighttime sleep becomes even more important. Most

Fig. 13-6 Children develop personal tastes in clothing as they get older and enjoy having the opportunity to choose some clothes for themselves. How can parents teach responsibility for caring for clothes?

Dressing and Choosing Clothes

Four-, five-, and six-year-olds are usually able to dress by themselves. Some may need help with complicated fasteners such as shoelaces or buttons down the back.

Many children have difficulty figuring out which clothes match. Parents can help a child learn about matching colors and clothes by helping the child select coordinating outfits ahead of time and storing them together.

Comfort, durability, and economy remain the guidelines for choosing clothes.

Parenting Q&A

What Is the Best Way to Handle Bedwetting?

It is not unusual for children who have learned to use the toilet to occasionally wet the bed at night. According to the National Institute of Health, more than seven percent of boys and three percent of girls wet the bed at age five. Either the child's bladder is not large enough to hold urine during the night, or the child is not awakened by the feeling of a full bladder. Sometimes the cause is an infection in the urinary tract. Here are some tips for dealing with bedwetting:

- **Treat bedwetting accidents casually.** Shaming or scolding a child doesn't help.
- **Make sure the child understands that the wetting is not his or her fault and that it will eventually stop.**
- **Reduce the amount of fluid the child drinks before bed.**
- **A small percentage of children continue to wet the bed as they get older, but almost all stop by the time they are teens.** Children need continued support and reassurance that they will outgrow the problem.

THINKING IT THROUGH

1. How are children older than five likely to feel when they wet the bed at night?
2. If you were a parent whose child has had episodes of wetting the bed at age six, how would you respond if someone invited your child to sleep over?

---

children this age need ten to twelve hours of sleep each night. In order to ensure this amount of sleep, parents and caregivers need to decide on an appropriate bedtime. If the child has to wake up early for school or child care, an early bedtime is best. This can often be hard on parents who work all day and don't have much time to spend with their children. However, it is important to keep in mind that a well-rested child will be healthier and happier than a tired and irritable one.

Children this age are generally more cooperative about going to bed. Some use delaying tactics, but many actually ask to go to bed. After saying goodnight and perhaps looking at a book or listening to soft music for a short while, most go to sleep easily. Some children may need conversation, companionship, or the comfort of a stuffed toy or favorite blanket to sleep. Reading bedtime stories continues to be a way that parents can nurture children and encourage an interest in books and reading. Ongoing bedtime rituals remain comforting to many young children.

Toileting

By their fourth birthday, most children have few toileting accidents—either at night or during the day. When accidents do occur, it is often because the child is concentrating on an activity and forgets to go to the bathroom. Sometimes a child is in a new place and feels uncomfortable asking where the bathroom is. A child who has been dry at night may wet the bed again in response to stress or changes. If bedwetting recurs, put the child back in training pants at bedtime for a while. In some cases, a toileting accident is an indication that the child has an illness or an infection. If these problems with toileting persist, consult a physician.

In most cases, the following steps can help minimize accidents:

- Before leaving home, make sure the child uses the bathroom.
- When arriving at a public place, point out where the bathroom is and remind the child to ask to use it.
- Keep an extra outfit available in the event of an accident. Handle the situation quietly without calling unnecessary attention to it.

When they begin school, some children may suffer from constipation or sometimes wet their pants. The stress children sometimes feel in their new school and with their routine can cause these problems. Most children adjust to the school routine within a few weeks, although the adjustment period depends on the individual child. For some children, the problem may recur at the beginning of school for several years.

SECTION 13-2 Review and Activities

Reviewing the Section

1. What factors influence the amount of food a child needs?
2. Why is good nutrition important for children ages four to six?
3. Identify one nutrition challenge children face when they begin school.
4. Describe how weight problems are linked to nutrition and physical activity.
5. How does poor nutrition affect physical development?
6. List three self-care skills children can develop.
7. List a few reasons why toileting accidents might occur.

Observing and Interacting

Talk to a child who is between the ages of four and six about nutritious foods. Does the child know what kinds of foods are best to eat (nutritious) and which are not? What nutritious foods does he or she like to eat for meals and snacks? Summarize your interview in a report.

Career Opportunities

Speech-Language Pathologist

Some children have problems making or understanding sounds. Some struggle with speech rhythm difficulties, such as stuttering. Speech-language pathologists help them to communicate more effectively. They also help people who have trouble swallowing.

▸ Job Responsibilities

Speech-language pathologists use speaking or writing tests to find out what speech problems children have. Then they create a plan for working with them. They teach sign language to children who cannot speak and help other children make sounds more clearly. They also teach children how to change the pitch or speed of their speech. They advise parents on how to help their children practice speaking and keep careful records of their clients' progress.

▸ Work Environment

Speech-language pathologists work in schools, hospitals, private clinics, and nursing homes.

▸ Education and Training

Speech-language pathologists must earn a master's degree, pass an exam, and work a certain number of hours in order to become licensed.

▸ Aptitudes Needed

- Patience
- Excellent communications skills
- Teaching ability
- Optimism
- Commitment to patient care

WORKPLACE CONNECTION

1. **Thinking Skills.** Why would it be helpful for speech-language pathologists to take foreign language classes?

2. **Resource Skills.** What kinds of work experience would you need for this job?

SECTION SUMMARIES

- Children between the ages of four and six grow steadily, and their body shape changes. (13-1)
- Permanent teeth begin to appear around the age of six, replacing the primary teeth. (13-1)
- From four to six, children refine their gross and fine motor skills. (13-1)
- The eating habits children establish influence the eating habits and health they experience as adults. (13-2)
- Weight gain can result from poor eating habits. Physical inactivity is a major cause of overweight in children. (13-2)
- Four- to six-year-olds can wash and dress themselves and can help care for their own clothes. (13-2)
- Children between the ages of four and six may still have toileting accidents. (13-2)

REVIEWING THE CHAPTER

1. How does children's posture change during the period from four to six? (13-1)
2. What purpose do the first *permanent teeth*, the molars, serve? (13-1)
3. Why do some children continue to suck their thumbs? When does it become a problem? (13-1)
4. How do children's gross motor skills improve during this age span? (13-1)
5. Give at least four examples of activities that can help four- to six-year-olds improve their dexterity. (13-1)
6. What is hand preference? When is it usually established? (13-1)
7. Why is it important for parents to teach children this age about good nutrition? (13-2)
8. Analyze the factors that contribute to underweight in children. (13-2)
9. What are the two primary reasons that children may have problems with bedwetting? (13-2)

THINKING CRITICALLY

1. **Predicting Consequences.** Review the list on page 409 of immunizations usually required by schools. What might happen if immunizations were voluntary?
2. **Summarizing Information.** Suppose you worked at a child care center. Describe three steps you could take to help the children prevent toileting accidents.

MAKING CONNECTIONS

1. **Math.** Using the charts in Fig. 13-1 on page 410, create a graph to compare the average height and weight for boys and girls at ages four, five, and six. Summarize the differences.
2. **Reading.** Ask a librarian to recommend a book that would be suitable as a bedtime story for a four- to six-year-old. Read the book and report what aspects would make the book appealing to children.

APPLYING YOUR LEARNING

1. **Basic Skills.** Create a poster that a caregiver could use to help a child learn one self-care skill.
2. **Tie It Up.** How would you teach a five-year-old to tie shoelaces? Give a visual demonstration of the steps you would use. Be sure that a child would understand the words you use.
3. **Giving Advice.** Suppose you are an advice columnist. A parent writes in to say that her five-year-old is having toileting accidents. Write a letter in which you advise her on what to do.
4. **Nutritious Meals.** Imagine that you are the parent of a very active five-year-old. Plan three small meals or snacks that are nutritious and appealing to a child this age.
5. **Encouraging Healthy Behavior.** Write a list of ten things that parents could say to children to encourage good eating habits and physical activity. What could they do to promote these behaviors?

Learning from Research

1. Choose one of the following claims to investigate.
2. How is this research finding useful to parents of children ages four to six?
3. Summarize what you've learned about the effects of watching television on children ages four to six.

Television and Overweight. One research study found that children who watched two or more hours of TV per day were twice as likely to become overweight as children who did not. Has research been conducted that found the restriction of TV viewing results in normal weight for children, ages four to six?

Television and Food Intake. Research has found that TV viewing is associated with an increased intake of calories, especially from snack foods. Children who eat in front of the television tend to eat more fatty foods. Do you agree with this research finding? Why or why not?

Television and Food Commercials. In two consecutive weekends of watching children's television programs, researchers found that 37% of commercials were about food. The majority of those were for snack foods, followed by breakfast cereals, then fast food chains. Where else are children ages four to six enticed by food advertisements and displays of snacks, cereals, etc?

Section 14-1
Emotional Development from Four to Six

Section 14-2
Social and Moral Development from Four to Six

Emotional Development from Four to Six

Justin was unusually quiet as he walked to school with his mother. It was his first day, and he was both excited and fearful. His new teacher was there to greet them. As his mother talked with the teacher, Justin peered into the classroom and saw two of his friends from preschool. "Can I go and play with Scott and Dakota?" he asked. When the teacher said yes, he walked off, proud to be old enough for school.

Objectives

- Summarize general patterns of emotional development in children ages four, five, and six.
- Describe ways preschoolers and children in kindergarten use their imagination.
- Identify ways of responding to expressions of fear, jealousy, and stress in children ages four to six.
- Propose strategies for helping children gain self-confidence.

Key Terms

self-confidence
initiative
tension

General Emotional Patterns

The years between four and six are marked by increased independence. It is at this age that many children venture out of the home environment to attend preschool, daycare, and kindergarten. Perhaps for the first time, they find themselves with unfamiliar adults and large groups of other children. Each child responds to these challenges differently. There are, however, certain milestones that children in this age group generally attain.

Four Years

Most four-year-olds are still quite self-centered. They can be defiant, impatient, loud, and boastful. They might argue and be bossy with other children and even with adults. At other times, four-year-olds may be very loving and affectionate, because they need and seek the approval of parents and other caregivers. See Fig. 14-1.

Four-year-olds want to see themselves as separate from their parents or other main caregiver. They want to do things for themselves, such as washing and dressing, and they enjoy the feeling of independence that they get from doing these tasks.

The vocabulary and language skills of four-year-olds show marked improvements over those of toddlers. At this stage, children enjoy testing out the sounds of language and making up nonsense words. Four-year-old Marvin, for example, goes around chanting phrases like "Antsy, wantsy, pantsy," and then breaks into hysterical laughter. Children of this age might also try using "rude" words, just to see how adults react.

Four-year-olds have an active imagination, allowing them to enjoy a rich fantasy life. Because a four-year-old mind often cannot distinguish fantasy from reality, however, an active imagination can also lead to fears. Shadows in a dark bedroom, for example, can become a monster in the child's mind. Parents can help a child get over these fears by acknowledging them and talking about them.

Five Years

By the age of five, children have begun to view themselves as whole persons, with a body, mind, and feelings. They are eager to explore the larger world, but at the same time they may be fearful of unfamiliar people, places, and experiences.

Five is the age at which a child typically begins kindergarten. Not all children welcome that first day of school. See Fig. 14-2. When Katrina's mother brought her to the kindergarten classroom, Katrina clung to her mother's legs and begged not

Fig. 14-1 Four-year-olds can play and share with other children, but they can also be self-centered and bossy. What can caregivers do to help children manage these feelings?

to be left there alone. Katrina, like many five-year-olds, was afraid of being left alone in an unfamiliar situation. Children this age experience anxiety about the strangeness of the school setting and about unfamiliar routines. It's important to help children cope with their anxieties by listening to their concerns and offering love and support. Children who have attended a child care center or preschool may adapt more easily.

Five-year-olds are still emotionally impulsive. They want to wander around, talk, and play when the spirit moves them. It is in the school setting, where they must sit still, listen, and focus on a task, that they start learning to control these impulses.

At this age, children also begin to feel more empathy for others. This empathy makes them better able to play together and cooperate, because they can see another's point of view.

Six Years

As children turn six, they are likely to go through a period of emotional turmoil. Some are in school all day for the first time. They face the task of finding their status outside the home. At times they long to feel grown-up, but often they feel small and dependent. Six-year-olds crave praise and approval, and are easily hurt and discouraged.

Six-year-olds are often stubborn and quarrelsome. They are the center of their own universe, and try to please others only to win praise for themselves. They are often at their worst with their own parents. They may resent being given direction, and their first response is likely to be "No!"

Fig. 14-2 **Five is the age at which children typically begin kindergarten. Separating from parents or caregivers can be difficult for some children.** How can a teacher help put a child at ease?

At six, children experience rapid mood changes. They love and hate, accept and reject, smile and rage, sometimes for no apparent reason. At the same time, a six-year-old is beginning to experience deeper feelings of happiness and joy, leading to an appreciation of more activities. A six-year-old can enjoy music or dance lessons and organized sports. This is a good time to start a child on such activities. Learning new skills builds a child's sense of competence.

Specific Emotions

As children grow older they become better able to recognize and express a variety of emotions. At the same time, their growing feeling of competence as they master various tasks helps them to control their emotions. However, they continue to experience fears during the years from four through six, though the nature of those fears changes over time. See Fig. 14-3.

Self-Confidence

As children ages four to six accomplish tasks, learn new skills, and deal with unfamiliar situations, their **self-confidence**—belief in their own abilities—grows. Caregivers can help children develop self-confidence by providing continuing opportunities for them to learn. Children who feel self-confident in turn develop **initiative**—a motivation to accomplish more.

Fig. 14-3 **How might a four-year-old and a six-year-old react to a new baby in the family?**

Health & Safety

ADHD

Attention Deficit Hyperactivity Disorder (ADHD) is a condition that becomes apparent in some children in the preschool and early school years. It is estimated that between 3 and 5 percent of children have ADHD, or approximately 2 million children in the United States. The most common characteristics of ADHD are the inability to pay attention, hyperactivity, and acting on impulses. Because many children may have these symptoms, but at a low level, or the symptoms may be caused by another disorder, it is important that the child receive a thorough examination and appropriate diagnosis by a well-qualified professional. Parents can ask their pediatrician to refer them to a child psychiatrist who can diagnose and treat this condition. Although medication is often used as treatment, there has been recent concern about over-diagnosis and over-medication. A child with ADHD faces a difficult, but not impossible, task ahead. A child with ADHD needs help, guidance, and understanding from parents, therapists, and school in order to achieve his or her full potential.

One complicating factor at this age is the tendency of children ages five and six to see their world in terms of all or nothing. If a project doesn't go the way a six-year-old intends, the child may think, "I can't do anything right." The child's self-esteem and self-confidence slips. It is important to help children this age experience more successes than failures. The saying "success breeds success" is especially true when applied to six-year-olds.

Anger

The expression of anger changes more during early childhood than the expression of any other emotion. Toddlers show anger freely and without restraint, sometimes biting, kicking, and hitting. Preschoolers are less likely than toddlers to express their anger in physical violence. A four-year-old who is upset because her mother will not let her play outside is more likely to scream, "I hate you, Mommy!"

As children grow older, they use increasingly subtle ways to express their anger:

- **Four years.** An angry episode lasts longer in a four-year-old than in a younger child. Four-year-olds may still use physical violence, or they may threaten and attempt to "get even."

- **Five years.** Five-year-olds are more likely to try to hurt other children's feelings than to hurt them physically.

- **Six years.** Six-year-olds are even more hurtful with words. They tease, insult, nag, and make fun of others.

There are a number of reasons for these changes in the expression of anger. Frustration is a major cause of anger, and a child's tolerance for frustration generally increases with age. Also, some sources of earlier frustration are eliminated as the

LOOKING AT REAL LIFE

Danielle and her five-year-old daughter Lori are enrolled in a parent-child art class at the park district. Each week, the teacher introduces them to a new material and possible techniques to use in their artwork. The first week focused on drawing. Lori likes to draw and works very hard to stay within the lines when coloring her drawings—something she has observed her mother do. So the next week when they began to make little clay pots and Lori couldn't smooth out the walls of her pot the same way the teacher did, she pushed it away and said she didn't like art anymore. Danielle knew that many children Lori's age feel that there is a "right" or "wrong" way to create. Danielle suggested to Lori that they still play with the clay but build animals out of it instead. Lori was reluctant at first but began to enjoy making her favorite animals out of clay. Danielle praised Lori's efforts and told her she was a great artist. By next week's class, Lori was eager again.

▶▶**PERSONAL APPLICATION**

1. What are some ways in which you explore your own creativity?
2. How do you react when the result of something you've tried is not as good as you had hoped?

child's skills improve. Finally, by age six, children have better social skills, which can help them deal with situations that lead to anger. They can usually work in groups, for example, and recognize that some things belong to other people.

Disagreements with other children are the most common cause of anger. Although quarrels are still loud and verbal, five- and six-year-old children begin to conceal and disguise their feelings. Sometimes their methods of revenge are indirect. They may pretend indifference, sneer, or make sly remarks. Often they make exaggerated threats. Occasionally, they take their anger out on a scapegoat, such as a younger sibling, a pet, or a toy.

Criticism can also be a cause of anger. Six-year-olds don't like to be criticized.

Fig. 14-4 **Fear of the dark is common at this age.** What can parents do to help a child with this fear?

Children who are scolded for doing something wrong may "punish" a parent by breaking yet another rule.

Children vary greatly in how much anger they show and how they show it. Some variations depend on a child's temperament. Others result from the child's environment. Children tend to imitate the behavior of adults. Parents and other caregivers can teach children self-control by expressing their own anger in appropriate ways.

Fear

Imagination is a major emotional force in children from four to six, and many of their fears center on imaginary dangers. They may be afraid of ghosts or monsters. Many children of this age are afraid of the dark. Some may worry about the possibility of being left alone or abandoned. Fear of thunder and lighting is also common at this age. See Fig. 14-4.

Many children fear situations related to school. They may be afraid of being criticized by a teacher or teased by other children. Here are some ways that caregivers can help children deal with such fears:

- **Accept the fear.** Just listening and saying you understand can greatly help a fearful child. Never say that what the child fears doesn't exist. It is very real to the child.

- **Let the child express the fear without ridicule.** Children this age fear being made fun of. If they worry that they might be ridiculed, they may not be open about their fears.

- **Help the child feel able to face the fear.** Use talking and acting out to help the child learn to face the fearful situation. Reading a book together about another child who dealt with a similar fear might also help.

Sometimes, of course, a child's fear about a certain situation is justified. A bully at school, for example, could be a cause for real concern. In such cases, parents need to take action to deal with the source of the fear and give support and reassurance.

THE DEVELOPING BRAIN

Children's fears of the dark, nighttime monsters, and other perceived threats may be "hard-wired" in the brain. These fears are probably inherited from our early human ancestors, who genuinely had things to worry about when the light faded each day, such as nocturnal predators. American psychologist Steven Pinker says that irrational fears in adulthood are likely to be childhood fears that never went away.

Fig. 14-5 Habits such as biting nails or grinding teeth may be signs of stress and tension.

Jealousy

Sibling rivalry—jealousy of brothers and sisters—is common during this period. Some parents unintentionally make the problem worse. They may try to improve behavior by comparing one child to another. One father, for example, asked his daughter, "Why can't you be neat like your sister Selena? I never have to tell her to put her toys away." Comparisons such as this are rarely effective and may actually damage a child's self-esteem and undermine family relationships.

Children at this age sometimes express their feelings of jealousy by tattling, criticizing, or lying. Some may feel jealous and react by boasting.

Parents and other caregivers can help children work through jealous feelings by encouraging cooperation and empathy. It is best to avoid taking sides and to give children a chance to practice working out their own problems. Sibling rivalry tends to fade as children mature and find interests outside the home.

Children and Stress

Children, like people of all ages, experience stress, or **tension**. They may worry about everything from a fire in their home, to a stranger taking them, to a bully in the neighborhood. Their active imagination contributes to the stress that they experience.

Children's fears and worries may result in the mental or emotional strain of tension. Children may develop physical symptoms, such as stomachaches, headaches, and difficulty sleeping. They may cry, scream, or throw temper tantrums. Many preschoolers express tension by biting their nails, swinging their legs, or grinding their teeth. See Fig. 14-5.

Here are some ways to help preschoolers and children in kindergarten handle stress and reduce tension:

- **Look for the cause.** Ask children showing signs of stress to draw pictures of themselves. One preschooler whose parents had just divorced drew a picture of herself split in two. Alternatively, use a puppet or stuffed animal. Explain that the toy is not feeling happy, and then ask the child what the problem is. The child may describe his or her own problems.

- **Give children time to calm down.** If tension boils over into a tantrum or uncontrollable crying, call for time out.

Fig. 14-6 **One way to show respect for a child is to listen and respond to the child's concerns.** What are some other ways a parent can show respect for a child?

Send the child to another room, not for punishment, but for a brief time to be alone and calm down.

- **Provide opportunities to get rid of tension.** Give children a physical way of releasing stress. Have them jump up and down or take them to a park or playground where they can run around. Teaching appropriate ways to reduce stress now will be helpful throughout life.

- **Read a book about the issue causing stress.** There are books that deal with issues that can cause stress in children, from moving to a new home to facing someone's death. Reading a book together can help the child learn ways to handle the situation.

- **Maintain normal limits on behavior.** Some parents ease up on rules because they want to make life easier for a child feeling stress. Such an approach can actually backfire by confusing the child—and causing additional stress and tension.

Encouragement

Preschoolers have reached a stage in which they can start to take initiative and make some decisions on their own. According to psychologist Erik Erikson, those who are encouraged in these efforts gain self-confidence. Repeated discouragement or punishment, on the other hand, can lead to feelings of inferiority or inadequacy.

Parents and other caregivers can help preschoolers and kindergartners develop self-confidence in a number of ways:

Children Around the World

Raising a Child in Austria

In Austria, the government encourages parents to stay home to raise their children. By law, women are not allowed to work eight weeks before or after giving birth. This leave from work is fully paid. Families also receive financial support that allows one parent to stay home, often for years. Weekends are reserved for family time. Adults who relax and play show to children by example ways of alleviating and managing stress that may build up over a long week.

Until they are in the sixth grade, Austrian children come home from school, eat lunch, and then may spend the rest of the afternoon playing with friends, practicing sports, or learning an instrument. Most Austrian children learn to ski at a very young age, building their sense of competence and self-confidence.

Investigating Culture

1. What are the benefits of a "24-hour culture" like that of the United States?
2. What are the drawbacks?

- **Show respect for the child.** Express confidence in the child's abilities. Offer the child choices whenever possible, then show respect by going along with the child's decisions. When you make a decision, show respect by explaining your reasons rather than by saying, "Because I said so." See Fig. 14-6.

- **Offer honest praise and encouragement.** Try to catch the child doing something right, and then praise the action or accomplishment. Be specific. "I really appreciate it when you help clear the table after dinner." General comments such as, "Good job," tend to lose meaning over time.

- **Set the preschooler up for success.** Select activities that are challenging, but not overwhelming. Be sure the child has the ability to perform a given task to help avoid frustration and failure. Then give the child plenty of time and opportunity to practice.

- **Avoid stereotyping.** Give boys and girls opportunities to develop a wide range of skills, from making breakfast to learning how to drive screws or pound nails.

The best way to help preschoolers develop self-confidence is to give them opportunities to perform well. Children need to feel good about what they do. Internal satisfaction will go farther than praise from others in helping them develop self-esteem and from that, self-control.

SECTION 14-1 Review and Activities

Reviewing the Section

1. What are three main emotional differences in children ages four, five, and six?
2. How are *initiative* and *self-confidence* related?
3. Why are six-year-olds better able to control anger than four-year-olds? What is the best thing caregivers can do to help children express anger?
4. What is the relationship between imagination and fear in the mind of a preschooler?
5. How might preschoolers and kindergartners show that they are feeling *tension*? How should a caregiver respond?
6. How can caregivers help children develop self-confidence?

Observing and Interacting

Find a setting in which you can observe at least two preschoolers with a parent. Watch for the emotions they show. Note one emotion, the apparent cause, and how the child expressed it. Prepare an oral or written report.

Social and Moral Development from Four to Six

Children four through six years of age find themselves in an expanding world. As they begin preschool, kindergarten, and elementary school, they must learn how to interact with new people, make friends, and work and play in organized groups. They must also learn how to take direction and accept authority from adults outside the home. Increasingly, they must determine right and wrong and act accordingly.

Objectives

- Summarize general patterns of social development in children ages four, five, and six.
- Suggest strategies to help children resolve conflicts.
- Analyze the role of competition and cooperation in children's development.
- Develop guidelines for encouraging moral development in children.

Key Terms

peers
aggressive behavior
competition
moral development

General Social Patterns

A major task of the preschool, kindergarten, and early elementary school years is to develop social skills. As children spend more time outside the home, they need to refine their skills at getting along with their **peers**, other children of their age. Adult authority figures other than parents and main caregivers also gain more importance. Although the rate at which individual children learn social skills varies, there are general patterns common at each age.

Four Years

Four-year-olds form friendships with their playmates. Unlike toddlers, who tend to engage in parallel play, essentially playing by themselves, four-year-olds spend more time in cooperative play. They can play in groups of three or four, sharing toys and taking turns. Four-year-olds are often bossy and inconsiderate, however, so fighting may break out.

Although friends are important to four-year-olds, the family is still more important.

Children this age actively seek approval by making such remarks as "I'm good at drawing pictures, aren't I?" or "Look how high I can climb!" If things go wrong, they look to parents and other caregivers for comfort.

Five Years

Five-year-olds tend to be more outgoing and talkative than four-year-olds. They can play in groups of five or six, and their play is more complicated. Fights break out less frequently. When they do quarrel, five-year-olds typically resort to name-calling and to wild threats.

By age five, children have developed more respect for others' belongings. A five-year-old may still try to grab another child's toy, but such behavior is less common.

When children begin school, social acceptance by peers becomes more important. Five-year-olds are concerned about what their friends say and do. They do not want to be thought of as different, and they fear ridicule.

At about this age, some children begin to gossip about other children. Typically they talk about which children they consider to be friends or who has what toys. Gossip

Learning Through PLAY

Social Rules and Play

Playing a board game with a four-year-old can be fun, but at the same time very frustrating. Children delight in playing games, though they often create their own set of rules as they go along. In the preschool years, the world seems to revolve around a child in his or her eyes. As a child matures, the world seems to get bigger and include more people. Social rules become more important. Playing games allows a child to explore rules and why they are necessary. The child is able to see the world from another's perspective and is able to understand why rules are necessary for things to be fair.

Following Up

Would younger or older children be more concerned about fairness? Why?

Fig. 14-7 **By the age of six, children discriminate between types of friends. Best friends are likely to be children of the same sex.** Why are friendships at this age often marked by friction?

indicates what behaviors the children as a group value, and what actions they consider undesirable.

Six Years

The social relations of six-year-olds are often characterized by friction, threats, and stubbornness. Children this age want everything, and they want to do things their own way. They may not want to share their own toys, and they may be jealous of other children's toys.

Best friends at this age are usually children of the same sex, though six-year-olds play readily in mixed groups. See Fig. 14-7. They enjoy group play and organized teams for games. If they tire of playing, however, they will simply drop out of a game. They have no regard for team effort.

Resolving Conflicts

Children ages four through six spend a lot of time with other children. They may have to compete for toys, attention, or taking a turn on playground equipment. Such circumstances can lead to conflict.

Preschoolers might resort to **aggressive behavior**. This is hostile, and at times destructive, behavior that people display when faced with conflict. Such behavior usually erupts when they are angry or frustrated, and often results from conflicts over objects or control of space. Hitting, kicking, biting, and forcibly taking objects away from others are examples of aggressive behavior.

Children need to learn that aggressive behavior is unacceptable. Through their own example and through their teaching, parents and other caregivers can guide children in nonaggressive ways to express anger and resolve conflicts with their peers. See Fig. 14-8. Here are some suggestions:

- **Encourage children to talk about their feelings.** When Carla's father heard her lash out at her friend Erin, "You're ugly, and I hate you!" he had the girls sit down and tell what they were feeling. Carla admitted she was angry because Erin had used up all of her red markers. Erin told Carla how much the angry words had hurt her feelings.

- **Acknowledge the efforts of children to resolve conflicts.** Offer specific praise and encouragement, such as "You and Jeremy did the right thing in deciding to take turns playing on the swing."

- **Model appropriate behavior.** In your daily life, show appropriate ways to deal with anger and conflict. Studies show that many children who engage in acts of aggression were exposed to adults who used or condoned aggressive behavior.

Is Competition Good or Bad?

Not everyone has the same views about the role that **competition**—rivalry with the goal of outperforming others or winning—should play in children's lives. Some say that children benefit from competition because it stimulates individual efforts and promotes higher standards. Competition, they maintain, helps children gain a realistic view of their own abilities in relation to others. It helps children excel and prepares them for the adult world. See Fig. 14-9.

Fig. 14-8 Caregivers need to encourage angry preschoolers to talk about their feelings as a start toward resolving conflicts.

Fig. 14-9 **People differ about whether children should compete.** What is your opinion?

Others feel that competition is harmful to children because it instills the idea that success depends on the ability to outdo others. This mindset, they say, can lead to hostile relationships. In addition, competition can discourage initiative in those who rarely win because it points out their inadequacies and lowers their status and self-esteem.

Teamwork and Cooperation

Most preschoolers and kindergartners prefer cooperative play to competitive games. Children can actually engage in both kinds of play. They can play cooperatively in competitive games by working together with their teammates.

Children not playing at a particular time can cheer for their teammates. When they are playing, children can share in the game. For example, in a ball game, each child can have a turn.

Whatever the game, caregivers need to teach children not to compare themselves with others. Show them, instead, how to compare their skills today with their skills in the past. Is Carlos running faster than last month? Children can get a feeling of satisfaction from seeing improvement in their own performance.

The relationship between six-year-old Julia and her family was strained. Nothing seemed to please her. When she screamed and protested after her parents took her television privileges away, they relented. After her parents gave in to her demands, her behavior grew worse. At their wits' end, Julia's parents went in to see the school counselor.

"Our daughter is acting out all the time. How can we get her to change?" they asked. "Perhaps you need to ask what you can do to change the situation," the counselor advised. "Let's begin by looking at your expectations. It is reasonable to expect a six-year-old to follow the family rules or face the consequences, but it isn't realistic to expect her to be happy about the consequences. You want Julia to learn self-control by accepting the consequences of her actions. You need to accept that your daughter may be unhappy for a while, but stick to the limits you set. Right now, try letting her know that it is acceptable to have those unhappy feelings. There is a big difference between accepting feelings and accepting inappropriate behavior."

▸▸**PERSONAL APPLICATION**

1. Why do you think it's emotionally difficult for some parents to enforce the limits they have set?
2. How can you convey to a child that you understand his or her feelings, even if the child is behaving inappropriately?

Family Relationships

Relationships within a family change as a child advances from age four to age six. Four-year-olds feel close ties to home and want to feel important in the family. They are proud to show that they can help with chores. However, they often quarrel and bicker with their siblings.

Five-year-olds, too, delight in helping out at home. They now play much better with their brothers and sisters. They are usually protective and kind toward younger siblings.

Six-year-olds are less in harmony with other family members, in part because they are more self-centered. Their own opinions and needs come first. Six-year-olds commonly argue with adult family members. They can be rough and impatient with younger brothers and sisters, and may fight with older siblings.

Moral Development

Moral development—the process of learning to base one's behavior on beliefs about what is right and wrong—begins early in life. Toddlers learn the rules their parents and other caregivers set. At that stage, however, they don't understand the reasons behind the rules. They just learn that some actions—such as hitting another person—make their caregivers unhappy with them. They don't want to lose love and approval, so they learn to avoid those behaviors.

Preschoolers, on the other hand, are beginning to understand the reasons behind such rules. They are developing the beginning of a *conscience*—that inner sense of right and wrong that guides people's behavior and helps them make judgments about what is good and bad behavior. The rules that they learn in early childhood form the basis of their developing conscience.

Parenting Q&A

Why Do Young Children Lie?

Many children tell tall tales and exaggerate. Young children often confuse stories with reality. These are not deliberate deceptions. Adults can show the child that they know the difference by saying, "I will listen to your story, and then I need to know what really happened."

Sometimes a statement that sounds like a lie is really a misunderstanding. The child who says, "I did what you told me," may believe that a task is done, even though a parent may not agree. Sometimes children do tell deliberate lies.

Here are a few reasons why:
- To get attention from adults.
- To avoid punishment.
- To please others and not risk losing love.

Points to consider:
- Does the child know what's been said isn't true?
- What might be the reason that the child is lying?
- Do I need to get more information about the situation?
- Is the child asking for more attention?

Help children separate fact from fiction. Don't punish children when they are being imaginative. Children need to know that telling the truth is important because people rely on what others say in deciding how to act.

THINKING IT THROUGH

1. Describe a time you lied when you were younger.
2. What would you do if a five-year-old lied about taking a cookie?

Guidelines for Moral Development

Parents and other caregivers have a responsibility to help children develop a moral sense that will guide their behavior. Here are some suggestions:

- **Set clear standards of behavior.** Tell children, for example, "We do not take other children's toys. It is wrong to take something that belongs to someone else." Teaching children the reasons for rules helps them understand why the rules are important.

- **Respond to inappropriate behavior.** When rules are broken, deal with the problem immediately and appropriately. Repeat the rule and the reason for the rule.

- **Talk about mistakes in private.** Six-year-olds, especially, don't like to be criticized. Correcting their behavior in front of others may make them feel humiliated.

- **Understand that children will test the limits.** As children develop a moral awareness, they are likely to try disobeying or refusing to cooperate. This is a sign that they are beginning to understand what is acceptable and what is forbidden behavior.

- **Consider the child's age and abilities.** For example, at preschool, Crystal was playing at a shallow table filled with rice and containers. She started tossing the rice into the air and watching it land on the floor. The teacher reminded Crystal that she must keep the rice in the table, then handed her a broom and a dustpan to sweep up the mess. Crystal's teacher knows that children this age can't always remember the rules but will learn from the consequences of their actions.

- **It is a lifelong task to learn self-discipline.** It is unfair to expect perfection from children. Instead, help children learn from their mistakes—and recognize their steps in the right direction.

- **Continue to show love despite misbehavior.** Children need to know that, although you do not like what they did, you continue to love them. Separate the deed from the doer. See Fig. 14-10.

Modeling Moral Behavior

One of the best ways to teach children moral behavior is to model it in everyday actions. Children learn by following an example. If they are told that lying is wrong, but then hear their parents telling lies, they will be confused by the mixed message.

Fig. 14-10 **Children who have misbehaved need to be reassured that they are still loved.** Why is it important to separate the action from the child?

Guide Children's Behavior

Although most parents struggle with guiding a child's behavior, they know it's an important responsibility. Parental guidance makes a major difference in whether or not children grow up to be happy, well-adjusted people. Here are some ways to guide children effectively:

- **Build trust.** Maintain a routine to help children feel secure. Meet children's needs so they know that they can rely on others. Respond to their needs in a loving way so that they can count on you, no matter what.

- **Accentuate the positive.** Look for opportunities to give sincere compliments. Comment when children show positive behaviors such as patience, cooperation, kindness, and cheerfulness.

- **Build empathy.** Talking about feelings makes children more sensitive to others. Even preschoolers can understand that other children have feelings, too.

- **Respect fears and feelings.** Guide children's behavior by offering respect and reassurance. Even if fears are groundless, take children's feelings seriously. Be willing to listen and offer support.

- **Teach actions and consequences.** Use everyday situations to show that each action has a consequence. Explain that if children

angrily throw a toy, and it breaks, it won't be replaced. Soon they will start to avoid actions that result in negative consequences.

- **Encourage responsibility.** Assign a daily job. Doing a chore well helps children develop pride in themselves and contribute to the family.

- **Guide by example.** Be positive, helpful, and caring to encourage good behavior. Model ways to treat siblings, friends, neighbors, and relatives with kindness and respect.

YOUR TURN

Reassurance. Bedtime can bring fears. Some children are afraid of the dark, while others think there is a monster under the bed. What could you say to a four-year-old to help calm his or her fears?

Josh's dad, for example, was eating his dinner when the telephone rang. Josh's mother got up to answer the phone. "If that's someone for me," said his dad, "tell them I'm not at home."

"Dad, didn't you tell me that it's wrong to tell a lie?" asked Josh.

"That's right," said Josh's dad as he returned to his dinner.

"But didn't you just tell a lie?"

"Do as I say, not as I do," came the response.

The next time Josh's parents talked to him about what is right and wrong, he didn't take the message so seriously.

Moral behavior is learned behavior, but parents are not their child's only teachers. The influence of peers increases as children spend more time away from home. They pick up language and speech patterns from their friends and notice that other families live by different rules.

Television, movies, and other media also influence what children learn. As they gain independence, many children watch more television. Some of the shows they see may reflect values that run counter to those of their family.

Parents and caregivers are responsible for what children watch and how much they watch. One way to prevent television from having a negative effect is to limit television viewing. If children develop other ways of learning and playing, watching television is less likely to become a habit.

SECTION 14-2 Review and Activities

Reviewing the Section

1. How does the nature of play change between the ages of two and four?
2. Describe some situations that could cause conflicts among children ages four through six. Choose one of the situations and provide a positive strategy for helping the children resolve the conflict.
3. In what ways might children benefit from *competition*? In what ways might it be harmful?
4. Why might family members experience more friction with a six-year-old than with a younger child?
5. Name three strategies that caregivers can use to help children learn right from wrong.
6. How can parents reinforce their values when a child is exposed to the influence of the media and *peers*?

Observing and Interacting

Based on how you and your friends interact, how would you define "friend"? How differently do you think children of ages four, five, and six would define "friend"?

Career Opportunities

Family Court Judge

Family court judges decide who should get custody of children when parents divorce, how much money one spouse should pay to the other, how often parents are allowed to visit their children, and where abused children should live. They determine who should be allowed to provide foster care or adopt. When youth commit crimes, they decide what treatment or punishment they should receive.

▶ Job Responsibilities

Judges make sure everyone in the courtroom is treated fairly. They decide what evidence may be presented, settle disputes between sides, and interpret laws. Family court judges often try to arrange for help and treatment for troubled youth, instead of prison time. They try to keep families together whenever possible.

▶ Work Environment

Judges most often work in courtrooms and offices. They must also research past decisions about cases in law libraries.

▶ Education and Training

Family court judges need bachelor's and law degrees. They are usually required to have several years of experience, as well as knowledge of family and child problems.

▶ Aptitudes Needed

- Listening skills
- Intelligence
- Fairness
- Capacity to deal with stress
- Interest in the problems of children and families

WORKPLACE CONNECTION

1. **Thinking Skills.** What work experiences would be helpful for judges to have before working in family court?

2. **Resource Skills.** How could you learn about careers in law?

---

14 Review and Activities

SECTION SUMMARIES

- Children develop increased independence, curiosity, and boldness as they mature from ages four to six. (14-1)
- Children learn to express anger with words rather than physical attacks as they mature from ages four to six. (14-1)
- The rich imagination and fantasy life of preschoolers can lead to fears, such as ghosts and monsters. (14-1)
- The world of children four to six expands as they attend preschool, kindergarten, and elementary school, and interact with more people outside the home. (14-2)
- Children begin learning how to resolve conflicts in nonaggressive ways. (14-2)
- Caregivers can help children develop an internal sense of right and wrong. (14-2)

REVIEWING THE CHAPTER

1. Why is six such a difficult age emotionally? (14-1)
2. How should a caregiver respond to a five-year-old's fear of monsters? (14-1)
3. Why is it so important for preschoolers to feel *self-confident*? (14-1)
4. How is the way four-year-olds play together different from the way two-year-olds do? (14-2)
5. Compare the ways children relate to their friends at ages four, five, and six. (14-2)
6. Explain the likely reactions of a six-year-old who is corrected in front of others. (14-2)
7. What can a caregiver do to help a child learn to express anger in nonaggressive ways? (14-2)
8. In what ways can *competitive* games foster cooperation among children? (14-2)
9. Under what circumstances might a preschooler lie? (14-2)
10. How can parents use television to help a child develop acceptable morals and standards? (14-2)

THINKING CRITICALLY

1. **Making Inferences.** Is it possible for parents to treat all of their children equally at all times? Make up two different situations involving sibling conflicts, and explain how parents might deal with each one. Can they always prevent sibling rivalry?
2. **Drawing Conclusions.** On the basis of what you have read and what you know from personal experience, do you think that competitive games are helpful or harmful to children? Be prepared to defend your position in a class debate.

MAKING CONNECTIONS

1. **Social Studies.** Suppose you are part of a group of adults setting up a T-ball league for six-year-olds. Prepare a list of ten rules of behavior that you would want the children to follow. All of the rules must concern appropriate behavior, not athletic concerns.

2. **Writing.** Write a fable—a short story with a moral—about a six-year-old who only wants to do things his way and never listens to his parents. What lesson does he learn?

APPLYING YOUR LEARNING

1. **Analyzing Behavior.** Five-year-old Callie attends a child care center where you are a worker. Over the past three weeks she has begun to bite her nails. She also has started twisting her hair, and she cries very easily. You suspect that she is upset about something. What are some ways you could try to find out what is troubling Callie? If there is a family problem, how would you handle the situation?

2. **Modeling.** You are caring for a four-year-old who has trouble remembering to say "please" and "thank you." Give an example of how you can model good manners for this child.

Learning from Research

1. Choose one of the following research claims to investigate.
2. How is this research finding useful to children ages four to six?
3. Summarize what you have learned about how outside factors affect a child's social development.

Rating Systems. Rating systems have been developed to indicate the presence of violence or other objectionable material in television programs, movies, and video and computer games. Research one of these systems. Write a report on whether you think the system is effective. Give reasons for your opinion.

Etiquette. Research what various authors think are good manners in young children and at what ages the authors suggest children should learn various kinds of polite behavior. Note areas in which the authors agree or disagree. Explain why you agree or disagree with the author's views.

Stress and Tension. Locate a Web site that discusses sources of stress in children. Analyze the reliability of the advice based on when the site was last updated, the sponsor of the site, and the credentials of the person giving the advice.

15 Intellectual Development from Four to Six

Thoughtful Reading:

As you read this chapter:

- What do you wonder? Note each of your questions and the page number.
- What opinions do you have about what you read?
- Summarize what you read in a short paragraph.

Section 15-1
The Developing Brain from Four to Six

Section 15-2
Learning from Four to Six

The Developing Brain from Four to Six

Do you enjoy art, reading, or music? Think back to your early experiences in school. It's quite possible that your interest in these subjects first started when you were between the ages of four and six. At this time, children are exposed to new ideas and activities at school. These experiences have a significant impact on their growing minds. As repeated experiences reinforce pathways in the children's brains, skills and interests begin to emerge.

Objectives

- Evaluate the value of intelligence tests and discuss different kinds of intelligence.
- Identify signs of intellectual development in children four to six.
- Analyze Piaget's theory of preoperational thinking.
- Compare the thinking and learning theories of Vygotsky and Montessori.

Key Terms

intelligence quotient (IQ)
cultural bias
multiple intelligences

What Is Intelligence?

Many parents wonder how intelligent their children are. Will they do well in school, quickly learning to read and count? These skills build the basis for later work in school. How will their school experiences shape their lives?

Traditional Views of Intelligence

Educators use formal intelligence tests to try to assess children's thinking skills. The test results can help teachers, principals, and learning specialists understand and meet students' educational needs.

The first intelligence test was developed by French psychologist Alfred Binet (bee-NAY) in 1905. In 1916, Lewis M. Terman of Stanford University made a major revision of Binet's test. The revised test, commonly called the Stanford-Binet, became the standard instrument of intelligence measurement for many years. Today, it is just one of many tests used to measure intelligence in children.

Using results from the Stanford-Binet test, Terman developed a mathematical formula that could be used to give a child's intelligence a number value. This **intelligence quotient**, or **IQ**, is a number obtained by comparing a child's test results to those of other children the same age. The average child of any age has an IQ between 90 and 110. Those who score higher or lower than this average are said to be of above- or below-average intelligence.

Intelligence tests are composed of tasks and questions that correspond to what is expected of children of various ages. See Fig. 15-1. Two-year-olds, for example, can't read, so an intelligence test for that age group might include building a tower of blocks, identifying parts of the body, and fitting simple geometric shapes into corresponding holes.

Over the years, critics have pointed out that relying on intelligence tests to rank children's mental abilities has several drawbacks:

- No single test can give an accurate measure of a child's mental abilities. Some tests give greater weight to certain abilities and less weight to others.
- Factors that have nothing to do with intelligence, such as whether a child feels ill or stressed on the day of testing, can influence results. A child's previous experience with the kinds of tasks included in the test can affect test scores.
- Overall scores, such as IQ scores, don't tell us much about individual strengths and weaknesses. Two people with the same IQ may have very different abilities. It is important for the person giving the test to explain how the child scored on all measures. Some tests are composed of many subtests, each measuring different abilities.

Fig. 15-1 **Intelligence tests for young children can't rely on written questions and answers.**

Fig. 15-2 **Intelligence tests must be valid for children whose first language is not English.**

Educators must use intelligence tests cautiously. The National Association for the Education of Young Children (NAEYC), an association dedicated to improving the well-being of children from birth through age eight, warns that no decision about a child's placement in school should be made on the basis of a single test. Today, preschools and kindergartens are more likely to use several different techniques to gain an overview of a child's level of development in all areas, not just thinking skills. If the child falls outside the norms of development for his or her age, then an in-depth assessment of skills may be necessary so that educators can identify problem areas and plan appropriate activities.

In the late 1900s, some intelligence tests were criticized for **cultural bias**. This means that many of the test questions favored or gave an advantage to those from one culture over other cultures. Language differences can also affect test results. A child whose first language is not English may not earn as high a score as an equally intelligent child who has learned English from birth. New tests have been designed in response to these criticisms. They have been screened for cultural bias. Children may take them in their native language. The goal is for all children to be assessed fairly. See Fig. 15-2.

Multiple Intelligences

In recent years, psychologist Howard Gardner has presented a different way of looking at intelligence. He argues that humans have **multiple intelligences**— abilities in problem solving or creating materials that have value. He has identified eight such intelligences:

Fig. 15-3 Children high in bodily-kinesthetic intelligence are more likely to enjoy and be good at physical skills and sports.

- **Spatial intelligence** involves an understanding of the potential use of space, thinking in three-dimensional terms, and imagining things in clear visual images. Architects and landscape designers are among those who rely on this type of intelligence.

- **Musical intelligence** involves skill in performing, composing, and appreciating musical patterns.

- **Bodily-kinesthetic intelligence** has to do with the potential to use one's body to solve problems, using the mind to coordinate body movements. See Fig. 15-3.

- **Interpersonal intelligence** involves the potential to understand the intentions, desires, and motivations of others. This type of intelligence helps teachers, counselors, and religious and political leaders work more effectively with other people.

- **Intrapersonal intelligence** entails the capacity to understand oneself, including fears, hopes, and motivations. According to Gardner, it means having a good working model of ourselves and using it to regulate our actions.

- **Naturalist intelligence** entails recognizing, categorizing, and drawing upon the features of the environment.

Gardner believes that the intelligences usually operate at the same time and complement each other as people develop skills and solve problems. Each person has a blend of intelligences. Gardner believed that deciding how best to take advantage of each person's unique blend is a major challenge.

If caregivers recognize that a child is particularly high in one type of intelligence, they can provide the child with learning opportunities that not only build those strengths but also challenge the child and encourage interest in learning.

- **Linguistic intelligence** involves sensitivity to language, the ability to learn languages, and the ability to use language to accomplish goals. Gardner sees writers, poets, and lawyers as having high linguistic intelligence.

- **Logical-mathematical intelligence** consists of the ability to analyze problems using logic, perform mathematical operations, and explore issues scientifically. This intelligence is associated with scientific and mathematical thinking and research.

Signs of Intellectual Development

Researchers have identified intellectual skills commonly seen in children ages four, five, and six. Some of these are included in the "Developmental Milestones" chart, Fig. 15-4 below. When you read the chart, it's easy to see that a child's brain is able to handle increasingly complex skills over this time span. As you learn about various theories of intellectual development, check the chart to see if children's skills match each theory.

Piaget's Theory of Preoperational Thinking

Jean Piaget described the time between ages two and seven as the *preoperational period*. See Fig. 15-5 on page 458. Piaget believed that in this period, children are oriented inward and learn from concrete evidence, can only view the world from their own perspective, and can't think in abstract terms.

Four-, five-, and six-year-olds show the following signs of preoperational thinking:

► **FIG. 15-4 Developmental Milestones—INTELLECTUAL   Ages 4-6**

4 YEARS

- Speaks in complete sentences of five to six words
- Makes up stories
- Asks many *when, where, how,* and *why* questions

- Understands three-step directions
- Knows colors and shapes
- Understands *same* and *different, top* and *bottom*

5 YEARS

- Uses six- to eight-word sentences with correct grammar
- Understands about 13,000 words
- Learns alphabet and many letter sounds

- Recalls part of a story
- Counts up to ten objects and can sort by size
- Understands *above* and *below, before* and *after*

6 YEARS

- Reads words and simple sentences
- Writes simple words
- Solves problems more effectively

- Plays pretend games
- Has longer attention span
- Understands *right* and *left* and additional time concepts

Fig. 15-5 Piaget's Four Periods of Learning

Period	Characteristics
Sensorimotor Birth–2 years	Children learn through their senses and own actions.
Preoperational 2–7 years	Children think in terms of their own activities and what they perceive at the moment.
Concrete operations 7–11 years	Children can think logically but still learn best through experience.
Formal operations 11–Adult	People are capable of abstract thinking.

- **Make-believe play.** Children continue to learn through *imaginative play*, which is fantasy or dramatic play in which they may imitate real-life situations, as when they play house or school. See Fig. 15-6.

- **Use of symbols.** Children learn that objects and words can be symbols—that is, they can represent something else. A child this age can recognize that a stop sign means "stop."

- **Egocentric viewpoint.** Children continue to view the world in terms of their own thoughts and feelings. One five-year-old explained that grass grew so that she wouldn't hurt herself if she fell.

- **Limited focus.** The preoperational child makes decisions based on his perceptions, which are often limited. If you poured the same quantity of water in two containers—a tall one and a short, wide one—a child in this stage would say that the taller one contains more water. The child in this stage might also say that all apples are red, so green fruits cannot be apples.

Fig. 15-6 What skills might dress-up and make-believe play help children develop?

Vygotsky's Theory

Lev Vygotsky (1896–1934) was an influential Russian psychologist whose work differed somewhat from Piaget's. While Piaget maintained that the learning stages that children go through are a natural part of the human maturation process, just like gains in height and weight, Vygotsky believed that development is too complex to be divided into neat stages.

Vygotsky believed that learning is socially based. According to him, parents, teachers, and peers promote learning. Children play key roles in their own education and that of their peers. Learning takes place in, and is dependent upon, the social environment.

Vygotsky believed that teachers should collaborate with students rather than lecturing, and that students should collaborate with each other. A classroom based on Vygotsky's theories would provide clustered tables for teamwork and small group learning. Children of different ages would learn from each other, and teachers and students might take turns leading small group discussions on a reading, for example.

Montessori's Theory of Learning

Dr. Maria Montessori (1870–1952), studied children and developed her own theories about childhood learning. Today, Montessori's methods are used at approximately 4,000 Montessori schools in the United States and 7,000 around the world. In addition, many public and private schools use Montessori's ideas in some way, as do many parents.

Montessori believed that children would learn naturally if placed in a prepared learning environment containing the appropriate materials or "learning games." For

LOOKING AT REAL LIFE

Four-year-old Haley had always loved to take walks in the nearby forest with her father. Her dad noticed that she spent lots of time looking around her as she walked, and asked questions about the things she saw. She asked why the leaves changed color in the fall, where dirt came from, how trees, grass, and flowers grew, and why a heavy rain made big puddles.

Haley's father gave her a small shovel and rake for her birthday, and he took her to see the butterflies at the local zoo. Haley and her dad started a little garden in their yard. Haley learned to distinguish weeds from other plants in the garden. She watered the plants and pulled the weeds.

▸▸**PERSONAL APPLICATION**

1. When did you first begin to show an interest in a particular area? Did adults around you help you to pursue these interests?
2. What programs or classes are available in your area where young children can pursue special interests, such as dancing or painting? If you were to teach such a class, what area would it be in?

example, before they learn to write, children play games and engage in activities designed to strengthen the muscles of the hand and fingers. The Montessori method focuses on the development of the senses, language, and motor skills with a view to preparing a child's mind and body for further learning.

A Montessori classroom is designed to be an environment in which children can learn by themselves and from each other. It commonly has several "learning stations" arranged by subject area. The materials are all within children's reach, pictures on the walls are at children's eye level, and everything in the room has a place on a shelf or in a container. Teachers allow students a great deal of independence, never interrupting a student engaged in a task. Great respect is shown for a student's instinctive pursuit of individual learning. A four-year-old pouring water from a pitcher into cups is not "playing with a toy pitcher," because the pitcher is real and breakable, only child-size. If the child drops it, it breaks, and he or she learns that actions have consequences, and it's important to be careful. By using arm muscles and fingers, gross and fine motor skills develop. The child is also learning about the properties of water. A Montessori teacher would never say that this child is "playing," but rather "working." The use of the word "work" instead of "play" is designed to help children develop a sense of worth—the same pride in their work as adults experience from their jobs.

SECTION 15-1 Review and Activities

Reviewing the Section

1. What does an *IQ* score of 105 indicate about a child? What information does it not give?
2. Explain what *cultural bias* in intelligence testing means.
3. A ballet dancer who performs in time to music is using what types of intelligence?
4. Give at least three examples of intellectual skills at ages four, five, and six.
5. What is Vygotsky's theory of learning? How do his theories differ from Piaget's?
6. What do Vygotsky and Montessori's theories have in common?

Observing and Interacting

Design a classroom for first-graders to reflect Vygotsky's theories of social learning. If you were to design it to reflect Montessori's theories, what changes would you make? Create two diagrams of the classroom, labeling one "Vygotsky" and the other "Montessori." Each diagram should show where desks and learning materials should go.

Learning from Four to Six

Jorge came home from kindergarten, bursting with excitement about his day. "We have a real bunny at school now," he said, "And Miss Jackson said I can help take care of him! Today I cleaned his cage, and then I filled his water bottle, and then I got to feed him. He has special food to eat, and I gave him some." Jorge thrust a note into his mother's hand. "Look! Mary and I get to feed him every Wednesday! Can I bring some lettuce on those days?"

Objectives

- Suggest ways to help children learn from everyday experiences.
- Identify strategies to encourage children's interest in reading, art, and music.
- Explain how parents can help their children prepare for and adjust to kindergarten.
- Identify possible speech problems for children this age.

Key Terms

phonemes
alliteration
bilingual
finger plays

Helping Children Learn

Four- to six-year-olds are often excited about learning. Parents and caregivers can encourage this enthusiasm in many ways.

Learning from Everyday Life

Experiences, especially those shared with adults, form the basis for children's learning. Talking with children about their world and what they are doing encourages these interests. Positive comments, such as "Wow, the building you are making is so tall—and it has so many windows!" teach vocabulary and encourage feelings of self-worth. You can also ask children questions that help them think about their experiences in new ways and focus on the process of their play. Encourage them to organize their thoughts by asking questions like, "How did you do that?" and "What are you going to do next?"

Explanations and suggestions can also be helpful. You might explain in simple terms why water from a faucet can come out cold or hot. If a child grows frustrated trying to find room to put together a train set, you could suggest removing other toys from the floor to make the job easier.

Asking a child's advice is another effective technique for promoting learning. For

Parenting Q&A

How Much Television Is Too Much?

Most parents wonder how much television their children should watch and what programs are appropriate. Parents may wish to keep some facts in mind when making decisions about children and television.

From ages four to six, children's brains are rapidly developing and responding to stimulation. Watching television may affect their brain development. When children watch television they are missing out on other experiences, like forming relationships, getting exercise, and using their imagination. Children who spend a lot of time watching television are less active, which can lead to weight problems and other health problems.

Researchers strongly suspect that attention deficit disorders and weak problem-solving skills among children are related to watching too much television. Watching more television is associated with poorer academic performance, especially in reading.

While watching television is no substitute for reading or other activities that challenge the mind, some programs for children are educational and interactive. For example, many public television programs stimulate learning by encouraging imaginative play and posing questions that children can answer aloud at home. Parents should restrict children's viewing of programs that depict violence or contain material that is not appropriate to a child's level of development.

THINKING IT THROUGH

1. How can watching a lot of television affect a child's social skills?
2. What activities would you suggest to a six-year-old instead of watching television?

---

example, ask how to fold napkins for a meal and then fold them the way the child has suggested.

Trips and activities are important to learning. A ride on a bus, train, or plane can be an adventure that leads a child to discuss what's seen and ask questions. Nature walks are fun, too—and free. Everyone in the family can learn about the natural world by taking a close look at plants and animals.

Helping around the house provides great learning opportunities. Four- to six-year-olds can help sort laundry to be washed into lights and darks, set the table, and put their toys away. Helping around the house gives children a sense that they are part of the family and play an important role in it.

Appreciating Reading

Developing an interest in reading is important because books provide an opportunity to learn about and understand the world. Children who enjoy reading will find learning easier and more fun. Reading to young children regularly helps them associate books with enjoyment at an early age.

An important factor in learning to read is the ability to hear **phonemes** (FOH-neems), such as the *ou* in *house*, the smallest individual sounds in words. Rhyming words help develop phoneme awareness, so reading rhyming books to children is a good learning activity. When a book becomes familiar, stop from time to time and let the child fill in the sounds and words. When Jessica's mom reads, "Hey diddle, diddle, the cat and the..." Jessica shouts, "Fiddle!"

Another way to develop phoneme awareness is through **alliteration**—the repetition of certain sounds. Many alphabet books provide opportunities to use alliteration because they collect words that begin with the same letter. After children have learned the sound, they can begin to associate the letter with the sound, which is an important step in learning to read.

THE DEVELOPING BRAIN

Children between four and six are at the ideal age to learn not only their own first language but other languages as well. Exposure to other languages rewires the neurons in the still developing brain in such a way that a child's overall language abilities increase greatly.

Watching television isn't a substitute for reading. Studies have shown that children whose caregivers read to them have an easier time learning to read.

Research suggests that children who are **bilingual**, or able to speak two languages, find it easier to learn to read. They seem to understand that printed words convey a particular meaning sooner than children who speak only one language. This may give them an edge when learning to read.

Choosing Books

Young children love books and stories. When caregivers encourage this interest, children are more likely to read for pleasure as they grow older.

Most communities have public libraries that lend children's books. In some cases, children can get their own library cards. This symbol of being grown up helps children look forward to going to the library and choosing their own books.

How can you tell which books will appeal to children? The following questions will help you make appropriate choices:

- Are the pictures colorful, interesting, and easy to understand?
- Will the story appeal to the child's interests?
- Does the story include action that will hold the child's attention?
- Will the child understand most of the words?
- Does the book use descriptive language that brings the story to life?
- For younger children, is the story short enough to read in one sitting?
- If you are considering buying the book, is it sturdy enough to stand up to hard use?

What kind of books do four- to six-year-olds like? Many like stories about experiences that are different from their own. Through books, children who live in cities can learn about farm life and children who live in rural areas can experience subways, apartments, and other aspects of city life. See Fig. 15-7.

Children this age also enjoy humor, including funny rhymes and unusual situations. When they giggle over a picture of a horse in a bathtub, they show that they are beginning to separate reality from fantasy.

Introducing Art and Music

Art helps children express their feelings, develop fine motor skills, and express their creativity. Four- to six-year-olds benefit from working with many different art materials, such as modeling clay, crayons, paper, paste, paint, and scissors. Even dried macaroni can be strung into a necklace or painted and pasted onto a sheet of construction paper to make a design.

Children should be encouraged to experiment with art materials without being corrected or criticized. What matters to the child is the creative process. You can help children feel proud of their artwork by displaying it and sharing it with others.

When you talk to children about their artwork, you're not only fostering a sense of accomplishment, you're also helping develop their verbal skills. Ask, "How did you make that?" Rather than guessing what a picture represents, ask the child to tell you. Then find specific aspects of the work that you can praise. For example, you

Fig. 15-7 **Children love to go to the library and choose their own books.** Why do parents need to help children make their choices?

Playing Grown-Up

Between the ages of two and nine, children often engage in imaginative play, or "make believe." This kind of play aids intellectual development in many ways. In imaginative play, children act out imaginary situations, often imitating what they see in the adult world. After watching an adult bake a cake, a child may pretend to bake a cake for a favorite stuffed animal. After visiting a parent's workplace, a child may play "office" or "store." Children might also use fantasy play by drawing images from stories or films, perhaps acting out an explorer's voyage across the Atlantic Ocean. Most children show an interest in imaginative play at some time or another. Adults who provide opportunities for imaginative play do children a great favor.

Following Up

What materials could you provide for children who want to pretend to be detectives?

might say, "I really like the bright colors you used for the flowers."

The rhythm of music intrigues children, whether it's the thud of a ball bouncing on the sidewalk or the sound of footsteps. Children this age become more aware of rhythms and enjoy singing simple, repetitive songs. Many children are introduced to singing by **finger plays**, songs or chants with accompanying hand motions. "The Itsy, Bitsy Spider" is an example of a popular finger play.

The opportunity to play simple instruments helps develop children's interest in music. Children enjoy using bells, drums, tambourines, or almost anything that makes a noise. There is no need to buy instruments: old pans, bowls, and mixing spoons work just as well.

The School Experience

Because children attend school for many years, it is vital that they develop a positive attitude from the start. Parents and caregivers should plan carefully to make the transition from home to school as smooth as possible.

Preparing for School

Many parents place their children in a preschool so that they can become used to a school setting. In preschool, children learn to pay attention, take turns, sit quietly for a time, and interact with other children.

At age five or six, most children enter kindergarten. The standard for entering the public school system is usually when the child reaches his or her fifth birthday. Most systems have a cutoff date, such as September 1. If a child is five by that date, the child may enter kindergarten. If not, the child must wait until the following year. See Fig. 15-8.

Fig. 15-8 **The first day of school can be exciting, scary, or a mixture of both.** How would you prepare a child for the first day of school?

The question of when a child is ready to start school is a difficult one. Should a child of school age who would be among the youngest in the class wait another year before starting school? What about a child who doesn't seem ready? One study showed that even children with high intelligence had emotional problems if they began school before they were ready.

Another study, however, suggests that the opposite is true. In this research, children who started late had problems with behavior later in their school careers.

What, then, should a parent do? Many school systems offer screenings to help assess a child's readiness. Parents whose child is enrolled in preschool can talk to the child's preschool teachers. They can judge the child's readiness based on what they have observed. Parents can also talk with their child's pediatrician and look for certain signs. A child is ready for school if he or she can:

- **Communicate with adults.** A child must be able to talk to adults other than his or her parents and be understood.

- **Manage personal needs.** A child should be able to put on and take off his or her coat and shoes and use the bathroom without help.

- **Complete a task.** A child should be able to complete a task such as finishing a drawing or putting away supplies.

- **Listen attentively.** A child should be able to listen attentively to a story and answer questions about it.

- **Follow directions and take turns.** A child must be able to participate in activities and cooperate with classmates.

- **Be patient.** A child should be willing to wait for a request to be met or to have a question answered.

YOUR TURN

Making decisions. If you felt that your child was ready for school, but the child's preschool teacher did not, what could you do?

Many states require that a child have a physical exam before starting school. Parents also have to show that their children have had the immunizations the school requires. For more information on immunizations, see Chapter 20.

In the past, kindergarten was usually only a half-day long. Today, however, all-day kindergarten programs are very common. Research has shown that children in all-day kindergarten programs perform better in elementary school. Why do you think this is true?

Making the Transition

Starting kindergarten can be a major adjustment for a child, even one who has gone to preschool. The school is generally bigger than the preschool, and it includes children several years older. A child switching from a half-day preschool to a full-day kindergarten must adjust to the longer hours away from home. Many children entering kindergarten also begin riding a school bus for the first time.

Parents can help their children adjust to this new experience in several ways:

- Be sure the child knows his or her full name, address, and telephone number.
- Explain what to expect at school. If possible, visit the school together before the child's first day and meet the teachers. Some schools offer open house or orientation days for new students and their parents.
- Be sure that the child has plenty of rest by starting an earlier bedtime a few weeks before school begins.
- Let the child choose a lunch box or backpack and pick out the clothes to wear on the first day of school. This will help the child link the new school to feelings of increased independence.

- If possible, arrange to have the child play with future classmates before the first day of school. Seeing people they know helps reassure children in new situations.
- Above all, share positive feelings about school with the child.

Speech Development

By the time they start school, children have gained an extensive knowledge of language just by listening and talking at home. They probably don't know what an adjective is, but they can use adjectives confidently and correctly. As children grow older, their vocabularies increase and the sentences they use become more complex. However, children learn all the basic forms of language almost effortlessly in the preschool years.

Children ages four, five, and six typically show a rapid increase in their vocabulary. A normally developing six-year-old can understand and use approximately 2,500 words. See Fig. 15-9. Articulation (clear, distinct speech) improves dramatically in this period as well. By age six, children can correctly say 90% of the words they know.

Much of this improvement in speech depends on physical development. Some sounds are more difficult to make than others. The sounds represented by *b*, *m*, and *p* are produced simply by moving the lips. By three, most children can make these sounds. The *f* and *v* sounds, among others, involve both the lips and the teeth. Children may not master these sounds until age five. The most difficult sounds are those represented by *j*, *ch*, *st*, *pl*, *th* and *sl*. They require the smooth coordination of lip, tongue, and throat muscles. Some children may reach six or seven before "pwease" becomes "please."

Fig. 15-9 **By the age of six, children's language skills have reached the point where they can understand and enjoy a simple joke.**

Speech Difficulties

Although most children develop good language skills at home, some have problems with spoken language. They may have plenty of opportunities to listen and speak at home, but they may hear and use only a limited number of simple words. Children need to hear—and be encouraged to use—language that is specific and rich in detail. For example, rather than using the very general verb "go," encourage children to use a variety of descriptive verbs: The boys *race* across the field. Mom *jogs* every morning. The bugs *creep* down the tree. Some children have a head start. When parents and other caregivers begin talking to children from the time they are very young, it helps speech development. Describing what a child is seeing and doing builds vocabulary.

Children who don't speak English at home often face challenges when they begin school. They must learn English language skills and, at the same time, keep up with the class. Some schools have classes with bilingual teachers or aides for English-language learners. Children who move from one part of the country to another may also have difficulty because of differences in pronunciation.

Some children have physical problems that prevent normal speech. Others may be intellectually or emotionally delayed.

All these situations may cause children to have difficulties at school. They may not be able to understand the teacher or to make themselves understood. As a result, learning becomes more difficult. This situation may cause emotional problems as well. Classmates may be unkind to a child whose speech is different, even if the difference is simply an accent. Teasing and jokes can add to a child's sense of isolation. Whatever the cause, children with speech problems need special help—preferably before they begin school.

SECTION 15-2 Review and Activities

Reviewing the Section

1. Choose an experience—other than one mentioned in the chapter—that a caregiver could use to teach new skills to a child. Explain why this activity is well suited to a four- to six-year-old.
2. Give a specific example of how parents can encourage a child's interest in reading, art, and music.
3. Identify two steps parents can take to prepare children for kindergarten, and explain the reasons behind them.
4. What challenges might children whose first language is not English face at school? How can teachers help the child overcome these challenges?
5. What types of school activities might be challenging for a student with a speech difficulty? For each activity you list, list an alternative that is easier and teaches some of the same skills.

Observing and Interacting

Talk to a kindergartner about what school is like. What does the child like most? Note both what the child says and how he or she says it. Does he or she appear to be having any difficulty producing certain sounds? Write a report of your findings.

Career Opportunities

Toy Designer

Toys must be attractive enough to appeal to parents, interesting enough to capture a child's attention, safe, and easy to keep clean. New toys must not look like those already available, and they must function properly. Designing toys is challenging work!

▸ Job Responsibilities

Toy designers start with a concept for a new toy. They give toys names, draw plans for them, and determine how they can be created, either by hand or by machines. Many toys have complicated parts or motors. Toy designers may also work on the packaging and on advertising for their toys.

▸ Work Environment

Toymakers use computers for design and engineering. Competition to create a popular new toy is fierce. Some toy designers form their own companies but most work for large toy manufacturers.

▸ Education and Training

Recommended courses of study for future toy designers include: child psychology, industrial design, art history, children's literature, and fine arts. After earning a bachelor's degree, most toy designers apply for internships with toy companies.

▸ Skills and Aptitudes

- Creative drive
- Ability to use and understand technology
- Knowledge of children's likes and dislikes
- Sense of fun

WORKPLACE CONNECTION

1. **Thinking Skills.** How does spending time around children help toy designers?

2. **Resource Skills.** How could you observe how children use toys?

SECTION SUMMARIES

- Traditional intelligence tests take into account the ages of children but may put more emphasis on certain types of intelligence. (15-1)
- Howard Gardner identified eight types of intelligence. (15-1)
- According to Piaget's theory, children ages two to seven are in the preoperational period of thinking. (15-1)
- Vygotsky and Montessori introduced influential theories of learning. (15-1)
- Everyday life offers many opportunities for learning. (15-2)
- Caregivers who make reading a regular part of children's lives are encouraging them to enjoy books in the future and are promoting learning. (15-2)
- Children starting school can be helped to prepare for new situations. (15-2)
- Between ages four and six, children's language skills usually improve rapidly, but some children need help. (15-2)

REVIEWING THE CHAPTER

1. What is the goal of intelligence tests? On what grounds have they been criticized? (15-1)
2. Choose two of Gardner's *multiple intelligences*. Predict three professions other than those mentioned that someone high in each intelligence might choose. (15-1)
3. What are two ways that children learn during Piaget's preoperational period? (15-1)
4. Briefly outline the positive effects reading has on learning in general. (15-2)
5. Identify the benefits of having children explain the processes they use in creating art. (15-2)
6. List at least three abilities that a child must display before being allowed to enter kindergarten. (15-2)

7. How might engaging in imaginative play help a child prepare for the transition to school? (15-2)
8. What are two signs of language skills that children develop during this stage? (15-2)

THINKING CRITICALLY

1. **Creating Opportunities.** Suppose you are the parent of an only child. What are five ways that you could help that child develop his or her interpersonal intelligence?
2. **Making Inferences.** Five-year-old Sue and four-year-old Wendy are having a tea party for their dolls. In what type of play are they engaging? Give examples of how they might show the other characteristics of preoperational thinking at their tea party.

MAKING CONNECTIONS

1. **Social Studies.** Research the experiments that Piaget used to understand preoperational thinking. Choose one to demonstrate to the class, and explain what it means about preoperational thinking.

2. **Writing.** Imagine you are a parenting expert with a magazine column. A parent writes saying he wants to get his five-year-old son interested in reading, but it's hard to get him to sit still with a book. What would you advise him to do?

APPLYING YOUR LEARNING

1. **Identifying Skills.** Decide what intelligences are needed for the following tasks:

   - Writing an autobiography
   - Making and selling crafts
   - Writing songs to be used in television commercials
   - Painting landscapes

2. **Encouraging Learning.** Imagine that a five-year-old you know is drawing a picture of her family and where they live. Write a list of five comments you could make or questions you could ask to encourage the child's learning and promote positive feelings about herself.

3. **Assigning Appropriate Tasks.** Name five tasks you could ask a four- to six-year-old to do around the house. Beside each task, indicate what skills it would help the child develop.

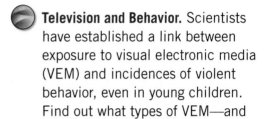

Learning from Research

1. Choose one of the following claims to research.
2. How is this information useful to parents of children ages four to six?
3. Summarize what you have learned.

Television and Behavior. Scientists have established a link between exposure to visual electronic media (VEM) and incidences of violent behavior, even in young children. Find out what types of VEM—and what level of exposure—are believed to be safe for children.

Social Interaction and Behavior. Research shows that the brain of a young child responds strongly to facial expressions of anger, hostility, or indifference, and that these responses correlate with rising anxiety levels. Identify situations in which children are exposed to facial expressions of this type. What strategies can parents use to reduce the anxiety these expressions produce in children?

The Developing Brain and Behavior. The developing brain needs stimulation of all five senses: taste, smell, sight, touch, and hearing. Research shows that experiences that stimulate more than one sense at a time are more easily retained in the long-term memory. Find out why children remember multi-sensory experiences better. Give examples of multi-sensory experiences.

The Child from Seven to Twelve

Chapter 16
Physical Development from Seven to Twelve

Chapter 17
Emotional and Social Development from Seven to Twelve

Chapter 18
Intellectual Development from Seven to Twelve

CHAPTER 16 Physical Development from Seven to Twelve

Thoughtful Reading:

As you read this chapter:
- Ask clarifying questions such as who, what, when, and where.
- Ask follow-up questions such as how and why.
- Find sources to answer all your reading questions.

Section 16-1
Growth and Development from Seven to Twelve

Section 16-2
Caring for Children from Seven to Twelve

Growth and Development from Seven to Twelve

From the ages of seven to twelve, children go through a period of major physical changes. A sudden spurt of growth adds to their height, and their bodies change in profound ways as they begin to take on the physical characteristics of adulthood. There are two significant stages during these years: middle childhood and the preteen years. Middle childhood runs from ages seven through ten. During this period, children build on the growth and skills that began in early childhood. Eleven- and twelve-year-olds are in the preteen years, poised to enter the path that leads to being an adult.

Objectives

- Describe average changes in height and weight between the ages of seven and ten, and for eleven- and twelve-year-olds.
- Explain the physical changes that take place at the beginning of puberty and their impact on children's lives.
- Analyze the benefits of regular physical activity.
- Identify why children's motor skills improve.

Key Terms

growth spurt
body image
eating disorder
scoliosis
menstruation

Height and Weight

From the ages of seven to ten, boys and girls grow in height an average of just over 2 inches (5.1 cm) per year. This is a slower average rate of growth than they experienced as preschoolers, toddlers, and infants. The gain in height is usually at a regular pace, but many children have **growth spurts**, periods when they grow very rapidly in a short time. For nine-year-old Ahmad, that meant needing longer jeans by November, even though his pants were new at the start of the school year.

The average rate of growth increases during the preteen years. It is during this time that many children go through *puberty*, the set of changes that result in a physically mature body that is able to reproduce. Girls tend to go through puberty a bit earlier than boys, and are often taller than the boys in their class at this time. Boys have larger average gains in height between the ages of 12 and 14, when they typically go through puberty. See Fig. 16-1 for average heights of boys and girls from seven to twelve.

During this period, growth takes place in different parts of the body at different times. Typically, the hands and the feet are the first to grow, followed by the arms and legs, and then finally the torso. Sometimes one part of the body—perhaps the nose—grows faster than other parts. This can cause embarrassment.

In terms of weight, boys and girls gain on average about 6½ pounds (2.9 kg) each year during middle childhood. During the preteen years, average annual weight gain is about 10½ pounds (4.7 kg) for girls and 9½ pounds (4.3 kg) for boys. Because puberty typically occurs in boys about two years later than girls, boys have a greater annual weight gain than girls after about age twelve.

Experts believe that heredity is the most influential factor in determining a child's ultimate height. When parents are considered to be below an average height, it is likely that their children will be short.

Nutrition is an important influence on a child's weight during these years. A child who eats foods low in fat and high in nutrients is less likely to have a weight problem than one who eats fatty foods that are low in nutrients. Physically active children are also less likely to be overweight.

Body Image

Some children—especially preteen girls—become sensitive about how they think their bodies look, or their **body image**. They may become self-conscious about the changing shape of their bodies. Too often, images of thin celebrities and models give them the impression that they must be thin to be beautiful. Some become overly concerned with their own weight, seeing themselves as overweight when they really are not. This, and other factors, can put preteens at risk for developing an **eating disorder**, a serious pattern of overeating or restrictive eating. Preteens may experience an unhealthy preoccupation with food and thinness. Eating disorders can have a devastating effect on the body and can even lead to death. For more on eating disorders, see page 486.

Fig. 16-1 Average Heights and Weights: Ages Seven to Twelve

Age	BOYS		GIRLS	
	Height / Inches	Weight / Pounds	Height / Inches	Weight / Pounds
Seven years	48	51	47¾	50
Eight years	50	56	50¼	56
Nine years	52½	63	52½	64
Ten years	54½	70	54½	72
Eleven years	56½	79	57½	82
Twelve years	58¾	89	59½	92

Fig. 16-1 The figures on this chart represent averages for each group. As during early childhood, children in middle childhood and the preteen years vary greatly in height.

Team sports give children the opportunity to have fun, be physically active, and learn teamwork and other skills. Individual sports, such as swimming, provide some of the same benefits. Children typically learn these sports in groups and often compete against others.

In both team and individual sports, there are ways to help maximize a child's overall enjoyment and benefit:

- **Choose a developmentally appropriate sport.** Children should only play sports for which they have the physical maturity.

- **Encourage playing for fun and for good health, not just to win.** Children benefit more when they are encouraged to play for fun and for individual skill development, rather than playing just to win. Look for a coach with this attitude.

- **Nurture good sportsmanship.** Respect for other players and the game should be one of the most important lessons a child learns. Respect for teammates and fellow athletes translates to respect for others in life.

- **Remind the child that everyone has good and bad days.** Prepare children for both failure and success in sports. If parents, coaches, and caregivers continue to encourage children, they are more likely to accept mistakes and continue enjoying sports and active play.

YOUR TURN

Behaving appropriately. Some parents behave inappropriately at youth sporting events. If you were helping coach a team of young athletes, how would you educate parents about the importance of being a positive influence at sporting events?

Fig. 16-2 **At some points during middle childhood, boys often experience growth spurts.** What other changes do they experience?

Proportion and Posture

During middle childhood, children tend to keep the same body type they had in early childhood. For example, a tall and lean five-year-old typically remains tall and slim through middle childhood. As seven- to twelve-year-olds grow, their proportions change: legs lengthen, adding height and bringing the head more in proportion to the body. Children also become stronger and develop greater muscle tone in their legs, arms, and torso. See Fig. 16-2.

Some older children and preteens develop curvature of the spine called **scoliosis**. The spine curves sideways, affecting posture. Scoliosis may be treated with exercise, a brace, or surgery.

Permanent Teeth

Most children lose all of their primary teeth between the ages of five and thirteen, and most of the permanent teeth appear at this time, too. As mentioned in Chapter 13, the first permanent teeth to emerge are the set of molars that appear around the age of six. Around age twelve, a second set of molars emerges behind the first set. A third set of molars—the "wisdom teeth"—appears later.

Onset of Puberty

Puberty usually occurs between the ages of nine and sixteen. Researchers believe that the start of puberty is related to heredity and nutritional factors. On average, however, puberty starts about the age of ten for girls and about one to two years later for boys. Significant physical changes trigger the onset of puberty. The *pituitary gland* begins sending out hormones that cause a number of profound physical changes in the body.

In both boys and girls, a significant growth spurt occurs during puberty in which they gain 25 percent of their total adult height. Hair appears under the arms and in the pubic area. Sweat and oil glands become more active, and a child can begin to experience body odor and acne.

Boys

In boys, facial hair begins to appear, and the voice deepens. Sometimes the deepening doesn't take place smoothly, and a boy's voice may occasionally "crack," or change tones, during the growth of the larynx and vocal cords. A boy's shoulders broaden, and his muscles grow larger. Also, a boy's sexual organs develop and become capable of reproduction.

THE DEVELOPING BRAIN

It is possible to hone one's fine motor skills with activities that teach the brain to control hand and finger movements to a high degree. One such activity is typing. The more a person practices typing, the better his or her fine motor skills will become.

Girls

Girls typically experience more profound changes at puberty. Their breasts begin to enlarge, their waist narrows, and their hips widen. The sexual organs develop and become capable of releasing mature eggs. Related to that change is the beginning of **menstruation**. This is the monthly cycle in which an egg is released and the uterus prepares for a possible pregnancy. Most girls begin to have menstrual periods about two years after puberty begins. The average age for menstrual periods to begin is now eleven or twelve, about a year earlier than past generations experienced. Girls' menstrual periods may be irregular at first, and not occur every month. Some girls experience discomfort and cramping with menstrual periods.

Motor Skills

In the years from seven to twelve, a child's motor skills improve greatly. As the body matures, the muscles gain strength. Children at these ages enjoy active play. Some take lessons to learn to swim and dance, and participate in gymnastics. Team sports are popular.

With the increase in muscular strength comes growing muscle control. Hand-eye coordination improves and both gross and fine motor skills become easier and smoother. More complex tasks become possible. For example, catching a baseball is a challenge for a seven-year-old, but a ten-year-old can manage it quite easily. Playing computer games can help children improve their fine motor skills.

SECTION 16-1 Review and Activities

Reviewing the Section

1. How does a *growth spurt* affect a child's body during puberty? Why do children sometimes feel awkward at this stage?
2. What are the average changes in height and weight per year during middle childhood? In the *preteen* years?
3. How might the physical changes a preteen experiences affect his or her body image?
4. How does the timing of puberty differ between boys and girls?
5. What benefits does a child gain from participating in sports?
6. Why do motor skills improve during this period?

Observing and Interacting

Talk to some adults you know to find out what they did between the ages of seven and twelve to stay physically active. Which of those activities do you think children would still enjoy today? What activities are most popular now?

Caring for Children from Seven to Twelve

During middle childhood and the preteen years, children experience increasing independence and tremendous physical and emotional growth. However, they continue to need adult guidance on topics such as nutrition and personal hygiene. Habits established during these periods often remain throughout life.

Objectives

- Explain how the Dietary Guidelines can help achieve good nutrition.
- Develop a plan of physical activity for school-age children.
- Identify ways to help prevent dental problems.
- Compare and contrast personal hygiene needs for an eight-year-old and a twelve-year-old.
- Explain what school-age children should be taught about personal safety.

Key Terms

fiber
sedentary activities
sealants
orthodontist

Nutrition

Good nutrition from a well-balanced diet is essential for growth, development, learning, and health. Children in middle childhood and the preteen years require good nutrition to grow, develop, learn in school, and feel their best. Such diets contain essential nutrients and a good balance of carbohydrates, fat, and protein. The Guidelines for Healthy Eating on page 154 and USDA's MyPyramid Plan can help ensure that meals and snacks incorporate an appropriate variety and amounts of foods that children need for a healthful diet, depending upon their age and activity level. See Fig. 16-3.

Dietary Guidelines

The Dietary Guidelines for Americans is another useful tool for children and adults. They present a more comprehensive plan for incorporating nutritious foods and physical

Fig. 16-3 **School-age children have greater independence in choosing the foods they wish to eat during the day. How can parents teach children to make healthy food choices?**

activity into daily life for good health. They include recommendations, such as:

- **Keep weight within a healthy range.** Balance calories from foods and beverages with the calories needed for growth and activity.

- **Be physically active each day.** Children and teens need at least one hour of physical activity most or all days of the week. Physical activity has both short-term and long-term health benefits for children.

- **Eat a variety of nutrient-dense foods and beverages.** Adopt a balanced eating pattern, including foods from the basic food groups.

- **Choose a variety of grains daily, mostly whole grains.** Foods made from whole grains help form the

foundation of a healthy diet. They provide **fiber** plus many nutrients. Fiber is an indigestible plant material that helps the digestive system work properly.

- **Choose a variety of fruits and vegetables daily.** Many children fail to get the recommended servings of fruits and vegetables. These foods contain essential vitamins and minerals, fiber, and other substances important for good health.

- **Limit the amount of fat in the diet.** No one needs a diet high in fatty or fried foods and snacks. Most fats that are eaten should come from fish, nuts, and vegetable oils, rather than from red meat sources.

- **Limit sugar and salt.** Choose and prepare foods and beverages with little added sugar and salt.

Parenting Q&A

How Can Parents Help an Overweight Child?

Parents of overweight children are often concerned about the health and emotional issues their children may face and are unsure of how to help. Here are some ways parents can offer support and guidance.

- **Consult with the child's pediatrician.** Ask the pediatrician to evaluate the child's weight, growth, and health. Discuss any health or emotional concerns. Ask for guidance on providing a healthy diet that will meet the child's nutritional needs.
- **Focus on health rather than weight.** Don't make losing weight the main issue. Explain to the child that eating healthy foods helps the body grow strong and provides energy for fun activities. Involve the whole family in a healthy eating plan.
- **Make a variety of healthy foods available.** Children should not be placed on restrictive diets. Provide a wide variety of healthy foods from all of the food groups, especially fruits and vegetables. Giving children choices makes them more willing to try new things.
- **Encourage regular physical activity and limit television viewing.** Excessive television viewing is linked to weight problems in children. Encourage the child to participate in physical activities he or she enjoys, whether it is a team sport, riding a bike, or hiking. Be a good role model. Be active daily and plan activities the whole family can participate in.
- **Offer unconditional love and support.** Overweight children sometimes develop a poor self-image. Caregivers should make it clear that the child is loved and accepted at any weight.

THINKING IT THROUGH

1. How might allowing children to help with food selection and preparation encourage them to try new foods?
2. Why is involving the whole family in any diet changes a good idea?

Making Food Choices

As children become more independent, they begin to make more of their own food choices. They may make or buy some of their own snacks and meals. Peers or the media may influence these choices, which often take place away from home. For example, Leah can choose from various foods offered at her school for lunch. When she brings a lunch from home, Leah sometimes trades the fruit from her packed lunch for cookies or chips.

Despite outside influences, family remains the primary influence on a child. Modeling good eating behavior is one of the best ways to teach a child good eating habits. Here are a few things that families can do:

- Eat meals together. Show by example that healthful eating habits include eating both the right foods and the right amounts. In other words, don't overeat.
- Serve varied, well-balanced meals that are low in fat, sugar, and salt.
- Stock the kitchen with a variety of nutritious foods for snacks.
- Limit sweets and deep-fried foods to special occasions. Dessert does not need to be served every day.
- Offer children smaller portions than an adult would eat. Never force them to "clean their plate." Instead, allow and encourage children to stop eating when they feel full.
- Make calcium-rich foods and beverages a part of a child's diet to help ensure strong bones.

Starting the Day Right

Breakfast is an important meal for both children and adults. It provides the vital fuel that people need to begin the day. Researchers have found that children who

Fig. 16-4 **Eating a healthy breakfast helps children concentrate at school and gives them energy.** Which food groups are especially important at breakfast?

eat breakfast have a greater capacity for learning and participation and a greater ability to concentrate, especially on tasks that require problem solving and creativity. Skipping breakfast can result in headaches, fatigue, and restless behavior, which interfere with classroom learning. See Fig. 16-4.

A healthy breakfast includes two servings from the grain group, one from the dairy group, and one from the fruit group. National school breakfast programs help provide this nutrition and ensure that all children can begin the school day the right way.

Eating Disorders

Although most children go through periods when they rebel against what is served at mealtime or sneak sugary treats from time to time, a small percentage of children begin to develop eating disorders. There are several types of eating disorders. They include:

- **Anorexia nervosa.** This is an intense fear of weight gain characterized by starvation techniques and severe weight loss.
- **Bulimia.** Bulimia involves periods of out-of-control eating followed by purging the body of food, often through vomiting.
- **Binge eating.** This disorder includes periods of highly excessive eating, followed by weight gain.

Fig. 16-5 **Increased sedentary behavior, especially television viewing, has significantly reduced the amount of physical activity among children.** What are some ways that parents can encourage children to spend more time pursuing physical activities?

Researchers believe that some children with eating disorders may be preoccupied with being thin due to a poor body image, or have psychological problems, such as depression or low self-esteem. Many strive to please others and feel that food is the one thing that they can control in their lives. Children with eating disorders need counseling from a trained professional. Parents shouldn't hesitate to consult a professional if they notice unusual eating patterns or sudden weight gain or loss in their daughter or son. If a child's friends notice a problem, they should tell a teacher or school counselor.

Physical Fitness

Compared to their parents, children today are less likely to walk or ride their bikes to school. Many are less fit than they should be, and they run the risk of becoming set in a pattern of inactivity that could result in health problems, especially when they are older. One reason for the decline in fitness levels is that children spend hours every day in **sedentary activities**, activities that involve little exercise, such as watching television or playing computer and electronic games. The hours children spend in front of a screen cut into the time that might otherwise be spent in physical activity. Parents and other caregivers make the best role models for healthy living by limiting their own television viewing and their children's time in front of screens, and by joining children in physical activities. See Fig. 16-5.

To promote physical fitness, parents should look for a variety of developmentally appropriate activities that their children might enjoy. When choosing possibilities, it's good to include activities that can be continued later in life, such as hiking, biking, swimming, dancing, skating,

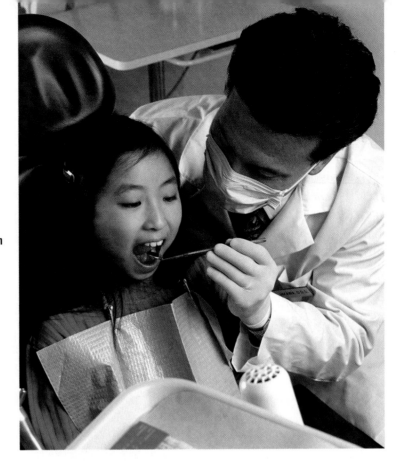

Fig. 16-6 As a child's full set of permanent teeth develops, dental check-ups and cleanings become an important means of preventing tooth decay. **What is another way to help prevent tooth decay?**

basketball, and tennis. Children need at least an hour of physical activity daily. Parents who remain physically active are role models for their children.

Sleep

Most children get busier as they get older. During the evening, school-age children have homework to complete, and perhaps a karate class or a music lesson. Getting to bed on time can be a challenge, but experts recommend enforcing a bedtime for school-age children. The National Sleep Foundation recommends that children get from ten to eleven hours of sleep nightly. It helps their performance in school, as well as their mood.

Caring for Teeth

By age seven, children may need reminders, but they can brush their own teeth at least twice a day and floss daily. A dental check-up and cleaning at least once a year is recommended to help prevent tooth decay. Sometimes fluoride treatments are given. See Fig. 16-6.

Tooth decay occurs when bacteria in the mouth produce acids that break down tooth enamel and expose the softer parts of the tooth. Bacteria produce acids from sugars that a person eats or drinks. As children get older, they have more access to sugary foods and drinks. Because of their negative health effects and link to tooth decay, sugary foods and sweet drinks should always be limited in a child's diet.

Health & Safety

Personal Safety, Ages Seven to Twelve

One of the biggest concerns of parents is the personal safety of their children. As children spend more time away from home and family, they are exposed to more dangers. The following safe practices can reduce the risks:

- Wearing protective gear during active play and sports.
- Knowing how to recognize trouble and get help in an emergency. Parents can play the "What If?" game, asking questions such as: *What would you do if you woke up at night and smelled smoke? What would you do if you heard scary noises outside your bedroom?*

- Paying attention to traffic. Carelessly darting from between parked cars or crossing streets against traffic can be dangerous. It's important to cross streets at corners only after checking for oncoming cars.
- Never getting in a stranger's car or going anywhere with a stranger. Adults don't usually ask children for help or directions.
- Running and yelling if approached in a threatening way.
- Taking the safest route if walking to school and knowing places along the way to go for help.
- Walking in groups. Parents may want an older child to walk with a younger child.
- Keeping doors locked when home alone.
- Never opening the door to a stranger when home alone, even to someone who is wearing a uniform.

Most of all, children should be taught to trust their feelings. If someone, including an adult, makes them feel afraid or uncomfortable, they should get away and tell a trusted adult.

> **Check-Up**
>
> How would you reassure a child who is constantly concerned about personal safety?
>
> _____

To prevent tooth decay, some dentists place **sealants** on children's teeth. Dentists usually place these thin, plastic coatings on permanent molars. They have proven an effective way to prevent decay.

Sometimes permanent teeth do not come in straight. This can sometimes cause problems with the way teeth fit together. If so, a dentist may refer the child to an **orthodontist**. This dental specialist can determine whether the child would benefit by having braces, separators, or retainers to straighten the teeth.

Personal Hygiene

Seven- to ten-year-olds are often unconcerned about good hygiene. It is not that they want to be dirty, they just simply can't be bothered to take the time to bathe or shower. To prevent battles over bathing, there are several things parents and caregivers can do.

- **Focus on the essentials.** Make sure that the child washes hands before eating and after using the bathroom.

- **Give choices when possible.** Let the child choose between showering and taking a bath. Give a choice of shampoo. Children, like adults, respond well to having control over decisions that affect them.

- **Send positive messages.** Comment on how refreshing a shower is, or how relaxing and warm a bath feels. This signals to children that bathing and showering bring benefits besides simply getting clean.

The lack of interest in hygiene often changes around age ten. At about this time, the physical changes of puberty increase the need for cleanliness. With puberty, the

Jerome started going through puberty before all his friends. Although he felt self-conscious about his new body hair and his cracking voice, he felt even worse about his acne. He scrubbed his face every day, but the acne persisted. Finally he decided to ask his parents for help. His father revealed that he, too, had a severe case of acne as a teen and he knew how it felt to be self-conscious about it. Jerome's dad suggested cleaning his face gently, then using a drying lotion at night. Touching or squeezing the blemishes should be avoided. Jerome's mom suggested visiting his doctor to ask about treatments that could help prevent acne from forming. Jerome felt relieved that there might be a way to minimize the problem.

▸▸ **PERSONAL APPLICATION**

1. Have you had acne? How did you feel about the condition?
2. How would you advise parents to bring up the subject of acne without embarrassing their children?

body produces more sweat, so preteens may develop body odor. In addition to a daily bath or shower, they may need to start using deodorant or antiperspirant and to change into fresh clothes after physical activity. Parents need to help preteens make this transition. Sometimes they are unaware of body odor.

During puberty, the oil glands in the pores of the skin produce more oil. At times the production can be excessive, resulting in acne and a greasy appearance to the hair. These problems usually go away over time, as the body's production of skin oil goes down. Encourage preteens to remedy the problem. Acne-prone skin should be washed twice a day with warm water and mild soap to help suppress outbreaks. Shampooing more frequently should help reduce oily hair.

Checkups and Vaccines

Annual checkups can help prevent illnesses. Before starting fifth grade children typically receive a tetanus and diphtheria booster, and sometimes an MMR (measles, mumps, and rubella) booster. Chickenpox and hepatitis B vaccinations are also strongly recommended before the age of thirteen. Children with weak immune systems or chronic lung conditions—such as asthma—should also receive annual flu shots.

SECTION 16-2 Review and Activities

Reviewing the Section

1. What are four of the recommendations included in the Dietary Guidelines for Americans?
2. Why is eating breakfast so important for children?
3. What are the three types of eating disorders?
4. Why is plenty of physical activity vital for seven- to twelve-year-olds? What is the recommended minimum length of time that should be spent on daily exercise?
5. Why might a dentist recommend *sealants* on teeth?
6. Identify at least four basic safety principles that children should be taught.
7. How are personal hygiene needs different for a preteen than for a seven- to ten-year-old?

Observing and Interacting

Observe preteens on the playground and how they spend their time with each other. How many are engaged in active play? How many are just sitting and talking? Evaluate how a teacher might encourage the less active group to engage in more physical activity.

Career Opportunities

Children's Activities Director for City Parks

Some cities have facilities that include beaches, picnic grounds, gardens, and swimming pools. Activities directors bring events such as concerts and art displays to the parks. They also plan events for children, such as concerts and educational programs.

▸ Job Responsibilities

Children's activities directors must begin planning events months in advance. They contact and make arrangements with performers. They decide how long the event should last and whether food and seats should be brought in. Children's activities directors make sure that events are appealing to children and safe for all involved.

▸ Work Environment

Children's activities directors for city parks typically work in offices, but they visit the parks often.

▸ Education and Training

Many activities directors study management of nonprofit organizations. They usually have backgrounds in recreation. In cities with large immigrant populations, it helps to know at least one language other than English.

▸ Skills and Aptitudes

- Energy
- Organizational skills
- Resourcefulness
- Ability to make budgets
- Imagination
- Sense of fun

WORKPLACE CONNECTION

1. **Thinking Skills.** What kinds of activities might appeal to children?

2. **Resource Skills.** Where could you volunteer to get experience in planning events?

SECTION SUMMARIES

- Most children grow steadily during middle childhood, but have occasional growth spurts. (16-1)
- Good dental hygiene practices are important because most permanent teeth come in between the ages of five and thirteen. (16-1)
- Puberty is a time of dramatic physical changes. (16-1)
- Children need to develop good eating habits during this period. (16-2)
- Regular physical activity is essential for good health. Lack of exercise is linked to weight problems in children. (16-2)
- Increased interest in personal hygiene often begins during the preteen years. (16-2)
- Personal safety is an area of concern for parents of children seven to twelve. (16-2)

REVIEWING THE CHAPTER

1. Why are preteen girls often taller than the boys in their class? (16-1)
2. At what ages does *puberty* usually start for boys and for girls? What gland in the brain triggers the start of puberty? (16-1)
3. When does *menstruation* usually begin? (16-1)
4. What physical changes occur between ages seven and twelve that may help a child's athletic skills improve? (16-1)
5. Give one Dietary Guideline and explain its importance to good nutrition and health. (16-2)
6. List at least three things that parents and caregivers can do to encourage good eating habits. (16-2)
7. How is lack of exercise related to increased obesity in American children? (16-2)
8. What type of dentist specializes in straightening teeth? (16-2)
9. What safety rules should children be taught to follow when they are home alone? (16-2)

THINKING CRITICALLY

1. **Drawing Conclusions.** Why are preteens often self-conscious about their bodies?
2. **Making Inferences.** Why do you think eating disorders are more predominant among females? Why might eating disorders be developing at a younger age?

MAKING CONNECTIONS

1. **Writing.** Pretend you write an advice column for children and teens. Write an encouraging response to a letter from an eleven-year-old boy who is bothered by being the shortest student in his class.

2. **Science.** The Dietary Guidelines recommend regular physical activity and limiting fatty, fried foods. These actions also help prevent obesity. Research the increase in obesity in the United States since 1980 and how obesity is linked to long-term health problems. Plot the increase on a graph and present your findings to the class.

APPLYING YOUR LEARNING

1. **Activity Planning.** You will be babysitting your eight- and nine-year-old cousins during the summer. The boys enjoy watching DVDs and playing video games. Outline five days of activities that you would plan to help them become more active.

2. **Encouraging Good Nutrition.** Imagine that you work at an after-care program for children in second grade through fifth grade. Plan at least six nutritious snacks.

3. **Eating Disorders.** Research two types of eating disorders. Share your findings with the class about the various disorders. Find out why some children and teens may develop them, and what effects these disorders have on those who have them and their families.

Learning from Research

1. Choose one of the following claims to investigate.
2. How is this research finding useful to seven- to twelve-year-olds?
3. Summarize what you've learned about how the age at which puberty begins affects health.

Puberty and Girls. In North America, the age of onset of puberty in girls has been decreasing by three or four months every decade since 1860. Scientists can't fully explain this phenomenon, but they believe that it is partly the result of better health and nutrition. What are some other explanations for the steady drop in the average age puberty begins for girls?

Puberty and Boys. Researchers have found that boys today are starting puberty earlier than boys of previous generations. What are some reasons for early development in boys?

Puberty and Television. According to research, drops in the hormone melatonin—a hormone that causes drowsiness—are associated with earlier onset of puberty in children. Researchers found that when children were not permitted to watch television, their bodies produced more melatonin. Are there alternative explanations for the link between television watching and earlier onset of puberty?

CHAPTER 17

Emotional and Social Development from Seven to Twelve

Thoughtful Reading:

As you read this chapter:

- Identify three phrases that remind you of background knowledge.
- Reread the passages.
- Write three "I connect to __?__ on page _____" statements about what you read.

Section 17-1
Emotional Development from Seven to Twelve

Section 17-2
Social and Moral Development from Seven to Twelve

Emotional Development from Seven to Twelve

Andrea's parents had a hard time describing her to others. When she was seven, Andrea often stayed in her room. By age ten, she had become more outgoing. Her parents were relieved that she was more cheerful and showed more affection. A year later, she changed again. She became moody and didn't want to spend time with her parents at all. There's nothing unusual about the emotional shifts that Andrea experienced. They are typical of the changes children go through between the ages of seven and twelve.

Objectives

- Identify signs that indicate a child's growing sense of self.
- Explain the link between competence and self-esteem.
- Identify strategies for helping children develop competence.
- Describe the emotional changes that occur between the ages of seven and twelve.
- Recommend strategies for living with children ages seven to twelve.

Key Terms

sense of self
sense of competence
gender identity
anxiety

A Sense of Self

 One of the most important changes that occurs between the ages of seven and twelve is the development of a **sense of self**. Your sense of self is your idea of who you are, based on your emotions, personality, and the ways you perceive the world. As they grow, children acquire the ability to think in more abstract terms. This affects the way they see themselves.

Compare the answers that were given by a five-year-old and a nine-year-old to a researcher's questions. The researcher asked the five-year-old girl whether she could become the family dog. The girl said no, but based her reasoning on physical traits. The dog, she said, "has brown eyes and walks like a dog." When a nine-year-old was asked whether she could become her brother, she answered no for a different reason: "I'm me and he's him. I can't change in any way 'cause I've got to stay like myself."

Children between the ages of seven and twelve recognize that they have a personality that is uniquely theirs. They see themselves as a mixture of many qualities—some based on physical appearance, others on talents or abilities. By age ten, children are able to see themselves as being highly skilled in one area and less so in another. By ages eleven and twelve, children also use personal qualities to define themselves: "I'm honest," or "I'm a good friend," or "I can be counted on."

They also see that they behave differently in different situations. Dionte always thought of himself as being friendly and outgoing until he went to a party at his cousin's house. The only person he knew there was his cousin, and he found it hard to begin talking to anyone else. "How can I be both friendly and shy?" he wondered. As he thought about it, Dionte realized that he is shy only with strangers and that his behavior is influenced by the situation he is in.

He also realized that different people might perceive him in different ways. To people he knows, he appears friendly and outgoing, but strangers might consider him quiet or even stuck-up. Dionte's ability to understand how others might see him offers a clear example of his growing thinking skills.

Developing a Sense of Competence

According to theorist Erik Erikson, the early school years mark the stage when children strive to develop a **sense of competence**—a feeling that they can be successful and meet most challenges. They do so by acquiring and improving a wide range of skills. In the classroom, these skills include reading, math, and writing. Outside the classroom, children may develop skills in sports, music, art, and crafts. Erikson believed that as children refine these skills, they see themselves as competent and develop high self-esteem. A child's feelings about his or her competence can have a real effect on the choices he or she makes and on his or her satisfaction later in life. Children with high self-esteem are more willing to try new things and to persevere at difficult tasks. In contrast, Erikson believed that those who experience repeated failures and disappointments begin to see themselves as inferior and incompetent. Children's beliefs about their competence can greatly affect their choices and their satisfaction in later life. For these reasons, it is essential that children ages seven to twelve experience more successes than failures. See Fig. 17-1.

Fig. 17-1 **Most children gain a sense of competence during their early school years.** What impact does that have on later success in school?

THE DEVELOPING BRAIN

Why do some children become more competent at mental tasks than other children their age? Are those individuals simply smarter than others? Some children do have a genetic inheritance that makes them better equipped to learn than most of their peers. But most people have far more intellectual capacity than they use. Growing up in a stimulating environment and determination to succeed are two other factors that can lead to success and feelings of competence.

Fig. 17-2 **Children need to experience the success that comes from mastering a skill. Those who have a particular talent should be encouraged to pursue it.**

Eleven-year-old Andrew went home to an empty house every day after school. His parents wouldn't let him have friends over, which he didn't mind much because he didn't have many friends. Unsupervised and with time on his hands, he often got into trouble. One day he was caught shooting a BB gun at cars in a nearby office parking lot and was given a stern warning. About a month later, someone scratched, "A loser was here" into the front door of the office building. It was Andrew. His way of identifying himself revealed much about his self-esteem.

Sound relationships with peers are an important ingredient in developing a sense of competence. As children grow from seven to twelve, their peers become much more important to them. They begin to let go of their total reliance on parents and start to depend on friends for help and reassurance.

Children ages seven to twelve are going through other changes that prepare them for the learning and mastery that lead to competence. Their brains develop connections that allow their memory to expand. Increased memory allows children to learn and understand more.

There are a variety of ways to help seven- to twelve-year-olds develop a sense of competence:

- **Help children focus on their strengths.** Ask them to make a list of the things that they are good at. Encourage them to develop special skills and talents. See Fig. 17-2.

- **Provide opportunities.** Include children in the work of the family. Doing chores can help them learn practical skills and contribute to the family.

- **Encourage learning.** Recognize the importance of learning. Make sure children have a quiet time and place to do homework and practice skills.

- **Establish reachable goals.** Help children break large tasks down into smaller parts. They can focus on accomplishing one part at a time, yet complete a larger goal.

- **Recognize successes.** Look for things children do well, and be specific in praise. "In that book report, you did a great job of explaining the plot."
- **Focus on the positive.** "You got twelve out of fourteen right on that math test. That's much better than you did on the last test."

LOOKING AT REAL LIFE

Margaret, the mother of eleven-year-old Hannah, was surprised at what she was hearing from her daughter's teacher. Mrs. Schwartz said that whenever she asked Hannah to do something, her response was, "I can't."

"I don't understand Hannah," said Margaret. "She seems confident. I know I have high expectations, but she's a bright child. If she gets Bs, I ask why she didn't get As. If she gets an A, I ask why it wasn't an A+, because I know that she could get those grades if she applied herself."

Mrs. Schwartz thought for a moment and said, "Maybe Hannah says she can't because she is becoming afraid of failing to meet others' expectations." She suggested that Margaret rethink the messages she was sending. Hannah might be feeling that nothing she did would ever be good enough to please her mother.

▶▶**PERSONAL APPLICATION**

Think of a time when someone put pressure on you. How did you respond?

Developing a Sense of Gender

An important part of a child's growing sense of self is **gender identity**—the awareness of being male or female. Gender identity is a complex process that begins in early childhood and is usually firmly fixed by about age four. In middle childhood and early adolescence that identity becomes stronger as children become more aware of their bodies and of gender differences. Between ages seven and twelve, children:

- Choose to spend more time with others of the same sex. Close friendships at this stage are almost always with children of the same sex.
- Show an increased desire to act and talk like others of the same sex.
- Tend to choose adults of the same sex as their role models, the people whom they admire and try to pattern their behavior after.
- Begin to explore relationships with the opposite sex late in this stage.

Emotional Changes

Children ages seven to twelve may sometimes feel that they are on an emotional roller coaster. One year they are typically withdrawn; the next year they're outgoing. One year they feel anxious; the next year they're carefree. These changes are a normal part of the emotional development that runs parallel to physical, social, and intellectual development. Emotional changes generally follow a pattern that varies from year to year.

Later Childhood

Between ages seven and ten, children generally progress from negative to positive—from unhappiness to happiness.

- **Age seven.** Seven-year-olds are typically withdrawn and quiet, and they tend to stay close to home. Many children this age worry a great deal about all kinds of issues. See Fig. 17-3. Some are particularly sensitive to what others say about them.

- **Age eight.** Eight-year-olds generally have a more positive attitude than at age seven. They are willing to explore and become curious about new things. They are lively and active—and often very dramatic. They might, for example, exaggerate when telling stories or describing their feelings.

- **Age nine.** Nine-year-olds tend to be absorbed in their thoughts. They can be very harsh about their own failings and even embarrassed by them. Some nine-year-olds keep their feelings hidden and show signs of anxiety and tension. At times, they may become completely absorbed in their own concerns.

- **Age ten.** By age ten, children are usually once again more positive and happy. Their growing sense of self and increasing feelings of competence help them focus on their strengths rather than their failings.

The Preteen Years

Puberty usually begins around ages eleven or twelve—the preteen years. The physical changes of puberty, brought about by the release of hormones, bring emotional changes as well. Preteens often feel and act awkward, and mood swings can carry them from happiness to sadness—and back again—in a matter of minutes.

Preteens tend to be very absorbed in their own thoughts and concerns. They may pay little attention to people other than their peers, who are extremely important to them. They crave group acceptance and

Fig. 17-3 **As they learn more about the world around them, seven-year-olds often become withdrawn and fearful.** What is another typical emotion at this age?

become anxious if they stand out in any way from their peers. They hate the thought of being "different."

It is not unusual for preteens to hide their true feelings behind a mask of not caring. This behavior is a sign of growing emotional control.

Specific Emotions

The emotional life of young children centers on the family. In older children and preteens, the focus shifts to the wider world. People and events outside the family have more impact on children's emotions than before. Children gradually gain better control of their emotions, expressing them in more socially acceptable ways.

Anger

Children at any age can feel angry—and let others know it. Even ten-year-olds, who are typically quite happy, show anger. When they do, though, it usually passes quickly. Depending on temperament and environment, some children become angry more often than others.

Anger can erupt at any time in moody preteens. Often the outbursts of anger are eruptions that boil over and pass quickly. A preteen may storm out of a room and slam a door but then return a little while later as if nothing had happened. See Fig. 17-4.

Many times, these outbursts have little to do with the event that seemed to trigger them. Courtney, for example, became very angry when her mother asked her to hang up her coat after school. Within minutes, though, she was cheerful. Courtney was really angry because her friends went shopping without her.

By age seven, children generally know that they should express their anger in socially acceptable ways. For example, they should use words to talk about their anger, not lash out verbally in an uncontrolled way that hurts others' feelings. They know that they should seek a compromise to settle their differences or turn away from the situation. On occasion, however, an older child may show aggression. It is important to avoid responding in the same way. Setting a good example is the best method of teaching a child. Here are some additional approaches that may work:

- **Teach the child how to gain self-control.** Counting to ten and taking deep breaths are two ways of helping an angry child learn to calm down.

- **Help the child learn nonaggressive ways to resolve conflicts.** Children who learn how to express their anger appropriately at home—perhaps with siblings—will be better equipped to settle conflicts at school.

- **Reward the child for controlling anger.** Saying something like "I'm proud of the way you responded to the teasing," reinforces self-control.

Fig. 17-4 **Angry outbursts over seemingly minor events are not uncommon during the preteen years.** Why do you think preteens sometimes find it hard to control their anger?

- **Help the child learn to use unrelated physical activity to work off anger.** Shooting baskets, running, or walking the family dog are all harmless ways to blow off steam.

Fear and Worry

All children have fears, but the nature of their fears changes. Seven-year-olds may still have some of their earlier fears, such as a fear of the dark. Look for easy solutions such as leaving a light on at night.

By age ten, the fears of earlier years have largely disappeared. As childhood fears disappear, however, new worries may take their place. News reports of terrorism, fatal car accidents, or natural disasters can set off worries in some older children and preteens. They may worry that such events will strike their families and need to be reassured that adults will take all the steps necessary to protect them. See Fig. 17-5.

Other worries that occupy this age group have to do with how others see them. Up to the age of ten, most children are concerned mainly with how adults see them. During the preteen years, however, the focus of these fears shifts toward the attitudes of their peers.

Fig. 17-5 **As children become more aware of the world, they become more aware of the dangers in it.** What might you do to help a child overcome fears?

Anxiety

Anxiety is a state of uncertainty and fear, often about an unspecified but seemingly immediate threat. A certain amount of anxiety, especially about specific problems or events, is normal. For example, anxiety about passing a major test or a parent's serious illness is understandable.

Excessive anxiety, however, can be a sign of an anxiety disorder. People who have an anxiety disorder frequently worry that something terrible is about to happen. Preteens or teens with an anxiety disorder can develop persistent physical symptoms such as tension headaches, nausea, or rapid heartbeat. Parents who suspect an anxiety problem should consult the family doctor or the child's pediatrician.

Envy and Jealousy

As older children become more aware of the world around them, they are apt to develop feelings of envy and jealousy. Envy is the feeling of wanting something another person has, to the point of feeling intense dislike for that person.

"I hate Erica," Kayla told her best friend. "She gets everything she wants. Now that her parents bought her a TV for her bedroom, I'm not going to talk to her anymore."

Jealousy is a complex emotion involving the fear that a loved one might prefer someone else. A seven-year-old might be jealous of a parent's attention to a sibling. A ten-year-old might feel jealous when a best friend spends more time with another friend. A preteen, learning to feel comfortable with the opposite sex, might feel jealous of a peer who seems to be at ease and to get all the attention. See Fig. 17-6.

At the middle school dance, for example, Nicholas was happy that he found the courage to ask Kristin to dance, and that she accepted. His happiness turned to painful jealousy, however, when another boy asked Kristin to dance and they danced several songs together.

Because children between the ages of seven and twelve are often acutely aware of their developing selves, absorbed with their feelings, and anxious to fit in with their peers, jealousy is very common.

Fig. 17-6 **In their anxiety to fit in and be accepted by their peers, preteens often experience feelings of envy and jealousy.** How can parents help preteens deal with these emotions?

Help a Child Work Through a Difficult Situation

Children these ages become less likely to confide in their parents. They can develop secret fears or worries. Interpersonal situations become more complex than those they may have experienced before. More than ever, they need guidance from caring adults to help them figure out how to deal with difficult situations. Those frequently in contact with children can become good listeners.

- **Establish genuine communication.** Accept each child as a unique individual. The child will sense your genuine interest and may become more willing to confide about any issues.

- **Take their concerns seriously.** Don't belittle or dismiss any fears or worries that cause children emotional distress. Let children know that you are available to talk about anything that is troubling them.

- **Put any worries into perspective.** Brandon worried constantly that his mother might die and that he would be left alone. When his mother had to take a plane trip for business, Brandon begged her not to go. His mother reminded him that plane crashes were much less likely than car accidents.

- **Try to determine how serious the problem might be.** Note any extreme feelings. Be aware of such danger signs as depression, feelings of hopelessness, or increased self-centeredness and lack of concern for others. Consult a professional for help in dealing with the situation.

YOUR TURN

Counseling. If you were a parent, caregiver, or teacher of a child who was constantly struggling with working through a difficult situation, do you think the child would benefit from seeing a counselor? Why or why not?

Living with Children Seven to Twelve

Children from seven to twelve can be difficult to live with at times. A quiet, withdrawn seven-year-old might not be willing to talk about his feelings. An eight-year-old girl, though cheerful, might cling to her mother. An eleven-year-old boy might be experiencing secret fears. Here are some tips for preventing minor emotional upsets from becoming major problems:

- **Be patient.** Remember that school-age children still don't have full self-control. When preteens show anger, it's often due to the difficulty they are having adjusting to the changes in their bodies.

- **Avoid taking it personally.** A child who is angry or upset may say nasty things to a parent or caregiver. Remember that children don't usually mean what they say in angry moments.

- **Help the child maintain self-control.** Make sure children understand that their behavior must stay within acceptable limits. Actions that break the rules need to be dealt with. If misbehavior is not serious, talking it through may be enough.

- **Listen attentively.** Ask the child to explain what happened and why. There may have been a valid problem. Even so, this doesn't excuse inappropriately expressed anger. Let the child know that you don't approve of the behavior, and discuss more appropriate options.

SECTION 17-1 Review and Activities

Reviewing the Section

1. What are two signs of a child's growing *sense of self*?
2. Explain why a *sense of competence* in school-age children is important to future success in life.
3. What are five ways to help children develop a sense of competence?
4. What is the typical emotional state of a child age seven? Eight? Nine? Ten?
5. What kinds of fears might a ten-year-old have? How can caregivers respond?

Observing and Interacting

Go to a local mall or other place you can observe older children and preteens. While you might not be able to determine the exact ages of the children you see, look out for typical behaviors that you read about. Record the behaviors you observe. Then try to estimate the ages of those you observed.

Social and Moral Development from Seven to Twelve

Between the ages of seven and twelve, a child's world expands and changes in significant ways. Gradually, children become less influenced by their parents and more influenced by their peers. At the same time, they develop new kinds of relationships at home and at school. They learn to stand up for themselves and take more responsibility for their decisions and actions.

Objectives

- Describe how friendships change during these years.
- Recommend strategies for resolving conflicts with peers and for dealing with bullying.
- Characterize changes that occur in family relationships as children gain more independence.
- Outline ways that caregivers can guide children's moral development.
- Analyze the effects of peer pressure and suggest ways of dealing with negative peer pressure.
- Identify ways children can assume more responsibility.

Key Terms

bullying
peer pressure
conformity

Relationships with Peers

As children grow, their friendships grow deeper. Because seven- to twelve-year-olds have a sense of self and are better able to communicate their thoughts and feelings, their friendships become more personal. Beginning around age seven or eight, children look for the following qualities in their friendships:

- **Loyalty.** Older children value friends who will stand by them when they are in a difficult situation or feeling low.

- **Trustworthiness.** Older children need to feel comfortable talking about their inner feelings, so they look for friends they can trust. They want friends who won't pass on personal revelations.

- **Kindness and understanding.** Children this age seek friends who will listen and be sympathetic to their feelings, which are often tumultuous.

- **Fun.** Most children look for friends whose company they enjoy and with whom they can have a good time.

Children this age still enjoy active, physical play with their friends, but they spend increasing amounts of time simply talking. Preteens who are close friends might spend an afternoon together, go home, and then call each other and spend an hour or more talking in the evening as well. See Fig. 17-7.

It is seven- to twelve-year-olds' development in other areas that brings about these changes. Intellectual growth makes deeper friendships possible. Because they can now think abstractly, older children and preteens can better understand how others see them. At the same time, they can more easily see other people's points of view and feel empathy for them. These new skills make it easier to relate to friends in a deeper way.

The physical and emotional changes of puberty also play a role in friendships. Preteens are curious about the changes they are experiencing and about their awakening sexuality. Talking to their friends helps them explore and think through these issues.

Peer Groups

For older children and preteens, acceptance by peers is closely related to high self-esteem. Children who feel that they "fit in" are more confident, more likely to make and keep friends, and more likely to succeed at school. Feelings of rejection by peers may negatively affect performance at school and family relationships.

Children at this age generally have a number of peer groups. They may include classmates, sports team members, and children who live in the same neighborhood. Adults can help them gain peer acceptance by teaching social skills and encouraging participation in group activities. Children who experience rejection by their peers may need professional counseling to prevent lifelong difficulties.

Making Friends

Tara and Nate were neighbors. They began playing together when they were two years old. When they were six, they played on the same soccer team. At age eight, however, Tara and Nate began to move in different directions. Tara began spending more time with her new best friend, Kari, and other girls from school. Nate would pal around with the boys.

Fig. 17-7 Older children value friends who will listen to their ideas and concerns.

Fig. 17-8 **At this stage, close friendships are almost always with others of the same sex.**

The experiences of Tara and Nate show how sex differences become important as children grow older. Young children play with children of either sex, though they often prefer playmates of the same sex. As children grow older they are more likely to become friends only with children of the same sex. This is true despite the fact that as puberty begins, they become more interested in and preoccupied with preteens of the opposite sex. See Fig. 17-8.

By age twelve, Tara began to see Nate in a whole new way. "I think he's really cute," Tara confided to Emily. "Why don't you tell him?" teased Emily. "Or maybe I will."

"Don't you dare," squealed Tara, "I would just die!"

One reason preteens avoid opposite-sex friendships is that such relationships raise questions of being romantically involved. Most eleven- and twelve-year-olds just aren't ready to take that step. They want to avoid the teasing they may encounter if they have a friend of the opposite sex.

The number of friends children have at this stage varies. Some children have many friends; some have several; and some have just one or two. The number of friendships may depend on the child's temperament. Some children enjoy being part of a large group. Others are more private and quiet and do not want or need many friends. Another influence is the child's social environment. Children who are in after-school programs, clubs, or teams have more opportunities to make friends and may have more for that reason. See Fig. 17-9.

There is no set number of friends that children should have. Still, some older children and preteens may "collect" friends. They use the number of friends they have as a way to measure their popularity. Those with fewer friends may feel that they are not liked.

In reality, the key to a healthy social life is not how many friends a child has, but rather whether the child has the social skills for forming and maintaining friendships. It's important to help and encourage children to build social skills and get involved in activities that interest them.

Resolving Conflicts with Peers

Just as the nature of friendship changes as children grow, so too does the nature of conflicts they face. While young children may have conflicts over toys, older children and preteens have conflicts over more complex issues.

Many conflicts among children arise from envy, jealousy, or gossip. Whitney, for example, heard a rumor that Caitlin had been spreading gossip about her. She confronted Caitlin and accused her of telling lies. Caitlin heatedly denied this, and a shouting match ensued. A crowd of girls soon gathered around them to watch.

Other conflicts may be based on emotional needs. Older children and preteens have a need to belong. Conflicts may arise if they feel excluded from a group or if they think someone is showing them disrespect.

In general, children at this stage should be able to use words to express their anger. Those who received guidance at an earlier age on how to deal appropriately with anger are more likely to have the necessary self-control. Occasionally, however, anger can lead to aggressive behavior. Preteen boys

Fig. 17-9 **Participating in a variety of activities presents more opportunities to make friends.** What other factors contribute to a healthy social life?

are more likely than girls to use aggressive behavior to express anger.

If a conflict looks as if it might escalate into violence, others need to intervene. Here are some guidelines for helping people in conflict resolve their differences:

- **Set some ground rules.** Establish an agreement to work peacefully toward resolution. Letitia and Katie stepped out of the group around Whitney and Caitlin and tried to calm them down. "Let's get to the bottom of this, but no more yelling or name-calling, okay?"

- **Listen to both sides.** Ask both people to give their side of the story, and listen carefully to what they say. Whitney was less concerned about the silly gossip—which no one believed—than about the idea that Caitlin didn't respect her. Caitlin was hurt that Whitney had so little trust in her. "I never said those things. How could you even think I would?" asked Caitlin.

- **Find common ground.** Find something that both people can agree on, so that they can move forward. Sometimes this is as simple as deciding to end the disagreement.

- **Reach a solution that is acceptable to both sides.** Win-win solutions, in which both parties gain something they want, are best because both people can feel good about the resolution. At first, Whitney wanted Caitlin to apologize, but Caitlin refused, saying there was nothing to apologize for. Finally, they agreed to apologize to one another for the situation and how it made them feel. "I'm sorry that the rumor made you feel I didn't respect you," said Caitlin. "I'm sorry that my reaction made you feel that I don't trust you," said Whitney.

Fig. 17-10 **Children who are confident and have close friends are rarely victims of bullies.** Why do you think this is true?

Dealing with Bullies

Bullying means directing aggression or abuse toward another person, usually someone weaker. It can take many forms, including pushing, shoving and other physical abuse, teasing, spreading rumors, and making offensive comments. Boys are more likely than girls to be bullies and to be the victims of bullies. See Fig. 17-10.

Bullying can cause both physical and emotional pain for victims. Unfortunately, children who are being bullied often don't tell their parents or other adults. They may fear that telling on a bully will only make the bullying worse.

Parents, teachers, and other caregivers need to be on the lookout for signs of bullying. They should suspect bullying if a child:

- Comes home with cuts, bruises, or torn clothing.
- Frequently "loses" lunch money and other valuable items.
- Does not want to go to school.
- Becomes unusually moody, withdrawn, and bad tempered.
- Is always anxious and has trouble sleeping.

An adult who suspects that a child is being bullied should question the child in a supportive way. The adult could ask how the child's day went and follow up with, "What was your favorite activity at school today?" and, "What was your least favorite thing?"

A child who is being bullied needs to be reassured that it's not his or her fault. Emphasize that no one has the right to bully anyone else. Report the situation to a teacher, principal, or school counselor. Schools usually take the problem of bullying very seriously.

Learning Through PLAY

Problem Solving Through Play

In the later elementary and early middle school years, children are learning more about themselves as individuals, as well as about their classmates. During this time, some children experience pressures and problems such as lying, cheating, or bullying. One way to help children work through these problems is to act out typical situations focusing on ways to prevent and deal with them. Involving children in the problem-solving process helps them develop the skills they will need throughout their lives. Acting out situations and modeling their resolution can give children ideas about how to handle situations if they arise again.

Following Up

How would you solve a problem that you were having with a friend?

Fig. 17-11 **Parents often have to work hard to maintain positive relationships with their preteen children.** Why do preteens tend to be critical of their parents' values?

Family Relationships

Given the number of changes occurring between the ages of seven and twelve, it's no surprise that family relationships change, too. As children move from dependence to greater independence, the complex relationships between children and their parents and siblings reflect that transition.

Family situations vary greatly. Some families have two parents in the home; others have only one. Some children live with a guardian or in a foster home. The main caregiver may be a person other than a parent. It might be a grandparent or other relative.

In many families, both parents work outside the home, affecting how much "family time" is available. The number and ages of siblings also affect family relationships.

Parents

As children grow older, their attitudes toward their parents typically change in the following ways:

- Seven-year-olds depend on their parents but often challenge parental authority.
- At eight, children tend to cling to their parents.
- By nine, children become wrapped up in their own thoughts and sometimes ignore their parents.
- Ten is generally a smooth year. Children are happier and more communicative.
- At eleven and twelve, as they begin to move away from the direct control and influence of parents, preteens may become quite critical of their parents' values.

The preteen years are often challenging for parents, no matter how healthy the family relationship. See Fig. 17-11.

When Samantha first moved to a new neighborhood and started at a new school, the group of girls who sat under the trees at recess wanted to be friends with her. They invited her over to join them. At first, being included felt great. After a while, though, the girls started daring each other to steal things. First it was a book from the school library. Then it was lipstick from the drugstore. When Samantha wouldn't steal the lipstick, the girls stopped talking to her. Soon almost no one in Samantha's class was talking to her.

▶▶**PERSONAL APPLICATION**

1. What options does Samantha have for dealing with the situation? What are the possible outcomes of each?
2. How difficult is it to stand up against peer pressure?

Siblings

Starting at age seven, children generally get along well with brothers and sisters who are much younger or much older. They are helpful and protective of children under two, and tend to respect and admire siblings in their late teens.

Seven- to twelve-year-olds often have difficult relationships with siblings who are closer to them in age. They tend to judge each other harshly and conflicts are common. Parents and other adults need to help close-in-age siblings develop empathy and a sense of cooperation.

Moral Development

As they spend more time outside the home, children more often face decisions about right and wrong that they must answer alone, without an adult to guide them. What will they do if a group of classmates teases someone for not being a good athlete? What will they say if a peer dares them to smoke a cigarette or to try drugs?

Parents, other adults, and older siblings all can help prepare children to make the right moral choices in a number of ways. For example, they can:

- **Set a good example.** Modeling moral behavior is the best method of teaching a child to act in a moral way.

- **Support the child's growing conscience.** Sometimes going along with the group may seem like a means to feeling accepted, even if the group is doing something wrong. Children need to be reminded that they will regret doing the wrong thing.

- **Talk about how to handle situations that might occur.** Discussing "what-ifs" ahead of time can help a child develop coping strategies for difficult situations.

- **Reinforce empathy.** Ask children to put themselves in another's place. How would they feel if they were the object of their group's teasing? Being able to feel empathy can deter a child from teasing or otherwise harassing another just to stay "in" with the group.

- **Use the child's sense of fairness.** Children in this age group value fairness. Encourage them to use that sense of fairness to lead them to the right decisions.

Fig. 17-12 **Showing conformity by dressing alike is usually harmless.** In what kinds of situations can conformity be harmful?

Peer Pressure

In the preteen years, children loosen their ties to parents and identify increasingly with peer groups. Being accepted by peers is of paramount importance.

Because of this, **peer pressure**—a social group's influence on the way individuals behave—becomes very strong. The desire to be accepted leads preteens to adopt the words, behaviors, habits, and ideas of others in their social group. In their drive for **conformity**—being like one another—they may dress alike, adopt similar hairstyles, and find other ways to show that they belong. See Fig. 17-12.

A child who is different from others in some way can have a difficult time during this period. A preteen who likes music that differs from what is currently popular or who dresses differently may be ridiculed and teased by others.

Peer pressure can be a powerful influence on a young person's life—for good or for bad. Those whose friends have positive values are more likely to stay clear of drugs, alcohol, and other risky behaviors. The urge to go along with dishonest or unethical actions can be equally strong. Older children and preteens are more likely to avoid or resist negative peer pressure if they:

- Join a peer group that shows positive moral values.
- Find others with similar hobbies and interests and spend time with them.

- Rely upon conscience to help make decisions about what is right and wrong.
- Try not to appear upset when teased by peers. People who tease are looking for a reaction. If there isn't one, they may stop.
- Talk about the problem with a parent or other trusted adult.

Parents and others who work with children can help them avoid the influence of negative peer pressure by giving their love and support.

Parenting Q&A

How Can Parents Teach a Child Tolerance?

No one is born with an intolerant attitude. Prejudice and intolerance are learned from others. Young children are ready to be tolerant of anyone. Parents need to make sure that they stay that way.

- **Tolerance is a moral issue that deals with fairness.**
- **As with any moral behavior, parents can teach by example, avoiding any behavior that signals prejudice.**
- **At work, home, or in public, parents can show that they are willing to get along with anyone who behaves appropriately.**

- **Parents can also help children to understand and respect the traditions of other cultures.** Parents can teach their children that all human beings deserve fair treatment.
- **Encouraging tolerance is a continuous process.** Children hear intolerant messages from many outside sources, including the media and peers.
- **Parents need to raise the subject of prejudice anytime the opportunity presents itself.** When parents repeat messages about accepting differences, children are more likely to retain them.

THINKING IT THROUGH

1. What would you do if a friend tells a joke that makes fun of a group of people?
2. Does tolerance mean that any behavior is acceptable?

Children Around the World

Lessons You Can Eat

Martin Luther King Jr. Middle School in Berkeley, California, has about 1,000 students and is home to a program called the Edible Schoolyard. Alice Waters, a chef, had the idea of creating a garden so that students could learn to take care of plants and cook foods they helped grow. Today, students learn how to plant seedlings, identify ripe fruits and vegetables, make new soil from decomposing plants, and gather eggs from hens.

Establishing a sense of competence is important for students this age. Assigning each student a daily job in the garden—such as chopping apples that will be pressed for their juice— enables them to reach goals. Students learn to take responsibility for their actions. In addition, chef Waters finds that students are more willing to try new foods that they have helped grow and prepare.

Investigating Culture

1. Does your school have outdoor education?
2. If not, how could you go about learning about gardening if that is something you are interested in?

Taking Responsibility

Children in this age group need to learn that with independence comes responsibility. They need "safe" opportunities to explore, test, and learn about their new responsibilities. Parents can help in many ways:

- Treating eleven- and twelve-year-olds less like children. Spend time talking and having fun.
- Allowing preteens to make low-risk decisions. Preteens need to rebel and test limits. Choosing how to decorate their room is a harmless way to do so.
- Encouraging them to think through the consequences of their decisions. If they don't do their homework, what will happen to their grades?
- Within reason, letting them experience the consequences of making "bad" decisions. Going to bed late means being tired all day. Spending an allowance early in the week means having no money at the end of the week.
- Negotiating family rules. Listen to any objections or special needs that a preteen might have. Make accommodations whenever practical.
- Sticking to the family rules. Breaking these rules calls for clear, effective consequences. Physical punishment is counterproductive and time-out usually does not work with this age group. Grounding and taking away privileges are the most effective ways to teach preteens that their behavior has consequences.

SECTION 17-2 Review and Activities

Reviewing the Section

1. Starting at age seven or eight, what characteristics do children look for in friends?
2. In what ways do friendships change during this period? How are these changes linked to changes in other areas of development?
3. How can adults help preteens resolve conflicts with peers?
4. How can adults help a child who shows signs of having been *bullied*?
5. What factors contribute to changes in family relationships during this period?
6. Explain how parents can help children make the moral choices as they gain more independence.
7. How can preteens use positive *peer pressure* to their advantage and resist negative peer pressure?
8. What is the link between independence and responsibility?

Observing and Interacting

Think of an occasion in which you saw peer pressure in action. Describe what took place. Was the result good or bad? If it was bad, what could have been done differently to change the outcome?

Animator

Animators create images for movies and television. Much of what animators create is for an audience of children and young people. In the past, they drew scenes by hand, but most use computers now. The number of applicants for animator positions typically exceeds the number of jobs available.

▶ Job Responsibilities

Animators sketch, create models, and lay out sequences of scenes in two or three dimensions (2D or 3D). They are artists whose drawings come alive with motion, facial expressions, and gestures. Animators work increasingly in 3D, the format used for many video games. Major movie studios are adding 3D departments to their animation divisions.

▶ Work Environment

Animators work in offices for television or movie-production companies, animation companies, or for themselves. They work on assignments that may last from as little as a few weeks to as long as two years.

▶ Education and Training

A bachelor's degree in fine arts or computer science, illustration, or graphic design makes candidates more attractive to employers. Those interested in computer-based animation should study engineering, computer science, and programming.

▶ Skills and Aptitudes

- Creativity
- Computer skills
- Talent for turning words into pictures
- Drawing skills

WORKPLACE CONNECTION

1. **Thinking Skills.** How would dance classes help someone who wanted to be an animator?

2. **Resource Skills.** What could you do to learn about the field of animation?

17 Review and Activities

SECTION SUMMARIES

- Between the ages of seven and twelve, children develop a sense of self. (17-1)
- Children with a sense of competence are likely to have high self-esteem and be willing to try new things. (17-1)
- Emotions play a major role in the development of children. (17-1)
- The focus of the child shifts from the home to the larger world. (17-1)
- Older children's friendships deepen and become more personal. (17-2)
- Peers become more important, but conflicts are common. (17-2)
- As children gain more independence, they need help making moral choices. (17-2)

REVIEWING THE CHAPTER

1. What does it mean to have a *sense of self*? (17-1)
2. By eleven and twelve, how do children define their personalities? (17-1)
3. How would a child with a *sense of competence* be likely to deal with failure? (17-1)
4. How can adults help children express their anger in appropriate ways? (17-1)
5. What social skills do you think a person needs to have in order to make friends? (17-2)
6. How and why does the nature of conflicts with peers change at this age? (17-2)
7. Why might a child be afraid to tell an adult that he or she is being *bullied*? How can an adult deal with the situation? (17-2)
8. How do seven- to twelve-year-olds' attitudes toward their parents change? (17-2)
9. Why do preteens need guidance in moral development? (17-2)
10. Give three examples of ways parents and other adults can help children take greater responsibility for their actions. (17-2)

THINKING CRITICALLY

1. **Analyzing Behavior.** When do you think the urge to conform begins? Do you think it continues into the later teen years? List some ways in which you and your friends conform and explain why.
2. **Drawing Conclusions.** Have you seen friendships change due to feelings of envy or jealousy? What do you think caused these feelings, and what could have been done to resolve conflict between the people involved?

MAKING CONNECTIONS

1. **Writing.** Write a short skit about a preteen boy who believes that a friend has betrayed him by telling a secret. The friend is actually innocent. The behavior of the characters should not be aggressive but should reflect what you've learned about preteens in the chapter.

2. **Social Studies.** Make a poster for a campaign aimed at stopping bullying in schools. Include examples of physical and emotional bullying. Illustrate ways that children can protect themselves from bullies.

APPLYING YOUR LEARNING

1. **Giving Advice.** Suppose a friend confides that her twelve-year-old brother is angry all the time and is upsetting the family. The brother seems to have no limits and even throws and breaks things. How would you advise your friend to handle the situation?

2. **Modifying Outcomes.** Develop three scenarios involving peer pressure and describe the outcomes. Switch papers with a classmate and create alternate endings for each scenario.

3. **Learning Social Skills.** Twelve-year-old Petra is new to your school. She just moved to this country from Germany. If she asked you what she needed to do in order to make friends in your community, what would you tell her?

Learning from Research

1. Choose one of the following research claims to investigate.
2. How is this research finding useful to parents of children ages seven to twelve?
3. Summarize what you've learned about bullying and its effects on preteens.

Bullying and Violence. According to research, preteens who bully watch more violent television and get into more fights at school. In addition, bullies are more likely to engage in violent behaviors later in life. Do you agree with this research finding? Why or why not?

Bullying and Power. Researchers have found that many bullies who hit, hurt, and humiliate other children have friends who also bully but have less power in the social group. These "lieutenants" don't bully others until the main bully is present. Why do researchers think this occurs?

Bullying and Bystanders. Researchers have found that teens who witness bullying may feel helpless and guilty for not reporting the incident or standing up to a bully. They have also found that witnessing bullying may influence students to model their own behavior after that of bullies. Do you agree with this research finding? Why or why not?

CHAPTER 18

Intellectual Development from Seven to Twelve

Thoughtful Reading:

As you read this chapter:

- Write down any questions you have about what you read.
- Identify at least three phrases that you question.
- Find answers in the text or in outside sources.

Section 18-1
The Developing Brain from Seven to Twelve

Section 18-2
Learning from Seven to Twelve

The Developing Brain from Seven to Twelve

The brain is the center of learning. As children advance from seven to twelve, brain development continues enhancing their ability to learn. Their intellectual development improves steadily, becoming capable of new ways of thinking. The emotional and intellectual needs of preteens differ from those of younger and older children. Educators created middle schools for preteens in an effort to address these special needs.

Objectives

- Identify signs of intellectual development in children seven to twelve.
- Contrast the thinking skills of seven-year-olds with those of preteens.
- Compare different theories of intellectual development as they relate to this age group.

Key Terms

transitivity
conservation
hypothetical

Signs of Increased Intellectual Growth

Advances in intellectual growth between the ages of seven and twelve are exciting to witness. Learned routines become automatic, so children are able to use their brain power for higher-level learning:

- **Memory.** Memory is central to all learning, and critical to success in school. People use both short-term memory and long-term memory to learn. For example, if you have studied for a test, you've memorized the necessary information. To do so, you brought information into your short-term memory to concentrate on it and then stored it in your long-term memory. You may forget all about that information until you get to the test. Once there, you recall the information by bringing it back into your short-term memory and answer the question. Then you let it go so that you can recall the answer to the next question.

Improvements in the way the brain functions allow older children and preteens to learn more and to use their knowledge more efficiently. For example, children in this period no longer count on their fingers. They can recall and apply basic mathematical operations, like adding and subtracting, almost automatically because they've done them so many times.

- **Awareness and curiosity.** Children from age seven to twelve also develop a keener awareness of themselves and those around them. They become better at planning their own behavior and at understanding their abilities and the abilities of other people. Children eight and older begin to recognize that a person can know someone else's point of view and figure out what that person is thinking. They show more concern about what people think of them.

In this stage, children begin to think of themselves according to their unique qualities—their feelings and beliefs—not just their physical features. They are able to strive to achieve a goal because they are learning to control their behavior. At school, they become increasingly independent in their learning. They can evaluate which learning strategies work best for them. They practice organizing their work so that they can complete longer-term projects. Preteens often develop interests that can last a lifetime, such as participating in sports, acting in plays, or loving to read. See Fig. 18-1.

- **Idealism and abstract thinking.** Young children judge whether something is right or wrong strictly by how much pleasure or pain it involves, such as whether they will be punished for a particular behavior. Older children and

Fig. 18-1 **Many preteens become more involved in learning as they study topics that spark their curiosity.**

Fig. 18-2 **Preteens often recognize and involve themselves in social issues, such as this food drive for needy people.** Why do preteens believe that there are simple solutions to social problems?

adolescents adopt moral standards that authority figures, such as parents, will approve of.

By the preteen years, children can recognize complex social problems such as prejudice or crime, but they don't understand why the problems are difficult to solve. For example, these idealistic children tend to believe that to prevent theft, thieves just need to stop stealing. They can't yet analyze their ideas to see if they are realistic. Nonetheless, their idealism can help them become involved in improving their world. See Fig. 18-2.

- **Attention span.** For reasons that are not yet understood, at about twelve years

old, preteens' attention span actually grows shorter. They tend to learn less because they can't concentrate as long. Their grades may drop at school, and test scores may decline.

Theories of How Children Learn

Questions about how and why thinking skills expand continue to interest child development professionals. Piaget's work was followed by some studies that built on his theories, along with others that contradicted his ideas.

Fig. 18-3 Piaget's Four Periods of Learning

Period	Characteristics
Sensorimotor Birth–2 years	Children learn through their senses and own actions.
Preoperational 2–7 years	Children think in terms of their own activities and what they perceive at the moment.
Concrete operations 7–11 years	Children can think logically but still learn best through experience.
Formal operations 11–Adult	People are capable of abstract thinking.

Piaget

As you learned earlier, Jean Piaget proposed a theory to explain how children's thinking skills develop. Of the four stages into which he divided childhood intellectual development, children from seven to twelve fall in the last two, as shown in Fig. 18-3.

Concrete Operations Stage

Most children begin to move into Piaget's concrete operations stage at about age seven. Their thinking works effectively on concrete, or actual, objects and tasks. They can generalize from their own experiences, but they can't yet understand abstract ideas. For example, a five-year-old probably couldn't draw a map of the route from home to a nearby playground visited regularly. An eight-year-old would be able to visualize the neighborhood and draw a rough map. However, a child this age would have difficulty imagining what route to take if the usual one was blocked and another had to be found.

During the concrete operations stage, children develop several important thinking skills that build a foundation for mastering their school work. These skills include:

- **Classifying objects.** In Piaget's preoperational stage, children as young as three can *classify* objects, or group them, according to one similar characteristic, such as shape or color. They can't sort by several categories, however. For example, they can't distinguish all the blocks in a set that are both red and square. By age seven, children are able to sort items by two or more different characteristics at the same time.

- **Placing objects in a series.** In the concrete operations stage, children can arrange objects in ascending or descending order, such as from largest to smallest. This requires the ability to compare objects mentally and to make logical connections between what they know and what they are learning. See Fig. 18-4.

- **Extending relationships.** Piaget said that children at this stage learn **transitivity**, or the concept that a relative relationship between two objects can extend to a third object. For example, if three is greater than two, and two is greater than one, then three must also be greater than one.

Fig. 18-4 **Older children become able to recognize and place objects in a complex pattern.** In which of Piaget's stages do children acquire this skill?

- **Conservation.** Piaget demonstrated that during his concrete operations stage, children also learn the principle of **conservation**. This means that they understand that an object has the same characteristics even if there is a change in the way it looks. To test this ability, Piaget showed children of different ages two balls of clay of equal size. He then rolled one ball into a long cylinder and asked the children whether one was larger now. Younger children thought that the longer piece of clay was larger because it seemed to take up more space. By age seven, children could see that the amount of clay had not changed.

Formal Operations Stage

At about age eleven, children begin to move into Piaget's formal operations stage. They develop the ability to think abstractly and to see different sides of an issue. Abstract thinking shows in a variety of ways, such as:

- Imagining **hypothetical** situations, or situations that might happen
- Solving problems by anticipating and preparing for different situations
- Debating issues
- Using "if … then" formulas to consider what they might decide to do under changing sets of circumstances
- Recognizing societal problems and understanding the complex reasons for them

A preteen who begins to show these types of thinking is likely to use them only selectively at first—not in all situations and not at all times.

Piaget theorized that the complex, multi-level framework of stages which he proposed was biologically based and universal. Each child experienced the stages, always in the same order. His ideas deeply influenced

Children's Museums

Traditional museums are typically filled with historical objects, paintings, and other treasures. Touching these items is usually not allowed. That's one reason children are sometimes less than enthusiastic about museum visits. Looking at seashells in a case behind glass doesn't give children the chance to experience them. In special museums designed especially for children, learning takes place through actual experience. Children might be able to touch a variety of real seashells and experience the differences in texture and size. They might experience how aspects of science work or learn through interactive displays. Children's museums are based on the belief that children learn best through actual experience.

Following Up

Choose something that would be featured in a children's museum exhibit. Identify five ways children could learn more about it.

several generations of parents and educators. However, other influential theories arose that offered other perspectives on the way children develop, including children from seven to twelve.

Lev Vygotsky (1896–1934)

Vygotsky's theory was that biological development and cultural experience both influenced children's ability to learn. He believed that children learned most, and best, from one another and from adults. For children ages seven to twelve, who are learning to evaluate themselves and others, this means that the more they interact with other people, the more they will learn. Working together with adults and teachers and receiving their guidance are important. So are peer and small-group learning in the classroom, and social activities such as clubs, team sports, and other events where children can interact and learn from watching and communicating with one another.

Maria Montessori (1870–1952)

In contrast to Vygotsky, Montessori stressed the importance of self-directed learning. She believed that teachers should provide the necessary resources for children to learn independently, and then intrude on the children's learning experience as little as possible. For seven- to twelve-year-olds, the Montessori classroom might offer a combination of language, history, geography, the sciences, and the arts. However, group lessons would be kept to a minimum as teachers allowed children to exercise their growing independence by exploring their interests in their own way. Real-life experiences are stressed. See Fig. 18-5.

Fig. 18-5 Montessori schools believe children learn best through real-world experiences.

Howard Gardner (1943–)

Howard Gardner, who proposed the theory of multiple intelligences, challenged Piaget by theorizing that knowledge is multifaceted. For example, a seven-year-old who is at a certain stage in understanding numbers may be at a different stage in spatial/visual development. See Fig. 18-6. Educators have supported Gardner's theories because they see their students learning and thinking in different ways every day.

Fig. 18-6 Gardner's theory of multiple intelligences takes the approach that children have different ways of learning. A child might be strong in visual-spatial intelligence but not as advanced in the verbal-linguistic intelligence.

The more students develop their different intelligences, the greater their skills and knowledge will become, according to Gardner. For children seven to twelve years old, this could mean offering school activities each day that support as many of their growing interests and abilities as possible.

The list that follows gives examples of activities that can encourage children from seven to twelve to develop their different intelligences:

- **Verbal-linguistic.** Write a story, act in a play, speak to the class about an issue important to students

Children Around the World

Analyzing the Media's Messages

Who is in charge of the media? What kind of picture does the media paint of our society and our world? Is it an accurate picture? These questions are the foundation of many media education courses. Some countries, such as Canada and Hungary, require that students take media education courses in which they analyze the media's messages. Teachers present material from newspapers, magazines, the Internet, films, and television. Teachers can show students how to look critically at the media and make comparisons between media outlets. Students can provide real-world examples. As our

world grows more complex, many feel that students need to learn how to analyze the media and its messages now more than ever.

Investigating Culture

1. In the United States, a few large corporations now own most of the traditional news sources (newspapers, television and radio stations). What effect might this have on the media?
2. Other than those given in the passage, offer a reason why it is important to analyze the media's messages today.

Fig. 18-7 **Some children have a high level of analytical intelligence.** How can teachers and parents encourage this ability in children?

- **Logical-mathematical.** Create a weekly budget, learn to play chess, conduct a science experiment
- **Visual-spatial.** Create a design, paint a neighborhood scene, diagram the school grounds
- **Musical.** Talk about how a piece of music "feels," practice playing an instrument
- **Bodily-kinesthetic.** Dance, practice sports, learn new crafts
- **Interpersonal.** Identify and help solve a class problem, lead a class project
- **Intrapersonal.** Create a comic book, start a blog or an online journal, create a class photo album.
- **Naturalist.** Visit a nature museum, report on how to save an endangered species

Robert Sternberg (1949–)

Sternberg's research suggested an answer to why some students who did well in school don't excel in the working world.

Others who experience success at working didn't excel in school. His theory proposed that people have three kinds of intelligence. Whether people are successful in a particular environment can depend on how strong or weak these intelligences are.

According to Sternberg, children, like adults, have varying degrees of these three types of intelligence. When parents, caregivers, and educators encourage all three, all children can demonstrate their talents, and schools can find ways to reward and encourage each student.

- **Analytical intelligence.** This involves the abilities to recall, recognize, analyze, compare and contrast, evaluate, and explain problem-solving strategies. Children with high analytical intelligence are often considered to be "smart" because they are good at the types of activities and tests given in schools, including intelligence tests. See Fig. 18-7.
- **Creative intelligence.** Sternberg believes that school programs are too often so focused on improving student

knowledge that they can hinder creativity. Creative intelligence is required whenever children imagine, pretend, invent, and design. Children high in creative intelligence might not follow directions well or score highly on tests.

- **Practical intelligence.** Children's practical intelligence helps them to apply experience or knowledge to solve a "real-world" problem. These "street smart" children can speedily assess a problem and the resources available, and then figure out the quickest and most practical way to solve it. These children might not be the top performers at school, but they have the potential to become tomorrow's leading managers, politicians, and businesspeople.

SECTION 18-1 Review and Activities

Reviewing the Section

1. In what ways are preteens idealists? What aspects of their intellectual development contribute to this idealism?
2. What thinking skills do children develop during Piaget's concrete operations stage?
3. In the context of intellectual development, what does the term *conservation* mean?
4. What does use of "if...then" reasoning indicate about a child's intellectual development?
5. In what significant way is Vygotsky's theory of learning different from that of Montessori?
6. Compare Gardner's and Sternberg's theories. How are they alike? How do they differ? How could an educator use each to help students succeed?

Observing and Interacting

Make a visit to a local toy store. What board games can you find that are appropriate for seven-year-olds? What board games are appropriate for twelve-year-olds? Using what you have learned about intellectual development, explain why the games you found for preteens were too difficult for seven-year-olds.

Learning from Seven to Twelve

At seven, Bryson spent hour after hour coloring. At ten, he was always flying by on his bicycle. By his twelfth birthday, however, he had become quite serious. His favorite birthday present was a computer time-travel game from his aunt, and the two of them were soon playing it. Bryson's ability to focus on more demanding tasks is typical of his age. He likes the challenge of learning about topics that interest him. During this age span, schools begin to test children like Bryson and his schoolmates to assess their intellectual development and knowledge through standardized tests.

Objectives

- Compare different learning methods that are effective for children ages seven to twelve.
- Identify characteristics of the middle school experience that make it particularly suited to preteen learning.
- Contrast the different types of standardized tests and describe how they are developed.
- Explain how standardized test scores are used.

Key Terms

learning method
peer learning
standardized test

Learning Methods

Young children learn skills primarily through imitating older children and adults. Seven- to twelve-year-olds are more and more capable of abstract thought and of more demanding work. Teachers present a variety of ways to learn, or **learning methods**.

Direct Learning

In their first years in school, children's learning is more activity based, using sensory aids such as finger paints, posters, play money, and games. In contrast, language-based direct learning becomes the more common form of instruction for older children.

Vince, Kirsten, and several of their seventh-grade classmates were working on a project for the Science Fair. Kirsten and Vince's group was having some trouble resolving its conflicts over how the project should go. Although Vince and Kirsten were supposed to be working together on a drawing of a single-celled amoeba, Vince was hoarding the markers. Keith, another group member, was trying to slack off and let the others take over, but Jared wasn't letting him get away with it. "Get the scissors and start cutting out the game pieces," he said. Sydney, a bright, hardworking girl who wanted to impress her teacher and classmates, had taken charge of writing an essay for the group. She was worried that Keith's lack of motivation would hurt the group's grade.

▶▶ **PERSONAL APPLICATION**

1. In this situation, some of the students are working very hard while others are not. What role do you usually play in a group?
2. If someone in your group weren't making much of a contribution, how would you handle the situation?

Children capable of direct learning can acquire facts and ideas by listening and reading. For example, the teacher might talk to the class about the Civil War and assign reading in the social studies textbook. The children must pay close attention to the teacher, and they must learn to take notes and read their textbooks more independently. Their progress in mastering these skills is gradual. How well they absorb the material can be measured in various ways such as tests, quizzes, and essays.

Peer Learning

Another learning method, known as **peer learning**, occurs when students observe and listen to one another. They work together in pairs, in small groups, or as a class on a project or task. One advantage of peer learning is that it provides an environment in which students may feel less awkward about asking questions or expressing confusion. Working on group projects helps students learn to work together cooperatively, communicate, and build time- and resource-management skills.

Independent Learning

Teachers also help students build the skills needed for independent learning. Assignments take more time, and they require a series of steps to complete. Independent learning allows students to both work on their own and to use the information they gather in a variety of challenging ways. It also prepares them for long-term assignments common in high school, college, and the working world.

A teacher may, for example, suggest an area of study, such as farming in North America, and have students choose a specific topic, perhaps crops of the American desert. Then students will get a week or more to complete the assignment. Students will research and select topics, collect materials, and continue their research, finally preparing a finished assignment.

A sixth-grade teacher might give specific directions for each step of the process. Students would complete each step by a designated time to meet the final deadline. Teachers may need to help students allocate their time between steps. Preteens may be given more responsibility in planning their work and meeting their deadlines.

Middle School—A Place for Transition

The typical school day of a fourth grader and that of a high school freshman are not at all alike. Fourth graders still perform best in the type of classroom setting used with younger children, with one teacher who is almost like a parent. This teacher leads them through most of their coursework and gives them personal, individual care and guidance. The children know all their classmates and spend most of their time in their familiar classroom surroundings.

On the other hand, high school students rotate from class to class all day with changing teachers and classmates. Their learning environment is impersonal compared to elementary school, and they are expected to do much of their work independently.

Developing New Independence and Social Skills

The period of time between fourth grade and high school can be very stressful for students as they begin to have new concerns and needs. They become increasingly aware of their changing bodies. At the same time, they are becoming more and more focused on what people think about them. They are more independent, yet this independence

may have led to greater responsibilities at home that may limit personal activities. They are developing social skills, but they aren't yet ready for the less personal high school setting.

Effective Middle Schools

Educators continue to debate what are the best educational settings for preteens, but they do agree on some approaches to what can be a very stressful age. Middle school homeroom teachers offer the personal contact that early adolescents still need and function as someone familiar the students can go to with problems. The best middle schools have a low number of students per teacher or advisor, perhaps 10 to 1. These schools involve parents and community leaders in their classroom activities, and they integrate coursework from several classes/courses rather than offering disconnected classes in rigid time frames.

At the same time that middle school educators try to personalize the school setting, they also try to offer an environment where students can enjoy being more grown up. Students may be able to pick some of their subjects. They can choose new friends. More challenging academic work can increase their confidence in their ability to learn. All these positive aspects of the middle school can create a comfortable bridge to high school.

Measuring Students' Intellectual Development

Schools often rely on tests to evaluate how well students are developing intellectually and how much knowledge they

How Much Should I Help My Child with Homework?

Some children are excited about having homework, while others are not. When children start to have homework, parents and caregivers have to make almost as many adjustments as the child does. They also need to decide just how much help to give. Here are some ways to find the right balance:

- **Avoid doing too much.** Most parents know that they shouldn't do their children's work for them, but it's tempting to lend a hand. Try helping the child think through the assignment and decide how to tackle it. Preplanning is a valuable life skill.
- **Offer help when it is really needed.** If a child can't figure out how to do a problem, you may be able to help by showing how to solve one that is similar.

- **Supply materials and help with organization.** Providing supplies such as notepads and pens shows that you see homework as important. Help organize the study area. For example, color-coded folders can help a middle school child organize work by class or by project.
- **Allow time for a break after school.** Children may need time to play or participate in other activities after school. This gives children a mental break before focusing on studying again.
- **Above all, be there.** It is wonderfully reassuring for a child to have a trusted adult available while doing homework. In addition, keeping an eye on the homework session offers opportunities to help children learn time-management skills.

THINKING IT THROUGH

Are there any disadvantages of having an adult help with homework?

---

are acquiring. Schools periodically give **standardized tests**—tests that allow educators to tell how students are performing intellectually when compared to the thousands of other students who have taken the same test. Many states mandate standardized tests to students in order to measure their learning achievement. These tests are also used as an indicator of how well the schools are meeting the learning needs of their students.

Fig. 18-8 **Schools use standardized achievement tests to determine what knowledge a child has acquired.**

Testing Students' Ability and Knowledge

Standardized tests have a special usefulness in assessing how well children are able to learn, and how much they have learned. Most seven- to twelve-year-olds take standardized tests in one or more grades. See Fig. 18-8.

Creating Standardized Tests

Teams of scientists and educators design standardized tests for schools. Along with the tests come exact instructions for giving and scoring them. Before standardized tests are ready for use, they are repeatedly tested with students and revised. This effort guarantees that the tests have three properties that are necessary to make them good tests.

- **Validity.** A standardized test is valid when it measures what it is supposed to measure. For example, if a test is supposed to measure reading comprehension, enough time has to be given for the students to complete reading the selections and answering the questions.

HOW TO

Stay Involved in a Child's Education

Parents who get involved in their child's education send the message that school counts. Here are some ways they can do so:

- **Meet the staff.** Many schools have a back-to-school night for visiting children's classes and meeting the teachers. Teachers describe the curriculum, plus their expectations and rules.

- **Talk to the teachers personally.** Many schools also schedule one-on-one parent-teacher conferences.

- **Read messages sent by the school.** Teachers and principals often send important information about the school and activities there. They may mail or e-mail the information or have the students take it home.

- **Review the child's homework.** Parents can judge a child's performance by reviewing homework. Looking at assignments that have been graded helps to identify areas that need improvement.

- **Help out with school activities.** Parents can volunteer to help in the class or for field trips and special activities.

- **Join the parents' group.** Parents can learn about the school and offer constructive suggestions.

- **Talk to the child.** Parents can stay involved simply by talking to their child about school. Encourage students to describe the work they did that day and any important events that took place.

YOUR TURN

Communication. Many children answer "Nothing" or something vague such as "Just stuff" when asked what they did in school. If you were a parent, how would you ask about your child's day in school to be sure to get an answer that has real information?

- **Reliability.** Standardized tests must be consistent. The test is reliable if it can be given to the same age group, again and again, with similar results.

- **Practicality.** Standardized tests must be practical for schools to be able to use them. They cannot be difficult to give, and they must be quick and relatively easy to score. They must also be affordable.

Kinds of Standardized School Tests

There are many kinds of standardized tests. Three kinds that are given to children from seven to twelve include tests that measure how well they can learn, how much they have already learned, and what they might have a special ability or interest in learning.

- **Learning ability tests.** Learning ability tests are designed to help educators predict how well a student might do in a particular learning situation. All the students taking the test answer the same set of questions. Their scores are then compared.

  Learning ability tests go by several names, including intelligence tests, mental ability tests, scholastic aptitude tests, and academic aptitude tests.

  Most tests require students to read questions and write answers. A student with highly developed language skills may earn a higher score than a student with highly developed musical skills. Having a higher IQ on this one test does not mean that the top scoring student is smarter. The second student's learning ability is just different.

- **Achievement tests.** Achievement tests are used to help measure what students have actually learned about a particular topic or subject. Standardized achievement tests are the most prevalent standardized test used in schools. They give educators a sense of the progress students are making in acquiring knowledge. A certain score on these types of tests may be required for graduation.

- **Aptitude and interest tests.** Aptitude and interest tests offer important measures of people's talents and preferences. A student who scores high in mathematical aptitude might strive to become an engineer or a scientist. Another name for interest tests is *interest inventories*. Students select what they like best from different groups of ideas, activities, or situations. Patterns in their answers are analyzed to see where their interests are strongest.

Uses and Misuses of Standardized Tests

While standardized tests provide useful indicators of how students are developing intellectually, they have important limitations. They are estimates that measure only a small sample of a student's abilities or achievements. Even with tests of considerable reliability, scores can vary due to factors such as the age of the test taker and conditions at the test's location. Many critics argue that standardized tests do not accurately assess the intellectual development of minority and disadvantaged students as well as English language learners, no matter how "culture fair" and "culture free" the test makers claim them to be.

Teachers feel pressured to have their students get high test scores. They are sometimes criticized for teaching only what is going to be on achievement tests, ignoring opportunities to share other important information with students that would enliven their studies.

In spite of the criticism, however, most educators still believe that standardized testing is necessary. Along with teacher tests, it remains the best way for a teacher to keep informed about what students need and how to best help them develop intellectually.

SECTION 18-2 Review and Activities

Reviewing the Section

1. What is direct learning? How is it different from the most common method of learning used for children below age seven?
2. Devise three assignments a teacher might make to encourage independent learning.
3. In what ways is the middle school approach to education different from that used in elementary school and high school? Why is the middle school approach appropriate for preteens?
4. Why do schools use *standardized tests*? What are the three properties their tests must have to be good tests?
5. What do intelligence tests measure? Is it possible for a student to have a different IQ score, depending on the test? Explain your answer.
6. How do achievement and aptitude tests differ? If you had to pick which you'd prefer to score high on, which would you pick? Why?
7. Imagine education without standardized testing. Create two lists showing what would change and what would stay the same. Pick the world in which you'd rather go to school and tell how your school experience would be.

Observing and Interacting

Join four or five students who will interview their families and friends about standardized testing. See how many kinds of tests these people know about and how important they think they are. Draw conclusions about how complete and accurate their understandings are about the tests and the scores. Combine and share your findings.

Gymnastics Coach

Gymnastics is a popular sport. We watch as gymnasts hurtle through the air, twisting and turning somersaults. The moment of performance represents just a tiny part of the work of the gymnast. Coaches work hard training gymnasts to improve their flexibility, balance, and strength.

▸ Job Responsibilities

Most gymnastics coaches are former gymnasts, so they understand routines and can teach them. Coaches instruct gymnasts in performing safely and artistically. They help athletes cope with anxiety about performing. Coaches show athletes how to train their bodies and avoid injury by eating healthy foods and practicing routines.

▸ Work Environment

Some gymnastic coaches form businesses to train athletes, while others work for schools, recreation centers, and universities. Some coach individual gymnasts, while others coach teams in competition.

▸ Education and Training

Most gymnastics coaches hold bachelor's degrees in exercise science. Courses in sports psychology are also helpful. It is important for gymnastics coaches to learn first aid and resuscitation skills in case an athlete suffers an injury.

▸ Skills and Aptitudes

- Knowledge of gymnastics
- Ability to teach routines
- Energy
- Physical endurance and strength
- Interest in working with young people

WORKPLACE CONNECTION

1. **Thinking Skills.** How would being a gymnast yourself help you if you became a coach?

2. **Resource Skills.** How could you get experience coaching?

18 Review and Activities

SECTION SUMMARIES

- In middle childhood and the preteen years, children make many advances in their intellectual abilities. (18-1)
- Children move from the concrete operations stage to the formal operations stage at about age twelve, when they become capable of abstract thinking. (18-1)
- Among those who developed important theories about intellectual development in the twentieth century are Piaget, Vygotsky, Montessori, and Gardner. (18-1)
- Different methods have been developed to test knowledge and intelligence. (18-1)
- Direct learning, peer learning, and independent learning are different modes of learning that are appropriate to children ages seven to twelve. (18-2)
- Middle school programs are specially designed to meet the educational and emotional needs of preteens. (18-2)
- Between the ages of seven and twelve, students begin to take standardized tests that are specially designed to measure their intellectual performance and aptitudes. (18-2)

REVIEWING THE CHAPTER

1. How have seven-year-olds advanced in their ability to classify? (18-1)
2. How is the ability to put objects in a series linked to *transitivity*? (18-1)
3. How does having more awareness of how they learn help children learn? (18-1)
4. Explain why Piaget said that putting objects in a series and understanding *conservation* were advances in mental abilities. (18-1)
5. Give two reasons why children in this age group may need a break after school is over before they begin their homework. (18-2)
6. Name six things parents can do to increase their involvement with their child's school. (18-2)
7. In what ways is middle school different from elementary school and high school? (18-2)

THINKING CRITICALLY

1. **Drawing Conclusions.** Why do you think that children in these ages have a stronger sense of awareness and curiosity?
2. **Making Inferences.** If hypothetical thinking is so advantageous for children, why don't they use it more often when they first acquire the skill?

MAKING CONNECTIONS

1. **Social Studies.** With a partner, prepare for a debate about learning. One of you will argue that Gardner's multiple intelligences theory is more accurate, and the other person will argue that Sternberg's intelligence theory is.

2. **Writing.** Create a dialogue between a parent and his child's teacher discussing why the child often hands homework in late. Include specific actions that they might take to help the child.

APPLYING YOUR LEARNING

1. **Testing.** Devise a new experiment to test one of the four mental abilities children acquire in Piaget's concrete operations period. Describe how you would test this ability.

2. **Analyzing Behaviors.** Identify which multiple intelligences are displayed by children who engage in the following behaviors (there may be more than one):

   - Spends a lot of time working alone on carpentry projects.
   - Organizes a nature hike.
   - Volunteers at a local day care center.
   - Likes to make up songs.

3. **Interpersonal Skills.** Imagine you are a middle school teacher about to have a conference with the parents of one of your students. What would you say to help them become more involved in the student's learning?

Learning from Research

1. Choose one of the following claims to investigate.
2. How is this finding useful to parents of preteens?
3. Summarize what you've learned about how math anxiety may affect learning.

Math Anxiety and Short-term Memory. According to research, people who have high levels of math anxiety show less short-term memory capacity. Investigate whether math anxiety is the cause of short-term memory capacity loss.

Math Anxiety and Gender. Researchers have found that girls and boys show similar levels of math anxiety in elementary school. However, girls show more math anxiety than males in high school and college. Girls begin to doubt their ability to do math around the time of seventh grade. What do researchers believe leads to lower girls' confidence about math skills?

Math Anxiety and Testing. Students with math anxiety become anxious and may perform poorly on tests. Students with math anxiety may also feel anxious during math class, while doing homework, as well as while taking tests. What are some possible causes of math anxiety?

Additional Topics of Study

Chapter 19
Adolescence

Chapter 20
Children's Health and Safety

Chapter 21
Family Challenges

Chapter 22
Child Care and Early Education

Chapter 23
Careers Working with Children

CHAPTER 19 | Adolescence

Thoughtful Reading:

As you read this chapter:
- Ask questions about what you are reading.
- Identify new information you learn from what you read.
- Connect what you read to your personal experiences.

Section 19-1
Physical Development of Adolescents

Section 19-2
Emotional and Social Development of Adolescents

Section 19-3
Moral Development of Adolescents

Section 19-4
Intellectual Development of Adolescents

Physical Development of Adolescents

The term adolescence has a number of meanings. Generally, it refers to the complex time of life when a child begins to mature into an adult. In that sense, the ages of adolescence vary from person to person. It may begin at age 11 or 12. In this chapter, adolescence refers to the teen years, ages 13 to 19.

Objectives

- Compare and contrast the physical development of males and females.
- Describe the changes associated with the sexual development of males and females.
- Assess the importance of nutrition, hygiene, exercise, and sleep during adolescence.

Key Terms

estrogen
testosterone

A Time of Many Changes

The teen years are among the most challenging for teens and their families. Adolescents experience many changes, including coping with fluctuating emotions, handling new social situations and influences, and using new intellectual abilities. However, the physical changes associated with adolescence are the most obvious signs that a teen is moving toward adulthood.

Physical Development During Adolescence

Adolescence is a time of rapid growth in height and weight and of physical changes throughout the body. Both males and females grow taller and become stronger. At the same time, they mature sexually, experiencing the body changes brought on by puberty. While this phase marks the development of sexual characteristics, puberty also includes other kinds of physical change that occur at this time of life. Powerful hormones in the body bring on the physical changes of adolescence.

Once the changes of puberty begin, they continue with a rush that can be confusing and even a bit scary, especially when teens or preteens aren't prepared. Their only information may come from their friends, who may not be reliable sources. Parents need to prepare their children before puberty begins and reassure them that this type of physical growth is normal. A delay in puberty is also usually normal.

Figure 19-1 shows the physical changes that take place during adolescence. At the beginning of this stage, most young teens still look like children. By the end, they are clearly adults.

Height and Weight

Charts showing average heights are less helpful during this stage because individual growth patterns are so variable. During puberty, it's not unusual for a teen to grow 3 to 5 inches (7.6 to 12.7 cm) in height each year for several years. While many girls begin this growth spurt earlier, boys soon catch up. By about age 16, males are often bigger and stronger than most females of the same age. Many teens reach their full adult height by age 16.

To image-conscious teens, size matters. Those who go through puberty early may feel uneasy while at the same time being the object of their peers' envy. In many sports, players who are larger tend to have an advantage. Cultural expectations also shape teens' feelings about size. In this country, for example, it's more acceptable to be a small adult female than a small male.

Male Physical Development

Between the ages of 11 and 18, a typical male will double his weight from 75 pounds to 150 pounds (34 kg to 68 kg). In the same time span, he will grow about 14 inches (36 cm).

Eighteen-year-old Marcus is average for his age. At nearly 70 inches (178 cm) tall, Marcus weighs 150 pounds (68 kg). His shoulders are wider than they were a few years earlier, and he has become noticeably more muscular.

Fig. 19-1 **Significant physical changes between ages 13 and 19 are easy to see.**

Female Physical Development

Gina's growth has been typical for an adolescent girl. As an 11-year-old, she was 57 inches (145 cm) tall and weighed 80 pounds (36 kg). By the age of 14, she was slightly smaller than the average 14-year-old boy—63 inches (160 cm) tall and 110 pounds (50 kg). Now at age 15, she has grown about another inch (3 cm) and has gained 8 pounds (3 kg).

Girls usually don't grow much taller after about age 15. While many young women are taller, the average height for females in late adolescence remains just slightly over 5 feet 4 inches. Many girls do, however, gain some additional weight—the average female weighs 125 pounds (57 kg) at age 18. Of course, few teens are exactly average.

Sexual Development

Some of the most significant changes in adolescence are those of sexual development. As teens experience rapid growth spurts, girls develop physically into women and boys progress physically into men. During this time, teens become capable of sexual reproduction. Girls' bodies release eggs, and boys' begin to produce sperm.

Female Sexual Development

As you learned in Chapter 16, girls generally begin to mature sexually by the age of 11 or 12. At this time, they experience rapid growth. They also undergo the outward changes associated with sexual development. Menstruation begins about two years after breasts begin to develop. The beginning of menstrual periods indicates that a girl's body has increased its production of the hormone **estrogen**. The ovaries produce estrogen. These are two small glands located next to the uterus, the organ in which a baby develops in a pregnant female. The ovaries also produce eggs, the female reproductive cells.

LOOKING AT REAL LIFE

As they were walking home from school, Adam noticed his brother Jack was angry. When Adam asked him what was wrong, Jack yelled, "Forget it! I don't want to talk about it!" So Adam left him alone for a while. Later that evening, Adam tried to talk to him again. Jack said, "I hate school. I'm never going back. I'm the shortest kid in the class, and I always get picked last for sports. On the field, the other boys yell, 'Hey, Jack, short-stack!' The older boys are always saying they're going to beat me up." Adam asked Jack if he wanted him to let the boys know that if they picked on his brother, they'd have to answer to him. "No! Don't do that!" moaned Jack. Adam reminded his brother that he'd been the shortest boy in his class just a few years earlier. "There's more to you than your height," Adam said. "You tell funny jokes, and you have a lot of friends. Don't worry. You'll grow, just like I did," said Adam. Jack managed a little grin as he teased, "Yeah, now you're a giant!"

▸▸**PERSONAL APPLICATION**

1. Have you ever been self-conscious about your appearance?
2. What made you feel better about yourself?

Usually every 28 to 32 days, an ovary releases one ovum, or egg. If the ovum is not fertilized by a male sperm cell, it dissolves and drains out of the body along with a bloody discharge, the menstrual flow. Thus the menstrual cycle is the way the female body discards an unfertilized egg each month and then replaces it with a new one. An average menstrual period lasts from three to seven days.

Some girls experience irregular periods when they first start to menstruate. An erratic menstrual cycle is usually nothing to worry about. In the great majority of cases, a girl's cycle evens out within a year or so. However, if menstrual periods are extremely irregular, or if they are painful or prolonged, she should see a physician.

Girls entering puberty may experience weight gain because the addition of body fat is one of the effects of estrogen. The young teen is becoming a woman, and her body is beginning to round out. See Fig. 19-2.

Male Sexual Development

Boys, on average, mature sexually about two years later than girls. Between the ages of 13 and 15, boys' genitals become larger, and their testes, or testicles, begin to produce sperm. The sperm are the male reproductive cells.

Additional changes are caused by **testosterone** (tes-TAHS-tuh-rone), a hormone produced by the testicles. Testosterone levels in a boy's body begin to rise rapidly at the beginning of puberty. A boy has reached puberty when he experiences *ejaculation*, the ejecting of *semen*. Semen is fluid that contains sperm. The first ejaculation often occurs while he is sleeping.

Fig. 19-2 **During puberty, parents can help to reassure teens about the changes that are happening in their bodies. How much do parents need to tell young adolescents about their sexuality?**

HOW TO

Encourage Good Nutrition and Self-Image

With their busy schedules, teens often don't take good care of themselves. It often seems easier to grab a snack than to sit down for a well-balanced meal. Adequate sleep and exercise may also be neglected. It's not surprising that low self-esteem is so common among teens. There is a relationship among these factors. Here are some ways to turn the situation around:

- **Choose good nutrition.** The body needs breakfast to get the body and mind going, but it is the most skipped meal. Starting the day with a nutritious breakfast can boost achievement.

- **Exercise regularly.** Any type of exercise, done regularly, can improve fitness and give a feeling of well being.

- **Think positively.** Everyone has some good features—an interesting face, a strong body, or a great pesonality. Those who concentrate on their good features instead of real or imagined imperfections stand out for their positive attitude.

- **Look inside.** It's common to worry about what others think, but the solution isn't to just follow the crowd. Having the courage to be an individual makes it easier to see and appreciate the best qualities in others.

- **Be strong.** Make decisions independently. Teens who have a good self-concept can withstand peer pressure because they believe in themselves. Their strength comes from within, not from what others say about them.

YOUR TURN

Confidence. Most people would like to have confidence. What advice would you give to a friend who wanted to become more confident?

Fig. 19-3 **The quality of a person's diet is determined by dozens of individual food choices each day.**

Healthy Habits

Health and hygiene needs change somewhat during adolescence. However, making wise food choices, keeping clean, exercising, and getting enough sleep are still the keys to good health.

Nutrition

Puberty and related growth spurts have an impact on nutritional needs. A balanced diet of nutritious foods is needed to fuel growth, as well as normal body processes. Teens typically consume more calories than usual during growth spurts.

Eating right means not only avoiding foods high in fat, sugar, and salt, but also taking sensible portions. Overeating, especially of high-calorie foods, can lead to obesity. Parents can help by making nutritious food choices available, setting a good example, and paying attention to portion sizes. In the Hasegawa household, for example, bowls of food are not set on the table for family members to help themselves. Instead, Mrs. Hasegawa serves each person a plate of food with reasonable portions. If her sons are still hungry, they ask for seconds. See Fig. 19-3.

Hygiene

Personal cleanliness routines become more important in adolescence. Perspiration odor and oily skin and hair are common problems. Fortunately, most

Fig. 19-4 **Having good hygiene habits can help teens feel more confident.** What are some habits for good hygiene?

Fig. 19-5 **Getting moderate exercise on a regular basis is important for staying healthy and preventing obesity.**

teens care about their appearance and how they are perceived by others. Regular baths or showers remove dirt, sweat, and dead skin cells. Deodorant or antiperspirant helps control body odor. Clean clothes help present a fresh image. See Fig. 19-4.

Exercise

A moderate amount of daily exercise is important for everyone, including teens. It builds strong bones and muscles and benefits the heart and blood vessels. Unfortunately, nearly half of young people in the United States between the ages of 12 and 21 don't exercise on a regular basis. Physical inactivity sets the stage for possible obesity and the development of other health problems later in life.

There are some ways teens can add exercise to their daily routine. Doing so helps the body cope with stress and strengthens muscles, including heart muscles. See Fig. 19-5.

Sleep

Everyone needs adequate sleep. The body, especially the brain and nervous system, restores itself during sleep. Teens need at least eight and one-half hours of sleep every night, but most only sleep about seven hours. They tend to go to bed late and then find it difficult to get up in the morning.

The negative effects of too little sleep include the following:

- Difficulty concentrating in school and lower grades.
- Becoming irritated more easily and losing emotional control.
- Impaired coordination and slower reaction time.
- Decreased resistance to illness.

Some teens take on too many extracurricular activities or hold part-time jobs during the school week. Others spend late nights on the computer or watching television. Good choices, time-management skills, and a regular sleep schedule can help teens get enough rest.

THE DEVELOPING BRAIN

Scientists have conducted many experiments on sleep deprivation, keeping subjects awake for several days and observing them closely. The frontal cortex of the brain—which controls speech, memory, and the ability to solve problems—relies on sleep to function properly. After three days, most people in these studies had difficulty thinking, hearing, or seeing clearly.

SECTION 19-1 Review and Activities

Reviewing the Section

1. Describe the roles of *estrogen* and *testosterone*.
2. Why is good nutrition especially important for teens?
3. Why is it important for adolescents to get regular exercise? What are the dangers of little or no exercise?
4. Why do teens need to pay more attention to hygiene than younger children?

Observing and Interacting

Between adolescent girls and adolescent boys, who do you think has a more difficult experience in terms of physical changes and development? Why? Discuss your view with other classmates. Do you have similar opinions? Summarize in writing your opinions and those of your classmates. Did this discussion change your opinion or understanding?

Emotional and Social Development of Adolescents

As teens move toward adulthood, they work to establish their individuality. They typically become more attached to their friends and more independent from their families. These and related changes can cause tension between teens and their parents.

Objectives

- Analyze the factors that help an adolescent establish a personal identity.
- Summarize theories of identity development.
- Recognize possible emotional problems and suggest a course of action for dealing with them.
- Assess the role that peers play during adolescence.
- Explain the importance of social interaction.

Key Terms

personal identity
identity crisis
depression
bipolar disorder

Emotional Development of Adolescents

Adolescence is the time of life when a person asks, "Who am I?" and tries to answer that question. While it is often a period of confusion, it can also lead to a strong sense of self.

Teens find that their emotions become more powerful, difficult to control, and can even be frightening. They must learn to control their emotions, but sometimes they struggle to do so. When teens' emotions become too overwhelming, they may need the help of friends and family to cope.

Forming a Personal Identity

During early adolescence, young teens begin to develop the mental capacity to form ideas and opinions that are theirs alone. They see that these ideas and opinions may differ from those of their family and friends. In this way, they begin to experience a strong **personal identity**, a sense that they are unique individuals. They begin to understand that their ideas, attitudes, and opinions are what form their personality. At this stage, adolescents are forming the personality that they will present to the world as adults.

As they develop a personal identity, teens grow more concerned with what their peers think of them. Some become self-conscious and self-absorbed. Young teens, in particular, tend to worry about their physical appearance.

Later in adolescence, teens' sense of personal identity strengthens. They become more adept at understanding others' feelings, and their personalities often show more compassion and responsibility. See Fig. 19-6.

Influences on Identity Development

Social and cultural influences strongly affect the formation of a personal identity:

- **Family.** Even though teens sometimes rebel against parental authority, family continues to be an important influence. Some teens and their parents maintain close emotional ties through this period. Other teens become especially close to another family member, perhaps a brother or sister or grandparent. To parents it may sometimes seem that their teen is rejecting the family's values and beliefs. This may be true in the short term. However, an adult's personal identity usually incorporates much of what he or she learned while growing up.

- **Peers.** A teen's classmates and friends are forming their own personal identities. Those in a peer group often adopt the tastes and beliefs of more popular members. More confident teens evaluate those ideas and beliefs, accepting some and rejecting others. In this way, they can form a strong identity that is their own.

- **The future.** By mid to late adolescence, teens have to start thinking about their lives as adults. By planning for a career or further education, they can start to see themselves as unique and independent individuals in the adult world.

Fig. 19-6 **Because teens are better able to understand others' problems and needs, many are willing to volunteer their time for community and charitable projects.**

Theories of Identity Development

Many researchers have studied how adolescents form their sense of self. Leaders in this field of study include Erik Erikson (1902–1994) of the United States and James Marcia (born 1937) of Canada.

- **Erikson's Identity vs. Confusion.** Erikson noted that even the most well-adjusted adolescent may experience some confusion about identity or sense of self. He and other psychologists considered this normal because adolescence is the time of life when teens strive to discover who they are. However, Erikson acknowledged that this confusion can become a serious problem for some teens.

  Erikson believed that social and cultural influences have a strong effect on how adolescents develop a sense of self. He believed that one of the most significant of these influences is peer pressure—the influence of friends in the same age group. Erikson held that conforming too rigidly to one's peers' attitudes and opinions can prevent a teen from finding a strong identity through personal exploration. He called the resulting confusion about one's personal identity an **identity crisis**.

- **Marcia's Identity Processes.** James Marcia elaborated on Erikson's theory by offering ways for adolescents to solve their identity crisis. Marcia believes that there are four paths to a sense of personal identity, and that most teens explore several of these paths.

  On the first path, adolescents accept the values of their parents and other respected adults without questioning those values. On the second path, teens are unsure of their values. They are determined to find an identity, but they are still in the process of developing it.

LOOKING AT REAL LIFE

Cameron grinned and waved his new driver's license as he walked in the house. He had been confident he would pass the test and already had planned to drive his friends to a game on the weekend. But when he asked to use the car, his parents said no. They told him he was still too inexperienced to drive the family car without an adult along. Cameron was angry and humiliated. He had bragged to his friends that he would be driving them. He had to call and tell them that his parents wouldn't let him drive. Cameron refused to speak to his parents for two days. He felt they treated him like a child, and he was determined to make sure they understood how upset he was.

▶▶**PERSONAL APPLICATION**

1. Have you ever had an experience with your parents similar to Cameron's? What was your reaction to your parents' decision?
2. Put yourself in Cameron's parents' place. Why might they have made the decision they did?

On the third path, adolescents have no clear sense of identity and they aren't attempting to find one. On the fourth path, adolescents have solidified their values and have developed a sense of identity. These individuals may redefine this identity in adulthood, but they have made choices they are comfortable with for the time being.

Handling Emotional Difficulties

Adolescence is a very emotional time of life. Ideally, its pleasures include making new friends, learning new skills, and becoming active at school and possibly in the community. However, life doesn't always go smoothly. Sometimes the pressures of school, family, social life, and physical changes can be difficult to handle.

Everyone goes through difficult times. For teens, emotional ups and downs are normal. But sometimes significant emotional problems do occur. Recognizing the symptoms of emotional problems in a teen is an important step in preventing those problems from leading to serious consequences.

Depression

Feeling disappointed or sad from time to time is common, but there is an important difference between temporary sadness and true **depression**. With depression, feelings of intense sadness last for long periods of time and prevent a person from leading a normal life. See Fig. 19-7.

Depression can result from the loss of a loved one, family problems, the break-up of a close friendship, or failure in school. It can also be linked to the accumulation of smaller problems. An adolescent's feelings of being unable to cope with such stressful situations can be unbearable.

Females have a higher risk of depression because of hormonal changes, but they are more likely to seek help for depression than males. Some warning signs of depression include the following:

- Feelings of sadness most or all of the time.
- Feelings of emptiness.
- Lack of energy.
- Difficulty concentrating.
- Loss of interest in social activities, school, or activities that were formerly pleasurable.
- Unexpectedly poor grades.
- A change in eating or sleeping habits.

If these warning signs are ignored, there are risks for further consequences.

Anyone who sees signs of depression in a teen should act. Friends can tell the teen's parents, school counselor, or other responsible adult. Consulting a family physician or school counselor is a good first step. If the depression persists, the parents should consult a mental health professional.

Fig. 19-7 **Teens sometimes sink into depression if their lives are not going the way they want them to.** How can you help a friend who is suffering from depression?

Anxiety

Many people who suffer from depression also show signs of anxiety. A large number of people, adolescents included, experience this heightened feeling of uneasiness, fear, or uncertainty. Although there are different types of anxiety, all involve varying degrees of worry. Some possible traits of anxiety include fear of social situations, shortness of breath or racing heart, sadness, difficulty sleeping, and panic attacks. Ashley, who suffers from anxiety, avoids elevators, crowded areas such as movie theaters, and parties where there will be strangers. She knows being in such places makes her feel faint.

Teens who experience excessive worry should talk to a guidance counselor or doctor about the problem. If anxiety sufferers turn to alcohol or drugs as coping mechanisms, they can easily develop substance abuse problems.

Bipolar Disorder

Mood swings and other emotional changes are a normal part of growing up. Sometimes, though, mood swings go beyond what's normal for most teens. Some teens exhibit extreme changes in mood. One week or month they may be *manic*—outgoing and so full of energy that their friends are amazed. The next week, they are depressed and withdrawn, again causing others to wonder what's going on. This pattern of extreme changes in mood is characteristic of **bipolar disorder**.

Bipolar disorder (formerly called manic depression) can affect people of nearly all ages. It affects males and females about equally. Scientists aren't sure what causes the condition, but they think it results mostly from chemical imbalances in the brain.

During the manic phase of the disorder, the individual may experience exaggerated happiness and optimism, racing thoughts and speech, and reckless behavior. See

Fig. 19-8 **Irresponsible behavior, such as reckless driving or spending, can be a sign of bipolar disorder. Some signs include intense mood swings, from great happiness to deep depression and back again.**

Fig. 19-8. In the depressive phase, the individual may have feelings of guilt or worthlessness, a loss of energy, and an inability to take pleasure in anything.

The cycles of manic behavior and depression can each last for weeks or months, but sometimes they are much shorter in length. The periods of abnormal behavior may be separated by a time when the person acts more normally. Although there is no cure for bipolar disorder, it can be managed with medication and supportive treatment.

Social Relationships in Adolescence

During adolescence, teens explore their independence and self-expression through their social relationships with friends. Adolescents may hang out with their friends, talk to them on the phone, and then communicate online—all in the same day. Parents may wonder how they find so much to talk about. At the same time, teens may begin to rebel against the authority of their parents and other adults, whom adolescents may regard as stifling their self-expression.

The Push for Independence

Teens naturally want more freedom, which parents are often reluctant to grant. Parents want to protect their children from the dangers and disappointments that more freedom brings. As one mother put it, "Nick can't remember to pick up his dirty socks or take his homework to school. The idea of his roaming around on that motorcycle he wants to buy is very scary. My goal is to keep him alive and well—even if he hates me for it." Parents want teens to prove they are ready for more independence. Teens don't see the need to do so.

Teens want to spend more time with friends and less with family. These opposing positions can lead to friction and arguments at home.

Teens' tendency to begin questioning adult wisdom and authority also causes tension. All of these changes in attitudes and actions can cause friction between teens and adults.

Peer Influences on Social Development

Peers play an important role in teens' social development. As adolescents become less dependent on parents and other adults, most become more involved with peers.

Peer Groups

There may never be a time in life when the need for acceptance is greater than during adolescence. Not making the volleyball team or not being invited to a classmate's party can be devastating. As they form their identity, teens may place great importance on the acceptance and admiration of their peer group.

During this time, there is a tendency for teens to conform to the ideas and behavior of the group. They may listen to the same music and watch the same television shows. This is especially true in the early teen years.

An adolescent's conformist behavior can upset parents, who worry that teens will forget their many years of careful guidance. Such worries are often unfounded. Often, a teen seeks out a peer group that shares some of the same values.

Romantic Involvement

During adolescence, most teens gain experience being part of a couple through dating relationships. Young teens may spend more time thinking about their appearance and how to be noticed than actually dating. The rise and fall of romantic relationships can bring emotions that are difficult to control. However, such experiences give teens a better idea of what to look for in someone to marry. Some teens do marry, especially older teens, but marrying young does increase the risk of divorce.

Close Friends

The most important peers in a teen's life are a select few. These close friends are the individuals with whom teens share their secret dreams and fears. A teen will tell things to a best friend that he or she would never confide to a parent or other adult.

Parenting Q&A

How Much Independence Should a Teen Be Allowed?

The need to move toward independence is a major concern of teens. Understanding the importance of this need can help parents better respond to teens' concerns.

Teens typically want to spend more time with their friends without adult supervision. They enjoy practicing adult skills, such as driving, and want to explore the world on their own. Parents sometimes worry that lack of supervision can lead to reckless or even illegal behavior, sexual activity, and possibly pregnancy. They may also worry about a teen's safety while driving alone, or that a teen with too much freedom will neglect schoolwork.

Teens need to experience a reasonable amount of independence. That's how they learn the consequences of their decisions as they transition to young adulthood.

When a teen asks for more freedom, parents should consider:
- Has the teen usually been responsible, well behaved, and truthful?
- Do I know and trust the teen's friends and their families?
- Does the teen drive safely and understand all traffic laws?
- Is he or she doing well in school?

If parents answer yes to all of these questions, they should consider increasing a teen's privileges. However, it should be clear that these privileges will be taken away if any serious trouble results. This understanding will be a strong incentive to use the newly won independence in a responsible way.

THINKING IT THROUGH

1. Do you remember when you got your first taste of independence as a teen? What happened?
2. How would you react if you were a parent and your teen abused his or her privileges?

Having at least one close friend helps a teen navigate the trials of adolescence. Because friends are free to speak their minds with one another, adolescents can learn from a close friend how to alter their behavior or ideas. More importantly, they can do so without the fear of rejection present in a larger group of peers. Having a best friend also gives adolescents someone to "sound off" to about things that are worrying or angering them.

Opportunities for Social Interaction

As adolescents move into their middle and late teens, they typically become involved in more social activities. These activities can be both for pleasure and in service of the community.

Having a Good Time

There are many ways teens can have fun. These range from parties and time with friends, to sports and after-school activities. School and community organizations such as student government and the Boys and Girls Clubs provide opportunities for new friendships. Taking part in such activities isn't just enjoyable; it's a vital part of becoming a well-adjusted person. An individual who reaches adulthood without having engaged in a variety of activities may have to work harder to develop social skills than people who were social as teens.

Making a Social Contribution

It is also valuable for teens to become involved in activities that aid their communities. Some teens help out in hospitals, with charity events, or on environmental projects. There are always organizations and programs seeking volunteer workers. Groups such as the Family, Career and Community Leaders of America (FCCLA) can give teens opportunities to design and carry out community projects.

SECTION 19-2 Review and Activities

Reviewing the Section

1. Define *personal identity*. How does it develop during adolescence?
2. Describe the theories of Erik Erikson and James Marcia on how teens establish a personal identity.
3. Give two examples of serious emotional problems that can affect teens. Describe at least three characteristics of each.
4. As a parent or teacher, what would you do if you suspected a teen had an emotional disorder? As a friend?
5. Why are teens likely to conform to the behavior of others in their peer group?
6. What do teens learn from being involved in social activities?

Observing and Interacting

Observe a group of peers at school. Note how what particular group members say and do influences others in the group. In what ways are the teens similar? In what ways are they different? Record your findings.

Moral Development of Adolescents

During their adolescent years, teens must develop a moral compass to guide them through life. Peers, family, community, and the media—all play a role as teens develop their own ideas about right and wrong. Moral development guides teens' behavior as it gives them a greater awareness of the rules of society. Not surprisingly, some teens test the limits and make unwise choices.

Objectives

- Explain the meaning of the term "moral compass."
- Summarize Kohlberg's theory of moral development in adolescents.
- Identify social and cultural influences on moral development.
- Explain the potential consequences of a lack of strong personal values.

Key Terms

morality
moral maturity
popular culture

Developing a Moral Compass

As they leave childhood behind, adolescents look forward to taking their places in the adult world. Part of the quest for adulthood involves developing **morality**—a sense of right and wrong that guides decisions and actions.

Morality is based on values. A person's set of values may be referred to as a "moral compass." Like the instruments that help hikers find their way and avoid getting lost, values give direction to life. They help people make decisions that are right for them and avoid losing their way.

Moral development is an important part of the maturing process. Teens who develop a reliable moral compass are more likely to make positive decisions and less likely to be lured into negative behaviors. Those who don't are more likely to make poor choices and find themselves at odds with society's rules and laws.

Kohlberg's Levels of Moral Development

One of the most prominent theorists on the subject of moral development was American psychologist Lawrence Kohlberg (1927–1987). Kohlberg believed that moral development takes place in stages and that awareness of other people increases at each stage.

According to Kolhberg, there are six stages of moral development. At the first stage, the notion of what is right and wrong is quite simple, and is based on the idea of law and order. The individual obeys rules to avoid being punished, and doesn't hit for fear of being hit in return.

At Kohlberg's second stage, the level of morality is egocentric: what is right is what benefits the self.

In the third stage, the individual seeks to do what is right in order to gain the approval of others.

The individual in the fourth stage of moral development seeks to abide by the law and fulfill his or her duty. The individual recognizes that a safe society must have rules of behavior, so the person accepts and agrees to the rules that have been decided by others. See Fig. 19-9.

Kohlberg did not believe that all adults reach the fifth stage of moral development. At this stage, the individual better understands the feelings of others and develops a genuine interest in their welfare. The individual becomes more aware of belonging to a family and community and having social responsibilities. He or she recognizes that moral principles are based on individual values and are tied to the need to uphold a system of moral laws for the good of society.

To reach Kohlberg's sixth and highest stage of moral development, or a state of **moral maturity**, a person must be able to recognize and respect other people's points of view. The individual is concerned whether the rules of society are just and fair. Individuals at the sixth stage make decisions based on equal respect for all people.

According to Kohlberg, each stage represents a milestone in moral development. Most people who reach the higher stages do so during adolescence and adulthood.

Social and Cultural Influences on Moral Development

Moral development is an ongoing process that occurs within the context of a person's family, community, and society as a whole. As teens determine what is important to them and strive to establish their own value system, the influence of others—both positive and negative—grows more important.

Fig. 19-9 As teens develop a strong set of values to guide them, they often join with others who share the same values.

Peer Group Pressures

Peer groups can have an enormous influence on teens' moral development. Because teens are still discovering who they are and what is important to them, they look to their peers for approval and guidance. Peers also help teens clarify their values by discussing what's important and providing feedback. Positive peer influence helps teens build stronger convictions and behave according to their values.

Teens who are desperate to become more popular or to gain acceptance can be highly susceptible to negative peer pressure. In their insecurity, they may look up to peers who "break the rules" and show little regard for their own well-being or that of others. Instead of condemning immoral or illegal conduct, these teens imitate it in the hope of gaining praise and acceptance from others. That's how many teens get involved in drugs, drinking, sexual activity, shoplifting, and other negative behaviors that they later regret.

Fig. 19-10 **A popular movie (or music) can send messages.** Do you think today's movies (or music) are more likely to influence teens positively or negatively? Why?

Popular Culture

Teens' moral development is also heavily influenced by the **popular culture**, or the culture that prevails in modern society. Today, the media tend to dominate popular culture. Television, movies, music, magazines, and advertising all portray behaviors and can influence perceptions of right and wrong. See Fig. 19-10.

The media sometimes present negative behaviors in ways that may seem glamorous to adolescents. A successful rock star uses vulgar language. A popular movie shows violence as an acceptable means of resolving differences. Advertisements for alcohol suggest that people really have more fun when they drink. Television programs present rude, immoral, selfish, and antisocial behavior as amusing and harmless. Impressionable teens who are trying to establish their own identities need critical thinking skills to interpret the messages they receive from the media.

Family and Community

Parents have the primary responsibility for teaching their children moral values and helping them develop an accurate moral compass. Schools reinforce the basic values a society needs to function, such as honesty and cooperation. Many families and individuals also draw on their religious faith for moral guidance. Some teens seem to reject the values of their parents, but over time most come to recognize the importance of a healthy system of morality

"I never know what to expect from my fourteen-year-old son," said Yvonne. "One minute, Tyrell is hugging me before he leaves for school and telling me he loves me. The next minute, he's making fun of his sister's singing and telling me I need clothes that don't make me look so much like an 'old lady.' When I confront him about it, he always shrugs and says, 'Mama, you know I was just joking.' He spends a lot of time in the basement alone instead of being with his family."

▶▶ **PERSONAL APPLICATION**

1. As a teen, do you ever feel critical of your parents and siblings?
2. How could you help your family understand and deal with your mood swings?

that all can live by. Parents who practice what they preach and who live according to their professed values are more likely to have a positive influence.

Open and honest communication within the family helps teens learn values. Parents who discuss core values such as honesty and responsibility within the context of daily life can help teens see the role these values play in keeping families and societies functioning. Teens also learn more about values by being given more responsibility within the family. As they make their own choices—and their own mistakes—they can learn from each experience.

Some teens do, of course, break the rules and get into trouble. Parents who know or suspect that a teen is engaging in morally unacceptable behavior need to confront the teen. Even though teens may be reluctant to communicate with their parents about such problems, it is their parents' responsibility to help them change their inappropriate behavior.

Teens learn moral responsibility within the community, too. Every community has expectations and rules to follow. Teens discover that they must follow the rules or suffer the consequences. Gradually they also recognize the reasons behind rules and laws. As they learn to respect the rules of society, teens become better prepared to live successfully in that society.

Sometimes, despite a family's best efforts, a teen seems determined to pursue immoral and harmful behaviors. In such cases, the family may need to seek outside help. The teen might be more willing to listen to a favorite teacher than to family members. Some families choose to get assistance from a member of the clergy or a staff counselor. Teens with serious behavioral problems may need help from professional counselors.

Linking Behavior to Personal Values

A teen's personal values will guide his or her behavior. Teens who develop a strong value system early in the teen years are most likely to avoid negative behaviors and harmful experimentation. Those who give little thought to right and wrong are most likely to have problems.

Teens who mature early are most at risk for engaging in negative behavior. They look older than other teens their age, and for that reason are often pulled into older peer groups. Unfortunately, their mental and emotional maturity lags behind their physical maturity.

Sexual activity carries many risks for teens, including pregnancy and sexually transmitted diseases (STDs). Some STDs, such as chlamydia and gonorrhea, can be cured if they are caught early. Others, such as herpes and HIV/AIDS, are incurable. Teens who engage in sexual behavior run the risk of serious long-term consequences.

Other risky behaviors that can have consequences include drug use and crime. Teens who use drugs risk seriously damaging their health. Death rates are significantly higher for teens who use drugs than for those who don't. Teen drug users also run the risk of contracting HIV/AIDS because the disease can be transmitted through sharing needles. In addition, people who become addicted to drugs may resort to crime to support their drug habit. By abstaining from premature sexual activity, drugs, and other self-destructive behaviors, teens show they value and respect themselves.

Given the risks, negative influences, and potential problems teens encounter, it is hardly surprising that parents are concerned about helping them develop a good moral compass to guide their behavior. Teens need to learn at an early age that all behavior has consequences. Those who receive careful and caring guidance as they build their value system are most likely to stand up to negative peer pressure and media influences.

SECTION 19-3 Review and Activities

Reviewing the Section

1. What does "developing a moral compass" mean?
2. Explain Lawrence Kohlberg's theory of moral development as it applies to adolescents.
3. Why are some teens more likely than others to give in to negative peer pressure?
4. What can parents and other caregivers do to help teens develop positive values?
5. Why are adolescents who mature early at greater risk than other teens for engaging in risky behavior?
6. What risks do teens run if they don't have moral values to guide them?

Observing and Interacting

Give an example of a teen in the media who presents a positive message about moral values.

1. Was it difficult to find a positive example? If so, why?
2. Why do you think so much of what teens see and hear in the media does not support moral values?

Intellectual Development of Adolescents

Dramatic advances in brain development accompany the physical and emotional changes of the adolescent years. As their brains mature, teens start to think less like children and more like adults. They gain the ability to think in more complex and sophisticated ways. This ability enables teens to handle increasingly difficult mental tasks and to use better judgment.

Objectives

- Describe how the brain develops during the teen years.
- Compare theories of intellectual development in adolescence.
- Evaluate the impact of educational experiences on intellectual growth.

Key Terms

prefrontal cortex
amygdala
abstract thought

Getting Older and Smarter

In the early teen years, adolescents experience significant intellectual growth. This growth is due in part to changes in the brain and in part to the gains in education and life experience.

Changes in the Brain

 Recent advances in brain imaging techniques have made it possible for scientists to observe the changes that occur in brain functioning during adolescence. It is now known that the brain starts to grow again just before puberty. It then continues to mature for several years.

The part of the brain that undergoes the most dramatic changes is the **prefrontal cortex**—the part that sits just behind the forehead and controls planning, organization, prioritizing, and other complex thought processes. The growth and maturing of the prefrontal cortex makes it possible for teens to reason better and to control their impulses.

Until the prefrontal cortex is fully developed, teens tend to rely more on another part of the brain—the **amygdala** (uh-MIG-duh-luh), which controls fear, joy, and other emotional reactions. Teens have a tendency to use the emotional part of their brain more than the thinking part. This can lead to impulsive actions based primarily on instinct.

Interestingly, just as in earlier stages of development, the teen brain makes many more new connections than it actually needs. It then goes through a period of consolidation and "pruning" in which unused connections cease functioning.

Brain researchers say this process indicates that the adolescent brain is "a work in progress." They suggest that what teens do during this period of development can affect their thinking skills for the rest of their lives. Those who challenge themselves to develop their intellectual powers are more likely to develop strong brain connections and more advanced thinking skills. See Fig. 19-11.

Two Theories of Teen Intellectual Development

Many people have studied the intellectual growth of adolescents. Two leaders in this field of research were Jean Piaget and Lev Vygotsky.

Piaget's Stage of Formal Operations

Adolescents have reached the fourth and final stage of Piaget's four main stages of intellectual development. Piaget called this the stage of formal operations.

Fig. 19-11 The "use it or lose it" principle suggests that teens can increase their intellectual powers. How can teens take advantage of this opportunity?

This stage of intellectual growth begins at about age 11 and continues into early adulthood (though some psychologists argue that it ends at around age 15). During this period, young people become capable of **abstract thought**. This allows teens to consider what-if situations, to create sophisticated arguments, and to reason from different points of view.

Fig. 19-12 Piaget's Four Periods of Learning

Period	Characteristics
Sensorimotor Birth–2 years	Children learn through their senses and own actions.
Preoperational 2–7 years	Children think in terms of their own activities and what they perceive at the moment.
Concrete operations 7–11 years	Children can think logically but still learn best through experience.
Formal operations 11–Adult	People are capable of abstract thinking.

With their expanding intellectual abilities, young people can organize their thoughts and find solutions to everyday problems. They can also absorb information and apply it to their own lives. Thus they can start making intelligent decisions about their future.

Piaget has had a very strong influence on the field of child psychology, although some have criticized his theories. They argue that his four stages present too rigid a picture of intellectual development. Some of Piaget's critics also believe that he underestimated the influence of culture and social interaction on learning. See Fig. 19-12.

Vygotsky and the Influence of Social Interactions

Vygotsky differed from Piaget in that he placed a stronger emphasis on social interactions. He believed that children develop the ability to think by interacting with parents, teachers, and peers. In this way, they learn to think, gain mastery over their environment, and use language. He believed that language is the most important tool for influencing intellectual development. Younger children use it simply to communicate; adolescents use it as a kind of inner speech to guide what they think and do.

Vygotsky used the term *zone of proximal development* to explain his theory about the role of instruction in a child's learning. The zone of proximal development is the difference between what a child is capable of learning unaided and what the child could learn with the help of a parent or teacher or through collaboration with peers. It is a measure of learning potential. Vygotsky emphasized that only through collaboration with teachers and other students could students rise to the heights of their potential. See Fig. 19-13.

The Impact of Educational Experiences

Even though there are different theories about intellectual development, there can be no doubt that education has a profound

Fig. 19-13 **Vygotsky believed that children and teens could learn more through collaboration with teachers, parents, and peers. For this reason, he saw a clear connection between intellectual development and social interaction.**

impact on learning. This is true for students of all ages, but the school experience is particularly important for teens, given the changes that take place in the brain at this stage. Research has identified factors that influence how a student learns in school. These factors include the classroom environment, the degree of discipline and guidance at the school, and the involvement of parents.

A Positive Learning Environment

How would you describe the environment in your favorite class? It's not surprising that when the learning environment is positive and stimulating, more learning takes place. Students who respect their teachers are more willing to learn. Those who know that they won't be criticized for giving a wrong answer in class feel more comfortable about participating.

Health & Safety

Self-Destructive Behaviors

Adolescence is a time for trying new things. It is not uncommon for teens to experiment with drugs and alcohol. Some try them to fit in. Others do it because they are curious, or as a form of rebellion. Unfortunately, engaging in this kind of behavior can be harmful to one's health and safety. The use of drugs or alcohol can lead to aggressive behavior and health risks, such as seizures and vomiting. Overdosing on drugs or alcohol can be fatal.

When students feel at ease in the classroom, they generally have a more positive attitude about school. This usually translates into more learning when compared with similar students who have negative feelings about school.

The Role of Parents

Although teens often seem embarrassed by their parents, they do want their parents' support. Caring parents do more than simply make sure that their teen goes to school every day and does the required homework. They ask questions about schoolwork, offer suggestions for completing assignments, assist their children as needed, and attend school functions.

Parents also need to emphasize the importance they place on education. If teens fail to complete homework or skip school, parents need to get to the root of the problem and find ways to resolve it. Regular attendance and homework are essential parts of a good education, and a good education is a key to a fulfilling life.

SECTION 19-4 Review and Activities

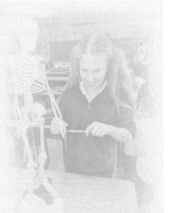

Reviewing the Section

1. Why is the brain of an adolescent said to be "a work in progress"?
2. What kind of thinking is possible during Piaget's stage of formal operations?
3. What did Vygotsky mean by the term "zone of proximal development"?
4. What does a "positive learning environment" mean, and why is it important?
5. How do educational experiences influence intellectual growth?
6. What can parents do to enhance intellectual development in their teen children?

Observing and Interacting

Consider your high school classes. Do you feel that you learn better, as Vygotsky believed, in a small group setting in which you collaborate with peers? Do your teachers lecture or do some allow you and your classmates to present lessons or lead discussion?

Camp Counselor

Camps provide experiences for children that may not be available in their hometowns. A camp counselor might sleep in a tent or a cabin, teach horseback riding or swimming, lead singing sessions, and toast marshmallows by a fire.

▸ Job Responsibilities

Camp counselors are responsible for the health, safety, and well-being of a group of campers. They set a good example, teach skills, counsel, and ensure that campers are successful in their activities. They also develop educational programs and enforce camp rules.

▸ Work Environment

Different kinds of camps operate in the United States: day camps, overnight camps, religious camps, and camps that serve children with special needs.

▸ Education and Training

Being a camp lifeguard or arts and crafts teacher requires specialized knowledge, but being a camp counselor generally requires someone who is adaptable, enthusiastic, and well-organized. Camp counselors must relate well to others—particularly children—and maintain their good humor under stress. Most positions involve knowledge of the outdoor environment.

▸ Skills and Aptitudes

- Ability to model good behavior
- Patience
- Friendly attitude
- Knowledge of principles of health, safety, and nutrition
- Teaching ability

WORKPLACE CONNECTION

1. **Thinking Skills.** If you wanted to work in camps all year, what kinds of work could you do?

2. **Resource Skills.** How could you learn a skill to teach at camp?

SECTION SUMMARIES

- During adolescence, the physical changes that occur due to puberty are completed. (19-1)
- It is important for adolescents to practice good personal hygiene, eat well, exercise, and get enough sleep. (19-1)
- An important part of adolescence is establishing a strong personal identity. (19-2)
- During the teen years, peers become an increasingly important part of life. (19-2)
- Kohlberg believed that moral development takes place in stages. (19-3)
- Social and cultural influences affect moral development. (19-3)
- Changes in the brain during adolescence enable teens to reason better and control impulses. (19-4)
- In Piaget's stage of formal operations, teens become capable of abstract thought. Vygotsky believed that social interactions are essential for learning. (19-4)
- Positive educational experiences contribute to intellectual growth. (19-4)

REVIEWING THE CHAPTER

1. What hormones are involved in male and female sexual development? (19-1)
2. Why are good nutrition and sleep important in the teen years? (19-1)
3. How are the identity theories of Erik Erikson and James Marcia related? (19-2)
4. What are the advantages of having a close friend? (19-2)
5. Give examples of positive values which might be part of a person's "moral compass." (19-3)
6. What occurs during the third stage of Kohlberg's stages of moral development? (19-3)
7. What is the connection between personal values and behavior? (19-3)
8. Why are teens more likely than adults to act on instinct? (19-4)
9. Why do you think a positive and stimulating classroom setting helps one's intellectual growth? (19-4)

THINKING CRITICALLY

1. **Drawing Conclusions.** Why can the teen years be both the most difficult and the most rewarding period of life for many people?
2. **Making Inferences.** What qualities or characteristics do you think allow some teens to get along well with others while remaining true to their own opinions and beliefs?

MAKING CONNECTIONS

1. **Writing.** Write a persuasive essay to convince other teens about the potential dangers of blindly following the crowd.

2. **Science.** In general, do you think that thin, average, and overweight teens eat different portion sizes compared to one another? Do you believe that eating more nutritious foods makes a difference? With a partner, create a hypothesis of the eating habits of teens for each weight category. Discreetly observe and take notes on the eating habits of four anonymous students of each weight group during lunchtime. Report your combined findings in a chart. Does your hypothesis hold true? What other possible factors are involved in weight?

APPLYING YOUR LEARNING

1. **Health Check.** Write down, as best you can remember, how many hours you have slept in the past three days. Are you getting as much sleep as your body needs? If not, what changes could you make in your habits?

2. **Analyzing Behavior.** Brainstorm a list of possible reasons why teens may be unpleasant to others or engage in negative behaviors. Based on one of your possible reasons, write a dialogue in which you persuade a peer to change his or her negative attitude.

Learning from Research

1. Choose one of the following claims to investigate further.
2. How is this finding useful for teens and their parents?
3. Summarize what you've learned about sleep deprivation and its effects on teens.

Sleep Deprivation and Hormones. According to sleep experts, sometime in late puberty, the teen body secretes the sleep-related hormone *melatonin* later than before. This means that teens may feel fully alert later into the evening, making it physically more difficult for them to get up in the morning. How might teens best deal with this hormonal change?

Sleep Deprivation and Emotions. According to Dr. William Dement, a leading sleep expert, lack of adequate sleep (9 hours and 15 minutes for teens) can impair teens' judgment. Long-term sleep deprivation can lead to depression. How might teens cope with feelings of depression brought on by lack of sleep?

Sleep Deprivation and Learning. Research shows that during slow-wave and REM sleep, the connections between nerve cells become stronger, and new skills are reinforced. Getting adequate rest *after* learning a new skill may be more important than sleeping enough the night before an exam. What implications does this have on test preparation?

CHAPTER 20 Children's Health and Safety

Thoughtful Reading:

As you read this chapter:
- Make a prediction about what you are reading.
- Visualize what you are reading and describe it.
- Reflect by writing four sentences about what you have read.

Section 20-1
Childhood Illnesses

Section 20-2
Accidents and Emergencies

Childhood Illnesses

When a child gets sick, parents and other caregivers need to know what to do. They need to be able to recognize common childhood illnesses and distinguish between minor conditions and those that need medical attention. They should also know how to comfort a sick child. Equally important, parents and caregivers should know how to prevent illness when possible.

Objectives

- Explain how regular checkups and immunizations can help prevent illness.
- Outline the causes, symptoms, and treatment of childhood allergies and asthma.
- Discuss effective ways to care for and comfort a sick child.

Key Terms

asthma
communicable diseases
contagious

Regular Health Care

Children, like adults, should have regular medical checkups. Health problems can often be detected in their early stages during a checkup. Early detection followed by early treatment may prevent a minor condition from becoming serious. In addition, checkups can assure parents that their children are developing normally. See Fig. 20-1 on page 576.

During their first year, babies should be examined regularly. After the first year, healthy children need checkups less frequently but at least once a year. Because these checkups are so important, many local health departments have free or inexpensive clinics that provide examinations and medical care for children who do not have their own pediatrician.

If a child shows symptoms that cause concern, parents or caregivers should call the child's doctor. In younger children, fever, lack of energy, prolonged diarrhea, constipation, vomiting, or difficulty breathing all warrant a call to the doctor. In older children, symptoms to bring to a doctor's attention include fever, persistent cough, vomiting, severe headache, or dizziness.

Immunization

To *immunize* is to protect a person against a particular disease. People can be protected from many **communicable diseases**—diseases that are passed from one person to another—by being immunized.

The most common way to immunize people is to administer a *vaccine*. A vaccine is a

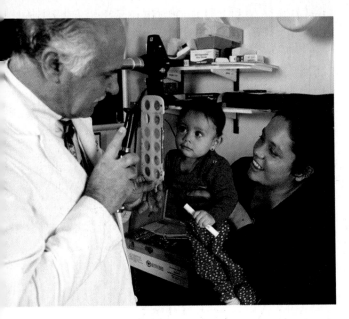

Fig. 20-1 **Regular checkups go a long way toward keeping a child healthy.**

small amount of a disease-causing agent that is introduced into the body so that a person can build resistance to it. After getting a vaccine, a person's body produces antibodies, substances capable of fighting off germs for that disease. For example, if Monica gets the vaccine for chicken pox at twelve months of age, she has the antibodies to fight it if she is later exposed to the disease.

Figure 20-2 shows what immunizations a child should receive and when. Parents are responsible for making sure their children get the immunizations they need at the right times. They should keep a record of each child's immunizations.

Many states require all children to be immunized for certain diseases before they enter school. Many also require that children in child care centers be immunized. In fact, children under the age of five are most likely to develop complications from the diseases, so parents should not wait until their children start elementary school to have them immunized.

Some parents worry that a vaccine could harm their child. In extremely rare cases, a child does have a bad reaction to a vaccine. Parents should discuss these concerns with their child's doctor. In most cases, the chances of getting the disease are much greater than the chances of having a bad reaction to a vaccine.

Common Childhood Conditions

Two conditions—allergies and asthma—are becoming increasingly common among children. Most children can live normal lives with these conditions as long as they receive proper medical care.

Allergies

An allergy is an extreme sensitivity to one or more common substances. Children may have allergic reactions when they eat or drink certain foods or inhale certain airborne particles. Foods that commonly cause allergic reactions in babies and children include milk, grains, eggs, shellfish, nuts, fruit juices, chocolate, and food additives. Airborne substances that can cause reactions include pollens, dust mites, molds, air pollution, and tobacco smoke. Symptoms of an allergic reaction may be mild, such as a rash, a runny nose with clear drainage, or itchy eyes. Some allergic reactions, however, may be serious or even life-threatening. Sometimes, for instance, the air sacs in the lungs may become constricted, cutting the flow of oxygen in the body.

More than one-third of the children in the United States develop some type of allergy. Specific allergies are not inherited, but the tendency to be allergic seems to be. If both parents have allergies, their child has a 70 percent chance of having at least one.

Fig. 20-2 Schedule of Immunizations

Age	Birth	1 mo	2 mo	4 mo	6 mo	12 mo	15 mo	18 mo	24 mo	4–6 yrs	11–12 yrs	13–18 yrs
Vaccine												
Hepatitis B	HepB #1	HepB #2[b]			HepB #3[b]				HepB[a b]			
Diphtheria, Tetanus, Pertussis (DPT) 4-dose series with boosters		DPT #1	DPT #2	DPT #3		DPT #4				DPT #5	Booster	Booster[c]
H. Influenza type B		HiB #1	HiB #2	HiB #3	HiB #4[b f]							
Polio		Polio #1	Polio #2		Polio #3[b]					Polio #4		
Measles, Mumps, Rubella						MMR #1[b]				MMR #2	MMR #2[b]	
Varicella (chicken pox)						Varicella[b]			Varicella[b g]			
Pneumococcal		PCV #1	PCV #2	PCV #3	PCV #4[b]			PCV[b]				
Influenza					Influenza (yearly)[d]							
Hepatitis A									Hepatitis A[e]			

Notes

Blue indicates that if child did not receive a dose of vaccine earlier, she or he can receive it during the period in blue.

a: If the child did not receive the Hepatitis B vaccine earlier, the three-dose series should be given during this period.

b: Can be given any time during this period.

c: Tetanus and diphtheria boosters should be repeated every 10 years after this.

d: Influenza vaccine is recommended yearly for children older than 6 months who have certain risk factors, including asthma, HIV, and other diseases. The vaccine is also recommended for healthy children between 6 and 23 months of age.

e: Hepatitis A vaccine is recommended for children and adolescents who live in high-risk areas or belong to high-risk groups.

f: May not be necessary if a certain brand of vaccine was given in the first two doses.

g: Second dose should be given before the age of 12.

Note: This information is periodically reviewed and updated. Check the Web sites of the Centers for Disease Control (www.cdc.gov/nip/acip) or American Academy of Pediatrics for the most current information.

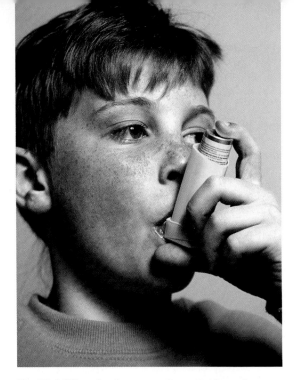

Fig. 20-3 **Wheezing from an asthma attack can be controlled with an inhaler which delivers medicine to the lungs.**

Allergies can't be cured, but their effects can often be prevented. For example, a child who is allergic to a specific food can avoid that food. One who is allergic to pollens can be encouraged to play indoors during peak pollen periods.

If an allergy causes severe problems, a series of allergy tests can determine which specific substances are causing the problems so that they can be avoided in the future. Medication or injections are used to control allergies.

Asthma

A growing health problem among children in this country is **asthma**. This condition causes the lungs to contract more than they should, narrowing the air passages and making it difficult to breathe.

Asthma attacks can be brought on by an allergic reaction. They may also be caused by a cold or the flu, physical activity, or exposure to cold air, smoke, or other irritants. Signs that a child may be having an asthma attack include coughing, wheezing, rapid breathing, and shortness of breath.

Children with asthma can take medication to open their airways and breathe more easily. A doctor must prescribe the medicine. Some medicines are taken every day to prevent asthma attacks, while others are taken to relieve an attack when it happens. Older children can be taught to give themselves their medication when they need it. See Fig. 20-3.

Caring for a Sick Child

All children get sick from time to time. Caregivers need to recognize the symptoms of common illnesses. Of course, parents shouldn't hesitate to call the doctor's office. Often, a nurse assesses the symptoms, consults with the doctor, and determines if the child should be seen. Figure 20-4 provides detailed information about some childhood diseases.

Caring for a sick child may involve little more than keeping the child inside and comfortable for a while. Recovery from many childhood illnesses takes only a few days. It may also be important to keep the child away from other children during the **contagious** period of an illness. This is the time when a child can pass the illness on to someone else. In general, children with a fever should not go to school or to a child care setting.

Children may need medicine to relieve pain or to reduce fever. Never give aspirin to a child with a fever. Some children with a fever who take aspirin develop a serious illness called Reye syndrome. Also, be sure to use only children's medicines recommended by the doctor, not those meant for adults.

Fig. 20-4 Identifying and Treating Diseases

Disease	Signs	Treatment
Chicken Pox	A red, itchy rash appears first, usually on the head and back. It may spread to cover the entire body. The rash begins as small bumps that look like pimples. These develop into fluid-filled blisters, which break open, leaving sores that become dry, brown scabs. Fever usually rises no higher than 102°F (39°C).	Rest in bed during initial stage. Give acetaminophen to relieve fever. Keep the child cool in loose clothing. Apply calamine lotion to relieve itching, or cool baths with baking soda or oatmeal added. Usually lasts 7 to 10 days. Marks left on the skin may take 6 to 12 months to fade.
Common Cold	Stuffy or runny nose, sneezing or coughing, mild fever, sore throat, diminished appetite.	Encourage rest and plenty of liquids. Give acetaminophen to reduce fever. Recovery takes 7 to 10 days.
Ear Infection	An infant may pull at the ear and cry; an older child is likely to say that the ear hurts. During the infection, there may be some temporary hearing loss. There is usually a fever.	See a doctor, who may prescribe an antibiotic. For a fever, use cool baths and acetaminophen.
Influenza (Flu)	Sudden onset of fever, chills, shakes, nausea, tiredness, and aching muscles. After a few days, a sore throat and stuffy nose may occur. The disease may last as long as a week.	Encourage rest and plenty of liquids. Doctors may prescribe antiviral medications for certain strains of flu. They may reduce the severity of the symptoms and shorten their duration.
Strep Throat and Scarlet Fever	Sudden onset, with headache, fever, sore throat not accompanied by runny nose or congestion, painful swallowing, white patches on the tonsils, loss of appetite, and fatigue. In scarlet fever, a rash of fine red dots usually appears within 24 hours. The rash is seen first on the neck and upper part of the chest before spreading. When it fades, the skin peels.	See a doctor, who will prescribe antibiotics for a positive throat culture. The child should rest in a warm, well-ventilated room. Throat lozenges and iced drinks can help reduce pain. Patients usually recover in a week. (The rash is the only sign that differentiates scarlet fever from strep throat.)

"I'm sooo bored," seven-year-old Tanner complained to his mother. Tanner was recovering from strep throat and this was the second day of school he had missed. "I just saw the school bus. Chase is home. Can't I have him over for just a little while? I feel fine!" he begged. Tanner's mother knew he was telling the truth. He was feeling fine for now, but when the acetaminophen wore off, his fever would be back and he would feel tired again. "You'll have to wait a few days to have anyone come over, Tanner. You wouldn't want Chase to get strep throat too, would you?" As much as Mrs. Ridgeway hated to miss another day of work, she knew that Tanner would have to stay home from school at least another day. Their doctor advised parents to keep children home for 24 hours after a fever was truly over and not just being controlled by medication. "Tanner, we've got time to watch a movie or play a game before I make supper. Or we could open that new sand art kit that you got for your birthday. What do you want to do?"

▶▶ **PERSONAL APPLICATION**

When was the last time you were sick? Did you think you were better only to realize that the feeling was temporary? Why do you think it's important for people to stay home from school and work when they're sick?

Comforting a Sick Child

It's important to maintain a calm and cheerful manner around a child who is sick. Treat the illness matter-of-factly while remembering that the child may need some extra love and attention.

Children who are very ill don't have much energy and may spend a lot of time sleeping. Children who have only a mild illness, however, and those who are recovering after a serious illness, may get restless and easily bored. Quiet play, especially with a caregiver, helps pass the time.

Children's behavior and needs during illness depend on their age. Infants may sleep much more than usual and tend to want lots of physical comforting. Children between one and three are usually very active and may have trouble staying in bed. Doctors might allow them to play quietly in the house if they feel up to it. Older children can often help take care of themselves. They usually enjoy reading books, doing puzzles, and playing games like checkers while they are recovering.

Going to the Hospital

A hospital stay can be a difficult experience for a child. Children may fear that they will never go home, or that they will be hurt, or will die. They may be frightened by unfamiliar doctors and nurses.

Parents can prepare their child for a hospitalization, unless it's an emergency. They can explain in simple terms what to expect. If possible, parents should take the child to tour the hospital. They may be able to see patient rooms, operating rooms, and recovery rooms. When the child is admitted, these things are already familiar and therefore less frightening.

Provide Good Nutrition During Illness

A sick child needs encouragement to eat small, frequent meals. Poor appetite during an illness is normal. If you have had the flu, you probably remember that eating was the last thing on your mind. The same response occurs in babies and children, but their smaller bodies can't go as long without food and liquids. There are some ways to provide the nutrition children need when they are sick:

- **Give the child more liquids.** Children need liquids to avoid *dehydration*—the depletion of essential body fluids. One liquid is a sugar and mineral (glucose-electrolyte) solution, which can be found in most drugstores. Breast-feeding for babies should not be interrupted.

- **Encourage the child to eat.** Children who are ill often aren't interested in eating. Keep offering foods the child likes, a little at a time and as often as possible. *Clear liquids* are often prescribed. These include water, chicken broth, fruit juices, and gelatin without fruit.

- **Don't force the child to eat.** One or two days of low food intake won't harm a child, as long as he or she gets enough liquids.

If illness and poor appetite persist for more than a few days, a doctor should be consulted. The child isn't fully recovered from an illness until he or she weighs about the same as before the illness began.

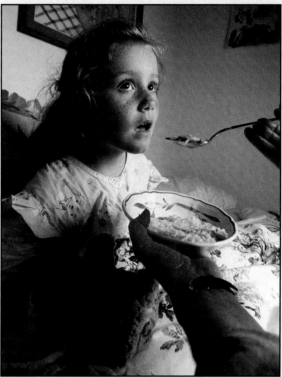

YOUR TURN

What are some ways to make food and liquids more appealing to a child who isn't interested in either?

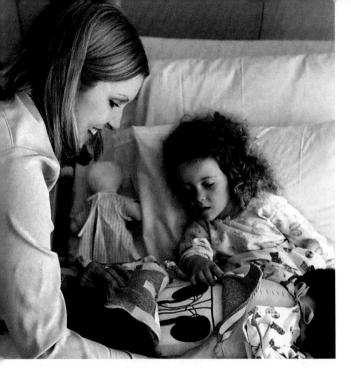

The Hospital Stay

Hospital staff recognize that children are more at ease and may recover more quickly if a parent stays with them. Some hospitals provide a cot in the child's room so that a parent can sleep nearby. Other hospitals have rooms with space for both the child and a parent. Even when there are no such arrangements, parents can often visit their child any time. See Fig. 20-5.

While in the hospital, a child may need many tests and forms of treatment. When the child asks, "Will this hurt?" the parent should answer truthfully. Although parents may not want to upset the child, it is actually more helpful to say something like, "Yes, it will hurt for a while, but then you will feel much better. It's all right for you to cry when it hurts, if you feel like it."

Fig. 20-5 Children are usually allowed to bring special items to the hospital to make their stay more comfortable, such as a special toy or blanket.

SECTION 20-1 Review and Activities

Reviewing the Section

1. Why should children have regular medical checkups?
2. What are antibodies and what is the purpose behind producing them by vaccination?
3. What is an allergy? Give three examples of substances that might cause an allergic reaction.
4. What signs indicate a possible *asthma* attack? What is one way to treat asthma?
5. Why should a sick child be kept away from other children during the *contagious* period of a disease?
6. Would a doctor prescribe an antibiotic for a cold? For an ear infection? Explain.

Observing and Interacting

Visit the Web site of a hospital in your community or region that serves children. Make a list of the special services the hospital offers for young patients and their families.

Accidents and Emergencies

A caregiver's most important responsibility is to keep children safe. Young children, in particular, simply don't know what can harm them. While caregivers can protect children from many hazards, accidents still happen. Caregivers need to be prepared for possible emergencies. Anyone who cares for children should know basic first-aid skills.

Objectives

- Describe how to prepare for the possibility of a fire.
- Outline the steps to follow in an emergency situation.
- Describe appropriate first-aid procedures for common childhood injuries.
- Identify the rescue techniques to use in life-threatening situations.

Key Terms

fracture
sprain
abdominal thrusts
convulsion
hives
shock
rescue breathing
cardiopulmonary resuscitation (CPR)

Safety

To keep children safe, caregivers need to know what to expect. Each age has its particular hazards because children of different ages have different interests and abilities. Special "Health and Safety" features throughout this textbook highlight these dangers. Infants, for example, will chew on almost anything and run the risk of choking, suffocation, or poisoning. Toddlers are so mobile that they can quickly get into dangerous situations if not watched constantly. Preschoolers and older children need frequent safety reminders from watchful caregivers. Safety both in and around vehicles is essential for all children.

If you care for children in their own home, one possible emergency you need to pre-plan for is a fire. Locate all outside doors. Note escape routes from various parts of the home. Find out whether the home has smoke detectors and a fire extinguisher. Ask whether the parents have an escape plan for a fire. If so, have them review it with you.

If a fire does break out, remember that the children are your first responsibility. Lead or carry them to safety. Then call the fire department.

Guidelines for Fast Action

Even if you don't spend a great deal of time with children, you should be prepared to act quickly in an emergency. Fast action can make the difference between minor harm and more serious injury. Memorizing the following five steps will help you if an accident does occur:

1. **Stay calm.** A soothing approach will help reassure the child and keep your thoughts clear.
2. **Evaluate the situation.** Is the injury minor or serious? Can you handle it on your own, or do you need someone else to help?
3. **Provide comfort.** Offer words of comfort if the injury is minor, along with treatment. If the injury is serious, keep the child warm until help arrives. Don't move the child.
4. **Call for help if necessary.** If you don't know what to do or the child is seriously injured, call for help. Keep a list of emergency numbers on hand. In many communities, you can get help by calling 911. Know how to contact an ambulance service, the child's doctor, and nearby hospitals. The parents of any child in your care should provide you with all the relevant phone numbers.

Learning Through  PLAY

Bicycle Safety Classes

While bike riding is fun, it also raises serious safety concerns. Every child who rides a bike should know and practice safe bike-riding techniques. Some park districts, schools, and bicycle shops offer bicycle safety classes for children of various ages. Learning the "rules of the road" is very important. Knowing which side of the street to ride on and signaling to make a turn are just two of these rules. In addition, a bike rider should always wear a protective helmet. This helps shield the brain if a crash or an accident occurs.

Following Up

What bike paths and other options for safe riding are available near your home?

When you call for help, give the child's age and state your name and your relationship to the child. Give the address of your location. Describe the problem clearly, answer any questions, and then follow instructions.

5. **Give basic first aid.** If you know what to do, provide the necessary treatment. If you're not sure how to handle the injury, keep the child comfortable and wait until help arrives.

First Aid

General first-aid guidelines for a variety of childhood injuries appear on the pages that follow. Reading about first aid is no substitute, though, for getting practical, hands-on training. If you plan to take care of children, contact the American Red Cross for information about first-aid training classes.

Bleeding

Many common injuries involve bleeding. To prevent the spread of disease, child care workers are advised to wear disposable gloves when giving first aid to a bleeding child.

• **Minor cuts or scrapes.** To stop the bleeding, place a clean cloth or gauze pad on the cut and apply firm pressure until the bleeding stops. Then clean the area with mild soap and warm water. Dry the wound, and apply an antiseptic ointment or solution. Cover the wound with an adhesive bandage or sterile gauze. See Fig. 20-6.

Fig. 20-6 **You can treat minor cuts by gently cleaning the cut, applying an antiseptic, and then covering it with a bandage.** What should you do if a child receives a more serious cut?

• **Deep cuts or wounds.** If the bleeding doesn't stop, or if the wound seems very deep, seek medical attention immediately. Continue to try to stop the bleeding until help arrives. Don't try to use a tourniquet—a bandage that cuts off the blood supply to a portion of the body. This could seriously harm the victim.

• **Nosebleeds.** Have the child sit or stand and lean slightly forward over a sink or bowl. Squeeze the lower half of the child's nose with a tissue for about ten minutes, then release your hold and check if a clot has formed and the bleeding has stopped. If not, apply pressure again for ten minutes. If you can't stop the bleeding, get medical help.

Bumps and Bruises

Minor bruises can be treated for ten minutes with a cold pack or even a bag of frozen vegetables. Place a towel between the cold pack and the child's skin. A bruised arm or leg should be kept elevated for a while. A fall resulting in a hard blow to the head can be serious. Seek medical help right away if a child loses consciousness, becomes drowsy or irritable, complains of a headache, or vomits.

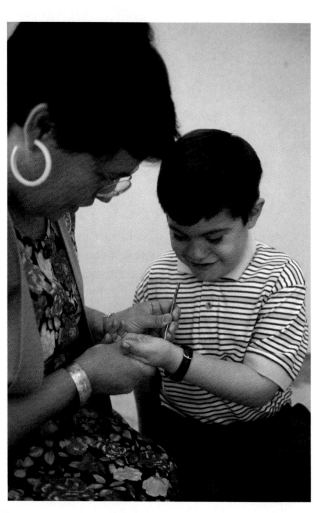

Fig. 20-7 **Pulling gently and smoothly on a splinter helps to remove it in one piece.**

Fractures and Sprains

A **fracture** is a break or crack in a bone. A **sprain** is an injury caused by sudden, violent stretching of a joint or muscle. Both may cause pain, swelling, and bruising. It's often difficult to tell a fracture from a sprain without an X ray.

If you suspect that a child has a fracture or a sprain, don't move the child until you know how serious the injury is. This is particularly important if the injury is to the head, neck, or back. Movement can cause further damage. Call for qualified medical help.

For a mild sprain, elevate the injured area and apply cold packs to help reduce swelling. If the pain persists, check with a doctor about further treatment.

Splinters and Thorns

A splinter is a tiny piece of wood, metal, glass, or plastic that becomes embedded in the skin. Thorns are treated like splinters. Although splinters are usually not dangerous, they do hurt and can cause an infection.

If the splinter is sticking out of the skin and is small, you can use tweezers to remove it. Sterilize the tweezers in boiling water or in the flame of a candle or match. Pull evenly on the exposed part of the splinter to remove it, then put antiseptic and a bandage on the wound.

If a splinter is just under the surface of the skin and is not glass, you can remove it with a sterilized needle and tweezers. Use the needle to break the skin and expose the end of the splinter. Grasp the end of the splinter with the tweezers, and gently pull it out. Clean and cover the wound. See Fig. 20-7.

Large, deeply embedded splinters, glass splinters, and those in the eye can be more serious and should be removed by a medical professional.

Burns

First aid for a burn depends on the cause of the burn and how serious it is. All but small surface burns are serious because they may cause shock, infection, or scarring. Burns are classified by degrees.

- **First-degree burns are mild and may turn the skin pink or red.** There are no blisters or peeling. First-degree burns may be caused by too much sun, hot objects, hot water, or steam. Put the burned area under cold water, or cool it with a cold, wet cloth, then keep it dry and clean. Don't put ointment on the burn; it should heal rapidly. See Fig. 20-8.

- **Second-degree burns are red and form blisters.** They can be caused by sun exposure or hot liquids and flames. If the burned area is small, cover it with a clean, wet cloth and take the child to see a doctor. If the burned area is large, cover the child with a blanket or clean sheet and call for emergency help.

- **Third-degree burns leave the skin blackened or white.** These burns don't always cause pain because nerve endings may have been destroyed. They can be caused by flames, extremely hot objects, or electricity. Immediate medical care is essential. Get the child to the hospital as quickly as possible.

- **Chemical burns.** Household products, such as drain cleaners and disinfectants, can burn the skin. Always check the directions and cautions on product labels. Using protective gloves, wash off

Fig. 20-8 **Cooling a first-degree burn quickly stops its spread.** What is the difference between first-degree and second-degree burns?

the affected area immediately and thoroughly with cool water. Remove any clothing with the chemical on it, unless the clothing has stuck to the skin. Seek immediate medical attention.

- **Electrical burns.** These burns may be deep, but they often appear to be minor, leaving only a small black dot on the skin. Cool the burn with water, and cover it with a clean, smooth cloth. Have the child lie down with legs elevated and head turned to one side to prevent shock. Call emergency services.

Choking

Choking occurs when a person's airway becomes blocked by a piece of food or some other object. Young children are particularly prone to choking because they tend to put all kinds of objects, including small toys, into their mouths. If the object isn't removed, air will not reach the lungs and the person could die.

A choking child may wheeze or make high-pitched noises or gurgling sounds. An inability to speak, breathe, or cry and a bluish tint to the face are other signs of choking.

If a child is choking, you must act quickly. For a choking infant, follow the steps shown in Fig. 20-9. For children older than one and for adults, use **abdominal thrusts**, a technique of quick upward thrusts into the victim's abdomen that force the air in the lungs to expel the object. Figure 20-10 illustrates the technique.

The amount of pressure to use depends on the age and size of the choking person. Too much pressure can harm a child. Get training in using abdominal thrusts before you need to use the technique.

Fig. 20-9
Rescue Technique for Choking Infants

Step 1: Place the infant stomach-down across your forearm, using your thigh or lap for support, and hold the infant's chest in your hand and jaw in your fingers.

Step 2: Point the infant's head downward and give up to five quick, firm blows to the infant's back with the heel of your hand.

If this procedure fails to expel the object that is causing the choking, follow these steps:

Step 3: Turn the infant face up. Lay the infant on your thigh or lap, and support the infant's head with your hand.

Step 4: Using your other hand, place two fingers on the middle of the infant's breastbone just below the nipples. Give up to five quick downward thrusts.

Step 5: Continue giving five back blows followed by five chest thrusts until the object is dislodged or the infant loses consciousness.

If the child does lose consciousness or starts to turn blue, immediate cardiopulmonary resuscitation (CPR) is needed. Have someone call 911, and begin CPR if you have been trained. Also, look into the infant's throat. If you can see the object that is causing the choking and think you might be able to grasp it, try to remove it with a finger.

Convulsions

A **convulsion**, or seizure, is a brief period during which muscles suddenly contract, causing the person to fall and twitch or jerk. Most convulsions last less than five minutes. There are many causes of convulsions. In infants and toddlers, the most common cause is a high fever.

During a convulsion, don't move the child but move any hard objects out of the way. Don't try to restrain the child or stop the movements. Loosen any tight clothing, especially around the neck. If the child vomits, or if saliva builds up in the mouth, turn the child onto his or her side or stomach to help drain the fluids. Don't attempt to put anything into the child's mouth.

Focus on bringing the fever down by applying cool washcloths to the forehead and neck. After the convulsion is over, give the child acetaminophen. If the

Fig. 20-10
Rescue Technique for Choking Children and Adults

If the victim is standing or sitting:

Step 1: Stand behind the victim. Make a fist with one hand and place it, with the thumb toward the victim, just above the child's navel.

Step 2: Grasp the fist with your other hand.

Step 3: Thrust your fist upward and inward quickly. Repeat the technique until you dislodge the object.

If the victim is unconscious:

Step 1: Position the victim on his or her back, and look inside the mouth. If you can see the object, use a sweeping motion with your index finger to remove it.

Step 2: If not, kneel over the victim, place the heel of one hand in the middle of the abdomen just above the navel, and place your other hand on top of the first hand.

Step 3: Give five quick thrusts, pressing your hands in and up.

Step 4: Open the victim's mouth again, and sweep the area again to try to remove the blockage.

Step 5: Repeat these steps until the object is expelled or help arrives.

Step 6: If the victim stops breathing, begin CPR if you have been trained in this technique.

seizure lasts more than five minutes, or if the child remains confused or groggy, call emergency services for further instructions. See Fig. 20-11.

Animal or Human Bites

Many young children suffer bites, mostly from household pets or from other children. For a bite that doesn't break the skin or a small puncture wound, wash the area with soap and water and flush with water for several minutes. Apply antibiotic ointment and give acetaminophen for pain relief if necessary.

If the wound is more serious and is actively bleeding, apply pressure to stop the bleeding, and then elevate the area of the bite. If the wound is bleeding heavily and the child cannot move or is too weak to stand, apply pressure to the wound and call emergency services. If the animal that bit the child was a bat, fox, coyote, skunk, or raccoon, call the local health department so that the animal can be caught and tested for rabies. The child must be given shots to prevent the disease after being bitten by an infected animal.

Any bite that punctures the skin carries a risk of infection. Cat bites, in particular, tend to cause infection. The site of a bite should be checked for several days. If the bite becomes infected, medical help is needed.

Insect Stings and Bites

The greatest risks from stings and bites are allergic reactions and infections. Any child known to be allergic to bee stings should be taken to a doctor immediately after being stung. Other symptoms after a sting that require immediate medical attention include wheezing, tightness in the chest, vomiting or dizziness, and heavy perspiration. A severe allergic reaction called *anaphylactic shock* can cause the airway to swell shut and a person to die. You should also seek help if a child is stung in the mouth or breaks out in blisterlike sores called **hives**.

You can remove a bee's stinger by scraping it with a blunt-edged object, such as a credit card. Wash the area with soap and water, and apply a cold pack. Give acetaminophen for pain. Watch

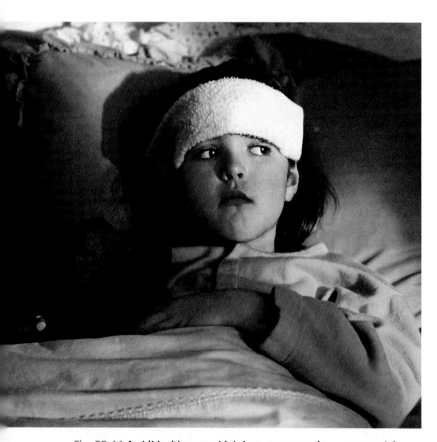

Fig. 20-11 **A child with a very high fever may experience a convulsion. Applying a cool washcloth to the forehead can help reduce a fever.**

the site for signs of infection over the next few days.

Ticks are small insects that cling to the skin and may carry diseases. If you find a tick on a child, use tweezers to grasp the tick as close to the skin as possible. Then pull the tick off in one smooth motion. Wash the area well with soap and water.

Mosquito, ant, and chigger bites are annoying but not usually dangerous. A paste of baking soda and water or calamine lotion will generally relieve itching. Using witch hazel or rubbing alcohol on the spot will also provide relief. See Fig. 20-12.

Poisoning

Children are inquisitive and don't readily comprehend danger. Young children tend to put things in their mouth. This combination of factors can lead to poisoning. Recognizing that a child has been poisoned isn't always easy. The following symptoms may indicate poisoning:

- Inability to track movement with the eyes
- Burns or stains around the mouth
- Strange-smelling breath
- Difficulty breathing
- Unconsciousness
- Fever
- Rash
- Burning or irritation of the eyes or blindness
- Choking, coughing, nausea, dizziness

If you believe a child has swallowed, breathed in, or touched poison, call the nearest hospital or a poison control center. Be prepared to describe what poisoned the child; how the poison was taken; if the child has vomited; the child's age, weight, and height; and any health problems the child has. Keep the container that held the

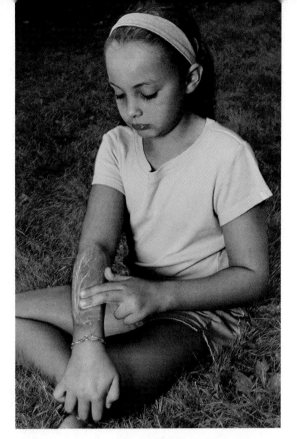

Fig. 20-12 **You can relieve itching from insect bites by dabbing them with calamine lotion or an anti-itch preparation.**

poison with you when you call so that you can answer any questions about it. Follow the directions you receive. Take the container with you if you are told to take the child to the emergency room. Figure 20-13 on page 592 gives examples of poisons and lists the ways children usually come into contact with them.

Shock

When a person suffers a severe injury, loses a great deal of blood, or is severely burned or poisoned, the body may go into **shock**. Important body functions, including breathing and heartbeat, are impaired. Symptoms of shock include cool, clammy skin; a rapid and weak pulse; shallow

Fig. 20-13 Common Household Poisons

Kind of Poison	Examples	Type of Contact
Medicines	Painkillers, stimulants, sleeping pills, aspirin, vitamins, cold medicines	Swallowing
Cleaning Products	Ammonia, automatic dishwashing detergent, laundry detergent, bleach, drain and toilet-bowl cleaner, disinfectant, furniture polish	Swallowing, contact with skin or eyes, inhaling
Personal Care Products	Shampoo, conditioner, soap, nail polish remover, perfume, after-shave lotions, mouthwash, rubbing alcohol	Swallowing, contact with skin or eyes, inhaling
Gardening and Garage Products	Insecticides, fertilizers, rat and mouse poisons, acids, gasoline, paint thinner, charcoal lighter fluid, antifreeze	Swallowing, contact with skin or eyes, inhaling
Plants	Some wild mushrooms, English ivy, daffodil bulbs, rhubarb leaves, holly berries, poinsettias, poison ivy and poison oak	Swallowing, contact with skin or eyes

breathing; and enlarged pupils. Sometimes a person in shock loses consciousness.

Shock can be serious and must be treated quickly. If you suspect a child is in shock, seek medical help immediately. Lay the child down on a soft surface and raise the feet higher than the head. Loosen tight clothing, and keep the child warm until help arrives.

Rescue Techniques

When a child stops breathing, or when a child's heart stops beating, immediate and correct action is vital. Learning rescue techniques will enable you to respond quickly—and possibly save a life.

Rescue Breathing

Rescue breathing is a procedure for forcing air into the lungs of a person who is not breathing. In children, breathing may stop as a result of drowning, choking, serious head injury, poisoning, or other emergency situations. If the brain is deprived of oxygen for five minutes, brain damage may result. Longer periods without oxygen usually result in death. The technique to use with infants and small children is shown in Fig. 20-14. Child care workers should wear gloves and use a protective face mask when using this technique. You can learn more about rescue breathing in a rescue training class.

Fig. 20-14
Rescue Breathing for Infants and Small Children

If you determine that a child is not breathing, send someone to call 911 and follow the steps below. If you are alone and no one hears your call for help, continue the following steps for one minute. Then make the 911 call yourself.

Step 1: Place the child face up on a firm surface. Turn the child's head to one side and clear the mouth of any fluid or foreign matter. If there is an object caught in the child's throat, use the procedure for choking described on pages 588–589. You should remove the object only if it is visible and loose.

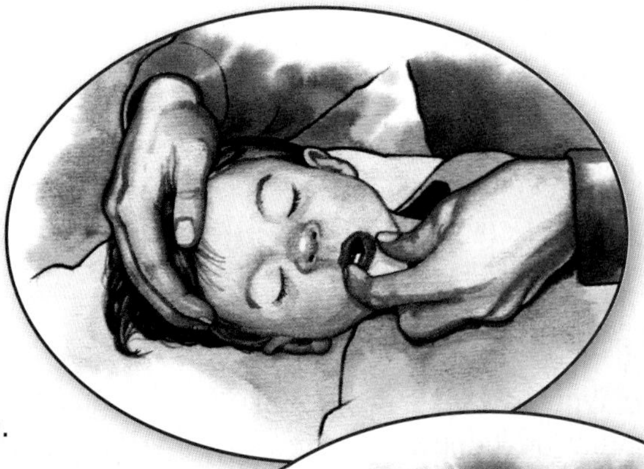

Step 2: To open the child's airway, lift the child's chin with one hand and push down on the forehead with the other.

Step 3: Take a breath, cover the child's mouth with your mouth, and pinch the nose closed. Keeping the child's chin lifted, give one slow breath. If you see the child's chest rise, remove your mouth and let the child's lungs expel the air. Then repeat the breathing. If the chest does not rise, position the head, as in Step 2, and attempt another breath. If the second breath does not make the chest rise, use the procedure for choking described on pages 588–589.

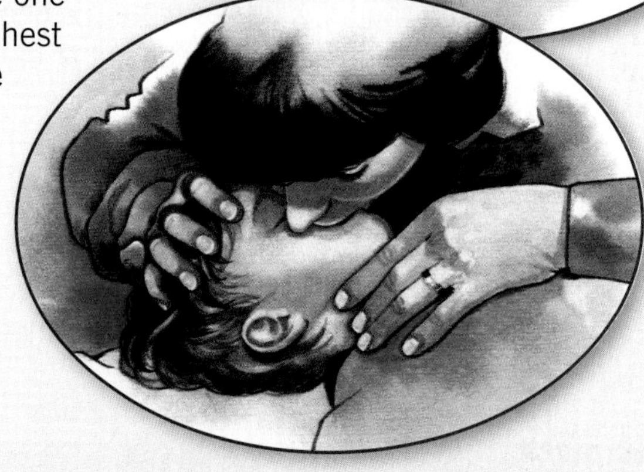

Step 4: If the child is still not breathing and there are no signs of life, CPR, which combines chest compressions with rescue breathing, should be started immediately.

Cardiopulmonary Resuscitation (CPR)

Cardiopulmonary resuscitation (CPR) can save the life of a child who has stopped breathing and whose heart has stopped beating. The technique combines rescue breathing with chest compressions to restore breathing and circulation. The technique used for infants and children is different from that used for adults. Only people who have received training from a certified instructor can perform CPR. Many communities offer training programs. For information, call your local chapter of the American Red Cross or the American Heart Association.

SECTION 20-2 Review and Activities

Reviewing the Section

1. What steps would you take to be prepared in case a fire broke out where you were caring for children?
2. List five guidelines for responding to an accident or injury.
3. When you call for help in an emergency, what information should you give the operator?
4. How should you treat a nosebleed?
5. Briefly describe the three degrees of burns. Give an example of how you would treat a burn in one of the categories.
6. What should you do if you think a child has been poisoned?
7. What action should you take to help a choking toddler?
8. What is *rescue breathing*? Under what circumstances would rescue breathing be needed?

Observing and Interacting

Visit a park or playground, and observe a group of children playing. Identify any potential hazards you notice. What types of injuries or accidents might occur at the playground? Write a list of first-aid guidelines that you think should be posted at the park or playground.

Emergency Medical Technician (EMT)

A woman is in labor. A child falls into an icy creek. A cut on a boy's finger won't stop bleeding. When people call for help, emergency medical technicians (EMTs) rush to the scene. When they arrive, they are expected to know what to do—and to do it quickly.

▶ Job Responsibilities

In many communities, 911 operators dispatch EMTs and other helpers. Once EMTs arrive, they decide what the patient needs. They gather information from others on the scene and then provide emergency care. During the trip to the hospital, they monitor the patient's signs of life and give additional care if necessary. At the hospital, they report what they did and observed. After each trip, they replace supplies, check equipment, and decontaminate their vehicles if the patient had a contagious disease.

▶ Working Conditions

EMTs never know where their work will take them. They must be fit enough to bend and kneel and strong enough to lift patients. The work can be stressful: speed is critical, the hours are irregular, and many of the patients are in distress. However, EMTs find it rewarding to help the injured and critically ill. Many thrive on the fast pace and challenge.

▶ Education and Training

EMTs are trained at four levels: basic, intermediate 1 and 2, and paramedic. An EMT's level of training determines what he or she can do.

▶ Skills and Aptitudes

- Empathy
- Agility
- Strength
- Emotional stability
- Energy
- Interest in medicine

WORKPLACE CONNECTION

1. **Thinking Skills.** How might you learn how to cope better with stress?

2. **Resource Skills.** If you wanted to become an EMT, how could you find out about training programs available in your area?

Review and Activities

SECTION SUMMARIES

- Regular checkups allow health problems to be detected early. (20-1)
- Immunizations against certain diseases produce antibodies that fight off the germs that cause them. (20-1)
- Children who have allergies and asthma can take steps to avoid the causes and treat the symptoms. (20-1)
- Caregivers should know the general steps to follow when a child gets sick or injured. (20-2)
- Appropriate first aid for common childhood injuries depends on the severity of the injury. (20-2)
- The rescue technique to use with a person who is choking depends on the victim's age. (20-2)
- Rescue breathing is needed for someone who stops breathing. CPR combines rescue breathing with chest compressions. (20-2)

REVIEWING THE CHAPTER

1. What are some of the signs that a younger child needs to see a doctor? (20-1)
2. What is a *communicable disease*? (20-1)
3. Give four examples of foods and other substances that commonly cause allergic reactions. (20-1)
4. What are the signs of an *asthma* attack? How should attacks be treated? (20-1)
5. What medicine can be given to a child to reduce pain and fever? (20-1)
6. A child in your care sustains a minor cut. What should you do? (20-2)
7. What should you do when you suspect a child has a *fracture* or *sprain*? (20-2)
8. What should you do if a child in your care appears to be in *shock*? (20-2)
9. Explain how to perform *rescue breathing* on infants and small children. (20-2)

THINKING CRITICALLY

1. **Analyzing Information.** Why do you think infants have much more frequent checkups than older children?
2. **Drawing Conclusions.** You are taking a group of children on a campout. As a leader, what skills should you have?

MAKING CONNECTIONS

1. **Writing.** Write a guide sheet with at least ten ideas of activities that could be used with children who are recovering from an illness. Organize the ideas according to appropriateness for children of different ages.

2. **Math.** After reading the chapter, determine what first-aid supplies you should keep in your home. Price the products at a store. Compare the total cost to the cost of a ready-made first-aid kit. Which would you buy? Why?

APPLYING YOUR LEARNING

1. **Determining Treatment.** How would you treat these injuries?

   - A small cut that continues bleeding after you have applied pressure to it for 10 minutes
   - A small burn that has formed a blister
   - A mosquito bite

2. **Recognizing Sequence.** With a partner, describe the different steps for rescuing an infant or four-year-old child who is choking. Write each step on an index card, but don't number the steps. Shuffle your cards and exchange your set for your partner's cards. Each of you should put the cards in the correct order.

3. **Organizing Information.** Develop a form you could take with you and complete when you care for children. Include space for all information you should have on hand.

Learning from Research

1. Choose one of the following claims to investigate.
2. How is this finding useful to parents and other caregivers?
3. Summarize what you've learned about extreme risks to children and how to avoid them.

Drowning. Most children drown in swimming pools, lakes, ponds, or oceans. Is this claim true or false? Explain why this is true or false and what can be done in an emergency. What precautions can be taken to avoid drowning?

Poisoning. More than half of all poisoning cases reported to poison control centers involve children older than six. Is this claim true or false? Explain why this is true or false and what can be done in an emergency. What precautions can be taken to avoid poisoning?

Bicycling Accidents. Most deaths from bicycling accidents are the result of head injuries. Is this claim true or false? Explain why this is true or false and what safety precautions can be taken by children when riding a bicycle.

Thoughtful Reading:

As you read this chapter:
- What do you wonder? Note each of your questions and the page number.
- What opinions do you have about what you read?
- Summarize what you read in a short paragraph.

Section 21-1
Family Stresses

Section 21-2
Exceptional Children

Section 21-3
Child Abuse and Neglect

Family Stresses

Simon stared out the window. It was a sunny day, but he didn't want to go outside. Nothing sounded like fun. Simon missed his dad, his grandparents, and his school friends. He even missed the dog who had lived next door. His mom and sister seemed excited about their move, but Simon was having a hard time adjusting.

Objectives

- Identify possible signs of stress in children.
- Give examples of situational stress that families may encounter.
- Recommend ways to help children and adolescents cope with family challenges.

Key Terms

regression
situational stress
addiction
support groups

Children and Stress

In difficult times, children can be more vulnerable than adults. They may lack an understanding of events, as well as effective coping skills. Parents can help children during hard times by listening patiently and accepting their feelings of anger, grief, and sadness. Children are often much more aware of parents' worries than their mother or father realizes. It helps when parents are able to appropriately acknowledge their own emotions and provide an example of how to cope.

Possible Responses

Children react to stress in a variety of ways, but age is a factor. Figure 21-1, "Signs of Stress in Children and Teens," on page 600 shows how children of various ages may show stress.

When times are tough, adults should observe children closely for any of these signs. It's important to be alert for changes in behavior or **regression**—the temporary backward movement to earlier stages of development. If a toilet-trained child begins having accidents, for example, it may be a sign of stress.

Fig. 21-1
Signs of Stress in Children and Teens

In children under age 5:
- Excessive attachment to parents
- Fear of being left alone
- Increased sensitivity to loud noises
- Eating problems
- Uncontrollable crying

In children ages 5–11:
- Disturbed sleep
- Headache, nausea, or other physical problems
- Pretending to be ill to avoid going to school
- Fighting
- Poor school performance

In older children ages 11–14:
- Withdrawal from others
- Depression
- Aggression
- Confusion
- Acting out—stealing, fighting
- Sleeping too much

In teens:
- Anxiety or panic attacks
- Irritability and moodiness
- Physical symptoms, such as stomach problems, headaches, or chest pain
- Sleeping problems
- Sadness or depression
- Overeating
- Drinking alcohol, smoking, or taking drugs

Situational Stress

Stress can come from the environment a child lives in or from certain circumstances and changes. This type of stress is called **situational stress**. Some of the stress factors that have the greatest impact on a child's daily life include parents' divorce, moving, family financial problems, substance abuse by a family member, illness, and the death of a loved one. The way the parents handle the situation has a huge impact on the child's stress level. One of the worst things a parent or caregiver can do is to say "You shouldn't feel that way." Instead, they should first *accept* the child's feelings and use them as a starting point for trying to offer help. A child's other caregivers can also play a part in helping the child cope.

Moving

Moving to a new community, and sometimes even to a different neighborhood, interrupts friendships, affects school performance, and disrupts activities. Moving can be especially difficult for older children because of the importance they place on peer relationships.

Adults can help children by explaining why a move is necessary and by including them in making decisions. After the move, parents should help their children get involved in activities that allow them to meet others their age. They might sign up for swimming or art lessons, and check out other group opportunities, such as story hour at the library. Caleb's parents signed him up for T-ball and a summer day camp. By the time school started, Caleb already knew several children who would also be in first grade at his new school.

Financial Problems

Family money problems can stem from a variety of factors. Unemployment, gambling, shopping addiction, illness and medical bills, and poor money management are just a few. As leaders of the family, parents often set the tone for their children's comfort and stress levels. When families are struggling with finances, parents should make a special effort not to argue about money in front of children or take out their worries on them. Now a young adult, Jane recalls the summer her family spent camping in a park. A few years later she learned that the family's fun "adventure" had occurred because they were homeless. Because she and her siblings were young and their mother's attitude was positive, the children were spared the stress that might have been expected.

When money is scarce, older children may worry about what will happen to them. Without spending money, adolescents may be concerned about loss of status in their peer group. However, it's important that parents not hide money problems from older children. Parents need to be clear about possible consequences of the problems and the need to cut back on spending.

Divorce

Research has shown that children experience the effects of divorce at the time of the breakup and for decades afterward. When children of divorce grow up, many face greater fears that their own relationships will fail. Yet children suffer much less when parents make a joint effort to help them adjust to the new family situation.

Parents should tell their children together about their divorce and discuss where the children will live. Children often blame

Fig. 21-2 When parents divorce, children should feel free to talk about their feelings, even when they are negative.

themselves for the failure of their parents' marriage, so parents must emphasize that the children did nothing wrong. Parents should remind children of their love for them frequently.

Some children ask questions, some cry, and some appear not to react at all when they learn their parents are divorcing. Parents should accept any reaction, including none at all.

Most children want to know how the divorce will affect them, wondering, "Where will I live? Can I still go to camp this summer? Will I go to a new school?" It's important that parents be honest with children about possible outcomes and involve children in decision making. Parents should never give children false hope that parents might get back together. See Fig. 21-2.

Parents should resist the urge to spoil children who are feeling sad. It is also important not to confide in children or place them in the middle of arguments. This unfairly makes them feel that they have to take sides. In fact, they desperately need the love of both parents to get through this time.

Many children show behavior problems after their parents' breakup. Even children who appear happy on the surface may be hiding their pain to keep parents from worrying.

Substance Abuse

Some people develop an **addiction** to a substance, such as alcohol, cocaine, crack, or prescription drugs. They become dependent on the substance, often feeling that they can't live without it. Substance abuse causes serious problems for families.

Some adults who abuse substances hurt their families with words or physical violence. Often, they are emotionally unavailable. Some parents lose their jobs because of their dependence on the substance, or even turn to crime in order to support their addiction.

Even though they're aware of a substance abuse problem, family members don't always want to admit it. They sometimes help the addict hide the problem or take on that person's responsibilities. Sometimes they try to rescue the addict, or react so strongly that the focus turns from the addict's behavior to the family member's reaction.

Most substance abusers become skilled at hiding the evidence of their problem from others. In order to get better, however, they and their families must confront the problem. Nagging or threatening a substance abuser won't help. Substance abusers won't seek help until they are ready. Usually, this happens when the consequences of the behavior become especially painful, as when they lose their jobs or their families.

In the meantime, family members should take steps to protect themselves. **Support groups** give people a chance to explore and accept their feelings. See Fig. 21-3. They come to realize that they aren't alone with their problems. There are several well-known groups, such as Al-Anon (for the families and friends of alcoholics) and Nar-Anon (for the families and friends of narcotics abusers). Anyone who has a friend or family member who is abusing alcohol or drugs can join these groups at no cost. Families can draw on the strength and experience of other people in similar situations. Adolescents might also talk to a school counselor, trusted teacher, or religious leader.

Fig. 21-3 Support groups help not only substance abusers but also their friends and family members. How might you find a group in your community?

Help a Child Cope with Divorce

Divorce changes children's lives forever. It's the responsibility of both parents to minimize the impact whenever possible and help children adjust to changes. Here are a few tips for helping children cope:

- **Keep things as normal as possible.** Maintain routines, including family mealtimes and rules of behavior.

- **Maintain ties.** Help children stay in touch with their friends and members of both sides of the family. Encourage visits, calls, and e-mails to help maintain these important relationships.

- **Create a special place.** If the child must move, help the child personalize his or her space in the new home. Have children keep personal belongings in each parent's home if they go back and forth frequently.

- **Develop new traditions.** Holiday activities may change. Children may spend holidays with only one parent or with a newly blended family. Invite children to invent new holiday traditions while maintaining some old favorites.

- **Watch for changes.** Observe changes in the child's behavior, school performance, and temperament. If a child withdraws or shows a major shift in behavior, visit the pediatrician or a counselor.

- **Work with the school.** Make the child's teacher aware of the situation. Many schools offer professional resources, referrals, and even lunch groups to help children cope.

YOUR TURN

Support. Imagine that a family moved in next door to you. If you learned the parents were newly divorced, what could you do to help the children, who are seven and ten, adjust to their new situation?

Illness

When a family member is ill, the rhythms of family life are upset. Children need an honest explanation of what is happening geared to their ability to understand. When the illness is minor, children can be reassured that the person should soon be well again. If the illness is serious or the person is dying, adults should tell children the truth in a calm, reassuring way. They might be told, "The doctors are doing everything they can to help Aunt Laura feel better." See Fig. 21-4.

Children sometimes have irrational fears or false beliefs about illness. They may worry that they are somehow at fault, or believe that a disease like cancer is contagious. Adults should reassure them that nothing they did caused the illness. Unless the disease is communicable, the child should be assured that no one else in the family will come down with it. A child may also misunderstand what is said. One four-year-old overheard that someone had "died in bed." It took her parents days to figure out why she cried hysterically at bedtime.

Death of a Loved One

Children's grief, like that of adults, is a complex set of emotions that may include fear, anger, despair, agitation, and guilt. While each child grieves differently, the age of the child influences his or her reaction. Researchers have found that two factors—children's level of development and religious or cultural background—influence their views of death.

Children's ages influence their reactions to death, but even toddlers can sense emotional upset in the family.

- **Children under three** cannot understand more than a brief separation and may react to a death in the same way they react to a parent's weeklong vacation.

- **Children ages three to five** think that death is like sleep—you are dead, and then you wake up and are alive again. As a result, they may seem unfeeling when a person dies, not understanding that death is permanent.

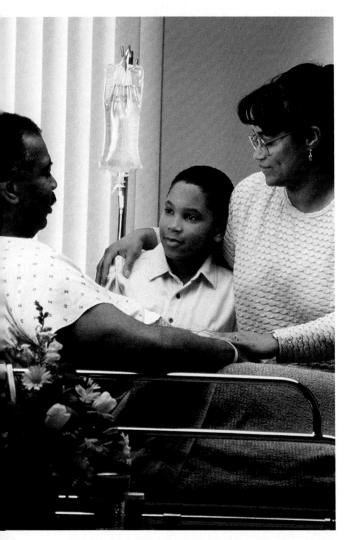

Fig. 21-4 **Most hospitals permit children to visit family members.** Are there situations when it may be best to not have children visit?

- **Children ages six to nine** may believe that angry words or thoughts caused death. They may fear that other family members will abandon them. Most children this age recognize that death is final, but they may not understand that it happens to everyone.

- **Preteens** may still feel that the person died because of some bad deed. They may feel angry toward the person who died or toward other family members.

- **Teens** may assume too much responsibility for financial or other family concerns. They understand the finality of death and its impact on the family.

Helping Children Cope

By age five, many children have had some contact with death, by seeing a dead bird or losing a beloved pet, for example. They may not fully understand what has happened, but they will have reactions to the loss. There are a number of ways that parents can help children cope with the loss of a loved one.

Funerals and memorial services are rituals that allow people to vent feelings and to honor the deceased person. When children want to go, experts believe they should be allowed to attend these services. See Fig. 21-5.

Very young children need simple explanations about death, such as the loss of functions like eating, sleeping, thinking, or feeling.

Religion and Spiritual Beliefs

Religion and spiritual beliefs are a source of comfort to many people who have suffered a loss. Beliefs offer explanations and give meaning to life and death. Letting children know that things are the way they are supposed to be, according to the family's spiritual beliefs or faith, can help them feel secure. Parents should let children know that some pain is a part of living and that it will lessen in time.

Fig. 21-6 **A healthy response to a family member's death is to keep memories alive through photos and stories.**

Death of a Parent

The death of a parent is probably the most tragic thing that can happen to a youngster. A child whose parent dies needs support for an extended period. Many children react with guilt. The child may think, "I wasn't always good when he wanted me to be," or "I wasn't quiet enough when she was sick." Even infants go through a period of excessive crying and searching for a parent who has died.

Parents should reassure children that, no matter what happens, they will always receive loving care. If asked, parents should talk to their children about who would take care of them in the very unlikely event of their death.

Experts say that children whose parents have died or are dying need three things:

• Someone to meet the child's emotional and physical needs

• Reassurance that they will always be loved and cared for, no matter what happens

• Explanations that are appropriate for their ages

Child therapists recommend telling children the truth when death is near and allowing them to say goodbye. Children should be allowed to visit the dying parent.

Some people mistakenly believe that it's best to avoid talking about the deceased person. Actually, the opposite is true. See Fig. 21-6. When a parent dies, the surviving parent should encourage children to express their grief by drawing pictures or talking. If the child has fears, adults should deal with them. Older children and teens should not be placed in an adult role with adult responsibilities.

Healthy children sometimes ask, "When will I die?" Often, they simply want to know *if* they will die. Parents can say that while every living thing dies, most people live a long time. They can also be told that people eat nutritious foods and wear seat belts in order to live a long life.

Suicide

Some people feel overwhelmed by their problems, overcome by depression, or irrationally angry at others, and decide that taking their own lives is the solution. Sadly, some of the people who attempt suicide are children and teenagers.

When an adult commits suicide, children who are old enough to understand should be told. Adults can stress that there are many ways of getting help and dealing with problems that aren't harmful to anyone.

Anyone who is thinking about suicide should seek help from a parent, friend, doctor, or counselor. Many survivors of a suicide attempt say that they later realized that their problems had other solutions. Warning signs of suicide include talking about suicide or giving away possessions. If you know anyone who is doing these things, talk to a school counselor or another adult. Most people who commit suicide are depressed. With modern treatment options, they can find hope again.

Older children and teens who know someone who committed suicide may wonder if they could have done something to prevent it. They may feel betrayed or abandoned. These feelings are a normal part of the grieving process.

Grieving takes time. Talking to a professional counselor can help. Finding a way to accept and express intense feelings is also important. Survivors can do something positive that they believe the person would have wanted them to do.

SECTION 21-1 Review and Activities

Reviewing the Section

1. Why are children more vulnerable to stress than adults?
2. Define *situational stress*. What are the most common reasons for this type of stress?
3. Identify three signs that early adolescents (ages 11–14) may be under a great deal of stress.
4. Identify at least three things parents can do to help children adjust to divorce. List three things they should *not* do.
5. What might help a teen cope with a parent's substance abuse or serious illness?

Observing and Interacting

Ask your parent or an adult friend if he or she has gone through a stressful time.

1. Was the stressful time the result of an event, such as a move or a death in the family? If so, what happened?
2. What did other people say that helped during this time? What didn't help?

Exceptional Children

When a family has a child who has a disability or is gifted, modifications are needed. Parenting, family life, education, and interaction with the world must undergo adjustment. Children with disabilities and those who are gifted are called "exceptional" because their needs vary from those of the "average" child in some ways. Most children with physical, mental, or emotional disabilities need special adaptations in some aspect of their lives. Gifted children need additional stimulation. Parents, teachers, and other caregivers are all challenged to meet the individual needs of each child.

Objectives

- Compare different types of disabilities.
- Explain current approaches to education for children with special needs.
- Summarize what types of help are available to families raising children with special needs.
- Identify the traits typically exhibited by gifted children.

Key Terms

gifted
learning disability
dyslexia
ADHD
ADD
mental retardation
autism
autism spectrum
  disorders (ASD)
inclusion

Children with Special Needs

Some children who have needs significantly different from those of the average child are often said to have special needs. These children fall into two general categories—those with disabilities and those who have special abilities. Some children have special needs when a health condition or disability affects their ability to function in some way. The attitude of their parents and other caregivers has a profound impact on their future. Like all children, they want to experience success and feel good about what they do. While disabilities and health conditions vary greatly, the general goal is to help children with special needs become as independent as possible by involving them in family and school life. When they participate in daily chores and fun activities, children discover how much they can do.

Gifted children, those who have special abilities in one or more areas, may present challenges for parents, teachers, and other caregivers. Sometimes it can be difficult to keep them motivated and help them reach their potential. See Fig. 21-7.

Types of Disabilities

Disabilities may result from difficulties with mobility, vision, or hearing. Some disabilities affect a child's ability to learn, speak, or express emotions. Some problems are apparent at birth; others may not be discovered for months or years. Some children have a disability that is clearly apparent, but many have so-called *invisible disabilities*—disabilities that people might not notice right away. Children with a learning disorder, for example, or those with diabetes, have invisible disabilities. Some of the most common types of disabilities, visible and invisible, are described here.

Learning Disabilities

A **learning disability** interferes with a child's ability to learn, listen, think, speak, read, write, spell, or do math. Children with a learning disability often have average or above-average intelligence, but they achieve below their potential because of the difficulties they experience with learning. Learning disabilities result from disorders in the brain and central nervous system. Most learning disabilities are detected in children when standardized testing begins, between the ages of seven and twelve. Early diagnostic testing, followed by intervention using special teaching methods, is critical to their educational success.

Fig. 21-7 **Gifted children sometimes don't get top grades in school. They may find school boring or their talents may be in other areas.**

Dyslexia, which prevents a child from understanding printed symbols in a normal way, is an example of a learning disorder. A child with dyslexia may be very intelligent but have trouble processing visual information. Letters and numbers may be reversed or absent, so children with dyslexia may have difficulty with reading, writing, spelling, and math. They may find it hard to understand directions and distinguish left from right.

Attention Deficit Hyperactive Disorder

ADHD, attention deficit hyperactive disorder, is a behavioral disorder that may be accompanied by learning disabilities. Children with ADHD often fail to finish what they start, don't seem to listen, and are easily distracted. They may always be active and have trouble staying in their seats. Some show signs of a lack of emotional control. Parents and teachers learn special teaching methods that may be useful with students with ADHD. Medication is often prescribed for many children with ADHD, but the practice remains controversial. **ADD**, attention deficit disorder, is similar to ADHD, but doesn't involve hyperactivity.

Speech and Language Impairments

Speech and language impairments interfere with a child's ability to communicate. A child with a speech disorder may have difficulty making certain speech sounds or modulating the volume or quality of the voice. A child with a language disorder may find it difficult to understand and use words correctly, making it difficult for the child to express ideas or follow directions. Some speech and language disorders are associated with hearing impairment, mental retardation, and brain injury. In many cases, though, the cause is not known.

Because speech and language are so important to learning in general, it is important that children with these impairments receive help at an early age. Speech-language pathologists can work with teachers and parents to help individual children get effective therapy.

Mental Retardation

Children with **mental retardation**, also known as cognitive impairment or developmental disability, have below-average intelligence and skills. Besides problems with thinking and learning, children with mental retardation may have difficulty paying attention, remembering,

communicating, and interacting with others. Levels of mental retardation range from mild to profound. There is no cure.

Mental retardation may result from a genetic disorder, brain damage, poor prenatal care, or a variety of factors. In many cases, the cause is unknown.

Down syndrome is an example of a genetic disorder resulting in varying degrees of mental retardation. Children with this condition also have distinctive physical features. *Fetal alcohol syndrome,* a condition that affects children born to some mothers who drank alcohol during pregnancy, is another disorder characterized by developmental delays, mental retardation, and physical abnormalities.

Children with mental retardation have lifelong limitations, but with effective parenting and the right approach to their education, they can experience success. The goal is to help them become as independent as possible. Many are able to learn living and job skills that enable them to live alone or in a group home and to earn a living. See Fig. 21-8.

Serious Emotional Disturbances

Children with serious emotional disturbances generally exhibit one or more of the following characteristics:

- Inability to learn that cannot be explained by other factors
- Inability to build or maintain satisfactory relationships with others
- Inappropriate behavior or feelings
- General unhappiness or depression
- Irrational fears

Troublesome emotions and behavior may have to do with a child's stage of development, but in some cases, a child's behavior indicates a more serious problem. Initially,

Fig. 21-8 **Programs such as the Special Olympics provide tremendous opportunities for exceptional young people.**

parents may deny there is a problem and hope the child outgrows it. If a serious problem is suspected, though, the child should be evaluated promptly.

Treatment options include counseling for the child, the parents, or the entire family. Psychiatrists, psychologists, family therapists, and some social workers are trained to help children with emotional difficulties and their families.

Autism and Autism Spectrum Disorders

Autism is a disorder that affects a child's ability to communicate and interact with others. It is one of the most common developmental disorders, affecting about one child in 500. Autism affects about four times more boys than girls, although no one knows why. It usually appears during the first three years of life.

Autism is one of a group of disorders collectively known as **autism spectrum disorders (ASD)**. Children who have one of these conditions may exhibit many of the symptoms or very few. Among the traits associated with autism and ASD are:

- Resistance to change
- Absence of empathy
- Little or no eye contact
- Repetition of words or phrases
- Repetitive movements and play
- Difficulty focusing and inability to remain attentive
- Distress without apparent cause
- Loss of skills already learned

THE DEVELOPING BRAIN

About 10 percent of people with autism are called autistic savants. Some of these individuals have a compulsive interest in some narrow activity—the memorization of sports trivia, for example. Others develop an amazing ability in a certain area, such as music or mathematics. One common mathematical skill among savants is known as calendar calculation. Savants with this ability can mentally calculate the day of the week that any given date fell on, or will fall on, over a span of tens of thousands of years. Scientists don't understand how the brains of autistic savants can do such things.

While symptoms of autism and ASD vary widely, parents should seek help if their child doesn't babble or coo by 12 months, is overly attached to a single toy or object, or becomes withdrawn and unresponsive. Children who are diagnosed early and who receive appropriate therapy do better in the long run.

Hearing and Visual Impairments

Some children with hearing impairments are totally deaf; others are hard of hearing, meaning that they can hear some speech with the help of a hearing aid. Communication skills vary. Some children with hearing impairments can speak, but others cannot.

Children with visual impairments may be totally blind or may have very low vision. It can be hard for them to follow traditional classroom instruction since so much teaching is visual.

Physical Disabilities

Physical disabilities take a wide range of forms. They may range from mild to severe involvement. Some may be present at birth while others may develop over time or result from an injury.

Normal daily routines that others take for granted can be difficult or impossible for people with disabilities. Children with coordination problems may need assistance with bathing, eating, and getting ready for school. Some children with disabilities need regular physical therapy or specialized equipment. All children with physical disabilities need patient and understanding caregivers who can help them learn how to perform basic activities and enjoy greater independence. See Fig. 21-9.

Educating Children with Special Needs

The educational needs of children with disabilities vary. Some can function in a regular classroom and need no special adaptation. Others need individualized attention but can be placed in a regular classroom. Those with certain disabilities require specialized education in programs designed to meet their specific needs. Many children receive help from teachers who are specially trained to work with students with learning disabilities. A teacher might give both spoken and written directions, for example, to help children who have trouble with reading. Some students with disabilities have teacher assistants who attend class with them.

Fig. 21-9 **Physical therapy is important for some children with physical disabilities.**

Parenting Q&A

What Rights Do Children with Disabilities and Their Parents Have?

The Individuals with Disabilities Education Act (IDEA) specifies the rights of children with disabilities and their parents. These rights include:

- Children have a right to a free public education that meets their needs.
- Parents or caregivers must be notified if a school system plans to evaluate a child or change the child's school arrangement.
- Parents have the right to request that the school evaluate a child.
- Children must be retested at least every three years and their school situation must be reviewed at least every year.
- Children can be tested in the language they know best. Parents must be spoken to in the language they know best.
- Parents can request to see the child's school records.
- The school must draw up an educational program specifically for the child, and parents can take part in the process of developing that plan.

THINKING IT THROUGH

1. Why is it important to review a child's educational program each year?
2. How does IDEA guarantee parents an active role in a child's education?

The Individuals with Disabilities Education Act (IDEA) ensures that children with disabilities receive a free public education that meets their needs, including a written plan for each student's education, taking into account his or her abilities. The plan is called an Individualized Education Plan, or IEP.

The law also requires schools to make every effort to place children with disabilities in regular classrooms while receiving special education services. This approach is called **inclusion**, or mainstreaming. Education experts believe that it benefits both children with special needs and children without those challenges. It allows them to learn together, develop empathy, and improve communication and social skills.

About 50 percent of American students served by IDEA have been classified as having a specific learning disability, such as dyslexia. Almost 20 percent have a speech or language impairment. Slightly more than 10 percent receive special education services because of mental retardation. Another 8 percent or so have emotional disturbances. There are also thousands of children who have autism, orthopedic impairments, and

Fig. 21-10 **Many children with special needs are educated in a regular classroom.** What law ensures that these children receive the education they deserve?

hearing and visual impairments, but they represent a relatively small percentage of the students receiving special education services. Some children have multiple disabilities. See Fig. 21-10.

Raising Children with Disabilities

The responsibilities and demands of raising a child with disabilities or serious health conditions can seem overwhelming. Many parents have difficulty accepting that their child has a disability. They may regret that their child won't be able to do some of the things they imagined. They may feel guilty about devoting more time and energy to the child with special needs and fear that they are shortchanging other family members.

Support for Families

Support groups for parents of children with disabilities can help. When they meet, members of these groups share advice and solutions to everyday problems. Members keep each other up to date on research and treatments. They can also help parents meet their children's emotional needs. Children who get emotional support from their caregivers are more likely to view themselves in a positive light.

Hundreds of organizations exist to help children with special needs and their families. Some financial aid is available for parents who meet certain income guidelines. State funds may offer money for testing and treatment for children with disabilities. Community agencies may also make funds available.

No two children, including children with the same disability, are exactly alike. Some will find it easier to learn self-care skills such as dressing, bathing, and using toilet facilities than others. Some may need help with just a few tasks, while others need greater assistance.

Parenting a child with special needs is just as rewarding and important as parenting any other child. Parents and caregivers who know what they can reasonably expect of a child with special needs at different ages and stages are more likely to see the child reach his or her full potential.

Gifted Children

 Gifted children show, or have the potential to show, exceptional ability in one or more areas. They might, for example, have a special talent for music, art, mathematics, or language. Some gifted children are highly creative. They may have the potential to invent new technologies or develop new ways of solving problems.

Identifying Gifted Children

It is not always easy to identify gifted children. Children who talk and read early, have large vocabularies, and retain information about what they read or observe may be classified as gifted. Such traits do not always show up in gifted individuals, however. Many brilliant people develop language abilities fairly late.

On the other hand, some gifted children can be identified very early in life. They may learn to walk and talk early. Some display advanced skills in writing, coloring, or building. As they grow older, they often have wide-ranging interests, preferring to interact with adults rather than with other children, and showing awareness of serious issues such as world hunger.

Despite their special ability, not all gifted children are high achievers. Some don't have the patience to complete tasks that seem unimportant to them. They may be bored in the classroom, in part because they may be able to perform two or three grades above their actual grade level. They may question classroom procedures or give unexpected answers to questions. Some gifted children who aren't challenged at school grow frustrated and become poor students.

Special Programs

In school districts that offer programs for gifted children, students may be tested to determine if they qualify. These tests sometimes fail to identify all gifted children, however, especially those who don't perform well in class or who have limited language abilities.

Some gifted students feel isolated and misunderstood. While they benefit from playing with a variety of children, they also need time with other gifted learners. They need stimulation and challenges so that they can make the most of their abilities. They also need to be accepted and to feel good about what makes them different. They need to be valued for themselves, not just for their special abilities.

SECTION 21-2 Review and Activities

Reviewing the Section

1. What does the term "invisible disabilities" refer to? Why do people need to be aware of them?
2. What kinds of difficulties would a child with *dyslexia* experience?
3. What traits are associated with *ADHD*?
4. What traits are associated with *autism* and *ASD*?
5. How does the policy of *inclusion* benefit children with disabilities and children without them?
6. What kinds of support are available to those raising a child with a disability?
7. How can caregivers help *gifted* children make the most of their abilities?

Observing and Interacting

Interview a teacher in your area who works with students with special needs. What is a typical day like in the teacher's classroom? How do the teacher and other staff members make sure the needs of all students are met?

Child Abuse and Neglect

Hundreds of thousands of children become the victims of child abuse and neglect each year, often at the hands of their parents. Most victims, however, never come to the attention of authorities. Their abusers may have threatened them with harm if they tell someone, or they may feel intense guilt for things that aren't their fault. Emotional and physical scars can last well into adulthood and can affect the overall health of former victims, as well as their future relationships with others.

Objectives

- Define child abuse and describe the four types of maltreatment.
- Analyze the signs of abuse in children and adolescents.
- Summarize common reasons behind abuse and maltreatment.
- Explain what can be done to prevent child abuse.

Key Terms

addiction
   counselors
mandated reporters
crisis nurseries

Types of Maltreatment

The federal Child Abuse Prevention and Treatment Act (CAPTA) defines maltreatment, and so does each state. Generally speaking, however, the government recognizes four major types of maltreatment:

- **Physical abuse.** This means intentionally causing an injury to a child. This includes hitting, burning, shaking, or otherwise harming a child.

- **Neglect.** Both physical and emotional neglect are possible. Neglect means failing to provide for a child's basic needs, whether they be for food, water, a place to live, or love and attention.

- **Sexual abuse.** This category includes any inappropriate sexual behavior with a child, including touching or taking photographs.

- **Emotional and verbal abuse.** This mean rejecting children, blaming them, or constantly scolding them, particularly for problems beyond their control.

Death is the most tragic consequence of maltreatment. More than 1,000 children die in the U.S. each year because of abuse or neglect. Over half of all victims of child maltreatment are victims of neglect. Neglected children may fail to develop mentally and physically at the same rate as their peers. Physically abused children may bear physical scars or become permanently disabled. All abused children suffer emotionally. They often feel lonely, unloved, guilty for no reason, and unworthy of care and attention. These feelings may persist into adulthood and cause problems in relationships.

Signs and Symptoms of Child Abuse and Neglect

When abuse or neglect occurs, there are usually signs in both children and adults. Neglected children are often absent from school, steal food or money, have poor personal hygiene, and lack protective clothing for wet or cold weather.

Physically abused children may have bruises, broken bones, or burn marks that cannot be explained. This is not always the case, though. Not all physical abuse leaves marks on visible parts of the child's body, such as the face or arms. Some abusers intentionally leave no marks when they hurt children.

Children who are sexually abused sometimes run away, refuse to participate in physical activities, and exhibit sexual knowledge beyond their normal level of development.

Emotionally abused children often show aggression, act inappropriately like an adult (bossing other children), or like a very young child (rocking back and forth). See Fig. 21-11.

Who Abuses Children?

An adult in the home is most often to blame for physical abuse. Statistics indicate that mothers abuse children more often than fathers do.

In sexual abuse cases, however, it is most often another relative or a family friend who harms the child, not a parent.

People who abuse children often have difficulty controlling their impulses. While many parents feel frustrated when a child is crying or whining, people who abuse children often act without thinking. Abusers often feel depressed, extremely anxious,

Fig. 21-11 Signs of Maltreatment	
The following are signs that children may be being mistreated:	**The following are signs that adults may be mistreating children:**
• Learning problems that cannot be explained • No adult supervision • Withdrawal from others • No desire to go home after school or other activities • Fearfulness, as though waiting for something bad to happen • Changes in school performance or behavior • Has untreated medical conditions	• Sees the child as bad or worthless • Makes frequent demands that the child cannot achieve • Asks teachers to use physical discipline if the child misbehaves • Denies child's problems in school or at home • Sees the child as a burden • Rarely looks at the child

or overwhelmed. In many cases, they were abused themselves as children and they don't know how to discipline children in a constructive way. Abuse may come from only one parent. The other parent may deny that it's happening. Sometimes, only one child in a family is targeted for abuse.

Why Does Abuse Occur?

Children are *never* responsible for the abuse or harm that others inflict on them. Some children, however, are more vulnerable to maltreatment than others. See Fig. 21-12. Children with physical and mental disabilities are more likely to be abused. Younger children are neglected more often, and they are more likely to die of maltreatment. When children are sexually abused, the abuse most often occurs before age seven. Girls are more often the victims of sexual abuse than boys are.

Immature mothers who have children at a young age are more likely to abuse children. So are people who live in poverty and have few resources to help with child care and other responsibilities. Child abusers may be socially isolated or stressed due to unemployment. However, abuse can occur in households of any income or education level, ethnicity, or religious background. In families with domestic violence where one parent abuses the other, children are more likely to be hurt as well.

Fig. 21-12 **Children who are abused often feel unloved and lonely.** Why might some children be more at risk to abuse than others?

Abusive parents often don't know enough about child development to have reasonable expectations. Some expect even very young children to obey them promptly or remember rules given earlier. If abusers get help, they can learn what to expect from children of various ages and how to nurture them.

Fig. 21-13 **Abusers can undergo counseling to learn how to stop their harmful behavior.** What are some other options to support parents?

to help substance abusers—are now offering help to parents through state departments of child welfare. These counselors are trained to help abusive parents who are also addicted to drugs or alcohol. See Fig. 21-13.

What Can Be Done?

Abusing or neglecting children in any way is illegal. People who work with children, including teachers, doctors, nurses, and counselors are required by law to report maltreatment if they see evidence of it. These people are called **mandated reporters**. See Fig. 21-14. While others may not have a legal obligation to report abuse, they should contact child protective services agencies as soon as they suspect it. Every state has a child welfare agency.

Studies have shown that a large percentage of child maltreatment cases involve substance abuse. When parents become dependent on alcohol and other drugs, they neglect their children's needs. When parents abuse substances, they are often emotionally unavailable and can be violent due to the effects of drugs. Substance abusers buy drugs with money that should have been spent on food and other basics for their children. Many problems—mental illness, depression, unemployment, and high stress levels—can go along with substance abuse. So many maltreatment cases involve substance abuse that social service agencies are working hard to manage these cases better. **Addiction counselors**—therapists trained

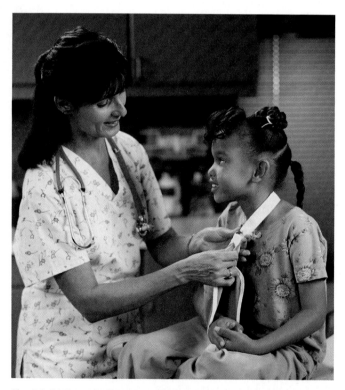

Fig. 21-14 **People who work with children are required by law to report maltreatment if they see evidence of it.** What other things can be done to prevent child abuse and protect the victims?

When an agency hears a report of possible child abuse, it sends someone to investigate. If the child is thought to be in danger, the court may place the child in a foster home. If there is a history of abuse, or if the child has severe injuries, parents may be arrested and charged with crimes. Ultimately, their parental rights may be terminated and their children may never live with them again.

Putting abusers in prison gives children temporary protection but doesn't solve the problem. In most cases, abusers undergo treatment and counseling to understand the reasons for the abuse and to end it.

Most abusive parents must learn how to care for their children and treat them in loving ways. Several programs are available to help them. Members of Parents Anonymous, one of the best-known groups, support each other as they work to change their behavior.

Some communities have **crisis nurseries**, child care facilities where troubled parents can go when they have nowhere else to turn. Many are open 24 hours a day and provide short-term free child care. Crisis nurseries provide children with a safe environment. Using a crisis nursery gives parents a chance to cool off and cope with their frustrations, anger, and problems without hurting their children. These facilities often also provide parenting classes, counseling, and job training.

Treatment for Abused Children

Children who have been abused are usually treated through counseling sessions with mental health professionals who have experience with victimized children. Counseling involves helping people make sense of their feelings and behavior and improving interactions with others.

Counselors who work with abused children have many goals, including:

Miranda was nine when she started going to counseling with Dr. Mitchell, a psychologist. She had been abused from age six to eight, and she had been having anxiety, feelings of guilt, and sleeping problems. Dr. Mitchell helped Miranda recognize that adults, not children, are responsible for healthy parent-child interactions. This helped ease Miranda's feelings of guilt about the abuse. Dr. Mitchell taught Miranda some ways to cope with her sad feelings and established a plan for her safety, including choosing supportive people in her environment whom she could turn to when she felt insecure.

▶▶**PERSONAL APPLICATION**

1. Why might it be difficult to talk to a counselor about a problem?
2. What does your school counselor do when she or he believes that a child is being abused?

- Protecting children from further harm
- Improving family communication
- Encouraging healthy friendships between children and their peers
- Teaching mistreated children to take care of themselves and make choices that help keep them safe
- Helping children have realistic expectations of parents who have problems
- Providing a safe place to express anger, disappointment, and sadness

Counseling may take many forms and should be appropriate to the child's age.

Many counselors use techniques that allow young children to express their feelings about abuse through play. Each affected person, including the victimized child, the abusers, and other family members, may be involved in individual counseling. Treatment may involve the child victim and the non-abusive parent, or it may involve the whole family with the goal of bringing everyone back together. If reuniting the family is the goal, the abuser must first acknowledge responsibility for the abuse and make a commitment to change.

In order for children to feel free to talk to their counselors about anything that worries them, counselors agree not to tell parents anything without telling the child first. They cannot, however, keep secrets regarding the child's safety from the parents. Counselors won't tell anyone outside the family about what happens in sessions unless the child is in danger or the family requests a release of information.

Many family problems are related to poor parenting skills and lack of knowledge about child development. Classes like the one you are taking give parents—and future parents—more realistic expectations about children and what it takes to care for them properly.

SECTION 21-3 Review and Activities

Reviewing the Section

1. What are the four types of child maltreatment?
2. List five possible signs of abuse in children.
3. Name several characteristics common in people who abuse children.
4. How are substance abuse and child abuse linked?
5. Who are *mandated reporters* and what responsibilities do they have?
6. How might understanding child development help prevent abuse?

Observing and Interacting

Talk to a counselor, social worker, teacher, or police officer about why people find it difficult to report suspected cases of child abuse. What particular problems might a person have in reporting abuse? Describe what you would say and do to encourage a close friend to report suspicions of child abuse.

Wildlife Educator

Many people rarely have contact with animals other than family pets. The role of the wildlife educator is to teach people about animals: how they behave in the wild, how to stay safe around them, and how to preserve the places where they live.

▶ Job Responsibilities

Wildlife educators give talks at schools using live animals or replicas. They talk about animal species that are endangered. Wildlife educators create materials—brochures, videos, exhibits, and guided tours—to teach people about wildlife. They answer questions about animals. Some also help raise money for wildlife preservation.

▶ Work Environment

Wildlife educators often travel to speak at schools. They work in zoos, aquariums, museums, nature centers, and parks. They often work when others have time off—including weekends. Some work part time or volunteer.

▶ Education and Training

People who want to be wildlife educators should study biology, natural resource management, forestry, and education. Gaining experience in public speaking is also helpful. Most wildlife educators have a college degree.

▶ Skills and Aptitudes

- Curiosity about nature
- Ability to teach
- Love of animals
- Public speaking skills
- Physical strength

WORKPLACE CONNECTION

1. **Thinking Skills.** How do wildlife educators help children get over a fear of animals?

2. **Resource Skills.** How could you get experience working with animals?

CHAPTER 21 Review and Activities

SECTION SUMMARIES

- Most families face stressful situations at times. When they occur, children may need extra support. (21-1)
- Children should be told about problems honestly and in a way suited to their age level. (21-1)
- Disabilities that affect children range from physical to learning to emotional. (21-2)
- Federal law requires that public schools meet the needs of children with disabilities. (21-2)
- Early diagnosis and treatment help children with disabilities reach their potential. (21-2)
- There are four types of child abuse and maltreatment. (21-3)
- Treatment and counseling can help abusive parents learn to stop patterns of abuse. (21-3)

REVIEWING THE CHAPTER

1. What are two examples of *regression* in children? (21-1)
2. How should children be told that their parents are divorcing? (21-1)
3. Why are *addictions* so devastating to family life? (21-1)
4. Compare and contrast how children of different ages understand death. (21-1)
5. How does the Individuals with Disabilities Education Act benefit children? (21-2)
6. When should a child who learns to walk and talk early be considered *gifted*? Explain. (21-2)
7. Which type of maltreatment involves children not receiving enough food and adequate shelter? (21-3)
8. What are possible emotional traits of people who abuse children? (21-3)
9. What is the duty of a *mandated reporter*? What responsibility do others have if they suspect child abuse? (21-3)

THINKING CRITICALLY

1. **Drawing Conclusions.** Which do you think would be better for a child, living in a home in which the parents often fight or having the parents divorce? Why?
2. **Making Inferences.** Why do you think many families don't consider seeking outside help when they are dealing with a problem?
3. **Analyzing Behavior.** Children with disabilities are more likely to be abused than children without disabilities. Why do you think that is true?

MAKING CONNECTIONS

1. **Writing.** Write a story about a child whose family is dealing with a major issue, such as moving, divorce, illness of another child in the family, death of a close relative, or substance abuse.

2. **Science.** Choose a topic from the chapter to research, such as depression, substance abuse, or autism. Look for scientific research that links these conditions to the brain. Share your findings with the class.

3. **Social Studies.** Stage a debate in which you argue for or against the idea that parents who abuse children should lose all rights of custody for those children.

APPLYING YOUR LEARNING

1. **Positive Messages.** Write a list of appropriate and comforting things to say to a person whose relative or family pet has just died.

2. **Interpersonal Skills.** Suppose a student new to the school is in two of your classes. She seems shy. What are four practical things you could do to help her feel more comfortable? How might your answers be different it you were in sixth grade?

3. **Internet Search.** Search online for information about Rett's Disorder. Whom does Rett's Disorder strike most often? What are its symptoms?

Learning from Research

1. Choose one of the following research claims to investigate.
2. How might the research finding you chose be useful to people who help maltreated children?
3. Summarize what you've learned about the consequences of child maltreatment.

Homelessness and Maltreatment. Studies show that homeless adults are more likely to have been maltreated in childhood than adults who are not homeless. Identify one research study that supports this premise and one that refutes it.

Emotional Health and Maltreatment. A long-term study showed that as many as 80 percent of people who were maltreated in childhood developed at least one mental health disorder by age 21, including eating disorders, anxiety, and depression. Identify one research study that supports the link between anxiety and child maltreatment and one research study that refutes it.

Crime and Maltreatment. A National Institute of Justice study showed that people who were maltreated as children were more likely to be arrested as juveniles. They were also more likely to commit violent crimes as adults. Identify one research study that supports the link between crime and child maltreatment and one that refutes it.

22 Child Care and Early Education

Thoughtful Reading:

As you read this chapter:

- Ask clarifying questions such as who, what, when, and where.
- Ask follow-up questions such as how and why.
- Find sources to answer all your reading questions.

Section 22-1
Child Care Options

Section 22-2
Participating in Early Childhood Education

Child Care Options

On his way to work each day, Luis takes his son, Alberto, to the Sunny Day Child Care Center. At the end of her workday, Alberto's mother, Elena, comes to get him and brings him home. Luis and Elena, just like millions of others, rely on substitute child care. The reasons for the growing number of children in substitute child care are many, as are the child care options available.

Objectives

- Analyze the reasons people need substitute child care.
- Compare and contrast the different types of substitute care.
- Determine the questions parents should ask when choosing substitute care.

Key Terms

child care center
in-home care
family child care
nanny
license
accreditation
play group
parent cooperative
Head Start

The Need for Substitute Care

More and more parents have come to rely on other people to care for their children at least some of the time. Why is there such a demand for substitute care? There are many reasons, including:

- In many two-parent families, both parents work outside the home. When parents have jobs, their children usually need substitute care.
- Many children live with a single parent who has a full-time job. Parents in this situation need full- or part-time care for their children.
- Some parents who care for a child at home feel that the child could benefit from regularly spending time with a group of other children. They place their child in a child care setting for some time each week.

Types of Substitute Care

Parents who need substitute care have a variety of options. All provide the child with physical care and a place to play.

Some place greater emphasis than others on education. Substitute care is provided in two general settings. Some services are offered in a home. Others are provided in a **child care center**, a facility in which a staff of adults provides care for children.

THE DEVELOPING BRAIN

Studies show that nurturing and supportive child care outside the home can promote a child's brain development. For optimal brain development, children need a stimulating environment, individualized attention, and exposure to language.

Home-Based Care

Many young children receive **in-home care** from a caregiver who comes to their home. **Family child care** is similar, but takes place in the caregiver's home. Parents may choose home-based care because they feel a home setting may be easier for their children to adjust to. Home-based care may also be convenient for parents, it may be located closer to home, and the hours may be more flexible. Some parents like this arrangement because the child care provider is a relative, friend, or neighbor—someone they know and trust. See Fig. 22-1.

Home-based care usually involves a smaller group of children than center-based care. For this reason, many parents prefer home-based care for infants or other children who need a lot of individual attention. There are three main types of home-based care.

- **Care in the child's own home.** Many parents have their child cared for by someone who comes to their home. In-home care is convenient, but it can be costly. Also, the child may not have a chance to play with other children. Some families hire a **nanny**—a person trained to provide child care. The nanny may live with the family or come to the home daily. Although this arrangement is fairly expensive, a nanny can offer reliable and stable care at almost any time of day.

- **Family child care.** Another option for parents is family child care. In this situation, a child care provider cares for a small group of children in his or her own home. The group often includes the

Fig. 22-1 More and more parents today use substitute care for their children in other people's homes. What are some advantages of home-based care over center-based care?

provider's own children. Family child care offers children the comfort of a home setting with opportunities for social interaction. Also, because the group size is small, the child care provider can give the children individual attention. Family child care usually costs less than in-home care.

Some states require child care providers to have a **license**, which means they are registered with the state and meet health and safety standards. See Fig. 22-2. A license does not indicate the quality of the care provided, however. Some family child care providers go a step further and earn **accreditation** from a recognized organization such as the National Association for Family Child Care (NAFCC). Only those who meet strict standards for quality child care can receive a certificate of accreditation.

- **Play groups.** Some parents and children take part in a **play group**. In this arrangement, parents take turns caring for one another's children in their own homes. A play group is similar to family child care, but it involves a number of different homes and different caregivers. Most play groups involve no fees because the work is shared. This type of care is best suited for parents who don't work full time but who want their children to have the opportunity to socialize with other children.

Center-Based Care

In child care centers, several adults care for one or more groups of children. Centers vary widely in their hours, their fees, and the ages of children they accept. They also differ in the activities, equipment, and play areas provided, and in the training and experience of the staff.

Fig. 22-2 People who run home-based child care programs may be required to get a license from their state. Why do you think some states insist on licensing for child care providers?

Some child care centers are businesses run for profit, while others, called nonprofit organizations, charge fees that just cover expenses. Still others are funded by the city, state, or federal government. Finally, some centers are run by businesses that offer child care as a benefit to their employees or customers.

Each state has an agency that licenses child care centers. A center must meet minimum health and safety requirements in order to be licensed. The license also limits the number of children a center may accept, depending on space, facilities, and number of people on the staff.

Professionals in the child care field have created a system to recognize centers that meet high standards. Child care centers can choose to join the National Association for the Education of Young Children (NAEYC). Members apply to the association for accreditation. This involves a review of the facility's staff, programs, and environment to see if they meet the association's strict criteria. See Fig. 22-3.

Parents can choose from several center-based child care options.

- **Child care centers.** Child care centers primarily serve children whose parents work outside the home. The typical center offers children a variety of activities. Some centers emphasize specific learning activities, while others allow more time for informal play. Usually there is a daily routine with time set aside for meals, naps, and indoor and outdoor play. Child care centers may offer half-day or full-day programs. Most child care centers are designed for children two years old and older, although some provide care for infants and young toddlers.

- **Parent cooperatives.** In a **parent cooperative**, or co-op, child care is provided by the parents of the children in the co-op. The parents take turns staffing the co-op, which is usually in a facility other than a home. A preschool teacher or another qualified child care provider may organize the program and guide the parents. A co-op program costs considerably less than a child care center. It may not be an option, however, for families in which both parents work full time.

Fig. 22-3 NAEYC Staff-to-Children Guidelines

The National Association for the Education of Young Children (NAEYC) is dedicated to improving the professional care and education of children from birth through age eight. NAEYC recommends that child care centers meet the following minimum ratio of child care providers to children. In general, the total number of children in a group should be no larger than two times the ratio of staff to children. That is, there should be no more than 8 infants, 12 toddlers, or 20 children ages three to five years in a group.

Ages	Number of Staff	Number of Children
Infants (birth–12 months)	1	4
Toddlers (12–24 months)	1	4–5
Toddlers (2–3 years)	1	6–7
Preschoolers (3–5 years)	1	10
Kindergarteners (5–6 years)	1	12
School-age children (6–12 years)	1	15

Fig. 22-4 **Preschool helps to prepare children for kindergarten.** What are some useful skills that children learn in preschool?

- **Preschools.** Preschools provide educational programs for children ages three to five. They typically offer activities that help children develop in all areas. The staff usually includes one or more teachers and a number of assistant teachers. Preschools usually offer half-day sessions from two to five days a week. Some centers offer both child care for younger children and preschool programs for three- to five-year-olds. A growing trend is for children to attend a pre-kindergarten program the year before kindergarten. See Fig. 22-4.

- **Specialized preschools.** Some preschools provide specialized programs that differ from the traditional approach. Montessori preschools, for example, use special learning materials and follow the ideas of Maria Montessori, an Italian educator. (See Chapter 15 to learn more about Montessori's theory of learning.) Children are encouraged to learn by exploring and experimenting and are given the freedom to move from one activity to another as they wish. Another example is called High/Scope. This program encourages children to learn through active experiences with people, material, and events rather than through direct teaching.

- **Head Start centers.** The **Head Start** program is funded by the federal government. It provides locally run child care facilities designed to help lower-income and disadvantaged children from birth to five years old become ready for school. Most Head Start centers have half-day sessions. Head Start offers a variety of activities. It also provides children with meals, health care, and social services. Parents are expected to be actively involved in the Head Start program. See Fig. 22-5.

Care for Older Children

Many parents wonder at what age their children can be left unsupervised. Child care experts advise against leaving children twelve and under home alone. This means that many parents and other caregivers need substitute care for their school-age children before and after school and during school holidays, breaks, and summers.

Some children go to the home of a neighbor or relative. Others depend on before- and after-school programs run by schools or religious or community groups. Such programs offer a safe place where children can have a snack, do their homework, and enjoy supervised activities.

Finding child care for school holidays and summer vacation can be more difficult. Fortunately, parents and other caregivers know in advance when school holidays will occur, so they can make plans well in advance. Often parents take their own vacations from work during the school holidays. Few parents can take the entire school holidays off, however, so they need to find ways to fill the gaps.

- Some parents arrange to share child care with several other families.
- High school and college students on similar school schedules are often available to provide in-home care.

Fig. 22-5 Why would Head Start programs want to include infants, as well as older children?

HOW TO

Tell if a Child Is Doing Well in Child Care

Parents want to know if their child is happy and doing well in child care. They can:

- **Look for bonding.** Children need time to adapt and warm up gradually. After an adjustment period, look for a bond to develop between the child and staff.

- **Ask for updates.** Sometimes caregivers will answer questions or give feedback at the end of the day or by appointment. Find out how the provider thinks the child is doing. Child care professionals often can give insight about a child's development.

- **Talk to the child.** Of course, the child is the best source of information if he or she is old enough to talk. Ask questions about activities, meals, and playtime. What is the child learning? With younger children, a reluctance to stay with the caregiver, especially if it lasts beyond the first few minutes, could indicate a problem.

- **Take time to observe.** Visit the child care center or home. Many allow parents to just drop in. Some centers have a one-way mirror for observation. Parents can see how their child acts on a typical day.

- **Get involved.** If possible, volunteer for special parties or help with field trips.

- **Be aware.** Although most child care experiences are positive, be aware of possible warning signs. Listen if a child complains about being bullied, mistreated, or ignored by the staff. Check it out and take any appropriate action.

YOUR TURN

Conferences. When meeting with a child care provider, it's a good idea to prepare questions. If you were the parent of a three-year-old in preschool, what kinds of questions would you ask a child care provider?

Fig. 22-6 **Many organizations offer after-school care for school-age children.** In what ways would this care differ from that provided for younger children?

- Often the programs that offer before- and after-school care also offer care for school holidays. Some also offer some summer programs.
- Museums, zoos, parks and recreation departments, Girl Scouts and Boy Scouts, and other community organizations may offer day camps and other programs for longer breaks and summer vacation.

Parents looking for holiday child care need to ask the same questions they would ask when looking for any other kind of substitute care. Safety, provider training, and child-to-adult ratios are still very important. See Fig. 22-6.

Fig. 22-7 **Parents need to visit each home or child care center they are considering before choosing one.** What should they look for when they first arrive?

Choosing Substitute Child Care

There are many factors to consider when choosing substitute care for a child. Foremost is the quality of care. In addition, the cost, convenience, qualifications of the caregivers, and the facilities and activities provided are all considerations. See Fig. 22-7.

What to Look For in Substitute Care

When parents start searching for care, it's helpful to use an organized approach. Figure 22-8 on page 636, "Questions for Evaluating Child Care," provides a list of important considerations. The questions are tailored to a child care center, but they could be adapted to other situations as well. Because the quality of care has such an impact on a child's well-being and development, it's important to put in the time and effort to find the best choice.

As a child grows, parents may need to make new child care arrangements. Mary put two-year-old Todd in family child care because she liked the idea of a home setting. When Todd turned four, however, she moved him to a preschool program so that he could start to prepare for kindergarten. A child's behavior could signal a need to change, too. If a child suddenly begins to cause trouble at child care, it may be because he or she is bored. Perhaps the activities are no longer interesting or challenging. If a child begins to cry regularly when being dropped off at child care, this could be a sign that a child no longer feels comfortable in that setting.

Fig. 22-8 Questions for Evaluating Child Care

These are questions parents or other caregivers might consider when evaluating substitute care options. Parents should ask some of the questions directly. Other questions require parents to observe the facility and the providers. How could this list be adapted to provide a record of a visit to each facility?

Aspect of Care	Questions to Consider
The Child Care Provider	• Does the number of children per adult meet NAEYC criteria? • What education, training, and experience do providers have? • How long have providers worked at this facility? How often are new providers hired? • What safety and first-aid training do providers have? • How do providers ensure that children are released only to authorized persons? • What arrangements are made if a provider is ill? • Do the providers seem to enjoy caring for the children? Are there joyful interactions between the children and the providers?
The Facility	• Does the physical space in the facility match NAEYC criteria? • Is the facility licensed and/or accredited? • Are both indoor and outdoor areas safe, comfortable, and clean? • If meals or snacks are provided, are they nutritious? Are they served in a clean area? • Are sleeping areas separate from noisy areas? • What happens if a parent must pick a child up late? • Does each child have a place for his or her belongings? • Is there a clean diaper-changing area for infants and toddlers? • Are the toilets and sinks clean and easy to reach? Can children reach clean towels, liquid soap, and toilet paper?
The Program	• Do providers guide children's behavior in appropriate ways? • Are the policies in writing? If so, ask for a copy. • Are rules reasonable for the children's ages? • Are the toys suitable for the children's ages? • Are activities varied and matched to the children's levels? • Do children have time for self-directed free play? • Is there a regular method for the provider to report to parents? • Do the children seem involved and happy? • If you were a child, would you like to spend time here? • What is the policy for sick children?

Issues Specific to Home-Based Care

Home-based care generally operates on a smaller scale than center-based care and involves fewer caregivers. For these reasons, parents considering home-based care for their children need to ask some additional questions.

- **How many children does the provider care for?** Most experts recommend that a family child care home have no more than six children per adult, including the child care provider's own children. This number should be even lower if infants and toddlers are part of the mix. A child care provider working alone should handle no more than two children younger than age two. See Fig. 22-9.

- **Is there a back-up plan for illness or vacations?** What happens when the family child care provider must be gone? Are there arrangements for someone to fill in? Parents need a back-up care plan.

- **Who else will be in the home?** Parents need to know who else will be around their children. They should ask about children, teens, or other adults who live in the home. Who are they, what are their backgrounds, and how might they interact with the children?

- **Are there both quiet and active times for children?** Children need a good mix of planned activities and informal play. Children shouldn't simply sit in front of the television much of the day or be left without supervision.

- **What if there is an emergency?** In most home-based care settings, there is only one adult child care provider. To deal with emergencies—such as an injured child who needs medical attention—the provider should have someone on call who can fill in at short notice.

Fig. 22-9 Parents need to find out how many children a home-based child care provider will be caring for. When there are fewer children, each child gets more individual attention.

The Cost of Substitute Care

While quality of care is the primary consideration in choosing child care, cost is also an important factor. The cost of child care varies significantly depending on the type of care and where it is located. In major cities, for example, families may pay more than $1,000 per month for a single toddler at a child care center. In general, the least expensive child care option is care provided by family and friends. Nannies are usually the most costly choice. Center-based care is usually more expensive than home-based care, but the cost varies widely from place to place. The age of the child needing care is also a factor. Care of infants is typically more costly than for preschoolers.

No matter what the cost, however, it adds up. Depending on the parents' working hours, children may need substitute care for nine or ten hours a day, five days a week.

In two-parent families, when earnings are compared to child care and other job-related costs such as transportation and clothing, it is sometimes less expensive for one parent to stay at home and provide care.

Sources of Information

How can parents locate potential sources of substitute care? Community groups, libraries, and local government agencies can supply listings. Groups such as Child Care Aware, NAEYC, and Nation's Network of Child Care Resource and Referral offer listings for many areas. All three groups have Web sites that provide easy access to their referral services and other information, including a lot of helpful information for parents and caregivers and links to other reputable Web sites. Many parents find substitute care by asking friends for referrals.

It is essential that parents visit each home or child care center they are considering before choosing one. This takes time, but it allows them to see the facility and the child care providers firsthand. In fact, taking the child to visit can help a parent see how the child responds to the place and the people and how the child care providers respond to the child.

Anyone considering a substitute care option should ask for references. Any child care provider—whether a center or a home-based provider—should be willing to give the names and phone numbers of parents whose children attend. These parents can say how long they have been using the service and describe the strengths and weaknesses they have observed.

Children are a precious resource and a responsibility. Parents must do everything possible to ensure their children are receiving quality care.

SECTION 22-1 Review and Activities

Reviewing the Section

1. Give three reasons why parents might need substitute care for their children.
2. What are the main differences between home-based care and center-based care?
3. What is the difference between a *child care center* and a *parent cooperative*?
4. For what ages is a preschool appropriate?
5. Why does the NAEYC recommend a greater number of care providers for younger children than for older children?
6. Why is it so important for parents to ask questions of prospective substitute child care providers?

Observing and Interacting

With a partner, write an interview between a parent and a director of a child care center. Determine the twelve most important questions for the parent to ask. Act out the interview for the class.

Participating in Early Childhood Education

While you are studying child development, you may have an opportunity to visit an early childhood classroom. Perhaps you will observe the children to better understand their development and behavior. You might be a volunteer helping the child care staff. You might also work with children as part of your course work. No matter what your role, understanding how such programs are organized and the roles, responsibilities, and concerns of the staff will make your experience more rewarding.

Objectives

- Describe the benefits of having learning centers in early childhood classrooms.
- Identify procedures that promote health and safety in early childhood classrooms.
- Evaluate the role of planning in providing appropriate learning experiences.
- Assess methods for promoting positive behavior in the classroom and dealing with misbehavior.

Key Terms

learning centers
circle time
free play
transitions

The Early Childhood Classroom

If you visit an early childhood classroom, you will notice that it is carefully designed to meet children's varied needs. It takes a special kind of environment to promote the physical, social, emotional, and intellectual development of young children.

First, the classroom environment needs to be child-size. Chairs should allow children to sit with their feet touching the floor. Having shelves within reach allows children to reach and return materials on their own. Posters and other wall decorations should be at the children's eye level. Drinking fountains, sinks, and other facilities should also be accessible.

A child-size environment promotes independence. The children are able to use materials without having to ask adults for help. This promotes feelings of success and self-sufficiency. Figure 22-10 on pages 640–641 shows one arrangement of learning centers in an early childhood classroom.

Fig. 22-10

Learning Centers in the Early Childhood Classroom

1 Block Center. This area may include small and large blocks, building logs, trucks and cars, and people and animal figures. Placing a rug or carpeting on the floor in the block center cuts down on noise.

2 Dramatic Play Center. This area provides children with opportunities for make-believe play. It can include clothes for dressing up, a play kitchen, and materials that can be used to play office or grocery store.

3 Music Center. The music center can include musical instruments such as tambourines, finger cymbals, triangles, and drums. It can also include a piano or keyboard and CDs.

4 Math and Science Center. In this area, children can learn math concepts such as matching, sorting, classifying, and counting. They can also learn about colors, sizes, and shapes. Children can also explore their world using science tools such as magnifying glasses, scales, and magnets. Specimens of natural objects—rocks, leaves, and perhaps a hamster—help children experience the world around them.

5 Computer Center. Children can learn basic computer skills. A wide variety of educational software programs help children practice specific skills.

6 Language Arts Center. This area includes materials related to speaking, listening, reading, and writing. It should be a quiet area with good lighting and comfortable chairs or pillows.

7 Active Play Area. Children exercise their large muscles in the active play area. It can include streamers for tossing; bean bags; areas for climbing, tumbling, and sliding; and a work bench for hammering.

8 Art Center. The art center allows children to be creative and exercise their imaginations through drawing, painting, and working with clay and fabric. It should include paper, scissors, glue, crayons, paints, chalk, clay, and fabric. There should be smocks for children to wear when they work with these materials.

9 Director's Office. Large, one-way observation windows allow the program director to handle paperwork and meet with parents while viewing the children. Sometimes parents use this observation area to check on their child's progress.

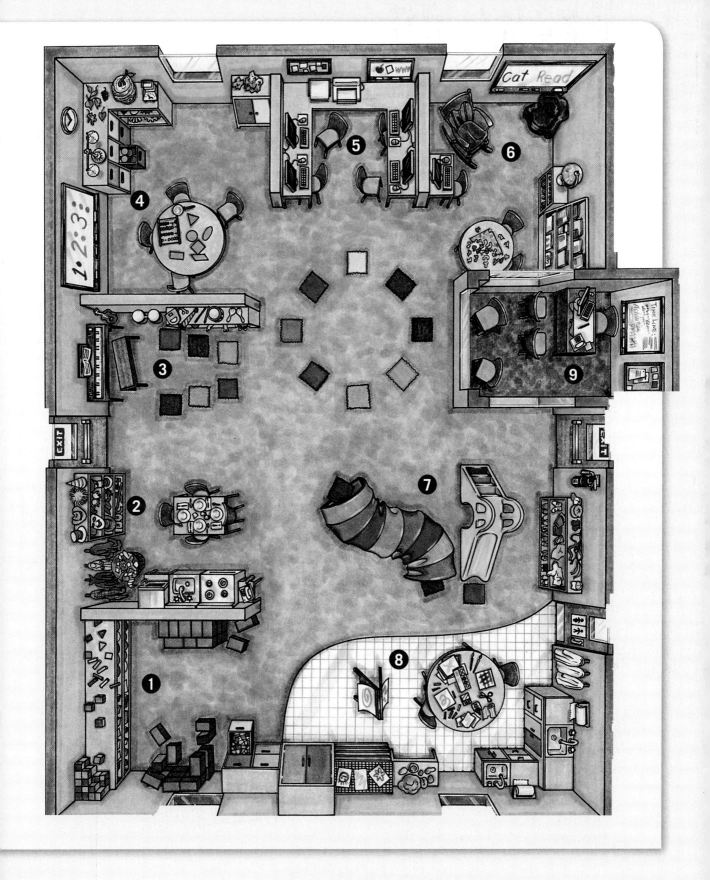

Learning Centers

Early childhood classrooms are usually divided into **learning centers**—areas designed for certain types of play and learning. Learning centers allow children to make choices. They can explore different areas of knowledge and develop skills through hands-on experiences. Learning centers provide a structure for the way children move through their day.

Classrooms differ in the number and types of learning centers they include. Other classrooms may have more or fewer learning centers.

Early childhood educators use guidelines such as these when designing a classroom and setting up learning centers:

- Use low shelves, colored floor coverings, wall decorations, or storage containers to separate learning centers.
- Separate noisy centers from quiet centers.

Children Around the World

Child Care in Denmark

In many countries in Europe, access to child care is considered a right rather than a privilege. In Denmark, for example, the government provides funding for child care for all children beginning at birth. The care is free for parents who can't afford to pay. Child care for very young children doesn't include specific learning goals, but rather emphasizes play and the development of social skills. There are usually three child care workers for every ten children, and at least one of the workers must have a teaching degree. Parents' boards meet monthly to discuss how child care facilities are operated. Danish employers accommodate parents' schedules. It is acceptable, for example, for parents to leave work so that they can pick their children up from child care on time.

Investigating Culture

1. What does providing child care beginning at birth indicate about a country's culture?
2. What might be some benefits and drawbacks of providing child care for all?

- Place the art center near a source of water. The floor should be easy to clean if it gets wet.
- Leave a large, open area for large-group activities, such as dancing or story time.

Health and Safety

Ensuring the health and safety of the children in the classroom is the most important responsibility of teachers and other child care providers. They must follow health care routines to prevent illness, make sure the environment is safe, and supervise play.

Health Care Routines

Health care routines prevent the spread of illness. Early childhood classrooms usually have strict policies regarding illness and attendance. For example, many early childhood programs don't allow sick children to stay in the classroom. They also ask that sick children be free of fever for at least 24 hours before returning to the classroom.

As children enter the classroom, staff members look for obvious signs of illness, such as a runny nose or fever. Children who are sick or become sick in the classroom will not be allowed to stay with the group. The child's parent or another caregiver will be called to pick the child up. If a major illness, such as chickenpox, occurs, all parents should be notified.

Parents or other caregivers should receive a written copy of the center's health policies. Having the rules in writing helps to prevent misunderstandings about when children should stay home and how illnesses will be handled if they occur when the child is in the classroom.

Fig. 22-11 **Frequent hand washing helps prevent the spread of illness.** How can young children be encouraged to wash their hands regularly?

Careful hand washing is one of the best ways to prevent the spread of illness. Hands need to be washed after using the toilet, after blowing the nose, and before cooking, eating, or playing with materials such as clay. Children should be taught to wash their own hands thoroughly with warm water and soap and to dry them with a clean paper towel. See Fig. 22-11.

Child care providers also must wash their own hands often, especially after helping children in the bathroom and before preparing food. This helps protect everyone's health and sets a good example for the children.

Other good health habits that care providers can teach children include:

- To blow and wipe their noses and to dispose of the tissue.
- To cover their mouths when they cough.
- To use only their own comb, brush, or headwear—never those of another child.
- To avoid sharing food and eating utensils.

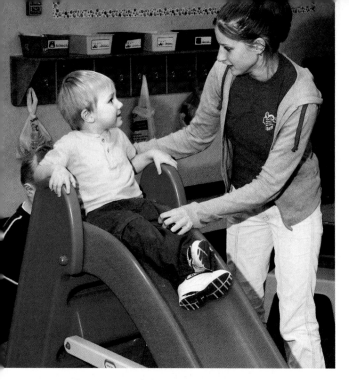

Fig. 22-12 **Equipment must be chosen with care, taking into account children's ages and abilities.** Why might an area that is safe for toddlers be hazardous for infants?

Safety

To keep children safe, child care providers must create a safe environment, practice and teach safe behaviors, and know what to do in an emergency. A safe environment takes into account the age and developmental levels of the children using it. See Fig. 22-12. Playground equipment suitable for preschoolers, for example, could be hazardous for younger children.

The classroom and outdoor play areas, and all equipment, should be inspected regularly for possible safety hazards such as uncovered electrical outlets or cords, and broken toys.

An important part of keeping children safe is to provide close supervision at all times. There should always be an adequate number of adults present to watch the children in each area. If there is an emergency,

Health & Safety

Food Safety Routines

To prevent cases of food-related illness, child care workers need to follow careful routines when handling food. Their main concerns are to keep eating areas clean and to store foods at safe temperatures.

Eating areas should be thoroughly washed with warm water and food-safe disinfectant both before and after the children eat. Food scraps or germs from children's hands could contaminate other foods set in the same place. The sponges or cloths used to clean these surfaces also need to be cleaned and disinfected regularly.

A child care center that serves meals and snacks must follow strict standards when preparing and serving food. Centers that serve food must be licensed and are subject to regular safety and sanitation inspections.

Check-Up

Observe the cafeteria in your own school. Write an evaluation of its attention to food safety routines.

Fig. 22-13 **Circle time is a time for learning together.** What are some activities that might take place during circle time?

an adult should stay with the children in the classroom while another adult goes for help.

Planning Appropriate Activities

Planning plays an important role in providing appropriate learning experiences for young children. The daily schedule should provide a variety of types of activities. Activities also need to provide opportunities in each area of development. Of course, activities must be appropriate to the age and skill levels of the children, too.

Play Builds Learning

Young children learn primarily through play. When planning activities for them, it is important to remember that the more involved the children are and the more realistic their experiences are, the more they learn. For example, reading children a story about a fire truck can help them learn about fire safety and community helpers. However, reading the book becomes a much more powerful learning tool when followed by a trip to the fire station and a chance to climb aboard a real fire truck.

Of course, children can't go on field trips every day, so care providers need to find other ways to help them experience what they are learning. Children need play experiences that focus on these areas of development:

- Thinking and problem solving
- Movement of large and small muscles
- Creativity, including music, dance, art, and dramatic play
- Relationships with others

Children need a variety of activities that involve different experiences. When several children sit at a table and work on separate puzzles, they are playing individually alongside one another. If they work on the same puzzle, they practice teamwork and getting along with others. Sometimes children play alone, such as when they look at a book by themselves. When the teacher reads the book to the group and they talk about it, they experience the same book in a different way. Children also play in small groups, perhaps dressing up and pretending to be a family. A teacher can guide group music or movement activities. The entire class may also come together at **circle time**, when they share their experiences in show-and-tell or listen to a story together. See Fig. 22-13.

The Daily Schedule

The daily schedule is the plan for how children will spend their time in the early childhood classroom. A good schedule for young children features a balance of active and quiet activities, small- and large-group activities, and teacher-directed and child-selected activities. (Time when children can choose any activity they want is often called **free play**.) Here is a sample schedule for a three-hour session for four-year-olds:

8:30-8:45	Arrival and free play
8:45-9:15	Circle time
9:15-9:45	Learning centers
9:45-10:00	Toilet and hand washing
10:00-10:15	Snack
10:15-10:45	Outdoor play
10:45-11:15	Learning centers
11:15-11:30	Group time and goodbyes

A good daily schedule allows time for **transitions**, periods during which children move from one activity to the next. During a transition, the children need to

Learning Through  PLAY

Play in a Montessori School

What is a morning like in a typical child care facility? A child might spend 15 minutes at the science center and then 15 minutes at the language arts center. Then the child might be able to play for 15 minutes in the center of the room. However, all early childhood centers are not structured in this way. In a Montessori early childhood room, you would also find learning centers, but they would be called work areas. And children are free to move from area to area at their own will. That is, they do not wait for a caregiver to tell them to move to a different area. The Montessori method of teaching is named after Italian educator Maria Montessori. Her philosophy of education was that when children play purposefully—for example, as they play with math manipulatives—they are learning.

Following Up

What would the role of the teacher be in a Montessori school?

Fig. 22-14 **Written activity plans help a teacher plan appropriate and successful activities.** What other functions do activity plans serve?

conclude one activity, put their materials away, and get ready for the next activity. Children should always be warned a few minutes ahead of time that they will soon have to make a change. This helps them mentally prepare for the change and encourages cooperation.

Developing Activity Plans

A daily schedule outlines the children's day in general. The lead teacher then plans the specific activities that children will do in the learning centers and during circle time and other group times. There are at least two types of forms that many teachers use to write these plans.

The first form—the planning chart—works from the daily schedule. This form lists the activities that will take place in each learning center during the day. Roger teaches in a preschool and he is preparing a weeklong planning chart based on the daily schedule shown on page 646. His students are currently learning about communities, so he is planning activities for each learning center that relate to this topic in some way. For example, he will have vehicles used by various community workers added to the block

center, and he will have dress-up clothes for different community members in the dramatic play center. Roger plans to read stories about communities during circle time.

The second form, an activity plan, allows teachers to record detailed information about each planned activity. On this form, teachers include specific information under the following headings:

- Title of the activity
- Objective, or purpose, of the activity
- Type of activity (for a learning center, small group, or large group)
- Materials needed
- Procedures
- Evaluation—a recap of the success or problems with the activity

The forms teachers use to plan activities are less important than the fact that they make careful plans. Writing plans ahead of time helps teachers think through the appropriateness of each activity. It also provides a list of materials needed so that the activities can be set up before children arrive. Written plans can be filed for future reference and reuse. They are also an excellent way to show parents what their children do each day. See Fig. 22-14.

The equipment and materials used in the early childhood classroom must be safe, durable, and appropriate for the age group that will use them. Glue sticks, for example, are more appropriate than liquid glue for younger children because they are easier to use. Here are some questions to ask yourself when choosing materials for an early childhood classroom:

- **Are they safe?** Edges should be rounded rather than sharp. Paint and other art materials must be non-toxic.

- **Are they durable?** Materials and equipment should be able to withstand prolonged and rough use by a large group of children.

- **Are they easy to clean?** This is more important in the classroom than at home because materials are used by many children.

- **Are they appropriate?** Materials should be appropriate for both boys and girls and for their ages. In addition, they should be free of stereotypes.

- **Are they effective?** Children should be able to learn basic concepts while using the materials.

- **Are they versatile?** Items that have more than one use are usually good choices.

- **Will they hold a child's interest?** Materials should encourage children's active play rather than passive participation.

- **Are they enjoyable?** Children should have fun when using the materials.

YOUR TURN

Interacting. You are buying art materials for a preschool. Identify two items you might buy. How well do they meet the guidelines for selection? Describe three ways each might be used as a learning tool.

Fig. 22-15 **When positive behavior is stressed, children are more likely to be cooperative.**

Promoting Positive Behavior

For a classroom to function smoothly, teachers need to promote positive behavior. They must let children know what is expected of them. They must also model good behavior and use positive reinforcement when children behave appropriately. At the same time, they need strategies for dealing with unacceptable behavior in a safe and nurturing manner.

Setting Classroom Expectations

Teachers should describe expected behaviors in positive terms. That is, they should tell the children what they *should* do—not what they *shouldn't* do. Each expectation should also have a clear purpose and be appropriate for the age of the children involved. The younger the child, the shorter the list of expectations should be.

When children are old enough, it's a good idea to involve them in establishing classroom expectations. You might open the discussion by asking what they already know about appropriate behavior at home or in their community. Then they can come up with some of their own ideas for classroom expectations and the reasons why each is necessary. When children are involved in this process, they feel more ownership in the classroom and they are more likely to meet expectations. See Fig. 22-15.

As a child care provider, Paige knows that one of her tasks is to help children learn what is expected of them. Paige makes sure that the children follow her directions and those of the other adults in charge. "Sometimes," she says, "I have to remind the kids to return the playground equipment when the five-minute whistle blows. Some of them don't want to come back inside." Paige uses time-outs when children misbehave. She says, "Today one of the children kept poking another child with her paintbrushes. I had to ask her to leave the activity and take a time-out. After a while, I asked her what she needed to do in order to come back. She said that she needed to say 'sorry' to the classmate she poked. She did that, and she was allowed to paint again."

▶▶ PERSONAL APPLICATION

1. Do you believe that time-outs are effective for young children? Why or why not?
2. Give an example of misbehavior that you think wouldn't qualify for a time-out and tell how you would handle it.

Here are some examples of reasonable expectations for an early childhood classroom:

1. **Keep your hands to yourself.** This discourages hitting or pushing.
2. **Always walk when you are inside the building.** This prevents accidents from falls.
3. **Put things away when you are finished.** This keeps the room well organized and allows children to find materials when they want them.
4. **Use your inside voice in the classroom.** This prevents the classroom from being too noisy.
5. **Be a friend to others.** This promotes cooperation and builds a pleasant atmosphere.

Using Positive Reinforcement

Children enjoy being recognized and rewarded with attention. They tend to repeat behaviors that are rewarded. To make this technique effective, however, teachers must be sincere in their response to a child's behavior. If they give only automatic or inattentive comments and praise, the children won't see them as rewards. Teachers must also be consistent. If Clay is praised for cleaning up after himself, then Maya and Alexandra should be praised for the same action.

Being a Good Role Model

In the classroom, the teacher's own behavior has a powerful influence on children. Children are more likely to do what their caregivers do. If teachers want the children to use inside voices, then they, too, must use a quiet voice indoors. If

Fig. 22-16 **When children misbehave, they need to be told what they are doing wrong, why it is wrong, and what they should do instead.**

teachers want children to treat each other with kindness, they should show kindness to the children and to their coworkers.

Dealing with Misbehavior

Of course, children will behave in unacceptable ways from time to time. All adults in the classroom need to know in advance how they will handle such situations. The children should also understand what will happen if they misbehave. Cases of misbehavior must be handled consistently in each situation and with each child.

In most cases, a simple statement of what the child should do is an effective way of dealing with misbehavior. If Jesse is using his voice too loudly, for example, he should be reminded of the expectation regarding noise level in the classroom: "Jesse, please use your inside voice. Others can't hear well when you are shouting." In other situations, a child may be offered a choice of more acceptable activities. If Jackie is not playing well in the block center, she might be told, "Jackie, you may choose to go to the dramatic play center or the art center. You can't stay in the block center because you keep taking Emilio's blocks." Notice that each example includes an explanation of why the child's behavior was unacceptable. See Fig. 22-16.

For some types of unacceptable behavior, a stronger response is necessary. Behavior that could hurt other people or damage property must not be permitted at any time. Children who exhibit this type of behavior should receive an immediate and consistent response. One effective approach is to give the child a time-out—a set time away from the activity or other children. (For more information about time-outs, see page 95.) When a time-out is used, the caregiver should continue to show the child that he or she is cared for but that the actions aren't acceptable.

SECTION 22-2 Review and Activities

Reviewing the Section

1. What are the benefits of dividing early childhood classrooms into different kinds of *learning centers*?
2. Why do child care centers need written policies concerning sick children?
3. Why is regular hand washing, by children and adults, particularly important in a child care setting?
4. What are three of the ways care providers can ensure that the child care environment is safe?
5. How does writing activity plans help teachers educate young children?
6. Describe one way a teacher can encourage positive behavior in a classroom.

Observing and Interacting

Visit a child care center. Describe the overall environment and behavior that you observe. What kinds of learning centers are there? How are activities organized? How do the children interact with one another and with the care providers? What is your overall impression of the center?

Child Care Worker

Today, with the majority of parents working outside the home, the demand for child care workers is higher than it has ever been. Child care workers help children develop physically, emotionally, socially, and intellectually. In homes, child care centers, and preschools, they make sure that the children in their care are safe and nurtured.

▸ Job Responsibilities

Child care workers supervise children and make sure they get exercise, play, and relaxation. They may also be responsible for planning activities and providing healthy meals and snacks. They answer children's questions and teach basic lessons.

▸ Work Environment

As a child care worker, you might work in your own home or the home of someone else, in a child care center, community center, religious center, or even an office building. Some stores, workplaces, and gymnasiums offer child care so that parents can shop, work, or exercise while their children play.

▸ Education and Training

If you want to be a child care worker, you need at least a high school diploma. It also helps to have plenty of babysitting experience with children of different ages. Studying early childhood education or child psychology in college can open the door to higher-paying job opportunities.

▸ Skills and Aptitudes

- Energy and enthusiasm
- Gentleness and compassion
- Patience
- Interest in child development
- Teaching ability

WORKPLACE CONNECTION

1. **Thinking Skills.** Give an example of how a child care worker could help children develop social skills.

2. **Resource Skills.** Find out how child care workers can advance to higher-level jobs.

CHAPTER 22

Review and Activities

SECTION SUMMARIES

- Many parents rely on substitute care for their children. It may be provided in a home- or center-based setting. (22-1)
- Home-based care options include in-home care, family child care, and play groups. Center-based care options include child care centers, parent cooperatives, preschools, and Head Start centers. (22-1)
- When choosing substitute care, it's important to carefully evaluate choices. (22-1)
- A typical early childhood classroom includes different learning centers that concentrate on particular areas of learning. (22-2)
- Child care providers' primary responsibility is for the health and safety of the children in their care. (22-2)
- A daily schedule and written plans help ensure appropriate learning experiences for children. (22-2)
- In an early childhood classroom, rules and positive reinforcement help promote appropriate behavior. (22-2)

REVIEWING THE CHAPTER

1. What are three reasons parents might use substitute care? (22-1)
2. Why do some parents prefer home-based child care? (22-1)
3. Why is the ratio of child care providers to children important? (22-1)
4. What is the difference between a *child care center* that is *licensed* and one that is *accredited*? (22-1)
5. Identify two options for parents for school holiday child care. (22-1)
6. Give four examples of *learning centers*. (22-2)
7. List three practices that help maintain health in the classroom. (22-2)
8. Give an example of how children learn through play. (22-2)
9. What is the purpose of an activity plan? (22-2)
10. List five factors to consider when choosing materials for an early childhood classroom. (22-2)
11. What methods can early childhood classroom staff use to teach children appropriate behavior? (22-2)

THINKING CRITICALLY

1. **Analyzing Information.** Which five questions would you rank as most important when evaluating substitute child care? Explain.
2. **Making Inferences.** Why is it more effective when setting rules to tell children what they should do, not what they shouldn't?

MAKING CONNECTIONS

1. **Writing.** Imagine that you are starting your own home-based child care service. Write a brochure describing your services.

2. **Math.** Suppose you were to start a child care business in your home. You will take care of four children and charge $30 a day per child. You pay $80 a week for meals. You also spend $675 on equipment. How much money will you have made after a year, assuming you take two weeks off for vacation and the children come five days a week, including holidays?

APPLYING YOUR LEARNING

1. **Special Programs.** Use the Internet or other resources to find out more about Head Start, Montessori preschools, or High/Scope preschools. What are the programs like? What do children need in order to enter each program? What roles do parents play? Write a one-page summary of your findings.

2. **Interpersonal Skills.** Suppose that you are a teacher in an early childhood classroom. The children are busy working in the learning centers. You have one child who is not sharing the supplies in her center. You have already pointed out her unacceptable behavior once, but she has continued the behavior. What approach would you take toward the child?

Learning from Research

1. Choose one of the following areas to investigate.
2. How is this research useful to people who work in early childhood classrooms?
3. Summarize what you have learned from your research about child care and early education.

Health in Early Childhood Classrooms. Choose one childhood health issue to research. Develop a list of procedures that could be followed by early childhood staff to address that health issue in the classroom. Then create an activity plan for teaching young children about that health issue.

Computer Use in Early Childhood Classrooms. Research the various ways computers are used in early childhood classrooms. What impact might these uses have on small and large motor skill development? Identify the new technology being developed for early childhood classrooms of the future.

Quality Care in Early Childhood Classrooms. Several studies have found that the quality of care a child receives plays a major role in his or her development. Describe the characteristics of quality care provided in early childhood classrooms. Evaluate its effects on child development.

23 Careers Working with Children

Thoughtful Reading:

As you read this chapter:

- Identify three phrases that remind you of background knowledge.
- Reread the passages.
- Write three "I connect to ___?___ on page _____" statements about what you read.

Section 23-1
Preparing for a Career

Section 23-2
Beginning Your Career

Preparing for a Career

Josie knows that she wants to work with children, but she doesn't know what her options are. She needs to gather information that will help her make a decision. A good place to start is with an understanding of the working world.

Objectives

- Compare different levels of jobs and the education and training required for each.
- Evaluate various methods of gathering information about careers.
- Describe the benefits of gaining work experience.
- Identify the factors to analyze when researching careers.
- Summarize the types of skills needed for career success.

Key Terms

entry-level job
paraprofessional
professional
entrepreneur
aptitude
internship
job shadowing
service learning
work-based learning
lifelong learner

Career Options

Choosing a career may seem like a very difficult decision. There are so many jobs to choose from. How do you know where to begin? Most people start by choosing a career area or career field—a group of similar careers. Later, when they have learned more about the career field, they can choose a specific career to prepare for.

Taking a class in an area of interest is a good way to explore career options. Perhaps you are taking this class because, like Josie, you are interested in working with children. The knowledge and skills you have gained in this class will help prepare you to make a choice that is right for you.

Opportunities for Working with Children

Those interested in working directly with children often choose careers related to child development or child care. A pediatrician, for example, specializes in medical care for children. In-depth knowledge of child development and medicine are required.

Fig. 23-1 People who work with children need an understanding of child development. How would that understanding help this person do her job?

A lead teacher in a child care center depends on knowing about how children develop to plan appropriate activities and care. Look for the "Career Opportunities" features throughout this book for profiles of additional careers that involve working with children. See Fig. 23-1.

Levels of Jobs

Within a career area, there are usually jobs available at several levels. These levels correspond to the amount of education and training required and the degree of responsibility the job carries.

- **Entry-level jobs** are the kinds of jobs many people take when they first enter a career area. Most people, however, don't stay at this level. With more experience, and perhaps more education, many move up to jobs that carry more responsibility. After he received his high school diploma, Russell took an entry-level job at a child care center so that he could explore his interest in helping children. Within a few years, and after earning a degree from a four-year college program, he had moved into a lead teacher position at the center.

- A **paraprofessional** has some education beyond high school that trains him or her for a certain field. Many jobs at the paraprofessional level require a related degree from a two-year college. An assistant teacher in a preschool, for instance, is a paraprofessional.

- A **professional** has a position that requires at least a degree from a four-year college or technical school in a particular area of study. Many professionals have a more advanced degree, such as a Master's degree, and years of experience. Professionals may be in charge of programs or supervise entry-level workers and paraprofessionals. Kindergarten teachers are professionals.

A School Where Teachers Fly to Work

If you lived on Out Skerries Island, in the Shetland Islands off the coast of Scotland, you would get a lot more attention from your teachers than you might want. The school there has only two students, who are brothers, and six teachers. The brothers cost the most to educate of any students in Great Britain. It costs over $100,000 a year to teach the two boys, because three of their teachers are flown in every week from another island. If the boys' school closed, they would have to take a long journey by ferry and taxi to another school. The boys' lives are a mix of new and old. In keeping with traditional practices on the islands, the boys have learned how to catch lobsters, mend nets, and repair boats. They've also learned to shear sheep for their wool. The modern world hasn't left the boys behind, though. They keep in touch with friends on other islands through e-mail and text messaging on cell phones.

Investigating Culture

1. What aspects of island life do you think you would enjoy?
2. What aspects would you find difficult?

Opportunities for Entrepreneurs

Most people work for someone else—an elementary teacher works for a school district, a toy designer works for a manufacturer. Others choose to be self-employed or to own their own business—to be **entrepreneurs** (AHN-truh-pruh-NURS). An entrepreneur's life can be both exciting and challenging. Because entrepreneurs have no boss, they get to make the rules, set their own schedules, and make the decisions. However, they also assume all the risks of the business and often end up working very long hours.

People who are self-employed need to be self-motivated, self-disciplined, good problem solvers, and willing to work hard. Entrepreneurial opportunities related to children include owning a child care business, writing children's books, and providing entertainment for children's parties.

Evaluating Interests, Aptitudes, and Abilities

To make a decision about a career to pursue, consider how well you would "fit" that career. Some careers may sound exciting, but when you look at them more closely, you might realize that they wouldn't be right for you. As you explore various career choices, you need to consider them in light of your own interests and values, aptitudes, and abilities.

- **Interests and values.** If you work toward a career that doesn't match your interests, it could set you up for years of unfulfilling work. Your interests might include areas of study that you enjoy, such as psychology or science, or activities that you enjoy, such as photography or music. You also need to consider your values, or what is important to you. Do

Fig. 23-2 **The Internet is a great resource for career information.** What career information sites are you already familiar with?

Fig. 23-3 **There are many opportunities for finding out more about career areas.**

you want a career that pays a high salary? Are you concerned about gaining satisfaction from your work? Are you willing to work weekends or long hours, or is time with family and friends more important?

- **Aptitudes.** An **aptitude** is a natural talent or potential for learning a skill. What kinds of learning come most easily to you? Perhaps you have a natural ability to communicate with young children or an aptitude for learning new computer applications. High school counselors have tests that you can take to help you determine what your aptitudes are. It's a good idea to consider careers that match your strengths. See Fig. 23-2.

- **Abilities.** You already have many skills that will be useful in the working world. Identifying what those skills are can help you make career decisions. As you begin

to take on more responsibilities, you can expand and improve your abilities—both those specific to career areas that interest you and general skills, such as effective communication, computer literacy, teamwork, and reliability. These general skills are useful in any career.

Finding Career Information

Another important part of career decision making is research. Learning more about areas that interest you will help you narrow your career choices.

Gathering Information

You can gather information from a variety of sources. Online sources, libraries, and people can all be helpful. See Fig. 23-3. The Internet can put you in touch with trade and professional organizations, government resources, job listings, and people working in various careers. Most libraries have excellent career information resources. These two government publications are available in print and online:

- *The Occupational Outlook Handbook*, which gives detailed information on hundreds of jobs.
- *The Occupational Outlook Quarterly*, which updates information on career trends every three months.

Probably the best way to find out what a career is really like is to talk to people who are in that career. After all, who knows better than a teacher what the day-to-day life of a teacher is like? You can ask school counselors, teachers, relatives, and friends about possible contacts in specific career areas. Most people are happy to share information about their careers.

Gaining Work Experience

You can learn a lot about a career—and about yourself—by working. Summer work and part-time jobs are good ways to get started. Another way to learn about a job is through an **internship**, in which you work for little or no pay while you gain experience and receive supervision.

You might also be able to arrange to do **job shadowing**—observing someone in his or her job. This process involves contacting someone whose career interests you and arranging to spend time at work with that person, following the person around like a shadow. You'll also be able to ask the person questions about his or her job. Your guidance counselor may be able to help you make arrangements for job-shadowing experiences.

Another way to learn about a career is by volunteering. Many organizations—especially those that operate on limited funds—welcome volunteers. See Fig. 23-4. The opportunities may be temporary or longer term. Arielle volunteers as a children's storyteller at her local library once a month, while Jared volunteers as an assistant for children's activities at a city park each weekend. Guidance counselors often have a list of organizations looking for volunteers. Community centers are also a good resource for volunteering opportunities.

Although volunteers are not paid for their work, volunteering offers a great experience. It may even lead to a paying job. One added benefit of volunteering is

Fig. 23-4 **You can gain valuable work experience by volunteering or taking part in a service learning program.** What are some benefits of getting work experience while you are still in school?

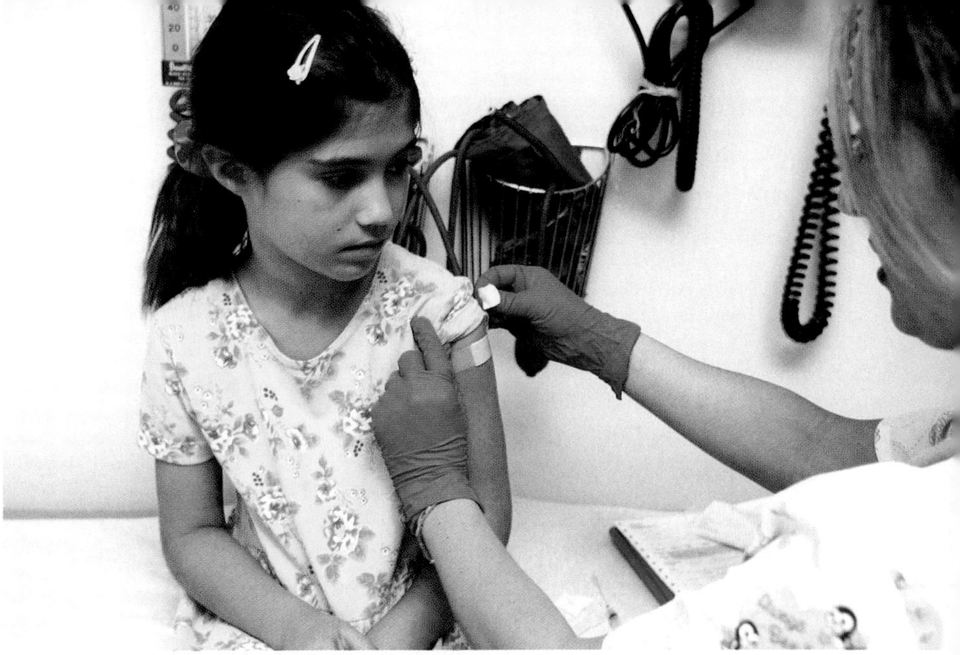

Fig. 23-5 **Some jobs require long hours. For example, a doctor's office doesn't close until all patients have been seen.** Why might some people have a problem with that type of schedule?

the satisfaction of helping others in the community. In addition, colleges and employers are impressed by people who make the effort to help out in their community through volunteer work.

Some school programs offer direct work experience. Schools with **service learning** programs have students volunteer in their community as a graduation requirement. Schools with **work-based learning** programs offer students the opportunity to combine in-school and on-the-job learning.

Work experience offers another benefit besides a feel for what it's like to have a job. You may meet people who know someone in the career area that interests you. Supervisors and co-workers may also be willing to serve as references whom a prospective employer can contact for information about your skills and character.

Analyzing Careers

Knowing where to look for career information is one thing, but then what? Here are eight factors to analyze when delving deeper into your career search:

- **Tasks and responsibilities.** What does a worker in this career do? Is the work the same every day or varied? Is the pace fast or slow? How much control does a worker have over the work?

- **Work with people, information, or technology.** Each career tends to emphasize one area over another. A reading teacher works mainly with people. An editor of children's books works mainly with information. A designer of children's clothing works mainly with technology.

- **Work environment.** The work environment is the physical and social surroundings at the workplace. Camp counselors work outdoors; nurses work indoors. Some people work alone; others work in teams. Which kind of environment is most appealing to you?

- **Working hours.** Many people work from 9:00 in the morning to 5:00 at night, but many others work different hours. See Fig. 23-5. Some jobs require weekend and holiday work. Many jobs require overtime or travel. What is acceptable to you?

Twenty-year-old Patrick has worked in a drop-in center for runaway and homeless teens for four years. He loves the job. When new clients come in, he makes sure they have a meal, learn their way around the center, and get counseling if they need it. Patrick knows that he wants a career that involves helping people, so three years ago he enrolled part time at a nearby community college and studied for an associate's degree in human services. He will finish his degree in a few months and is considering whether he should continue his studies. With a bachelor's degree in social work, he would be eligible for higher-paying jobs with more responsibility. Best of all, he'd have the flexibility to work with different groups of people. He could even work as a school social worker or probation officer. On the other hand, it would mean going to college full time and giving up his current job. It's a difficult decision.

▶▶PERSONAL APPLICATION

1. Have you made a decision about your education after high school?
2. How could you find more information about two- and four-year colleges?

- **Aptitudes.** Compare the aptitudes needed for a career with your own aptitudes. How well do they match?

- **Education and training.** Although many people gain experience on the job, they need the right education to land that job in the first place. What education and training are required for the careers that interest you? School counselors, libraries, and the Internet all offer information about education and training opportunities beyond high school and ways to pay for them.

- **Salary and benefits.** Income generally increases with training and education. Income also tends to rise as workers gain experience. A first-year paraprofessional can expect to earn less than a co-worker with five years in the same job. Many employers offer benefits such as health insurance, retirement plans, and paid vacation time in addition to salary.

- **Career outlook.** What do experts think will happen to this career in the future? Will the demand for the career grow or shrink? Answers to these questions affect how easy it will be to find a job in certain career areas. Many sources estimate future trends for various jobs.

Preparing for Career Success

Some people simply take whatever job comes their way. While this approach sometimes works out, it's much smarter to think carefully about the career you would like and then work to achieve it. After all, you'll spend most of your waking hours at work. Wouldn't it be better if that work were satisfying, challenging, and worthwhile?

Setting and Achieving Goals

Career goals are like a road map to your future. As with other goals, you need both long-term and short-term career goals. If you decide that you want a career as a kindergarten teacher, that's your long-term goal. Getting there will take years and require many smaller achievements. To reach your long-term goal, you'll need short-term goals—specific actions to achieve in the next few days, months, or year. Without short-term goals, it's less likely that you will achieve your long-term goal.

Lynette's goal was to become a physical therapist. With that long-term goal, she set a short-term goal of working with children on a daily basis to make certain she would like that aspect of the career. Through her job as a camp counselor, she met that goal.

Fig. 23-6 In most careers, workers need to periodically upgrade their skills. Think of a job for which this would be important.

Developing Skills for a Lifetime

Preparing for a career involves more than learning about careers and setting goals. You also have to prepare yourself for the working world. In the past, people often stayed in the same career—sometimes at the same company—all their lives. Today this isn't the case. People tend to change careers several times.

To succeed in today's working environment, you need to be flexible and willing to change. You also must commit to being a **lifelong learner**, willing to learn new information and acquire skills throughout your working life. These qualities will make you a more effective worker and a valued employee. See Fig. 23-6.

Now is the time to build the skills you will need for future employment. Some of these skills require training related to a specific career. Others are more universal skills that every worker needs to be successful. You can start building these universal skills right now:

- **Personal qualities.** Employers look for employees who are enthusiastic, committed, responsible, respectful, and willing to take initiative. Personal integrity and taking pride in one's work are also high on their lists.

- **Interpersonal skills.** Employees must get along with co-workers, supervisors, and customers. They must have leadership skills and work well in teams made up of people from diverse backgrounds.

- **Basic skills.** To succeed at work, employees need to be able to solve math problems. Strong communication skills—verbal, nonverbal, written, and electronic—are also key to positive relationships on the job.

- **Thinking skills.** Employers need workers who are able to learn, reason, think creatively, make decisions, and solve problems.

- **Management skills.** Employees must be able to set goals and use available resources—information, time, materials, skills, and people—to get the work done efficiently. Being well organized is important to managing well.

- **Technology skills.** Most jobs require the ability to use computers. For many jobs, technology skills are classified as "basic skills." Many other careers require highly specialized training in technology.

SECTION 23-1 Review and Activities

Reviewing the Section

1. What is the difference between a *paraprofessional* and a *professional*?
2. Why should you evaluate your interests, *aptitudes*, and abilities when researching careers?
3. What sources of career information can you find on the Internet?
4. Describe two different ways of gaining work experience.
5. List eight factors to analyze when researching careers. Underline the three that you consider the most important.
6. Why do you need both short-term and long-term career goals?
7. Why is *lifelong learning* more important today than it was in the past?

Observing and Interacting

Choose two of the universal skills needed for a worker to be successful. Then choose someone whose job you observe in everyday life, such as a teacher, mail carrier, or store clerk. Explain how the person uses the skills that you chose to perform his or her work.

Beginning Your Career

Lucy's just finished a two-year degree program at a nearby community college. She's both excited and nervous about starting her career. She's looking forward to the challenges of working with young children and finally being on her own. Sometimes, though, she feels overwhelmed by finding a job. As with all major goals, it's best to break down job hunting into a series of steps that you can accomplish one at a time.

Objectives

- Compare different ways to find job openings.
- Describe the purpose and contents of a résumé, cover letter, and job application.
- Summarize the steps to take for a successful interview.
- Assess which career skills are needed for success in any workplace.
- Identify guidelines for leaving a job.

Key Terms

networking
job fair
résumé
cover letter
ethical
unemployment benefits
COBRA

Looking for a Job

A few people are lucky. They find themselves in the right place at the right time and are hired for their dream job. Others are fortunate to have an internship or a part-time job turn into a full-time position. Most people, however, must devote a considerable amount of time and effort to their job search. They spend time finding job openings, contacting employers, interviewing, and following up.

You should plan to invest time and energy in your own job search. After all, you will be spending many hours at work each week. Isn't it worth making the effort to make sure you find the right job for you?

The key to a successful job search is organization. A notebook or computer file used to record names, addresses, and dates is one way many people keep track of their job search. For instance, Will uses his computer to record the dates he responds to newspaper ads, the dates employers contact him, the times and locations of his interviews, and the dates he sends follow-up letters.

Finding Job Openings

The Internet and classified ads from the newspaper are excellent ways to find job openings, but they are not your only resources. Finding a job often begins with a tip from a friend, relative, or acquaintance. That is why it's a good idea to spread the word that you are job hunting. The more people who know that you are looking for a job, the better.

For example, MacKenzie's neighbor has a sister who is a Girl Scout leader. She knows that the organization will be looking for a new staff member soon. Brendan's roommate knows of an opening for a teacher at the preschool where his girlfriend works. The practice of using personal and professional contacts to further your career goals is called **networking**. Many people find that networking is the best way to find a job. See Fig. 23-7.

Another way to find out about job openings is to attend a **job fair**. At a job fair, employers with current or future job openings meet with prospective employees. Sometimes community colleges or universities sponsor such events. You may not land the perfect job by attending a job fair, but you will be able to make valuable contacts by meeting some employers.

Preparing a Résumé

A **résumé** is a concise document that summarizes your career objectives, education, work experience, and accomplishments. It's like a personal advertisement to show prospective employers.

Fig. 23-7 When searching for a job, it's a good idea to tell as many personal and professional acquaintances as possible. What names could you include in your network of contacts?

You should create your résumé on a computer. See Fig. 23-8. Many word processing programs provide sample résumés with different layouts, typefaces, and designs. Find a sample that fits your needs and customize it with your own information. Figure 23-9 on page 670 shows the sections that are traditionally included in a résumé.

The first section of the résumé—the objective—is made up of one or two sentences that state the type of position you are seeking. It should convey a sense of purpose and direction. It's a good idea to customize the objective for each potential employer or job listing.

In the section on education, list the schools you attended starting with the most recent, along with any degrees, honors, or awards you have received. If you have received several honors or awards, you could list them separately under "Honors."

For the remaining sections of your résumé, consider carefully what you want to include and emphasize. If you don't have much work experience, focus on your skills. If you have done volunteer work, be sure to include that. After all, volunteering shows that you are responsible, caring, and an active community member. You might also include information about any committees or projects you have worked on.

Here are some additional tips for preparing an effective résumé.

- Be concise, keeping the résumé to one page if possible. Two pages is the maximum length.
- Be truthful. Don't misrepresent your work history, accomplishments, or education.
- Use action verbs to describe accomplishments. Consider these possibilities: achieved, developed, coordinated, produced, led, and conducted.

Fig. 23-8 **A computer is a powerful tool for finding a job. It can be used to find job openings, locate information about employers, and develop a résumé.**

- Proofread the document carefully. Have someone else proofread it, too. Poor grammar or misspelled words could cause employers to eliminate you from consideration.
- Keep it simple. Don't clutter your résumé with pictures, extra graphics, or a fancy format.
- Ask any references for permission before including their names and contact information. References may be listed on your résumé or on a separate page.
- If an employer requests that your résumé be sent by e-mail, ask for formatting guidelines.

Fig. 23-9
Sample Résumé

Desiray T. Minter
6412 W. Main Street
Asheville, NC 28810
828-555-1234
DTM@anymail.com

Objective:	To work with children as a teacher's assistant in a Bilingual Education program.
Education:	Ashton Community College, Asheville, North Carolina Associate in Applied Science, Child Development, 2007
	Whittier High School, Asheville, North Carolina High School Diploma, 2004
Skills:	Excellent organizational skills Fluent in Spanish and French Able to work independently or on a team

Experience:

2004–Present	**Photography Assistant** Angelface Photography Studio, Asheville, North Carolina Assist children's photographer with studio sittings; schedule appointments.
2002–2004	**Foreign Language Tutor in Spanish and French** Tutored four to five high school students each semester.
1999–2001	**Counselor** Far Hills Equestrian Camp, Greenville, North Carolina Supervised eight campers each session.

Honors:	FCCLA State Vice President of STAR Events, 2006 American Legion Award, 2006 National French Honor Society
Membership:	Family, Career and Community Leaders of America (FCCLA) 4-H (Chairperson of Horse Leader's Conference)

References available upon request.

Writing a Cover Letter

An employer may receive dozens, or even hundreds, of résumés in response to an ad placed in a newspaper or on the Internet. An interesting **cover letter**, or introductory letter sent with a résumé, could set yours apart from the rest and result in a request for an interview.

A cover letter provides an opportunity for you to make a good impression. Your cover letter should highlight your relevant talents and skills, prompt the employer to read the résumé, and ultimately result in an interview. Figure 23-10 shows a sample cover letter.

Here are some key points to keep in mind when writing a cover letter:

- Highlight your skills and background but don't repeat everything in the résumé.
- Limit the letter to one page.

Fig. 23-10
**Sample
Cover Letter**

6412 W. Main Street
Asheville, North Carolina 28810

June 15, 2007

Ms. Michelle Hansen
Director, Human Resources
School District 184
Asheville, North Carolina 28810

Dear Ms. Hansen:

I am replying to the ad on the *Asheville Citizen-Times'* web site seeking a teacher's assistant for the Bilingual Education program at the Early Childhood Education Center. I believe that my skills are an excellent match for this position.

As a high school and college student, I enjoyed courses in child development. I have been successful working with children of all ages—as a camp counselor, tutor, and active member of FCCLA and 4-H. Currently, my job as a photography assistant involves working with preschool and grade school children.

My other main interest is foreign languages. In 2006, I had the opportunity to participate in a month-long exchange program in Mexico. I speak Spanish fluently and have four years of credit in French. As a language student at Whittier High School, I frequently assisted with special events in an elementary school program for English-language learners.

I am available for an interview any morning of the week. The best time to reach me at home is before noon. My telephone number is 828-555-1234. My e-mail address is DTM@anymail.com. Thank you for your consideration.

Sincerely,

Desiray T. Minter

Desiray T. Minter

- Tailor the letter to fit the particular situation. If you're answering an ad, for example, be sure to address the requirements cited in the ad.
- As with the résumé, make sure your spelling and grammar are flawless.
- Try to address the letter to an individual rather than "To Whom It May Concern."

It's often possible to call the employer to obtain the name of a contact person or the person's title. This information may also be on an employer's web site.
- Use high-quality white or cream paper and sign your name legibly in black ink.
- Include a cover letter when sending a résumé by e-mail.

Greg looked in the mirror and straightened his tie. He was nervous about going on an interview. Although he had just received a four-year degree in physical education, he still wasn't sure at what level he wanted to teach. His career counselor at school suggested that he start applying for a variety of jobs to see what was available.

That day, Greg was on his way to an interview for an elementary physical education teacher position. He arrived a bit early and went to the school office to check in. The secretary told him to take a seat. As Greg waited, he looked over the copy of his résumé that he had brought. The principal already had one, but his counselor recommended always taking an extra. Greg also had copies of several letters of references from jobs he held in college.

The principal called Greg into his office and talked with him for about an hour. He asked Greg about his education, his experience, and his desire to teach physical education. Then he took Greg on a brief tour of the school. After the interview, Greg thanked the principal for his time and shook his hand. He told the principal that he hoped to hear from him soon.

▶▶PERSONAL APPLICATION

Have you ever gone on an interview? If so, were you nervous? What kinds of things did you do to prepare?

Filling Out an Application

Most employers ask applicants to fill out a job application. An application is a screening tool that helps employers determine which applicants deserve further consideration. Follow these tips for filling out an application:

- If you have an appointment, arrive on time or a few minutes early.
- Be well groomed and neatly dressed when you go to fill out the application.
- Read and follow the directions on the application carefully. If it is an electronic application, make sure you know how to use the computer before you start.
- Print neatly or type carefully, and answer questions truthfully and as positively as possible. If a question does not apply, write "NA," for "not applicable," in the space.
- Some applications ask for salary requirements. "Negotiable" is a tactful way to respond.
- Bring your job search notebook or printouts from your computer file, and a copy of your résumé. You will need specific information about your educational background and work history.
- Most applications ask for an availability date. If you're not currently working, write "Immediately." If you have a job and must give notice, write "Upon two weeks' notice."

Interviews

The thought of a job interview makes some job seekers nervous. You're less likely to feel uneasy if you prepare well for each interview. Think of the interview as your chance to show the interviewer that you are more than a name on a piece of paper.

Here are some suggestions to help you through the interview process:

- **Dress appropriately.** Try to match your outfit to the job. Feeling that you are dressed appropriately will help you feel confident. Avoid very baggy or tight clothing and keep jewelry to a minimum. See Fig. 23-11.

- **Prepare.** Learn as much as possible about the company before the interview. Study the employer's web site. Talk to people who are familiar with the employer. Review the list of commonly asked interview questions in Fig. 23-12 on page 674 and prepare possible answers.

- **Rehearse.** Practice for the interview with a friend or relative. Remember to show you have a positive, upbeat attitude. You might want to videotape the process and then look for ways you could improve your performance.

- **Arrive early.** Allow for possible traffic delays and arrive a few minutes early. If possible, do a trial run the day before the interview to make sure you know where you have to go and to see how long the journey takes.

- **Greet the interviewer.** Shake the person's hand firmly and make eye contact. Try not to appear anxious or overly eager.

- **Listen carefully.** Pay attention to the questions you are asked. Don't attempt to change the subject or interrupt the interviewer.

Fig. 23-11 **Your appearance counts at a job interview, so be sure to dress appropriately.** What are some other ways you can prepare for an interview?

- **Ask appropriate questions.** When the employer asks if you have any questions, focus on the nature of the job, its responsibilities, and the work environment. Try to fill any gaps in your knowledge about the position. Don't bring up the topic of salary and benefits at a first interview unless the interviewer brings it up first.

- **Leave gracefully.** Thank the interviewer and voice your interest in the job as you shake hands to leave.

Fig. 23-12 Commonly Asked Interview Questions

"What are your weaknesses?" Can you answer that question? Before going to a job interview, prepare replies to common interview questions:

1. What are your strengths?
2. What are your qualifications for this position?
3. Why would you like to work for this company or school?
4. What do you want to be doing in five years (or ten years)?
5. How would a past teacher or employer describe you?
6. Why did you leave your last job?
7. What rewards are the most important in your career?
8. Why did you choose this career?
9. How do you work under pressure?
10. What two or three accomplishments have given you the most satisfaction?
11. What is a major problem you have encountered at school or on the job? How did you deal with it?
12. How creative are you? What are some examples of your creativity?
13. Have you worked as part of a team? What were the pluses and minuses of the experience?
14. Why should we hire you?
15. You seem under-qualified for this position. Are you?
16. What is the hardest job you have ever done?
17. What questions do you have about the job or this company?

If a company is interested in hiring you, it may require you to undergo a drug test or submit to a background check. Many jobs today—especially positions in early childhood education and care—require this kind of screening. In many states, candidates who are found to have drug problems or who have been convicted of a crime against a child will be rejected.

Following Up After an Interview

Many job seekers become frustrated with the waiting game they must play after an interview. It may help if you remember that the interviewer might have additional candidates to see before a decision can be made. If the interviewer says that he or she will be in touch within two weeks, you should wait that length of time. After that, it's permissible to call and politely ask about the status of the application. A good way to approach this situation would be to say, "Could you please tell me what the next step is in the hiring process?" The employer might want you to come in for a second interview, or you might be told that someone else has been hired.

While you might be tempted to ask why you didn't get the job, it's better to be gracious in accepting the news. The employer is not obliged to explain his or her decision. It's better to learn from the experience of the interview and move on. If you felt that certain aspects of the interview did not go well, practice ways of handling them better next time.

Evaluating a Job Offer

You might think that the most important factor in deciding whether to accept or reject a job offer is the salary. Of course, adequate compensation is important, but there are other factors to consider.

Fig. 23-13 An entry-level job may not pay very much, but it provides an opportunity to gain valuable experience and skills.

Perhaps the company is one that could provide a bright future. Many employees have started at entry-level positions simply to "get their foot in the door" at a desirable company or school. If there is potential for advancement, avoid thinking that the job is not good enough. Remember that in the early years of your career, you are building experience and a work history. See Fig. 23-13.

When an employer makes a job offer, you don't have to give an answer immediately. It's permissible to ask for a day to think about the offer, but you should not put off the decision for too long. If it's a difficult decision, make a list of the pros and cons. The pros are the benefits that go along with the paycheck, such as health insurance and the opportunity to gain experience. The cons are the disadvantages of the job, such as a long commute or weekend hours.

If you're offered a job but feel that you would want to move on as quickly as possible, it may be best not to take it. Changing jobs frequently would not look good on your résumé. Always be gracious when turning down a job offer. You might want to apply for another position with the same employer at another time.

Write a Follow-Up Letter After an Interview

Within 24 hours after an interview, it is appropriate to write a follow-up letter. You can mail your letter or use e-mail. In either case, keep your language formal and businesslike. If more than one person interviewed you, send a separate letter to each. Make sure the letters are different for each person. Here are some points to cover in the letter:

- **Refer to information you gathered in the interview.** This builds a personal bridge back to the person receiving the letter. It also serves as a reminder and clarification of that information.

- **Thank the person for his or her courtesy and time.** This shows good manners.

- **Include any points that you may have forgotten to mention.** Turn any concerns or objections that came up during the interview to your advantage.

- **If you promised to send any other information, include it with your letter.** Prospective employers may request letters of reference, transcripts, or other additional information.

- **Tell them you will call to check about the job.** Sometimes the interviewer will tell you when to call. If not, wait about ten days.

YOUR TURN

Correspondence. Compose a letter to follow up after an interview. Instead of expressing your continuing interest, you must tell the interviewer that you are no longer interested in being considered for the job. How can you do so tactfully? Why might you write a follow-up letter if you don't want a job?

Fig. 23-14 **Supervisors appreciate good team players who want to contribute to the success of an organization.** How do communication skills contribute to teamwork?

Building Career Skills

Beginning a new job is an exciting time. You will learn new skills and practice those you have already acquired. Whether you are working with the Head Start program, at a private school, or at a children's museum, there will be new people to get to know.

A positive attitude and an eagerness to help out will pave the way to success in any workplace. See Fig. 23-14. Show that you are willing to work hard, you care about the quality of your work, and you can get along with others, including difficult people. Here are just a few of the skills that will help ensure success at any job:

- **Communication skills.** The way you speak, listen, and write will have an impact on your success in the workplace. Make an effort to speak clearly, listen carefully, and write clearly and concisely.

- **Relationship skills.** Whenever a group of people must work together, there is potential for conflict. Learn to respect differences, work cooperatively as part of a team, and resolve conflicts before they get out of hand.

- **Leadership skills.** Leadership involves making decisions, acting fairly, and supervising and inspiring others. Leadership skills are necessary for many of the careers that relate to children. After all, children look to the adults in their lives for guidance and leadership.

- **Teamwork.** To work effectively as part of a team, you need to be able to follow rules and do what is expected of you. Good team players are dependable, responsible, and honest. They know that the whole team will benefit if they all do their best.

Fig. 23-15 **Employees can gain valuable insights during a performance evaluation.** How can these evaluations help people advance in their careers?

- **Managing multiple roles.** Throughout your career, you will have a variety of roles. It will be necessary to juggle work, family, social, and community obligations. Learning to prioritize, manage your time effectively, and handle stress can help you feel in control of the demands on your time.

- **Learning from performance evaluations.** Wherever you work, you will have periodic performance evaluations. During the evaluation, your supervisor will comment on what you have been doing well and point out areas that need improvement. You may be given, or asked to develop, goals for the following year. Working to improve in these areas should help you advance in your career. See Fig. 23-15.

- **Continuing to learn.** In most careers, you need to continue to learn in order to advance. One way of doing this is to take advantage of opportunities for continuing education. Some employers are even willing to pay for all or part of the costs. Continuing education can take the form of attending conferences or workshops, earning credentials through a professional organization, or taking college classes. Many colleges and universities now offer courses that can be completed online.

- **Ethical practices.** Being **ethical** means doing the right thing. In the workplace, it means being honest, following the rules, and reporting violations of the rules. Following ethical practices is particularly important in child care settings. It is essential that parents can trust and rely on the people who care for their children.

Leaving a Job

Most people today don't stay in the same job until retirement. In fact, it's highly likely that you will change jobs—and perhaps careers—a number of times during your working life. You need to know, therefore, how to make the transition from one job to another as smooth as possible.

It's usually not a good idea to quit one job before you have another one lined up. After all, you don't know how long it will take to find another job and you probably need to keep earning. Besides, many employers are more interested in potential employees who are currently working. As you seek new employment, you should do it on your own time, however. It's unethical to use work time to interview for another job. It's also wrong to use company time to write or print résumés and cover letters or to contact prospective employers.

Employee's Responsibilities

When you leave a job, you should make every effort to leave under the best possible circumstances. Follow any established procedures for notifying your employer of your intent to resign. It's normal to put your resignation in writing. Give as much notice as possible so your employer can find a replacement. A two-week notice is typical. See Fig. 23-16.

Continue to do your job well up to the time you leave. If you're asked to train a replacement, strive to give that person the best possible start. After all, you might cross paths with some of your co-workers in the future. You might even want to return to the same employer later in your career.

Fig. 23-16 **When you leave a place of employment, try to leave on the best possible terms. You might need to ask your former supervisor for a reference. You might even want to return one day.**

Employer's Responsibilities

Employees don't always leave their jobs because they want to. Employers can terminate employment as well. In some cases, people lose their jobs because they don't perform satisfactorily. In other cases, such as when business is slow, jobs may be cut through no fault of the employees.

If you lose your job, you may be entitled to claim **unemployment benefits**—funds paid by individual states to unemployed people who are actively seeking employment. Employers are also responsible for paying into the fund that provides for unemployment benefits.

You may also be able to keep any health insurance that you received through your employer. Under **COBRA** (Consolidated Omnibus Budget Reconciliation Act), you can stay in the same insurance plan that you had as an employee for up to 18 months, but you have to pay the entire cost of the premiums yourself.

Jason had been running the youth fitness area at Lakeview Health and Racquet Club for two years when he was laid off by his employer. Although Jason's evaluations had been excellent, the club's membership declined when a new fitness center opened nearby, and Lakeview simply could not afford to keep him on the payroll. Naturally, Jason was worried about how he would pay his bills without a job. Luckily, he could receive unemployment benefits while he searched for new employment. If Jason had simply quit his job, he would not have been eligible for unemployment compensation.

Jason also learned that he could keep his health insurance, thanks to the COBRA law. The monthly premium was costly, but it was considerably less than buying insurance as an individual.

Jason was encouraged when he heard a statement that many others who have suffered job setbacks have found to be true: "Sometimes when a door closes, a window opens." Jason had a feeling that there was an even better position waiting for him. Now it was his job to find it.

Ongoing Employability

As you move along your career path, be sure to remember the keys to early employment success. Commit yourself to excellence. Continue learning. Do all that you can to show that you are reliable, flexible, honest, and responsible. Show that you have what it takes to succeed in the world of work!

SECTION 23-2 Review and Activities

Reviewing the Section

1. What resources could you use to find job openings?
2. What could a job seeker with little work experience emphasize on his or her *résumé*?
3. What is the purpose of a *cover letter*?
4. Give three tips for filling out a job application.
5. How should a job seeker follow up after a job interview?
6. When evaluating a job offer, what factors should you consider besides salary?
7. Choose one of the career skills listed in this section that you would like to work on. Identify at least one practical way to do so.

Observing and Interacting

Interview three people and ask them how they found their current jobs and any other jobs they have had. Ask them for suggestions on finding a job, getting an interview, and what they did to prepare for the interview. Then write a summary describing what you learned.

Kindergarten Teacher

How would you like to give children the enthusiasm for learning? Kindergarten teachers introduce students to concepts they will build on throughout their lives. They teach children how to take turns, share, and treat others with respect. Kindergarten teachers can build an enthusiasm for learning that will stay with children for years to come.

▶ Job Responsibilities

Kindergarten teachers are responsible for planning lessons and activities. They often use hands-on activities, like making letters out of clay to teach the alphabet. They read books aloud, make learning tools, and even dance, sing, and do artwork. Kindergarteners have a short attention span, so lessons must be lively.

▶ Work Environment

A kindergarten classroom is a bright, colorful place with students' work decorating the walls. Kindergarten teachers work with children individually, in small groups, and as a class during the day. They must encourage appropriate behavior. Teachers must evaluate students' progress and give feedback to their parents.

▶ Education and Training

Kindergarten teachers need to complete a bachelor's degree and an approved teacher-training program. Public school teachers must be licensed. Kindergarten teachers are usually licensed to teach preschool through third grade.

▶ Skills and Aptitudes

- Patience
- Creativity
- Ability to motivate children
- Recognition of children's academic and emotional needs
- Organizational skills

WORKPLACE CONNECTION

1. **Thinking Skills.** Being a teacher requires the ability to inspire trust and confidence. How can you develop this ability?

2. **Resource Skills.** How could you get experience teaching or mentoring young people?

SECTION SUMMARIES

- Within career areas, there are usually entry-level, paraprofessional, and professional jobs. (23-1)
- You can gain work experience through part-time work, volunteering, service learning, and work-based learning. (23-1)
- When analyzing careers, there are eight factors to consider. (23-1)
- Certain skills, including decision-making, management, and technology skills, are needed for success in almost any workplace. (23-1)
- Sources of job openings include the Internet, newspapers, other people, and job fairs. (23-2)
- Résumés and cover letters serve specific purposes in the job search process. (23-2)
- Learning and building new skills helps lead to workplace success. (23-2)

REVIEWING THE CHAPTER

1. Identify four resources for learning about career areas. (23-1)
2. What are some of the benefits of gaining work experience through part-time or volunteer work? (23-1)
3. Why should you consider the work environment and working hours when analyzing a career? What else should you consider? (23-1)
4. What is *networking*? Identify three groups of people who could be part of your job search network. (23-2)
5. What types of information should you include in your *résumé*? In your *cover letter*? (23-2)
6. Describe four ways of preparing for a job interview.
7. On a new job, how could you demonstrate that you have a positive attitude? (23-2)
8. How much notice should you give when leaving a job? (23-2)

THINKING CRITICALLY

1. **Making Inferences.** What personal qualities do entrepreneurs need? Why are these important? What personal qualities are *not* suited to entrepreneurship?
2. **Analyzing Information.** When analyzing careers to see if they might suit you, which aspects would you study first? Why?

MAKING CONNECTIONS

1. **Writing.** Assume that you go on two interviews and receive two job offers on the same day. How would you go about comparing the two offers? Develop a list of at least ten factors you would need to consider before making a decision. Rank the factors from the most important to the least important.

2. **Social Studies.** Interview people who have worked at least ten years in a field you are interested in. Ask them how the field has changed during that time. What are the most significant changes? What predictions can you make about the job market in the future, based on your research?

APPLYING YOUR LEARNING

1. **Analyzing Behaviors.** Why do you think most employers prefer to interview potential employees who are currently working rather than those who are unemployed?

2. **Assessing Interests.** Evaluate your personal interests and aptitudes in relation to the skills needed for a specific career that involves working with children. Does this type of career seem like it might be a good fit for you? Explain your reasoning.

3. **Interpersonal Skills.** Work with a partner to develop and present a mock interview for a specific job. Create a list of skills and tasks for the job. Ask questions based on those in Fig. 23-12 on page 674.

Learning from Research

1. Choose one of the following areas to investigate.
2. How is this research useful to people who are making decisions about their careers?
3. Summarize what you have learned about career options using one of these learning experiences.

Job Shadowing. Research information about job shadowing. Note the purpose of job-shadowing experiences and the age levels at which it is used. How does job shadowing help students choose a career path? What are the advantages of this type of experience?

Service Learning. Research service learning on the Internet. Identify schools that have service-learning programs. Note the specifics of the program and examples of volunteer projects students have worked on. What are the advantages of this type of experience?

Work-Based Learning. Research information on work-based learning. Identify schools offering work-based learning programs that combine on-the-job learning with classroom learning. Find out how a work-based learning program works and give examples of where students received on-the-job training. What are the advantages of this type of experience?

GLOSSARY

(The numbers in parentheses indicate the Chapter and Section in which the term is introduced.)

A

abdominal thrusts. A technique in which quick, upward thrusts with the heel of the hand into the abdomen are used to force air in the lungs to expel an object caught in the throat. (20-2)

abstinence. Avoiding sexual activity completely. (2-2)

abstract thought. Capacity to consider "what-if situations," to create sophisticated arguments, and to reason from different points of view. (19-4)

accreditation. Recognition from an organization that indicates that a person or program has met certain standards.

ADD. A behavioral disorder that may be accompanied by **learning disabilities** and is characterized by difficulty in concentrating and following through on something one has started. ADD is similar to **ADHD**, but ADD does not involve hyperactivity. (21-1)

addiction. A dependence on a substance such as alcohol or drugs. (21-1)

addiction counselors. Professionals trained to help substance abusers. (21-3)

ADHD. A behavioral disorder that may be accompanied by **learning disabilities** and is characterized by difficulty in concentrating and following through on something one has started. Some people with ADHD are always active and have trouble staying still. They may also show signs of a lack of emotional control. (21-1)

adolescence. The complex time of life when a child begins to mature into an adult, approximately between the ages of 13 and 19. (1-2)

age appropriate. Things that are suitable for the age and individual needs of a child. (9-3)

aggressive behavior. Hostile, and at times destructive, behavior that some people display when faced with conflict. (14-2)

alliteration. The repetition of certain sounds. (15-2)

alternative birth center. Facilities for childbirth that are separate from hospitals and provide a more home-like environment for **labor** and **delivery**. (5-3)

ambidextrous. Able to use both hands with equal skill. (13-1)

amniocentesis (AM-knee-oh-sen-TEE-sis). A prenatal test performed by withdrawing a sample of the **amniotic fluid** surrounding an unborn baby. Cells from the **fetus** that are in the fluid are tested for birth defects and other health problems. (4-3)

amniotic (AM-knee-AH-tik) **fluid.** Liquid that surrounds and protects the developing baby in the uterus. (4-1)

amygdala (uh-MIG-duh-luh). The part of the brain that controls fear, joy, and other emotional reactions. (19-4)

anecdotal record. An observer's reports of a child's actions, usually concentrating on a specific behavior or area of development. *See also* **developmental checklist, frequency count, running record.** (1-3)

anemia. A condition caused by a lack of iron in the blood. Symptoms include shortness of breath, fatigue, and rapid heartbeat. (5-1)

antibodies. Substances produced by the body to fight off germs. (7-2)

anxiety. Uncertainty or fear about an unspecified, but seemingly immediate, threat. (17-1)

Apgar scale. A system of rating the physical condition of a newborn shortly after birth using five factors: heart rate, breathing, muscle tone, response to stimulation, and skin color. (6-2)

aptitude. A natural talent or potential for learning a skill. (23-1)

articulation. The ability to use clear, distinct speech. (12-2)

asthma. A condition that causes the lungs to contract more than they should, narrowing the air passages and making it difficult to breathe. (20-1)

attachment. The bond between two people, such as between a child and a parent or other primary caregiver. (8-1)

attention span. The length of time a person can concentrate on a task without getting bored. (9-2)

autism. A developmental disorder that affects a child's ability to communicate and interact with others. (21-2)

autism spectrum disorders (ASD). A group of disorders characterized by the following traits: resistance to change, absence of empathy, little or no eye contact, repetition of words or phrases, repetitive movements or play, difficulty focusing, an inability to remain attentive, distress without apparent cause, and loss of skills already learned. (21-2)

autonomy. Independence. In children, autonomy may mean bathing and dressing themselves and eating independently. (11-2)

axon (ACKS-on). The connection between **neurons** that transmits instructions from the cell body to another neuron. *See also* **dendrites, neurons.** (9-1)

B

baseline. A count of behaviors an observer makes before any steps are taken to try to change the behavior. (1-3)

bilingual. Able to speak two languages. (15-2)

bilirubin. A substance produced by the breakdown of red blood cells. (6-3)

bipolar disorder. A psychiatric disorder characterized by extreme changes in mood, from highly energetic to depressed and withdrawn, sometimes fluctuating rapidly. (19-2)

birth defect. An abnormality, present at birth, that affects the structure or function of the body and may threaten a baby's health. (4-3)

blended family. A family formed when a single parent marries another person who may or may not have children. (3-1)

body image. How people feel about their own physical appearance. (16-1)

bonding. Forming emotional ties, such as those between parents and their child. (6-3)

bullying. Aggressive or abusive behavior directed toward another person, usually someone weaker. (17-2)

C

cardiopulmonary resuscitation (CPR). A rescue technique that combines **rescue breathing** with chest compressions to restore breathing and circulation. (20-2)

caregivers. Parents, guardians, and others responsible for caring for children. (1-1)

cause and effect. One event is caused by another. For example, infants learn that, by crying, they can get their needs for food and comfort met. (8-2)

cervix (SIR-viks). The lower part of the uterus. (6-1)

cesarean (si-ZARE-ee-uhn) **birth.** The delivery of a baby through a surgical incision in the mother's abdomen. (6-1)

child care center. A facility in which a staff of adults provides care of children. (22-1)

childproof. To take steps to protect a child from possible dangers in the home or early childhood classroom. (9-3)

chorionic villi (CORE-ee-ON-ik VI-lie) **sampling.** A prenatal test that uses a sample of the tissue from the membrane that encases the fetus to check for specific birth defects. (4-3)

chromosomes (CROW-muh-soams). Tiny, threadlike structures in the nucleus of every cell that carry hereditary information. (4-2)

circle time. Period in an early childhood classroom when an entire class comes together to share experiences or listen to stories. (22-2)

COBRA. A law ensuring that former employees can keep the health insurance they received through their former employer for 18 months. They must pay the entire cost of the premiums themselves. COBRA stands for the Consolidated Omnibus Budget Reconciliation Act. (23-2)

colic (COL-ick). A condition in babies that results in extended periods of crying. (8-1)

colostrum (cole-UH-strum). The first breast milk a mother produces. It is high in protein and calories and helps protect babies from illness. (6-3)

communicable diseases. Illnesses that are passed from one person to another. *See also* **contagious**. (20-1)

competition. Rivalry with the goal of outperforming others or winning. (14-2)

conception. The process by which a **sperm** cell reaches the **Fallopian tube**, and penetrates and fertilizes an **ovum**. This results in the beginning of a pregnancy. (4-1)

concepts. General categories of objects and information. (9-2)

confidential adoption. In this type of adoption, the birth parents don't know the names of the adoptive parents. There is no exchange of information after the baby is adopted, and the access to information about birth parents is limited by law. (2-2)

confidentiality (CON-fuh-den-shee-AL-uh-tee). Protection of another person's privacy by limiting access to personal information. (1-3)

conformity. Dressing or acting like one another. (17-2)

conscience. An inner sense of what is right and wrong that prompts good behavior and causes feelings of guilt following bad behavior. (3-2)

conservation. A principle that means that even if an object changes in its presentation, its characteristics are the same. (18-1)

contagious. The period when a person may pass an illness on to someone else. *See also* **communicable diseases**. (20-1)

contractions. The tightening and releasing of the muscle of the uterus during labor to move the baby through the birth canal. (6-1)

convulsion. A seizure or a period of unconsciousness with uncontrolled jerking or twitching of muscles. (20-2)

cooperative play. Playing with another child including interaction and cooperation. *See also* **parallel play.** (11-2)

cord blood. Blood left behind in the **umbilical cord** and **placenta** following birth. It contains **stem cells.** (6-1)

cortex (CORE-teks). Part of the brain's cerebrum. Its growth permits more complex learning. (9-1)

cover letter. An introductory letter sent with a **résumé** when applying for a job. (23-2)

cradle cap. A skin condition in infancy known for yellowish, crusty patches on the scalp. (7-3)

creativity. A mental ability that involves using the imagination to produce original ideas. (12-1)

crisis nurseries. Child care facilities where troubled or stressed parents can leave their children for a short time if they have nowhere else to turn. (21-3)

cultural bias. Favoring or giving advantage to people from one culture over people from another culture. (15-1)

custodial parent. The parent with whom a child resides after a divorce. (3-1)

D

---

delivery. The birth of a baby. (5-3)

dendrite. Branchlike features at the end of each **axon** that receive messages from other **neurons.** (9-1)

depression. Feelings of intense sadness that last for long periods of time and prevent a person from leading a normal life. (19-2)

deprivation. Not having critical needs met due to an environment that does not provide what is necessary for physical, emotional, and intellectual well-being. (3-2)

depth perception. The ability to perceive objects as three-dimensional, not flat. (7-1)

developmental checklist. A list of skills children should master or behaviors they should exhibit at a certain age. *See also* **anecdotal record, frequency count, running record.** (1-3)

developmental milestones. Key skills, such as learning to walk, used to check a child's progress against average development. (7-1)

developmental tasks. Challenges that must be met or skills to be acquired during different stages of life. (1-2)

developmentally appropriate. Toys, activities, and tasks that are suitable for a child at a specific age. (10-1)

dexterity. Skillful use of the hands and fingers. (10-1)

diaper rash. A skin condition that includes patches of rough, irritated skin in the diaper area. Sometimes, painful raw spots also develop. (7-3)

dilate. To open wider. (6-1)

directed learning. Learning that results from being taught formally or informally. (12-1)

DNA (deoxyribonucleic acid). Complex molecules that make up the genes that carry the blueprint for a person's creation. (4-2)

dominant gene. In a gene pair, this is the stronger gene and is the one more likely to be expressed as a physical trait. *See also* **genes**, **recessive gene**. (4-2)

Down syndrome. A genetic disorder caused by an extra **chromosome** that results in distinct physical features and varying degrees of **mental retardation**. (21-2)

dyslexia. A learning disability that prevents people from understanding printed symbols in a normal way. (21-2)

E

eating disorder. A serious pattern of overeating or restrictive eating. (16-1)

embryo. The name for the developing baby from about the third week of pregnancy through the eighth week. *See also* **fetus**, **zygote**. (4-1)

emotional development. The process of learning to recognize and express feelings and establish a unique personal identity. (8-1)

emotional maturity. Being responsible enough to consistently put someone else's needs before your own. (2-1)

empathy. The ability to understand how another person feels. (11-1)

entrepreneurs (AHN-truh-pruh-NURS). Workers who are self-employed or own their own businesses. (23-1)

entry-level job. A position for beginners in a field. It requires limited education and training. (23-1)

environment. People, places, and things that surround and influence a person, including family, home, school, and community. (1-2)

estrogen. A **hormone** produced by the **ovaries**. The beginning of **menstruation** indicates that a girl's body has increased its production of this hormone. (19-1)

ethical. Doing the right thing. (23-2)

extended family. Type of family that includes a parent or parents, at least one child, and other relatives all living together. (3-1)

F

failure to thrive. A condition in which babies fail to grow and develop properly because of a lack of love and attention. (8-1)

Fallopian tube. A tube that connects the **ovary** to the **uterus**. (4-1)

family child care. A child care situation in which an adult cares for a few children in his or her own home. *See also* **in-home care**. (22-1)

fetal alcohol effects. A condition less severe than **fetal alcohol syndrome**. It causes damage to the developing baby, but to a lesser degree. (4-4)

fetal alcohol syndrome (FAS). An incurable condition found in some children of mothers who consumed alcohol while pregnant. It includes a wide range of physical and mental disabilities that last a lifetime. (4-4)

fetal monitoring. Watching an unborn baby's heart rate for indications of stress during labor and birth. (6-1)

fetus (FEE-tuhs). The stage of development that begins around the eighth or ninth week of pregnancy and lasts until birth. *See also* **embryo**, **zygote**. (4-1)

fiber. An indigestible plant material that helps the digestive system work properly. (16-2)

fine motor skills. These skills involve the smaller muscles of the body, such as those in the fingers. They require small, precise movements, such as using scissors or writing. Also called small motor skills. *See also* **gross motor skills**. (7-1)

finger plays. Songs or chants with accompanying hand motions. (15-2)

fixed expenses. Payments, such as rent or taxes, that generally can't be changed. *See also* **flexible expenses**. (5-2)

flame resistant. Something that will not burn as quickly as other materials. (10-2)

flexible expenses. Costs such as food, clothes, and entertainment that can be reduced if necessary. *See also* **fixed expenses**. (5-2)

fluoride. Strengthens the hard outer coating, or enamel, of teeth to help prevent decay. It is often added to drinking water and toothpaste or applied to teeth. (13-2)

fontanels. Open spaces found in a baby's skull where the bones have not yet joined together permanently. These allow a baby's head to change shape to fit through the birth canal. (6-2)

formula. A mixture of milk substitutes, water, and essential nutrients that can be fed to a baby. Formula comes in liquid or powdered form. (5-2)

foster children. Children, typically from troubled families or those in difficult circumstances, who are placed in the temporary care of another person or family. (3-1)

fracture. A break or crack in a bone. (20-2)

free play. Period when children in an early childhood classroom can choose any activity they want to do. (22-2)

frequency count. A tally of how often a certain behavior occurs. *See also* **anecdotal record, developmental checklist, running record**. (1-3)

G

gender identity. The awareness of being male or female. This complex process begins in early childhood and is usually firmly fixed by about age four. (17-1)

genes. The parts of **chromosomes** that determine a human's inherited characteristics. *See also* **dominant gene, recessive gene**. (4-2)

genome. The complete genetic blueprint of a person. (4-2)

gestational diabetes. A form of diabetes that occurs only during pregnancy and usually goes away after the baby is born. (5-1)

gifted. Describes people who have special abilities in one or more areas. (21-2)

gross motor skills. These skills involve the large muscles of the body, such as those of the leg and shoulders. They have to do with the ability to make large movements, such as jumping and running. Sometimes called large motor skills. *See also* **fine motor skills**. (7-1)

group identification. A feeling of belonging with others that becomes important to children between the ages of four and six. (13-2)

growth chart. A chart that shows the average heights and weights of children at different ages. (7-1)

growth spurt. Periods when children grow very rapidly in a short time. (16-1)

guidance. Using firmness and understanding to help children learn how to control their own behavior. (3-2)

H

hand-eye coordination. The ability to move the hands and fingers precisely in relation to what is seen. Needed for skills such as cutting. (7-1)

Head Start. A program funded by the federal government that provides locally run child care facilities to lower-income and disadvantaged children from birth to five years old. It is designed to prepare children for school. (22-1)

heredity. The biological transfer of certain inherited characteristics from earlier generations. (1-2)

hives. Blisterlike sores caused by an allergic reaction. (20-2)

hormones. Powerful body chemicals that produce specific results. In **puberty**, some hormones activate the physical and emotional changes teens experience as they become sexually mature. (2-2)

human life cycle. Stages of human development that present different challenges to be met or skills to be acquired. (1-2)

hygiene. Personal care and cleanliness. (10-2)

hypothetical. Considering something that might happen. (18-1)

I

identity crisis. Confusion about one's identity that results from failing to find a strong identity, or sense of self, through personal exploration. (19-2)

imaginative play. Fantasy or dramatic play which imitates real-life situations. (9-2)

imitation. Learning by watching and copying others. (12-1)

immunizations. Shots of a small amount of a dead or weakened disease-carrying germ given in order that the body may build resistance to the disease. *See also* **vaccine**. (7-3)

incidental learning. Unplanned learning, as when a child happens to push a button on a musical toy and discovers that this action causes music to play. (12-1)

inclusion. Also known as mainstreaming. This refers to practices based on a law requiring schools to make every effort to place children with disabilities in regular classrooms while receiving special education services. (21-2)

incubator. A special enclosed crib, generally used for **premature** babies, in which the oxygen supply, temperature, and humidity can be closely controlled. (6-1)

infertility. The inability to become pregnant. (4-2)

in-home care. Care for children in their own home. *See also* **family child care**. (22-1)

initiative. Motivation to accomplish more. (14-1)

intelligence. The ability to interpret and understand everyday situations and to use prior experiences when faced with new situations or problems. Also defined as the capacity to learn, which is shaped by heredity and environment. (12-1)

intelligence quotient (IQ). A numerical score that indicates, based on a test, whether a person's **intelligence** is average or above or below average for his or her age. (15-1)

intergenerational. Describes relationships between those in younger and older age groups. (3-1)

internship. A job in which a person works for little or no pay while gaining work experience and receiving supervision. (23-1)

interpretation. In observing children, the analysis an observer forms and expresses about what was observed. (1-3)

J

jaundice (JAWN-diss). A condition that occurs in over 50 percent of newborns and causes the baby's skin and eyes to look slightly yellow. It is caused when the liver cannot remove enough **bilirubin**. (6-3)

job fair. An event where employers with current or future job openings meet with prospective employees. (23-2)

job shadowing. Observing someone in his or her job. (23-1)

L

labor. The process by which the baby gradually moves out of the **uterus** and into the vagina to be born. (5-3)

lactase. An enzyme that helps in the digestion of lactose, a sugar found in milk. (5-1)

lactation consultant. A breast-feeding specialist who shows breast-feeding mothers how to stimulate adequate milk flow and how to position babies properly so they can nurse. (6-3)

lactose intolerance. A condition in which milk and milk products cause abdominal pain and gas. (5-1)

lanugo (la-NEW-go). Fine, downy hair that may be present on the forehead, back, and shoulders of a newborn. (6-2)

learning centers. Areas in an early childhood classroom designed for certain types of play and learning. (22-2)

learning disabilities. A problem that interferes with a person's ability to learn, listen, think, speak, read, write, spell, or do math. (21-2)

learning methods. Different ways of learning. (18-2)

legal guardian. A person who is designated by the courts to assume responsibility for raising a child. (3-1)

license. A registration with the state that indicates that child care providers meet certain health and safety standards. (22-1)

lifelong learner. A person who is willing to learn new information and acquire new skills throughout his or her life. (23-1)

low birth weight. A weight of less than 5 pounds, 8 ounces (2.5 kg) at birth. (4-4)

M

malnutrition. The effects of lack of enough food or adequate amounts of needed nutrients. In babies, it is linked to poor brain development, which can lead to learning difficulties. (7-2)

mandated reporters. People who work with children, including teachers, doctors, nurses, and counselors, who are required by law to report maltreatment of children if they see evidence of possible abuse. (21-3)

manipulate. To work with the hands. (9-3)

maternity leave. Time off from a job that allows a woman to give birth, to recover, and to care for a new baby. *See also* **paternity leave**. (5-2)

math readiness. The level of knowledge of basic math concepts, such as number recognition, needed for learning math. (12-2)

menstruation. The monthly cycle in which blood is released from the uterus after ovulation if an **ovum** has not been fertilized. (16-1)

mental retardation. Also known as cognitive impairment or developmental disability. Children with mental retardation have below-average intelligence and skills. Levels range from mild to profound. (21-2)

midwife. A person trained to assist women in childbirth. Midwives must have training in normal pregnancy and birth and must pass a certification exam before they can practice. (5-3)

miscarriage. The natural death of a developing baby before the 20th week of pregnancy. *See also* **stillbirth**. (4-3)

moral development. The process of learning to base one's behavior on beliefs about what is right and wrong. (14-2)

moral maturity. Psychologist Lawrence Kohlberg's sixth and highest state of moral development, in which people are able to recognize and respect other people's points of view. (19-3)

morality. A sense of right and wrong that guides decisions and actions. (19-3)

multiple intelligences. Abilities in problem solving or creating materials that have value. Howard Gardner has identified eight intelligences. (15-1)

myelin (MY-uh-lin). Waxy, protein-based substance that coats **axons**, making it easier to transmit information from one **neuron** to another. (9-1)

N

nanny. A person trained to provide child care who may live with the family or come to the home daily. (22-1)

negative reinforcement. A response aimed at discouraging children from repeating an inappropriate or unacceptable behavior. *See also* **positive reinforcement**. (3-2)

negativism. Doing the opposite of what others want. This behavior is normal for toddlers. (11-1)

neonatal period. The first month after a baby is born. *See also* **postnatal period**. (6-3)

networking. Using personal and professional contacts to further career goals. (23-2)

neural pathways. Links between **neurons** that "wire" the brain so that the brain can control different body functions and thinking processes. (9-1)

neuron. Nerve cell. *See also* **axon**, **dendrite**. (9-1)

neuroscience. The modern study of the brain. (12-1)

neurotransmitters (NOOR-oh-tranz-mih-terz). Chemicals released by axons that attach to **dendrites** with certain kinds of receptors. (9-1)

night terrors. Type of sleep disturbance that occurs during the first few hours of sleep, when children are deeply asleep. Children may be very upset but unable to explain what's wrong. In the morning, they usually remember nothing of the incident. (10-2)

NREM sleep. A cycle of sleep in which rapid eye movement doesn't occur. (11-1)

nuclear family. Type of family that includes a mother and father and at least one child. (3-1)

O

object permanence. The concept that objects continue to exist even when they are out of sight. (9-2)

objective. Using facts, not personal feelings and prejudices, to describe events or things. (1-3)

obstetrician. (ahb-ste-TRISH-un). A doctor who specializes in pregnancy and childbirth. (5-1)

open adoption. Adoption in which the birth parents and adoptive parents know something about each other. (2-2)

orthodontist. A specialized dentist who can determine whether children would benefit from having braces, separators, or retainers to straighten the teeth. (16-2)

ovum (OH-vum). A female cell or egg needed for reproduction. (4-1)

P

parallel play. Playing near, but not actually with, other children. This behavior is characteristic of 18-month-olds. *See also* **cooperative play**. (11-2)

paraprofessional. A worker with an education beyond high school that trained him or her for a certain field of work. (23-1)

parent cooperative. A **child care center** in which care and opportunities for socialization and learning are provided, on a rotating basis, by the parents of children in the program. Often a child care professional guides the program. (22-1)

parenting. Caring for children and helping them grow and develop. (2-1)

parenting style. The way parents care for and discipline children. (3-2)

paternity. Legal identification of a man as the biological father of a child. (2-2)

paternity leave. A period, usually 12 weeks, of unpaid family or medical leave from work offered to new fathers. *See also* **maternity leave**. (5-2)

pediatrician. A doctor who specializes in treating children. (5-2)

peer learning. A learning method that involves students observing and listening to one another. (18-2)

peer pressure. A social group's influence on the way individuals behave. (17-2)

peers. People close to one's own age. (14-2)

perception. The ability to learn from sensory information. (9-2)

permanent teeth. The set of 32 teeth that gradually replace the **primary teeth**. These teeth will not be naturally replaced by another set. (13-1)

personal identity. A sense of oneself as a unique individual. (19-2)

phobias. Abnormal fears. (11-1)

phonemes (FOH-neems). The smallest individual sounds in words, as in the *ou* in *house*. (15-2)

placenta (pluh-SEN-tuh). The tissue that connects the developing baby to the uterus. It is rich in blood vessels that allow nutrients and oxygen to flow to the baby. (4-1)

play environment. A comfortable space with no dangers and with toys that are safe and interesting. (8-2)

play group. An arrangement in which parents take turns caring for one another's children in their own homes. (22-1)

popular culture. The practices that prevail in modern society and influence teens' behaviors and moral development. (19-3)

positive reinforcement. A response that encourages a particular behavior. *See also* **negative reinforcement.** (3-2)

postnatal period. The period following a baby's birth. *See also* **neonatal period.** (6-3)

postpartum depression. A condition in which new mothers may feel very sad, cry a lot, have little energy or interest in the baby, and, in extreme cases, may think about harming the baby. (6-3)

preeclampsia (pre-ee-CLAMP-see-ah). Condition characterized by high blood pressure and the presence of protein in the mother's urine. It can deprive the developing baby of adequate oxygen and nutrition because of reduced blood flow in the **placenta.** (5-1)

prefrontal cortex. The part of the brain that undergoes dramatic changes in adolescence. Located just behind the forehead, it controls planning, organization, prioritizing, and other complex thought processes. Its growth and maturation make it possible for teens to reason better and to control their impulses. (19-4)

prenatal development. The baby's development during a pregnancy. (4-1)

prepared childbirth. Reducing pain and fear during the birth process through education and the use of breathing and conditioning exercises. (5-3)

preschooler. Children from age three to about age five, when most start going to school. (10-1)

professional. A person with a position that requires at least a degree from a four-year college or technical school in a particular area of study. (23-1)

proportion. In child development, this refers to the size relationship between different parts of the body. (7-1)

puberty. The set of changes that result in a physically mature body that is able to reproduce. (16-1)

R

---

reading readiness. Learning the skills necessary for reading, including letter recognition and the understanding that letters of the alphabet combine to form words on a page. (12-2)

recessive gene. In a gene pair, this is the weaker gene and the one less likely to be expressed in a person's physical traits. A person must inherit two recessive genes (one from each parent) for the same recessive trait in order for it to be expressed. *See also* **dominant gene.** (4-2)

reflexes. Instinctive, automatic responses, such as grasping, sneezing, or sucking in infants. (7-1)

reflux. A condition in which partially digested food rises in the throat. (8-1)

regression. The backward movement to an earlier stage of development, as when a toilet-trained child begins having "accidents." (21-1)

REM sleep. A sleep cycle characterized by rapid eye movement. (11-1)

rescue breathing. Procedure for forcing air into the lungs of a person who isn't breathing. *See also* **cardiopulmonary resuscitation.** (20-2)

résumé. A concise document that summarizes career objectives, education, work experience, and accomplishments. (23-2)

Rh factor. A protein that may or may not be found in the blood. Without treatment, problems may result when a mother's Rh factor differs from that of her developing baby. (5-1)

rooming-in. Refers to the practice of allowing a baby to stay with his or her mother in her room during the entire hospital stay after birth. (6-3)

rubella. German measles. (4-4)

running record. A method of writing observations in which the observer writes down everything observed about a child or group for a set period of time. *See also* **anecdotal record, developmental checklist, frequency count.** (1-3)

S

scoliosis. A curvature of the spine that affects posture. (16-1)

sealants. Thin, plastic coatings on permanent molars that are an effective means of preventing tooth decay. (16-2)

sedentary activities. Activities that involve little or no exercise, such as watching television or playing computer and electronic games. (16-2)

self-centered. People who think about their own needs and wants, not those of others. (11-1)

self-concept. How people see themselves. (11-1)

self-confidence. Belief in one's own abilities. (14-1)

self-discipline. The ability to control one's own behavior. (3-2)

self-esteem. Self-worth, or the value people place on themselves. (1-2)

sense of competence. The feeling that one can be successful and meet most challenges. Children acquire this sense by developing and improving a wide range of skills. (17-1)

sense of self. An idea of who one is, based on temperament and personality. (17-1)

sensorimotor period. Psychologist Jean Piaget's first stage of learning, from birth to about age two. During this period, babies learn primarily through their senses and their actions. (9-2)

sensory integration. The process by which the brain combines information taken in through the senses to make a whole. (10-1)

separation anxiety. A fear of being away from parents, familiar caregivers, or the normal environment. (11-1)

sequence. A step-by-step pattern. (1-2)

service learning. School program in which students volunteer in their communities as a graduation requirement. (23-1)

sexuality. Refers to a person's view of himself as a male or female. (2-2)

sexually transmitted disease (STD). Disease spread from one person to another through sexual contact. Also called sexually transmitted infection (STI). (2-2)

shaken baby syndrome. A condition that occurs when someone severely shakes a baby, usually in an effort to get the baby to stop crying. The syndrome can lead to brain damage, including **mental retardation**, cerebral palsy, or blindness. (7-2)

shock. A condition in which important body functions, including breathing and heartbeat, are impaired because of a severe injury or loss of blood. (20-2)

sibling rivalry. Competition between brothers and/or sisters for parents' affection and attention. (11-1)

SIDS (Sudden Infant Death Syndrome). Also known as crib death, this is the unexpected death of an infant with no obvious cause. The baby dies during sleep, without crying out, and with no evidence of a struggle. (7-2)

single-parent family. Type of family that includes either a mother or father and at least one child. (3-1)

situational stress. Stress that comes from the environment a child lives in or from certain circumstances and changes. (21-1)

sleep deprived. Lacking adequate sleep. (11-1)

social development. The process of learning self-expression and how to interact with others. (8-1)

socialization. The process by which young children learn to get along with other people, first in their own families, then in other groups. (11-2)

speech-language pathologist. A specialist trained to detect and correct speech, language, or voice problems. (12-2)

sperm. Male cell needed for reproduction. (4-1)

sphincter (SFINGK-tur) **muscles.** Muscles that help regulate elimination from the bowels. (10-2)

sprain. An injury caused by sudden, violent stretching of a joint or muscle. (20-2)

standardized test. Test that allows educators to tell how students are performing intellectually when compared to a large group of other students who have taken the same test. (18-2)

stem cells. Cells capable of producing all types of blood cells. They can be used to treat serious blood-related illnesses in humans. (6-1)

stillbirth. The death of a developing baby after the 20th week of pregnancy. *See also* **miscarriage.** (4-3)

stimulating environment. A place in which babies have a wide variety of things to see, taste, smell, hear, and touch. (7-1)

stimulation. Activities that arouse a baby's sense of sight, sound, touch, taste, and smell. (1-2)

stranger anxiety. In babies, a fear of unfamiliar people, usually expressed by crying. This behavior develops sometime during the second half of the baby's first year. (8-2)

stuttering. Serious speech difficulty that occurs when a person speaks with sporadic repetition or prolonged sounds. True stuttering can be identified by the rhythm, pitch, and speed of speech, which is rapid, forced, short, and sharp in sound. (12-2)

subjective. Relying on personal opinions and feelings, rather than facts, to judge events. *See also* **objective.** (1-3)

support groups. Groups of people in similar circumstances who gather to share their feelings so that each member can draw on others' strength and experience. (21-1)

surrogate (SIR-ug-get). A substitute. Often refers to a woman who becomes pregnant in order to have a baby for another woman. (4-2)

symbolic thinking. The use of words and numbers to stand for ideas. (9-2)

synapse (SIN-ap-suhs). Tiny gaps between **dendrites** where messages are transmitted from one **neuron** to another. (9-1)

synthetic fibers. Fabrics made from chemicals, rather than from natural sources. (10-2)

T

teething. The process, sometimes painful, by which teeth push their way through the gums. (7-3)

temper tantrums. Incidents in which children release anger or frustration by screaming, crying, kicking, pounding, or holding their breath. (11-1)

temperament. A person's unique nature, which determines how he or she reacts to others and to the world. (8-1)

tension. Mental or emotional stress. (14-1)

testosterone (tes-TAHS-tuh-rone). A hormone produced by the testicles. Levels of this hormone rise rapidly at the beginning of puberty. (19-1)

time-out. A short period of time in which a child sits away from other people and the center of activity. (3-2)

toddler. One- or two-year-old child. (10-1)

toxoplasmosis (TOX-o-plaz-MO-sis). An infection caused by a parasite. It can cause blindness, hearing loss, and disabilities in babies if pregnant women are infected. It can also cause miscarriage or stillbirth. (4-4)

transitions. Periods in an early childhood classroom during which children move from one activity to the next. (22-2)

transitivity. The concept that a relative relationship between two objects can extend to a third object. (18-1)

trial-and-error learning. Learning that takes place when a child tries several solutions before finding one that works. (12-1)

typical behaviors. Ways of acting or responding that are common at each stage of childhood. (1-1)

U

ultrasound. A procedure in which sound waves are used to make a video image of the unborn baby. (4-3)

umbilical cord. A long tube that connects the baby to the **placenta** and transmits oxygen and nourishment from the mother's blood to the baby. (4-1)

unemployment benefits. Funds paid by individual states to unemployed people who are actively seeking employment. (23-2)

uterus. The organ in a woman's body in which a baby develops during pregnancy. (4-1)

V

vaccine. A small amount of a dead or weakened disease-carrying germ that is injected so that the body can build resistance to the disease. (7-3)

vernix. A thick, white, pasty substance covering babies in the uterus that protects them from constant exposure to amniotic fluid. It is made up of the fetus's shed skin cells and secretions from the glands. (6-2)

W

weaning. Changing from drinking from the bottle or breast to a cup. (7-2)

work-based learning. School program that offers students the opportunity to combine in-school and on-the-job learning. (23-1)

Z

zygote (ZY-gote). The fertilized human egg. *See also* **embryo, fetus.** (4-1)

CREDITS

Cover Design: Squarecrow Creative Group

Interior Design: Squarecrow Creative Group

Cover Photo: Corbis, Ariel Skelley

Photo Credits:
Ann Garvin 326
Articulate Graphics, Joel and Sharon Harris 281, 282, 283
Circle Design, Carol A. Spengel 106, 107, 108, 109, 110, 111, 182, 183
Comstock Images 308, 309
Ken Clubb 546, 588, 641
Corbis 219, 382, 417, 504, 516, 619, 634, 656, 682
  Paul Barton 149, 590
  Peter Beck 487
  Annie Griffiths Belt 200
  Ralph A. Clevenger 509
  Steve Cohen 199
  Philip James Corwin 222
  C/B Productions 441
  Laura Dwight 146, 176, 234, 278, 279, 287, 306, 452, 458, 472, 525
  Jim Erickson 70, 100
  Randy Faris 439, 448, 495
  Jon Feingersh 99
  Tom Grill 482, 490, 502, 505
  Bob Gomel 443
  GoodShoot 506
  Charles Gupton 11, 483
  John Henley 46, 68
  Robert Holmes 43
  Image 100 500
  R.W. Jones 436
  Reed Kaestner 421
  Ronnie Kaufman 303, 369, 428, 450, 551, 598, 624
  Michael Keller 105, 113
  Jetta Klee 485, 486
  Rob Lewine 488
  Robert Maass 623
  Don Mason 253, 265

Stephanie Maze 395
Tom & Dee Ann McCarthy 345, 429, 434, 438, 606
Raoul Minsart 211
Gail Mooney 659
Kevin R. Morris 30
Helen Norman 457
Gabe Palmer 13, 74, 161, 170, 353, 419, 456, 614, 658
Jose L. Pelaez, Inc. 12, 31, 56, 135, 168, 187, 208, 209, 213, 223, 224, 245, 250, 252, 276, 386, 507, 585, 677
Mark Peterson 64
Steve Prezant 342, 378, 415, 424
ROB & SAS 256
Bob Rowan 264
William Sallaz 539
Chuck Savage 542, 543
Norbert Schaefer 49, 112, 406, 407
Ariel Skelley 13, 92, 122, 132, 190, 194, 226, 263, 333, 466, 467, 480, 617, 622, 681
Tom Stewart 432, 511, 612, 620, 657, 666
Jerry Tobias 216
Doug Wilson 7, 215
Jennie Woodcock 212, 273
Custom Medical Stock Photo NMSB 140
Dan Grossman, Stony Creek Studio 589, 593
David R. Frazier Photolibrary Inc. 75
Design Office 226
Getty Images 179,189
  Altrendo 120
  Barros & Barros 21, 26, 79
  Bruce Ayres 53, 171, 174
  Brand X Pictures 248
  David Buffington 202
  Paul Chesley 318
  Comstock Images 241, 346, 422
  C Squared Studios 167
  Mel Curtis 497

Digital Vision 355, 642
E. Dygas 63
Hoby Finn 346
Kevin Fitzgerald 491
Natalie Fobes 385
Tracy Frankel 6, 158
Larry Dale Gordon 153
Paul Harris 71, 82
Peter Hendrie 338
Thomas Hoeffgen 88
HMS Images/Harry Sieplinga 52
William Howard 114, 121
Ken Huang 47, 57
Jonathan Kirn 321, 338
Regine Mahaux 5, 51
Geoff Manasse 331
MedioImages 310, 340
Laurence Monneret 133, 142
National Geographic 319
Rosanne Olson 24
Lori Adamski Peek 513
Photodisc 496
Whit Preston 435
Richard Price 620
Ken Reid 35, 42
Gabrielle Revere 84
Tamara Reynolds 600
David Sacks 117
David J. Sams 323
Stephen Simpson 77, 476, 492
Don Smetzer 494, 518
Stone/Catherine Ledner 237
Stone/Michael Rosenfeld 247
SW Productions 59, 83, 94, 98, 240, 388, 501
Thinkstock 206, 207, 499
Arthur Tilley 54
Camille Tokerud 371
Julie Toy 508
Terry Vine 199
Simon Watson 381, 391
Ross Whitaker 327, 329
ImageState 195, 202
  Laurence Mouton 384
Index Stock
  Bill Bachmann 127
  Benelux Press 81

Vic Bider 87
Cheryl Clegg 27, 34
Gary Conner 78
Tomas del Amo 148
Diaphor Agency 361, 376
Kent Dufault 141
Spencer Grant 582
Grantpix 347
Richard Kasmier 23
Bill Keefrey 6, 118
Elfi Kluck 159
Omni Photo Communications, Inc. 400
Jacque Denzer Parker 362
photolibrary.com pty.ltd 344
Hoa Qui 364
RuberBall Productions 165, 343, 360
Nancy Sheehan 393
Scholastic Studio 10, 351
SW Productions 18, 19, 605
Masterfile 315
Rolf Bruderer 474, 475
Burazin 328
Peter Christopher 359
George Contorakes 102, 103
Kathleen Finlay 95
David P. Hall 314
Dan Lim 9, 354, 392, 402
David Mendelsohn 203
Tim Pannell 236
David Schmidt 477, 481
George Shelley 86
Ariel Skelley 5, 25, 72, 380, 404, 599, 607
Lloyd Sutton 337
Mark Tomalty 184
Wei Yan 235
Kevin May 37, 39, 40, 85, 377, 626, 627, 631, 632, 638, 639, 643, 649, 652, 654
Photo Researchers
Alex Bartel 181
Mark Clarke 151
CNRI 131
Tony Craddock 134
Tracy Dominey 188
Claude Edelmann 108
Simon Fraser 196
LA/B.C./Aigo 129
G. Moscoso 108

Richard T. Nowitz 192
Saturn Stills 103, 144, 175
PhotoDisc 7, 17, 20, 43, 44, 89, 99, 163, 203, 249, 305, 332, 339, 350, 403, 449, 491, 517, 539, 623, 653
Nick Koudis 143
LEGO Systems Inc. 471
PhotoEdit
Bill Aron 348, 536, 647, 676
Bill Bachman 257
Billy E. Barnes 175
Robert Brenner 396, 446, 628
Michele D. Bridwell 73
Cleve Bryant 226
Peter Byron 377
Jose Carillo 13, 353, 611
Myrleen Ferguson Cate 10, 90, 223, 260, 269, 293, 297, 312, 347, 349, 365, 366, 367, 453, 460, 529, 553, 560
Cindy Charles 255
Paul Conklin 648
Gary Conner 9, 394, 510
David Kelly Crow 334
Bob Daemerich 13, 93, 455, 609, 661 675
Deborah Davis 254
Mary Kate Denny 11, 442, 550, 561, 563, 565, 602, 629, 646
Lon C. Diehl 232, 437, 644
Kayte M. Dieorna 259
Laura Dwight 230, 244, 269, 280, 286, 363, 389, 398, 413, 454
Amy Etra 91
Kathy Ferguson-Johnson 372
Tony Freeman 62, 96, 299, 317, 336, 356, 390, 523, 535, 583, 594, 595, 645, 653, 667, 680
Spencer Grant 12, 139, 266, 268, 274, 284, 368, 420, 425, 520, 527, 528, 540, 549, 665, 668, 678
Jeff Greenberg 258, 408, 426, 526, 554, 637
Robb Gregg 567
Will Hart 571

Richard Hutchings 197, 503, 584, 651
Bonnie Kamin 578
Christina Kennedy 267, 290
Dennis MacDonald 566, 570
Tom McCarthy 575, 582
Cathy Melloan 608, 616
Robin Nelson 574, 596
John Neubauer 449
Michael Newman 8, 9, 10, 12, 22, 23, 63, 67, 143, 180, 216, 221, 225, 227, 233, 238, 239, 255, 260, 261, 262, 270, 275, 290, 294, 301, 305, 322, 339, 357, 373, 403, 416, 430, 440, 447, 461, 464, 465, 470, 521, 522, 527, 530, 548, 550, 576, 586, 587, 603, 633, 663
Dwayne Newton 557
Jonathan A. Nourok 220, 231, 531, 538,
Mark Richards 517, 581, 634
Nancy Sheehan 249, 288, 295, 311, 320, 399
Frank Siteman 591, 662
Susan Van Etten 325, 335, 660
Dana White 562, 679
David Young-Wolff 226, 242, 243, 254, 273, 296, 299, 303, 304, 316, 349, 409, 414, 418, 431, 469, 471, 479, 515, 544, 545, 552, 556, 569, 572, 601, 669, 673
Phototake
Dr. Yorgos Nikas 106
Richard T. Nowitz 130
Super Stock
Francisco Cruz 147, 160
Jiang Jin 172, 185
ThinkStock 58, 66, 178, 204
Courstesy of the USDA 154

Note—Models and fictional names may have been used to portray characters in stories and examples in this text.

INDEX

A

Abstinence, 60, 62–63, 119, 684
Abstract thought, 684
  from ages seven to twelve, 522–523
  in adolescence, 567
Accidents and emergencies, 583–594
  first aid for, 585–592
  guidelines for fast action, 584–585
  rescue techniques for, 592–594
  safety and, 583, 584
Accreditation, 629, 684
Achievement tests, 537
Acquired immune deficiency syndrome
      (AIDS), 60, 61, 141, 142, 565
Active listening, 82
Actor in children's theater, 43
Adaptability, 260
ADD (attention deficit disorder),
      610, 684
ADHD (attention deficit hyperactivity
      disorder), 432, 609–610, 684
Addiction, 602, 684
Addiction counselors, 620, 684
Adolescence, 32, 545–570, 684
  emotional development in, 553–557
  independence in, 559
  intellectual development in, 566–570
  moral development in, 561–565
  physical development in, 545–548
  social relationships in, 557–560
Adoption, 66, 74–75, 120
  confidential, 66
  open, 66
Adoption consultants, 99
Adults, rescue technique for choking, 589
Advice, asking child's, 461–462
Affection from ages one to three, 353–354

Age-appropriate, 296, 684
  physical activities and, 419
  toys and, 298–299, 398–399
Aggressive behavior, 684
  from ages four to six, 441–442
Aging population, 77–78
AIDS, 60, 61, 141, 142, 565
Al-Anon, 602
Alcohol, 136
  pregnancy and, 133–134
Allergies, 237, 576, 578
  food, 232, 235, 576
Alliteration, 463, 684
Alpha-fetoprotein (AFP), 130, 131
Alternative birth centers, 173, 684
Ambidextrous, 414, 684
American Sign Language, 301
Amniocentesis, 131, 684
Amniotic fluid, 110, 180, 190, 684
Amniotic sac, 110, 180, 181
Amygdala, 566, 684
Analytical intelligence, 529
Anaphylactic shock, 590
Anecdotal records, 38, 684
Anemia, 149, 685
  sickle cell, 125
Anger
  in ages one to three, 349–350
  in ages four to six, 433–434
  in ages seven to twelve, 500–501
Animals
  bites from, 590
  safety and, 245
Animators, 517
Anorexia nervosa, 486
Antibodies, 230, 247–248, 685
Anxiety, 685
  in ages seven to twelve, 501
  in adolescents, 557

separation, 351–352, 358

stranger, 266–267, 270

Apgar scale, 192–193, 685

Aptitude and interest tests, 537

Aptitudes, 661, 664, 685

Art, introducing to ages four to six, 464–466

Articulation, 400–401, 685

Artificial insemination, 120

Associations, making, 289

Asthma, 578, 685

Attachment, 685

building bonds of, 255–258

Attention from ages one to three, 384–385

Attention span, 289, 685

from ages seven to twelve, 523

Australia, preventing infant death in, 247

Austria, raising a child in, 437

Autism, 611, 685

Autism spectrum disorders (ASD), 611–612, 685

Autistic savants, 611

Autonomy, 371–372, 685

Awareness from ages seven to twelve, 522

Axons, 282, 285, 381, 685

B

Babbling, 302

Babies. *See* Infants

Baby blues, 201–202

Baby bottle decay, 313

Baby talk, 352

avoiding, 301–302

Bandura, Albert, 29

Baseline, 38, 685

Bathing of infants, 240–242

Bedtime routines for first year, 228

Bedwetting, handling, 423

Behavior

aggressive, 441–442

dealing with inappropriate, 93–98

guiding children's, 88–98, 447

learned, 270

linking, to personal values, 564–565

promoting positive, 649–652

self-destructive, 569

typical, 22

Belittling, 97

Bicycle safety, 421

classes for, 584

Bilingual, 463, 685

Bilirubin, 196, 685

Binet, Alfred, 453

Binge eating, 486

Bipolar disorder, 685

in adolescents, 557

Birth. *See* Childbirth

Birth certificate, 198

Birth control pills, 119

Birth defects, 685

causes of, 126–128

prevention and diagnosis of, 128

types of, 123–126

Birth plan, 172

Bites, 590

animal, 590

human, 375, 590

insects, 590–591

Bleeding, 585

Blended families, 73–74, 685

Bloody show, 179

Bodily-kinesthetic intelligence, 456, 529

Body image, 478

from ages seven to twelve, 478

Body shape

of newborn, 216

from ages four to six, 410

Body systems in embryonic stage, 107

Bonding, 195–196, 197, 685

Books, sharing, 86

Bottle-feeding, 164, 165, 198, 231, 233, 264

Brain

changes in the, 566

developing, 28, 153, 191, 214, 257, 283, 289, 435, 463, 497, 552, 628

functions of, 282–283

of newborn, 191

organization of, 284–287

parts of, 282

size of, in children, 27

stimulating development in infant, 286

structure of, 280–283

study of, 279–280, 381–382

Brain stem, 282

Breast-feeding, 164, 165, 196, 198, 201, 232–233, 264

case for, 230–231

Breath, shortness of, 151

Breech presentation, 113, 184

Bribing, 96

Bronfenbrenner, Urie, 29

Bruises, first aid for, 586

Budget, making, 166, 168–169

Bulimia, 486

Bullying, 509–510, 685

Bumps, first aid for, 586

Burns, 245

first aid for, 587

preventing, 335, 336

Burping of infants, 233–234, 261–262

C

Caffeine, 134, 136, 137

Calcium, 154, 155, 156

Camp counselor, 571

Carbohydrates, 153

Cardiopulmonary resuscitation (CPR), 594, 685

Career opportunities

actor in children's theater, 43

adoption consultants, 99

animators, 517

camp counselor, 571

child care workers, 653

child development researcher, 305

child life specialist, 339

children's activities directors for city parks, 491

emergency medical technician (EMT), 595

family court judge, 449

genetic counselor, 143

gymnastics coach, 539

kindergarten teacher, 681

obstetric sonographer, 175

parent educator, 67

pediatrician, 249

pediatric nurse, 203

play therapist, 403

puppeteer, 377

speech-language pathologist, 425

storyteller, 275

toy designer, 471

wildlife educator, 623

Careers

analyzing, 663–664

beginning, 667–680

building skills for, 677–678

evaluating interests, aptitudes, and abilities for, 660–661

finding information on, 661–663

gaining work experience, 662–663

impact of children on, 53

learning about opportunities in, 22

opportunities for entrepreneurs, 660

options in, 657–661

preparing for success in, 664–665

Caregivers, 22, 686. *See also* Parents

Car seat safety, 169

Cause and effect, 273–274, 289, 382, 686

Cell division, 106–107

Center-based care, 629–632

Cerebellum, 282

Cerebral palsy, 124, 226

Cerebrum, 282

Cervical cap, 119

Cervix, 179, 182, 686

Cesarean birth, 113, 187–188, 201, 686

Chemical burns, 587

Chicken pox, 140–141, 579

Child abuse and neglect, 617–622

preventing, 620–621

reasons for, 617–622
signs and symptoms of, 618–619
treating, 621–622
types of maltreatment, 617–619
Child Abuse Prevention and Treatment
Act (CAPTA), 617
Childbirth
cesarean, 113, 187–188
options for, 171–174
premature, 188–189
preparing for, 111, 113
Childbirth education classes, 171–172,
185
Child Care Aware, 638
Child care centers, 628, 630, 686
evaluating child in, 633
teacher in, 658
Child care in Denmark, 642
Child care options, 627–637
substitute care as, 627–638
Child care workers, 653
Child development
influences on, 30–31
self-esteem in, 34
theories about, 28–29
Child development researcher, 305
Childhood
comparing past and present, 23–25
as crucial, 27–28
development beyond, 32–33
illnesses in, 575–582
views of, 23
Child life specialist, 339
Childproof, 297, 686
of home, 335
Children. *See under* Emotional
development; Intellectual
development; Moral development;
Physical development; Social
development
around the world, 30
benefits of studying, 21–22
care for older, 632, 634
developing self-esteem in, 33

exceptional, 608–616
foster, 76
gifted, 609, 615–616
giving directions to, 89
guiding behavior of, 88–98
keeping safe, 41
making difference in lives of, 21–26
meeting needs of, 83–87
observing and interacting with, 35–42
overweight, 484
rescue breathing for, 593
rescue technique for choking, 589
special needs, 608–614
stress and, 599–600
studying, 27–34
Children's activities directors for city
parks, 491
Children's museums, 526
Children's theater, actors in, 43
Child therapists, 606
Chlamydia, 61, 141
Choking, 232, 245, 300, 336, 587–588
rescue techniques for, 588, 589
Chorionic villi sampling, 132, 686
Chromosomes, 114, 686
errors in, as cause of birth defects,
127–128
Circle time, 645, 686
Cleft lip/palate, 124, 128
Climbing, 337
Climbing equipment, 421
Clothes
for infants, 237–239
for ages one to three, 322–323,
331–333
for ages four to six, 422
safety and, 245
COBRA (Consolidated Omnibus Budget
Reconciliation Act), 679–680, 686
Cocaine, 134, 137–138
Colic, 263–264, 686
Color blindness, 127
Colostrum, 196, 686
Common cold, 579

Communicable diseases, 575–576, 686
Communication
    developing, in infant, 300–304
    between infants and caregivers, 256
Competence, sense of, in ages seven to
        twelve, 496–498
Competition, 686
    from ages four to six, 442–443
Conception, 105–106, 686
Concepts, 686
    development of, 294
        in first year, 294–295
        in ages one to three, 383–384
Concrete operations stage, 524–525
Condom, 119
Confidential adoption, 66, 686
Confidentiality, 41, 686
Conflict resolution
    from ages four to six, 441–444
    with peers, 508–510
Conformity, 686
    peer pressure and, 513
Conscience, 88, 686
    from ages four to six, 444
Consequences, exaggerating, 98
Conservation, 525, 686
Consistency in guidance, 98
Contagious period, 578, 686
Contractions, 180, 181, 184, 687
Convulsions, 589–590, 687
Cooperation from ages four to six, 443
Cooperative play, 363, 439, 686
Cord blood, 186–187, 687
Cortex, 282, 687
Cover letters, 670–671, 687
Cradle cap, 242, 687
Creative intelligence, 529–530
Creativity, 687
    from ages one to three, 390, 391
Crib
    choosing, 167
    safety of, 164
Crisis nurseries, 621, 687

Crowning, 183
Crying, 300
    comforting and, 261–264
    responding to, in infant, 229
Cultural bias, 455, 687
Cultural influences on moral
        development, 562–564
Curiosity
    from ages one to three, 391
    from ages seven to twelve, 522
Custodial parents, 73, 687
Cuts, first aid for, 585
Cystic fibrosis, 124, 127, 191

D

Death
    from child abuse, 617
    of loved one, 604–605
    of a parent, 606–607
Dehydration, 581
Delivery, 171, 687
Dendrites, 282, 283, 284, 381, 687
Denmark, child care in, 642
Dentist, first visits to, 313–314
Depression, 52, 687
    during pregnancy, 160
    in adolescents, 556
    postpartum, 202
Deprivation, 84, 687
Depth perception, 217, 687
Development, 209. *See also* Emotional
        development; Intellectual
        development; Moral development;
        Physical development; Social
        development
Developmental checklist, 38, 687
Developmentally appropriateness, 314,
        687
Developmental tasks, 32, 687
Development milestones, 210, 687
    in intellectual development, 290, 389,
        457

in physical development, 222–223, 315, 412

in social development, 268–269

Dexterity, 317, 318, 687

Diabetes, gestational, 150

Diapering, 242–244

Diaper rash, 242, 687

Diaphragm, 119

Diet, influence on teeth, 313

The Dietary Guidelines for Americans, 482–483. *See also* Guidelines for Healthy Eating.

Difficult situation, helping child work through, 503

Dilation, 182, 184, 687

Directed learning, 383, 687

Direct learning, 531–532

Disabilities, types of, 609–612

Divorce, 601–602, 603

DNA (deoxyribonucleic acid), 114, 117, 687

Dominant genes, 115, 116, 127, 688

Dominant inheritance, 127

Down syndrome, 124, 127–128, 131, 610, 688

Dramatic play, 293, 457, 640–641

Dress, comparing past and present, 25

Drugs, during pregnancy, 134–138

Duchenne muscular dystrophy, 127

Dyslexia, 609, 688

E

Ear infection, 579

Early childhood, role of environment, 31

Early childhood classroom, 639–652

daily schedule in, 646–647

guidance in, 649–652

health care routines in, 643

learning centers in, 640–643

materials in, 648

misbehavior in, 651–652

planning activities for, 645–647

safety in, 644–645

Eating. *See also* Nutrition, Guidelines for Healthy Eating, 154

Eating disorders, 478, 486, 688

Economic changes, 78

Ecstasy, 134

Education. *See also* School(s)

childbirth, classes, 171–172, 185

comparing past and present, 24

experiences of, 568–570

staying involved in child's, 536

Effacement, 182

Ejaculation, 548

Electrical burns, 587

Embryo, 107, 687

Embryonic stage, 107, 110

Emergencies. *See* Accidents and emergencies

Emergency medical technician (EMT), 595

Emotional abuse, 617, 618

Emotional adjustments, 52

Emotional changes in ages seven to twelve, 498–499

Emotional development, 253, 688

of infants, 253–265

attachment in, 255–258

climate in the home, 264–265

crying and comforting, 261–264

temperament in, 258, 260–261

from ages one to three, 343–360

developing positive self-concept, 355, 357

evaluating emotional adjustment, 357–358

general patterns, 343–349

individual differences, 354–355

managing misbehavior, 356

sleep, emotions, and behavior, 358–360

specific emotions, 349–354

from ages four to six, 429–438

encouragement and, 436–438

patterns in, 429–431

specific emotions in, 432–435
stress and, 435–436
from ages seven to twelve, 495–504
emotional changes in, 498–499
living with children and, 504
sense of competence in, 496–498
sense of gender in, 498
sense of self in, 495–498
specific emotions in, 499–504
working through a difficult situation, 503
in adolescence, 553–557
formation of personal identity, 553–555
handling emotional difficulties, 556–557
influences on identity development, 554
theories of identity development, 555
comparing social development and, 253–254
Emotional health during pregnancy, 159–160
Emotional maturity, 54, 688
Emotional needs, 84, 85–86
of new mother, 201–202
Emotions in infancy, 254
Empathy, 354, 688
Employability, ongoing, 680
Encouragement from ages four to six, 436–438
Energy level, 261
Entrepreneurs, 688
opportunities for, 660
Entry-level jobs, 658, 688
Environment, 688
as cause of birth defects, 126–127
influence on child development, 30–31, 213–214, 312
influence on health, 334, 336
influence on intelligence, 382
interaction with heredity, 128
play, 272
Environmental tobacco smoke, 334

Envy in ages seven to twelve, 502
Epidural blocks, 185, 188
Episiotomy, 186
Erikson, Erik, 28, 29, 256, 436, 555
Estrogen, 547, 688
Ethics, 678, 688
Exceptional children, 608–616
Exercise
in adolescence, 551
for new mother, 201
prenatal, 157
Expectations, having reasonable, 48–49
Experiences of infant, 212
Exploration, difference between play and, 273–274
Extended family, 77, 688

F

Face-to-face interactions in play, 262
Failure to thrive, 256–257, 688
Fallopian tube, 105–106, 688
Falls, 245
preventing of, 335
False labor, 181
Families
balancing work and, 169–170
blended, 73–74
building strong, 80–82
challenges for, 598–607, 614, 624–625
extended, 74, 77
functions of the, 71–73
influence on identity development, 554
joining, 74–76
moral development and, 563–564
nuclear, 73
other children in, 162
play as a, 72
single-parent, 73
sources of support, 79–80
trends affecting, 77–79
two-income, 78
Family, Career and Community Leaders of America (FCCLA), 560

Family child care, 628–629, 688
Family conflict, handling, 81–82
Family court judge, 449
Family doctors, 172
Family life cycle, 76
Family planning, 119. *See also* Abstinence
Family relationships, 511–512
  from ages four to six, 444
Family stresses, 599–607
Fats, 153
Fears, 52
  from ages one to three, 348, 350–352,
    358
  from ages four to six, 434–435
  from ages seven to twelve, 501
  of the dark, 322, 435
  on illnesses, 604
Feedback
  need for consistent, 271
  providing positive, 297
Feeding. *See also* Nutrition
  decisions about, for infant, 164, 165
  infants, 230–237
Fetal alcohol effects, 134, 688
Fetal alcohol syndrome (FAS), 133–134,
    610, 688
Fetal development. *See also* Prenatal
    development
  month by month, 108–109
Fetal monitoring, 180, 688
Fetal position, 113
Fetal stage, 110–111
Fetus, 110, 688
Fiber, 683, 688
Financial concerns, 55–56
Financial problems, 601
Fine motor skills, 689
  in first year, 219, 221
  from ages one to three, 316–318
Finger plays, 465, 689
Finland, parents in, 75
Fires, 336, 583
First aid, 585–592
  for animal or human bites, 590

for bleeding, 585
for bumps and bruises, 586
for burns, 587
for choking, 587–588
for convulsions, 589–590
for fractures and sprains, 586
for insect stings and bites, 590–591
for poisoning, 591
for shock, 591–592
for splinters and thorns, 586–587
First-degree burns, 587
Fixed expenses, 166, 689
Flame-resistance, 322, 689
Flexible expenses, 166, 689
Fluoride, 420, 689
Follow-up letter, 676
Fontanels, 191, 216–217, 689
Food allergies, 232, 235, 576
Food Groups. *See* Guidelines for Healthy
    Eating
Food poisoning, 232
Foods
  introducing solid, 235
  safety of, 644
Forceps, 186
Formal observation, 39
Formal operations state, 525–526,
    567–568
Formula, 164, 689
Foster children, 76, 689
Foster homes, 621
Fractures, 689
  first aid for, 586
Fraternal twins, 118
Free play, 646, 689
Frequency count, 38, 689
Freud, Sigmund, 29
Friends
  close, 558
  imaginary, 367
  making
    in ages one to three, 364–365, 367
    in ages seven to twelve, 506–508
Frustration, 52, 344

Fulghum, Robert, 71–72
Fun, 505
Funerals, 605

G

Galinsky, Ellen, 50
Gardner, Howard, 455–456, 527–529
Gender identity, 689
  in ages seven to twelve, 498
Genes, 114, 312, 689
  dominant, 115, 116, 127
  recessive, 115, 116, 127
Genetic counseling, 129–130
Genetic counselor, 143
Genetic diseases, 117
Genetics, 114–116
Genetic testing, 123
Genetic traits, 116
Genital herpes, 61, 141, 565
Genital warts, 61
Genome, 114, 689
German measles, 139–140, 150
Germinal stage, 106–107
Gestational diabetes, 150, 689
Gifted children, 609, 615, 689
  identifying, 615
  special programs for, 616
Gonorrhea, 61, 141
Gossip, 440–441
Grief, 604–607
  dealing with, on loss of an infant, 122
Gross motor skills, 689
  in first year, 219, 220–221
  from ages one to three, 316
Group B streptococcus, 141
Group identification, 422, 689
Growth, 209
Growth charts, 214, 689
Growth spurts, 477, 689
Guidance, 88, 689
  consistency in, 98
Guidelines for Healthy Eating, 154,
    327, 415, 420
Gymnastics coach, 539

H

Hand-eye coordination, 690
  from ages four to six, 411
  from ages one to three, 318–319
  for first year, 224
Hand preference from ages four to six,
    413–414
Harlow, Harry, 255–256
Hazardous substances/chemicals, danger
    to unborn infant from, 138–139
Head Start, 632, 690
Health
  comparing past and present, 24
  environmental influences on, 334, 336
  of infant, 212
Health care. *See also* Medical checkups
  early childhood classroom routines for,
      643
  expenses of, 166, 168
  for infants, 246–248
  for new mother, 201
  during pregnancy, 147–150
  regular, 575
Health considerations, 55
Health insurance, 166, 173
Hearing impairments, 612
Hearing in first year, 218
Heartburn, 151
Height
  in adolescence, 546
  from ages four to six, 409–410
  from ages one to three, 312
  from ages seven to twelve, 477–478
Hemophilia, 127
Hepatitis B, 61, 141
Heredity, 114, 115, 690
  as cause of birth defects, 127
  influence on child development, 30,
      210–211, 311–312
  influence on height, 215
  influence on intelligence, 382
  interaction with environment, 128
  in tooth quality, 313

Heroin, 134
High/Scope, 631
Hitting, from ages one to three, 375–376
Hives, 590, 690
Holiday child care, 634
Home-based care, 628–629
  issues specific to, 637
Home-pregnancy tests, 147
Homework, helping child with, 534
Hormonal implants, 119
Hormonal injections, 119
Hormonal patch, 119
Hormones, 59, 690
Hospital
  cesarean birth in, 188
  delivery of baby at, 173–174
  neonatal intensive-care unit (NICU) in,
    199, 200
  neonatal period in, 196, 198–199
  sick children in, 580, 582
Human bites, 590
Human immunodeficiency virus (HIV),
    60, 61, 565
Human life cycle, 32, 690
Hydrocephalus, 125–126
Hygiene, 690
  for ages one to three, 328–333
  from ages seven to twelve, 489–490
  in adolescence, 550–551
Hypothetical situations, 525, 690

I

Idealism, from ages seven to twelve,
    522–523
Identical twins, 118
Identity crisis, 555, 690
Identity development
  influences on, 554
  theories of, 555
Illnesses, 604
  for ages one to three, 334
  nutrition during, 581

Imaginary friends, 367
Imagination, from ages one to three, 389,
    390
Imaginative play, 293, 457, 690
Imitation, 383, 690
Immunizations, 575–576, 690
  for infants, 246–248
  for ages one to three, 334
  for ages four to six, 409–410
  for ages seven to twelve, 490
  schedule of, 577
Implantation, 107
Incidental learning, 382–383, 690
Inclusion, 613, 690
Incubator, 189, 690
Independence, encouraging, from ages
    one to three, 371–372
Independent learning, 532–533
Individual differences, from ages one to
    three, 354–355
Individualized Education Plan (IEP), 613
Individuals with Disabilities Education
    Act (IDEA), 613
Infant mortality, 247
Infants. See under Emotional development;
    Intellectual development;
    Newborn; Physical development;
    Social development
  arrival of, 179–189
  avoiding dangers to, 133–142
  basic supplies for, 163
  bathing, 240–242
  burping, 233–234, 261–262
  carrying, 257
  clothes for, 237–239
  delivery of, 172
  dressing, 237–239
  environment and, 31
  feeding, 230–237
  handling, 225–227
  health and wellness, 240–248
  losing, 122
  medical care for, 246–248

name of, 187
playing with, 213
reading to, 302
rescue breathing for, 593
rescue technique for choking, 588
room for, 164
safety of, 245
stimulating senses of, 293–294
teeth of, 244, 246
Infections
  danger to unborn baby from, 139–142
  ear, 579
Infertility, 120–121, 690
Influenza, 579
Informal observation, 39
Inhalants, 134
Inheritance, 497
In-home care, 628, 690
Initiative, 432, 690
Insect stings and bites, 590–591
Intellectual development
  in first year, 278–304
    brain development in, 279–287
    communication in, 300–304
    concept development in, 294–295
    developmental milestones in, 290
    learning in, 288–289, 296–297
    Piaget's theories and, 291–293
    play in, 297–300
    speech in, 303–304
    stimulating senses in, 293–294
  from ages one to three, 381–402
    attention in, 384–385
    brain development in, 381–391
    creativity in, 390, 391
    curiosity in, 391
    developmental milestones in, 389
    guiding learning in, 395–397
    imagination in, 389, 390
    intelligence in, 382
    learning methods in, 382–383
    memory in, 385–386
    perception in, 387
    play activities and toys in, 397–399

readiness for learning and, 392–394
    reasoning in, 387–389
    speech development in, 399–402
  from ages four to six, 453–470
    art and music in, 464–466
    development milestones in, 457
    intelligence in, 453–456
    learning in, 461–470
    Montessori's theory in, 459–460
    Piaget's theory of preoperational
      thinking in, 457–458
    play in, 465
    reading in, 463–464
    school experience in, 466–468
    signs of, 457
    speech development in, 468–470
    Vygotsky's theory in, 458–459
  from ages seven to twelve, 520–538
    learning methods and, 531–533
    learning theories and, 523–530
    measuring, 533–538
    signs of increased intellectual
      growth, 521–523
  of adolescents, 566–570
    changes in the brain, 566–567
    impact of educational experiences,
      568–570
    theories of, 567–568
Intellectual needs, 84, 86–87
Intelligence(s), 453, 690
  analytical, 529
  creative, 529–530
  defined, 382
  multiple, 455–456, 527–529
  practical, 530
  traditional views of, 453–464
Intelligence quotient (IQ), 453, 454, 690
Intensity, 260
Interest inventories, 537
Intergenerational interaction, 78, 690
Internet safety, 513
Internship, 662, 691
Interpersonal intelligence, 456, 529
Interpretation, 41, 691

Interviews, 672–674
    commonly asked questions in, 674
    following up on, 674, 676
Intrapersonal intelligence, 456, 529
Intrauterine device (IUD), 119
Invisible disabilities, 609
In vitro fertilization, 120–121
Iron, 155

J

Jaundice, 196, 691
Jealousy, 52
    from ages one to three, 352–353
    from ages four to six, 435
    from ages seven to twelve, 502
Job application, filling out, 672
Job fairs, 668, 691
Jobs
    evaluating offer of, 675
    leaving, 679–680
    looking for, 667–677
Job shadowing, 662, 691

K

Kindergarten, entering, 430–431, 466
Kindergarten teacher, 681
Kindness, 505
Kohlberg, Lawrence, 561
    levels of moral development, 561–562

L

Labor, 171, 179–186, 691
    coping with, 185
    early signs of, 179–180
    false, 181
    first stage of, 182, 184
    inducing, 181
    pain relief during, 185
    premature, 180
    second stage of, 183, 184, 186
    third stage of, 183, 186–187
    transition during, 182, 184

Lactase, 156, 691
Lactation consultants, 198, 691
Lactose intolerance, 156, 691
Lanugo, 192, 691
Large motor skills. See Gross motor skills
Late adulthood, 33
Learning
    from everyday life, 461–462
    in the first year, 288–289, 296–297
    guiding, 395–397
    methods of, 382–383, 531–533, 691
    play in building, 645
    readiness for, 392–394
    theories on, 523–530
Learning ability tests, 537
Learning centers, 640–643, 691
Learning disabilities, 609, 691
Legal guardian, 74, 691
Length of infant, 215
License, 629, 691
Lifelong growth and development, 32–34
Lifelong learners, 665, 678, 691
Lightening, 113, 179
Limits, setting, 90–92
Linguistic intelligence, 456
Listening, 297–298, 504
Logical-mathematical intelligence, 456, 529
Love
    from ages one to three, 353–354
    comparing past and present, 24
    threatening to withhold, 87
Low birth weight, 137, 691
Loyalty, 505
LSD, 134
Lying, 445

M

Mainstreaming, 613
Make-believe play, 457
Malnutrition, 236–237, 691
Management skills, 56–57, 62, 64, 166–169, 666, 677–678
Mandated reporters, 620–621, 691

Manipulating, 299, 691
Marcia, James, 555
Marijuana, 134, 137–138
Maternity clothes, 157
Maternity leave, 169, 691
Math readiness, 394, 692
Meal appeal for ages one to three,
    327–328
Media, analyzing messages of, 528
Medical checkups. *See also* Health care
    for ages one to three, 333–334
    for ages seven to twelve, 490
Memorial services, 605
Memory
    in ages one to three, 385–386
    in ages seven to twelve, 521–522
Memory games, 386
Menstrual cycle, 105, 106, 548
Menstruation, 481, 547, 692
Mental retardation, 610, 692
Middle age, 32
Middle school, 533
Midwives, 172, 173, 692
Milia, 192
Minerals, 152–153
Misbehavior
    dealing with, 356, 651–652
    unintentional, 93
Miscarriage, 122, 692
Mobiles, 293–294
Mobility, 77
Montessori, Maria, 527, 631, 646
    learning theory of, 459–460
Montessori schools, 459–460, 527, 631,
    646
Mood, 261
Moral development, 692
    in ages four to six, 444–448
    in ages seven to twelve, 512–516
    in adolescence, 561–565
        developing a moral compass, 561
        Kohlberg's levels of, 561–562
        linking behavior to personal values,
            564–565

social and cultural influences on,
    562–564
Morality, 561, 692
Moral maturity, 562, 692
Morning sickness, 150
Moro reflex, 220
Mother, postnatal care of, 201–202
Motor skills
    in first year, 219–221
    from ages one to three, 314–318
    from ages four to six, 411, 413
    from ages seven to twelve, 481
Motor vehicle safety, 338
Moving, 600
Multiple births, 118
Multiple intelligence, 455–456, 527–529,
    692
Multiple sclerosis, 287
Muscular dystrophy, 125
Music, introducing to ages four to six,
    464–466
Musical intelligence, 456, 529
Myelin, 282–283, 285, 287, 692
MyPyramid, 327, 415, 482

N

Nanny, 628, 692
Nar-Anon, 602
National Association for Family Child
    Care (NAFCC), 629
National Association for the Education of
    Young Children (NAEYC), 455,
    629, 630, 638
    staff-to-children guidelines, 630
Nation's Network of Child Care Resource
    and Referral, 638
Natural family planning, 119
Naturalist intelligence, 456, 529
Nature, 30, 210
Negative reinforcement, 94–96, 692
Negativism, 344–345, 692
    from ages one to three, 362–363

Neglect, 617. *See also* Child abuse and neglect

Neonatal intensive-care unit (NICU), 199, 200

Neonatal period, 196, 198–199, 692

Networking, 668, 692

Neural pathways, 280, 291, 692

Neural tube, 107

Neurons, 28, 279–280, 282, 283, 284, 381, 692

Neuroscience, 382, 692

Neurotransmitters, 283, 692

Newborn. *See also* Infants
at birth, 190–192
bonding with, 195–196, 197
examining, 192–194
physical changes in, 193
records of, 194
tests for, 194

Nicotine, 134

Nightmares, 358–359, 692

Night terrors, 322

Non-English speakers, 469

Nosebleeds, 585

Notes, taking, during observation, 40

NREM sleep, 359–360, 692

Nuclear families, 73, 692

Nurture, 30, 210

Nutrition
during illness, 581
during pregnancy, 152–156
for infants, 211, 230, 236–237
for ages one to three, 324–328
for ages four to six, 415–417
for ages seven to twelve, 482–486
for adolescents, 549, 550
for new mother, 201

O

Obesity, 177

Objective observations, 36, 37, 693

Object permanence, 292, 693

Observation records, types of, 36–38

Observations, 35–42
actions during, 39
objective, 36, 37
reasons for, 35–36
subjective, 36, 37
taking notes during, 40
using, 41–42

Obstetrician, 148, 172, 693

Obstetric sonographer, 175

Older children, care for, 632, 634

Open adoption, 66, 693

Organized sports, emphasizing enjoyment in, 479

Organs in embryonic stage, 107

Orthodontist, 489, 693

Outdoor safety, 421

Over-the-counter drugs during pregnancy, 135–136

Overweight child, role of parents in helping, 484

Ovulation, 105

Ovum, 105–106, 114, 548, 693

Ovum transfer, 121

P

Pacifiers, 264

Parallel play, 361, 362, 439, 693

Paraprofessionals, 658, 693

Parent(s)
adolescents and, 570
custodial, 73
death of, 606–607
in helping with homework, 534
role of, in helping overweight child, 484

Parent cooperatives, 630, 693

Parent educator, 67

Parenthood
challenges of, 51–53
changes brought by, 50–53
decision making about, 54–55
desire for, 55
preparing for, 161–164
rewards of, 53

single, 65, 73
stages of, 50
teen, 58–66
Parenting, 447–457, 693
balancing school with, 64
developing skills in, 49–50, 83–98
as learning process, 47–48
responsibilities, 33, 47–54, 71–73, 80–82, 83–87
Parenting styles, 87, 693
Paternity, 62, 693
Paternity leave, 169, 693
Patience, 504
Pediatrician, 249, 657, 693
choosing, 164–166
Pediatric nurse, 203
Peer groups, 506, 558
pressures of, 563
Peer learning, 532, 693
Peer pressure, 59, 513–514, 693
Peers, 439, 693
conflict resolution with, 508–510
influence on identity development, 554
influence on social development, 558
relationships with, 497, 505–506
Perception, 288, 387, 693
Perceptiveness, 260
Performance evaluation, 678
Permanent teeth, 410, 480, 693
Persistence, 260
Personal identity, 553, 693
forming, 553–555
influences on development of, 554
Personal safety, 488
Personal values, linking behavior to, 564–565
Personality, 31, 258, 260–261, 354–355, 366
Pet protection, 338
Phobias, 351, 693
Phonemes, 463, 693
Phototherapy, 196
Physical abuse, 617
Physical activities, encouraging, 419

Physical development
of infants, 208–248
developmental milestones in, 222–223
during first year, 214–221, 224
influences on growth and development, 210–214
patterns of, 209–210
from ages one to three, 310–338
developmental milestones in, 315
health, illness, and safety, 333–338
height and weight in, 312
hygiene, 328–333
influences on growth and development, 311–312
motor development in, 314–319
nutrition needs and eating in, 324–328
proportion and posture in, 312–313
sensory integration in, 320
sleeping and, 321–322, 324
teeth in, 313–314
transitions in routines, 323
from ages four to six, 408–424
bedwetting in, 423
developmental milestones in, 412
hand preference in, 413–414
height and weight in, 409–410
motor skills in, 411, 413
nutrition for, 415–418, 420
physical activities in, 419, 421
play in, 413
posture and body shape in, 410
self-care skills in, 420, 422–424
sleeping in, 422–424
teeth in, 410, 420
thumb sucking in, 410
weight problems in, 418
from ages seven to twelve, 476–490
body image in, 478
checkups and vaccines, 490
height and weight in, 477–478
hygiene in, 489–490
motor skills in, 481

nutrition in, 482–486
organized sports and, 479
personal safety in, 488
physical fitness in, 486–487
proportion and posture in, 480
puberty in, 480–481
sleep in, 487
teeth in, 480, 487, 489
during adolescence, 545–548
exercise in, 551
height and weight in, 546
hygiene in, 550–551
nutrition in, 549, 550
self-image in, 549
sexual development, 547–548
sleep in, 552
Physical disabilities, 612
Physical fitness from ages seven to twelve, 486–487
Physical needs, 84–85
of new mother, 201
Piaget, Jean, 29, 291, 523, 524
periods of learning of, 383, 524, 568
on concrete operations stage, 524–525
on formal operations state, 525–526, 567–568
on preoperational thinking, 457–458
on sensorimotor period, 291–292
theories of, 291–293, 383
Pituitary gland, 282
PKU, 125
Placenta, 110, 693
Planning chart, 647
Play
activities in, 397–398
board games and, 440
in building learning, 645
changes in, 317
children's museums and, 526
comparing past and present, 25
cooperative, 363, 439
difference between exploration and, 273–274
face-to-face interactions in, 262
family, 72

free, 646
imaginative, 293
with infants, 213
in intellectual development, 297–300
make-believe, 457
memory games in, 386
parallel, 361, 362, 439
playing grown-up, 465
problem solving through, 510
roles in, 413
sensory, 293
social development through, 270–272
toys in, 23, 398–399
Play environment, 272, 693
Playground equipment, safety and, 644
Play groups, 629, 693
Play therapist, 403
Poisoning, 245, 336, 591, 592
food, 232
Popular culture, 563, 693
Positive body language, 82
Positive difference, making a, 48
Positive learning environment, 569–570
Positive reinforcement, 92–93, 650, 694
Postnatal period, 195–202, 694
care of mother in, 201–202
Postpartum depression, 202, 694
Posture
from ages one to three, 312–313
from ages four to six, 410
from ages seven to twelve, 480
Practical intelligence, 530
Practicality of standardized tests, 537
Preeclampsia, 150, 694
Prefrontal cortex, 566, 694
Pregnancy, 565
alcohol and, 133–134
discomforts of, 150–152
early signs of, 147
emotional health during, 159–160
medical care during, 147–150
month by month, 112–113
nutrition during, 152–156
personal care and activities during, 157
physical changes in, 113

reducing stress during, 158
teen, 55, 60, 62–66
weight gain during, 156
Pregnant teens, nutrition for, 155
Premature birth, 188–189
Premature infants, caring for, 199–201
Premature labor, 180
Prenatal development, 104–142, 694
conception in, 105–106
defined, 106
embryonic stage in, 107, 110
genetics and, 114–116
germinal stage in, 106–107
month by month, 108–109
preparing for birth, 111, 113
problems in, 122–132
Prenatal tests, 130–132
Preoperational period, 457–458
Prepared childbirth, 171–172, 694
Preschoolers, 311, 694
Preschools, 631
in France, 395
specialized, 631
Prescription drugs, during pregnancy,
135–136
Preteen years, 499, 511
Privileges, loss of, 95
Problem solving through play, 510
Professionals, 658, 694
Proportion, 694
from ages one to three, 312–313
from ages seven to twelve, 480
in child development, 216–217
Protein, 152, 154, 156
Puberty, 545, 548, 694
onset of, 480–481
Punishment, effective use of, 93–94
Puppeteer, 377
Pyramid, Food, 327, 415, 482

R

Reading
appreciating, 463
choosing books for, 463–464
to infants, 302

Reading readiness, 393–394, 694
Reasoning, from ages one to three, 387–389
Recessive genes, 115, 116, 127, 694
Recessive inheritance, 127
Reflexes, 281, 694
in first year, 219–220
Reflux, 264, 694
Regression, 599, 694
Regularity, 261
Relaxin, 186
Reliability of standardized tests, 537
REM sleep, 359–360, 694
Rescue breathing, 592, 694
for infants and small children, 593
Rescue techniques, 592–594
Resource management skills, 56–57
Respiratory syncytial virus (RSV), 246
Responsibility, taking, 516
Rest. See Sleep
Résumé, 694
preparing, 668–670
Reye syndrome, 578
Rh factor, 149, 694
Role models, being good, 90, 650–651
Roles, play and, 413
Romantic involvement, 558
Rooming-in, 198, 695
Rooting reflex, 220
Rubella, 139–140, 150, 694
Running record, 36, 694

S

Safety, 583
car seat, 169
childproofing of home, 335
for children ages one to three, 336–338
in early childhood classrooms, 644–645
food-related hazards, 232, 644
in handling newborns, 226
for infants, 245
Internet, 513
in learning, 297
outdoor, 421
personal, 488
water, 245, 337

Scarlet fever, 579

School(s), 466–468. *See also* Education
  balancing, with parenting, 64
  middle, 533
  Montessori, 459–460, 527, 631, 646
  preparing for, 466, 468
  readiness for, 467

Scoliosis, 480, 695

Sealants, dental, 489, 695

Second-degree burns, 587

Sedentary activities, 486–487, 695

Self, sense of, in ages seven to twelve, 495–498

Self-care skills, teaching in ages four to six, 420, 422–424

Self-centeredness, 344, 695

Self-concept, 695
  developing a positive, 355, 357

Self-confidence, 695
  from ages four to six, 432–433, 436–438

Self-control, 504

Self-destructive behaviors, 569

Self-discipline, 88, 368, 695

Self-esteem, 695
  helping children develop, 33
  role of, in development, 34

Self-feeding, 236
  from ages one to three, 325

Self-image in adolescence, 549

Semen, 548

Sense of competence, 496–498, 695

Sense of self, 495–498, 695

Senses, 281

Sensitivity, 260

Sensorimotor period, 291–292, 695

Sensory dysfunction, 320

Sensory integration, 695
  from ages one to three, 320

Sensory play, 293

Separation anxiety, 351–352, 695
  from ages one to three, 358

Sequence, 28, 695

Serious emotional disturbances, 610–611

Service learning, 663, 695

Serving sizes, from ages one to three, 326

Sex chromosomes, 115–116

Sexual abuse, 617, 618

Sexual development during adolescence, 547–548

Sexuality, 695
  teen, 58–63

Sexually transmitted disease (STD), 60, 61, 119, 141–142, 565, 696

Shaken baby syndrome, 226–227, 695

Shared values, 81

Sharing, promoting, from ages one to three, 373–375

Shock, 591–592, 695
  anaphylactic, 590

Shouting, 96–97

Sibling rivalry, 695
  from ages one to three, 352–353
  from ages four to six, 435

Siblings, 512

Sick children, 578
  comforting, 580
  in hospital, 580, 582

Sickle cell anemia, 125

SIDS (Sudden infant death syndrome), 138, 227, 228, 695

Single parent family, 65, 73, 695

Situational stress, 600, 696

Skerries Island, Scotland, teaching in, 659

Skinner, B. F., 29

Sleep
  for first year, 227–229
  from ages one to three, 321–322, 324
  from ages four to six, 422–424
  from ages seven to twelve, 486–487
  in adolescence, 552
  for new mothers, 201

Sleep deprivation, 359–360, 552, 696

Sleepiness during pregnancy, 150–151

Slides, 421

Small motor skills. *See* Fine motor skills

Smell in first year, 218

Social development, 253, 696

comparing emotional development and, 253–254

of infants, 266–274

   developmental milestones, 268–269

   difference between exploration and play, 273–274

   learned behavior and, 270

   signs of, 266

   stranger anxiety and, 266–267, 270

   through play, 270–272

from ages one to three, 361–376

   developing social skills in, 366

   encouraging independence in, 371–372

   general patterns in, 361–364

   guidelines for guidance in, 368–371

   making friends in, 364–365

   possible behavioral problems, 375–376

   promoting sharing in, 373–375

   setting limits, 370–371

from ages four to six, 439–448

   conflict resolutions in, 441–444

   family relationships in, 444

   moral development in, 444–448

   patterns in, 439–441

Social influences on moral development, 562–564

Social interactions

   influence of, 568

   opportunities for, 560

Socialization, 361, 696

Social needs, 84, 85–86

Social relationships in adolescence, 557–560

   close friends in, 558–559

   opportunities for social interaction, 560

   peer groups in, 558

   peer influences in, 558

   romantic involvement in, 558

Social Security number for newborn, 199

Spanking, controversy over, 97

Specialized preschools, 631

Special needs, children with, 608–609

   educating, 612–614

   raising, 614

   rights of, 613

   types of disabilities, 609–612

Speech and language impairments, 610

Speech development

   from ages one to three, 399–402

   from ages four to six, 468–470

   milestones for, 303–304

Speech-language pathologists, 400, 425, 610, 696

Sperm, 106, 114, 696

Spermicide, 119

Sphincter muscles, 330, 696

Spina bifida, 125–126, 128

Spinal cord, 282

Splinters, first aid for, 586–587

Sprains, 696

   first aid for, 586

Standarized tests, 534, 696

   creating, 535

   kinds of, 537

   uses and misuses of, 537–538

   validity of, 535

Stanford-Binet test, 453–454

Stem cells, 187, 696

Stereotyping, avoiding, 438

Sternberg, Robert, 529–530

Stillbirth, 122, 696

Stimulating environment, 213–214, 696

Stimulation, 27, 696

Storyteller, 275

Stranger anxiety, 266–267, 270, 696

Strangers, 421

Strep throat, 579

Stress

   family, 599–607

   from ages four to six, 435–436

   children and, 599–600

   reducing, during pregnancy, 158

   situational, 600

Stuttering, 401–402, 696

Subjective observations, 36, 37, 696

Substance abuse, 602

Substitute care, 627–638
   choosing, 635, 637–638
   cost of, 637–638
   need for, 627
   questions for evaluating, 636
   sources of information on, 638
   types of, 627–634
Sucking reflex, 219
Suffocation, 245
Suicide, 607
Sun, infants and, 245
Sunburn, avoiding, 338
Support sources of, 62, 64, 79–80, 122,
      602, 614, 696
Surrogate mother, 121, 696
Swings, 421
Symbolic thinking, 293, 696
Synapses, 283, 696
Synthetic fibers, 332
Syphilis, 61, 141

T

Taegyo, 159
Taste, in first year, 218
Tay-Sachs disease, 126, 127
Teamwork, from ages four to six, 443
Technology, 79
Teen marriage, 65–66
Teen parenthood, 58–66
Teen pregnancy, 55, 60, 62–66
Teen sexuality, 58–63
Teeth
   care of
      from ages one to three, 313–314,
         329–330
      from ages four to six, 410, 420
      from ages seven to twelve, 487
   infant's, 244, 246
   permanent, 410, 420, 480
Teething, 244, 697
Television, time spent watching, 289, 416,
      448, 462

Temperament, 397
   in infants, 258, 260–261
Temper tantrums, 345, 374, 435, 697
Tension, 435, 697
Terman, Lewis M., 453
Testosterone, 548, 697
Thalamus, 282
Thalidomide, 135
Third-degree burns, 587
The Thirties, 32
Thorns, first aid for, 586–587
Thumb sucking, 264
   from ages four to six, 410
Time-out, 95–96, 697
Tobacco, 137
Toddlers, 311, 697
Toileting from ages four to six, 424
Toilet teaching, from ages one to three,
      330–331
Tolerance, teaching, to children, 514
Tooth decay, 420
Touch, 294
   in first year, 218
Toxoplasmosis, 140, 697
Toy designer, 471
Toys
   age and, 298–299, 398–399
   choosing, 299–300
   choosing safe, 336
   comparing, 23
Traditions, forming, 80
Traffic, 421
Training pants, 331
Transition, 646, 697
   during labor, 182, 184
   managing, in child's routines, 323
Transitivity, 524, 697
Trial-and-error learning, 383, 697
Trust, building, through care, 258, 259
Trustworthiness, 505
Twins, 118
Two-income families, 78
Typical behaviors, 22, 697

U

Ultrasound, 131, 697
  labor and, 180
Umbilical cord, 110, 173, 190, 216, 697
Understanding, 505
Unemployment benefits, 679, 697
Unintentional misbehavior, 93
Uterus, 105–106, 697

V

Vaccines, 247, 575–576, 697. *See also*
        Immunizations
Vaginal implant, 119
Validity of standardized tests, 535
Values
  sexuality and, 59–60
  shared, 81
Varicella, 140–141
Varicose veins, 151
Vegans, 156
Vegetarians, 156
Verbal abuse, 617, 618
Verbal-linguistic intelligence, 456, 528
Vernix, 192, 697
Very late adulthood, 33
Vision in first year, 217–218
Visual impairments, 612
Visual-spatial intelligence, 456, 529
Vitamins, 152
Voice in first year, 218–219
Volunteering, 662–663
Vygotsky, Lev, 29, 459, 526, 568

W

Water safety, 245, 337
Weaning, 235, 697
Weight
  of premature baby, 188
  of infant, 215
  from ages one to three, 312
  from ages four to six, 409–410
  from ages seven to twelve, 477–478
  in adolescence, 546
  gain of, during pregnancy, 156
Weight problems, 418
Wildlife educator, 623
Work
  balancing family and, 169–170
  comparing past and present, 24–25
Work-based learning, 662, 663, 697
Work experience, gaining, 662–663
Workplace changes, 78–79
Worry, 52
  in ages seven to twelve, 501

X

X chromosomes, 115–116
X rays, danger to unborn infant from, 138

Y

Y chromosomes, 115–116
Young adulthood, 32

Z

Zone of proximal development, 568
Zygote, 106–107, 397